THE PAPERS OF
WOODROW WILSON
VOLUME 5
1885-1888

SPONSORED BY THE WOODROW WILSON
FOUNDATION
AND PRINCETON UNIVERSITY

THE PAPERS OF
WOODROW WILSON

ARTHUR S. LINK, *EDITOR*

JOHN WELLS DAVIDSON AND DAVID W. HIRST
ASSOCIATE EDITORS

JOHN E. LITTLE AND WILLIAM M. LEARY, JR.
ASSISTANT EDITORS

JEAN MACLACHLAN, *CONTRIBUTING EDITOR*

Volume 5 · 1885-1888

PRINCETON, NEW JERSEY
PRINCETON UNIVERSITY PRESS
1968

INTRODUCTION

THIS fifth volume of *The Papers of Woodrow Wilson*, covering the period from July 1885 through August 1888, records dramatic and momentous changes in Wilson's professional career, intellectual development, and personal life.

Those who have assumed that *Congressional Government* represented the apex of Wilson's political thought and writing will be interested in the mutations and new thrusts in Wilson's intellectual development revealed herein. The young scholar, not yet thirty years old, begins the studies and lectures in administration that will make him the pioneer student in this field in the United States. He writes the first draft of a projected comprehensive treatise on the development of modern democracy. Self-taught in German, he discovers the world of German scholarship in political science and law. He sets to work on the book that will be published as *The State* in 1889. So complete is the documentary record that we can literally see Wilson's mind in operation—how it probed, deployed, organized materials, and moved from one level of knowledge and sophistication to another.

This volume also chronicles the first three years of Wilson's career as a teacher, at the new Bryn Mawr College. Documents and Editorial Notes disclose Wilson planning and developing what he conceived to be the appropriate curriculum in history, political science, and economics. Descriptions of his lecture notes and extensive samples of these notes show the kind of work that he did in the classroom. The documents also reveal why Wilson's three years at Bryn Mawr were years of discontent as well as of promise. Finally, the materials herein set the record straight, once and for all, concerning the circumstances of Wilson's resignation from the college in 1888.

This volume also chronicles the beginning of life together for Woodrow and Ellen Wilson. Fortunately for later generations, they were separated for extended periods between 1885 and 1888. Their letters, printed in entirety insofar as they are known to be extant, record and reveal their growing mutual love, details of their daily lives, the births of their first two daughters, and the expanding nexus of relationships that constituted their social world.

There have been no editorial innovations in this volume. As in previous ones, the Editors have reproduced texts *verbatim et lite-*

ratim, to use J. Franklin Jameson's phrase, repairing them only when absolutely necessary for clarity and using the editorial *sic* only in the case of words repeated in the original.

For special assistance in the preparation of this book, the Editors are particularly obliged to various individuals at Bryn Mawr College: President Katharine McBride, for permission to reproduce letters from the Presidential Files and extracts from the Minutes of the Executive Committee of the Board of Trustees; Professor Arthur P. Dudden, for searching the Bryn Mawr College Archives and supplying letters and information concerning Wilson's course work; and Miss Janet M. Agnew, Head Librarian, and her assistants, for answering numerous inquiries and furnishing the photographs relating to Bryn Mawr in the picture section.

A host of other individuals contributed materials and information. The Editors thank especially Miss Frieda C. Thies, Curator of Manuscripts, the Milton S. Eisenhower Library of The Johns Hopkins University, for help in finding documents relating to Wilson and the Hopkins; Dr. John W. Spaeth, Jr., Archivist of Wesleyan University, for information and documents concerning Wilson's call to that institution; and M. Halsey Thomas, Archivist of Princeton University, for almost daily help.

The Editors again express their appreciation to Mrs. Bryant Putney of Princeton University Press for copyediting and other assistance.

The Editors here record the death of Clifford P. Gehman, who worked for almost seven years transcribing Wilson's shorthand, on January 5, 1968, at the age of ninety-two. Although Mr. Gehman was eighty-four when he began this work, he transcribed hundreds of pages of Wilson's shorthand drafts of letters, speeches, and essays, as well as a student diary and marginal notes in books and on documents. His letters to the Editors reflected his enthusiasm for his work and an appreciation of its historical importance. On one occasion he wrote that Wilson's notes enabled him to "get the feel of the man, in the words, the penmanship, the choice of outlines. Surely he was highly concentrated, to put it in one way. No left, no right, just straight ahead. Without the shorthand he would have been a different man." Mr. Gehman had a distinguished career as a shorthand reporter, and the work that he did for the Wilson Papers was a fitting climax of his career and a lasting contribution to Wilsonian scholarship.

The Editors are pleased to record that this volume embodies the work of Colonel James B. Rothnie, U.S.A., Ret., who has joined Miss Marjorie Sirlous in the additional transcribing of Wilson's shorthand.

THE EDITORS

Princeton, New Jersey

April 10, 1968

CONTENTS

Introduction, vii
Illustrations, xvii
Abbreviations and Symbols, xix

The Papers, July 2, 1885–August 31, 1888

ILLUSTRATIONS

Following page 388

TEXT ILLUSTRATIONS

ABBREVIATIONS

ALI	autograph letter initialed
ALS	autograph letter(s) signed
API	autograph postal initialed
APS	autograph postal signed
att(s).	attached, attachment(s)
EAW	Ellen Axson Wilson
ELA	Ellen Louise Axson
enc(s).	enclosed, enclosure(s)
env.	envelope
hw	handwriting or handwritten
hwL	handwritten letter
hwLS	handwritten letter signed
JRW	Joseph Ruggles Wilson
JWW	Janet Woodrow Wilson
LPC	letterpress copy
TCL	typed copy of letter
tel.	telegram
TLS	typed letter signed
WW	Woodrow Wilson
WWhw	Woodrow Wilson handwriting or handwritten
WWsh	Woodrow Wilson shorthand
WWT	Woodrow Wilson typed

ABBREVIATIONS FOR COLLECTIONS AND LIBRARIES

Following the National Union Catalogue of the Library of Congress

CtY	Yale University Library
DLC	Library of Congress
MdBJ	The Johns Hopkins University Library
MH	Harvard University Library
MiU-H	University of Michigan, Michigan Historical Collection
NIC	Cornell University Library
NjP	Princeton University Library
NN	New York Public Library
NNC	Columbia University Library
NPV	Vassar College Library
PBm	Bryn Mawr College Library
RSB Coll., DLC	Ray Stannard Baker Collection of Wilsoniana Library of Congress
ViU	University of Virginia Library
WC, NjP	Woodrow Wilson Collection, Princeton University Library
WP, DLC	Woodrow Wilson Papers, Library of Congress

SYMBOLS

⟨   ⟩   matter deleted from manuscript by Wilson
and restored by the editors

[Sept. 8, 1884]   publication date of a published writing; also
date of document when date is not part
of text

[*Sept. 8, 1884*]   latest composition date of a published writing

THE PAPERS OF

WOODROW WILSON

VOLUME 5

1885-1888

THE PAPERS OF
WOODROW WILSON

From Henry Crew[1]

Dear Wilson: Baltimore, Md., July 2–1885.

I stopped this A.M. in the final throes of packing to strike a bargain with a Druid Hill Ave. Jew for those clothes of yours. Notwithstanding I told him I never would take a cent less than $10.00, he seemed inclined to give me only $6.00—which the same I enclose in cash as the best I could do.

The scissors & case the old Jew found in some of your pockets & brought back to show me that he was an honest man even if he did deal in secondhand clothing: I send them thinking possibly you may have some associations with them.

Well, I suppose I'll be the nine hundred and ninety ninth one to offer congratulations, but nevertheless—Here's to you both! May you live long and prosper! . . .

                    Very hastily & sincerely   Henry Crew.

ALS (WP, DLC).
  [1] A.B., Princeton, 1882; Fellow in Physics at the Johns Hopkins in 1884-85, who roomed at Wilson's boardinghouse at 8 McCulloh Street.

From Charles Baker Wright

Dear Wilson: Akron, O., July 8, '85.

I was thrown into the editorial tread-mill almost immediately after getting here and have been toiling up its inclined plane ever since till last Saturday. Then our managing editor, whose place I was supplying, came back from his vacation and I am free again. I meant to have written you long ago. I should have done so at the same time I wrote President Battle,[1] withdrawing from his list of candidates. You see it was this way: a letter came one day from the president of Middlebury College,[2] at Middlebury, Vermont, inviting me to the English chair of that institution, giving favorable terms and so on and urging me to come. Then came a letter from President Gilman, also urging me to accept if I had fully determined not to be back at the University. I found it to be an old, though small, college and of good standing. It didn't seem good policy to throw it over for a 1:49 chance elsewhere, yet I gave up the N. C. possibilities with a good deal of regret. The

Rev. Thomas Hume, of Norfolk, Va.,[3] got it, it appears. I see by the reports that your friend Phillips is in, as is also Love.[4] I needn't say anything about your own kindness in the whole matter; you know my "sentiments" on the subject. . . .

There is no need of wishing you the happiest of happy summers, for I am sure you are having it.

Very heartily,   C. B. Wright.

ALS (WP, DLC).

[1] Kemp Plummer Battle, President of the University of North Carolina. Wilson had apparently nominated Wright for a professorship in English at the University.

[2] Probably Cyrus Hamlin, who resigned the presidency of Middlebury College on July 1, 1885. He was succeeded by Ezra Brainerd.

[3] Professor of English Language and Literature at the University of North Carolina, 1885-1902.

[4] William B. Phillips was named Professor of Agricultural Chemistry and Mineralogy; James Lee Love, Assistant Professor of Pure Mathematics.

From Melville R. Hopewell

Tekamah, Neb, July [9] 188[5]

I address you at Wilmington—supposing a letter will reach, & not knowing your present whereabouts—

Have sold grass for 85 on NE 1/4

SW 1/4 10-21-11 for	$7.00
fees	2.00
N. Y. Dft. inclosed	5.00
to your order,	

Truly   M. R. Hopewell

P. S. Have had some parties, asking prices of your lands, others who would like to lease for a term of years, for pasture purposes, with privilege of fencing, & removing fence at end of lease. Let me know what you think.   M. R. H.

ALS (WP, DLC).

From Janet Woodrow Wilson

No. 12 East 16th Street

My precious boy,   New York City July 13th 1885

We received your welcome letter two or three days ago. My impulse was to answer immediately—but really I did not care to write you from Peekskill. The truth is we were horribly "taken in" in our venture there. . . .

I know nothing about those rooms you speak of in the eight

room cottage, but I remember those on the lower floor were considered very desirable. I hope you are having pleasant weather now[.] It is too bad to be shut up by rain while in the mountains. Much as you enjoy each other under such circumstances, you can do that as well, and enjoy the beautiful walks besides, when the sun shines. The idea of your studying German! That sounds very unromantic, but you are wise. Has dear Ellie[1] managed to get sleep enough yet, I wonder! I hope you will both be able to gain flesh in the mountains. Do try to get quite well, dear. If you can be well and strong, I shall have no fears for you. You are bound now to make health your first consideration. I am so thankful that your own chosen little wife is *all* your own now—for you will not be lonely and depressed anymore.

Your dear father is remarkably well—and his spirits are evenly cheerful. I am so glad that I came with him. We have enjoyed the passed ten days immensely in spite of the drawbacks at Peekskill. Write when you can, dear—and beg dear Ellie to write. Is she going to sketch some of the views at Arden, I wonder? Your father joins me in warmest love to both our dear children.

Most lovingly   Your Mother

ALS (WP, DLC).

[1] The reader is reminded that this is a continuing series, and that persons referred to by familiar names and diminutives who have appeared in earlier volumes are identified in the Index of this volume under the form of the name used.

From Reginald Lane Poole

Dear Sir: ·   Oxford 17th July 1885.

In sending you this prospectus I am desired particularly to request the favour of your support to the scheme. Our hope is to make the 'Historical Review' representative of all the historical work of English-speaking nations, and we count very much upon the assistance of scholars on your side of the Atlantic. I shall be grateful if you will kindly inform the Editor or me whether it is within your power to help us, and if so in what departments: for it is not only in the way of regular articles that most valuable assistance may be given, but also by recording and commenting on the appearance of new books, especially of books which are likely to escape the notice of historical scholars who are not also bibliographers.

I remain, dear Sir, yours faithfully

Reginald Lane Poole, Sub Editor.

ALS (WP, DLC) with WWhw notation on env.: "Ans. Aug. 9/85." Enc.: printed prospectus for *English Historical Review*.

From Marion Wilson Kennedy

My dearest Woodrow: Little Rock, July 19th [1885]

We were *very* glad indeed to receive your very satisfactory letter last week. Do you know you are the only one who has written us *any* description of the wedding yet? I flattered myself that they would all be so sorry for Ross and me, away off here, that, for once in our experience, we would be *overwhelmed* with letters! How sadly was I mistaken! Annie wrote me a note, which I received yesterday, telling us of your and Ellie's whereabouts, and of Father and Mother's destination. As she was getting ready to go away for the summer herself, she thought she hadn't time to write more than a hasty note. . . .

Judge Martin[1] has just sent back your book, and besides expressing his own admiration of it, he says that Judge Bearden,[2] —one of our candidates for U. S. Congress—, says *if* he is elected he intends to get that book and *study* it. I wonder if Ellie,—the dear sister I long so to see—, is as proud of you as *I* am, Woodrow? She can't possibly be much more so. Of that I am firmly convinced. The household here are quite well, unusually so for this season. Little Woodrow[3] is much more nearly well than he has ever been in warm weather before. Ross is gaining flesh slowly, since he quit using tobacco altogether. Do you smoke yet?

We are going to spend our summer quietly at home, we hope— and will look eagerly for letters from you all, as our only means of excitement. Please don't fail us. Kiss dear Ellie many times for us both, if it isn't *too much trouble*. With warmest love to you both, from Ross and self,   Your sister   Marion.

ALS (WP, DLC).

[1] Joseph W. Martin of Little Rock, previously and subsequently judge of the Sixth Circuit Court of Arkansas.

[2] Judge John T. Bearden, who failed to win the Democratic congressional nomination in the Third Arkansas District.

[3] Her son, Wilson Woodrow Kennedy, born in 1879.

From Robert Bridges

Dear Tommy: [New York] July 19 '85

Today I have had shipped by express the "Works of Jefferson" 9 vols and Lalor's "Cyclopaedia of Political Science" 3 vols, which the boys commissioned me to send to you on their behalf. I write this note so that if the books are delayed you may know that they are on the way. "A History of Virginia" has also been sent, by mail.[1] An envelope containing the names of the donors accompanies the box.

I sincerely hope that we have not duplicated anything which you already possess. If so—an exchange can easily be arranged.

The reunion was an unprecedented success. Fifty of us sat down at the table. The pleasantest feature of it to me was the reunion of the old crowd. Pete and you only were missing—(and Pete got down with his wife over Sunday.) We had very pleasant rooms, and a club room in the same house. You may imagine that very little sleeping was done except by Daniel (the Sage of Marshfield) who could not be disturbed. Talcott appointed himself a committee to keep the boys awake. He crowned his efforts about 4 o'clock Tuesday morning by upsetting Doctor's cot and putting the mattress on top of him. We all made it pleasant for the Cow.

Every now and then some one would say "Tommy ought to be here to make the thing complete." It was the only drawback. The dinner was fine and the fellows never more genial. Old clique feelings are very much softened. The boys were never so patriotic as now. We are still remembered at Princeton. All the classes and the Glee Club came around to cheer us.

Ridge did not get very tight, and spoke for the "Western Men" until his "counsel," McFee, told him to sit down.

Talcott has been with me for several days—just went home this morning. He is the same old boy—and is developing in the right way. I never saw him look so well.

I wish you all joy and happiness. My kindest remembrance to Mrs. Wilson.   Your friend   Bob Bridges

ALS (WP, DLC) with WWhw notation on env.: "Ans. July 1885." Encs.: personal cards from eight of WW's classmates: Webster, Lee, Henderson, Talcott, Woods, Mitchell, Bridges, and Godwin, and printed "Sexennial Reunion Song" by Robert Bridges.

[1] The books mentioned in this paragraph were H. A. Washington (ed.), *The Writings of Thomas Jefferson* (9 vols., New York, 1853-55, reprinted several times); John Joseph Lalor, *Cyclopaedia of Political Science, Political Economy, and of the Political History of the United States* (3 vols., Chicago, 1881-84); and John Esten Cooke, *Virginia, A History of the People* (Boston, 1883). The Lalor and Cooke volumes are in the Wilson Library, DLC.

From James E. Rhoads

My dear Friend,   Bryn Mawr, near Philadelphia, 7 mo 20, 1885.

With this I send form of application for a fellowship in History for 1886-87.[1] I have hesitated to offer any encouragement to this lady from doubts as to the possibility of her having had the necessary preparation for the fellowship.

Very truly thy friend,　James E Rhoads

ALS (WP, DLC) with WWhw notation on env.: "Both Ans. July 27/85." Enc.: L. B. Shriver to WW, July 18, 1885, ALS (WP, DLC), informing WW of a reception to be given by the trustees and faculty of Bryn Mawr College on September 23, 1885, to mark the opening of the college.
1 From Mary E. Whipple. See J. E. Rhoads to WW, Aug. 15, 1885.

From Addie C. Wildgoss

Haverford College P. O. July 24th [1885]

Mr. Wilson,

I regret to say that very recently I have been obliged to abandon my project of the cottage on the Bryn Mawr Coll. grounds, owing to two of the professors who had engaged rooms with me, proposing, as they think, to do better by themselves, in taking the adjoining cottage & forming a club for the professors. This left me a certainty of yourself only and probably another gentleman which would not justify me in the risks and care of the undertaking.

We can accommodate you with a very delightful room, with a small one as Study at our own house at Haverford. Your expenses will be the same covering car fare to & from Bryn Mawr. The distance between the two stations is only three minutes, making in all from our house nine or ten. Will you favor me with an early reply.　　　　　　Very truly Yours　A. C. Wildgoss

ALS (WP, DLC) with WWhw notation on env.: "Ans. July 28/85."

From Melville R. Hopewell

Dear Sir　　　　　　　　　Tekamah, Neb, July 24 1885

I wrote you sometime since, inclosing a small draft for grass, sold from your land.

I now hand you Dft for 4.00 less Ex[.] My fee 1.00 being 5.00 for 20 acres grass on NE 1/4 SW 1/4 10-21-11.

I believe I also asked if you would sell this 80 or any of your land? I have had one or two inquiries for price of late, also one man wanted to lease a ½ section for pasture? Hoping to hear from you　　　　　　I am truly Yours　M. R. Hopewell

ALS (WP, DLC) with WWhw notation on env.: "Ans. Aug. 4/85."

From Janet Woodrow Wilson

Our very dear children,   New York City–Monday July 27–'85
I have been startled this morning by the recollection of the fact that your month at Arden Park is almost at an end–and yet we have not heard anything of your further plans. It has been so very hot here during the last two weeks, that we have been able to do nothing beyond trying to keep quiet–and thinking as little as possible. . . .

Tuesday) You have probably heard that Annie, Josie, and the little boys,[1] expected to leave Columbia on yesterday for the Warm Springs. Josie will remain there only one week–then join us here. We have decided to remain where we are another week after this–and then we may go to Saratoga for a little while–but we have not made any settled plan beyond next week. We started out last week one day in search of the number suggested by dear Ellie –but finally found we were looking in the wrong direction–and have not tried again. We have concluded that it will be better to remain where we now are–as we probably could not do better.

I need not tell you that we have thought and talked about you a great deal. We are so glad to think of your happiness in each other. I love to think of you in that beautiful place–of your happy wanderings from day to day.

I must not stay to scribble more–for papa is waiting for me to walk out with him. It is decidedly cooler this morning. God bless you both. We love you with all our hearts.

Yours lovingly   Mother & Father

ALS (WP, DLC) with WWhw notation on env.: "Ans. Aug. 3/85."
[1] George and Wilson Howe.

From Addie C. Wildgoss

Mr. Wilson,   Haverford College P. O. July 30th [1885]
Both rooms have a bright pleasant outlook. They are not communicating but adjoining; the smaller one is a hall room, with one large window facing the S. E. The dimensions are 14 by 9 feet (fourteen by nine). It has been used as a double room and that in the summer. The large room is eighteen and a half feet either way, has three large windows one opening on the West. There is a large closet in the hall adjoining & belonging to these rooms. In the large room there is a wardrobe or rather a closet. The rooms are furnished but if you prefer anything of your own there is no reason why you should not send it on. Your desk or such pieces in the study we have not, and while sending one you

may prefer to send all. Our furniture is very simple. I am confident that you cannot be more pleasantly situated than here. You need not lack ventilation or privacy in your rooms, because by curtaining off the hall, the two rooms can be thrown as it were into one. Will you please let me know your decision as soon as possible, as there are some arrangements to make should you desire to come early in Sept.[1]

Very Sincerely Yours   A. C. Wildgoss

ALS (WP, DLC) with WWhw notation on env.: "Ans. Aug. 3/85" and the sentence, "Nominations constitute the 'personal' column of the Senate's docket," which appears in the essay, "Courtesy of the Senate," printed at Nov. 15, 1885.

[1] Wilson decided to rent these rooms in spite of Dr. Rhoads' offer, made in his letters of August 15 and 20, 1885, of housing on the college grounds. That this was true is evident from several freight invoices addressed to Wilson or Miss Wildgoss and describing goods shipped from Savannah, Baltimore, and New York to Haverford. (See Ocean Steamship Company of Savannah to Addie C. Wildgoss, Sept. 5, 1885; Philadelphia, Wilmington, and Baltimore Railroad Company to WW, Sept. 14, 1885; James Fitzgerald to WW, Sept. 16, 1885; Adams Express Company to Addie C. Wildgoss, Sept. 16, 1885; and Pennsylvania Railroad Company to WW, Sept. 18, 1885, all in WP, DLC.)

The Wilsons arrived in Haverford probably around the middle of September. However, the arrangement with Miss Wildgoss did not work out (Wilson, in a letter to Ellen of May 9, 1886, referred to "that trying stay at Haverford"), and the Wilsons moved to rooms in the "Betweenery," one of the college-owned cottages on the Bryn Mawr grounds, on about October 19, 1885. (Stockton Axson to EAW, Oct. 17, 1885, ALS [WP, DLC], addressed to Haverford, was forwarded to Bryn Mawr on October 19.) The "Betweenery" was situated between the "Deanery," the Dean's residence, and the "Greenery," another cottage across the way. The Wilsons lived in the "Betweenery" until the autumn of 1887. See Edith Finch, *Carey Thomas of Bryn Mawr* (New York, 1947), pp. 164-65.

From Charles Andrew Talcott

My dear Tommy: Utica, N. Y. Aug. 3. 1885

Your letter of June 9th did not reach me until my return from Princeton. I left for Princeton early in the morning of June 12th and your letter reached Utica the same day. I did not return home until too late to write before your wedding, so I celebrated the 24th of June as a sort of holiday, regretting however that I was not at Columbia to give you the moral send off mentioned in your letter. We all missed you very much at Princeton but I need not say we often thought of you and spoke of you and wished sincerely for your great happiness. I was particularly disappointed in not seeing you because I had looked forward to meeting you there and was not aware of your intentions until I reached Princeton.

I think you would have enjoyed the reunion heartily. There were seven of us in two rooms; dress parades at all hours of the day and undress parades at all hours of the night, wonderful exhibitions by Bridges of great muscular developement; imaginary

surgical operations performed on Hiram's vertebral wart, the old friend of our earlier days. This last pleasure was somewhat marred by the seasons of remorse through which Dr. Mitchell passed after each operation; "won't I catch it when I get back to Baltimore," he would say; and then rehear[s]e imaginary explanatory conversations with which to beguile the entire Woods family, when assembled to pass judgment upon him. But these clouds were quickly dispelled and I have a very strong suspicion that Hiram enjoyed these delicate attentions to our old friend the wart as much as any of us. Mr. Webster's philosophical calm was undisturbed during our sojurn. Lee had just become engaged and was happiness personified; and I felt when I left that I knew Henderson better than I ever did before. We had a very pleasant time all in all and the only element needed to make the pleasure more complete was your presence there. On my way home I stopped in New York a few days with Bob, enjoying them greatly. I hope time will not bring duties so absorbing that these pleasant gatherings will be forgotten and lost sight of and that the sentiment of those earlier days which even now lingers so sweetly in mind & memory will survive the cares, the disappointments and struggles which it may be our lot to encounter. I must either close or spoil another sheet. Excuse my formality in concluding this incoherent epistle, but you must recollect this is my first letter since your marriage & I am not quite tame yet. With warmest regards
                   Yours sincerely as ever   Charles A. Talcott

ALS (WP, DLC).

To Reginald Lane Poole

Dear Sir: [Arden, N. C., Aug. 9, 1885]
    I have received your letter of the 17th of July, accompanying the circular of the projected 'English Historical Review.' I appreciate very highly the desire of the projectors, expressed in yr. letters, to secure my support for the scheme, and I shall be sincerely glad to render any assistance that may be within my power. There is undoubtedly a very clear need of such a Review, and no one who desires as much as I do to see a strong English Historical Review established could refuse cordial support to any serious attempt to found one.
    My time will be so much occupied for some years to come that I fear I cannot be either a frequent contributor; and, as my special studies are for the most part confined to the fields of administration and Am. Constitutional history, I fear that any original mat-

ter I may have to offer will not often be quite of the sort most acceptable. I shall however be glad to put myself at the service of the editors for reviewing or critical work; and shall interest myself in supplying such bibliographical and other items of interest as may come under my view.

With heartiest interest in the undertaking, I remain, dear Sir,
Yours sincerely   W. W.

ALI (draft) (WP, DLC).

From Janet Woodrow Wilson

New York City—No. 12 East 16th Street
My darling Son,   Tuesday August 11th [1885]

I am distressed to hear of James Bones' faithlessness. Please write to him at once—and tell him that the sum due has been turned over to you, and that you really need it—so that you must beg him to remit immediately. How can a good man be so faithless as to his promises?

Josie arrived in New York last Thursday morning—about a week earlier than was first proposed. . . .

We have given up all idea of going to Saratoga—and will likely remain where we are, till the last week of this month. Your father thinks we must be in Clarkesville not later than Sep. 1st—so as to get the house ready for occupancy before the session opens—as far as possible.

Please let us know as soon as you can the particulars of your plans. How long will you be in Morgantown(?)[1] First of all, when will you leave Arden Park? I think you are very wise to remain at Arden Park as long as you can—while you are so comfortable. I need not say that we will be sorely disappointed at not seeing you before we go West. But perhaps we may get a sight of each other yet.

We had a letter from dear Annie this morning. She wishes to come on by the 14th. I have bespoken a room for her in this house—so' that we will be together for awhile again. . . .

With warmest love for your precious self and dearest Ellie
Yours   Mother.

ALS (WP, DLC) with WWhw calendar for August and September 1885 on an enclosed sheet.

[1] Woodrow and Ellen had accepted an invitation to visit Elizabeth Adams Erwin and her husband, Hamilton, in Morganton, North Carolina, after leaving Arden. See Elizabeth Adams Erwin to ELA and WW, June 19, 1885, and Elizabeth Adams Erwin to EAW, Aug. 8, 1885, both ALS (WP, DLC).

From James E. Rhoads

My dear Friend,   Bryn Mawr, near Philadelphia, 8 mo 15, 1885.

With this I send the Thesis just presented by Mary E Whipple. It was necessary for her to write rather hastily, but she quotes no authorities except a newspaper or two, and her paper gives evidence of less historical study than that of the lady whose application we laid aside. But I do not wish to prepossess thy mind too much before thou hast examined the paper.

It is now practically certain that we can offer thyself & wife comfortable board in one of the cottages near the college buildings, at the rate of $16. a week for the 2 rooms & board.

     Cordially thy friend,   James E Rhoads

Within a week we shall decide upon this arrangement if it be made & it is almost assured.

ALS (WP, DLC).

From Martha Carey Thomas

My dear Mr Wilson,   Blue Ridge Summit, Pa. Aug. 15, 1885

We have at last, I think, found the proper candidate for the fellowship in history. Several months ago Miss Bancroft,[1] professor of French in the Northwestern Univ. Evanston, Ill., wrote to me for advice in regard to studying in Paris asking at the same time some questions about Bryn Mawr. She mailed me an historical thesis, which she had presented at Syracuse Univ. for the degree of doctor of philosophy, and after reading it I enclosed her a blank of application for a fellowship and several programs. I met her by appointment a few days ago in Phila. and she has, it seems, asked the advice of several historians, among them Professor James[2] of the Univ. of Penna., and has decided to apply for a fellowship at Bryn Mawr, deferring thus her going abroad until the following year. She began her historical studies six years ago and has resigned her professorship in the Northwestern Univ. because history has become her chief interest. She was graduated from Syracuse Univ. in 1877 and took her M.A. as well as her Ph.D. in history. She sent her dissertation to fifty historians and received letters from all except two; among them President [Andrew D.] White wrote to her and has been very kind in advising her about her historical work. I am now of course only repeating her own statements. She said also that some professor—perhaps C. K. Adams, but I have forgotten whom she said—told her that the historical seminary of the Johns Hopkins had spent one evening in discussing her dissertation. You will perhaps remember it.

She is a woman of about thirty five years of age. I was favorably impressed by her. She seemed to me ambitious and energetic and it may be that she only needs an uninterrupted time for study and and [sic] a knowledge of good methods to do good work. I send by the same mail her thesis and a catalogue of the Northwestern Univ.

She has positively engaged to return to her present position for three months, that is, should she receive the fellowship she could not come to Bryn Mawr until the first of January; but if she seems to you desirable this need not prevent her receiving the appointment. I forgot to say that her great interest is constitutional history. She is not willing to apply formally for the fellowship until she knows whether her enforced absence during 3 months or any other fact would make it improbable that she could receive the appointment. She feels I think that her rejection, were it known, might be a disadvantage in her future work. As she has already held a professorship I thought her case somewhat unusual and promised to lay the matter before you. Will you consider it and tell me what you think? If you wish I will write to Pres. White. Pres. Rhoads can personally ask Prof. James' opinion. Miss Bancroft will be [in] Ocean Grove for the next three weeks; she is extremely anxious to have the matter decided before she goes back to the west.

I have met Miss Whipple and she seemed to me a very undesirable candidate. She has had little literary training and her method of teaching history was, I thought, very far from satisfactory.

Asking you to give my kind regards to Mrs Wilson whose acquaintance I hope soon to have the pleasure of making

           I am   Sincerely yours   M. Carey Thomas

ALS (WP, DLC).

  1 Jane Marie Bancroft, Ph.D., Syracuse University, 1880, and Dean of the Women's College and Professor of French Language and Literature at Northwestern, 1878-85. After holding the fellowship in history at Bryn Mawr in 1886, she did further graduate work at the University of Zurich and the Sorbonne. She married George O. Robinson in 1891 and afterward devoted her energies and money to various philanthropies.

  2 Edmund J. James, Professor of Public Finance and Administration in the Wharton School of Finance and Economy of the University of Pennsylvania.

From James E. Rhoads

My Dear Friend,   Bryn Mawr, Penna 8/20. 85.

With this I send the thesis of Miss Bancroft. It seems to me much the best yet offered—well-written giving evidence of general culture and of historical ability with the power of independent thought.

We have no[w] arranged for a housekeeper to take the two cottages on the College premises and can offer Mrs Wilson & thyself two comfortable rooms at $16. per week board for both. I think this is at once the cheapest and most convenient accommodation you can find. With kind regards to Mrs Wilson,

I am truly thy friend,   James E Rhoads

The Boarding House at Haverford Miss Wildgosses' is about a mile from the college, & in bad weather the walking will be difficult.

ALS (WP, DLC).

To Martha Carey Thomas

My dear Miss Thomas,   New York,[1] Aug. 29/85

Your letter of the 15th of August, after some wandering, has found me here. I have had time to examine Miss Bancroft's essay on the Parl. of Paris, and am inclined to agree with you in thinking that we have found in Miss B. a suitable candidate for the historical fellowship. I remember hearing the essay reviewed at one of our Seminary meetings in Baltimore.[2] It is by no means true that an evening was devoted to it. It was simply 'reported upon,' as all pamphlets of this kind are there; and I remember that, in the five or ten minutes wh. Dr. Jameson gave to it, he spoke rather severely of one or two rather extraordinary errors in Miss Bancroft's argument which his wonderful memory had enabled him to detect. In choosing such a subject Miss B. was guilty of the singular indiscretion of entering the lists with some of the greatest scholars of Europe in a contest over an exceedingly knotty question.

Still, this need not obscure the fact that Miss B. gives evidence of very great industry and considerable culture. I think that, under the circumstances, the fellowship should be given to her, though I regard the fact that she cannot be in Bryn Mawr before the first of Jan'y as a very grave drawback to her candidacy.

I shall write to Dr. Rhoads as soon as possible about this matter and about Miss Whipple.

Mrs. Wilson wishes me to thank you for your kind message, and joins me in warmest regards,

Very sincerely Yours,   Woodrow Wilson

ALS (President's Files, PBm).

[1] Woodrow and Ellen, after their visit with the Erwins, had gone to New

York, probably to be with Dr. and Mrs. Wilson before they left for Clarksville.

2 See the Minutes of the Seminary of Historical and Political Science, Oct. 17, 1884, Vol. 3.

EDITORIAL NOTE
WILSON'S TEACHING AT BRYN MAWR, 1885-86

Wilson set forth his plan for a two-year course of study for history and political science students at Bryn Mawr in the copy that he supplied for the first college catalogue for 1885-86, months before he began his teaching career.[1] Moreover, in the spring and autumn of 1886 he wrote out detailed reviews of what he had actually done in the classroom in 1885-86 and added a revealing description of his methods and objectives.[2] So fully descriptive is the latter that the Editors can do little more than to add a few details and to guide the reader through the documentary record.

Bryn Mawr opened its doors on September 21, 1885, with thirty-five undergraduates and seven graduate students enrolled. Wilson began the first semester with eight majors in history, the second with seven, one having failed.[3] His sole lecture course during the academic year was one in ancient history, which Wilson viewed as the foundation of his two-year course of study. In the Bryn Mawr catalogue for 1885-86, Wilson had announced two consecutive one-semester courses—the first on Greece, the second on Rome. However, he intimated in his commentary in the autumn of 1886 that in fact he had given Greek and Roman history throughout the year 1885-86 on alternate weeks. The Bryn Mawr records and Wilson's own grade records indicate that he had already decided to use this plan by the time that the college opened.[4]

The extant record gives us a fairly clear picture of Wilson's course during his first year of teaching at Bryn Mawr. In four lectures on about September 24, 25, 28, and 29, he first introduced his students to the field of history, revealing his own emphases and interests significantly while expounding upon the usefulness of historical study.[5] Next Wilson gave lectures on the sources of Greek and early Roman history.[6] During the balance of the first semester, he proceeded, as he put it in the description written in the autumn of 1886, to alternate weekly between Greek and Roman history until he reached the

1 Printed at Feb. 3, 1885, Vol. 4.

2 See "Wilson Reviews His Course Work at Bryn Mawr," printed at June 1, 1886, and "Wilson's Description of His Courses at Bryn Mawr," printed at Nov. 27, 1886.

3 He listed their names and grades for the entire academic year 1885-86 on several pages in the pocket notebook described at Sept. 21, 1885.

4 The Bryn Mawr "Register of Students, Vol. I" (bound ledger book, PBm) shows Wilson's students taking both Greek history and Roman history throughout the two semesters of 1885-86; and Wilson gave separate (and often different) grades for the two courses in the fall semester.

5 The notes for these lectures are printed at these dates in this volume.

6 The notes for his lecture on the sources of early Roman history are printed at Oct. 1, 1885. It seems reasonable to assume that he gave a comparable lecture on the sources of Greek history, even though the notes for this lecture have not survived.

point, mid-way in the second century B.C., "where Greek history is merged into Roman by conquest."

For this first semester course in Greco-Roman history, notes for only five of the lectures in Greek history have survived.[7] However, Wilson gave a clear description of his coverage during the first semester in the review that he wrote in the autumn of 1886. Moreover, pages 30 through 99 of the first edition of *The State* seem to consist of his Greco-Roman history lectures in revised form.

We have a complete set of notes for Wilson's lectures during the second semester, from early February through early June of 1886.[8] These lectures began with further Roman conquests during the republican era and ended with the establishment of the new "Roman" empire under Charlemagne. There are notes on twenty-four topics in this group. Each was probably written for a single lecture, even though Wilson met his class five times a week, or about sixty times, during the second semester. His letters during the spring of 1886 indicate that he used many class periods for student reports. As the titles of these lectures reveal, Wilson put heavy emphasis on the constitutional and administrative aspects of Roman history, although some of them were brief chronological outlines drawn from standard authorities like Mommsen. Wilson drew upon these second-semester lectures when writing pages 99 through 164 of *The State*.

Wilson's only graduate student at Bryn Mawr during 1885-86, Jane Bancroft, did not arrive at the college until January 1886. Instead of offering formal courses for this single student, Wilson gave her frequent tutorials in European and American political history, emphasizing the Constitutional Convention of 1787, Hamilton's writings, and Marshall's decisions.[9] Wilson's letters to his wife in early June 1886 reveal that he was then meeting Miss Bancroft for an hour every day.[10]

The reader should bear in mind that the lecture notes printed in this and following volumes were prepared only as guides for lectures. Wilson often presented them as synopses and then went on to elaborate, point morals, and draw students into the discussion.[11]

[7] They are printed at Oct. 15, 1885. It is of course possible that these notes were the only ones that he composed for his lectures on Greek history.

[8] They are described at Feb. 9, 1886.

[9] See WW to Lucy M. Salmon, Sept. 8, 1886, and Jane Bancroft Robinson to R. S. Baker, Feb. 1, 1926, RSB Coll., DLC.

[10] e.g., WW to EAW, June 3, 4, and 7, 1886.

[11] For student reminiscences of Wilson as a lecturer at Bryn Mawr, see Leah Goff Johnson to R. S. Baker, March 27, 1926; Mary Tremain to R. S. Baker, Jan. 21, 1926; and Helen A. Scribner to R. S. Baker, March 13, 1926, all in RSB Coll., DLC.

Pocket Notebook

[c. Sept. 21, 1885-c. Aug. 1, 1888]

Inscribed on cover (WWhw):

"Woodrow Wilson, Bryn Mawr 1885"

Contents:

(a) WWhw and WWsh class rolls and grade records for Bryn Mawr students, 1885-87.

(b) WWhw lists, "Books missing: Oct. 30, '85," and "Books to be disposed of," including names of recipients.

(c) Page with WWhw nom de plume, "Edward Coppleston."

(d) WWhw list of certain contributors to Marquardsen's *Handbuch*, described in n. 2 to the book review printed at April 17, 1887.

(e) WWsh brief memorandum about the supremacy of principle over individual self-interest.

(f) WWhw lists of publishers, stores, servants, books, friends, and other persons.

(g) WWhw "Visiting List."

(h) WWhw citation of article in *Revue des Deux Mondes.*

(i) WWhw list of monies received from grass leases in Nebraska, April 11, June 15, and Aug. 18, 1887.

Pocket notebook (WP, DLC).

Notes for Four Lectures on the Study of History

I.   [c. Sept. 24, 1885]
The "Preliminary Age."   (*Analysis*

Almost all recorded history, which is not the history of savages, is the history of nations. Back of the age of history lies a vast "Preliminary Age" compared with whose extent the age of recorded history is short, compared with whose antiquity all recorded history is modern. It is necessary to suppose such a period of preparation in order to account for the existence of nations. Of course nations are new. Their existence presupposes a degree of civilization such as cannot conceivably have been primeval, a regard for law such as we know to have been of late development. Civilization, as we know it, can be traced back to such small beginnings that we can be sure that in the times quite beyond our view its growth was still nearer the rudiments. It is not conceivable that useful or necessary arts once known should h've been lost. Progress lies in the growth of man's ability to make more of himself and to make more out of nature; and such ability, once acquired, is too immensely valuable to be forgotten.

In order to account for the existence of nations, therefore, and of the differences between nations, we must suppose isolated groups in the 'Preliminary Age.' In order to the progress of man there must be the cooperation of *men*; there must exist cooperative groups of men held together by "a felt union of heart and spirit." Such groups could be produced only by the operation of "the authority of 'customary law'," and the development of such an authority required the isolation of groups. They must lie apart in order that their habits, their social union, may crystalize. In this stage, therefore, *trade* is an evil, *war a good*. War was an ab-

solute necessity on the part of each group that other groups unlike itself might be kept at a distance. War, consequently, was
universal. And in this war groups with the best customary law,
with the best family organization, the best religion, prevailed.
Hence, when society emerges into the light of history we find the
patriarchal form of government almost everywhere. So universal
does it seem that we are apt to conclude that it was the common
type of society for all branches of the race. But so much evidence
to the contrary has lately been brought to view (Bibl.)[1] that it is
evident that we were led into error by the fact that the patriarchal
type was *victorious*. Other types were driven out of the choice
places of the original seats of the race and forced to hide them-

[1] Accompanying these notes for lectures is a WWhw bibliography, on a sepa-
rate page, listing, in the following order, Charles F. Keary, *The Dawn of History:
An Introduction to Prehistoric Study* (New York, 1879); George Rawlinson, *The
Origin of Nations* (London, 1877); Walter Bagehot, *Physics and Politics* (New
York, 1873); William E. Hearn, *The Aryan Household* (London, 1879); Lewis
H. Morgan, *Ancient Society* (New York, 1877); John F. McLennan, *Studies in
Ancient History, Composing a Reprint of Primitive Marriage* (London and New
York, 1886); and the "Works" of Sir Henry Maine and Herbert Spencer. Refer-
ences are to the first American edition or, if there was none, to the first Brit-
ish edition. Wilson evidently had an advanced copy of McLennan's *Studies in
Ancient History*; or perhaps it was published in 1885 under an 1886 copyright.
Wilson presumably listed and described the above books at this point in the
lecture.
    Wilson's mention of the "Works" of Herbert Spencer, the first such reference
in documents reflecting Wilson's own research and reading, raises the question
of his acquaintance to this date with the founder of social Darwinism. We are
fortunately not without considerable evidence on this point.
    The first reference to Spencer in the Wilsonian record is in the shorthand
notes that Wilson took in Professor Lyman H. Atwater's course in the history
of civilization in the spring term of Wilson's senior year at Princeton. However,
Atwater apparently made only a passing reference to Spencer. (See the class-
room notes in the scrapbook described at Jan. 1, 1881, Vol. 2.) Wilson's first extensive exposure to the English social philosopher came at the Johns Hopkins.
Davis R. Dewey gave a brief report on *The Principles of Sociology, The Study
of Sociology, The Man versus the State*, and the first volume of *Social Statics* in
Dr. George S. Morris' course in the philosophy of the state on November 5, 1884.
A transcript of Wilson's notes on this report is printed at that date in Volume 3.
Morris followed with his own systematic review of Spencer's works in lectures on
November 12 and 19. Transcripts of Wilson's notes on these lectures are printed
at these dates in Volume 3. In addition, Professor Herbert B. Adams, in his
course on the history of politics, discussed Spencer briefly in a lecture on sovereignty on February 18, 1885. (See the first classroom notebook described at
Oct. 8, 1884, Vol. 3.)
    How much or how little of Spencer that Wilson read between the autumn of
1884 and the late summer of 1885, it is impossible to say. His inclusion of Spencer's "Works" in the bibliography listed at the beginning of this note is no certain evidence that he had read any of them.
    References in future volumes will show that Wilson did occasionally read,
cite, and quote from Spencer. However, it is a fact of no little significance that
Wilson apparently never owned any of Spencer's works. At least none remains
in the Wilson Library in the Library of Congress. It is perhaps more significant
that Dr. Ely, who introduced Wilson to the study of modern economics, apparently never mentioned Spencer in either his undergraduate or his graduate
course in political economy. The editors have not found any reference to Spencer
in the notes that Wilson took in these courses. His notebooks for them are described in Volume 2 at October 3 and December 6, 1883.

selves in obscure corners or pushed on into unoccupied continents. The best institutions very early went out and 'possessed the earth.'

The customary law which was the crystalizing force in such groups grew, probably, by the power of imitation—imitation of successful characters and the repetition of accidentally successful rites and practices. It was possibly the result of haphazard experiment. Once formed, it was all-powerful; every member of the group had to conform, or incur the severest penalties. The group had donned a strait-jacket of observance.

Objects and Methods of Study.

To 'learn history'? *No*—but to learn *from* history. The primary object of study at this stage is to arouse genuine living interest in the subjects of study.

An acquired taste. But one easily acquired.

Do not burden the mind.

Let the primary object of preparation be to understand, not to remember merely. It is sufficient to *see* particulars, details; landmarks must be remembered—there is no other means of keeping to the right road.

Let the paramount object of recitation be reproduction of ideas and impressions—of author's thoughts. Style—ancient Athens

This does not mean, of course, that our object should be entertainment alone. The proper study of history is full of grave effort; but that effort may be made charming.

It may be made so by projecting our own life, the life of our own minds into it. The diagram and the pins. Look into ancient times as if they were our own times, and into our own times as if they were not our own. Suppose that you had yourself wished to thrust Pericles from power, or that Socrates were the grandfather of your college-mate. School your imagination to live the ancient life. Here is the object and use of class reports and of the supplementary lectures proposed

II.   [c. Sept. 25, 1885]
Nations.

The "competitive examination of constant war" promoted general progress by making the best drilled and the best bred groups of men predominant. These war-surviving groups were the *stocks* from which nations sprang. But differing nations sprang from the same stock; Greeks and Romans were of a common parentage. What created the difference—*what are nations*? None of the simple outward conditions of existence, such as difficulties or advantages of soil and influences of climate, explain the diversities amongst nations. Nations totally unlike have arisen and lived under exactly similar outward conditions. We may acknowledge that *race*-making forces are beyond our ken; but cannot we make something out of the *nation*-making forces? Again *imitation* seems the most probable, because the most capable, factor. "A national character is but the successful parish character." (See Newman, 23) There has been, in each instance, "a partial permission of selected change," "an unconscious imitation and encouragement of appreciated character." "The more acknowledged causes, such as change of climate, alteration of political institutions, progress of science, act principally through this cause."

Imitation may result in various ways—according, it would seem, to the earliest forms of a nation's political institutions. There are many stationary nations, whose civilization seems to have been arested—*petrified*, as it were—just as they had become prepared for higher progress. Higher progress came only where there was internal change, and internal change was conditioned principally by political habit. A subordinate element of internal change was *mixture of races*. This, when one race did not altogether absorb the other, produced either variety of character or tasselations of caste. But political conditions were vastly the most important.

III.   [c. Sept. 28, 1885]
Influence of Discussion.

Discussion has been the chief means of throwing off the yoke of customary law, and discussion has strengthened into habit only or chiefly where there has been *government by discussion*. It is thus that internal change has depended so largely upon political institutions. The old, undebateable law was a law of *status*; the new, debated law is a law of reason, of consent, of contract. And this difference is the whole difference between stagnation and progress. We find, in the stationary, customary civilizations of the East, that everything which does not rest upon *status* rests upon individual will. In the changeable, progressive civilizations of the West everything rests upon consent, upon the convictions of the common thought of each nation. The only nations which have made history worth the studying are those which have mixed *counsel* with their principles of political rule—in which from the earliest times elders have freely advised them in the presence of freemen who were at liberty to cry out in assent or in disapproval.

Discussion, once admitted, can with difficulty be thrust out or silenced. It "takes, but does not give." (*"Discuss" a fowl*) But the forms of government which admit discussion must invite a discussion of *principle* or even they cannot provoke growth. The chief nations of history—the nations, namely, which early surrounded their kings with councils, and those councils with listening crowds—did invite contests over principles, as, first of all, notably, over the division of conclusive authority between the few and the many. Should the assent or disapproval of the listening crowd be imperative or not? The Middle Ages witnessed "a return to the period of authoritative usage and an abandonment of the classical habit of independent and self-choosing thought." The car of progress was again set in motion by a reassertion of the popular element in society.

Discussion of guiding principles of government was at first necessarily confined to small states. In them it took its rise and had its early growth. Without printing or any of the modern facilities for the transmission and circulation of thought all discussion must be *heard*—it must be possible for all the free population to come together into one assembly. This is the significance of the small city states of Greece and of the small city states of medieval Italy.

IV.   [c. Sept. 29, 1885]

The Value of Discussion.

The best part of what is now called political liberty owes its existence to discussion. Discussion has been the mother and nurse of all free governments. "A free state means a state in which the sovereign power is divided between many persons, and in which there is a discussion among those persons." And the characteristics of a free state are just those which discussion is surest to produce: namely, order, tolerance, and an active intelligence.

There is a modern tendency to decry discussion, under the contemptuous name of 'talk'; but talk which concerns itself with principles cannot be too much encouraged. (1) It means the substitution of reason for force, and thus of order for anarchy. It creates a disposition to hear both sides and to yield to the voice of the majority. (2) It offers prizes to intelligence by bringing all the faculties into active play. (3) It developes that type of intellect which is the highest of all—namely the "speculative intellect" —by conditioning success on the better argument, on the use of clear-sighted reason, and so compelling a right use of the faculties. (4) Its detective processes discover the truth. (5) It begets tolerance—a very modern product. (6) It turns the old vigour of the race, which once went to produce eager, restless, oftentimes rash action, into channels of clear creative thought, and so produces that calmness without sluggishness and that deliberation without weakness, that "animated moderation," in action which the uncivilized man knows nothing of, but which is the perfect flower of social growth.

WWT MSS. with WWhw emendations (WP, DLC).

Notes for a Classroom Lecture

[c. Oct. 1, 1885]
Sources of Early Roman History.

Roman history did not begin to be written until within about two hundred years of the Christian era (about three hundred years after Herodotus, 484). At that time (the second Punic War) annalists began to write. Of these *Fabius Pictor* and *Cincius Alimentus* were the earliest. They were contemporaries, and wrote, in Greek, accounts of their own times, to which they prefixed brief narratives of the previous history of Rome. Similar annals were written in Latin a little later by *Porcius Cato*. Following these men came a host of like chroniclers, of whom it is worth while to remember *Valerius Antias* as Livy's chief authority.

Contemporary with the first annalists were two *poets*, *Naevius*, who composed an epic on the first Punic War, and *Ennius*, who composed an epic on the second Punic War. Like the annalists, these poets filled their works with the traditions concerning the early history of their city. Poets and annalists alike seem to have agreed upon a body of tradition common to the belief of all Romans. None of them had wit enough to invent,—and, had they invented, they would not have agreed even in substance. Whence did they obtain materials for their accounts of times before their own?

(1) From oral tradition—and oral tradition, though always unreliable because of the accumulation in it of sources of error, may have been less unreliable then when it was a main dependence than it is now when everything may be committed to writing and there is no need to trust the memory. Besides, the Roman, like the Eng., constitution had a slow and orderly growth which gave paramount importance to precedent and so gave great things over in trust to tradition and made it of the utmost importance to public men to cultivate a lively knowledge of the past.

(2) From the traditions of the *Senate*, wh. was a body of members chosen from the No[bility]. and so a body of continuous life, with unbroken traditions and a membership composed of those who had taken the most active part in public affairs.

3) From the records of the sacerdotal corporations. The Augurs were intimately connected with every pub. undertaking—and the pontiffs were official interpreters of the law and annalists of the national history. From very early times down to the time of the Gracchi (131 B.C.) the Pontifex Maximus, the head of the pontifical college, yearly wrote down the most remarkable events of each 12-month and published them on wooden tablets for the information of the people. "These tablets were preserved in the *Regia*, the official dwelling of the chief pontiff, near the temple of Vesta, in the Roman forum." On them were recorded, doubtless, ecclesiastical rather than laical events, but they must still have preserved a thread, however thin, of narrative of the greater facts of the national life. They noted, probably, such events as were considered manifestations of the divine will, as, for instance, pestilences, dearth, famines, inundations, earthquakes, eclipses, foreign wars and civil disturbances.

(4) From other public documents, such as official lists of the annual magistrates, books of law precedents, books of rules and regulations for different public functionaries, and census lists.

(5) Laws and treaties cut on stone or engraved on metal tablets—especially the 12 tables of the Decemvirs.

(6) Public monuments bearing inscriptions.

All public records were probably either partially or totally destroyed at the time of the Gallic invasion (390 B.C.); but they were possibly in large part restored, from memory and other sources afterwards. The 12 tables of the Decemvirs especially, being fundamental to the whole law of the State, were doubtless readily and exactly reproduced.

(7) Family records. Every Roman family had a distinct corporate life of its own and was characterized by an intense pride & a high spirit which gave life and prominence to its separate traditions. Busts, or masks, of the most distinguished members of each family were kept in the *atrium* of the common residence and upon these were inscribed the offices held and the chief public services rendered by the deceased. Elaborate funeral orations reciting the virtues of the dead and the history of the family were pronounced in public whenever a member of the family died. To supply materials for these 'laudations' fam. records were kept. These were probably kept from the earliest time at wh. writing

came into common private use, i.e. from the beginning of the repub.—and frequently recurring laudations would keep alive a sufficient memory of the contents of these records to admit of their being reproduced after the Gallic inroad. Falsifications due to fam. pride &c of course limited the value of these records but they were of more value than any other of the sources mentioned. They constituted the chief materials of the annalists, and were manageable by them because the highest power of the State was so often for long periods together in the hands of a few great fams. that the archives of these fams. would be to all intents and purposes state pub. archives.

WWhw MS. (WP, DLC).

From Richard Heath Dabney

My dear "Tommy":   New York. Oct. 9th, 1885.

I feel almost ashamed to write to you at all, after allowing so long a period to elapse before answering your exceedingly interesting & most welcome letter,[1] and thanking you for the great treat, and, if possible, still greater instruction, which I derived from the perusal of your "Congressional Government."

But I know that you will be lenient with me when I tell you that both letter & book reached me just after my arrival in Heidelberg, to which town I had gone for the express purpose of being quiet and settling down to five months of very hard work—the home-stretch of my race for "Ph.D." And you will be still more inclined to be easy on me when I say that during a large part of my stay there I wrote only postal cards even to my father. I have always loathed the process of cramming up for an examination, and I had about as rough a time of it for this one as ever in my life; for while History, when studied rationally, is an intensely interesting subject, there are few subjects which are so infernally boring to cram up for an *examination*. You can therefore bet your bottom dollar that I was immensely relieved to have the load off my mind when, on Aug. 1st, I succeeded in getting the degree. As my sole reason in attempting it was that I believed it would be easier to obtain a position more easily with than without a degree, I felt no elation at the fact that I had the right to attach if I chose, in future, the caudal appendage of "Ph.D." to my name; but I *did* feel powerfully glad that I was at length done swallowing dates etc. by the bushel.

Well, old fellow, you can hardly imagine my delight at reading your book & the able & just criticisms upon the same; although

I must say that I was not in the least surprised at your writing so masterly a work—having always believed firmly that you were destined to become a darn sight "bigger man than old Grant." But for all that, I am very glad indeed that my predictions concerning you were realized so very *soon*. Many a man—in fact the immense majority of men—would be proud indeed to write such a work at the age of forty-five; but there are few indeed who could write it at your age. Nor must you suppose that I say this on account of my friendship for you. I say it, I believe, as entirely free from bias as did the reviewers of the book. I shall not go into details of criticism & tell you what points about it especially pleased me, but will simply say that I entirely agree with your opinion—which is a *new* one—that the great trouble about our system of government is that both Power & Responsibility are spread over far too great an area—that is, divided up among a host of Standing Committees instead of being concentrated upon a Cabinet Ministry. This is the central thought of the work, and it is in my humble opinion a true one, and of immense importance. I repeat, therefore, what I said in my postal card from Heidelberg: "Bully for you!" I sent my copy to Charley Kent (who has of course returned it to me since) in Göttingen, while I was in Heidelberg, and he, too, liked it immensely, as I need hardly say.

But, to change the subject: let me congratulate you most heartily upon having secured a charming wife—that is, if you carried out your intention of getting married in June. Give her my best regards, & tell her that I don't think she will be offended at my saying that, however lovely and attractive she may be, she has a husband who is in every way worthy of her. . . .

Your sincere friend   R. H. Dabney.

ALS (WP, DLC) with WWhw notation on env.: "Ans. Oct. 28/85."
  [1] WW to R. H. Dabney, Feb. 14, 1885, Vol. 4.

From Raymond Landon Bridgman[1]

Sunday Times Office,
My dear sir,   Boston, Mass., Oct. 10, 1885.

Your name has been mentioned to me among those likely to give favorable consideration to the following plan:

I am thinking of getting a syndicate of leading dailies to take articles once a week of about a column each from the best writers upon the leading problems of national life and government. But it is necessary to secure the writers first, so the papers may know whether it is best to enter the arrangement. In Boston I have already secured Col. Carroll D. Wright, Gen. H. B. Carrington, Hn. F. B. Sanborn and Mr. Gamaliel Bradford. I hope to get so many writers that no one will be called upon very often. Such a series of articles, I think, can be made of much value in the popular discussion of the leading issues of the times. Should you like to have your name added to my list of writers, provided papers enough can be secured to enable me to give a fair price?

Very truly yours,   R. L. Bridgman.

ALS (WP, DLC) with WWhw notation on env.: "Ans. Oct. 20/85."
 ¹ A newspaper correspondent and author of many books.

Notes for Lectures on Greek History

[c. Oct. 15-c. Dec. 1, 1885]
Reforms of Solôn (Solon 638-558)

Drako had given to Athens fixed, definite law: Solôn gave it a fixed and definite constitution. The reforms of Solôn, as usually described, are of two kinds: *political* and *economical*. About the first there seems to be little room for serious doubt; concerning the second various views of varying credibility may be held.

(A) There can be no substantial doubt about his having
  (1) Divided the citizens into four classes (Pentacosio-medimni, Hippeis, Zeugitai, Thetes) according to their wealth, giving citizenship to all, but admitting to offices of importance only Eupatrids possessed of enough wealth to make them *Pentacosiomedimni*; about his having
  (2) Constituted out of the four tribes a Probouleutic ('preconsidering') Senate of 400, chosen from the Eupatrids by the Ekklesia and charged with the duty of preparing all matters to be brought before the latter body, as well as with the duty of summoning and managing its meetings; about his having
  (3) Given to the Ekklesia the privilege of electing and overseeing the Archons; or about his having
  (4) Enlarged the jurisdiction of the Areiopagos by giving it a certain censorship over private morals.
(B). But the evidence is by no means so clear as to the economic reforms attributed to Solôn. The whole question turns upon the amount of credence we vouchsafe to our

chief witness, Plutarch, who wrote, indeed, with Solôn's own account of his work before him, but who may have carried back into the times of the Solonian reforms economic ideas which were of much more recent date. When he wrote it was six hundred years since Solôn's memorable archonship. In the fragments of his writings remaining to us, Solon 'distinctly mentions three things': in this connection (1) The removal of certain pillars from the land. "(2) The enfranchisement of the land. (3) The protection, liberation, and restoration of the persons of endangered or enslaved debtors." By Plutarch and the writers who follow him these statements are interpreted to mean that the small landholders of Attica had borrowed money on mortgage; that they had pledged for their debts not only the land but also their own persons; and that Solôn removed from the land certain stone pillars set up as evidences of mortgage, thus cancelling one evidence of debt, prohibited all forfeiture of personal liberty for debt, thus destroying the other satisfaction of the creditor, and liberated all who were then enslaved because of debt. He is said besides to have debased the coinage for the relief of the richer debtors whose lands and persons were not in danger.

For the debasement of the coinage there is no direct evidence; and the chief objections to the other parts of this view are that it presupposes, without sufficient, indeed without any, proof, the existence of a very modern system of borrowing on mortgage, and that we find mortgages much more in favour at a little later time than they would have been had they been so violently broken up by Solôn.

A more plausible interpretation of these reforms seems to be that the actual cultivators of the soil of Attica held their land by a very precarious tenure of the great Eupatrid owners and were liable to be reduced to actual slavery by these landlords whenever for any reason they failed to pay their rent; and that Solôn, besides liberating men thus enslaved and forbidding all similar slavery in future, removed the pillars which marked the ownership of the Eupatrids and thus gave the small cultivators a chance to acquire inalienable rights to the soil.

(B.C. 509) *Reforms of Clisthens* (Kleisthenes)

Kleisthenes was the creator of democracy in Athens. He destroyed the exclusive political power of the Eupatrids and grafted upon the constitution planted by Solôn the largest popular rights. He was the greatest of Athenian constitutional reformers.

(1.) Setting aside the four great historical tribes as political units, he divided the whole free population of Attica into ten tribes, giving to each the name of a national hero who became its tutelary divinity. These tribes he divided into *demes* or cantons, so distributed that the demes of each tribe, instead of being contiguous, were scattered throughout all Attica. The statues of the ten tutelary heroes of the tribes were erected in the Agora of Athens itself, and it was there that the scattered demes of a tribe met whenever a tribe came together for any purpose.

(2.) He changed the number of Senators from 400 to 500, and caused them to be chosen yearly, by lot, from the whole body of citizens, 50 from each tribe. The Senate also became a permanent body, exercising some of the administrative and judicial functions until that time belonging to the Archons. The office of Senator was the only office thrown open to all citizens indiscriminately by Kleisthenes. All other offices were opened to all who belonged to the first 3 classes of the Solonian property classification, but remained closed to the fourth, or Thetic, class.

(3.) The Ekklesia was made to meet at fixed periods, at least ten times a year, and the greatest freedom of speech was guaranteed to it. It chose every elective officer.

(4.) The collective body of the people exercised, under the name *Heliaea* (a sort of judicial session of the Ekklesia), jurisdiction over all public crimes. Jurisdiction over the graver private crimes remained with the Council of Areiopagos, and lesser crimes, as well as all private causes, continued to be judged by the six mesne archons, the *Thesmothetae*.

(5.) Direction of military and naval affairs was transferred from the Archôn *Polemarchus* to ten Strategoi, or generals, chosen yearly by the Ekklesia, one from each tribe. The Polemarch still, however, shared command in the field, where he was at first given honourable precedence.

(6.) Instituted *Ostracism*.

Kleisthenes broke the ascendency of the Eupatrids by his new tribal division; prevented a rehabilitation of the old local factions of Mountain, Plain, and Shore by his separation of the deme of each tribe; and by means of the O guarded against revolution, thus giving his reforms time to take root and a constitutional, law-abiding spirit time to grow.

The Invasion of the Persians

Before the close of the 6th century, B. C., Persian conquest swept over Asiatic Hellas to the W. shores of the Aegean, and the ambition of Darius was impatient to push even further E.; but the intrigues of three Greeks seem to have been the immediate cause of the invasion of Greece itself by the Persians. These three men were Demokedes of Kroton, Histiaeus of Miletus, and Hippias of Athens.

1. *Demokedes of Kroton.* Kroton was one of the earliest towns of the classical world to produce great physicians, and of her physicians Demokedes was one of the best known. Seeking his fortune through his profession in various parts of Hellas, he at last came into the service of Polykrates of Samos. Upon the murder of Polykrates by the Persian satrap Oroetes, he fell into the hands of the Persians and was sent as a slave to Susa. There he was fortunate enough to be of great service to Darius by curing him of a hurt which had baffled the skill of the Persian quacks. Darius loaded him with gifts and overwhelmed him with favours; but his slavery, though made splendid and luxurios, was still complete, for Darius was determined not to part with so valuable a doctor. Demokedes wanted liberty more than all the honours and luxuries of the Persian court. In order, ∴, to secure his own freedom, he risked the freedom of his nation. He had wrought a great cure upon Atossa, the most influential of the wives of Darius, and he induced her, by way of showing her gratitude, to turn the ambitious schemes of Darius away from Scythia, whither they were then looking, to Greece and gain his consent to sending a small body of his trusted friends to visit the free cities of Hellas under the guidance of Demokedes, for the purpose of gathering information about the resources which might invite conquest. The spies were sent out; Demokedes led them to Italy, escaped from them at Kroton[,] incited the people vs. them, and they returned, robbed and maltreated, to Susa. Both the interest and the passion of Darius were thus aroused against Greece. (Grote, chap. 34)

2. *Histiaeus of Miletus.* But Darius was still bent, first of all, upon an expedition against the Scythians, who, some hundred yrs. before, had put a slight upon the dignity of Persia. Marching through Asia Minor with an immense host, he crossed the Propontis and the Danube on bridges which he had compelled the Greeks to build for him, and set out on a fatal campaign into Scythia. He intended to return into Persia by another route. He, ∴, left the Ionians in charge of the bridge across the Danube

with instructions to destroy it if he did not retreat to it within 60 days. Among these Ionians were Miltiades, despot of the Thrakian Chersonese and Histiaeus despot of Miletus. The 60 days elapsed and Darius had not returned. Some Scythians, however, appeared with the news that Darius had met with desperate reverses and was in full retreat, and with the assurance that the Ionians had only to destroy the bridge in order to secure his utter destruction and their own freedom. But Histiaeus induced his companions to save the Persian power as a prop to their own despotisms. He was rewarded eventually with a splendid slavery at Susa such as Demokedes had endured. Like Demokedes, he jeoparded the liberty of his nation to further his own schemes for gaining liberty and power. The Ionian revolt came to a head at his suggestion. Athens lent her aid to the revolt; and again the anger and ambition of Darius were directed towards Greece. (Grote, chap. 34, text-book, chap. VII, Cox's 'Greek Statesmen,' chaps. on *Aristagoras* & *Miltiades*)

3. *Hippias of Athens.* The definite aim and final impulse of the invasion probably came from Hippias, the expelled tyrant of Athens. Foreseeing the possibility of evil days, Hippias had, before his expulsion, prepared a way for making favour with the Persian masters of Asiatic Hellas by giving his daughter in marriage to the son of the Lampsakene tyrant, Hippoklos, who was very firmly established in the confidence of the Persian court. He had, moreover, early prepared for himself a retreat at Sigeion, an Athenian settlement in the Thrakian Chersonesus, over which he had set first the uncle of Miltiades of Marathon and now Miltiades himself. It was to Sigeion that he betook himself when driven from Athens. He did not at once set afoot his projected intrigues with the Persians. He looked for aid in securing his restoration first of all to Sparta and her Peloponnesian allies. Sparta had very quickly discovered that she had been tricked by the Alkmaionids and the Pythian priestess & had done herself great disservice in assisting to expel the Peisistratid dynasty from Athens, and was now quite ready to retrace her steps in the matter, could she but secure the cooperation of powerful enough allies. A congress of the strongest Peloponnesian states was accordingly called to meet in Sparta in the interest of Hippias and Hippias himself appeared to plead his case. Sparta strongly seconded him. But the Corinthians indignantly refused to take any hand in the proposed restoration; Sparta would not take the field alone; and so the congress broke up, and Hippias, disappointed, turned again to his intrigues in Asia. So notorious were his trea-

sonable negotiations with Artaphernes, the satrap of Lydia, that the Athenians themselves sent an embassy to Sardeis to countermine his plans. This was the second time they had undertaken the mistaken enterprise of enlisting Artaphernes on their behalf. Their first embassy had been worse than a failure. Anticipating from the first the possible designs of Hippias, they had seven years before (509 B.C.) sent to seek a Persian alliance. They had been told that Dareios wd. assist no one who did not send him earth and water as tokens of subjection. The ambassadors had, in their rash eagerness, agreed to accept these humiliating terms. But the Athenians had scornfully refused to regard this base promise of their representatives, and the affair had issued only in ill feeling on both sides. Despite this sad miscarriage of the first negotiations, however, Athens sent commissioners a second time to Artaphernes, in 502 B.C., laid the whole case concerning Hippias before him, and urged every argument of reason and diplomacy to dissuade him from aiding the expelled and disgraced tyrant. But Hippias had played his selfish game well. Artaphernes told the Athenians imperatively, and with something more than a covert threat, that they must restore Hippias. They flatly refused, and went home under the conviction that war had virtually been declared. Considering themselves now open enemies of Persia, they soon after lent their aid to the Ionian revolt, and so increased the debt of wrath owed them by Dareios. "About twelve years later Hippias stood with a Persian host on the field of Marathon." (See Cox's 'Greek Statesmen' ch. on *Peisistratos*.)

[The Peloponnesian War]

The Peloponnesian war destroyed the only strong germs of national union among the Greeks, and so may be taken as an epitome of Greek history. It sums up the strongest force in Greek politics, the force, namely, of disintegration. There was no Greek nation. Hellas was an aggregation, not a union, of Greek towns. Each of these eagerly preferred the weakness of independence to the strength of confederation. Of course the only hope of abiding political power and national independence for the Greeks lay in permanent combination. The Persian invasions, by making united action imperative, had first made it possible; the Delian Confederacy promised to make it permanent, for at least a large part of the Hellenic world.

The pressure of formidable enemies without had forced the cities of continental Greece to act together for the common defence, and so the Persians had been repelled. But, though driven back from Greece itself, Xerxes was still master of the Hellenic states of Asia Minor, and he must be pushed back finally from the Aegean, if Greece was to be permanently safe from his arms. Consequently all the maritime cities of the Aegean must keep together. The Confederacy of Delos was therefore formed, and Athens was placed at the head of it. She had been the real head of Greece at Marathon and Salamis and Mycalê. She now became acknowledged leader in the new confederacy. Her naval power made it impossible for Sparta to cope with her in expeditions beyond sea. She only had adequate means for carrying the war into Asia.

The pact under which the new league was formed was to be permanently binding. Secession was understood among the confederates to be treason to the common cause, and to create a case for coercion. The coercion was to be applied by Athens. Whether in keeping the Persians in check or in keeping the confederates together, Athens and Athens alone was to exercise the armed force of the Confederacy. But the lesser states of the league were disinclined to war, and commuted the services owed by them for money contributions. Athens was thus made the only *acting* member, as well as the controlling and compelling member, of the Confederacy. Confederacy, therefore, gradually, almost imperceptibly, but quite naturally slid into Athenian Empire. It was not the ambition of Athens, but her Pan-Hellenic sympathies, which led to the formation of the Confederation; nor was it Athenian ambition which changed confederacy into empire. First and last, during all this greatest period of Grecian history, Athenian leadership was the only genuine bond of Pan-Hellenism. With its rise Grecian history culminates; with its fall, Grecian history begins to decline.

The Peloponnesian war again broke Hellas into fragments. It restored Spartan leadership, which was a leadership merely of force. We shall find Spartan leadership speedily giving place in turn to Theban supremacy, and that to Macedonian empire, which is to prove but a preparation for Roman conquest.

Supremacy of Thebes (371-361)

The supremacy of Thebes may be taken as a type of all non-Athenian rule in Hellas. Her government was not confederate but coercive, not for common Grecian ends, but for selfish Theban ends. The aims of Athenian empire had been Athenian, but they had been more than that: they had been Hellenic as well. Athens had been the head of a close league of self-government communities which she had kept together by guaranteeing them their own local govts., and freedom from foreign interference, whether from Persia or Sparta. Thebes, like Sparta, knew no other means of keeping her hold upon her allies but by putting garrisons in their citadels. She could not organize dominion. This explains the fact that her supremacy began and ended with the personal ascendency of Epaminondas. He impersonates Thebes during the only period at which Thebes deserves our serious attention. In moderation of counsel and unselfishness of motive Epaminondas was like our own Washington; in accomplishments he was like no one so much as Perikles; in military genius he was the prototype of the great Napoleon. He was able to keep life in Theban power for a time by doing what was very un-Theban, by domineering her subject states as little as possible, by being content, so far as practicable, with the position of peremptory arbitrator amongst them, by keeping the power of Thebes always ready rather than by making it continually felt. This was distinctly the policy of Epaminondas, not of Thebes. Thebes ruled like a monarchy with direct coercion; Epaminondas would have had her rule like a democracy, as Rome did rather than as Spain does, by considerate headship rather than by compulsive mastery.

The death of Epaminondas at Mantineia left Greece without a head: for it left Theban power nerveless and helpless and there was no other city powerful enough to take her place. Sparta was without resources and without capable leaders, and Athens, the only state which had ever promised to have a greatness larger than the greatness of her leaders, a strength which did not die with her generals, was still only half recovered from the ruinous desolation of 404. The collapse of Theban power left Greece again helplessly disintegrate, in just that situation of city against city, jealousy everywhere, but strength to wreak spite nowhere, which was to make Macedonian conquest easy. The young Philip had lived as a hostage in Thebes during the stirring times of Theban supremacy: he may have seen, even then, that his own great fortunes were being prefaced by the struggle which he was witnessing. Theban supremacy was the last glory of central Greece.

Must not fall into mistake of taking Athens as typical of Greece.

Democratic empire vs. monarchical empire—*Eng.*, *Rome*. Athens, tho. she understood empire better than the other cities, did not understand it perfectly.

v. Grecian colonization.—*French* & *Spanish* colonization.

What was of Epaminondas was not Theban. Theban supremacy in so far as it was Theban (Orchomenus) was only a little worse than the Spartan.

Even Epaminondas less wise than Perikles—witness attempt to establish naval power for Thebes.

Collapse at Mantineia

New Athenian Empire—weakness. Mistake in removing the check upon Macedon furnished by Olynthian league.

Comparative degeneracy of Athenian democracy—the absolutism of the δημος, unbalanced by Senate or Areiopagos. Latter filled with *lot-archons*, &c.

WWhw MSS. (WP, DLC).

From Robert Bridges

Dear Tommy: New York Oct 21–1885

I have just finished using the scalping knife on a Boston novel, a little ceremony which I honestly enjoy.[1] The whole lot of them are lacking in vigor, and honest American sentiment and faith. I look for the new day in the South and West (perhaps in Pennsylvania.) But, as Bromley of the *Tribune*[2] once said to Clarence Cook, I have "scraped up the gore and feathers," and am in a peaceful frame of mind for a long delayed talk with you. . . .

Here I sit and read or write at least five evenings in the week. I have all the extra work which I can conveniently do, and some which I have long planned which I cannot get at. The opportunity, I doubt not, will present itself. If it does not I will make it. . . .

This is a very "scrappy" letter, resembling the *Condensed Despatches* in the *Eve Post*. However, I expended my energy on the Boston novel.

Let me hear from you soon. It is a busy world, and our interests are divergent, but the old friendship never. Remember me kindly to Mrs. Wilson.

Your friend   Bob Bridges

ALS (WP, DLC) with WWhw notation on env.: "Ans. Dec. 20/85."

[1] Bridges was referring to William Dean Howells' *The Rise of Silas Lapham*. His unsigned review appeared in the Saturday supplement of the New York *Evening Post*, Oct. 24, 1885. Bridges conceded that Howells' characterization of Lapham was brilliant but deplored the novel's lack of "inspiration."

[2] Isaac Hill Bromley, on the editorial staff of the New York *Tribune*, 1873-82 and 1891-98.

From Raymond Landon Bridgman

Sunday Times Office,
Dear sir,   Boston, Mass., Oct. 22, 1885.

Should the newspapers favor my scheme as cordially as the writers with whom I have corresponded, a beginning will certainly be made, but I have not secured yet as many writers as I wish before submitting the plan to the papers. When that is done and as soon as enough favorable replies have been received to warrant me in going on, I will inform each one who has agreed to write. As it will be near or during the session of Congress at that time, I shall like, for the earlier articles, something upon important pending legislation, such as the silver coinage, or the national bankrupt law, or the tariff, or our Indian relations, or matter of like importance. I shall ask for voluntary contributions as soon as convenient from specialists on those topics, but shall probably have to make particular requests for the first three or four articles, so the scheme may be put promptly in motion. . . .

Among the writers now secured are Col. Carroll D. Wright, Gen. H. B. Carrington, F. B. Sanborn, Gamaliel Bradford, Prof. W. G. Sumner, Prof. W. T. Harris, Col. T. W. Higginson, Prof. Alex. Johnston, Prof. Richard T. Ely, President J. H. Seelye (if possible), S. David Horton, Prof. John B. McMasters, Prof. Henry C. Adams, the Rev. A. E. Winship (the Mormon question), Prof. F. W. Taussig and the Rev. R. W. Memminger of Charleston, S. C.
Very truly yours,   R. L. Bridgman.

ALS (WP, DLC) with WWhw notation on env.: "Ans. Oct. 26/85."

To Raymond Landon Bridgman

Dear Sir: Bryn Mawr, Pa., 26 Oct./85

Your favour of the 22nd received. I am quite willing to come under your plan as you have outlined it. I have never made a *specialty* of economic questions, and could, consequently, enter upon the discussion of such matters as the coinage, bankrupt laws, and the tariff, not as a specialist, but only as a student of the practical applications of political science to state policy—as a student, that is, of practical politics, of statecraft. My special preparation lies in that direction, and I shall be glad to avail myself of your plan, should it be successfully realized, to throw what light I can upon the constitutional and political bearing of national questions.
Very sincerely Yours,   Woodrow Wilson

ALS (WC, NjP).

To Richard Heath Dabney

My dear Heath,   Bryn Mawr, Pa., 28 Oct., 1885

Your thrice welcome letter w'd. have been answered long ago, if Mrs. W. hadn't been sick[1] and all my leisure time, consequently, given diligently to nursing her. What a letter that was for true dramatic effect! Written in New York! It was worth three written in Germany just for the suggestion it brought that mayhap I *might*, by some delightful turn of fortune, see your dear old 'phiz' soon again, oh thou illim'table idiot, thou very ass! Lippitt, Lippitt, Lippitt! Getting you back on the same continent again is almost as good as getting you back on East Range.[2] It seems like *neighborhood* after having the Atlantic between us.

Yes, my dear fellow, I did indeed carry out my purpose of marrying in June and a wonderfully happy man I am for it—happier than I ever dared to hope I should be. I was desperately in need of such a companion as Mrs. W. makes to turn my thoughts away from morbid contemplation of my own frames of mind and still more morbid weighings of the value of my own thoughts. I needed to be absorbed by somebody else—and I am. My mind and heart alike expand under the new influences.

But that's rhapsody enough for one letter. Say what I might, you wouldn't take my diagnosis of the case for a scientific one. I can do nothing but ask you to credit my assurance that, in any view of the matter, this is incontestable, that the *treatment* has proved absolutely successful. The treatment is, you must allow, the test of the diagnosis.

And now, old fellow, for what you say of "Congressional Government." For your generous praise I am sincerely grateful; it made me gladder than I know how to tell you, because I know that you would not utter it unless you meant it, and I am gladder to have you mean it than I know how to say. But for your agreement with the views of the book I am more than grateful. Nothing could gratify me more. If agreement had been the burden of the other letters I have received about the little volume, I should be a very proud and hope-full chap, I can tell you. For, if ever any book was written with fulness and earnestness of conviction, with purpose of imparting conviction, that book was: and, in my view, the extent to which it realizes that purpose is the standard of its success. Of course I should like to be able to believe that it was to stand as a permanent piece of constitutional criticism by reason of some depth of historical and political insight: but its mission was to *stir* thought and to carry irresistible practical suggestion, and it was as such a missionary that it carried my hopes and ambitions with it. I carefully kept all advocacy of particular reforms out of it, because I wanted it to be, so far as I could make it such, a permanent piece of work, not a political pamphlet, which couldn't succeed without destroying its own reason for being; but I hoped at the same time that it might catch hold of its readers' convictions and set reform a-going in a very definite direction. So that, your agreement is the greatest, the most substantial, the most valued compliment you could pay me—and I should like to wring your hand for it!

I am sincerely glad to hear of your Heidelberg Ph.D. You are altogether right about its market value—it is a highly valuable, almost indispensable, ticket of credit, label of quality. I am afraid I shall sooner or later feel the lack of a like stamp. It ought to be— it will be—capital for you; and, if you find any difficulty in getting a position, it will be only because history is taught in such a ridiculously, such a shamefully small number of colleges in this country. Of course I shall keep my eyes open on your behalf for next year.

I haven't left myself time to speak of my work here. I can say, however, that I am enjoying it, improving under it, and find the girls interested and intelligent. More another time. Write to me whenever you can, whatever you will.

As ever,   Your very sincere friend,   Woodrow Wilson

ALS (Wilson-Dabney Correspondence, ViU).
   1 Ellen was having a difficult time during her first pregnancy.
   2 Here Dabney inserted "He meant *West*." The reference is to Wilson's room at the University of Virginia.

To Walter Hines Page[1]

My dear Mr. Page,   Bryn Mawr, Pa., 30 Oct., 1885
   I trust that you will pardon my delay in answering your kind letter of Oct. 7. The task of setting in motion the department of history in a new college and the serious illness of my wife have combined to deprive me of all leisure, and so have cut me off from all letter-writing.

I thank you very much indeed for your appreciative reference to my book, and I am sincerely glad to hear that you have a special appetite for serious political and economic study. Here I have no associates who are more than mildly interested in the topics I care most for, and I assure you that the conversation you wish for, about 'half a hundred topics' suggested by "Cong. Govt." would delight me beyond measure. It would give me a chance to let off some of the enthusiasm I am just now painfully *storing up* in enforced silence. I am afraid that I cannot often find time to get away to New York; but I shall take pleasure in looking you up, should I go there.

I am just about to write to Dr. Ely, the Sec'y of the new Economic Association, and I will take great pleasure in mentioning your name for membership. I shall also ask him to see that a circular of the publications of the Dept.[2] be sent you. In moving I have lost sight of the one I had, else I should send you that, with the Constitution &c. of the Economic Association which I shall send with this letter.

I have been put upon the Association's Committee on Local Govt. Have you no thoughts that might be serviceable in that field? But, whether you have or not, I shall be glad to hear from you whenever you can write to me.

Very sincerely Yours,   Woodrow Wilson

ALS (Page Papers, MH).

[1] Page had recently left Raleigh to engage in newspaper work in New York, principally for the New York *Evening Post*.

[2] That is, the Department of History and Political Science of the Johns Hopkins.

From Joseph Ruggles Wilson

Very dear Son—   Clarksville, Novr 4, 1885

How often we think about you—how often we speak of you—you cannot guess: still less with what tenderness our hearts whisper together concerning you:—and then, never a thought is directed youward but that has a wing which bears it equally towards dear Ellie—for truly you are both as one to us.

Then, why do we not write more frequently? A conundrum hard to solve, and I may as well " ' 'tup." In fact you must not ask such posers even "into yourself"—for we hear them all the same (among the echos of our own consciences, perhaps?) and, hearing, are troubled.

Yet, truth to tell, we have been surpassingly busy since our Tennessee advent—and, for that matter we still are steeped to the lips in domesticities and collegisticies:—for, having just gotten moved (although never snugged) we are preparing, ahem! to move again. In all this I might think your dear mother's experience a tough and ever tougher one, were she not always wearing the smile which a heart of courage lends to fortitude. Her pluck is immense. For weeks her own cook (and the best we have ever had: I write it with a loving tear) amid all the elements of con-

fusion which she alone was, every hour, reducing to order as by
a miracle—this, in a house almost as mean as a house could be
whose outlook upon vacancy is rivalled only by its dreary inlook
—with callers many, long-sessioned, and inane many a time (herself not being able to call anywhere the while)—each night going
to bed tired, pressed by the necessity for a day-light rising—&c.
&c—she yet has made all things bright by her illuminating patience! Help me to feel proud of her, you two younglings who
would be so glad to help *her* in every way! I am far from complaining in her behalf: that were a heresy. When *she* complains,
then may *I* complain—and that will be—never. Although I do think
that, like Mark Tapley,[1] at Eden, she has had occasion to adjudge
it meritorious to be jolly. And, when she reads what I have thus
written, she will emphatically let drop one heavy word, nonsense!
Meaning thereby that she doesn't in the least understand—so unconscious is her ripe goodness!

As for myself—to make a long and sharp descent—my days are
too well filled with work to admit a chink for the grumbling which
otherwise would become habitual. I have, it is true, only one class-
hour per diem—yet, to prepare for this, hoc labor est both diurnal
and nocturnal. The circle of my students is composed of ten likely youths, to whom theology is a wilderness, but out of the thickets
whereof they are slowly emerging into patches of surprising day.
As a science it is a wonderful study, but a *study* sure enough: and
I am trying to make it step by step so clear as that my young men
will suppose I know very little about it!

Josie is moving through his studies at an even pace, which will
get faster and surer when his mind is fairly awake to their importance[.] Meanwhile he is doing well and ever well-er. Every
body likes him, besides, and he seems to like every body (almost)[.] Last month he achieved "excellent" from every professor
save one who gives such long lessons (in mathematics, algebra,
viz) as to render it well nigh impossible for him to keep up with
a class ahead of him to start with.

Next week we expect to begin fixing up our new and very pretty
and most eligible home—a full account of which I leave to the
facile pen of materfamilias.

Be sure that we were greatly moved by your report of dear Ellie's illness—but, somehow, we knew that it would come out all
right—especially as she, too, is a brave little woman who will not
succumb until she must. Your last letter reassured us.

I wish you could find time to give us a minute account of your
work, and its prospects.

This is a long letter for *me* to write. I am compelled now to close—and I quit with assurances of more love for you both from us all than can be put into syllables.   Your affc   Father.

ALS (WP, DLC).
¹ A character in Dickens' *Martin Chuzzlewit*.

From Elgin Ralston Lovell Gould[1]

My dear Wilson: Washington, D. C., Nov. 9 1885.

I have been intending to write to you for the last six weeks, but have had scarcely any opportunity of doing so. I am occupied every day from 9 A.M. to nearly midnight with my professorial duties and my report to the gov't. embodying the results of my summer's investigations.

I had a busy summer of it and learned more than in any other two years of my life. I met and became acquainted with representatives of all classes in Belgium and Germany, from nobility and ministers of state down to the humblest laborer. I am happy to say that I succeeded in almost everything I set out to accomplish, in fact as the Bureau of Labor informed me, far more than they expected could be accomplished. I have received the highest praise for my work from the Hon. C. D. Wright, Com. of Labor —the highest praise he could give any one. Don't think me egotistical for mentioning this, but I only do so to old friends. I never worked so hard before in my life and I was never so highly rewarded in Knowledge to my self, in anything I ever before undertook. I came back however with the firm conviction that the most useful part of economic study is gleaned from observations of the forces actually at work in practical business life. I hope for an opportunity of having a long talk with you on these questions.

While abroad, I became intimately acquainted with Emil de Laveleye. After a conversation with him upon American institutions etc., I presented him with a copy of your book. He was very much interested and praised it in the highest terms. He came to talk it over with me four or five times afterwards. You will doubtless be pleased to know that he intends to write for a forthcoming number of the "Nineteenth Century," an article on "Recent Phases of Democracy in the United States"[2] on the basis of your book and as a companion to his recent article on the same subject as applied to Switzerland. This will be a fine European boom for you. I thanked him much on your behalf and encouraged the idea. If you could send me a couple of copies of your book now, I could make use of them in Berlin and Ghent much to your advantage.

I met this summer Mr. G. Harrison Smith, Vice-Consul General at Berlin, an old Virginian friend of yours. I also had the pleasure of a call from Mrs. Rennick the other evening.

I congratulate you on your marriage and wish you every success in your labors.   Yours faithfully,   E. R. L. Gould

ALS (WP, DLC) with WWhw notation on env.: "Ans. Nov. 11, 1885."

[1] Born Oshawa, Ontario, August 15, 1860. A.B., Victoria College (later part of the University of Toronto), 1881; Ph.D., the Johns Hopkins, 1886. Did research for the Bureau of Labor, 1885-92; lecturer at the Johns Hopkins, 1892-97, and at Columbia University, 1901-1902. Professor of Statistics, University of Chicago, 1895-96. Eminent authority on the social conditions of workers. In 1896 he organized a corporation in New York to build low-cost housing and was active in various reform and civic movements. Died August 18, 1915.

When he wrote this letter, Gould was teaching in a Washington high school and had just spent the summer in Europe conducting certain investigations for the Bureau of Labor headed by the distinguished statistician, Carroll D. Wright.

[2] De Laveleye's article never appeared in the *Nineteenth Century*.

To Albert Shaw

My dear Shaw,   Bryn Mawr, Pa., 11 Nov., 1885

I had to write to Dr. Ely in order to answer your question[1] about the time at which the history of the American economists might be expected.[2] My contribution to it was complete before I left Baltimore in June; but Dewey and Dr. Ely have found their plans constantly changing and their work steadily growing with the changes of plan, until now they cannot promise to be ready for going to press before next Spring. The question which I am now trying to get Dr. Ely to answer is, whether or not my mss. is still suited to fit the place originally intended for it. I am much too busy here to hope to find time to recast what I wrote for him: but I am quite willing to put my material at his disposal and step out of the role of author into that of one who lends his aid and gets thanks in the preface.

I am glad to hear that you are making such rapid strides in the matter of salary, but I must say that I am sorry to hear that those strides involve being "tremendously busy." I know that you do the very best of editorial work, and I am by no means inclined to underrate the influence of a mammoth weekly like the *Tribune*:[3] but I wish, my dear fellow, most devoutly, as I know you yourself do too, that you were within sight of a chance to write something of permanent value and influence in politics or economics. Tell me the minute you have the faintest hope of having such an opportunity, that I may rejoice with you.

The young women here have begun their work finely—and I

am enjoying my occupations here, so far, very thoroughly. I am really learning some history.

As ever,   Your very sincere friend,   Woodrow Wilson

TCL (in possession of Virginia Shaw English).
    1 Shaw's letter to which Wilson was replying is missing.
    2 See the Editorial Note, "Wilson's 'History of Political Economy in the United States,'" Vol. 4.
    3 Shaw was still an editor of the *Minneapolis Daily Tribune*. Perhaps he was chief editor for the Sunday edition.

EDITORIAL NOTE
WILSON'S FIRST WRITINGS ON ADMINISTRATION

Wilson's reference in his letter to Elgin R. L. Gould of November 11, 1885, to "work upon Comparative Systems of Administration"[1] is the earliest evidence in the correspondence in the Wilson Papers of the beginning of Wilson's writing in the field of administration.

Wilson had been introduced to this subject by Dr. Richard T. Ely at the Johns Hopkins in the second semester of the academic year 1884-85.[2] Ely, in his brief survey course, had concentrated upon bibliography, the emerging science of statistics, and methods of administration in Great Britain, Germany, and France. Wilson seems to have profited most from Ely's bibliographical references and commentaries, for we find Wilson later returning again and again to his notes taken in Ely's lectures for bibliographical guidance. However, it seems reasonable to assume that Ely's lectures were most significant for Wilson because they stimulated him to begin to think about the assimilation of European administrative systems into the American democratic polity. However that may have been, Wilson left no record of his developing ideas on this subject between the early months of 1885 and November of that same year. He seems to have focused his thoughts for the first time when he sat down, in early November, to write the article, "Courtesy of the Senate," printed as the first of the following documents, for he used this subject as a springboard for a discussion of the larger problem of how democracy could make professional civil servants responsible to public opinion without impairing their efficiency.

Wilson's first article addressed exclusively to this question was "The Art of Governing." One can only conjecture about the catalyst of this new thrust in Wilson's thought, but it seems to have been his reading of Johann Bluntschli's *Politik als Wissenschaft*, the third volume in Bluntschli's *Lehre vom Modernen Stat* (Stuttgart, 1876), which Ely had discussed extensively in his lectures.

In any event, Wilson first put his thoughts on paper in a brief preliminary essay or outline entitled "Notes on Administration." It is printed as the second of the following documents. Wilson then wrote out a first draft of "The Art of Governing." He later interleaved about

    1 The quotation is from E. R. L. Gould to WW, Dec. 15, 1885, answering Wilson's missing letter of November 11, 1885.
    2 See WW to ELA, Oct. 6, 1884, n. 1, and the classroom notebook described at Oct. 10, 1884, both in Vol. 3.

two thirds of its pages into the first draft of his famous article, "The Study of Administration," published in 1887.[3] Next Wilson wrote out a revised second draft of "The Art of Governing." It is printed as the third of the following documents.

"Notes on Administration" and "The Art of Governing" were, without any doubt, written between November 1, 1885, and November 1, 1886. However, certain clues indicate strongly, perhaps conclusively, that Wilson wrote these two pieces at about the same time that he composed "Courtesy of the Senate." First, there is his reference in his letter to Gould to his work on comparative systems of administration. Second, the handwriting of "Notes on Administration" and of both the first and second drafts of "The Art of Governing" is Wilson's script of late 1885 and very early 1886, becoming, among other things, more compact and angular. Comparison of the handwritings of "Notes on Administration" and of the two drafts of "The Art of Governing" with the handwriting of the first draft of "The Study of Administration" leaves little doubt that the former were written in late 1885 and the latter in late 1886.

The progression from "Notes on Administration" to the final draft of "The Study of Administration" is another example of Wilson's method as a writer. From an essay or outline in which he set down his first thoughts, he wrote the more elaborate piece, "The Art of Governing." He does not seem to have tried to publish it, although he may have given it as a speech about which we have no evidence. Nearly a year later, when given an opportunity to present a major paper before a scholarly audience, Wilson went back to "The Art of Governing" and used long portions of it in his new essay, "The Study of Administration."

The three essays printed below make it clear that Wilson's concept of administration was still quite inchoate in late 1885, and that he was in process of working toward a definition of the field that would be relevant in a democratic political system. He achieved this definition in "The Study of Administration," but, as materials in this and following volumes will reveal, "The Study of Administration" was merely the foundation upon which he would build in the future.

[3] See the Editorial Note, "Wilson's 'The Study of Administration,'" and "The Study of Administration," printed at Nov. 1, 1886.

Three Essays on Administration

[c. Nov. 15, 1885]

The "Courtesy of the Senate"

What is euphemistically called the "courtesy of the Senate" hardly deserves so soft a name. It is in fact a very sorry, unseemly thing. It is part of the etiquette of political management, one of the proprieties of the perfected caucus. This "courtesy," if established by invariable wont, would require, that, whenever a nomination is sent in by the President of the United States to the Senate, the wishes of the senators from the State in which the duties of the office affected are to exercised should be conclusive as to concurrence or rejection; provided, of course, that this privilege be not extended in its fulness to any senator who is not of the President's own party. It could be applied only with great embarrassment in a Senate whose majority were not of the President's party. A different code of "courtesy" would have to be devised in such a contingency.

There is, of course, a respectable side to senatorial "courtesy." Otherwise, it could never have gained a footing in so respectable a body. It has a garb which would naturally commend it to grave and discreet men; and in that garb it unquestionably first won recognition in the Senate. If a federal appointment is to be conferred in New York, it will probably be conferred on a New-York man; and it is pretty safe to conclude that the senators from New York will know more about the candidate than their fellow-members know. It is natural that their opinion as to his fitness should carry great weight. It may be safe in many cases to regard it as conclusive. But this is not "courtesy:" it is mere common-sense, and in no sense exclusively senatorial. The "courtesy" arises when such opinions of individual senators concerning appointments have been accorded, by tacit custom, a *right* to control as conclusive. The common-sense is acceptable and commendable; the "courtesy" is dangerous, and in the end will assuredly become corrupt.

Of course the most open enemy of senatorial "courtesy" is that principle of civil-service reform which is fast becoming regnant in our national politics. As the conquests of that principle advance, this doubtful practice of the Senate must disappear. Here comes into view one of those curious constitutional sinuosities, which have been, and apparently must ever be, so frequent in our national politics. The Senate's supervision of nominations is constitutionally imperative, and yet the logical outcome of decisive competitive examination in all grades of the civil service must be to make the performance of that duty by the Senate eventually merely nominal as regards all non-political offices. The odd feature of the case is, that these facts occasion little or no embarrassment in our political growth. By common consent, civil-service reform must grow, and stretch its branches far and wide, even though its roots do spread themselves in such a way as inconveniently to encroach upon and cramp certain constitutional principles. That ingredient of "time" is accordingly already apparent, which is to push the "courtesy" of the Senate into the background as an antiquity. Its interest will soon be little more than historical, so far as the Senate itself is concerned.

But the "courtesy" of the Senate must, for a long time yet, be worth looking into by every student of practical politics. As a sample of like practices in other spheres, its importance is only too likely to endure. In the matter of supervision of executive appointments, the pattern of the federal constitution has been reproduced, not only in State constitutions, but even in city charters. The "courtesy" of the Senate is but the biggest type of a practice extending throughout almost all our political systems, great and small. Wherever one set of persons is charged with superintending, with an absolute right of veto, appointments made by another authority outside themselves, a similar "courtesy" finds quick growth.

The same sort of courtesy exists, for instance, in most city councils, with whom rests the power of confirming or rejecting nominations made by the city's mayor; and it exists in them with much more vigor, with much more stringent force, than it has ever attained in the Senate. The ordinary townsman, who is not schemingly active in municipal affairs, must make a decided effort if he would understand the perfected pettiness of that business of patronage which controls the administrative side of the town's corporate life. No function of city government, not even the sweeping of the streets, is too humble to come within the view of its minute and inflexible rules. The mayor practically appoints no one of his own free choice. If he attempts to appoint a lamplighter in Ward No. 1, who is not a personal friend and political adherent of the councilman from that ward, his nominee is sure to be rejected. Every councilman knows that his place in the council can be retained, his hand in politics be kept, only by securing offices for the men who have managed his own nomination in the primaries; and all councilmen combine accordingly to prevent in Ward No. 1 what would be fatal to themselves if done in their own wards. So long as primaries can be managed, every councilman feels that it is out of the question to act upon any nomination without regard to the management of them. Ward politics must determine ward appointments, and not ward appointments only, but so far as possible all others, great and small, within the city's gift.

This is, speaking by close analogy, the "courtesy" of the town council. The only thing that ever, even for a time, breaks the usage is public opinion. The publicly approved merit of some officer of long service, or of honestly won popularity, suffices, oftentimes for long periods together, to assure him of repeated nominations and confirmations; and, during those constantly but irregularly recurring seasons of active and conscientious popular interest in the reform of town administration, numerous merit appointments are made with prompt docility by mayor and council. But generally public opinion does not care to trouble its head about the small things of town administration. Though it may sometimes demand an efficient mayor or an honest and capable city treasurer or assessor or superintendent of police, it seldom, if ever, inquires into the antecedents or abilities of under-officials of the rank and file of the service. Its virtuous attempts to see things worthily and efficiently done seldom disturb the tenure of the city-hall janitor or of the crossing-sweeper. The "courtesy" of the council, by no means scorning small things, steadily and quietly controls the filling of these humbler posts, however often it may be postponed in the filling of the bigger places.

Evidently, therefore, the "courtesy" obtaining in the small confirming councils of which the country is full is likely to last much longer in its obscure sphere than can that of the Senate in its prominent sphere. The "courtesy" of the Senate labors under the disadvantage of affecting, for the most part, only big places. It could never, therefore, be either so thorough or so habitual as the similar practice of a town council. Federal offices are naturally very conspicuous offices; and amongst federal offices, those whose filling is supervised by the Senate are the most conspicuous. Nominations constitute the "personal" column of the Senate's docket. "Man," said Goethe, "is properly the *only* object that interests man," which is another way of saying that gossip is natural; and senatorial action on nominations furnishes the most tempting food for political gossip. Very earnest men discuss principles, and often succeed in interesting others in those principles; but interest in the characters and careers of men is spontaneous. *Embodied* principles—principles, good or bad, which make a figure in known characters—are the only principles which make interest for themselves. Accordingly, the action of the Senate on nominations never goes long unwatched, and senatorial "courtesy" must be very sly if it would be active.

Considering, therefore, the interruptions which such a practice must constantly suffer in the Senate, perhaps the "courtesy" of a town council should be taken as the principal (because the least variable) type, and the Senate's merely as a subordinate example. An invariable rule is scientifically more serviceable than a rule with constant exceptions. At any rate, the "courtesy" of the Senate is not only illustrated by practices prevalent in town councils and other like overseers of executive choice, but the importance of discussing it consists in that likeness. It is interesting, as I have already said, as the biggest example of what many lesser political bodies are constantly doing with the most pernicious administrative results. It points, in a conspicuous sphere, a political moral, which is to be quite as plainly read in numberless narrower spheres. It is the biggest "sum" of its kind in our book of political problems; but there are scores of smaller ones just like it, and if any thing more difficult to solve.

Abuses such as are represented in these problems simply open wide again the question, How is patronage best controlled? Patronage is best directed by competitive tests uniformly and impartially applied, no doubt; but there must be some one authority—there had best be some one person—who is ultimately responsible for all abuses. You give responsibility an underground passage when you run it through the counsels of a consulting body like the Senate or a town council; and you must perform in each case the impossible task of digging away the whole superimposed mountain before you shall discover how the stream was made up, which finally issues forth. The attention which public opinion gives to federal nominations strengthens the hands of the President; but there is seldom any such support to be had by the city mayor, who is held responsible for bad administration without being vouchsafed the means of really controlling it. He has to use the indifferent, unsound tools put into his hands by other men with aims of their own, and those aims not generally the aims of efficient administration. We cannot get good mayors on such terms. Skilled, capable workmen will not do themselves the injustice of using this old-fangled machinery, of mistaken invention.

What shall we say, then? That we much prefer trusting one man at a time with power of appointment? By all means. We can punish or reward one man at a time easily and with clear justice. A crowd of men, a committee, a board, a council, a senate, it is impossible to punish, and undesirable to reward. The best limitation of executive power of appointment is to be found in clear responsibility and the advice of a board of civil-service examiners. The justice of public examination is to be preferred to the "courtesy" of private consultation.

Bryn Mawr College.   Woodrow Wilson.

Printed in the Boston *Citizen*, i (Feb. 1886), 1-2.

[c. Nov. 15, 1885]

Notes on Administration

Neither the practice nor the theory of administration has ever been reduced to a science either in this country or in England.

There may be much difference of opinion as to the *need* for a perfected theory; but there can be no difference of opinion as to the need for a perfected practice.

The Germans and French have done most in developing a *science* of administration. May this not be because administration has been made for them by a supreme central authority, so that they have been able to stand aside and speculate about it? We have had no local administration bidden and controlled by a central head, but have had to make our administration for ourselves, piece by piece, now a little and again a little—from hand to mouth —and have been too busy about the work to stop to speculate about it. A theory of navigation is useful to sailors—but they haven't time to think much about it in a high wind, much less to construct the like for themselves—that must be done on land—in a house.

Perhaps the task of developing a science of administration for America should be approached with a larger observance of the *utilities* than is to be found in German or French treatment of the subject. The *administration* should be subservient to the *politics* (to adopt Bluntschli's distinction), the theoretical avowedly only a reason for the practical, statesmanship first, doctrine second— the what-to-do always pressing on to the how-to-do-it.

We must have a new machine of government—a machine which may have *thought* for one of its motive powers, by having officers through whose interest in the public thought, and capacity for catching it, is to be controlled.

Men cannot be got to vote for principles—they may be counted on to vote for *men* with alacrity: the problem is to make them vote for men who embody principles.

One great difficulty about discussing administration is that we cannot point out clearly to everybody just where it resides in the various departments of any practicable government without descending to particulars so numerous as to confuse and so furnish no elucidation. No lines of dermarcation can be run between the great departments which everybody knows without being run up hill and down dale—over heights of distinction and through dense jungles of statutory enactment—hither and thither around 'ifs' and 'buts,' 'whens' and 'howevers,'—until they are altogether lost to the common eye which does not know how to use a telescope of logical discernment.

Then, too, administration wears such various shapes and garbs that not everybody can tell it when he sees it. A great deal of administration goes about *incognito* to most of the world.

I suppose that no great discoveries of method are to be made in administration. Constitutions are new, but administration is as old as government. It has been experimented in from the beginning. Now the purpose of it has been the execution of the will of a tyrant, again the execution of the will of the governed. But the organization for the one purpose may, if effective, serve—at least as a model—for the other.

The historical method of even greater use in the study of administration than in the study of constitutions. The will of a despot—wilful, changeful, whimsical—cannot be termed a constitution. A constitution embodies the idea of constant, ascertained *law*)

"Liberty depends infinitely more on administration than on constitutions" (Lieber) [Niebuhr]. But not the *security*, the guarantee, the life, of liberty—only the practical facilitation of its exercise. No: not so much as that. Liberty no more consists in easy functional movement than intelligence in the ease and vigor of the limbs of the body. Liberty consists in enlightened, *authoritative* public opinion—consists in the realization of the purposes of active, directive popular thought. Liberty lives and moves and has its being in self-government. Because subjection is without *chains* and is lightened by every easy-working device of considerate, paternal administration, it is not transformed into liberty.

Method of *Study*: One benefit of the comparative method in studying administration (or anything similar) is, that it brings before the mind *novel* forms and organizations. We are too used to the appearance and methods of our own system to see its true significance: perhaps the Eng. system is too much like ours to be used to the best advantage in illustration. It is best, ∴, to turn to a careful examination of the French and German systems.

WWhw in notebook inscribed on inside front flyleaf (WWhw): "*Comparative Public Law Notes*" (WP, DLC).

[c. Nov. 15, 1885]

The Art of Governing

I begin with an apparent paradox, which everyone who thinks will allow to be a simple fact: We have so much to do with government that we do not trouble ourselves to consider how it might best be conducted. We do not study the art of governing; we gov-

ern. What I mean is what everybody knows, that we are a practical people whose aptitude for self-government is the fruit of
many centuries of experimental drill. And all the observant world
has admitted that we have profitted much by the drill, that we
have been enviably free, astonishingly progressive, and notably
happy

But we have made the mistakes which excessively practical
people are apt to make, and we have suffered many embarrassments which we might have escaped had we done more of our
own thinking. There is the old example—growing more notable
the older it gets—of what Montesquieu did for us. The English
monarchy had grown to be a splendid instrument of liberty, and
it had grown under our supervision—for at the time I speak of we
were Englishmen—but the world is inclined to think that we did
not know wherein its excellence consisted until Montesquieu examined it and told us. Then it was plain enough, and Montesquieu's bit of analyzing stood us in good stead. We took care to
write his greater principles into every constitution we drew up
on this side the sea: and in none did we follow him more rigidly
than in the greatest of all, the Federal Constitution itself. But we
did not follow him like philosophers; we had no thought of re-
examining his principles to see if they really held good for all
cases. We simply accepted them, and, like practical men, thought
that if they were good to use at all they were good to use in their
plain literal meaning.

This was unfortunate: for it seems to me perfectly clear that,
since he wrote in a time which did not know the people as an
actual and active sovereign authority, Montesquieu did not hit
upon exactly the right devices for practical popular government.
When he said that it was essential for the preservation of liberty
to differentiate the executive, legislative, and judicial functions of
government and not to suffer them to be united in the same
hands, he was thinking of an undemocratic state in which the
executive ruled for life by hereditary right and not by virtue of
popular election; in which judges held their offices by executive
appointment; and in which only the legislators had any appearance of having sprung from the ranks of the governed. And he
did not *say* that it was essential to liberty to separate, to *isolate*,
these three great functions of government. But we understood
that he did say this, and we judged that what was good for a English monarchy limited by the power of an aristocracy would be
quite as good, even in an exaggerated form, for an American democracy limited by federal conditions. We counted ourselves obe-

dient to this great principle, therefore, when we so separated our executive, legislative, and judiciary as to prevent all intimacy of aim and coöperation of effort between them. We multiplied authorities, and so obscured responsibility and excluded efficiency.

It might seem, therefore, that, though so skilled and successful at conducting government, we are so unskilled at reading its philosophy that we are apt to misunderstand its meaning when it is pointed out to us. We do not take naturally to interpretation at first hand, and are, consequently, awkward at applying second-hand interpretations. Still, though Montesquieu wrote in French, he used a language of politics, of government, which was our own. His text and example were English institutions. We could scarcely read him much amiss; and we did not read him very much amiss. His philosophy, if new to us, was at least a domestic article, woven out of raw materials of our own production. It was no foreign creed. It went into our constitutions with an air of being at home there. It was an *English* constitutional principle.

But the period of constitution-making is passed now. We have reached new territory in which we need new guides, the vast territory of *administration*. All the enlightened world has come along with us into these new fields, and much of the enlightened world has realized the fact and is preparing itself to understand administration. But this 'much' does not include our own race. There is a science of administration, but it is not of our making. It is a foreign science, speaking very few words of the language of English or American political principle. It employs only foreign tongues, it utters none but what are to our minds alien ideas, its examples, its conditions, its aims are almost exclusively grounded in the histories of foreign races, in the precedents of foreign systems, in the lessons of foreign revolutions. It has been developed by German and French professors and is consequently everywhere adapted to the needs of a compacted state and made to fit highly centralized forms of government: whereas, to suit our purposes, it must be adapted, not to a simple and compacted, but to a vast and multiform, state & made to fit highly decentralized forms of government. It must be Americanized, not in language only, but in thought, in principle, in aim as well, before it can be of any use to us in the solution of our own problems of administration in town, city, county, State, and nation. It must learn our constitutions by heart, and get the bureaucratic fever out of its veins. It must drink less beer and inhale more American air. But have it we must, even if it be necessary to import it and give it new ideas.

And its foreign birth and rearing are not such formidable obstacles to its domestication here as they might have been once. We can nowadays discern a tendency, long operative but only of late days predominant, towards the adoption of the same general principles of government everywhere. Governments are tending to become alike. Monarchies are being put into the straight-jackets of popular constitutions; and republics are manifesting some inclination to go part of the way to meet monarchies by strengthening their executives. The Czar plainly cannot have personal comfort and safety until he consents to share with his subjects the power which he at present nominally and precariously possesses: and the mayor of New York has had additions made to his power which the mayor of Boston may well envy, and yet will surely get.

And there may be said, too, to be a tendency, dimmer and not so steadily impulsive, but still clearly distined to prevail, towards the equally great principle of confederation. There is to be wide union, with divisions of prerogative instead of universal centralization of power; cooperation with individual independence. There are tendencies towards a common governmental type, and that type the American

Still all this is in the future: both local liberty and international federation. Local liberty must come first; and for how few countries is this first step possible! The Czar might sign and promulgate to-morrow a constitution full of grants of popular representation and parliamentary privilege without getting much nearer to a system of government like the English, which he would doubtless be copying, than he is to-day. He could not decree the existence of a governing public opinion: and, consequently, he could not create a free government all at once if he would. In every civilized nation there is, I suppose a strong body of public opinion. People must think in these days when there is so much to think about and when information flows everywhere in such free and accessible currents; and there must be an interchange and, as a result, something like a wide community of opinion. But it is one thing to think and quite another to think habitually in Acts of Congress. The essential difference between free governments and unfree governments lies in the *authority* which public opinion invariably has in the former and often or always lacks in the latter and Germany and France, as well as Russia, still stand as examples of the unfree when judged by this radical test. Who has ever found German or French writers upon government thinking much of public opinion as controlling the progress of reform? Who has ever found American or English writers on government thinking of anything else but public opinion as controlling public affairs?

The continental writers look always for executive initiative. They count upon seeing the great central bureaux writing themselves out new methods and new forms. It is a very 'close' corporation which controls administration. The people do not mould government, as we and our neighbours do—or can do if we choose—government is made without consulting them, by the King and his ministers, where there is a King, by the President and his ministers, where there is not a King. Public opinion is, perhaps, an aid when it approves; but it is certainly an impertinence for it to interfere. Dr. Bluntschli—that most modern of Germans—was at the pains of writing a book to create in Germany a public opinion which might come to rule in matters of government. He regretted seeing the people leave the understanding of governmental principles alone as none of their concern. He begged that, not professors but common active people would read his book and try to have opinions about the matters of which it speaks. There seems to me to be more than one touch of the pathetic in all this. It is not—to our ways of thinking, at least—a cheering sight to see government made a thing to be determined upon by autocratic officials and talked about only by doctors of philosophy in scientifically arranged treatises. We would exchange a good deal of science for a little self-government.

But we must borrow the science, nevertheless, or at any rate the useful, helpful parts of it; and we can do so with ease and profit if only we read this fundamental difference of condition into all its essential tenets. We must filter it through our constitutions; we must put it over a slow fire of criticism and distil away its foreign gases. For administrative questions are now very pressing questions.

WWhw MS. (WP, DLC).

EDITORIAL NOTE
WILSON'S FIRST TREATISE ON DEMOCRATIC GOVERNMENT

"The Modern Democratic State," printed following this note, was a milestone in Wilson's career as a publicist and scholar. Between the writing of "Cabinet Government in the United States" in early 1879 and completion of *Congressional Government* in late 1884, Wilson had concentrated his thought upon the functioning of the British and American governments. To be sure, he had often generalized, even more in "Government by Debate" than in *Congressional Government*, about democratic government and its prerequisites. But he had always used such generalizations to reinforce his argument that enlightened and educated public opinion could best be rallied, led, and organized for action through the vehicle of Cabinet government. To be sure, also, he never lost his passion for Cabinet government. But "The Modern Democratic State" marked a turning point in the direction of his *major* scholarly and political concerns—away from preoccupation with particular constitutional forms toward much broader subjects. "The Modern Democratic State," the first written evidence of this change of direction, in fact signaled the beginning of what would become Wilson's long and systematic study of the origins, development, and problems of democracy in the modern world.

Of course Wilson had undergone two years of intensive preparation at the Johns Hopkins. There he had been exposed to and trained to some degree in the new scientific historical method. He had absorbed both Herbert Baxter Adams's and Richard T. Ely's disdain for theoretical and general historical, political, and economic writing unsupported by evidence, and their emphasis upon the origins and organic evolutionary development of institutions. But the catalyst of "The Modern Democratic State" seems to have been Wilson's reading or re-reading—perhaps during the summer of 1885—of some of the works of Sir Henry Maine, Herbert Spencer, Bagehot's *Physics and Politics*, and other writers while preparing his lectures on the study of history for his Bryn Mawr students.[1]

Looking back four years later, Wilson remembered his purpose in beginning "The Modern Democratic State" with utter clarity. As he wrote on December 28, 1889, in his Confidential Journal (described at October 20, 1887):

"It was in keeping with my whole mental make-up, therefore, and in obedience to a true instinct, that I chose to put forth my chief strength in the history and interpretation of institutions, and chose as my chief ambition the historical explanation of the modern democratic state as a basis for the discussion of political progress, political expediency, political morality, political prejudice, practical politics, &c—an analysis of the thought in which our age stands, if it examine itself. It is a task, not of origination, but of interpretation. Interpret the age: i.e. interpret myself. Account for the creed I hold in politics. Institutions have their rootage in the common thought and only those who share the common thought can rightly interpret them. No man can appreciate a parliament who would not make a useful member of it (e.g. Carlyle)[.] No one can give a true account of anything of which he is intolerant. I find myself exceedingly tolerant of all institutions, past and present, by reason of a keen appreciation of their reason for being—*most* tolerant, so to say, of the institutions of my own day which seem to me, in an historical sense, intensely and essentially reasonable, though of course in no sense *final*. Why may not the present age write, through me, its political *autobiography*?"

We do not know precisely when Wilson began to write "The Modern Democratic State," but it was almost certainly after the first of October 1885. Nor can we be absolutely certain about his method, as the documentary evidence in the Wilson Papers in the Library of Congress is undated and scattered. This, however, is how he seems

[1] See "Notes for Four Lectures on the Study of History," Sept. 24-29, 1885, n. 1.

to have proceeded: He first wrote out a brief outline.[2] Not satisfied with it, he some time later prepared a fuller outline.[3] Next he did additional reading, taking notes on and copying quotations from Johann Kaspar Bluntschli, *Allgemeine Statslehre* (first part of his *Lehre vom Modernen Stat*); Elisha Mulford's *The Nation: The Foundations of Civil Order and Political Life in the United States*; Thomas Erskine May's *Democracy in Europe: A History*; Thomas Carlyle's *Heroes and Hero-Worship*; and Herbert Spencer's *Political Institutions* (Part 5 of *Principles of Sociology*). At the same time, and perhaps meanwhile, he wrote out drafts of paragraphs and other random personal reactions and observations.[4]

Wilson then began to compose his text on half pages or sheets, writing, as the manuscript reveals, very rapidly with frequent use of abbreviations. When he completed it, probably on about December 1, 1885, it consisted of Parts I, II, and III, on 121 numbered sheets. These he sent to his father soon afterward, and Joseph Ruggles Wilson suggested, among other things, the addition of a preface "to state, at the very outset, *what* it is you mean to treat of; and then *how* it is you mean to treat it."[5]

Wilson's letter to Robert Bridges of December 20, 1885, reveals that he was at this very time in the midst of writing what he called his "Preliminary," or the preface that his father had suggested.[6] At the same time, Wilson also heavily revised both the main body of the text and the "Preliminary." His changes were not always made carefully, and the Editors have tried to establish what might be called the latest version of the text, without, however, repairing incomplete footnotes and sentences or filling out abbreviations.

Reading "The Modern Democratic State" reminds one of Wilson's remarks about himself in his letter to Ellen Axson of February 13, 1885:

"The fault of my mind is that it is creative without being patient and docile in learning *how* to create. I am like one who would play upon the piano, not only without any knowledge of the laws and theory of music, but with only a superficial acquaintance with notation and no practice at all in the management of the fingers; like one who would solve the mysteries of astronomy before getting further than the easier processes of arithmetic; like one who would build a house of such odds and ends of material as happen to be at hand, and on the first vacant spot to be found. . . . A few glimpses of a great subject are enough to set me to sketching a treatment of it elaborate enough to fill a volume. I at once buy a blank-book and begin to ac-

[2] It is a loose page entitled "The Democratic State" (WP, DLC).

[3] On two loose pages entitled "*Nature of Mod. Dem. State*," *ibid.*

[4] These research notes and memoranda are in two envelopes labeled (WWhw) "The Modern Democratic State, (2) Its Nature" and "The Modern Democratic State (3) Its Structure," in WP, DLC. Both envelopes also contain notes and memoranda of a later date. In addition, there are a number of memoranda on loose pages in WP, DLC, not in these envelopes. Some of them are printed following this Editorial Note.

[5] JRW to WW, Dec. 12, 1885.

[6] Wilson seems to have typed a complete draft of the "Preliminary" on his Caligraph and then to have written out another draft in longhand, retaining, however, eighteen typed pages in the total of forty-four in the "Preliminary."

cumulate matter (principally thoughts without facts) for a treatise. I should make a capital hack-writer!"

These strictures would seem to characterize very aptly Wilson's first effort to write a general treatise on government. Actually, Wilson's ambitions in this particular instance were forcefully restrained by his realization of his own limitations. "The Modern Democratic State" was in Wilson's mind nothing more than a first draft and effort to put thoughts into words—in short, a framework to build upon. "The writing I have been doing," he wrote to Bridges on December 20, 1885, "has not yet taken definite enough shape to be described. I am feeling after the real conditions which make popular institutions workable, and the most practicable means whereby they can be made and kept healthy and vigorous. If I have 'bottom,' I'll come out all right: if not, I'll decline upon something of more modest dimensions." This, in fact, is what he did with the text of "The Modern Democratic State." No doubt he realized that, after beginning a general treatise, he had ended by writing a fairly detailed analysis only of democracy in the United States. That he was aware of this structural defect seems evident from the fact that he published "The Modern Democratic State" in revised form as an article entitled "Character of Democracy in the United States" in 1889.

However, the ambition to write a "*novum organum* of political study"[7] continued to burn in the young scholar. He laid out his plan in grander form in a letter to Horace E. Scudder of Houghton Mifflin on May 12, 1886.[8] He incorporated some of the introductory and concluding portions of "The Modern Democratic State" into the opening and concluding chapters of the textbook, *The State*, published in 1889. But *The State* was not the grand treatise on the historical development of democratic government that he still wanted passionately to write. He returned to the projected study, which he had meanwhile begun to call "The Philosophy of Politics," briefly in 1891, sketching out an elaborate analysis and outline to supplement "The Modern Democratic State,"[9] and perhaps taking some additional notes.[10]

For various reasons Wilson went no further on "The Philosophy of Politics." One of them certainly was the fact that he devoted most of his spare time in the 1890's to turning out literary essays, articles, and books in order to augment his income as a professor at Princeton. But there was a more important reason for postponement of "The Philosophy of Politics": Wilson, throughout the decade, embodied the knowledge and insights that he derived from his additional work in political science in his graduate course on administration at the Johns Hopkins and in his undergraduate courses on law and jurisprudence at Princeton. The deeper he got into these subjects, the

[7] As Wilson called it in WW to Frederick Jackson Turner, Jan. 21, 1902 (Turner Papers, MH). Horace E. Scudder apparently first used the phrase in a slightly different form in H. E. Scudder to WW, June 6, 1886.

[8] For the immediate background of this letter, see WW to H. E. Scudder, May 12, 1886, n. 2. See also WW to Albert Shaw, May 29, 1887.

[9] It is printed at Jan. 12, 1891, Vol. 7. A second, briefer outline is printed at Aug. 28, 1892, Vol. 8.

[10] Some of the notes in the envelopes referred to in n. 4 may have been taken at about this time.

more he must have come to realize that he was not yet prepared to write a *"novum organum."*

By January 1902, however, he was ready to embark upon the great undertaking that he hoped would give immortality to his name. "I was forty-five three weeks ago," he wrote to Frederick Jackson Turner in the letter cited above, "and between forty-five and fifty-five, I take it, is when a man ought to do the work into which he expects to put most of himself." Only six months later he was elected President of Princeton University. In spite of new careers and duties from this time forward, the hope of writing "The Philosophy of Politics" died slowly. Even while he was President of the United States, Wilson often referred to it as a project for his retirement.

In the case of "The Philosophy of Politics," ambitions deferred of course meant ambitions never fully realized. But separate, substantial fragments were completed and will be put together in later volumes. "The Modern Democratic State" was the foundation. Indeed it was more than this: it was the ideological framework from which Wilson never seriously deviated. Future volumes will include the general chapters of *The State*, essays in which Wilson incorporated his understanding of the laws and principles of historical political development, and, above all, his notes for his lectures on administration, law, and jurisprudence. Altogether, they will give ample evidence of what "The Philosophy of Politics" would have been had circumstances ever permitted Wilson to write it.

Memoranda for "The Modern Democratic State"

[c. Dec. 1-Dec. 20, 1885]

I have conceived the (perhaps whimsical) purpose of combining Montesquieu, Burke, and Bagehot. Montesquieu often plays with his subject, but with a subtle mockery: he should play with it with the more manly, though equally pointed, humour—with the unflaging vivacity and the wide-eyed tolerant look straight upon life—of Bagehot. Both these masters in politics, however, lack the solemn seriousness of Burke, his full-voiced eloquence, his ardent, high-strung consciousness of the weight, the beauty, the delicacy of liberty. Combined, the three men stand for all that has force in political thought.

Alternative Titles:

The Life of States
The Life of Institutions
The Spirit of Institutions
Basis and Life of Institutions

Democracy has been in the main perhaps sufficiently analyzed. Indeed it was itself a searching analysis—of the ultimate residence of sovereignty and the intimate nature of the state. What remains unaccomplished is its SYNTHESIS. For lack of proper synthesis [it] limps and is threatened with incapacity for the great social undertakings of our modern time.

Its synthesis includes more than its *organization*. That has proved difficult and has as yet been but imperfectly accomplished: but a further than formal synthesis is needed. Organization in order to be adequate must rest on completely clarified and thoroughly assayed, verified principle. A synthesis of principle must precede a synthesis of form and function.

It is indicative of the steadiness of our habit (the naturalness with wh. the expedient seems with us to be the constitutional) that we can break constitutions without either destroying or losing respect for them.

Individualism: One dare not be so individual in social activity as in art, e.g., dare not outrun or shock the common habit; dare not *innovate*. Such is not the task of leadership.

Ages of the State

(1) Ancient (family and Gr. and Roman commonwealths) adult as a corporate, infant as a component, being.
(2) Middle Age: adult as to individuals *of some* classes, with influences, such as local privilege (German) and Xnity maturing individuals.
(3) Modern Age: fully adult U. S.
Immigration so much infantage.

Divorcement of *morals* & *politics*
(α) Machiavellianism
(β) Separation Ch. & S.
(γ) Secularization
(δ) Recognition of politics as a sphere of moral action. God is not the head of the state; but he is the Lord of the individual and the individual cannot be moral who is immoral in *public* conduct.

The *puberty* of peoples: It is noteworthy how sincerely and instinctively the Greeks admired Sparta and the Italians Venice; and apparently the chief ground of the admiration in each case was that the Spartans or Venetians possessed in their politics that stability which comes of knowing one's own mind and acting accordingly—that they were *adult*, i.e., in their self-possession and clear-sighted conservatism, holding to an even tenor of once-for-all plans.

The justness of the admiration is quite another qu.

The Family: solid, despotic, natural cooperation in wh. the individual is subordinate:—the Ancient State: same thing expanded; individual still subordinate, but nevertheless with fine field for the display of individuality:—The Roman State: its evolution from ancient state into imperial forms and ideas:—The Medieval State: the individual tied, not to the state, but to *men*: —The Modern State: the individual free—but still a member of the corporate political organization; now adult, neither lost in the family (as at first), nor sunk in the state (as of old), nor gravitating towards Rome, nor tied to an overlord, but acting as a *thinking member* of the body politic, not now of its instruments merely, but of its constituted will-power.

The Democratic State the adult state.

The true limitation to universal suffrage is limitation of *direct* control. The people should not govern; they should elect the governors: and these governors should be elected for periods long enough to give time for policies not too heedful of transient breezes of public opinion. The power of the people ought to be the power of *criticism* and of choice upon *broad* questions.

Preliminary

Need for *synthesis*:

Analysis already effected by Democracy:

- (a) residence of sovereignty in the people
- (b) 'natural rights of man'
- (c) as regards organization
    - (a) election and responsibility to people
    - (β) division of responsibility
    - (γ) local autonomy

Prominence of *negative* features in this analysis.

⟨⟨These principles of *Rousseau* and *Montesquieu*, the one extracting thoughts from mere speculation; the other deriving maxims from monarchical rather than republican practice.⟩⟩ From both alike we have derived a false tendency of reaction against authority.

Individual as opposed to *organic* conception of state life resulting from this analysis

Series of syntheses suggestible:

(1) Organic conception: Written constitutions &c. have

held us away from this conception and kept us to a mere *formal* idea of state existence. Would the nation not still exist if the Const. and the rest were suddenly swept away? (2) If organic, personal: if personal, must have means of self-expression through personality (thr. persons of trusted leaders) and abolish forever *impersonal* action, aggregate legislation, subdivided responsibility, &c—*atomistic action*.[1]

WWhw pencil MSS., loose pages (WP, DLC).
 [1] The above are samples of various memoranda that Wilson seems to have made at some stage during the composition and revision of "The Modern Democratic State."

A Treatise

[c. Dec. 1-Dec. 20, 1885]

The Modern Democratic State

Preliminary

Those who fathered modern democracy would doubtless be not a little disappointed with the degree and nature of its success. It is not what they promised it would be. Although it has now finally established its respectability among the polities of the world, it has done so at what would have seemed to them a ruinous cost [and] great sacrifice. It has lost its early ideality. More openly liked by statesmen and more tolerantly discussed by jurists, it is less confidently loved by revolutionists and reformers. It has proved, under the proper conditions, a practicable principle of govt: but its fathers promised that it would be a universal deliverance, the single principle and crown of government. Instead of political salvation, the world has extracted from Democracy nothing greater than much instructive and helpful political experience. For Democracy has received long, open, and severe test of its qualities: and all who are in haste to perfect the world have cooled towards it. In its youth self-conscious, self-confident, strenuous, it grows in its middle age slow, cautious, uncertain, anxious. It is now plain to everyone that its inspiration is of man, and not of God. The construction of govt. is not a matter of inspiration; reform is not a matter of invention.

All this was to have been expected: it is of the commonplace of the history of doctrine. Never a doctrine arrogated to itself absolute truth and perfect nutritiousness for all men alike but was eventually convicted of being only relatively true, and nutritious only under certain conditions and for certain persons.

That great political nostrum, Sovereignty of the People, excellent though it be for many diseases of the body politic, has proved no panacia, equally curative of all ills; and even when the proper conditions for its application have been supplied, it has not proved a remedy suitable to be applied without great caution. Disappointing as the fact may be, it has proved only a relative, not an absolute, good.

By common consent, nevertheless, modern democracy still stands first among the few polities which are for the future. If stripped of all false claims to recognition, it still has many solid claims remaining. It is, indeed, more than ever a matter of deep moment to the world whether the Democratic State prove a success or a failure. If not the cap-stone, it must in any case be the foundation of the future structure of politics. Men cannot turn back to the systems which they have rejected; advance or catastrophe is their alternative: and if a democratic polity based on individual initiative prove a failure, they will, apparently, be tempted to grope on, in the doubtful light of Socialism, towards a democratic polity based on communal initiative. Democratic in any case the future system must be.

If, ∴, democracy be a thing of limitations and yet a foundation to be built upon, there is the greater need that the builders of politics definitely ascertain just what its limitations are, the exact points of its strength and its weakness. There is a pressing necessity that earnest heed be given to the abiding principles of democracy; in order that we may get, in such wise that it may always firmly be kept, a competent conception of 3 things: (a) of the nature peculiar to the modern democratic state, (b) of the organization necessary to it, and (c) of the aims proper to it.

Such a conception has never yet been framed. Much as the world has seen of democratic experiments, the sustaining principles of the ordinary active life of democracy still lack thorough synthesis. Discussions of the abstract principles which it has been the hope and aim of democracy to realize have not sufficed to guide us in organizing democracy; and our statements of the principles to which it has in fact given reality have but imperfectly connected democracy's habits and achievements with democracy's self. Contrasts between its actual career, and its ideal character as conceived beforehand by ardent reformers, have been let stand as lessons in human fatuity instead of being put in their true place as lessons in the laws of political development: have served as weapons of polemics rather than as items in the slowly enlarging syllabus of proofs that the social organism, like the physical, has its order and its law of evolution,—an order in wh. democracy may be seen to be but a single term.

Why has democracy been a cordial and a tonic to little Switzerland and big America, while it has been as yet only an quick intoxicant or a slow poison to France and Spain, a mere maddening draught to the South American states? Why has England approached democratic institutions by slow and steady stages of deliberate & peaceful development, while so many other states have panted toward democracy through constant revolution? Why has democracy existed in Am., and in Australia virtually from the first while other new states have utterly failed in their efforts to establish it? What *is* democracy that it should be possible to some, impossible as yet to others? Answers to such ques. as these will serve to show the only truly significant thing now to be discovered concerning democracy: its place and office, namely, in the process of political development. What is its relative function? its position and power in Politics viewed as a whole?

Democracy is, of course, wrongly conceived when treated as merely a body of doctrine. It is a stage of development. It is not created by aspirations or by new faith; it is built up by slow habit. Its process is experience, its basis old wont, its meaning national organic oneness and effectual life. It comes, like manhood, as the fruit of youth: immature peoples cannot have it, and the maturity to which it is vouchsafed is the maturity of freedom and self-control, and no other. It is conduct, and its only stable foundation is character.

A particular form of government may no more be adopted than a particular type of character may be adopted: both institutions and character must be developed by conscious effort and through transmitted aptitudes.

The variety of effect produced by its principles, ∴ , upon different nations and systems, and even upon the same nation at different periods, is susceptible of adequate and instructive explanation. It is not the result of accident merely or of good fortune manifestly, that the English race has been the only race, outside of quiet, closeted Switzerland,—the only, i.e., race standing forward amidst the fierce contests of national rivalries—that has succeeded in establishing and maintaining the most liberal forms of popular govt. It is, on the contrary, a perfectly natural outcome of organic development. The English alone have approached popular institutions *through habit*. All other races have rushed prematurely into them through mere impatience with habit: have adopted democracy instead of cultivating it.

Modern theoretical democrats set out to establish an equality which history had at no time foreseen or promised; they have succeeded in establishing not that, but new proof of the organic nature and structure of the State, of which history has from the first contained unnumbered evidences. By their very failures they have laid bare the invariable causes of failure in politics: in trying to hurry political development they have made plain why it must be slow. They have revealed its law and process.

It is this natural, as distinguished from the expected, result that stands in need of full exposition: and the exposition given it ought to be at once of historical and philosophic completeness and of practical use. It has not enough concerned English writers on politics to keep habitually outside party questions, as Burke often did, and make plain to the world, which is now so generally inclined to imitate English institutions, just what it is that England has accomplished in the development of the State that she and her offspring should now be leading the world in politics. Liberal government, it must be acknowledged, has been least suggestively expounded where it has been most successfully practiced. One of the most prominent features of that sagacious conservatism which has enabled the English race to combine order with progress has been its aversion from treating principles of government as open questions,—its fear of any taint of *a priori* weakness. We have thought to run no risk of shaking effective political purposes by questioning too curiously the conceptions underlying them, or by exposing too bluntly the whole fact of our experience in putting political principles into practice.

The practice of government is, nevertheless, the best school in which to acquire a true working philosophy of government: wherever popular government has had its chief incidents, there it should find its chief expounders. Englishmen should explain English success. Moreover the sort of political philosophy of which the world now stands in need is not the theoretical philosophy which already exists and which practical statesmen distrust, but business-like philosophy suitable for plain men which as yet awaits creation but wh. when created statesmen must accept. It should be considered the business of English political investigation to supply elements of thought which will also be elements of reform and so of progress. The characteristic of their thought ought to be, not scientific aloofness, but *practical interiorness* of view. This method should be historical, comparative,—the method of fact. Democracy owes it to itself to be scientific,—not, however, for speculative but for practical purposes. It is itself the result of history, not of theory, a creation of experience rather than of speculation; and it ought to be careful to reap the full benefits of history, to know thoroughly the experience of which it is the out-come. Such investigation ought surely to prove congenial to Eng-lish practical tastes; and the general conclusions to which it may give rise ought surely to commend themselves to practical re-formers as eminently worthy of being applied in concrete cases.

The historical view of government is in any case the only fully instructive view; in the case we are considering—the case of his-tory's latest political fruit, democracy,—it is the only view not utterly barren. Only history can explain modern democracy either to itself or to those who would imitate it. I conceive that the real significance and value of American institutions, which still of course remain the most advanced types of successful democracy, lie not so much in what they originated as in what they fulfilled: and it is only by extending those lines of development which can be clearly traced backwards through the normal evolutions of politics in the past that they can make further permanent ad-vances. We have not broken with the past: we have, rather, un-derstood and obeyed it. In that has lain the chief source of our strength; and the moment we lose our hold upon the lessons of experience and begin to imagine ourselves free to originate novel devices in government, at that moment we shall lose also our knack at succeeding.

At the same time we should take every pains to avail ourselves to the utmost of our successes and to understand what freedom of movement they have secured us; otherwise we shall lose our habit of advancing. The object of all political thought should be action. It should never counsel a timid standing still for fear of possible mistakes: it should always point out the way of progress. It ought to teach that wise sort of boldness which can afford to make mistakes because it knows what is essential and guards that from risk while it ventures all else for the sake of liberty and a freer course for reform. It ought, in brief, to produce a philos-ophy of statesmanship.

The most thorough way of understanding ourselves, then, lies thr. an intimate acquaintance with the long processes of our breeding. There are no individual discoveries to be made in poli-tics as there are in astronomy or biology or physics; society grows as a whole, and as a whole grows into knowledge of itself. Society is an organism which does not develop by any cunning leadership of a single member, but with slow maturity and all-round adjust-ment, being led at last into self-consciousness and self-command by those who best divine the laws of its growth. Those who speak of the state as simply 'all-of-us' talk as if government had had no history: as if they had but just now discovered, or were just now re-inventing it. What government is has ceased to be a matter of speculation, has ceased to be a tenet of philosophy and has become a mere qu. of fact.

Of course it is no more a qu. of easily explored fact than is the qu. of the origin of species, and no one man can assume to be the world's master in explaining government. The difficulties of the subject have been much enhanced by reason of the supreme interest it has excited. It has been so much written about that it is almost impossible to approach it without preconceptions; it is everywhere a topic of such vital practical importance that it is almost impossible to approach it without personal or party prejudices. When our judgments have not been predetermined by our acquaintance with political speculation[,] by our ardor for a particular reform or by our ignorance of historical facts, they are in danger of being warped by the heats of the subject itself. Doubtless entire dispassionateness in treating it is not to be hoped for —even from oneself.

Government is not however, on the other hand, something which has passed away and been overlaid by the glosses of those who have striven to clear up traditions concerning it. It is not an Aryan migration or a Draconian code. It is with us to-day, in possession of as much vitality as it ever had; though in most places it has found the times grown so much better that it has assumed a mildness of manner and a gentleness of disposition which were not in its earlier days habitual with it. It has also drawn much nearer to the people and has become one of the ordinary instead of one of the awful concerns of life. It has doffed its pageantry and come down to mix with the vulgar interests of the common citizen. But it has not grown simply with age and condescension. Its tasks, if more commonplace, are also more numerous than they ever were and vastly more complex. Its very commonness, besides, has given it an air of ordinary business which has made it seem much more easily intelligible than it really is.

Still, its history is plain enough through all the periods which are of practical importance to ourselves: and the history of democracy is the philosophy of democracy. To adopt the too usual view that democracy is for all peoples alike an abnormal form of government, a reaction against more compact forms of the state, a frequently recurrent phase of transition from one kind of centralized political organization to another, is to mistake growth for

disease. There is almost nothing in common between popular reactions such as took place in France at her great Revolution and
the development of a government like that of the United States or
Switzerland. Democracy in Europe, outside of Switzerland, has
acted always in rebellion, as a destructive force: it can scarcely
be said to have had, even yet, any period of organic development.
It has built such temporary govts. as it has had the opportunity
to erect upon the old foundations and out of the discredited materials of centralized rule, elevating the people's representatives
for a season to the throne but securing to the people themselves
almost as little as ever of everyday local self-govt. Democracy in
America, on the other hand, and in the Eng. colonies, has had,
almost from the first, a truly organic growth. There was nothing
revolutionary in its movements: it had not to overthrow other
polities: it had only to organize itself. It had, not to create, but
only to expand self-government. It did not need to spread propa-
ganda: it needed nothing but to methodize its ways of living.

It was this democracy, the natural growth of transplanted Eng.
politics, that was to serve as the norm of social development for
other races less habituated to orderly change than the English
race; and it is this democracy which, having been unhappily
confounded with popular aspirations of every kind elsewhere, has
never received adequate explanation; which still waits to be put
in its place as a type, not of exceptional political revolution, but
of normal political growth.

Our view of these important facts, of the naturalness and
necessity of our institutions being in the main what they are, has
been considerably obscured by certain indirect consequences of
the fact that we have *written constitutions* at the foundation of
our whole structure of government. Our governments are still
chartered govts: as their first privileges were granted by the king,
so their present prerogatives were granted by the people. Our
constitutions, moreover, directly derived most of their important
provisions from the charters of the colonies: the gifts of power
from the Crown were only expanded and systematized in the gifts
of power made by the sovereign people. There was thus in each
case the deliberate erection of one kind of government in preference to another: the process was distinctly a process of conscious
choice, a process of discretional construction. Here, if anywhere,
it might seem, was a case in point for Locke or Rousseau, a case
of *contract*, of the debated selection by bodies of free men of the
particular sort of government that suited them. It was quite natural, ∴, that we should look upon our constitutions as new and

definite creations, and that we should accept concerning them such conventional ideas, of contract and the like, as tallied with such theories.

While it is the essence of the historical method to regard govts. as, in a certain important sense, growths, as steps sometimes consciously but always quite logically taken in a long course of more or less regular development, it is the suggestion of written constitutions, that govts. are distinct creations, which, if they do not actually depart from the lines of previous precedent and tendency, are at least definitive,—tendencies commanded by the deliberate choice of constitution-makers to stand still—to assume such and such final shapes.

Historical criticism of one kind our federal constitution has had in fullest quantity; but it has been criticism which sadly lacked perspective. The circumstances which induced and those which accompanied the formation of the Constitution, together with contemporary views as to its proper interpretation, have been set forth with abundant fulness. Such discussions have, in fact, constituted the great body of that splendid expository writing on the Constitution which has been one of the chief ornaments of our scholarly literature. But of historical criticism of the sort which seeks the place of the Constitution in the general scheme of governmental development the ages through and the world over there has been scarcely any. Our constitutions have been to most writers documents in American history, products of American sense, but not except in a very vague way the outcome of long processes which began in the politics of quite other systems than our own. Like the royal grants and charters from which they sprang, our constitutional arrangements have been made to wear a[n] appearance of deadness in the absence of any exercise of an external creative will; of political developments as were most in favour when our governments were formed. We, moreover, hedged our constitutions about with so great difficulties of amendment that they were made to seem, in conception at least, *final* creations: our fundamental laws were, so to say, put in *mortmain*. Our national life has been made to seem the manufacture of lawyers.

It was natural that in such an atmosphere, the organic nature of our national existence, and the organic connections between our political life and the life of the old-world systems, should be but dimly perceived. We have been too much dominated by the theory that our government was an artificial structure resting upon contract only. The nation has again and again been treated of as merely a colossal crowd composed of 'all-of-us.' Many of the greatest struggles of our constitutional history—and ours has been pre-eminently a *constitutional* rather than political history—have turned upon debates as to the exact extent to which we were bound together by the mere ligaments of law. It may be open to qu. whether we have even yet accepted the fact that the real foundations of political life in the United States are to be found elsewhere than in our constitutions.

And yet, if all thought of the controversies which have hitherto raged as to the legal character of the Union be put aside, it is evident that there is a national unity and purpose amongst us which rest upon unwritten laws higher than any constitutions and of which our constitutions are but a particular expression. The federal Constitution is, indeed, the formal basis of the Union, and its provisions while they stand must be held inviolable. We are not to substitute for it in practice abstract conceptions of national unity which we may consider, with whatever warrant, the reason of its being, but which are, nevertheless, not embodied in its language. It is the imperative law of political action for the nation. But it can be changed; and there is a law greater than it which cannot be changed,—a law which makes the Constitution possible, without which the Constitution would be but a dead letter; a law which is the supreme rule of the national life. This is that law written on our hearts which makes us conscious of our oneness as a single personality in the great company of nations; conscious of a common interest, a common vocation, and a common destiny:—not only a "spirit of '76," but a spirit for all time.

If we could conceive the Constitution swept utterly away, together with the whole system dependent upon it, by some legerdemain of fortune which should touch nothing but laws and the forms of constitutions, leaving us in possession of all else—our resources, our energies and our character—would the Union go with it? Is the Constitution the only actual bond which keeps us from falling apart into atoms? Is the general government a mere bundle of States bound together only by the frail thong of contract? Is it not true, rather, that the Constitution is but the formal symbol of a deep reality of national character? Justly revered as our great Constitution is, it could be stripped off and thrown aside like a garment, and the nation would still stand forth clothed in the living vestment of flesh and sinew, warm with the heart-blood of one people, ready to recreate constitutions and laws.

And all this because our success inheres in our history, in our experiences as a Teutonic race set apart to make a special Eng. character[.] When political institutions come to be viewed in their true historical proportions and perspective, it will be seen that it has not been without reason that Americans have regarded their system of government as standing at the front of the world's progress and politics; but probably we have hitherto insisted too much on the least significant proofs of our leadership. Our best claims upon the world's attention will appear when, ceasing to stop at the analysis and history of our constitutional law, we penetrate further, to the analysis of our constitutional being and discover in full historical light the true genesis of our form of government, and, by consequence, the general principles which lie at the foundation of all practicable government by the people. The present trend of all political development the world over towards democracy is no mere episode in history. It is the natural resultant of now permanent forces which have long been gathering, which brought modern lights out of mediaeval shades, and which have made the life of the most advanced nations of our day the wide, various, vigorous, complex, expanding thing that it is: the forces which have been substituting for success founded upon hereditary position or class privilege success founded upon individual merit. If what is best in these tendencies is to be advanced, to the exclusion of what is chimerical, mistaken, artificial, arbitrary, it is thoroughly worth while for American writers heartily in sympathy with the practical spirit of democracy, to endeavor to turn the world's thought, with their own, to broader outlooks and larger conceptions than have hitherto prevailed concerning the essential nature, organization, and aims of the Democratic State.

I. Nature of the Modern Democratic State.

In its most modern sense, as used by practical thinkers of today, Democracy means a form of government wh. secures absolute equality of *status* before the law, and under which the decisive, final control of public affairs rests with the whole body of adult males amongst whom the largest liberty of opinion, of discussion, and of political choice prevails. More briefly, it is govt. by universal popular discussion. Most briefly, it is govt. by public opinion.

The word has come to be used in this sense when applied to great systems of govt. only since the rise of the govt. of the United States. The creation of the conditions precedent to such democracy manifestly belongs to the long processes of historical de-

velopment. Govt. by discussion comes as late in political, as scientific thought in intellectual development.

It is a form of state life which is possible for a nation only in
the adult age of its political development. A people must have
gone through a period of political tutelage which shall have prepared them by gradual steps of acquired privileges of self-direction for assuming the entire control of their affairs. Long and
slowly widening experience in local self-direction must have prepared them for national self-direction. They must have acquired
adult self-reliance, self-knowledge, and self-control, adult soberness and deliberateness of judgment and sagacity in self-government, adult vigilance of thought and quickness of insight. When
practiced, not by communities, but by nations, democracy, far
from being a crude form, is possible only amongst peoples of the
highest and steadiest political habit. It is the heritage of races
purged alike of hasty, barbaric passions and of patient servility to
rulers, and schooled in temperate common counsel. It is an institution of political noon-day, not of the half light of political
morning. It can never be made to sit easily or safely on first
generations, but strengthens through long heredity. It is poison
to the infant, but tonic to the man. Monarchies may be made: but
democracies must grow.

The conditions precedent to democracy are sufficiently clear to
be set forth with some degree of definiteness. One of the most
important of these conditions is that there should be the greatest
possible freedom of discussion and the broadest possible diffusion
of enlightenment among the people. This condition is the more
interesting at the present time in view of the fact that it is approaching realization in so many of the nations of the world.
The strength and diffusion of democratic thought is the most
striking political fact of the present century; and there is an almost universal expectation that democratic practice will everywhere follow hard upon democratic opinion. The causes which
have bestirred such thoughts and purposes are the same that have
extended the intellectual awakening of the times from the studious classes to the working classes. The serious forces of democracy will be found, upon analysis, to reside, not in the disturbing
doctrines of eloquent revolutionary writers, not in the turbulent
discontent of the pauperized and oppressed, but in the elevation
of the masses by the various educational influences of the last
hundred and forty yrs. to a plane of understanding and of intelligent, orderly purpose more nearly on a level with the average
man of the hitherto governing classes. The movements towards

democracy which have mastered all the other political tendencies of our own day are not older than the middle of the last century: and that is just the age of the now ascendant movement towards systematic popular education. In the United States where popular govt. has had its steadiest and most assured supremacy, popular education had its earliest development, and has now its most spontaneous support. Its desirability and its efficacy have become as trite and self-evident here in political thought as the universal regulative force of gravitation have become in astronomical discussion.

Organized popular education is, after all however, only the sowing of the seed in separated plots. Each school is only a single seed-bed, more or less isolated from the similar beds of the national or communal system—which is a system rather in idea than in compactness of organization. Each little group learns by itself. Unless there were powerful influences afoot which gave each separate community more or less direct touch of the affairs and thought of all other communities, its learning, however uniform might be the methods of instruction everywhere, would take and retain a distinct local colour, and would be narrowed and minimized by a petty, purblind local application. It would in reality know only itself. But within the time during which popular education has been growing the most powerful forces for the diffusion and intercommunication of thought and information have been developing with equal rapidity. Through commerce and the press steady trade-winds have sprung up which carry the seeds of education and enlightenment, wheresoever planted, to every quarter of the globe. No scrap of new thought can escape being borne away from its place of birth by these all-absorb[ing] currents. No idea can be kept exclusively at home, but is taken up by the trader, the reporter, the traveller, the missionary, the explorer, and is given to all the world, in the newspaper, the novel, the memoir, the poem, the treatise, till every community may know not only itself and its neighbours, but all the world as well for the small price of learning to read and keeping its ears open. All the world, so far as its *news* and its stronger thought are concerned, is fast being made every man's neighbour.

Carlyle touched one of the great truths concerning modern democracy when he declared it to be the result of *printing*. In the newspaper press a whole population is made critic of all human affairs: democracy is "virtually extant," and "democracy virtually extant will insist on becoming palpable extant." Looked at in the large, the newspaper press will be seen to be a type of democracy, bringing all men without distinction under comment made by any man without distinction; every topic reduced to a common standard of news; everything noted and argued about by everybody. Nothing could give surer promise of popular power than the activity and alertness of thought which is made through such agencies to accompany the training of the public schools. The activity may often be misdirected or unhealthful, may sometimes be only feverish and mischievous, a grievous product of narrow information and hasty conclusion; but it is none the less a growing and potent activity. It at least marks the initial stages of effective thought. It makes men conscious of the existence and interest of affairs lying outside of the dull round of their own daily lives. It gives them a nation, instead of a neighbourhood, to look upon and think about. They catch glimpses of the international relations of their trades, of the universal application of law, of the endless variety of life, of diversities of race, of a world teeming with men like themselves and yet full of strange customs, puzzled by dim omens, stained by crime, ringing with voices familiar and unfamiliar.

And all this men can get nowadays without stirring from home, by merely spelling out the print that covers every piece of paper about them. If they throw themselves for any reason into the swift and easy currents of travel, they find themselves daily brought face to face with persons native of every clime, with practices suggestive of whole histories, with a thousand things which challenge a curiosity in satisfying which they enlarge their knowledge of life and alter their previous conceptions.

But the influences of the press, of travel, and of commerce, of the innumerable agencies which nowadays send knowledge and thought in quick pulsations through every part of society, do not necessarily mould men for effective personal endeavour. They may only confuse and paralyze his mind with their myriad stinging lashes of excitement. They may only strengthen the impression that 'the world's a stage' and that no one need do more than look on through his ready glass, the newspaper. They overwhelm him with impressions, but do they give stalwartness to his manhood; do they make his hand any steadier on the plow, or his purpose any clearer with reference to the duties of the moment? They stream light about him, it may be; but do they clear his vision? Is he better able to see because they give him countless things to look at? Is he better able to judge because they fill him with a delusive sense of knowing everything? Activity of mind is not strength of mind. It may show itself in mere dumb-show; it

may run into jigs as well as into strenuous work at noble tasks.
A man's farm does'nt yield its fruit the more abundantly in its
season because he reads the world's news in the newspapers. A
merchants shipments do not multiply because he studies history.
Banking is none the less hazardous to the banker's capital and
taxing to his powers because the best writing of the best essayists
is to be bought cheap.

Nothing establishes the democratic state save trained capacity
for self-government, practical aptitude for public affairs, habitual
soberness and temperateness of united action. But the influences
which make all sources of information common to all men alike,
which scatter broadcast the world's thought and the world's news,
are sure to put an end to the conditions under which the many
will receive without question the thought of a ruling few and to
create that dem. thought which is one presage of the dem. state.
They extend the reaches of public opinion. They multiply infinitely the number of the voices which must be heeded in legislation or in executive policy. They incline every man to clear his
throat for a word in the world's debates. They popularize everything that they touch. In the newspapers there is but little concerted between the writers; little but piecemeal opinion is created
by their comment and argument; there is no common voice
amidst their counsellings. But the aggregate voice thunders with
tremendous volume; and that aggregate voice is 'public opinion.'
Popular education and cheap printing vastly thicken the ranks of
thinkers everywhere that their influence is felt, and by rousing
the multitude to take knowledge of the affairs of govt. directly
prepare the time when the multitude will so far as possible take
charge of the affairs of govt. And it is only when such interest in
affairs has been rendered common and habitual that democracy
is possible, in any sphere wider than the communal.

'Why is democracy coming?' Because practical political education is everywhere spreading and all nations which have not
reached are entering or nearing the adult age of their political
development.

The successful operation of democratic institutions depends
upon several all-important conditions: as (1) Upon homogeneity
of race and community of thought and purpose among the people.
There is no amalgam in democracy which can harmoniously unite
races of diverse habits and instincts or unequal acquirements in
thought and action. That must be done by the single, steady, compulsive hand of a monarch or of a small governing body[.] Authority, not common counsel, must compound nations. A nation
once come to maturity and habituated to self-government may

absorb alien elements, as our own nation has done and is still doing; but Norman and Saxon must be fused by the fire of conquest, and the gap between Austrian and Hungarian must be bridged by a throne. Homogeneity is the first requisite for a nation that would be democratic.

The second requisite is that the nation should not only feel itself an organic, homogeneous body, but should also be accustomed or at least prepared to *act* as an organic body. Democracy is the sovereignty of the people made real. Consequently its existence is dependent upon several all-important conditions: as (1) Upon a sense of unity, of community of thought and purpose, among the people. No nation which has recently been held in a deadening bondage is capable of democracy; (2) upon a habit of concerted purpose and cooperate action. The nation which is to try democracy successfully must not only feel itself an organic body, but must be accustomed to *act* as an organic body. Not Parisian mobs, but national majorities must make and unmake governments. (3) upon a habit of orderly agreement and peaceful authority on the part of the body of the people. Not a habit of revolution, but a habit of resolution must constitute the political life of the nation.

Such a govt. really constitutes the people sovereigns. But their sovereignty is of a peculiar sort, unlike the sovereignty of a king or of a small, easily concerting group of men. It is judicial, not creative. It passes judgment, or gives sanction; it does not direct. It furnishes standards, not policies. Popular govt. is 'govt. by the people'; but govt. in the sense of control, not govt. in the sense of conduct of policy. Questions of govt. are infinitely complex questions, and no multitude can of themselves form clear-cut, comprehensive, consistent conclusions concerning them. And yet without such conclusions, without single and prompt purposes, govt. cannot be carried on. Neither legislation nor administration can be done at the ballot-box. The people can only accept the governing act of representatives. They do not and cannot originate measures of policy; they acquiesce in policy which a few have originated. They do not even suggest policy. They approve the suggestions of a very small number chosen from their midst. They do not, in any adequate sense of the word, govern, therefore; for government is the conduct of the state. It consists in the origination and prosecution of policy. It is action, volition, not mere ratification of measures, not mere acquiescence in action. The people govern in the same sense in which the Senate may be said to make treaties.

It is a deeply significant fact that only the United States and a few other govts. begotten of the Eng. race have yet furnished examples of successful democracy of the modern type. England herself is close upon democracy. Her backwardness in entering upon its full practice is no less instructive than the forwardness of her off-spring as to the conditions prerequisite to democracy. She sent out to all of her colonies which escaped the luckless beginning of being made a penal settlement, comparatively small, homogeneous, populations of pioneers with strong instincts of self-govt. and no materials out of which to build govt. otherwise than democratically. She herself, meanwhile, retained masses of population never habituated to participation in govt.[,] untaught in political principle either by the teachers of the hustings or of the school-house. She has had to approach democracy by slow and cautious extensions of the franchise to those prepared for it; her better colonies were born in democracy and had to receive all comers into its pale. She has been paring down exclusive privileges and levelling classes; they have always been asylums of civil equality. They have assimilated new, she has prepared old, populations.

And, through democracy thus genuinely grown, the cycle of Aristotle is impossible. For this democracy—this modern democracy—is not the rule of the many, but the rule of the *whole*. It is the nation come to its majority, conscious of its authority, and in clear sight of its aims. It is the nation not mature only but experienced in self-conduct and alert to maintain its independence. Democracy is truly government by the whole—for the rule of the majority implies and is dependent upon the coöperation, be it active or passive, of the minority. It is the peculiar beauty and characteristic strength of democracy that minorities do cooperate. There acquiescence is not a mere bowing to necessity or to force. It is a conscious act of the judgment nearly akin to actual agreement.

In modern democracy, the δημος is vastly wider than in the ancient republics. Now the *whole people* is included, either directly or by representation. It is Ochlocracy. England, long a republic, is now fast becoming a democracy.

A true conception of democracy is inseparable from the organic theory of the state.

This innate principle of union is of course not peculiar to ourselves. It is the principle which has built government up from its beginnings in the primitive groups of families & tribes; which has welded kindred races together, has given conquest of its final triumphs and state systems their only guarantee of endurance.

There are relations in which men invariably have need of each other, in which common coöperation is an absolutely indispensable condition of even tolerable existence. But that is not the whole ground of govt. and the state. They are formed as naturally, as much without deliberate choice, as is the family. Men have pressing need of each other in the higher undertakings of industry and the wider enterprizes of trade. But in these things they can and do exercise a choice. The divisions of labour and the combinations of commerce are matters of deliberate arrangement. The organization of government and the growth of the state are not. Society can exist without joint-stock companies; it cannot exist without government. Neither the family nor the state is an optional association; all other coöperative combinations of men are optional. The family and the state are not conveniences merely; they are necessities. The functions of both alike end where the mere convenience and advantage of combination begin. They are natural; all other unions are optional, artificial. They supply the necessary conditions for the highest development of man's nature. Churches, clubs, corporations, fraternities, guilds, partnerships, unions have for their end one or another special enterprise for the development of man's spiritual or material well-being. These are more or less advisable: the family and the state are indispensable. The ties of kin and the dependence of youth constitute the amalgam and object of the family; the state founds itself upon the instinctive associations of maturity. The discipline of the family cannot be endured by the man. But neither can he endure isolation. To stand apart from his fellows is to be but half a man, to live a life maimed, desolate, incomplete. His nature demands commerce of sentiment, community of aim. He may have a family of his own, but that is not enough. His family is but a part of himself. He must have other connections, connections which bring him into coöperation with wills altogether different from his own, connections of elevating comity and bracing competition, of common resolve and honorable equality. He cannot realize the highest possibilities of his faculties without the associations of society and the equal subordinations of government.

The limit of state functions is, consequently, the limit of necessary coöperation, the limit beyond which combination ceases to be imperative. This limit is not susceptible of being clearly drawn; but neither is it indistinct. The bounds of family association are not indistinct because they are marked by the immaturity of the young and the parental and filial affections. The rule that the state should do nothing which is possible or natural to optional associations is a sufficiently clear line of distinction between govts. and corporations. Those who regard the state as an optional, conventional union—a mere partnership—open the doors wide to socialism. If there is no natural, essential difference between states and corporations, there is no limit but that of mere convenience or policy to the functions of the state. Unless the state has a nature which is defined by that invariable, universal, immutable mutual interdependence which runs beyond family relations and cannot be satisfied by family ties, we have absolutely no criteria by which we can limit—except arbitrarily—the activities of the state. The criterion supplied by the native necessity of state relations banishes such license of state enterprise. The state, for instance, may not supervise private morals because they belong to the sphere of separate, individual responsibility, not of mutual dependence. Thought and conscience are private. Opinion is optional. The state may intervene only where common action, uniform law, are indispensable. Whatever is merely convenient is optional. Churches are spiritually convenient. Joint-stock companies are capitalistically convenient. When the state constitutes itself a church or a business company it becomes a mere monopoly. It should do nothing which is not in any case both indispensable to social life & necessarily monopolistic.

It is the proper object of the family to mould the individual, to form him in the period of immaturity in the practice of morality and obedience. This period of subordination over, he is called out into an independent, self-directed activity. The ties of family affection still bind him; but they bind him with silken, not with iron bonds. He has left his 'minority' and reached his 'majority.' It is the proper object of the state to give leave to his individuality, that it may add its variety to the sum of national activity. Family discipline is variable, selective, formative. It must lead. But the state must not. It must create conditions, not mould individuals. Its discipline must be invariable, uniform, impersonal. Family methods rest upon individual inequality: state methods upon individual equality. The family order rests upon tutelage; state order upon franchise.

Differences between ancient and modern democracies:

(1) In ancient, a substratic, non-citizen class which often proved a sleeping volcano.

(2) In the modern, the *commonness* of govt.—its entire openness to criticism by all, and its possible conduct by all,—the absence of distance, exclusiveness, or mystery about it. No hallowed sanctity about it.

Erroneous as it is to represent government as only a sort of commonplace business, little elevated above merchandizing, and to be regulated by counting house rules, the favour easily won for such a view nowadays is very significant. It means self-reliance in govt. It gives voice to the eminently modern democratic feeling that govt. is no hidden cult, but a common everyday concern of life, even if the biggest such common concern.

Modern democracy is widely different from ancient or mediaeval democracy in both its character and its prospects because of the adult nature of modern social life. In that society childish fears have been outgrown, youthful anxieties conquered, and mature agreement has replaced too hasty impulse. In Rome a class monopolized knowledge of the laws[,] a class blocked the avenues to property, a priestly college doled out religious directions as from a private store. In Greece oracles overawed, and facility of change sapped with instability. In both an excluded non-citizen class menaced order with breach and all society with ruinous upheaval. In neither were there the myriad-eyed presses of our modern states to tell everyone everywhere the smallest movements of private enterprize or public design. In our democratic states of to-day there run throughout the land accessible to everyone as copious streams of information and thought as were in Athens to be approached only by those who could find places in the knots gathered about Sokrates in the market place, those who could pay the fees of the Sophists, or those who could stay from their employments to hear the orators in the Agora. Men nowadays know what is going on the world over and have their views steadied by largeness of foundation, broadened by extent of horizon. It is easy to concert movements over vast areas, to have one national pulse for immense organisms. It is impossible to hatch in a corner plots which will affect more than a corner. With life everywhere, it is impossible to snatch power over a whole people by taking possession of its central govt. offices. To hold Washington would be as useless to an usurper as to hold Duluth. The nation cannot be corrupted, and we have ceased to fear a Caesar.

That nation whose military force consists only of a standing army distinct from the body of the people may suffer irretrievable defeat on a single field; but a nation whose people are its army cannot be defeated at all. To secure one victory a hundred more must quickly be added. Lexington was but the first skirmish. So with a people whose political drill and habit reach all alike. Self-govt. cannot be usurped. There is no single throne, but a throne at every polling-booth. Little but confusion of thought can result from using the Grecian and Roman republics as antetypes of the democracy of the modern world. Every difference of condition and form separated their democracy from ours. In comparing the two, only the most watchful and accurate distinctions of times and institutions and circumstances can preserve us from confusing error: and these only if they be kept constantly in view. Modern democracy can learn much from ancient, but only if particular points of antique practice and special features of antique precedent be used as illustration; not if old-time systems be taken as prototypes.

The democracy of the modern state is based upon the full recognition and ungrudging establishment of individual rights as peers of the rights of the state; the democracy of Greece knew no rights but the rights of the state. Even Roman republicanism saw the distinction but dimly. The democracy of the modern state is utterly incompatible with slavery in any form, and denies all class subordination. Its citizenship is as wide as its adult population. The citizenship of the ancient state, on the contrary, never stretched farther than to a minority of its adult subjects. It was, at widest, an exclusive privilege. There were slaves under the heel of the state: there were even freedmen who could never hope to gain the franchise. Class subordination was of the essence of the real constitution of the body politic.

I take it to be a conception absolutely prerequisite to any competent study of the development of the modern state that the democracy which is now becoming dominant is a *new* democracy, new not only in those fundamental particulars and formal diversities which I have already pointed out, but informed with a life and surrounded by controlling conditions altogether modern.

Aristotle, erecting a philosophy of politics upon generalizations rooted in the changeful fortunes of Hellenic states the old world over, conceived a cycle of degeneracies and revolutions through which every state of long life had an inevitable tendency to pass. The first ruler of every state was naturally the monarch, the single strong man with sovereign power. He would usually hand on his kingdom to his children, and they might confidently be expected to forget those pledges and those views of the public good which had bound and guided him. Their sovereignty would sink into tyranny. Tyranny would meet its check at some Runnymede and the princely leaders of revolt, taking govt. into their own hands, would establish an aristocracy. But aristocracies, though often public spirited and just in their youth always decline into a dotage of oligarchy. Oligarchy is even more hateful to civil liberty, is even a graver hindrance to civil life, than tyranny. A class can devise injustice in greater variety than can a single despot: and their insolence is always quick to goad the many to hot revolution. Then succeeds the democracy. But democracy, too, has its old age of degeneracy, an age in which it loses its early respect for law, its first amiability of mutual concession. It breaks out into license and anarchy, and none but a Caesar can bring it back to reason and order. The cycle is completed. The throne is set up again, and a new series of deteriorations and revolutions begins.

The confirmations of this view in the history of Europe since the time of Aristotle have been striking and numerous enough to strengthen many modern writers in their inclination to rewrite Aristotle. Many theoretical politicians the world over confidently expect modern democracies to throw themselves at the feet of some Caesar.

It has been said by a French writer that the autocratic ascendancy of Andrew Jackson illustrates anew the long credited tendency of democracies to give themselves over to one man. The country is older now than it was when Andrew Jackson delighted in his power, and few can believe that it would again approve and applaud childish arrogance and ignorant arbitrariness like his: but even in his case, singular and ominous as it was, it cannot be overlooked that he was suffered only to strain the Constitution, not to break it. He held his office by orderly election; he exercised it within the letter of the law; he could silence not one word of hostile criticism; and, his second term expired, he passed into private life as harmlessly as did James Monroe. A nation that can quietly reabsorb a vast victorious army is no more safely free and healthy than a nation that could send such a Pres. as A. J. into seclusion at the Hermitage to live without power and die almost forgotten.

The new conditions of modern political life are not merely new conditions: they are new essences. They enter into the very blood of political systems. First amongst these conditions, there is the popular and territorial size of the modern democracy. Unlike the city democracies of ancient Greece and medieval Italy, it has a life which includes a whole nation. There is no field limit to its active citizenship. Unlike Rome it is not a single narrow state driving the world with looser or tighter rein, but a vast state with autonomous life in every part and yet a common life and purpose, with as many centres of self-directive energy as units of organization and yet with voluntary ardour and unhampered facility of coöperation—not a head organism with huge dependent parts, but itself a single giant organism with a stalwart, common strength and an abounding life in individual limb and sinew.

Added to this greater size and increased breadth of life the modern democracy has a fulness of knowledge of itself not inferior to that of the Athenian state. And not of itself only, but of the world outside of itself. This knowledge is not, however, the word of mouth information, the public gossip of the old republics. It is not derived from the lips of the partisan orator or from the indistinct speech of common rumour but from the newspaper. And this fact is immensely significant. We are nowadays so accustomed to hear and to repeat extravagant estimates of the influence of the press that the idea has become too familiar really to impress our imaginations. We all allow the greatness of the newspaper without thinking of it. And yet a little fresh thought upon the subject makes it very plain that the railway and the telegraph have enabled the editor to alter the whole aspect of politics and so compel the political writer to recast radically, if he would retain at all, the 'Politics' of Aristotle. The newspaper press delivers information about the world's doings and the world's thought to all parts of a great country within an outside limit of two days. Every free nation knows and thinks about the same things at the same time. And if in the nation thus equally informed and synchronously thinking that organization of democracy prevails which ensures political life to every local unit, an infinite variety of thought and impulse must make up the aggregate, the national whole, of thought and impulse. Thoughts which in one quarter kindle enthusiasm will in another arouse antagonism. Events which are fuel to the passions of one section will be but as a passing wind to the minds of another section. No single moment of indiscretion surely can betray the whole country at once. There will be whole populations still cool, self-reliant, and unaffected. Paris rioted away the liberties of France at the Revolution because it was only in Paris that there was any life. The rest of the country, never having had imperative thoughts of its own as to the way in which it should be governed, could not have them now. Never having had self-chosen means of expressing or executing its purposes heretofore, it could not originate them now. Having always waited upon the will of Paris, it waited still. It held its breath until Napoleon came.

But such a posture of affairs—such vagrant energy in a single part and paralysis in all other parts, of the body politic—is the very negation of the modern adult state. In that state, each smallest member may know as much of the progress and the exigencies of affairs as any other member great or small; each part has its own view of affairs and its own will about them. Revolutions have to take such states in detail. Evil passions, sinister views, base purposes do not and cannot sweep a nation as generous emotions sometimes do. Sedition cannot surge through the hearts of a wakeful nation as patriotism could. In such organisms poisons spread slowly: only healthful life has unbroken course. The sweep of any agitation for purposes unfamiliar or uncongenial to the customary popular thought is broken by a thousand obstacles. It may be easy to reawaken old enthusiasms, but it must be infinitely hard to create new ones, and impossible to surprise the people into unpremeditated action.

But this is not the whole significance of the size and diffused vitality of the modern democratic state. Time out of mind popular states have presented the phenomena of the many led by the few: the minds of the few disciplined by persuading, and masses of men schooled and directed by being persuaded. And doubtless this must always be the organization of democracy. But the bigness of modern states necessitates the exercise of this persuasive power of dominant minds in a way very different from that in which it was exercised in former times. "It is said by eminent censors of the press," said Mr. Bright on one occasion in the House of Commons, "that this debate will yield about thirty hours of talk, and will end in no result. I have observed that all great questions in this country require thirty hours of talk many times repeated before they are settled. There is much shower and much sunshine between the sowing of the seed and the reaping of the harvest, but the harvest is generally reaped after all."* And so it must be in all self-governing nations of to-day. They are not a single audience within sound of the orator's voice; but a thousand audiences. Their actions do not spring from a single thrill of feeling, but from slow conclusions following upon much talk. The talk must slowly percolate through the whole mass. It cannot be sent through them like the pulse which answers the call of a trumpet. A score of platforms in every neighborhood must ring with the insistent voice of the controversies; and, for a few hundreds who hear what is said by public speakers, many thousands must read of the matter in the newspapers, discuss it interjectionally at the breakfast table, desultorily in the streetcars, laconically on the streets, dogmatically at dinner. Through so many stages of con-

* Sp. i, 393.

sideration passion cannot possibly hold out. It gets chilled by overexposure. It finds the modern popular state organized for giving and hearing counsel in such a way that those who give it must be careful that it is such counsel as will wear well, and those who hear it handle and examine it enough to test its wearing qualities to the utmost.

II. Structure of the Modern Democratic State.

There are, besides, other differences between old-time democracies and our own which, though apparently differences only of form, go in reality much deeper than form. The modern democracy is constitutional. Organic laws prescribe its methods and determine its powers. The ancient democracy set no limits to the absoluteness of the state. It consequently knew nothing of that careful separation of political functions which distinguishes between executive, legislative, and judicial offices. Nor had it conceived of any of the great uses of popular representation. All citizens that chose might attend and vote in the popular assembly. Every burgher was a legislator: and not a legislator only but often executive and judge as well. That same assembly in which he gave his vote upon laws might also, on occasion, originate executive decrees, and was often called upon to sit, at once as judge and jury, in common cases at law. Such a system allowed only a narrow absolutism of direct popular vote such as could be exercised in none but small city states. It was of course utterly incapable of being stretched to the great uses of those magnificent constitutional popular states of to-day in wh. vast populations realize all the strength and liberty of self-govt. by means of a representative system which enables a wise people to legislate through its wisest men.

These are, of course, deeply fundamental differences. They destroy all real likeness of form, spirit, or aim which might otherwise be found to exist between ancient and modern democracy. The reality after which modern political movements are reaching out is the universal emancipation and brotherhood of man: the highest ideal of that Aristotelian philosophy of the state which went so far beyond the actual liberties about it was the perfect development of a selected portion of mankind. There were many men who were fit to be slaves; there were but a few who were strong to be free.

Common participation in the affairs of the nation does not, however, of itself constitute national political life, or democratic self-government. Local self-government is an essential part of the true conception of democracy. A nation is a living organism only when every part is tremulous with life. France became a republic in 1871, but not a democracy. The prefects of the provinces, the subprefects, the mayors of the greater towns continued to be appointed at Versailles. Public opinion acted upon these officials, indeed, through elected local councils; but not imperatively. The responsibility of the official had its face turned towards the national ministry to whom he owed his office. The life of the people manifested itself only in the greater movements of the common interests. Political activity had but a single channel. Its objects, too, were distant and roundabout. It was not individual, but aggregate. It had no daily exercise in self-direction; it was called upon only to make occasional efforts of nation-wide coöperation.

A democracy exists only where there is life of a very different sort. In it national affairs, though the highest and greatest, are not the most handled of its tasks. It turns to take direct part in them only occasionally; and when it does put its hand to them it does so with skill and confidence because its touch has been made sure and deft in the daily management of like things on a smaller scale. They are quick to comprehend the principles upon which the great ship of state is to be sailed because they have handled familiarly from day to day the small craft of county and town.

This principle is evidently of the most vital importance. Not mere universal suffrage constitutes democracy. Universal suffrage may confirm a *coup d'etat* which destroys liberty. Its democracy depends upon what and how many things it is applied to. There seems to me to be a deeply significant propriety in the usage by which we reserve for the local board which governs that original unit, the town, the name 'Common Council.' In it dwells the true life of common counsel. That is common counsel which reaches the smallest affairs of local politics before it stretches to the greater undertakings of the national weal.

Properly organized democracy is the best govt. of the few. This is the meaning of representative institutions. The national will centres and acts in the nation's representatives. Legislature and executive are the head and mouth of the nation. Judges are the spokesmen of its judgments. Elections transmit the forces of thought and purpose and sentiment from every part of the vast organism to these chief, these capital organs: and the democratic constitution is at its best only when these organs respond with quick sensitiveness to the suggestions of the body.

The balance, or want of balance, of democratic institutions depends upon the character of the few who act for the whole. If they merely register the impulses, the unmeasured judgments of the people, they are mere automata and can serve no healthful purpose. They must choose. They must judge. They must guide. No democracy can live without a leisured class capable of thinking on the problems of government and in a position to think upon them in the light of the most catholic learning: nor can it thrive without giving to the thoughts of such a class weight in the actual conduct of affairs. Those who act for it must have power (of tenure) to resist all hasty public judgments, but chance to disobey no long, final public judgments. And there must be clear means of seeing how far and by what measures the public thought is followed.

And the safety or hazard of such experimenting in the proper limitations of political coöperation must depend upon the organization of democracy. The evil of democracy is guaged by the chances it offers to demagogues: its good is measured by the opportunities it creates for honest statesmanship. Nothing could be conceived more favourable to the development of political genius than democracy properly organized. All history through[,] political liberty has been the foster-mother of genius. Literature and art have always found it their best patron. Political genius has not, however, always been able to derive quite the same advantage from political liberty that literary or artistic genius has derived from it. To the latter freedom of individual thought and expression was a soil of sufficient richness. They grew by being left free to grow. But political genius cannot develop its full strength unless special opportunities be opened to it in the institutions of government. It must be offered place in the government and recognition in its counsels. Otherwise men who could be great statesmen will become nothing more than caustic pamphleteers: or, if they do not care to dwarf themselves into doing in ink what they feel capable of doing in affairs, they do nothing. Their genius is snuffed out. Literary men and artists grow of themselves, if only room and pure air be provided them: statesmen must be cultivated. They can be gotten only by assured bounties of actual power.

It is not hard to point out the conditions which nurture and befriend the demagogue. They feed and grow fat on talk. If no task is required of them which will reveal their folly and impotence in action, they are safe in the possession of their sinister power. The thing is easily seen in the practice of both the British government and our own. Across the sea no one so tickles the ears of the populace with extravagant sympathy for radical programs or so boldly assails ministers with impracticable contradiction as the Opposition speaker; and nothing so speedily and effectually makes the apparent demagogue so sober, cautious, and discreet as elevation to responsible office with a seat on the opposite side of the house. In Congress it is always the minority which is endorsing catch-penny measures in the houses and uttering wild doctrines outside of them. The majority feels a trifle anxious about all its actions, and would fain show itself sensible of its responsibility. Compel the demagogue to try his hand at acts of Congress under conditions which make it impossible to fail without incurring the blame of failure, and you have either convicted him a fool or transformed him into a statesman.

The demagogue draws his sustenance of power from the affections of the people. They love his flattering talk, his plausible protestations of loyalty to them, his specious pretences of ultra-democratic principle. But it is not talk alone that is capable of winning their hearty adherence. Great action appeals with infinitely greater strength to their imagination and affections. Institutions which favour strong statesmanship under representative forms of govt. inevitably make the statesman stronger than the charlatan. He rallies about himself, not mobs, but parties. He binds men to himself not by a vague community of sentiment but by a definite and decisive oneness of purpose. The people feel a keen charm in the knowledge of the fact that, though he is powerful, his power is derived from them and is dependent upon their favour. They are conscious of being represented by him in respect to their greater and soberer aims. They gain in dignity as he gains in beneficent powers. To follow him is to realize the greatest possible amount of real political life.

In the organization of democracy, ∴, influence in the popular counsels should always lead to titular, recognized, formative power in the government of the state. No man high in the confidence of the people in political matters should be suffered to go long without the harness of office. This is the only specific against demagogery: and it is a sure specific. Nothing makes a man so contemptible in the common esteem as to be only a brawler and agitator, if he have a chance to be anything else. Institutions which make talk free but offer no opportunities for the people to find out whose talk it is that is translated into action, must in the long run wreck any democratic system.

It is common to charge democracy with creating demagogy. The charge is undiscriminating. If democracy is 'in opposition' then demagogues have their golden chance. If there be a contest between the powers that be and the people demanding to be themselves instated in the seat of government, then indeed the demagogue may sow and reap a very harvest of stormy power. The men who led the plebeans in ancient Rome, the Jacobite orators who harangued in the clubs of Paris, the men who fomented the Chartist disturbances in England furnish types of the true demagogue—the impudent, brawling fellow who is loud and indiscriminate in his denunciations of all who may be honoured for name or place, violent in his attacks upon all established order, base in his appeals to sordid interest and low passion. But these were men who were engaged merely in opposition and attack. They were those who led in the clamour for popular admission to political influence. They were mere leaders in discontent. Their opportunity was not in democracy but in the denial of democracy.

If democracy is 'in power' such fellows must look to themselves. The power of those who lead the people has only to be made the real power of responsible political rule, bringing upon them the centred trust, and, therefore, the concentrated gaze of the nation, in the conduct of public affairs, to prove the demagogue's leaden weight to drown him. It is agitation, not rule, which is his native element. When the people's will is the government's will he must handle its motive parts gingerly.

Such considerations bear directly upon that most commonly held of all objections against democracy, that it is a state ruled by mere plausible talkers. Since popular governments have unquestionably been almost uniformly more liberal in policy and more brilliant in action than any others, it is singular that it should be so persistently urged against them that they are the mere creatures of adroit dialecticians, whose very nature forbids their originating either solid counsel or stable conduct.

The idea must surely rest upon cases of degenerate democracy, and the heart of the argument must be that the degenerate democracy is the normal democracy. It might be admitted that ancient and medieval popular states were commonly subject to the distemper of putting their confidence in false men, however, without involving modern democracies in the same condemnation. For, whilst the methods by which parliamentary leaders to-day gain and keep their influence do not essentially differ from those which the leaders of non-representative states employed in earlier times for the same purpose, there is a difference between the two which redounds to the great advantage of the modern state. The modern politician has, as I have said, a vastly bigger mass of opinion to work upon. None but the finest mental batteries, with pure metals and unadulterated acids, can send a current through so huge and yet so rare a medium. There is less possibility of govt. by dialectics now because of the very breadth, because of the sheer extent of necessary concert in the modern state.

The constitution of modern society compels every action of the state to wait upon almost universal consultation. In the state of to-day, indeed, even more than in the ancient state, numbers rule. But these numbers are reached not through spoken but through written appeal. In every case there is a printed—that is, a studied and deliberate—interchange of thought. These are instrumentalities for the communication of opinion which are often alive with a quick circulation of thought and which are constantly capable of rapidly creating wide-spread sympathies of sentiment: but the heats of malign passion cannot spread without difficulty over such cool expanses of inked and published utterance. Plausibility is the mere tinsel of talk; and, amongst the infinitely various examinations to which it is sure to be subjected under such conditions it is sure to come under the eye of hundreds who will detect and expose its spurious kind.

There is a further advantage which the modern democratic leader has over the ancient. He can act within the limit of his endowments. He is not expected to *combine* wisdom in counsel and genius in action. In the ancient republics he did need this rare combination of faculties: and the fact that there was now and then a Themistokles who was as sovereign at Salamis as in the Agora is one striking proof of the extraordinary vigor and fecundity of the democratic state in its rawest form. Now we do not make such unreasonable demands upon human capacity. The man who is full of persuasive counsel is kept for his native uses —for forming the thought of the nation. The man whom nature has fitted for executive action is used in nature's way—he fights the battles or conducts the administration of the nation. Marlborough, Wolf, and Wellington, Washington, Lee, and Grant are witnesses of the abounding strength of democracy in the field no less than were Themistokles and Aristeides and Caesar; but they cannot be said to have been successors of such men. None but Washington could claim to be also a statesman. They served policies framed in their nation's councils by far different men. They were but the instruments of statecraft. They had not themselves hatched the wars in which they fought.

In another way the position of these modern generals as mere instruments of the state marks one of the capital differences be-

tween ancient and modern politics—that difference which makes
endless debate inevitable and indispensable, however it may tease
those who wish to see energetic and simple things done, and
which, consequently puts debaters at the head of the state. The
objects of the ancient states, namely, conquest and revenue, were
simple objects; the ends of the modern state, namely, civil liberty
and economic progress are infinitely complex. The thing most to
be feared is that they will be thought simple and pursued with
instant action. 'Thirty hours of debate many times repeated' are
hardly sufficient to unravel the tangled skeins of interest of which
every subject of state action must consist. Deliberation is everything, and to be had at any cost. Cromwells and Williams the Silent are to be debarred from authoritative direction at all hazards
—save in undertakings of war. States nowadays keep their statesmen busiest about internal affairs of peace. Administration waits
on legislation. It is the very nature of the state to be guided by
the better reason, rather than by the prompt *dictum*[.] To regret
'great rulers' is to deplore democracy and the modern world

III. End and Functions of the Modern Democratic State.

If democracy fulfil the best and most characteristic of its promises, its coming will be the establishment of the most humane results of the world's peace and progress, the substitution of agreement for command, of common rights of purposing for exclusive
rights of purposing—the supreme and peaceful rule of *counsel.*
The goal of political development is identical with the goal of
individual development. Both singly and collectively man's nature
draws him away from that which is brutish towards that which
is human—away from his kinship with beasts towards a fuller
realization of his kinship with God. The rule of counsel, the catholic spirit of free debate, is an earnest of the ascendancy of reason
over passion. Society has attained to its full manhood when it has
put away crude hasty action and has come to guide itself by the
slow resolutions of deliberate choice.

This manhood of society is the promise of democracy. Aristocracy promises the wisdom of a class; monarchy, the wisdom of
an individual; democracy, the wisdom of all. Its prerequisite,
therefore, is of course popular education. Practically, of course,
a universal diffusion of intelligence is impossible. Intelligence is
native, not acquired; and education is meant to train, not to create, it. But a certain start in education can be given to all alike;
&, though the level of uniform instruction must be a very low
one, so must also the part which all but the few who lead may

play in the counsels of a vast state be a very small one. Where the lowest level of education for all is still very far above illiterate ignorance, the highest pitch of culture for the few must be very high indeed. Where all minds are awake some minds will be wide awake. And such are the conditions of common counsel: a few minds to originate and suggest, many minds to weigh and appreciate; some to draw up resolutions, many to consider them. The limitations of the public meeting are the limitations of the nation's deliberations. Not everybody can lead: but everybody can have a voice in deciding results.

Government, furthermore, is not the only concern of men. To the mass of citizens it probably seems their least concern. Certainly they give to it but few of their thoughts—and those not the freshest and best. And, should they desire to do otherwise, it must prove not to be a matter of choice with them. Their marketing and house-cleaning, their bargaining and their ledger columns must stand between them and all large or leisurely thought. They are too tired and too teased by daily toil and care to have more than a few breaths of their life to give to public affairs. These practical necessities, no less than mental limitations, must always relegate the real conduct of the state to those who have leisure and commanding intelligence.

But these things which circumscribe counsel by no means empty it of its reality and power. Though only a few set the fashion for the public thought and for the rest of the nation their [there] are but small parts to take in choice of advice, the aggregate weight of this choosing general opinion infinitely outweighs the personal initiative of even the greatest leaders. Though the part of each be small the part of all is the ruling part. No man can think without affecting, however insensibly, the sensitive currents of public opinion. Like the wind, those currents blow where they list, and no man can tell whence they come or whither they go. But they are none the less governed by immutable laws of man's nature. In the great nations of the earth their season is as regular and their direction as steady as the trade winds which sweep their sure course across the oceans. Bold sailors may cross them athwart, but none may venture to go in their teeth. The men who suggest its resolutions to a nation do not hope for success unless they have first studied these great dominating currents of the public thought. They must follow awhile if they would learn how to lead at last. They first take counsel of the nation before they venture to ask it to take counsel of them. They have choice of means, but they have not choice of aims. The form of the thought may be individual, but its substance is of the common counsel.

Nothing seems more fully assured than that America will continue to be the theatre of the broadest developments of democratic practice. Nowhere else are there so few things to hinder the free action of social and political forces. It is not predominant power which makes government obeyed and respected in America, but civic principle. We are bound by common consent. Moreover we are not entangled by foreign alliances or saddled with standing armies. Both our energies and our resources are free for the tasks and privileges of peaceful development. Every circumstance invites us to attempt a uniform organization of the people for self-help and self-defence in order that, through that organization, we may work out purified and perfected types of democracy.

I have already endeavoured to indicate the true criteria of democracy, to put into words its meaning and spirit, to interpret its hopes and make clear its proper aims. It remains to point out its limitations

Democracy is the fullest form of state life: it is the completest possible realization of corporate, coöperate state life for a whole people. The limit of its benefits is the limit of the benefits of coöperation. The line at which individual initiative and enterprise should stop and state undertaking begin it is not possible for any one mind to trace; but the experience of the world is fast finding out the necessary spheres of coöperate activity, and with the advance of that experience to certain conclusions the idea of the state will become more and more clearly defined. The limit to the benefits of political coöperation is no more to be determined by abstract theory than is the limit to the benefits of commercial coöperation. It is to be found by experiment, as everything else has been found out in politics.

WWhw and WWT MS. (WP, DLC).

From Joseph Ruggles Wilson

My Beloved Woodrow—   Clarksville, Decr 12, 1885
I have read your "piece" all through, and with great care—I need not add, with very much pleasure. To say the truth furthermore, I must complain that it was not until I was far into the contents of your 90, (odd), sheets, the light dawned upon me as to what it was all about! The composition is certainly all that partiality—even mine—could expect—and surely the sentiment is, throughout, just and striking—*but* (that mean, inevitable *"but"*) as a whole it certainly is obscure. Were you to read it as a lecture—

or utter it as an oration—you could of course illumine its dark places as you went along—and could keep pointing out from the beginning whither it was all leading. To a reader, however who knows not where, in his ignorance, to place the emphasis—to make the pause—to broaden the smile—or contract the brow it produces an emotion of wonder as to the end of so much beauty of opening scenery—or what shall the house be which has such an imposing portico.

Would it not be well to state, at the very outset, *what* it is you mean to treat of; and then *how* it is you mean to treat it. In other words, could you not put the last of it first, "sorter"?

What shall I do with the sheets? Return them at once to you by mail or retain them until further notice?

Your dear mother and Josie join me in all degrees of love—to dear Ellie and yourself. We are glad to hear of her returning strength. I wonder couldn't she expend a wee bit of it in an occasional note to her fond parents—or is she doubtful as to her *handwriting*!
                        In love with you both   JRW.

ALI (WP, DLC) with WWhw notation on env.: "Ans. 14 Dec./85."

From Henry Randall Waite

                              American Institute of Civics
Dear Sir: Boston, Mass., Dec. 14, 1885.
In looking over letters relating to the Institute I am led to believe that I neglected to acknowledge the receipt of your very excellent article, on "The Courtesy of the Senate," please pardon the neglect. The article is in type & a proof will be sent if you desire. Your copy is so good however that this is perhaps unnecessary.   Cordially yours   Henry Randall Waite

HwLS (WP, DLC).

From Charles Kendall Adams

My dear Sir: Ithaca, N. Y., Dec. 14 1885
Accept of my thanks for your letter of the 11th instant. You are right in inferring that the policy outlined in my inaugural address has been adopted by the Faculty of the University.[1] We have given much time to the elaboration of details with a view to adjusting the new courses to the new requirements, and it is not a little gratifying, if not remarkable, that when we had completed the work after some eight or ten meetings, the new scheme was adopted unanimously.

I am sorry to have to say that our course in political science is still in a somewhat chaotic condition. By this I mean that it has been impossible to evolve a perfectly symmetrical course out of the condition of things that has existed here in the past. The historical side was very strong, but what may be called the political side was not very symmetrically developed. The course as it stands under the passage of the new law may be sufficiently described by saying that in the third and fourth years a student will be expected to take nine hours of work in courses specially characteristic of history and political science. The student will have come to his work with a fairly adequate preparation during the first two years. I hope that the freedom given to our methods by the new arrangement will permit of some adequate development on the political side. I take pleasure in enclosing a list of the courses in this department as they are now given in the University.

I am much interested in what you say concerning your own work. While I doubt not you will be interested in historical studies, I am sure that you will be of most service to the world by devoting yourself very largely to studies of a political character. I shall look forward with interest to any work that may come from your pen.

I am   Very Sincerely Yours   C. K. Adams

HwLS (WP, DLC).
[1] Dr. Adams had been formally inaugurated as President of Cornell University on November 19, 1885.

From Elgin Ralston Lovell Gould

My dear Wilson: Washington, D. C., Dec. 15th, 1885.

Stress of work and absence from the city during the Thanksgiving recess must account for my extreme dilatoriness in answering your very kind letter.[1] I certainly appreciated it and designed a far earlier reply.

I am much obliged to you for your prompt response to my request for copies of your book. They (4 copies) arrived in due time and have been severally designated to Geheimerath Dr. Engel—the great statistician—Regierungsrath Dr. von Studnitz, Sr. Hochwohlgeborn Consul W. Annecke—late German minister to China —and Professor Hector Denis. I thank you very much for your kind offer of a volume for myself, but I had already replaced the copy I presented to Prof. Emil de Laveleye. I would feel as much at loss, if I remained for any length of time without possessing a copy of the now classic "Congressional Government," as would the Eastern Shore Virginian, were he deprived of the omniscient annual almanac of the Baltimore "Sun." . . .

I am glad to hear that you are at work upon Comparative Systems of Administration.[2] It will form a most valuable sequel to your former work. Will you be able to get the material you need without visiting Europe? I should think personal observations would make an interesting compendium.

I find my own tastes drifting more and more in the line of economic studies. I shall make my life-work investigations in that line and after a time shall hope to produce something myself. My associations with practical men have brushed away some of cobwebs of theory and when I write it will be with a full knowledge of the practical operations of economic laws in the great world of commerce and industry. To ascertain and present truthfully facts and their operation, I conceive to be of much greater importance than the mysteries of so much theory.

I have recently become acquainted with Gen. Francis A. Walker, and this, with my intimate association with Mr. Carroll D. Wright has been of great educational value.

I am still much occupied with my report. It grows daily, but seemingly very slow. I shall be glad when it is finished.

With regard, I am,

Yours very truly,   E. R. L. Gould

ALS (WP, DLC) with WWhw notation on env.: "Ans. 1/13/85 [86]."
    1 Of Nov. 11, 1885, which is missing.
    2 See the Editorial Note, "Wilson's First Writings on Administration."

To Robert Bridges

My dear Bobby,   Bryn Mawr, Pa., 20 Dec., 1885

It is, nowadays, so seldom that I have all to myself a piece of time big enough for the composition of a 'sure enough' letter that your epistle of Oct. 21 has been cheated of an answer all this time by stress of affairs.[1] Mistakenly or not, as you will, I suffer my productive instincts to command me often, and much of my scant leisure time has been going into writing on governmental topics which I can't pretend to be teaching to the young ladies here. My thoughts return so persistently again and again to the examination of the realities of politics that I cannot claim them for my class work except by giving them leave sometimes to follow their bent. The writing I have been doing has not yet taken definite enough shape to be described. I am feeling after the real conditions which make popular institutions workable, and the most practicable means whereby they can be made and kept healthy and vigorous. If I have 'bottom,' I'll come out all right: if not, I'll decline upon something of more modest dimensions. For the last few days I've been engaged upon the thesis, that democracy is the highest and most essentially *adult* form of the state.

This is the most I can say now of my non-professional work. It will take more definite, describable shape after while.

The dark hint you drop as to work for which you mean to make an opportunity interests me supremely, old fellow—as previous epistolary and other remarks of mine about what you are assuredly cut out for doing will have prepared you to believe: but the hint method is very tantalizing! I hope the opportunity will be made soon.

Amen and amen, as to the Boston novel. I don't know why I am dissatisfied with it; but doubtless you do: and I should be a happy man to see deliverance come out of Pennsylvania *by your hands*! I'd throw my best hat to the housetops.

Yes, my dear fellow, I *am* quite sure that married life has infinitely more of happiness and inspiration in it than can be found in bachelor quarters: and to hear you utter the belief does my heart and my hope good! At the same time, you may be very sure that, if my slender means permitted my taking pleasure trips, those bachelor quarters of yours would infallibly draw me to New York without excuse or pretence of other errand. I often long for a renewal of our old comradeship more than I can tell you. The old love never dies down for a moment, but I can't keep myself from occasional heart-sickness now and again because of the dispersion of the old crowd and the necessity which keeps us apart. Good-night, Bobby. God speed you! Mrs. W. sends warm regards,

As ever   Your affectionate friend,   Woodrow Wilson

I'll send $1.oo to Wilder at once. Wish I could send more.[2] Don't you pass near us Xmas? If so, couldn't you give us a glimpse of you?   W. W.

ALS (Meyer Coll., DLC).

[1] Wilson was answering both R. Bridges to WW, Oct. 21, 1885, and R. Bridges to WW, Dec. 12, 1885, ALS (WP, DLC) with WWhw notation on env.: "Ans. Dec. 20/85."

[2] Wilson was responding to the following passage in Bridges' letter of December 12: "In my official capacity, as member of the class committee, I am requested to inform you that the Class of '79 is $56 in debt for printing the *Record*, and that the office of B. Wilder is haunted night and day by a printers devil, crying for more. We are making an effort to pay it off immediately, and will be glad to send you a copy of the *Record* at $1.

"No restrictions are placed on the amount which you may contribute to keep Wilder out of jail."

From Raymond Landon Bridgman

My dear sir,   Boston, Dec. 22, 1885.

A beginning will be made in the newspaper plan proposed last month and I inclose a list of the writers secured, with mention of the day of publication of the first four articles.

While Congress is in session I wish to give particular attention to matters pending there. Is there any leading national topic likely to be discussed at the session upon which you would like to write. If so, what, and by what date may I expect the article?

The Philadelphia Press is the nearest paper to you which has entered into the arrangement. Several papers have written that the articles would be too heavy for them to use. I hope to show that they are as readable as they are valuable and full of sharp points for the average newspaper reader.

Very truly yours,   R. L. Bridgman

ALS (WP, DLC) with WWhw notation on env.: "Ans. Dec. 24/85." Enc. missing.

Wilson's Memorandum of Janet Wilson's Land Holdings in Nebraska[1]

Date Dec. 29/85

[Description]	[Section or Lot]	[Town or Block]	[Range]	[Acres]
W ½ N E.1/4	4	21	11 E	80
S ½ N.W 1/4	4	21	11	80
E ½ S W 1/4	4	21	11	80
W ½ S E 1/4	4	21	11	80
W ½ N.E 1/4	9	21	11	80
E ½ W ½	9	21	11	160
N.W 1/4 S E 1/4	9	21	11	40
E ½ S W 1/4	9	21	11	80
N E 1/4 S E 1/4	22	22	11	40
W ½ S E 1/4	22	22	11	80
N W 1/4 N.E 1/4	27	22	11	40
S.E 1/4 N.W.1/4	27	22	11	40
				880

Taxes	59.19
	1.00
Hopewell–	60.19

WWhw MS. (WP, DLC).

[1] Wilson's memorandum was based upon a tax bill from Burt County, Neb., c. Dec. 29, 1885 (WP, DLC).

From Janet Woodrow Wilson

My precious Son: Clarksville Tenn. Jan. 4th 1886.

I fear you have been wondering at my long delay in answering your last letter. Well—it is true, that I am more busy than ever in my life before—and that, consequently, it is very difficult for me to find leisure for even a hastily pencilled note to my precious far-away children. But—in spite of my much work—if I had known *how* to answer—*what* to advise—I would have done so at once. If I could depend on my own health—or upon getting a competent nurse—or had any knowledge of the character of the medical element here—I would say *with all my heart*—if you *must* send our darling Ellie away from you—*anywhere—send her to me.* As matters are, the choice seems to be between Rome and Bryn Mawr. My dear boy—*can* you bear to send your little wife away from you? If you have a skilful physician near you, and a competent nurse as well, I would say, *keep her with you if possible.* The separation under such circumstances would be unendurable, it seems to me—unless absolutely unavoidable. If this is *not* possible, of course it will be best to send the dear girl to her kind uncle in Rome—where she will surely be well cared for. But oh, my dear boy, how will you bear it! . . .

Take courage. God loves you both, and will care for you. God bless you—darlings both. Papa & Josie join me in love unmeasured.   Yours as ever   Mother.

P.S. omitted. ALS (WP, DLC).

From Richard Heath Dabney

My dear Tommy: New York. Jan'y 11th 1886.

My delay in answering your most welcome letter is certainly no proof of my enjoyment of it, but I *did* enjoy it for all that—and immensely too. I am truly delighted to hear how contented and pleased you are with your new sphere of usefulness, and it warms up my cold, bachelor's heart no little to hear how you are revelling in the felicity of wedlock. It makes me feel powerfully like embarking upon the sea of matrimony myself, though I am afraid it will be a long time before I shall be able to do so. You are certainly to be congratulated upon having secured so sweet and congenial a companion, and I trust that the sickness from which she had been suffering when you wrote proved to be only a passing indisposition.

How about the History of Political Economy by Ely and yourself? Do you find time to work on it much in addition to your regular professorial duties? The more I think about "Congressional Government," the more convinced I am that you are right in attacking a form of government which distributes both power and responsibility in infinitesimal fractions over a host of committees. . . .

With regards to Mrs. W. I remain as ever

Sincerely yours   R. H. Dabney.

ALS (WP, DLC) with WWhw notation on env.: "Ans. Feby 8/86."

From Raymond Landon Bridgman

Dear Sir,   Boston, Jan. 11, 1886.

An article on the formation of a new national party would be very acceptable in my series. Just now when congressional matters are so engrossing, it would be difficult to find room for it, but I should be glad to use it later.[1]

Very truly yours,   R. L. Bridgman.

ALS (WP, DLC).

[1] Wilson eventually responded with "Wanted,—A Party," printed at Sept. 1, 1886.

From Daniel Collamore Heath

Dear Sir: Boston Jan'y 27. 1886

Yours of the 24th rec'd. We shall be glad to have your opinion of Miss Sheldon's Hist'y[1] after you have examined it sufficiently to discover its merits. We believe it is to work a revolution in methods of teaching this subject. As you will see by the enclosed slip, we are making a manual for the teacher wh. will greatly aid in its use.

We are happy to say that your article on the Courtesy of the Senate, will appear in the first number of The Citizen, a copy of which we hope to mail you in the course of a week.

Would it not be possible for us to get Martha Cary Thomas to write an article for us? And this suggests to me what I have long had in mind, viz. to write to both you & Miss Thomas to enquire whether you might not have in mind a text-book for the schools. Could you not make a text-book on Civil Government for the schools?[2] If not, would you not do me the favor to name the best man in your opinion for such work?

Respect. Yours,   D. C. Heath.

ALS (WP, DLC) with WWhw notation on env.: "Ans. Feby 8/86." Enc.: printed circular advertising *The Teacher's Manual for Sheldon's Studies in General History* and *Outline Map of the United States.*

1 Wilson seems to have written for an examination copy of Mary D. Sheldon, *Studies in General History. (1000 B.C. to 1880 A.D.). An Application of the Scientific Method to the Teaching of History* (Boston, 1885).

2 For the development of this correspondence, see the Editorial Note, "Wilson's Plan for a Textbook in Civil Government."

A Book Review

[February 1886]

The Greville Memoirs.*

It is easy to enjoy these Memoirs, but it is not easy to convey an idea of their interest to those who have not read them. The first part of Mr. Greville's journals, which was published in 1874, concerned the affairs of the reigns of George IV. and William IV.; the second part, now published, brings the gossipy and beguiling narrative down into the very modern times of Victoria: the times of Radicals and Reform Bills, of Chartism and Free Trade. Though the matter in these volumes is chiefly political, it is not all so, and all sorts of tastes may derive satisfaction from abundant matter of a very different sort. Mr. Greville always attended the races. He stakes his money and comments on the personal history and characteristics of jockeys quite as gravely and philosophically as he discusses Cabinet crises. He suffered his sense of duty to drag him to balls and other "events" of the London season; and his journal always receives his candid impressions of the persons he met on such occasions. He spreads upon the same pages, too, with the same sedate formality that is on all other subjects the habit of his pen, records of all his private conversations with interesting or important persons, accounts of all his little trips into the country, to see places worth seeing, to wait upon the Council at Windsor or at Balmoral, or to be guest to this, that, or the other notable person, at this, that, or the other attractive country-seat. It is all very entertaining and amusing, and all very satisfactory to the American opinion that the talk at Court is quite like talk anywhere else, albeit not quite so free or interesting, and that titled people are not less ordinary than untitled people. Mr. Greville never lacks information as to what is going on. It flows to him, quite as if nature intended it, from all quarters. "Yesterday morning John Russell sent for me. . . . He gave me an account of the strange state of things at Madrid, and of the confusion and quarrels which have followed this fine mar-

* *A Journal of the Reign of Queen Victoria, from 1837 to 1852.* By the late Chas. C. F. Greville, Esq., Clerk of the Council. New York: D. Appleton & Co.

riage the French have effected." "To-day (*the cook told me*) nearly four hundred people will dine in the castle." And so it goes. It
was evidently meant that this man should know everything.

But of course the interest and value of these memoirs centre in their dominant theme, the conduct of public affairs. These
are the writer's chief, because his professional, concern. It is
when writing about these that his journal-inditing genius seems
most at home. Both inside and outside politics, his choice is to
speak about persons rather than about things. His accounts of
what he has heard and what he has said are always excellent
reading of their kind; his accounts of what he has seen are often
almost meaningless. What is one to make of this, for instance?
"I left Troy in the morning and went to Tintern Abbey: most
glorious, which I could not describe if I would, but which produced on me an impression similar in kind and equal in amount
to that which I felt at the sight of St. Peter's." Quite a ledger-like
way of casting up a balance between the quantitative and quali-
tative value of aesthetic emotions, but not of much service to the
reader who has not before him the estimate of what and how
much the writer felt at seeing St. Peter's. But these descriptions
of ruins and country sides which Mr. Greville has avowedly not
attempted would in any case belong to that part of his journals
which would soonest have lost its interest by evaporation. The
things that he does well are the things we most care to have him
do for us. We can see Tintern Abbey for ourselves; but we cannot
see Lord John Russell and Palmerston and Peel; and Mr. Greville
is able to do us a service by showing us these historical person-
ages as they appeared behind the scenes of the public stage.

One circumstance that gives great value and interest to these
journals is, that this grave, sedate gentleman, time out of mind
"Clerk of the Council," was almost as stable a part of the government as the queen herself. His official life ran through a greater
part of three reigns, and kept him constantly at the centre of affairs. His office, not less enduring than the throne itself, was,
as one may state without proving, less pivotal than the throne;
so that its occupant, though very close to the principal actors in
politics, was not compelled to be so strenuous an observer of
events as the sovereign, and could watch ministries come and go
with more spontaneous impartiality. Like the queen, he had to
serve first one and then the other party; but he knew that he had
simply to record decisions, not to make them, and could submit
without rancor to functions which are apt to mortify a high-
spirited sovereign, who theoretically has something more than

clerical duties to perform. It was of course no chagrin to him to find himself no actor in affairs. He was content to be familiar with the exits and the entrances of those who were the chief actors.

Besides, in addition to having the best of official positions from which to observe politics and politicians narrowly, Mr. Greville had an excellent mental position from which to observe them impartially. He was no partisan. He had a warmer, more conscious love of country than the ordinary official, and less stiffness of thought. Too judicial to be a leader in political contests, too second-rate to be a leader in political conceptions, he was at the same time too sensible to misjudge himself a statesman, too modest to try to be more than an excellent servant of the Council. His only political passion is hatred of the Radicals. These he would by all means outwit: though we know that, not living till our day, he never saw a real Radical. Such a man, intelligent but not original, has of course left us no profound reflections concerning the political life about him; but, after all, we never expect profound reflections in a diary. They would be out of place there, because one would have to confess to the feeling that they were not spontaneous. It is the happy fortune of writers of journals, that neither originality nor learning is required from them. What we want in them is, not philosophy, but those best servants of philosophy, wide-open eyes and a faculty for getting first-hand impressions of men and things and for setting forth those impressions honestly and unreservedly.

Mr. Greville has such eyes and such a faculty, and the consequence is that we learn from him just those things about English government which our philosophy of politics needs when it turns its eyes towards England. He lays open to our view that part of government—much the largest part—which depends upon the personal qualities and foibles of ministers of state, much as a man of like character and training might do for our national government were he in a position to see daily, and so know familiarly, all the characters of the House and Senate Standing Committees—or were he Clerk of a Council of Chairmen. In reading such memoirs, one, as it were, sees government in undress; sees not the forms, but the *men* of government, with all their unsublime motives, limitations of judgment, and smallness of view, as well as with their stronger and higher attributes. By being thus dissected—or, rather, thus *vivisected*—it may seem to some that government loses much of its dignity; but students of politics who want the kernels of things, and not their husks merely, must rejoice in thus seeing the real thing, even though it be vulgar or mean. There is unquestionably much sound reason in making government appear as majestic and impressive as possible to those who have simply to obey it; but to those whose business it is to understand government, it ought to be presented without its wigs and robes and ceremonies.

And, after all has been said, it must be confessed by every unbiassed reader of Mr. Greville's journals that English politics are not belittled by what he tells us. They do not lose in the essentials of dignity. It is not all partisan selfishness. Honesty presides. There is much steady regard to principle and heed to conscience. And these better things are constantly helped on by Mr. Greville himself. A trusted friend and counsellor of men in both parties, he hears expressions of opinion and gets wind of plans from both sides; and he uses his opportunities with the utmost patriotism. Without breach of confidence with anyone, he exerts himself to prevent all needless friction between opponents; he bestirs himself to remove misunderstandings such as are likely to start party differences off on a false scent to the detriment of the state. On one occasion, for instance, he adroitly but honorably acquaints Sir Robert Peel and his fellow-leaders in opposition, with Lord John Russell's disposition to act with them against Chartist demands in spite of his apparent partisan stiffness—of course without Russell's knowledge,—and so moderates the whole tone of a great debate in Parliament which promised to make the breach between parties impassable; and again and again we find him performing like amiable offices of peace and equity, until he has won our warmest admiration.

The press has certainly in our day become a great revealer of private affairs. The private lives alike of individuals and of governments are being freely, not to say ruthlessly, laid open to the public gaze. Mr. Greville is as candid in speaking of the state as Mr. Froude in speaking of Carlyle. Nothing is kept back. Print and electricity are compacting the world into one vast community, in which governments, like individuals, are one's neighbors, about whom one may daily learn and retail spicy gossip. A man may get from the circulating library at his door all that books can tell him of existing systems of government. Easy and comparatively inexpensive journeys may bring him within reach of all the knowledge of such systems that can be gained from personal observation. His Grevilles will acquaint him with the home-life of governments, his morning papers with the daily wants of their public life. It is possible to know as much every day of London and Paris and Berlin as of Washington. The world is become an open laboratory in which one may almost hourly note the operation of social and political forces.   Woodrow Wilson.

Printed in the Chicago *Dial*, vi (Feb. 1886), 269-71.

Wilson's Revised Course of Study for Students in History and Political Science[1]

[*c. Feb. 1, 1886*]

HISTORY.

The courses indicated suggest the topical plan of instruction which is to be followed. The histories of Greece and Rome are taken as representative of ancient history, those of France and England as representative of mediaeval and modern history; and in following these special lines the work of the classes will consist largely in the preparation by individuals of reports on specific topics and important episodes in the histories studied. These reports will be founded, not only upon the text-books used, but also upon all the standard authorities available.

Constant text-book drill will be combined with instruction by means of frequent lectures, whose object will be to give life to the narrative of the text-book used in recitation, by recounting the most important contemporary events in the history of other countries, and by pointing out the chief and most memorable characteristics of the periods studied, as well as the philosophical connection of leading facts and tendencies. The general purpose of the lectures will be to group and explain facts separated in the narrative, and to keep the student mindful of the broad views of history to which the events in the lives of individual nations stand related.

The courses on the Italian Renaissance and the German Reformation will be lecture courses.

Each year's work will be introduced by a brief course of lectures on the philosophy of history and methods of study.

First Year.   Major Course.
(*Ancient History—Minor Course.*)

I. History of Greece. *Five hours a week on alternate weeks during the first Semester.*

In this course lectures are given on such topics as the reforms of Solon and of Cleisthenes, the causes of the Persian invasion, the character and influence of the Confederacy of Delos. As the history of the popular states of Greece turns largely upon the individual characters and influence of leading men, class reports are required on the antecedents, lives, and work of the principal statesmen, dramatists, and orators.

II. History of Rome. *Five hours a week on alternate weeks during the first semester and five hours weekly throughout most of the second semester.*

In this course the lectures deal with such topics as the sources of Roman history, the causes, means, and ends of Roman conquest, Roman provincial administration, agrarian troubles, the characters, aims and reforms of the Gracchi.

In both courses text-book drill is made prominent, but more especially in Roman history, because the internal history of Rome, down to the time of the empire, turns upon class struggles and consequent legal and constitutional reforms which can be mastered in no other way.

The plan of conducting work in both Greek and Roman history simultaneously, the two courses alternating with each other week by week, is adopted in order that the histories of the two countries may run parallel up to the point where Greek history is merged into Roman by conquest, with a view to enable the student when hearing lectures, to perceive for herself, contrasts and likenesses.

III. European history from the fall of the Western Empire to the establishment of the Empire of Charles the Great. *Lectures five hours a week during the last weeks of the second semester.*

Second Year
(Modern History—Minor Course.)

History of France. *Three times weekly, on alternate weeks throughout the year.*

History of England. *Three times weekly, on alternate weeks throughout the year.*

Italian Renaissance and German Reformation. *Twice weekly during the first semester.*

Lectures on special topics in American History. *Twice weekly during the second semester.*

The topics selected for the lectures on American history will be such as the following: the foundation of the colonies, the contest between England, Spain, and France for the possession of America, contrasts in colonial life and manners, the causes of the Revolution, the second war with Great Britain, the great westward migration, the Missouri compromise, the history of parties with especial reference to the rise and influence of the Federalist party.

Either year of the major course in History may be taken separately as a minor course.

Group. History and Political Science. Students that elect this group may take as required studies, instead of one year of science and one year of history, one year of science and one year of French, Italian or Spanish.

Two years of history may be taken without the course in political science by electing one year of history as a minor course, and a second year as a free elective.

POLITICAL SCIENCE.

First Year.   Major Course.

Elements of Political Economy. Text-book drill and lectures. *Three times weekly throughout the year.*

History of Political Opinion. Lectures and class reports. *Twice weekly throughout the year.*

Second Year.

English and American Constitutional History. Lectures. *Three times weekly throughout the year.*

History of Political Institutions. Lectures. *Twice weekly throughout the year.*

Group. History and Political Science.

Printed in *Bryn Mawr College. Program. 1886-87* (Philadelphia, 1886), pp. 30-32.
    ¹ For a description of Wilson's actual course work during his second year at Bryn Mawr, see the Editorial Note, "Wilson's Teaching at Bryn Mawr College, 1886-87," and "Wilson's Description of His Courses at Bryn Mawr College," printed at Nov. 27, 1886.

From David Starr Jordan

                              The Indiana University, Bloomington.
Dear Sir,   President's Room, Feb'y 1st 1886.

There is a possibility that our Chair of History may become vacant in June. Salary $1500 to $2000. Would such a position in a flourishing State Univ. in a faculty chiefly composed of young men of modern training offer any attractions to you? Please regard this communication for the present as confidential.

                    Very truly yours,   David S. Jordan.

ALS (WP, DLC) with WWhw notation on env.: "Ans. Feby 8/86."

Notes for Lectures on Roman History

[c. Feb. 9-c. May 15, 1886]

Notebook with WWhw title on first page: "Roman Conquest."
Contents:

(1) Notes, mainly in WWsh, for lectures on Roman history listed in WW's order, with composition dates when given: "*Roman Conquest*," with WWhw outline; "*Roman Provincial Administration during the Republic*"; "*Tiberius Gracchus B.C. 133*"; "*Agrarian Troubles in Rome in 133 B.C.*," Feb. 18, 1886; "*Gaius Gracchus (153-121)*," Feb. 23, 1886; "*Causes of the Decline of the Republic*," March 25, 1886, printed at this date; "*Marius and Sulla*," March 29, 1886; "*Conquest, Provincial Organization and the Municipal Constitution*"; "*Caesar's Constitutional Reforms*," April 2, 1886; "*Heterogeneous Character of the Empire*," April 28, 1886; "*Provincial Administration under the Empire*," April 29, 1886, printed at this date; "*Provincial Organization under the Empire*," April 30, 1886; "*The Army under the Empire*," May 3, 1886; "*The Flavian Emperors (69-180 B.C. [sic])*," May 3, 1886; "*The Soldier Emperors (180-284)*," May 4, 1886; "*Diocletian, Constantine, and the New Constitution*," May 5, 1886; "*The Eastern and Western Empires*," May 6, 1886; "*The Neighbours of the Empire in the 4th Century*," May 7, 1886, with WWhw bibliography; "*The Huns and the Alani*," May 10, 1886; "*The West Goths*," May 11, 1886; "*The Vandals*," May 12, 1886; "*Salian Franks and Burgundians*," May 13, 1886; "*East Goths and Lombards*," May 14, 1886; and "*The Franks from Chlodwig to Charles the Great.*"

(2) Loose pages of notes on a work in Roman history made by Ellen Axson Wilson.

Notebook (WP, DLC).

A Political Essay

[c. Feb. 10, 1886]

Responsible Government under the Constitution*

Our written constitutions are more or less successful generalizations of political experience, and they exercise much the same spell upon the mind that other confident, roundly put generalizations exert. Like other broad inductions, they commend them-

---

* Abbott Lawrence Lowell, "Ministerial Responsibility and the Constitution," *Atlantic Monthly*, LVII (Feb. 1886), 180-93, had subjected Wilson's arguments for Cabinet government to rigorous and searching criticism and asserted that institution in the United States of the system of ministerial responsibility was neither wise nor feasible. Wilson thereupon replied at once in this essay, apparently on his own initiative, since the letter of February 15, 1886, from Thomas Bailey Aldrich, editor of the *Atlantic Monthly*, acknowledging receipt of Wilson's manuscript, is the first letter from Aldrich in the Wilson Papers. For an account of Wilson's first meeting with and a biographical note on Lowell, see WW to ELA, April 24, 1886, n. 2. Wilson recast and published "Responsible Government under the Constitution" under the title of "Government under the Constitution" in *An Old Master and Other Political Essays* (New York, 1893), pp. 141-81. All other notes in this essay are Wilson's and have been numbered consecutively. [Eds.' note]

selves as whole truths, though they are in fact only partial truths. Wherever they have misread or let drop from their reckoning any one of the lasting conditions which go to make a system workable, they must prove to have promised more than they can possibly fulfill. Their tone of command does not at all alter the historic realities of government. Human nature, especially political human nature, remains the same; and written constitutions can stand for facts only within the limits of those universal conditions of government over which they have no reforming power. This is the ground for that contempt everywhere felt and expressed, outside of French national conventions, for *a priori* constitutions, for paper boats meant to be seaworthy ships of state. But, though written constitutions cannot create a new nature for government, they can and do create new forms of government; above all, they speak out with the utmost plainness definite purposes of government, and the striking forms or novel purposes which they develop catch and dominate men's thoughts. The reality of the new forms creates a violent presumption in favor of the reality of the substance which they are supposed to contain.

The limitation of written constitutions lies centrally in the fact that laws cannot enforce themselves. In one sense, all governments must be governments of men, not of laws. Laws can have no other life than that which is given them by the administration and obedience of men; and the way in which men naturally exercise power must constitute the essence of every system under which they exercise it.

These considerations apply with less force to the Constitution of the United States than to many others, domestic and foreign, that might be cited, because it was framed by exceptional men thoroughly schooled in the realities of government. But even the Constitution of the United States illustrates the congenital weakness of its family. Its weakness in some points is, indeed, all the more striking because of its great strength in all others. Its strength will be found, upon analysis, to lie in its definiteness and in its limitations rather than in any balance of its energetic parts. Sir Henry Maine, with his instinct for central facts, has recently put his finger upon the chief sinews of our system. "American experience," he says, "has shown that, by wise constitutional provisions thoroughly thought out beforehand, democracy may be made tolerable. The public powers are carefully defined; the mode in which they are to be exercised is fixed; and the amplest securities are taken that none of the more important constitutional arrangements shall be altered without every guarantee of caution and every opportunity for deliberation. . . . It would seem that, by a wise constitution, democracy may be made nearly as calm as water in a great artificial reservoir."[1] These facts of the distinctness of the provisions of our Constitution and the difficulties and delays thrown about its amendment are those which would naturally seem most striking to a qualified English observer, because of the capital contrast which they present to the chief features of the singular constitution under which he himself lives. The difference between our own case and that of Great Britain upon which we have most reason to congratulate ourselves is that here, because of our written Constitution, public opinion has definite criteria for its conservatism; whereas in England it has only shifting, uncertain precedent. In both countries there is the same respect for law. But there is not in England the same certainty that exists here as to what the law of the constitution is. We have a fundamental law which is written, and which in its main points is read by all alike in a single accepted sense. There is no more quarrel about its main intent than there is in England about the meaning of Magna Charta. But much of the British constitution has not the support of even a common statute. It may, in respect of many vital parts of it, be interpreted or understood in half a dozen different ways, *and amended by the prevalent understanding.*

It is significant in this connection that one of the most important and most esteemed of the many legal commentaries on our government is entitled Constitutional Limitations. In expounding the restrictions imposed by fundamental law upon state and federal action, Judge Cooley is allowed to have laid bare the greater meanings of our whole constitutional system. The "may-nots" and "shall-nots" of our constitutions give them their distinctive shape and character. The strength which preserves the system is the strength of self-control. These constitutional restraints express the all-determining characteristic of the people by whom they are accepted and obeyed. They rest upon the legal conscience —upon what Mr. Grote would have called the "constitutional morality"—of our race. We are above all things law-abiding. These prohibitions of the law do not assert themselves as taskmasters set over us by some external power. They are of our own devising. We are *self*-restrained.

This legal conscience constitutes, for instance, the only guarantee of that chief arrangement of our constitutional system, the division of powers between the state and federal governments.

[1] Popular Government (Am. ed.), pages 110, 111.

The integrity of the powers of the States has depended solely upon the conservatism, the conservative legal conscience, of the federal courts. State functions have certainly not decayed; but the prerogatives of the States have been preserved, not by their own forces of self-defense, but by the national government's grace of self-restraint. What curtailment their province might suffer has been illustrated in several notable cases in which the Supreme Court of the United States has confirmed to the general government extensive powers of punishing state judicial and executive officers for disobedience to state laws. Although the federal courts have again and again obeyed their legal conscience in restraint of the aggressions of Congress upon the States, they have also from time to time countenanced grave encroachments upon state powers; and their occasional laxity of principle upon such points is sufficiently significant of the fact that there is no *balance* between the state and federal governments, but only a customary "constitutional morality" on the part of the federal courts. The actual encroachments which the latter have permitted to themselves, under the pressure of strong political interest at critical periods, were not needed to prove the potential supremacy of the federal government. They showed how that potential supremacy would on occasion become actual supremacy; but they added nothing but illustration to the principle that there is no guarantee but that of conscience that justice will be vouchsafed a suitor when his adversary is both court and opposing litigant. So strong is the instinct of our governments to keep within the sanction of the law that even when the last three amendments to the Constitution were being forced upon the Southern States by means which were revolutionary, the outward forms of the Constitution were observed. But it was none the less manifest with what sovereign impunity the national government might act in stripping those forms of their genuineness. As there are times of sorrow or of peril which try men's souls, and so lay bare the inner secrets of their characters, so there are times of revolution which act as fire in burning away all but the basic elements of constitutions. It is then, too, in the case of constitutions, that dormant powers wake which are not afterwards easily lulled to sleep again.

Such was certainly the effect of the civil war upon the Constitution of the Union. The "implying" of powers, once cautious, is now become bold and confident. In the discussions now going forward with reference to federal regulation of great corporate undertakings and federal aid to education, there are a score of writers and speakers who tacitly assume the powers of the national government in such matters for one that urges a constitutional objection. Constitutional objections, before the war habitual, have now lost all prominence. And the source of every contemplated increase of federal function is legislation, of course. Congress stands at the front of all government, because it is the one motive, originating power set up by the Constitution. It is the single affirmative force of the system. The President appoints officers and negotiates treaties subject to the "Yes" of the Senate. Congress organizes departments, organizes the navy, organizes the army. It audits, approves, and pays expenses. It conceives and directs all comprehensive policy. All else is negation. The President says "No" in his veto; the Supreme Court says "No" in its restraining decisions.

It is the habit both of English and of American writers to speak of the constitution of Great Britain as if it were "writ in water," because nothing but the will of Parliament stands between it and revolutionary change. They fail to ask what it is that constitutes the will of Parliament. Parliament dare not go faster than the public thought. There are vast barriers of conservative public opinion to be overrun before a ruinous speed in revolutionary change can be attained. In the last analysis, our own Constitution has no better safeguard. We have, as I have already pointed out, the salient advantage of knowing just what the standards of our Constitution are. They are formulated in a written code, wherein all men may look and read; whereas many of the designs of the British system are to be sought only in a cloud-land of varying individual readings of affairs. From the constitutional student's point of view, there are, for instance, as many different Houses of Lords as there are writers upon the historical functions of that upper chamber. But the public opinion of Great Britain is no more a juggler of precedents than is the public opinion of this country. Perhaps the absence of a written constitution makes it even less a fancier of logical refinements. The arrangements of the British constitution have, for all their theoretical instability, a very firm and definite standing in the political habit of Englishmen: and the greatest of those arrangements can be done away with only by the extraordinary force of conscious revolution.

We are too apt to forget how much of our own institutions rests upon the same basis, upon no other foundations than those that are laid in the opinions of the people. It is within the undoubted constitutional power of Congress, for example, to overwhelm the opposition of the Supreme Court upon any question by an increase in the number of justices and a refusal to confirm any appointments to the new places which do not promise to change the opinion of the court. Once, at least, a plan of this sort was thought to have been carried deliberately into effect. But we do not think of such a violation of the spirit of the Constitution as possible, simply because we share and contribute to that public opinion which makes such outrages upon constitutional morality impossible by standing ready to curse them. There is a close analogy, as it seems to me, between this virtual inviolability of the Supreme Court and the integrity hitherto vouchsafed to the English House of Lords. There may be an indefinite creation of peers at any time that a strong ministry chooses to give the sovereign its now virtually imperative advice in favor of such a course. It was, doubtless, fear of the final impression that would be made upon public opinion by action so extraordinary, as much as the timely yielding of the Lords upon the question at issue, that held the ministry back from such a measure, on one notable occasion. Hitherto that ancient upper chamber has had in this regard the same protection that shields our federal judiciary. Here again it is Congress which is equipped for aggression. With it lies the potential, the virtual, supremacy.

It is not essentially a different case as between Congress and the Executive. What with the covetous admiration of the Presidency recently manifested by some alarmed theorists in England, and the renewed prestige lately given that office by the prominence of the question of civil service reform, it is just now particularly difficult to apply political facts to an analysis of the President's power. But a clear conception of his real position is for that very reason all the more desirable. While he is a dominant figure in politics would seem to be the best time to scrutinize and understand him.

It is clearly misleading to use the ascendant influence of the President in effecting the objects of civil service reform as an illustration of the constitutional size and weight of his office. The principal part in making administration pure, business-like, and efficient must, under any conceivable system of government, be taken by the executive. It was certainly taken by the executive in England thirty years ago; and that much in opposition to the will of Parliament. The prominence of our administration in administrative reform furnishes no legitimate illustration of the singularity of executive influence in this county.

In estimating the actual powers of the President it is no doubt best to begin, as almost all writers in England and America now habitually begin, with a comparison between the executives of the two kindred countries. Whilst Mr. Bagehot has done more than any other thinker to clear up the facts of English constitutional practice, he has also, there is reason to believe, done something towards obscuring those facts. Everybody, for instance, has accepted as wholly true his description of the ministry of the Crown as merely an executive committee of the House of Commons; and yet that description is only partially true. An English cabinet represents, not the Commons only, but also the Crown. Indeed, it is itself "the Crown." All executive prerogatives are prerogatives which it is within the discretion of the cabinet itself to make free use of. The fact that it is generally the disposition of ministers to defer to the opinion of Parliament in the use of the prerogative does not make that use the less a privilege strictly beyond the sphere of direct parliamentary control, to be exercised independently of its sanction, even secretly on occasion, when ministers see their way clear to serving the state thereby. "The ministry of the day," says a perspicacious expounder of the English system,[2] "appears in Parliament, on the one hand, as personating the Crown in the legitimate exercise of its recognized prerogatives; and on the other hand, as the mere agent of Parliament itself, in the discharge of the executive and administrative functions of government cast upon them by law." Within the province of the prerogative "lie the stirring topics of foreign negotiations, the management of the army and navy, public finance, and, in some important respects, colonial administration." Very recent English history furnishes abundant and striking evidence of the vitality of the prerogative in these fields in the hands of the gentlemen who "personate the Crown" in Parliament. "No subject has been more eagerly discussed of late," declares Mr. Amos (page 187), "than that of the province of Parliament in respect of the making of treaties and the declaration of war. No prerogative of the Crown is more undisputed than that of taking the initiative in all negotiations with foreign governments, conducting them throughout, and finally completing them by the signature and ratification of a treaty. . . . It is a bare fact that during the progress of the British diplomatic movements which terminated in the Treaty of Berlin of 1878, or more properly in the Afghan war of that year,"—including the secret treaty by which Turkey ceded Cyprus to England, and England assumed the protectorate of Asia Minor,—"Parliament never had an op-

[2] Mr. Sheldon Amos, Fifty Years of the English Constitution, page 338.

portunity of expressing its mind on any one of the important and complicated engagements to which the country was being committed, or upon the policy of the war upon the northwest frontier of India. The subjects were, indeed, over and over again discussed in Parliament, but always subsequent to irreparable action having been taken by the government" (page 188). Had Mr. Amos lived to take his narrative of constitutional affairs beyond 1880, he would have had equally significant instances of ministerial initiative to adduce in the cases of Egypt and Burmah.

The unfortunate campaign in the Soudan was the direct outcome of the purchase of the Suez Canal shares by the British government in 1875. The result of that purchase was that "England became pledged in a wholly new and peculiar way to the support of the existing Turkish and Egyptian dominion in Egypt; that large English political interests were rendered subservient to the decisions of local tribunals in a foreign country; and that English diplomatic and political action in Egypt, and indeed in Europe, was trammeled, or at least indirectly influenced, by a narrow commercial interest which could not but weigh, however slightly, upon the apparent purity and simplicity of the motives of the English government." And yet the binding engagements which involved all this were entered into "despite the absence of all assistance from, or consent of, Parliament."[3] Such exercises of the prerogatives of the Crown receive additional weight from "the almost recognized right of evolving an army of almost any size from the Indian seed-plot, of using reserve forces without communication to Parliament in advance, and of obtaining large votes of credit for prospective military operations of an indefinite character, the nature of which Parliament is allowed only dimly to surmise" (page 392). The latest evidence of the "almost recognized" character of such rights was the war preparations made by England against Russia in 1885. Add to such powers of committing the country irrevocably to far-reaching foreign policies, of inviting or precipitating war, and of using Indian troops without embarrassment from the trammels of the Mutiny Act, the great discretionary functions involved in the administration of colonial affairs, and some measure has been reached of the amount of power wielded by ministers, not as the mere agents of Parliament, but as personating the Crown. Such is in England the independence of action possible to the executive.

As compared with this, the power of the President is insignificant. Of course, as everybody says, he is more powerful than the

[3] Amos, page 384.

sovereign of Great Britain. If relative power were the principle of etiquette, Mr. Cleveland would not have to lift his hat to the Queen, because the Queen is not the executive. The prerogatives of the Crown are still much greater than the prerogatives of the presidency; but they are exercised, not by the wearer of the crown, but by the ministry of the Crown.

As Sir Henry Maine rightly says, the framers of our Constitution, consciously or unconsciously, made the President's office like the King's office under the English constitution of their time, —the constitution, namely, of George III., who chose his advisers with or without the assent of Parliament. They took care, however, to pare down the model where it seemed out of measure with the exercise of the people's liberty. They allowed the President to choose his ministers freely, as George seemed to have established his right to do; but they made the confirmation of the Senate a necessary condition to his appointments. They vested in him the right of negotiating treaties with foreign governments; but he was not to sign and ratify treaties until he had obtained the sanction of the Senate. That oversight of executive action which Parliament had not had the spirit or the inclination to exert, and which it had forfeited its independence by not exerting, was forever secured to our federal upper chamber by the fundamental law. The conditions of mutual confidence and cooperation between executive and legislature now existing in England had not then been developed, and consequently could not be reproduced in this country. The position and disposition of mutual wariness which were found existing there were therefore made constitutional here by express written provision. In short, the transitional relations of the Crown and Parliament of that day were crystallized in our Constitution, such guarantees of executive good faith and legislative participation in the weightier determinations of government as were lacking in the model being sedulously added.

The really subordinate position of the presidency is hidden from view partly by that dignity which is imparted to the office by its conspicuous place at the front of a great government, and its security and definiteness of tenure; partly by the independence apparently secured to it by its erection into an entirely distinct and separate "branch" of the government; and partly by those circumstances of our history which have thrust our Presidents forward, during one or two notable periods, as real originators of policy and leaders in affairs. In a word, the President has always been at least titular head of a great nation; and he has sometimes been the real master of its destinies. He has been powerful, however, only at such times as he has had Congress at his beck. While the new government was a-making,—and principally because it was a-making,—Washington and his secretaries were looked to by Congress for guidance; and during the presidencies of several of Washington's immediate successors the continued prominence of questions of foreign policy and of financial management kept the officers of the government in a position of semi-leadership. Jackson was masterful with or without right. He entered upon his presidency as he entered upon his campaign in Florida, without caring too much about constitutional warrant for what he was to undertake. In the settlement of the Southern question Congress went on all fours with the President. He was powerful because Congress was acquiescent.

But such cases prove rather the usefulness than the strength of the presidency. Congress has at several very grave crises in national affairs been seasonably supplied with an energetic leader or agent in the person of the President. At other times, when Congress was in earnest, our executives have either been overwhelmed, as Johnson was, or have had to decline upon much humbler services. Their negotiations with foreign governments are as likely to be disapproved as approved; their budgets are cut down like a younger son's portion; their appointments are censured and their administrations criticised without chance for a counter-hearing. They create nothing. Their veto is neither revisory nor corrective. It is merely obstructive. It is, as I have said, a simply blunt negation, oftentimes necessarily spoken without discrimination against a good bill because of a single bad clause in it. In such a contest between origination and negation, origination must always win, or government must stop. In England the veto of the Crown has not passed out of use, as is commonly said. It has simply changed its form. It no longer exists as an imperative, obstructive "No," uttered by the sovereign. It has passed over into the privilege of the ministers to throw their party weight, reinforced by their power to dissolve Parliament, against measures of which they disapprove. It is a much-tempered instrument, but for that reason all the more useful and flexible. The old blunt, antagonistic veto is no longer needed. But here it is needed, to preserve the presidency from the insignificance of merely administrative functions. Since executive and legislature cannot come into relations of mutual confidence and coöperation, the former must be put into a position to maintain a creditable competition for consideration and dignity.

A clear-headed, methodical, unimaginative President like Mr.

Cleveland unaffectedly recognizes the fact that all creating, originating power rests with Congress, and that he can do no more
than direct the details of such projects as he finds commanded
by its legislation. The suggestions of his message he acknowledges to have been made merely to satisfy his own conscience.
That they are not regarded by Congress he takes as a matter of
course, and does not stop even to regret. It is his duty to tell Congress what he thinks concerning the pending questions of the
day; it is not his duty to interest himself in the effect produced on
Congressmen.

A partial confirmation of these views comes from those who
oppose any such leadership of Congress by the executive as exists in England, on the ground of the increase of power which
would accrue as a result to Congress. It is said that such a
change would, by centring party and personal responsibility in
Congress, give to legislation too great a prominence; would make
Congress the object of too excited an interest on the part of the
people.[4] Legislation in Parliament, instead of being piecemeal,
tessellated work, such as is made up in Congress of the various
pieces contributed by the standing committees, is, under each
ministry, a continuous, consistent, coherent whole; and, instead
of bearing the sanction of both national parties, is the peculiar
policy of only one of them. It is thought that, if such coherence
of plan, definiteness and continuity of aim, and sanction of party
were to be given the work of Congress, the resulting concentration of popular interest and opinion would carry Congress over all
the barriers of the Constitution to an undisputed throne of illimitable power. In short, the potential supremacy of Congress is
thought to be kept within bounds, not by the constitutional power
of the executive and the judiciary, its coordinate branches, but
by the intrinsic dullness and confusion of its own proceedings.
It cannot make itself interesting enough to be great.

But this is a two-edged argument, which one must needs handle with great caution. It is evidently calculated to destroy the
work of any argument constructed on the principle that it is laws
which are effective to the salvation of our constitutional arrangements: for it is itself constructed on the opposite principle, that
it is the state of popular interest in the nation which balances the
mechanism of the government. It would, too, serve with equal
efficacy against any scheme whatever for reforming the present

<hr />

[4] See, for the best presentation of this view, a striking article on Ministerial
Responsibility and the Constitution, by Mr. A. L. Lowell, in the Atlantic Monthly
for February, 1886.

methods of legislation in Congress, with which almost everybody is dissatisfied. Any reform which would tend to give to national legislation that uniform, open, intelligent, and responsible character which it now lacks would also create that popular interest in the proceedings of Congress which would unhinge the Constitution. Democracy is so delicate a form of government that it must break down if given too great facility or efficacy of operation. No one body of men must be suffered to utter the voice of the people, lest that voice become, through it, directly supreme.

The fact of the overtopping power of Congress, however, remains. The houses create all governmental policy, with that wide latitude of "political discretion" in the choice of means for giving effect to their will within the sphere of the federal powers which the Supreme Court unstintingly accords them. Congress has often come into conflict with the Supreme Court by attempting to extend the province of the federal government as against the States; but it has never, I believe, been brought to book for any alleged exercise of powers as against its competing branch, the executive, —a fact which would seem to furnish proof of its easy supremacy within the federal field. Having by constitutional grant the last word as to foreign relations, the control of the finances, and even the oversight of executive appointments, Congress exercises what powers of direction and management it pleases as fulfilling, not as straining, the Constitution. Government *lives* in the origination, not in the defeat, of measures of government. The President obstructs by means of his "No;" the houses govern by means of their "Yes." He has killed some policies that are dead; they have given birth to all policies that are alive.

But the measures born in Congress have no common lineage. They have not even a traceable kinship. They are fathered by a score or two of unrelated standing committees: and Congress stands godfather to them all, without discrimination. Congress, in effect, parcels out its great powers amongst groups of its members, and so confuses its plans and obscures all responsibility. It is a leading complaint of Sir Henry Maine's against the system in England, which is just under his nose, that it confers upon the cabinet, a body which deliberates and resolves in strict secrecy,—and so reminds him of the Spartan Ephors and the Venetian Council of Ten,—the preliminary shaping and the initiation of all legislation. He commends, by contrast, that constitution (our own, which he sees at a great distance) which reserves to the legislature itself the originating and drafting of its measures. It is hard for us, who have this commended constitution under our noses, to perceive wherein we have the advantage. British legislation is for the most part originated and shaped by a single committee, acting in secret, whose proposals, when produced, are eagerly debated and freely judged by the sovereign legislative body. Our legislation is framed and initiated by a great many committees, deliberating in secret, whose proposals are seldom debated and only perfunctorily judged by the sovereign legislative body. It is impossible to mistake the position and privileges of the British cabinet, so great and conspicuous and much discussed are they. They simplify the whole British system for men's understandings by merely standing at the centre of it. But our own system is simple only in appearance. It is easy to see that our legislature and executive are separate, and that the legislature matures its own measures by means of committees of its own members. But it may readily escape superficial observation that our legislature, instead of being simply served, is ruled by its committees; that those committees prepare their measures in private; that their number renders their privacy a secure secrecy by making them too many to be watched, and individually too insignificant to be worth watching; that their division of prerogatives results in a loss, through diffusion, of all actual responsibility; and that their coördination leads to such a competition amongst them for the attention of their respective houses that legislation is rushed when it is not paralyzed.

It is thus that, whilst all real power is in the hands of Congress, that power is often unhinged and its exercise brought almost to a standstill. The competition of the committees is the clog. Their reports stand in the way of each other: and so the complaint is warranted that Congress can get nothing done. Interests which press for attention in the nation are reported upon by the appropriate committee, perhaps, but the report gets pushed to the wall. Or they are not reported upon. They are brought to the notice of Congress, but they go to a committee which is unfavorable. The progress of legislation depends both upon the fortunes of competing reports and upon the opinions held by particular committees.

The same system of committee government prevails in our state legislatures, and has led to some notable results, which have recently been pointed out in a pamphlet entitled American Constitutions, contributed to the Johns Hopkins series of Studies in History and Political Science by Mr. Horace Davis.[5] In the

---

[5] It should be said, however, that Mr. Davis does not attribute the constitutional tendencies he points out to committee government.

state legislatures as in Congress, the origination and control of legislation by standing committees have led to haphazard, incoherent, irresponsible law-making, and to a universal difficulty about getting anything done. The result has been that state legislatures have been falling into disrepute in all quarters. They are despised and mistrusted, and many States have revised their constitutions in order to curtail legislative powers and limit the number and length of legislative sessions. There is in some States an apparent inclination to allow legislators barely time enough to provide moneys for the maintenance of the governments. In some instances necessary powers have been transferred from the legislatures to the courts, sometimes to the governors. The intent of all such changes is manifest. It is thought safer to entrust power to a law court, performing definite functions, such as the granting of charters, for example, under clear laws and in accordance with strict judicial standards, or to a single conspicuous magistrate, who can be watched and cannot escape responsibility for his official acts, than to entrust it to a numerous body which burrows towards its ends in committee rooms, getting its light through lobbies, and which has a thousand devices for juggling away responsibility, as well as scores of antagonisms wherewith to paralyze itself.

Like fear and distrust have often been felt and expressed of late years for Congress, for like reasons. But so far no attempt has been made to restrict either the powers or the time of Congress. Amendments to the Constitution are difficult almost to the point of impossibility, and the few definite schemes nowadays put forward for a revision of the Constitution involve extensions rather than limitations of the powers of Congress. The fact is that, though often quite as exasperating to sober public opinion as any state legislature, Congress is neither so much distrusted nor so deserving of distrust. Its high place and vast sphere in the government of the nation cause its members to be more carefully chosen, and its proceedings to be more closely watched and controlled by criticism. The whole country has its eyes on Congress, and Congress is aware of the fact. It has both the will and the incentive to be judicious and patriotic. Newspaper editors have constantly to be saying to their readers, "Look what our state legislators are doing"; they seldom have to urge, "Look what Congress is doing." It cannot be watched easily, or to much advantage. It requires a distinct effort to watch it. It has no dramatic contests of party leaders to attract notice. Its methods are so much after the fashion of the game of hide-and-seek that

the eye of the ordinary man is quite baffled in trying to understand or follow them, if he try only at leisure moments. But, at
the same time, the interests handled by Congress are so vast
that at least the newspapers and the business men, if no others,
must watch its legislation as best they may. However hard it may
be to observe, it is too powerful in great things to make it safe
for the country to give over trying to observe it faithfully.

But though Congress may always be watched, and so in a
measure controlled, despite its clandestine and confusing methods, those methods must tend to increase the distrust with
which Congress is widely regarded; and distrust cannot but
enervate, belittle, and corrupt this will-centre of the Constitution. The question is not merely, How shall the methods of Congress be clarified and its ways made purposeful and responsible?
There is this greater question at stake: How shall the essential
arrangements of the Constitution be preserved? Congress is the
purposing, designing, aggressive power of the national government. Disturbing and demoralizing influences in the organism,
if there be any, come out from its restless energies. Damaging
encroachments upon ground forbidden to the federal government generally originate in measures of its planning. So long
as it continues to be governed by unrelated standing committees, and to take its resolves in accordance with no clear plan,
no single, definite purpose, so long as what it does continues to
be neither evident nor interesting, so long must all its exertions
of power be invidious; so long must its competition with the
executive or the judiciary seem merely jealous and always under-
hand; so long must it remain virtually impossible to control it
through public opinion. As well ask the stranger in the gallery
of the New York Stock Exchange to judge of the proceedings on
the floor. As well ask a man who has not time to read all the
newspapers in the Union to judge of passing sentiment throughout the country. Congress in its composition is the country in
miniature. It realizes Hobbes's definition of liberty as political
power divided into small fragments. The standing committees
typify the individuals of the nation. Congress is better fitted for
counsel than the voters simply because its members are three
hundred and twenty-five instead of ten millions.

There are several ways in which Congress can be so integrated
as to impart to its proceedings system and party responsibility.
It may be done by entrusting the preparation and initiation of
legislation to a single committee in each house, composed of the
leading men of the majority in that house. Such a change would

not necessarily affect the present precedents as to the relations between the executive and the legislature. They might still stand
stiffly apart. Congress would be integrated and invigorated, not the
whole system. To integrate that, there must be some common
meeting-ground of public consultation between the executive and
the houses. That can be accomplished only by the admission to
Congress, in whatever capacity,—whether simply to answer proper
questions and to engage in debate, or with full privileges of membership,—of official representatives of the executive who understand and are interested and able to defend the administration.
Let each of the houses impose what conditions of responsibility
it will upon its guiding committee; let the tenure of ministers
have what disconnection from legislative responsibility may seem
necessary to the preservation of the equality of House and Senate
and the separation of administration from legislation; but throw
light upon administration, and give it the same advantages of
public suggestion and unhampered self-defense that Congress,
its competitor, has, and constrain Congress to apply system and
party responsibility to its proceedings. Such arrangements would
constitute responsible government *under* the Constitution.

The establishment in the United States of what is known as
"ministerial responsibility" would unquestionably involve some
important changes in our constitutional system, as I have elsewhere[6] fully admitted. I am strongly of the opinion that such
changes would not be too great a price to pay for the advantages
secured us by such a government. Ministerial responsibility supplies the only conditions which have yet proved efficacious, in
the political experience of the world, for vesting recognized
leadership in men chosen for their abilities by a natural selection
of debate in a sovereign assembly of whose contests the whole
country is witness. Such survival of the ablest in debate seems
the only process possible for selecting leaders under a popular
government. The mere fact that such a contest proceeds with
such results is the strongest possible incentive to men of first-
rate powers to enter legislative service; and popular governments
need more than any other governments leaders so placed that,
by direct contact with both the legislative and the executive departments of the government, they shall see the problems of
government at first hand, and shall at the same time be, not
mere administrators, but also men of tact and eloquence, fitted
to persuade masses of men and to draw about themselves a loyal
following.

[6] Overland Monthly, January, 1884: title, Committee or Cabinet Government?

If we borrowed ministerial responsibility from England, we should, too, unquestionably enjoy an infinite advantage over the English in the use of it. We should sacrifice by its adoption none of that great benefit and security which our federal system derives from a clear enumeration of powers and an inflexible difficulty of amendment. If anything would be definite under cabinet government, responsibility would be definite; and, unless I am totally mistaken in my estimate of the legal conscience of the people of this country,—which seems to me to be the heart of our whole system,—definite responsibility will stablish rather than shake those arrangements of our Constitution which are really our own, and to which our national pride properly attaches, namely, the distinct division of powers between the state and federal governments, the slow and solemn formalities of constitutional change, and the interpretative functions of the federal courts. If we are really attached to these principles, the concentration of responsibility in government will doubly insure their preservation. If we are not, they are in danger of destruction in any case.

But we cannot have ministerial responsibility in its fullness under the Constitution as it stands. The most that we can have is distinct legislative responsibility, with or without any connection of coöperation or of mutual confidence between the executive and Congress. To have so much would be an immense gain. Changes made to this end would leave the federal system still an unwieldy mechanism of counteracting forces, still without unity or flexibility; but we should at least have made the very great advance of fastening upon Congress an even more positive form of accountability than now rests upon the President and the courts. Questions of vast importance and infinite delicacy have constantly to be dealt with by Congress; and there is an evident tendency to widen the range of those questions. The grave social and economic problems now putting themselves forward, as the result of the tremendous growth and concentration of our population, and the consequent sharp competition for the means of livelihood indicate that our system is already aging, and that any clumsiness, looseness, or irresponsibility in governmental action must prove a source of grave and increasing peril. There are already commercial heats and political distempers in our body politic which warn of an early necessity for carefully prescribed physic. Under such circumstances, some measure of legislative reform is clearly indispensable. We cannot afford to put up any longer with such legislation as we may happen upon. We must look and plan ahead. We must have legislation which has been definitely forecast in party programmes and sanctioned by the public voice. Instead of the present arrangements for compromise, piecemeal legislating, we must have coherent plans from recognized party leaders, and means for holding them to a faithful execution of those plans in clear-cut Acts of Congress.

Woodrow Wilson.

Printed in the *Atlantic Monthly,* LVII (April 1886), 542-53.

From Thomas Bailey Aldrich

Dear Sir: Boston. Feby 15, 1886.

I have read your paper with great interest, and shall give it a place in the April number of the *Atlantic*—which number I am now making up.

In the course of two or three days a proof of your article is to be sent to you. Do me the kindness to return it to this office with as little delay as possible.

Yours truly,   T. B. Aldrich.
Ed. Atlantic Monthly.

ALS (WP, DLC).

From Joseph Ruggles Wilson

My beloved Woodrow—   Clarksville, Tenn., Feb. 17, 1886

Your letter received to-day was a blessing to us all. We have had the sorriest weather (or weathers) and are longing for spring —but your voice—for such it seemed—came upon us like a breath from some fragrant summer morning: and now let slow winter do his worst!

We often and often, though, look in upon dear Ellie and yourself. Our peeps are indeed not so satisfactory as they would be were we to possess a picture of your rooms, with desk in place, work-table (Ellie's) and all else of importance in situ. Can the much-seaming little helpmeet spare an hour to pencil this needed help? No—don't ask her; she has more than enough to do! Ah, dearest son, we love, we love you both; and in a way that you will better comprehend one day.

Your mother and I have just been reading your "Citizen"[1] piece —shall I say with what pleasure? And that shorter article in "The Dial"[2] was in the best style. We are not fair critics, however. If you misspelled every other word, and mixed yr. figures with rhetorical paints that ran into each other every-which-way, we would admire!—and yet, I don't know[,] we are perhaps made more sensitive to your faults—when we see them—by the very strength and pride of our affection. You will certainly do the right thing if you can find time and command drudging patience for the *text-book* to which you refer. Text-books move the world, to say nothing of their *market-value*. There they serve to widen one's reputation, and are a kind of avaunt courier as towards a better position. By the way, I experienced a sort of pang when I read that you felt compelled to discourage the 'confidential' from Indiana.[3] Are you in truth *tied*—tethered—where you are, at that unpronounceable college?—for two years! Well—perhaps best. Should you forward me those books you speak of, I will be placed under a real obligation.

Tell me—what are your *church* relations? Not yet have you alluded to this subject. We, here, are as badly-off as we can be, almost—our preacher being McK.[4] cut into parts, and ours the smallest of these! It is well-nigh intolerable. But God is worshipped by us—and herein is our glory and our joy. . . .

God bless you both is the prayer of our hearts, all,

Your affc Father

This letter is almost as hard to read as "Cicero" which I am reading now. *Some* of the words have to be made out by their connection as in Latin.   Aff. "Dode"[5]

Dode is a very fine fellow—but he doesn't know a well-written letter when he has the luck to see one.

P.S. Your dear Mother rec'd Ellie's most welcome letter, & we were all able to read it without an expert.

When & where were you PhD'd?

ALS (WP, DLC).
   [1] "Courtesy of the Senate," printed at Nov. 15, 1885.
   [2] Wilson's review article, "The Greville Memoirs," printed at Feb. 1, 1886.
   [3] See D. S. Jordan to WW, Feb. 1, 1886.
   [4] Possibly the Rev. Dr. Luther McKinnon, President of Davidson College, 1885-88, formerly pastor of the First Presbyterian Church of Columbia.
   [5] This paragraph and subscription in handwriting of Joseph R. Wilson, Jr.

To Robert Bridges

Dear Bobby,   Bryn Mawr, Pa., 18 Feby., 1886

I have rec'd your letter of yesterday. Hurrah! I'm delighted, my dear fellow, that I am to have such a chance to see you; and the programme you announce will be perfectly satisfactory and convenient. I had no thought of going away for the holiday. Come as early on Sunday as you can. Mrs. W. too will be glad to see you.

In haste,   Yours as ever,   Woodrow Wilson

ALS (Meyer Coll., DLC).

From David Starr Jordan

Dear Sir,   Bloomington, Ind. Feb'y 24. 1886.

I am sorry to hear that you are so thoroughly out of our reach.

Your acquaintance is doubtless far more extensive than mine among young men in training for a Chair of History, and you have better means than I, of properly weighing the quality of their work.

I should be very glad indeed if you would suggest the name of some young and rising man, who has the right kind of stuff in him.[1]

Please regard this as confidential, for the present, as we have as yet no actual vacancy.

Very respectfully yours.   David S. Jordan.

ALS (WP, DLC) with WWhw notation on env.: "Ans. March 16/86."
[1] Wilson suggested Richard Heath Dabney (see R. H. Dabney to WW, March 28, 1886), and Dabney received the appointment.

Two Letters to Robert Bridges

Dear Bobby,   Bryn Mawr, Pa., 27 Feby., 1886

My recollection of what took place in the Georgia legislature with reference to a proposed vote of money for education is definite enough for use in conversation, but scarcely definite enough, I fear, for use in an editorial. I will detail just what I know, however.[1]

Dr. Orr,[2] the State Superintendent of Education, a very competent, thoroughly informed man, used to maintain, upon knowledge, that the State was abundantly able to double or treble its expenditure for schools. His yearly reports to the legislature doubtless still urge his old, unanswerable arguments to that effect. I happened to spend an hour or so in the gallery of the State Senate chamber one day[3] when a proposal to increase the appropriation for education was under discussion, as a consequence of Dr. Orr's active urging. Only a very small minority favoured the proposal. The majority thrust it aside with a resolution that the Representatives and Senators of the State in Washington be requested to do all in their power to secure a grant from the federal treasury in aid of education. I heard but one speech made in opposition to this begging resolution. It was a sturdy appeal to the self-respect and independence of the majority in view of what the speaker treated as the unquestioned ability of the State to support a school system of any dimensions. No one seemed to regard it worth while answering this speech—and the resolution was carried.[4] The whole proceeding impressed me as a shameless declaration of the determination, on the part of a well-to-do community, to enjoy the easy position of a beneficiary of the national govt. to the fullest possible extent.

Now, these are recollections of four years ago. The substance and spirit of the proceedings were exactly as I have represented; the *form* may have been quite different. I am willing, therefore, to have Mr. Clarke[5] use the substance of what I have said as testimony of the demoralization of Ga. in view of promised subsidies —though, my uncertainty as to particulars makes the details of my story worthless.

I am sorry that I cannot contribute something more definite; but of course Mr. C. would not care to use my testimony *in my words*.

I am interested to know your reasons for staying on the P[ost]. Warm regards from Mrs. W.,

Yours as ever   Woodrow Wilson

If Mr. C. sh. care to write to Dr. Orr, (Atlanta, Ga.) I have no doubt he would supply him with much more telling evidence
Yrs.   W. W.

Telegram just rec'd. Seems a shame to telegraph such indefinite stuff. But I obey.[6]   Yrs.   W. W.

[1] The New York *Evening Post* and the *Nation* had launched a campaign against the bill for federal aid to education re-introduced in the Senate on December 9, 1885, by Henry W. Blair of New Hampshire. Bridges, in his conversation with Wilson on February 21, 1886, had asked Wilson to write down his recollections of certain proceedings in the Georgia Senate in 1882, hence this letter.
[2] Gustavus John Orr, State Superintendent of Education in Georgia, 1872-87.
[3] It was November 13, 1882. See *Journal of the Senate of the State of Georgia at the Biennial Session . . . Commenced . . . Nov. 1, 1882* (Atlanta, 1883), p. 131.
[4] By a voice vote.
[5] Edward P. Clark, editorial writer for the New York *Evening Post.*
[6] Wilson's telegram is printed in WW to R. Bridges, March 2, 1886, n. 2.

Dear Bobby,   Bryn Mawr, Pa., 2 March, 1886
By some postal perversity, your note of Saturday did not reach me until dinner-time on Monday when it was too late for me to telegraph my demurrer to the use of my name in the paper.[1] It makes no great difference, except that I should have wished such

an adjective as 'shameless' replaced by some less slap-like word; and it makes one a little nervous to be made responsible in print for the hurried recital of an only half-recollected incident.[2] If the editorial is to be reproduced in the 'Nation,' please let my name be left out or the adjectives cooled down a little?[3]

I am glad to have been of any service in the matter. I fervently pray that the short-sighted scheme may be defeated! It would be an outrageous precedent.

Write me as soon as you can about your *Post* vs. 'Com-Adv.' decision.

Our experience together in Princeton has left a mighty good taste in my mouth.

Mrs. W. sends warm regards.

As ever   Yours affectionately,   Woodrow Wilson

ALS (WC, NjP).

[1] Bridges' note of February 27, asking permission for the New York *Evening Post* to quote Wilson's telegram to Bridges of the same date, is missing.

[2] Wilson was referring to an editorial, "Impressive Warnings," in the New York *Evening Post*, March 1, 1886. It was a blast against the Blair bill for federal aid to education, and it cited reports from the South to support its argument that the southern states had ample resources to maintain good educational systems. The editorial, after identifying Wilson as author of *Congressional Government*, a native Southerner, and stout opponent of the Blair bill, quoted his telegram as follows:

"In the winter of 1882-83 I spent some time in Atlanta, Ga., while the Legislature was in session. The project of Federal aid to education was already then being pushed. One day I dropped into the gallery of the State Senate Chamber for an hour, and chanced to find a discussion in progress upon a proposal to increase the appropriation for education, as Mr. Orr had urged that the State was so abundantly able to do. Only a small minority favored the measure for heavier taxation. The majority supported a counter-resolution that the Senators and Representatives of the State in Congress be requested to do all in their power to secure the passage of a law giving aid from the Federal Treasury to education in the States. I heard one speech made in opposition to this begging resolution. It was a sturdy appeal to the self-respect and independence of Georgians, in view of what the Speaker treated as the unquestioned ability of the State to support a school system worthy of so great and prosperous a commonwealth. No attempt was made by the majority to answer his argument, which, like Mr. Orr's plea, was indeed unanswerable. The majority kept silent and contented themselves with passing the resolution appealing for outside help to do what by their very silence they confessed they were able to do themselves. It was evident that no increase in the state appropriation for public education would be voted so long as there was the least prospect of aid from Washington. The whole performance impressed me as a shameless declaration, upon the part of a well-to-do community, of its deliberate determination to enjoy the easy position of a beneficiary of the national Government to the fullest possible extent, rather than to be independent and support a good school system by its own unaided efforts."

[3] His name was used, but his strictures were considerably "cooled down" in the summary of his remarks in "A Vicious Way of Legislation," New York *Nation*, XLII (March 11, 1886), 207-8.

From Edwin Robert Anderson Seligman[1]

Dear Sir,   Columbia College, New York, March 6 1886

You will notice by inclosed circulars, that we intend to begin the publication of a scientific periodical. It is our hope to make it the center of scientific thought in its particular domain, in America, and with this end in view we have invited the cooperation of leading specialists all over the country and in Europe. Representatives of almost every leading institution of learning have consented to the use of their names—among them professors of Harvard, Yale, Princeton, Cornell, Univ. of Pa., Amherst, Smith, etc. etc. Would you consent to the use of your name in conjunction with theirs in our prospectus? We sincerely hope so.

Of course one great object of enlisting the support of all specialists is to make the annual bibliography as complete as possible. We should thus be greatly indebted to you, if you would send from time to time, at your convenience, the name of any book in your department which you think would be of aid to students working in a similar field. A few words to indicate the character and value of the book would also be greatly appreciated by us.

Hoping that you may see your way to consent to the use of your name,

I remain   Yrs truly   Edwin R. A. Seligman

ALS (WP, DLC). Enc.: Printed prospectus of the *Political Science Quarterly*.
    [1] Lecturer in Economics at Columbia College and one of the editors of the new *Political Science Quarterly*.

From Janet Woodrow Wilson

My precious Son,   Clarksville Tenn. March 11th '86

I send you the enclosed letter from your Aunt Helen, because it tells of things you will be glad to hear. Please return it to me when you are through with it. I have been so anxiously longing to hear just what she tells of my dearly loved brother's state of mind. I thought I was quite prepared to hear of his death[1]— and imagined that I would be *glad*—for his sake. And this is true— in a measure. But ever since the news of his illness came, my mind has been going back to the days when we were everything to each other—has been filled with memories of his unceasing tenderness and kindnesses to me & mine. And now I feel that I have lost a *friend* whose like we will never meet. When those he loved were in *trouble*, his love for them shone most conspicuously. But I am glad he is at rest. I will not say more just now.

I am very anxiously anticipating the time to come, when your father will be off to the Assembly.[2] He is not well—and there is no doctor here that he is willing to consult, so that I long for the time when he can get away to see George.[3] I hope his fears as to his disease may prove unfounded. But he is certainly far from well.

The wind storm you write of did not reach us. I am sorry to hear that your rooms are not fitted for great cold—surely they ought to be so in that climate. This house is very close & comfortable. Coal is abundant & cheap. How I long for the day when you & dear Ellie will join us! Your presence will be such a delight to your father.

I send you the enclosed from the Nebrask Agent. Your father wrote enquiring something about the possibility of selling the land. I don't know exactly what. But *please write him that we are not anxious to sell at present.* Your father meant only to enquire if it was a good time to sell. I think it very undesirable anyway—*for we dont know how to invest the small sum we already have*—and the likelihood is it would be lost or spent. So I think we had better leave things as they are for the present—at least until land can be sold at decided advantage. I hate to add to your labors—but our common interests are involved—so I beg you to write at once, if possible.

Your father & Josie are both at college. God bless you both, dear children.   Most lovingly   Your Mother

ALS (WP, DLC). Encs.: M. R. Hopewell to JWW, Jan. 27, 1886, and tax receipt dated Tekamah, Neb., Jan. 27, 1886.
   [1] Joseph R. Wilson, Jr., to EAW, Feb. 28, 1886, ALS (WP, DLC), had sent news of the recent death of Thomas Woodrow, Jr.
   [2] The General Assembly of the southern Presbyterian Church met in Augusta, May 20-29, 1886.
   [3] Dr. Wilson had been complaining about severe pains in his knee and planned to go to General Assembly by way of Columbia, for treatment by Dr. George Howe, Jr., his son-in-law. See JWW to WW, Feb. 17, 1886, ALS (WP, DLC).

To Robert Bridges

Bryn Mawr, 14 March, '86

Alas, my dear Bobby, it can't be! The 'seductive' circular sent out by Billy Wilder[1] was enough—why did you tempt me with that letter of yours with its generous offer of entertainment, and of Lee and Talcott, and all! I've canvassed the matter thoroughly, both in the light of a purse depleted by recent large purchases of books and of my college engagements. The latter block me completely, as regards any absence which may not be put off till the end of the week. I have two exercises every day of the college week, one from eleven to twelve in the morning and the other from five to six in the afternoon. You see how the latter blocks me, even if the former did not—and I have been taking liberties of postponement and even omission with that afternoon class of late which may by no means be soon repeated.

No, no! Bobby, it cant be—I'd give my head if it could! Give my love to the boys, and keep much for yourself from
Your sincere friend, Tommy.

ALS (WC, NjP).
    1 It was an invitation to a meeting of Princeton alumni in New York on March 23, 1886. The circular is missing.

To Edwin Robert Anderson Seligman

Dear Sir: Bryn Mawr, Pa., 16 March, 1886.
    I have hesitated some time as to what reply to make to your kind letter of March 6th. I am by no means a prolific writer, and what I do write is not likely to take periodical form. Nor will it be exactly in the field of investigation, of original research, proper to the projected 'Political Science Quarterly,' but rather in the field of comparative politics—possibly in the field of political speculation. But, since I am asked to be a contributor, not to the main body of the magazine, but to the annual bibliography, I consent with all my heart to give it what aid I can in that line, and, if so much entitles me to a place on your published lists, to the appearance of my name in your prospectus. I wish the 'Quarterly' all success.
Very sincerely Yours,   Woodrow Wilson
P. S. If you use my name, please don't dub me Ph.D. I've never rec'd the title.   W. W.

ALS (Seligman Papers, NNC).

To Talcott Williams[1]

Dear Mr. Williams,   Bryn Mawr, Pa., 16 March, '86
    The 'extremely sorry' of my telegram was too brief an expression of my regret at not being able to accept your kind invitation to dinner at your club. Monday is my busiest day at the college here, and it is only by special arrangement made beforehand that I can get off then. I was genuinely disappointed that I was com-

pelled to forego the chance of meeting you again. Please accept my thanks for your kindness in thinking of me.

Very sincerely Yours,   Woodrow Wilson

ALS (in possession of Dorothy T. Walworth).
    [1] Managing editor of the Philadelphia *Press*.

To Robert Bridges

Dear Bobby,   Bryn Mawr, Pa., 17 March, 1886

What will you think of a revised version of my last letter? I strongly suspect that you were instrumental in procuring the special invitation[1] to the Alumni dinner sent me to-day through M. Taylor Pyne.[2] When you wrote me I thought of the project of attending merely as a frolic, and therefore concluded that I ought not to disarrange my appointments here just to serve my own pleasure and amusement. A special invitation bearing the signature M. Taylor Pyne suggests that the trip may have business bearings—may be made to have in the future, that is—by emphasizing my identity with the Princeton Alumni. At any rate, no harm will be done in that direction—unless I make a complete fizzle in my toast speech. I shall try to reach N. Y. by 3:20 Tuesday [March 23]—in which case I will join you at Eve. Post Office at 4—unless you instruct to the contrary.

As ever,   Yours affectionately,   Woodrow Wilson

ALS (WC, NjP).
    [1] About the invitation, see the Editorial Note, "Wilson's 'First Failure' at Public Speaking."
    [2] Moses Taylor Pyne, born New York, Dec. 21, 1855. A.B., College of New Jersey, 1877; LL.B., Columbia Law School, 1879. He served as general solicitor for the Delaware, Lackawanna and Western Railroad, 1880-92, and subsequently devoted his time to management of the Pyne family estate and trust funds. Trustee of Princeton University, 1884-1921, and generous benefactor of his *alma mater*. Died April 22, 1921.

To William Royal Wilder

My dear Wilder,   Bryn Mawr, Pa., 19 March, 1886

I am sincerely obliged for your cordial note of Wednesday. I have accepted the invitation to the Dinner—with many misgivings as to my *toast*. That, however, will be the only thing to mar my pleasure on the festive occasion: and seeing you and the other '79 men will be some compensation to me for missing the reunion last June. Prepare yourself for a big grasp of the hand from

Yours sincerely,   Woodrow Wilson

ALS (Meyer Coll., DLC).

From Edwin Robert Anderson Seligman

My dear Sir,   Columbia College, New York, March 19 1886

I regret that you should have misunderstood my letter. We shall be glad to have your cooperation not only in the bibliography, but also in the main body of the Quarterly. Articles in comparative politics or political speculation would be just as welcome as original historical work. We expect in fact to have some articles on political theories very shortly.

The articles need however not be mere "magazine" articles, as you apprehend. We shall certainly have some articles 50, 60 or even 70 pages long,—and some articles already prepared are about 130 pages,—to run through 2 or 3 numbers. So that articles may be made as long as desired,—and of course we wish nothing but *scientific* work. This is not to be a popular quarterly.

I hope therefore that you may see your way before long to contribute an article on any subject, pertinent to the scope of the Quarterly, that may approve itself to you. And we shall be glad to print your name as one of the probable contributors. We hope to get out the first number (about 150 pages) in a week or 10 days.   Yrs truly   Edwin R A Seligman

ALS (WP, DLC) with WWhw notation on env.: *"Ans* March '86."

To Edwin Robert Anderson Seligman

My dear Sir: Bryn Mawr, Pa., 21 March, 1886

I am afraid, from the contents of your letter of the 19th, that I must have expressed myself with great awkwardness in answering your kind invitation to coöperate with the editors of the 'Political Science Quarterly.' I heartily sympathize with the aims of the *Quarterly*, and when your first letter came my first impulse was to consent to any use of my name you might choose to make. I had already half promised, however, to contribute to one or two other publications; and, as I am a very slow producer in the absence of adequate 'protection' of leisure and safety from interruption, I thought that it would scarcely be honest to *promise* aid to anything but the proposed bibliography. I was, therefore, glad to find that you wanted assistance there principally: and I consequently hastened to accept your invitation on that basis. I did, however, as you show me, somewhat misunderstand the purposes of the Quarterly. I had supposed that it was primarily for 'original' work—i. e. original investigation—in history and political economy: for which I have no aptitude at all. Since it is to be broad enough in its aims to include comparative politics and political speculation, I shall be very glad to figure among probable contributors: and it will not be from lack of interest in the periodical, but only because of hindering plans previously made and great lack of speed in production, if I do not become sooner or later an actual contributor. Meanwhile, let me repeat, I shall keep an eye upon the interests of the bibliography.

Very sincerely Yours,   Woodrow Wilson

ALS (Seligman Papers, NNC).

From Daniel Collamore Heath

Dear Sir: Boston Mar. 22. 1886

I hope you will conclude to make the text-book on Civil Government & will write a little short announcement of it to go in our forthcoming catalogue, or if you prefer not to make any detailed statement concerning it that you will allow me to say that we have in preparation such a book by you. When it is once known that you are to make it, you will get many hints here & there, & we shall for you, as to just what the book should & should not contain. I think it would be a very easy matter for us to send out a circular letter of enquiry to some of the best teachers of the subject to guide us in the work if you cared for any such consensus. We are going to get many hints thro' The Citizen in reference to this work. There is an article in the Mar. number (which will reach you in a day or two) by Prof. James, Univ. of Penn. that will be interesting in this connection, & there are several articles announced that will also be suggestive. Of course you could take your time for making the book. We have found that a long announcement not only preempts the ground, but gives time for shaping the plan of the book to best accomplish its ends.   Very truly yours,   D. C. Heath & Co.

ALS (WP, DLC) with WWhw notation on env.: "Ans. March 30/86."

EDITORIAL NOTE
WILSON'S "FIRST FAILURE" AT PUBLIC SPEAKING

One cannot be absolutely certain that Wilson's speech before a banquet of the Princeton alumni of New York, printed below, was his "first failure" at public speaking, as some writers have inferred.[1] But there can be little doubt that the address was not only a fiasco

---

[1] e.g., R. S. Baker, *Woodrow Wilson*, I, 264.

but also nearly fatal to the realization of Wilson's strong ambition for a professorship at his *alma mater.*

As the letters just printed have shown, Moses Taylor Pyne, who made the arrangements for the affair, had asked Wilson to reply to the toast "The College and the Government." Wilson surely must have realized what kind of a speech would be appropriate for what he knew would be a boisterous affair. Yet ambition seems to have distorted his judgment when he composed his address. Clearly, he not only hoped to impress his audience with his forensic ability and profound learning but also decided to seize this opportunity to urge his fellow-alumni to establish the very chair that *he* hoped to occupy.

The affair was an annual dinner meeting of the New York Alumni Association at Delmonico's on March 23, 1886. The *New York Times* reported on the following day that "Orange predominated everywhere," and that from the balcony of the dining room hung "the orange and black banner won at the football games on last Thanksgiving Day, with the battered and dilapidated spheroid that the young athletes of Yale vainly tried to carry to the winning post." More than 250 enthusiastic alumni filled the main dining hall and adjacent rooms. "There never was a jollier reunion," the New York *Tribune* reported on March 24. Old friendships were renewed while the walls echoed with college songs and cheers and "tobacco smoke began to rise in thick clouds." So festive were the celebrants, continued the *Tribune* report, that the president of the Association, James W. Alexander, rapped long on the table before he could proceed with the introductions.

Alexander, after a few witty remarks, introduced President James McCosh, who spoke briefly on the progress of the college during the past year and outlined his plan for strengthening its curriculum. John K. Cowen, '66, next responded humorously to the toast "Our Sister Associations." Henry van Dyke then toasted "Alma Mater." His speech, the *Tribune* reported, was "punctuated with the applause and laughter of his hearers." An account of the banquet in *The Princetonian* of March 24, 1886, listed Wilson as the next speaker and provides the most substantial account of proceedings from this point onward:

"The toast 'The College and the Government' fell to Prof. Woodrow Wilson '79 of Bryn Mawr College. Prof. Wilson's speech may be designated as the solid food of the evening. It was a logical and practical statement of what the scholar should do in the government of the country. In conclusion, Mr. Wilson advocated the establishing of a Professor of Politics in our various colleges, to teach the theory and practice of government. The representatives of the alumni associations of Harvard, Yale and Columbia received more than one cheer as they rose to respond for their colleges. Mr. Edmund Wetmore paid the respects of 'Harvard' in a delightful and amusing way, and Mr. Depew spoke for 'Yale' with all the wit and point of which he is the master. His speech was loudly applauded. 'Columbia' was gracefully responded to by Mr. F. C. Hinrichs, who claimed Columbus for the founder of Columbia, and showed how the other colleges had received nourishment from his chosen *alma mater.* The last speaker, De Lancey Nicoll '74, assistant District Attorney of N. Y. City, was listened to carefully throughout. He very humorously pointed out how Princeton men, though acquainted with every institution throughout the land, had always kept out of one–the jail,– and had never been guilty of occupying the aldermanic chair in New York. With many hearty cheers, this successful and happy reunion of Princeton men ended at an early hour this morning."

Reports of the reaction to Wilson's speech have been based on reminiscences long after the event. Henry van Dyke wrote many years later that Wilson spoke for nearly an hour and "was so in earnest– he wanted so much to say what he had prepared,–that he could not stop in spite of the interruptions–in spite of the men going out–he just simply went ahead to the bitter end and finished it up."[2] Ray Stannard Baker, after repeating van Dyke's comments, added that Chauncey Depew "poked good-humoured fun at the deadly seriousness of the young professor." Baker also said that Depew's remarks cut Wilson "to the quick," and that Wilson considered his speech to have been a "far worse failure than it really was, and did not recover for years from the chagrin of it." It was, Baker wrote, the only time in Wilson's entire career that an audience laughed at him.[3] Baker's information about Depew's comments and Wilson's reactions to them apparently came from Robert Bridges in 1925.[4]

Van Dyke's and Bridges' reminiscences were inaccurate in some details. For example, van Dyke seems to have exaggerated in saying that Wilson spoke for nearly an hour. If Wilson stuck to his text, as van Dyke said he did, he could not have spoken for much more than twenty minutes. But Wilson himself later confirmed the essential accuracy of these latter-day reports. For example, speaking to the Princeton Alumni Association of Philadelphia on January 30, 1891, he said: "This is a solemn toast, and I am a solemn fellow–so solemn that I once, without changing countenance, emptied a very large dinner hall by an after-dinner speech, and did it quickly."[5] Wilson's obvious reference to the New York affair may have been somewhat exaggerated. No doubt there was a good deal of milling about during all of the speeches. But Wilson's statement suggests that a number of men did walk out on him.

That Wilson was intensely disappointed by the response to his address and realized that he had spoken in much too serious a vein is clear from his father's letter of April 5, 1886. In it Dr. Wilson assured his son that he had undoubtedly underrated the impression that he had made, and that *"more thoughtful* men" would remember what Wilson had said long after they forgot the "Chinese-cracker squibs of the laugh-producing anecdotist." Depew's speech on this occasion does not seem to have survived, but Wilson had probably identified him as the "anecdotist" and described himself to his father as the butt of Depew's remarks.

[2] Henry van Dyke, "Let's Square Ourselves with the World: Both Sides of Wilson," *Success,* IX (July 1925), 8.

[3] R. S. Baker, *Woodrow Wilson,* I, 265-66.

[4] R. Bridges to R. S. Baker, Dec. 5, 1925, RSB Coll., DLC.

[5] "College Work and the Legal Profession," printed at Jan. 30, 1891, Vol. 7.

Wilson made another revealing remark some three years after the affair. Princeton, in the autumn of 1889, was about to fill a new chair in political science, and Wilson's name was high on the list. Bridges, who was much involved, reported that there were some who doubted Wilson's suitability for the position because, for one thing, he was "too learned and deep to interest his students." This, Wilson replied, was certainly astonishing. "Would," he continued, "I *were* learned! It must surely be the influence of that unfortunate after-dinner prose of mine at the Alumni dinner."[6]

The text of Wilson's address printed below is from Wilson's manuscript. He obviously composed it at some time between March 18 and 22, 1886, and the copy is hastily written and filled with errors and emendations.

[6] R. Bridges to WW, Nov. 5, 1889, and WW to R. Bridges, Nov. 6, 1889, Vol. 6.

An Address to the Princeton Alumni of New York

[c. March 23, 1886]

There is an old subject called 'the scholar in politics[']—a theoretical subject of much interest, and admitting of endl[ess] treatment. It exerts its fascination upon the mind of the college-bred man at a very early stage in his career—indeed principally at that stage. And this for a very simple reason. In this country, at least, it is a subject for speculation rather than for laborious investigation. It is surrounded by the bewitching light of Utopia.

The 'working hypothesis' of this subject is a proposition which is true only if understood in just the opposite sense from that in which it is generally used by the undergraduate—and, for the matter of that, the graduate—authorities upon this great topic. That proposition is that the scholar in politics, if a true scholar, is different from anybody else in politics. The inference is that he is better equipped for his business than any other politician: and it is this inference which needs to be reversed. His equipment for public service is different from other men's—and it is much larger. But it is more likely to be an incumbrance than an aid. The average college man goes into public life with a certain stock of ideas about politics: the more thoroughly a college man he is, the stiffer and more absolute those ideas. I cannot enumerate them: but I can describe them. Taken in the bulk, they may be said to be *reasoned politics*: politics stripped of its rags of humanity, washed of its dust, and soberly attired in the cap and gown of academic logic.

Now the world, I admit, is governed by logic in the long run: but representative government—the only govt. *we* ever talk about

—is conducted not by long runs but by short. It is a matter of persuading a great many people to take hold of certain objects just at hand—not to run after certain distant objects on the logical horizon. There is nothing that the logician more abhors than prejudice; nothing seems so contemptible in his eyes as slow expediency. And yet prejudice elects more candidates and passes more bills than logic—and expediency, I cannot help thinking, is of greater dignity in politics. There are no parts of Burke upon which I more love to dwell than those in which he defends prejudice against the assaults of the rational and expediency against the haste of the radical. "We are afraid," he says, "to put men to live and trade each on his own private stock of reason, because we suspect that this stock in each man is small, and that the individuals would do better to avail themselves of the of the [sic] general bank and capital of nations and of ages. Many of our men of speculation, instead of exploding general prejudices, employ their sagacity to discover the latent wisdom which prevails in them. If they find what they seek, and they seldom fail, they think it more wise to continue the prejudice with the reason involved, than to cast away the coat of prejudice, and to leave nothing but the naked reason: because prejudice with its reason has a motive to give action to that reason, and an affection which will give it permanence. Prejudice is of ready application in the emergency; it previously engages the mind in a steady course of wisdom and virtue, and does not leave the man hesitating in the moment of decision, skeptical, puzzled, and unresolved. Prejudice renders a man's virtue his habit, and not a series of unconnected acts. Through just prejudice, his duty becomes a part of his nature."

What is this but a commentary on much of modern socialism? The programme of the average labour organization, made up of distorted bits of economic truth; mixed with many of the cut and dried formulas of rationalistic socialism, represents an attempt to replace in the mind of the laborer the virtues of patient industry and of reverence for law which had taken such deep root there with calculated policies which ignore law and would substitute the natural rights of man. It is a perilous attempt to train the unlearned and the undisciplined to "live and trade each on his own private stock of reason." Its success is due to the fact that it uses these theories of natural right which chime in with selfish desire and so establishes passion at the same time that it overthrows habit. If that success is to extend, it would seem as if the crew of our ship of state must succeed in wrecking her under the idea of thereby escaping the hardships of navigation.

But we must not conclude that because in this case passion masquerades in the garb of reason the carnival is to be broken up by logic. The scholar's stock of ideas, profound and rounded as they are, belong to that desparful category of the things that are not seen—and cannot be seen by those whom we most want to have see them. The only gateway to a solution of such difficulties is knowledge of affairs. The logic of events will always convince men of folly: the statesman must prepare the way for that logic to operate by temperate concession to intemperate demands. Politics is an experimental art. As a scholar Mr. Gladstone defends the union of church and state; as knowing affairs, he disestablishes the church in Ireland and forecasts disestablishment in England. The logic of Cobden and Bright, backed by the thunders of every political economist then esteemed, had to wait to be assisted to the repeal of the Corn Laws by a famine in Ireland. Logic is much too stiff a thing to fit into the grooves of the world. It must be made flexible by expediency.

You have seen already, of course, the conclusion to which I am coming. It is, not that the college is, but only that it might be, a great direct aid to govt. Its indirect contribution to good institutions is of course inestimable. It has been the gymnasium in which men's minds have received the agility and the strength which have and [sic] steadied them for the higher exercises of govt., as for the greater undertakings in all other spheres of thought. But the college might do more than merely prepare men to understand *anything*. It might give them some preliminary drill in the practical thought of this great *particular* thing, govt. And to some extent it is doing so. But in every college there is missing a professor of politics. (Of course I am speakly roughly: every speech like this must be as broad as it is short.) There is instruction almost everywhere, of one sort or another, in history, and in many institutions instruction in political economy, jurisprudence, and constitutional law sets the student in the way of understanding most of the permanent relations of modern political society. The largest endowments and most advanced administrations even provide lectures on current topics of governmental policy: and such lectures are within the province of the future professor of politics. But than [that] person himself is not yet in any of our faculties. Presently I shall describe the functions of such a teacher as I foresee them. First let me say that we are afraid of the word politics. We fear that it would make prudent parents stare and pish to see it in our catalogues. Some of the more earnest of us even nerve ourselves to adopt the uncouth word 'civics' amongst the respected words of our vocabulary. Or we seek to stow politics away in disguise under the broad but elegant 'umbrella' of 'political science.' Perhaps this is part of the prejudice of logic. Politics is largely an affair, as I have said, of management and expediency—of much else besides reason—and it may seem to some that nothing which does not rest entirely— or at least mainly—on reason ought to find a place in a college curriculum. But the management and expediency of general politics is not necessarily the management and expediency of ward politics. The secrets of the ward politician would find their properest relations of place and treatment in a work on criminal jurisprudence; under the heading, unpunished crime. To let them assume exclusive title to the Aristotelian word 'politics' wd. be to sin against all philosophy.

It would be one of the chief services of the professor of politics that he would by his very title reclaim this word from its unmerited disgrace. It would be his duties to know and expose these unsavory parts of his subject: but only as some of the vicious forces which had to be understood only to be overcome by the higher management of the political art. It would be his whole duty to throw the light both of theory and of practice upon the art of government: to expound govt. as an historical development and to dissect it as a living organism. Let me be more explicit. I understand politics as a subject for instruction to include the history of political institutions and of speculative thought about such institutions, but to include these, not as sufficient in themselves to supply precepts for present political action, but only as indispensably introductory to inquiry, through every available channel, as to the real forces now at work in politics and the actual operation of the governments of the world. This would be, not a study of systems merely, but also of the circumstances and spirit which make each system workable in its own country and amongst its own people. Sir Henry Maine's striking volume on *Popular Govt.* recently published, comes within this sphere of the professor of politics, though it knows rather too much of the outer and rather too little of the inner history of national life to touch the real springs of democracy.

Of course the professor of politics may easily get lost in the immense field which I have vaguely set apart for him—just as the political economist of the new, 'all-the-facts' school may get lost in his boundless universe of statistics and particulars. To the subject of politics as I have defined it, there belongs a limitless world of human circumstances: it must have Shakespeare as well as Mill and Bluntschli for its text writer. But there are sane and possible methods for threading even such a labyrinth: and there will always be much to say against the political education sought to be furnished by our colleges so long as they confine themselves to the detached subjects of political economy and constitutional law and do not seek to penetrate to the heart of the nation's—if possible, of *each* nation's—being, laying bare the springs of action and the intricacies of acquired habit, political morality as well as political forms, political prejudice and expediency, as well as political reason and rigid consistency.

Perhaps it is too early in the history of our colleges to speak of such an addition to their faculties: but it is certainly not too early in the history of our politics. The practical difficulties of popular government, as well as of govts. of all other sorts, have so enormously increased that study which does not elucidate the practical conditions and aptitudes of govt. contributes almost nothing to the political life of the nation. Our politics are too narrow, our politicians too egotistically content with learning only from themselves. There is no channel through which to avail ourselves of the lights of comparative politics, of the general bank and capital of nations in the exigencies which threaten. It would help greatly if we could have in our colleges chairs of politics which should bridge over the gulf between closet doctrine and rough, everyday practice. I ask you to drink to the future professor of politics: may he be no less a scholar for being studiously a man of the world!

WWhw MS. (WP, DLC).

To Talcott Williams

Dear Mr. Williams,   Bryn Mawr, Pa., 24 March, 1886
I have just returned from a short run to New York and find your kind invitation for to-morrow evening. I accept with pleasure. With many thanks and in much haste,
Very sincerely Yours,   Woodrow Wilson

ALS (NIC).

Notes for a Lecture on Roman History

March 25/86
Causes of the Decline of the Republic
(1) Lack of adequate constitutional machinery for the administration of the Empire. (A) The Senate was the only power

Wilson's shorthand notes for a lecture on Roman history

in the state capable of undertaking systematic executive direction. So long as the power of Rome was compact within Italy itself the Senate had maintained both dignity and wisdom in its government. From the first, however, there had been at least 3 elements of great weakness in its composition. It was too (a) numerous a body to maintain and sustain a course of action after the administration of the imperial city had stretched it beyond the sure simple pristine policy which sufficed for the government of Italy; and it was (β) too distinctly a class chamber to continue to administer affairs in the interest of all classes very long after it became a matter of personal interest to its members to do otherwise. These causes were sure, sooner or later, to destroy its influence and prestige and to destroy these was to destroy its power because (γ) the Senate was supreme by sufferance, not by definite law but only by constitutional practice. By the time it grew weak the people had grown strong[.] A *plebiscitum* could override senatorial decrees. (B) The democratic assembly, however, was not competent to succeed the Senate in administration, and the more the Empire extended the less possibility [possible] had it not [now] become for the assembly to govern, because then it became the populace of the city set over the population of an empire.

(2) There was no republican cure for this. The contests for citizenship made first by the Latins and then by the whole of Italy could issue in no systematic constitutional reform; if citizenship was gained it was still only the populace of the city which heard evidence in the sovereign assembly. There was no system of representation to couple citizenship with political power. Discontent necessarily continued throughout a land, throughout a world, governed by a single city.

(3) The Senate, besides being by its very nature incompetent to conduct well the affairs of the Empire, became truly demoralized by the temptations connected with so vast a power. The plunder of the world was too much for the Senate's virtue. Every man wanted some day to have a province and so could not bring himself to inquire too harshly into a member senator's administration.

(4) As the Empire extended and Roman merchants followed Roman armies, the Senate was brought face to face in the class surge, as Marius, and his unscrupulous ways. As masters of the commerce of the world and farmers of the revenue, the equestrian order came into active and most demoralizing competition with

the senatorial class and the political power which it gained was established as universal and as lively as that of the Senate.

(5) The economic ruin of Italy brought about (a) by the rapid spread of the system of slave labor, extended conquest adding continually to the number of slaves (β) the consequent growth of immense estates and the driving of small farmers to the capital (γ) the policy of the government in importing grain to feed the idle population of Rome and so ruining by such disastrous competition the grain-farmers of Italy still remaining to struggle against the slave system. Without a sturdy, well-to-do middle class the republic could not live. It was not to be long possible in a country of great landlords and no free labor.

(6) The strain of military power. Rome, as the single center of administrative life for the Empire could not withstand the vast armies which she raised for the maintenance of that Empire. When they struck at her own liberties she was defenseless.

(7) Meanwhile the staid, conservative, legal habit of the Roman people was being more or less broken in upon by the disturbing philosophy and weakening superstition of the East, by the subtlety of the Greek and the mysticism of the Asiatic. The old habits of government were breaking up as the old habits of thought fell away.   W. W.

Transcript of WWsh in notebook described at Feb. 9, 1886.

From Joseph Ruggles Wilson

My precious Son—   Clarksville, Tennessee, Mar 27, '86.

I have read your Atlantic Monthly article, and with deep satisfaction. The style is something of an improvement upon "Con. Govt" in the one respect of shortened sentences, which adds to vitality as also to perspicuity. The subject itself I of course must not pretend to understand, except as what good sense I possess shall enable me to enter into its merits. You assuredly make it clear, that Congress is substantially all in governmental administration in that, under our system it is bound to be nearly all whether so designed originally or not—and that, this being the case Congress ought to rule consistently which is not possible when unity is dissolved into fragments through the vice of committeeism: therefore it is high time to hit upon some better device such as harmonious party management via Cabinet leadership a la English. You handle the whole subject with the skill of a practised dialectician, and one who does not need to back away from ever so many Lowells. Keep up the discussion, one way or another, until the country hears and heeds: as some day not far off it will be compelled to do.

Have you been bestowing much reflection upon another live subject, viz, the relations of Capital and Labor; to ascertain whether it is necessary to write "*versus*" between the two terms. So far the whole discussion is a muddle; and to my short sight there seems to be no adjustment within existing horizons save in *boards of arbitration* authorized by law and with such simplifications of detail and evidences of fairness all around, as to be sanctioned by wide public opinion. The long-received doctrine of supply and demand, as a self-regulating see-saw, does not seem to meet this case where associated monopoly is so gigantic on the one side and on the other associated labor is comparatively so puny whilst at the same time so obstructive. Sed jam satis quoad hoc.

From dear Ellie's letter to Dode received yesterday we learn that you have been with the Princeton Alumni at Delmonicos. I am very glad that you went. Had you a profitable time? Did you orate? Please tell us *all* about it.

Our little world here rotates upon its noiseless axis with due regularity: its atmosphere colorless: its zones all temperate: its products unvaried and not yet ripe.

Dode's progress is quite promising—my class duties are as pleasing as they are difficult—your mother's home affairs in a fair way towards the smooth hill-top of their initial hardness. But that which never stands still whatsoever else may hang back, is our ever-augmenting love for the Bryn Mawr darlings towards whom our hearts yearn indescribably and (to resume the figure just dropped) with a warmer and warmer equatorial glow.

Please try not to be anxious about us should you not have as frequent letters as we ought to dispatch from week to week. Remember, as to us three, as we endeavor to remember as to you both, that no news is if not good news at any rate not *bad* news.

Once more ashamed of a poor letter but not being able to make it richer,

I remain for dear Ellie and dear you
Your affectionate Father.

P.S. I will not try to send a notice of your dear mother's love—or Dode's—to you each one severally and to both as one. Imagine it if you can!

ALS (WP, DLC) with WWhw notation on env.: "Ans. March 31/86."

From Richard Heath Dabney

Dear Tom: Lexington, Virginia. March 28th, 1886.

My father sent me your card and told me that you had called to see me in N. Y.—I need hardly say how sorry I am to have missed you; and I wish also to thank your [sic] for having so kindly recommended me to President Jordan of the Indiana University. I received a letter from him on Friday, in which he mentioned that there was likelihood of a vacancy in the Historical Department, and that a decision would be reached on June 5th. When I get back to N. Y. I will send him copies of my testimonials if he desires them, and shall await anxiously the decision. . . .

With regards to Mrs. W., I remain sincerely your friend

R. H. Dabney.

P.S. omitted. ALS (WP, DLC).

From Houghton, Mifflin & Company

Dear Sir: Boston, March 29th, 1886.

We enclose herewith our semi-annual copyright return of sales on your Congressional Government, with check for $36.12 in settlement. The account was addressed to you at Arden, N. C. on the 1st of Feb., on the supposition that you were there, and has only just come back to us through the Post Office. Regretting the delay, we are

Very truly yours,   Houghton, Mifflin & Co.

F. J. G.

TLS (WP, DLC). Enc.: Printed and handwritten sales and royalty statement, Feb. 1, 1886, showing the sale of 289 copies of *Congressional Government* between July 1, 1885, and January 1, 1886.

From David Starr Jordan

Dear Sir,   Bloomington, Ind. March 29, 1886.

I should like to ask this question.

Would you give favorable consideration to an election to our chair of History, the election to take place in June, your work to begin at the close of your contract with Bryn Mawr? This is, I believe, August 1st 1887. If this could be done, we could probably offer $1800, with fair prospect of an increase.

A similar arrangement was made by us with Dr. von Jagemann,[1] whom you know, no doubt. His work with us begins August 1st 1886.

You would doubtless find the social advantages here less than at Bryn Mawr, but I think that with us you would be able to reach a much wider circle of men.

I have faith in the future of this still backward state—as well as in the future of its University.

Very respectfully yours,   David S. Jordan.

ALS (WP, DLC) with WWhw notation on env.: "Ans. April 7/86" and WWhw figures.
¹ Hans Carl Günther von Jagemann, Professor of Germanic Languages.

EDITORIAL NOTE

WILSON'S PLAN FOR A TEXTBOOK IN CIVIL GOVERNMENT

Wilson's letter to D. C. Heath of March 30, 1886, printed following this note, signaled his decision to write his first textbook. The files of D. C. Heath and Company for this period have been destroyed. However, it is possible to trace the progress of the negotiations between Heath and Wilson from Heath's letters and other documents in the Wilson Papers, Library of Congress, not only to this point, but through subsequent stages. From various drafts in the Wilson Papers, it is also possible to see how the concept of the book developed in Wilson's mind until it emerged in fully matured form in *The State*. This note will cover only the first negotiations between Heath and Wilson and Wilson's plans for the textbook as they both progressed to about August 31, 1886.

Heath, in his letter to Wilson of January 27, 1886, suggested that Wilson and Martha Carey Thomas of Bryn Mawr collaborate on a textbook in civil government for "the schools." In a missing letter of February 8, Wilson seems to have replied that he was very interested but would prefer to write the book by himself, for the idea of a Wilson-Thomas collaboration was never mentioned again in the correspondence. Joseph Ruggles Wilson's letter to his son of February 17, 1886, also indicates that Wilson had decided to write the textbook. Heath, in his letter to Wilson of March 22, urged Wilson to make a final commitment and asked him to prepare a short description of the textbook to be included in the next Heath catalogue. Even though the documents relating to the next exchange are missing, it is obvious that Heath, soon after March 22, sent Wilson either the manuscript or proofs of the *Teacher's Manual* of Mary D. Sheldon's *Studies in General History*. D. C. Heath and Company published this manual soon afterward under Miss Sheldon's name, but it had been prepared in the Heath office by one Stetson.

Wilson replied to Heath's letter of March 22 on March 30, 1886. Only a partial reconstruction of this letter exists, but in it Wilson made a definite commitment to write the textbook, for, as he informed Herbert Baxter Adams on April 2, "I have, too, just engaged to prepare a work on Civil Government for D. C. Heath." Wilson included an outline of his textbook in a letter to his father on March 31. He may have included a copy of this outline in his letter to Heath of March 30. He also went on to comment on Stetson's manual and to describe the kind of textbook that he, Wilson, intended to write.

Heath seems to have had this portion of Wilson's letter typed and returned to Wilson on April 15 for his use in preparing the announcement for the Heath catalogue. Someone in the Heath office wrote *"Prospectus"* at the beginning of and *"Plan of Woodrow Wilson's Civil Government"* on the verso of the third page of this manuscript.

Wilson did subsequently prepare an announcement, probably when he visited Heath at his office in Boston on April 22 or April 26, 1886.[1] None of the Heath circulars or catalogues for this period seem to have survived, and the only text of Wilson's announcement that the editors have discovered is in the "Boston letter" to the New York *Evening Post*, printed in that newspaper on May 18, 1886, as follows:

"Messrs. D. C. Heath & Co. will publish a volume on Civil Government by Prof. Woodrow Wilson of Bryn Mawr College. It is not yet written, and will probably not be issued for a year. It is intended as a text-book for advanced classes in high schools and colleges, but it will be of value also to the reading public. The work will be in two parts—the philosophical and practical—and its scope is suggested in these words: 'A practical exposition of the Federal and State Governments of the United States, with concise comparative studies of Grecian, Roman, and the chief modern European systems of government, and introductory chapters on the probable origin and early history, the nature, forms, and functions of government, and a chapter on law.' It is expected to make the book a systematic study in comparative politics."

This description can mean only one thing—that Wilson, at some time between the beginning and about the end of April 1886, had jettisoned his plan to write a textbook for grammar schools and had conceived, at least in embryo, the book that was to become *The State*. One finds evidence that this was true in the following portion of Heath's letter to Wilson of July 19, written in reply to Wilson to Heath of July 14, 1886: "It suits me all the better to have your book progress slowly and surely so that when it is done it will be safer to the publisher as well as more creditable to the author. I believe your plan of having it 'grow' is by all means the right one. We have had many calls for a new book for the lower grades in Civil Government, similar for instance to the enclosed which comes in the same mail as your letter. Will you kindly return it, and give us if you can the name of a good man to prepare an elementary book, or would you like to prepare an elementary one after making the larger one?"

As D. C. Heath to Wilson of July 27 makes clear, Wilson replied on July 22 that he had reconsidered the matter and now thought that he would like to prepare the elementary textbook as well as the larger one.[2] The Heath catalogue, issued in August, included announcements of both books.[3]

Wilson seems meanwhile to have done no work on either textbook

[1] WW to EAW, April 23 and 26, 1886. The strongest evidence that Wilson prepared this description during this visit to Boston is a brief outline entitled "Origin of Govt," which Wilson wrote on the back of a piece of stationery with the letterhead of the United States Hotel, where he was staying in Boston. This is a WWhw Ms. in the WP, DLC. There is the additional evidence that there is no acknowledgment in the Wilson Papers by Heath of receipt of the description.

[2] See also WW to D. C. Heath, July 31, 1886.

[3] D. C. Heath to WW, Aug. 5, 1886.

during the late spring of 1886, so overwhelmed had he been by course
work and examinations at Bryn Mawr. But he set to work at preliminary reading and research in late June, after he and Ellen had settled down for the summer with the elder Wilsons in Clarksville.[4] He
seems to have written the first chapter of the elementary textbook
(following the outline printed at August 8, 1886) soon after receiving
Heath's letter of August 5. He wrote to Ellen from Little Rock,
where he was visiting the Kennedys, on August 16: "I read the
first chapter of the text-book to sister Marion and bro. Ross this morning." Printed at August 8, 1886, this first chapter gives a clear indication of the kind of grammar-school book that he intended to write.

Documents and notes in this volume and the next will reveal the
progress of Wilson's work on both the elementary and advanced
textbooks.

[4] The documentary remains in the Wilson Papers do not shed much light
on Wilson's reading and research during the summer of 1886. One small body
of notes, which he certainly wrote at this time, relates to various departments
of the federal and state governments.

To Daniel Collamore Heath

[Dear Mr. Heath:]   [Bryn Mawr, Pa., March 30, 1886]
I think Mr. S[tetson]. has done about as well as could be expected under the inconveniences of a method which, it seems to
me, only the greatest genius could successfully employ. The cardinal danger of that method of treatment is *vagueness*. Only
such genius as could kindle the imagination and vitally touch the
enthusiasm of children concerning questions of duty, of reverence, and of patriotism—catching hold upon them and holding
them to every theme by virtue of a subtle personality pulsating in
every sentence—could afford to treat of such matters in the abstract and by way of introduction. Generalities never have any
'glitter' even that will hold the eye of a child. The single means,
I believe, in which a child can be taken hold of effectually is by
means of his imagination—through his interest. If once you can
engage his willing attention you may be sure his mind lies wide
open to every sentiment, whether of duty or of patriotism, of
love or of devotion which your subject naturally makes prominent in its natural progress. There's nothing but waste of breath
in telling him to love what he is not vitally interested in.

In brief, the narrative and descriptive method seems to me infinitely preferable to the expository and didactic. Mr. Stetson has,
you observe, to advance by way of definitions and eulogies on
good citizenship—and I conceive definitions and eulogies on good
conduct to be the very hardest things in which to interest young
minds—or old minds either, for the matter of that.

My plan will be to *tell the story of government* first and let the lessons in duty follow as natural, inevitable conclusions. I shall expend the very best efforts of my reason and my imagination in striving to show how the government we have was born and brought up, what its family connections were and are, what its experiences have been—everything that promises to arrest the boys attention. I shall seek every illustration possible from the things that come within a boy's own life, and shall depend on my success in getting him thoroughly interested in the *thing*, government, for my later success in arousing his interest in the *idea*, government.

To come down to concrete particulars, these are the topics with which I shall begin:[1]

The system of govt. under which we live—a rapid, but vivid, outline of its character.

It took a long history to build up this structure: what was the character of that history, and how has it made our character and our politics different from those of other peoples?

The Germans and their institutions as seen by Caesar and Tacitus, as telling what we might have been had we been born soon enough!—what the Romans thought of the German institutions, and the success of the Germans against the Romans. How some boys in a school in Maryland developed institutions just like those of the Germans.

How the political life of these men, our ancestors, changed in Gaul and Britain.

The sort of Govt. that England came at length to have.

The sort she had when our forefathers came to this country, and the sort they wanted to establish in the New World.

The establishment and growth of the colonies—the towns in New England, the broad counties in Va., etc.

You probably will not want any more. I mean to reverse Mr. S's method by doing in the text what he asks the teacher to do: supply the flesh and blood of each topic.

[Sincerely yours, Woodrow Wilson]

TCL (WP, DLC).

[1] The Editorial Note, "Wilson's Plan for a Textbook in Civil Government," discusses the provenance of this reconstructed letter. There is a one-page WWhw outline, entitled *"The American State,"* of the balance of this letter in WP, DLC.

To Herbert Baxter Adams

Dear Dr. Adams,   Bryn Mawr, Pa., 2 April, 1886

Possibly President Gilman has already spoken to you of the matter concerning which I wrote him yesterday. If so, you will anticipate the question I want to broach here. It is with reference to the degree. My experience here has been quite what I expected it to be, as regards preparation for the degree examination. Class work has so absorbed my time and energies that I have found it practically impossible to undertake any systematic reading outside of my courses. Such reading as I would have to do for the degree would be so much of the same kind as that which I have to do for my classes that it would only have jaded me, had I tried to crowd it into my scant portions of leisure. I have, therefore, occupied that leisure with small pieces of work of another kind—with original work in which I could, as it were, stretch my limbs. I have, too, just engaged to prepare a work on Civil Government for D. C. Heath, into which I hope to put some of my best paces of thought and treatment, and which will, consequently, take up the greater part of my vacations for some time to come, so precluding still more completely special preparation for the degree tests. I had, in a word, determined to make my regular professional studies work me along towards such preparation, so that I might take the degree in a couple of years, say:—for I have all along coveted such recognition as a Ph.D. from the Hopkins would give me.

But I find, rather unexpectedly, that I need a degree *now*, that not having it operates as a sort of technical obstacle to my immediate promotion. This I must, of course, say confidentially. I am, consequently, driven to ask, frankly but with the sincerest hope that I may be understood to ask without the least taint of presumption, for a special consideration of my case. I know that men have received such degrees in the highest quarters for special work done quite aside from the regular requirements: and I have ventured to hope that the authorities of Johns Hopkins might be inclined, in view of the work, both in your dept. and in Dr. Ely's, that I have done, and the work which I stand pledged to do in the future, to make mine a case of special arrangement, somewhat as was done in the case of Shinn's A.B.

I shall write to Dr. Ely to the same effect, in the confidence that the fact that I spent almost all my effective time last year in special work under him may count in my favour in his eyes in connection with the present question.

I have spoken very plainly; but I am sure that you have understood the spirit and the motives in which I have written.

With sincerest regards,
    As ever   Yours respectfully   Woodrow Wilson

ALS (H. B. Adams Papers, MdBJ).

From Joseph Ruggles Wilson

My beloved Woodrow—   Clarksville, April 5th 1886.

If you had not wings outspreading for higher flights, I would advise you to "set up" as a model letter-writer, and to publish, along with specimens of your own composition, chapters of rules for guiding others in their efforts to achieve this most difficult art. I cannot tell you how pleasing to me, and to us all, are those effusions of your confidential love with which you charm our hearts and refresh our minds. In this, too, you are getting ahead of me—in this matter of epistolary excellence I mean, as well as in certain lines of study:—and, don't you presume to say me nay in this averment! Truth to tell, though, my precious son and friend, I *am* able to understand all that you *write*, whatever is the subject (and all that you publish) and am still competent to judge of the style of yr. composition. So, please to continue to send me any & everything you compose, if not for my criticism, for my delectation. I need not try to say how delighted I am at your progress as a thinker and as a public man, and also at the ability you possess to choose friendships and to fasten friends. God is certainly dealing lovingly with you, and I dare to say that He receives at your heart the tribute of a daily gratitude—as I am sure He does from ours, in yr. behalf.

I have read with great interest the outline you have suggested as touching the *text book*. It takes one's breath away to run over the vast field of matter which is here proposed for survey. And if you can find room in a moderately sized volume for a view—comparative and positive—of so many different governments: and, without clouding perspicuity by the condensation needful—you will have produced a superlative desideratum[.] I am confident, however, of your success if you give yourself sufficient time, for studying matter and perfecting arrangement. As to the "Origin of Govt.," let me suggest that not *very* many pages be occupied: i. e., the speculative theories thereanent might either be omitted altogether (as a discussion)—and after merely numbering and stating these, would you not do well just to set forth what *you* believe to be the true doctrine: thus ranking yourself as a quotable *authority*?—if authority can at all be claimed as to such a matter? You surely are right in determining to fish (by circular or otherwise) for nothing more than suggestive hints, touching not so much the subject-matter as the probable wants of the schools and colleges in respect to size of vol., questions, and answers, &c. Now that you are likely to be "in for it" I would make a *sale-*

able book as well as a highly instructive one. How I *wish* I could help you!

As to your alumni speech I have no doubt you underrate the impression it made. I grant that such speeches are hard to make —but if you succeeded in interesting the *more thoughtful* men, they will remember what you said—and you—after they have long forgotten the Chinese-cracker squibs of the laugh-producing anecdotist. Did you get a chance at McCosh, for a pow-wow? *If* you could get a foothold at Princeton! . . .

Love unbounded from all three of us to all two of you.

Your affectionate Father.

ALS (WP, DLC).

From Daniel Coit Gilman

My dear Sir   Johns Hopkins University. Baltimore, Ap. 5 1886

Your note of the 1st requires an official response, & before giving it I must consult the Board of Univ. Studies. Dr. Adams will probably write you informally & I hope that it will be possible to meet your wishes; but it is never possible for me to fore-tell the action of the Board.

Yours Sincerely   D. C. Gilman

ALS (WP, DLC).

To Robert Bridges

My dear Bobby,   Bryn Mawr, Pa., 6 April, 1886

I am deeply distressed to hear the unfavorable reports about your father's condition brought by your note of last week.[1] I know how terrible a strain it must be upon you to work along in the presence of your anxiety and in spite of your strong desire to be with him. I sincerely hope that better news has reached you ere this. You have my warmest sympathy, old fellow, as I am sure you know. I have thought of you more times than I could count since I saw your tired, anxious face for those two or three minutes two weeks ago; and only press of college duties has prevented my writing sooner.

I suppose that Lee has written to you meantime. I enjoyed his company up there in your delightful quarters immensely while I had it. Tired as we both were, I got a glimpse of one or two of the traits which make you love him. He is a splendid, genuine fellow. I wish I had known him better before. We luxuriated in your rooms and would have enjoyed them without drawback if you had not been missing. But, for me, the principal pleasure of the trip was taken away by missing you. My *motive*, as I told you before, was to identify myself with Princeton by speaking at the dinner—though I doubt now whether it was a very good business investment to make the speech I did—but it was *you*, and not the dinner, that I was expecting to *enjoy*. It seemed, somehow, to take the wind out of my sails not to find you.

I have been receiving repeated and urgent invitations to accept a place in the faculty of the Univ. of Indiana—which has just passed under a new and progressive administration. But I want a chair of Politics, not of History: and I don't want to go West.

It was very thoughtful of you to send me the Chicago editorial. It did interest me very much—and seems to me to contain a very clever suggestion.

Mrs. W. joins with me in sending warmest regards. As ever
Yours affectionately,   Woodrow Wilson

ALS (WC, NjP).
1 It is missing.

From Herbert Baxter Adams

Johns Hopkins University,
Dear Mr. Wilson: Baltimore, Apr. 7 1886
I have talked over the situation with Dr. Ely and Pres. Gilman & we all agree that there is no chance of any degree without examination before the Board of Univ. Studies. But this point is also clear to us all. There is no chance of your being plucked. Dr. Ely and I will conduct your examination, both written & oral, in a manner at once considerate & just. We understand the case and you may rest assured that it will be successfully tried. With Classical Hist. & what you know of France, England & the U. S. there will be no obstacle on my side of the house. Dr. Ely assures me that you are sound enough in Polit. Econ.

Therefore come on boldly the last of May or early in June & take two written examinations of three hours each
(1) Hist.
　(a) General i.e. Classical, French, etc.
　(b) Engl. Const
　(c) Amer.　　"
(2) Polit. Econ.
　(a) Gen. Principles

(b) Finance U. S.

(c) Amer. Pol. Econ.

(d) Socialism

After passing these formal examinations a day will be set for your appearance before the Board, for about one hour. *You will pass that ordeal very easily.* It will be time to ask for special consideration when you need it.

To comply with a very absurd law requiring all theses to be bound uniformly for preservation in the Library, your book, or rather two copies of the same, will have to be sacrificed to the formation of a Wilson Scrap-Book. If you wish, I will have this base job done & hand you the bill of damages.

Very cordially,   H. B. Adams

Dr. Ely approves of what I have said and answers your letter herewith.

ALS (WP, DLC) with WWhw figures on env.

To Herbert Baxter Adams

Dear Dr. Adams,   Bryn Mawr, Pa., 8 April, 1886

Thank you very much for your cordial letter of yesterday. Sorry a figure as I always cut in examinations, from sheer perversity of natural disposition, I could not ask more generous treatment as regards such ordeals than you and Dr. Ely promise. I will come, of course. I cannot tell just yet when I can get off with least disturbance to my duties here; but I think June will afford more days than May. If there is no present necessity for fixing definitely upon a time, I will wait till I can know exactly what my engagements here will be at the end of our term before asking for a definite appointment.

Yes, have the 'Wilson scrap-book' made, and I will pay the bill. I write to-night to the publishers to know if they have not unbound sheets of "Cong Govt.," which would serve the scrap-book purpose better than bound copies. If they have, I will have them send you sheets; otherwise, I will have ordinary copies sent and the work of mutilation may proceed in spite of board backs.[1]

Let me say again that I appreciate very deeply the interest you and Dr. Ely have shown in the 'case,' and the kind consideration which you have extended to a nervous fellow who can't for the life of him pull in ordinary harness. Please give my kindest regards to Dr. Ely.

Very sincerely Yours,   Woodrow Wilson

ALS (H. B. Adams Papers, MdBJ).
    1 Actually, Wilson had Houghton Mifflin send his ribbon copy of *Congressional Government* to the Johns Hopkins, and it was apparently this copy that he presented as his dissertation. It is in the Manuscript Department of the Milton S. Eisenhower Library, The Johns Hopkins University.

From Daniel Collamore Heath

Dear Prof. Wilson: Boston Apr. 15. 1886.
    Your favor of the 30th ult. came duly to hand. I have been waiting before replying to hear from Holt about the Godkin.[1] Enclosed is his reply,[2] which you may return to me if you please.
    The announcement of your book strikes me very favorably. It seems to me it could not be better. Of course it can be modified in any way it seems wise to you when you come to put it on paper. I will try & send you proof of the announcement before it shall go into our catalogue. The book will be of so high a grade that I can readily see that suggestions from others as to what it should & should not contain &c. could come but from very few men & should be of general rather than a specific character.
    We could supply you at cost with such domestic & foreign books as it would be necessary for you to have in constant use in preparing your book. We could easily obtain books for you from the Boston Public Library, & also from the Athenaeum in which I am a shareholder.
                              Very truly yours,   D. C. Heath.

ALS (WP, DLC) with WWhw notation on env.: "Ans. April 19/86."
    1 This correspondence concerned a book on American government, which E. L. Godkin had promised to write for the publisher, Henry Holt.
    2 Wilson summarized Holt's letter to Heath in WW to EAW, April 18, 1886.

Two Letters to Ellen Axson Wilson

                    On the train between Wash. & Phila 15 April, '86
My darling wife,
    I am leaving Wash. rather earlier than I expected, because there is no train between this (4.20 p.m.) and 10 to-night. I have, therefore, been driven to scribble my note on the cars.
    I saw Renick and together we went around to see various officials whom he knew to be interested in 'Cong. Govt.'—amongst others a Mr. Graves,[1] at the head of one of the bureaux, who is one of the biggest official guns. They were all extremely cordial and complimentary—especially Mr. Graves, who proved a most interesting man—and who 'would not have our acquaintance stop here but wishes in some way to continue it.' Altogether I felt quite

'set up' to find myself known in so many offices. I saw Gould, too, at the High School where he teaches, and took a sort of lunch, of milk and "apple-bread" with him there. Went over the school and found it very interesting and suggestive.

After ascertaining that [E.M.] Gadsden was off on a few days leave because his wife was being confined, and that she had just been delivered of *twins*, I did not try to find him. I knew he wd. not want to see any more company!

About two I went up to the Capitol and watched the House and the Supreme Court until time to come away to my train (the Senate was in 'executive session')—And that's the account of my day[2]

That, at least, is what I *did*: what I have *felt* since last night, I dare not say. Oh, my little queen, I probably haven't felt the worst of it yet—for I have not yet gone *home* and not found you *there*!—but I feel enough now to know what it means to be separated from you,—but, dear me, this is not setting a good example—I must go write on the Caligraph! Suffice it to say, for the present, that your sweet thought of last night has been more than fulfilled. I love you, oh I love you, with a yearning, ever-growing love which fills my heart even more insistently and clamourously while you are away than when you are with me! I love you, I love you, I love you!

How I hope that my darling has been getting on prosperously to-day and that she is nearing a happy arrival! My splendid, brave little wife! Love to Aunt Lou[3] and all.

Your own   Woodrow

[1] Edward O. Graves, Chief of the Bureau of Engraving and Printing.
[2] For a further account of Wilson's visit in Washington, see WW to R. Bridges, April 19, 1886.
[3] Wilson had accompanied Ellen to Washington, where she took the train for Gainesville, Georgia, to have her baby at the home and under the care of her aunt, Louisa Cunningham Hoyt Brown.

My precious, darling little wife,   Bryn Mawr, 16 April 1886

Lunch is over; now for my 'loaf' with you. I will not mention the differences between *this* method of loafing and that—say of Tuesday, for fear I might have to stop and write on the Caligraph in the midst of the enumeration. I will say only that you were never loved and yearned over more than you are at this present moment. My heart is full to overflowing of *you*—is full of you *only*. The excitements of going about and talking to all sorts of people, and seeing all sorts of things that demanded my attention kept the dull ache at the *bottom* of my heart yesterday in Washington. The night before, after leaving you, I felt simply dazed and as it were stunned. But to-day my love for you has eclipsed every other energy. I am simply and only *yours*—every other part of my identity has apparently disappeared. I am not unhappy, darling: I love you too much for that. I love you too much to pain you by *brooding* over your absence. But at last I seem to be finding out just how much and how truly you are my wife—*and my life*! I am only half myself away from you, though I still live *for* you as intensely as ever. I can't be *altogether* miserable in your absence because I know that it is only absence of body— that the heart that makes my life so bright and happy—which is my life's *self*—is with me. I can know what you *would* say, were you still here—and, oh, my darling, *that* makes me *so* happy!

I am going to town presently to have my overcoat mended at the sleeve-ends, so that I must say good-bye till tomorrow.

The telegram came.[1] My little treasure is really safely at her journey's end! Oh, how glad and thankful I am! God bless you, sweetheart! Love to all   Your own   Woodrow

ALS (WC, NjP).
  [1] It is missing, as are the two telegrams mentioned in the next letter.

From Louisa Cunningham Hoyt Brown

Dear Mr Wilson   Gainesville, Ga. April 16th/86.

I hope that ere this you have rec' the two telegrams: the first telling you of the safe arrival of dear Ellie Lou at my home, the sec' telling you of the safe arrival of your little daughter Miss Margaret Wilson, at 11½ O'clock to day. Mr Evans & Loula[1] took a carriage & met E. L at the Depot last night: she seemed cheerful & well & retired about ten O'clock: I sat in my room reading for a short time when I heard E. L. suddenly arise: I waited a few minutes when still hearing her moving about her room I went to her door & asked her if she was sick & she called me in: I soon found that she needed a physician so sent for Dr Bailey:[2] he gave her something to quiet her & left after a short time telling me to send for him if she grew worse and that she was not in labor: E. L. slept some and as she was not much sick at her earnest solicitations I laid down about two hours: when I awoke I found that her pains were increasing so I sent for Dr B. again.

Two of my lady friends were with us & Mrs Shepherd,[3] the widow lady I wrote to her of.

I never saw any lady bear the pangs of labor so heroically as the dear child did: she did not let a groan escape her, & would smile sweetly between the pains & kiss me so affectionately. The tears came into her eyes once & she says "I am not crying for the pain but for Woodrow." After I got the dear little babe dressed I took it to its mother for her to see & she gave it the first kiss. E. L looks perfectly overjoyed when she looks at & takes it in her arms. Little Margaret has large dark blue eyes & looks as bright as a month old baby. The babe is finely developed & not a deformity on it: I think it came just at the right time. . . .

Yours affectionately,   Aunt Lou.

ALS (WP, DLC).
[1] Mrs. Brown's daughter, Loula, and James Phillip Evans. They had been married on December 2, 1885.
[2] J. W. Bailey, M.D., of Gainesville.
[3] A nurse.

To Ellen Axson Wilson

Bryn Mawr, 17 April, 1886

Oh, my darling, my darling, what shall I say to you *now*! My little wife is a mother: the baby has come—little Maggie has come! Oh, my little queen, how full my heart is—how infinitely I love you and the baby! And how I envy the baby! She does not know yet what a delightful little mother she has—and she is to have the delight of making your acquaintance after the sweetest, most intimate fashion possible. How strange it all is—and how much would I give to see my wife and my baby! Of course she is too wee and too pink as yet to look like anybody but herself—but I shall not soon get over the disappointment if Aunt Lou don't write very shortly to say that the baby is just a wee bit copy of *you*. I have set my heart on having my little daughter the image of her mother. My natural, spontaneous, inevitable, father's love for her will be increased from year to year in proportion as she reproduces you in herself.

And so 'Beth's' wish, that I might hear unexpectedly that it was all over, was abundantly fulfilled. The news was *so* unexpected that I think it took about an hour for me to realize what had happened—and to get over my consternation at the thought that so terrible a strain had come upon my darling immediately on the heels of her long journey. I have not allowed my fears to contradict the "both doing well" of Aunt Lou's telegram; but it has taken all my resolution to let the telegram have the last word in the matter. Oh, how thankful I am that my precious one is in such loving, skilful hands! She will be safe there, if anywhere;

and I know that our God will rule in this matter with all wisdom and mercy. Oh, how I have prayed for you, my darling: and what a comfort it is to *know* the God to whom we pray!

Are you willing to share my love with the baby, sweetheart? It wont decrease your portion any to do so. Oh, I love you, I love you, I love you—and I love the baby almost as much as I love you. Kiss her for me as often and as hard as is safe. Love to Aunt Lou and to all. God bless you, sweetheart—my queen—my precious wife.   Your own   Woodrow.

ALS (WP, DLC).

From Louisa Cunningham Hoyt Brown

Dear Mr Wilson   Gainesville, Ga. Aprl 17th/86
As it is Saturday night & I am busy I only write a P. Card—to let you hear how the mother & babe are getting on. I am glad to tell you that both are doing just as well as they can do. E. looks bright & cheerful & the babe sleeps almost all day & night. She says she had a delightful trip & was feeling well all the way. She says to tell you that you must enjoy your Boston trip all you can as yr mind will now be less anxious. She sends much love; E. is a dear sweet patient it is a pleasure to wait upon her.

She likes her nurse very much.   L. C. B.

API (WP, DLC).

To Ellen Axson Wilson

My precious little wife,   Philadelphia, Pa., April 18, 1886.
Here I am at uncle Tom's[1] according to engagement. The rest have gone to afternoon service, inviting me to stay at home and rest. Having found a piece of paper (a 'scratch-book') and having, now that you are gone, a *pencil*, I proceed to rest by writing to you. It will rest and quiet me more to write to you than to do anything else I know of.

I received at [*sic*] letter last night from D. C. Heath, the publisher, saying that he was very much pleased with the proposed announcement of the text-book—'did not see how it could be better'—and that he could furnish me with books, domestic and foreign, at cost, and could borrow any I wanted from the Boston libraries. He also inclosed a letter from Henry Holt saying that Mr. Godkin's book on Govt. was not finished, and—between him and Mr. Heath—he didn't think it ever would be.[2] So the publisher is in a good humor and the field is clear.

How you make everybody love you, darling! Dr. Rhoads told Mrs. Coale[3] yesterday that Mrs. R[hoads] had been very anxious about the effects of your journey upon you and had upbraided herself after you were gone for not having yielded to her strong impulse and gone with you to Gainesville. She might have done so as well as not, she said; she thought of it the night she came to tell you good-bye; and she was so sorry she had not insisted. Isn't that nice? My! If I had known how the journey would hasten the baby's coming, nothing in the world could have prevented my going all the way myself.

It has been unspeakably hard, sweetheart, to go all this time without any particulars—with no news except that of the telegram! But I have been a real good, rational boy, knowing the possibilities of the mail, saying over and over again to myself "both doing well," and *making* that suffice to suppress the cries of my heart to know the particulars of how my darling had fared—and is faring. Oh, my love, my love, how infinitely I long for you— how [un]speakably I love you and our little daughter! Isn't that odd, sweetheart! *Our* baby! Oh, precious, how lovely your baby must be! What a time you will have keeping me from smothering her with kisses & caresses when once I get hold of her! Sweetheart, wont it help you to get well that I am loving you so intensely? Oh if I only *could* help you! My darling, my queen! It hurts me so to think of you weak and sick! I would give my life for you! I love you, I love you, I love you! Love to all.

Your own   Woodrow.

ALS (WP, DLC). Letter damaged.
   [1] The Rev. Dr. Thomas A. Hoyt.
   [2] Godkin never wrote the book.
   [3] Mary Anna Coale, proprietress of the "Betweenery."

From Loula Brown Evans

Gainesville Ga. April 18th/86

Cousin Ellie & little Margret are getting on nicely: feeling very well today. both send much love.

Lovingly   Your Cousin   L. C.

API (WP, DLC).

To Daniel Collamore Heath

Dear Mr. Heath,   Bryn Mawr, Pa., 19 April, 1886
   I am sincerely glad that you like the plan I have outlined for

the text-book; and I'm glad—for *our* sakes, at least—that Mr. God-kin's book is not forthcoming.

I intend to try to get up to Boston the latter part of this week, to see what the libraries contain that I shall want. If I can arrange the trip, you may expect a call from me, to talk over our plans a little.

I enclose Mr. Holt's letter.

Very truly Yours,   Woodrow Wilson

ALS (WP, DLC).

To Ellen Axson Wilson

Bryn Mawr, 19 April, 1886

My darling, precious, matchless little wife,

Yesterday went off *very* pleasantly at uncle Tom's—he had nothing to do in the evening, and so we three had a long, cosey, interesting talk till it was time to go and catch my 10:15 train —but, after all, it was not much of a *rest* day for me. It's hard work exerting oneself to talk to them, as well as to other people, especially when aunt Sadie does not give one time to think sanely. I should have been more tired after an unoccupied day of lone-liness spent out here, however. I am altogether glad I went.

I held an examination in Greek history on Friday—baby's sure —enough birth-day—according to program; to-day I lectured the class on the mistakes made on Friday; and to-morrow I shall com-plete the examination—I got only half through on Friday. Then vacation, and the business trip to Boston. After all, it *will* be a real business trip: for, now that I am to have the use of the Boston libraries, I *must* see what they have that I shall need.

So much for what I have been doing, and am about to do. Now for a hint as to what I have been *thinking*. I have been thinking that, although it's a terribly lonely, trying business, this of being separated from the sweet, noble little woman for whom I live, it's not half so bad as used to be the loneliness before we were mar-ried,—except that, for the time being, I am desperately anxious to hear how she is faring. For, before, there was *nothing* to rest and soothe me: I wasn't sure of the future; but now I am: her love rests and soothes and delights me only less than her pres-ence would. It fills my life and my work with a sort of conscious-ness of blessing—of assured comfort and strength—which is of untold value to me. And I've been thinking that, if ever a man was blessed in having a baby—and a baby *daughter*—I am: be-cause a baby—especially a little *maiden*—completes *your* life and

happiness as no other gift of our heavenly Father could—besides elevating my life by a new love and a new responsibility. Oh, my darling, my heart is so full. It will require a life-time with you to give it vent! My precious wife, my precious baby! I love, love, love, love you!   Your own   Woodrow
Love to Aunt Lou.

ALS (WC, NjP).

To Edwin Robert Anderson Seligman

Dear Sir,   Bryn Mawr, Pa., 19 April, 1886
   Your letter of April 17 has just reached me. I would cheerfully undertake the review you propose but for one very important fact. I am self-taught, and *recently* self-taught, in German, and, consequently, read it *slowly*. If I had from now to the first week in May, uninterruptedly, for the perusal and review of Gneist's book,[1] the time would be quite enough. But I am compelled to be away from home most of this week and about half of next week, on a business trip to Boston, and the time over and above the period of my absence would not be enough for such a reading and review as such a book should have.
   I am extremely sorry; but you see the imperative nature of my reasons. I am not disinclined—quite the contrary: I am only unable   Very truly Yours,   Woodrow Wilson

ALS (Seligman Papers, NNC).
   [1] Rudolf von Gneist, *Das englische Parlament in tausendjährigen Wandelungen vom 9. bis zum Ende des 19. Jahrhunderts* (Berlin, 1886).

To Robert Bridges

Dear Bobby,   Bryn Mawr, Pa., 19 April, 1886
   First for a piece of news. You are being addressed by a *father*. I have a little daughter three days old. She is not here. I have not seen her. Mrs. Wilson went South, to one of her aunts in Georgia, last week—and the baby was born the day after her arrival: two or three weeks before it was expected. The birth was unquestionably hastened by the fatigues of the journey; and I have been made desperately anxious by the circumstances, as you may suppose. But the news is that both mother and baby are doing well.
   And now for a bit of business: I escorted Mrs. W. as far as Washington, her only change of cars, and spent Thursday there. I found my former law partner, E. I. Renick, who is now an underpaid official in the Treasury, looking quite overworked and run

down. His physicians have ordered him to take a vacation; but he can't afford to do so unless he can get some vacation work. He has written numerous Georgia and Southern notes which have gone into the *Nation*'s 'Week'; and I promised to try to find out for him, through you, whether the *Nation*, or the *Post*, would care for anything like a correspondence from the South this summer as to the true feeling of the solid men of the section, the farmers and merchants, with reference to Cleveland's civil service reform policy. He feels, as I do, that papers like the Atlanta *Constitution*, though they may represent fairly well the opinions of politicians, do not represent anybody else on such questions. Renick thinks, from what he has heard through private sources, that the real public opinion of the South is staunchly in favour of Cleveland's course; and I think so too, so far as I am informed. Now, if interest isn't burning too low at present on the subject, would not that be a good thing to work up? Renick, I feel quite sure, is fully capable of the work, if it's wanted, and I knew it would be no harm to ask.

I sincerely hope that you have long ere this had final good news from your father. I have thought of him very often of late.

As ever   Affectionately Yours   Woodrow Wilson

ALS (WC, NjP).

Two Letters to Ellen Axson Wilson

My darling little wife,   Bryn Mawr, 20 April/86

Aunt Lou's letter, written the day baby came, reached me last night—my first particular news of the event of which my heart has been so very full these last four days! Oh, my darling! My brave, *splendid* darling! I have read aunt Lou's sweet letter till I know its simple account by heart—in more ways than one. That letter has carried me in a few minutes through all the anguishing sympathy with and all-absorbing love for my darling which would have possessed me through all the hours of her suffering, had I been with her! And I have felt all her own gladness at the baby's birth—our sweet, sweet little daughter! Oh, with what phase of love and sympathy has that letter *not* filled me! And that precious sentence that aunt Lou, with a true woman's choice, chose to repeat to me: "I am not crying for the pain, but for Woodrow"! I would not exchange that sentence for all the sweet things in our language! My darling! my little queen! How the tears have blinded me as I have read those words over and over again—because I was *not* there to comfort and help my sweet one: and oh, how inexpressibly happy the love that is in them has made me! The last thing I did before I went to sleep last night, the first thing I did when I woke this morning, the principal thing I have done ever since, when not under compulsion to work, has been to call you, aloud, by every sweet name known to our love vocabulary! Please thank and kiss aunt Lou for me for her letter—and tell her that the more she can and will repeat of what you say, the better for me. Oh, my lovely little pet, you are a perfect little witch, to manage to keep me so wonderfully happy at 'long taw.' In spite of the fact, of which I am so vividly conscious, that my life is *suspended* until I shall see you again, you make me absolutely happy—and almost as delighted with the baby as if I had her in my arms—by simply loving me! My blessed little wife! No trouble, however deep, no disappointment, however keen, can hurt me so long as I have you. You are my treasure, my strength! Kiss my little daughter for me—and my little *sister* Maggie[1]—and give a great deal of love from me to aunt Lou: and spend as much of the day as you can loving and thinking about   Your own   Woodrow.

[1] Ellen's sister, Margaret Axson.

My darling little wife,   Bryn Mawr, 20 April/86
    I must take the 9:48 to-morrow morning, so that I better write to-night the letter that I am to send you to-morrow. The train for Boston leaves Broad St. station at 11 A.M.; but there is no 10:18 from here, and the 9:48 is the best I can do. I shall be due in Boston at 8:05 P.M.—a pretty long day's ride! But I am quite well and in good trim, and shall stand it quite easily: because the Saturday and Sunday postal cards both came to-night, and their good news has set my heart on its feet again. Oh, my sweetheart, God has been *very* merciful and gracious to us! May he continue to bless my darling, and our precious little daughter!
    And so you have Mrs. Shepherd after all? I am *so* glad to know that you *like* her. That's almost half the battle. You would smile —I think I know the sort of smile it would be—if you could but know how eagerly and repeatedly I read the little messages from you on these postal cards. Ah, what a treasure the first letter *from you* will be—*all* of it a message from my little queen, and writ by her own hand! But you mustn't write that letter a single moment too soon (from the doctor's point of view), my sweet one,—do you hear?—for all I'm longing beyond all words for it. In the meantime, however, you may let the messages that are to

go into dear aunt Lou's letters grow in size with your strength. *Any* words from you are so precious to me just now. They seem to bring me a step nearer to my darling than I am when merely hearing *of* her: even though aunt Lou *does* seem so like *my* own dear aunt. What a debt of love and gratitude I shall owe her for her tender care of my treasures! Sweetheart, tell me as soon as you can, what *you* think of our baby. Can you send *that* in a message through aunt Lou, or cousin Loula? Or must you reserve it until you can have the pen yourself, and give free leave to your eloquence?

Eileen, I notice that that same gentleman I told you of before, whenever he passes that little stream in the hollow yonder, stops and says 'my darling' just as he did then—except that somehow there is nowadays a peculiar tremour in his voice when he utters the words, as if tears were rising in his heart—it must be for *gladness*, to judge by his smile and his eyes. *He is evidently in love*! It's an interesting case. Innumerable kisses to my darlings—and love to all.   Your own   Woodrow

Continue to send letters here. Mrs. C[oale]. will forward them.

ALS (WP, DLC).

From Ellen Axson Wilson

[Gainesville, Ga.,] April 21/86

I am allowed to write, my darling, just long enough to say that I *love love love* you, & to tell you how my heart aches to see you, & to have you see the baby. It is a little beauty, darling. Everyone says the prettiest little baby they ever saw, & so plump & healthy; so perfectly well. Ah how good our Heavenly Father is to us!—how tenderly He has cared for me!

I am just as well as can be,—"have never been sick yet" the nurse says. Both baby & I are considered perfect phenomenons in the way of "doing well." Every danger is over & I am *quite myself again*. So you must put aside all anxiety about me & celebrate my recovery by having a "grand old time" in Boston. Am so glad you can carry a light heart this trip. Goodbye my darling, my love, my *life*, my dear *dear* husband.

Your own little wife   Eileen.

They wont let [me] write again until the regular day, Monday. I got out a special license for this. *I love you* sweetheart.

ALS (WC, NjP). Enc.: Louisa C. H. Brown to WW, April 21, 1886, ALS (WC, NjP).

Three Letters to Ellen Axson Wilson

My darling wife,   Boston, Mass., 22 Apr. 1886

I arrived here safe and sound last night. It's now 10:25 A.M. I have not started out to see anybody or anything yet. But I shall so soon as I finish this letter. I can't do anything before having a little chat with my precious one.

The way I feel upon reaching this borough is an involuntary tribute to its fame. I feel that odd sort of excitement which I imagine the literary adventurers of Sam. Johnson's time used to feel upon reaching London. After all, there *is* more history, political and literary, connected with Boston and her surroundings, Cambridge and the rest, than about any other place in the country. It gives one a queer sense of elation to be here, which, I confess, I did not expect to feel. I am tempted not to make any *visits* at all, but just to go about and spy out the noted buildings and localities. If I did not have the fear of you before my eyes, I believe I should adopt that course. But you sent me here: & I must do your errands. I have not settled upon any program, so that I cannot tell you what I am *going* to do; but you may be sure that I will tell you each day what I *have* done—whom and what I have seen.

I am staying at the 'United States Hotel' where I am most pleasantly accommodated at $3.00 per day—better than we calculated.

My darling, I have a secret to tell you: The farther I get away from you—the more distractions crowd in upon my mind, the more you seem to me, the more my mind and heart overflow with thoughts and loves for you—the more conscious I am of how inseparably my life is bound up in yours. I shall carry you & the baby about in my heart to-day as a sort of source and store of smiles and joy. *You* shall make all my enjoyments double and treble. I love, love, love, love, *love* my precious wife and my sweet baby. Love to aunt Lou and all. Kisses for sister Maggie.

                    Your own   Woodrow.

My darling little wife,   Boston, April 23 1886. 10:20 A.M.

I am now ready to account for one day's proceedings. I went first to call on D. C. Heath. He is a very pleasant, open-faced, cordial, and yet business-like gentleman of about 35 or 40 yrs. We talked over the plan for the text-book a little, and then he took me around to the Athenaeum library and introduced me to the authorities—who turned me loose in the alcoves. That settled my fate for the morning. I stayed and looked over books till 2 o'clock.[1] Then, after dinner, I went over to Cambridge to the Harvard library, and, introducing myself to Mr. [Justin] Winsor, the librarian, settled my own fate for the afternoon, until turned out at five o'clock. I haven't found any books that will be specially helpful in my work, but I've begun to get a birds-eye view of what's been written—and how it has been written—which is quite suggestive.

In the evening I went to the opera.

This morning I shall first go to call on Mr. Scudder at H., M., & Co's—then to see Mr. Bradford (who appears in the Directory as 'stockbroker')—and Mr. Ross.[2] I have been putting off visiting them, because I fear that their invitations will at once destroy all my liberty. I *must* go to the Harvard library again to-day—by special arrangement. I am in a fair way to get permission to borrow the books I want there. Mr. Winsor seems well disposed.

I am feeling quite well, except for a little mutiny on the part of my bowels. If I could hear from my darling one, I would not mind that, or anything else of the kind; but, for some reason, though other letters have been forwarded to me by Mrs. Coale, none have turned up from Gainesville. Since my days are made up of love for you and our little one, nothing is so sure to disturb my serenity as the sligh[t]est cloud of anxiety about you and her. Oh, *how* I love you—oh, how I long to see our sweet little Maggie! But I'm coming sweetheart; our lives are 'sure-enough' one and the same—this is only a pause in them. You can live, for the time being, on the joy of your sweet motherhood *and* on hopes and thoughts of next June; and I can and do live constantly on those hopes and thoughts. How like a repitition of heart-experiences of *last* Spring—and yet how different! *Now* I *know* to what I come—then I only dreamed—with only half sufficiency—to what I was to come. The element of imagination *now* is how I shall feel as a *father*. I can't half realize that part of the program yet—though I do find myself eagerly and intensely loving that precious little daughter whom I have not seen. When I see her! Oh, darling, darling, what unfailing delight you bring me—my bride, my wife, my strength, my joy, my all! My little daughters mother. Love to aunt Lou, cousin Loula, sweet little sister—and for you and *our* Maggie, the whole heart of   Your own   Woodrow

1 Wilson's list of titles noted in the Boston Athenaeum Library, the Harvard University Library, and the Boston Public Library on April 22 and 23, 1886, is a two-page WWhw MS. (WP, DLC) on stationery of the United States Hotel.
2 Probably Denman Waldo Ross. See WW to ELA, April 20, 1885, n. 1, Vol. 4.

My darling wife,   Boston, April 24, 1886. 12.06 P.M.

Yesterday morning I went & called on Mr. Scudder at H., M., & Co's. He was out: so I spent another morning at the Athenaeum library, finding some books which, though in a 'furrin' language, will, I hope, be useful in my book-job. After dinner I called again *for* Mr. Scudder (as you would say)[.] 'He was out, but would be in within a few minutes. Wouldn't I like to see Mr. Houghton?'[1] I would. I was taken into a cherry-wood office and presented to a tall, somewhat rugged, but genial, hearty gentleman of about 65 years, I should say, who insisted on my staying until Mr. Scudder should come in. Mr. Scudder came in. We three talked pleasantly. Mr. Houghton invited me and Mr. Scudder to dine with him this evening, and me to go over the Riverside Press establishment with him this afternoon. We accepted. I am to meet him at 2:30—and to get away from him—some time before bed-time. I'll have a good time, though—because I've made up my mind to, and because my company will be agreeable. To resume: Mr. Scudder then took me and introduced me to Mr. Aldrich, who is a Saxon in colouring, briskly executive in manner, pithy and interesting in matter. He was very cordial. We talked of Mr. Lowell, my *Atlantic* opponent. Upon a sudden impulse, I asked Mr. Aldrich for a card of introduction to him, and posted off to make a call at his office. We were very glad to see each other. I found him really delightful. He is a young lawyer of just my age (we compared ages, quite like two boys). He is son of the manager, (and, I opine, owner) of the Lowell Institute. He is full of matter of the right sort: and our hour's conversation ran off as if it were but a tenth part so long.[2] I'll tell you the particulars of these little meetings after lunch some day—in one of the sweet days coming.

In the evening, being too fagged out to go to Cambridge, as I had intended, I went to the *Mikado* instead; and, upon returning to the hotel, found a note from Mr. Lowell inviting me to dinner to-day: but I was already promised to Mr. Houghton, you know.

This morning, under escort of one of the men in H., M., & Co's., I went to the great Public Library, was introduced to the authorities, and bewildered myself for a couple of hours— till coming away to write to my darling—looking over their vast catalogues and some of the books therein represented.

And now, with all my 'trapusing' around, have I lost sight of my dear ones for a moment? Not for a moment. With all my gadding about, my *heart* has remained, absolutely untravelled,

with you—and with that little precious possession whom I have
never seen, but who is part of me. Oh, I love, I love, I love you,
sweetheart, my precious one, my queen! You are all the world to
me. Love to aunt Lou, cousin Lou, little sister, and all

Your own   Woodrow

ALS (WC, NjP).
    [1] Henry O. Houghton, founder of the publishing firm.
    [2] Lowell, in May 1939, described the meeting as follows: "A few weeks later
there appeared in my office a tall, lantern-jawed young man, just my age. He
greeted me with the words: 'I'm Woodrow Wilson. I've come to heal a quarrel,
not to make one.'" Quoted in Henry W. Bragdon, "Woodrow Wilson and Lawrence Lowell," *Harvard Alumni Bulletin*, XLV (May 22, 1943), 595.
    It was the beginning of a long friendship and professional association. Lowell,
lawyer and educator, was born in Boston, Dec. 13, 1856. A.B., Harvard, 1877;
LL.B., Harvard, 1880. Practiced law in Boston, 1880-97. Lecturer at Harvard,
1897-99; Professor of Government, same institution, 1900-1909; President of
Harvard University, 1909-33. Chairman, executive committee of League to Enforce Peace, 1915-21; president, 1921-23. Author of many books, including *Essays on Government* (Boston, 1889); *Government and Parties in Continental Europe* (2 vols., Boston, 1896); *Public Opinion and Popular Government* (New
York, 1913); and *At War with Academic Traditions in America* (Cambridge,
Mass., 1934). Died Jan. 16, 1943.

From Ellen Axson Wilson

My own darling Woodrow,   [Gainesville, Ga.,] April 24/86
    I am so well & strong that they let me write a few lines again
today;—& now I have so much to say that I don't [know] what to
say first & what to keep for next time. But I *must* tell you about
the baby; she grows sweeter and prettier every day; she has the
lovliest little mouth & chin just like Maggie's & her head is *such* a
pretty shape, only she has my horrid high forehead; her eyes are
very dark blue at present—almost black—with very large iris; they
are set far apart & the space between them & the ear is very wide.
She has beautiful little ears by the way & a dear little baby nose,
—altogether it is a *lovely* little face if it *is* red. Her eyes are *so*
bright & she looks about in the most knowing way possible;—she
already knows the difference between me & other people & positively refuses to sleep away from me. She is very good, nurses
every three hours, goes to sleep at the breast, & sleeps till she is
hungry again. They ought to sleep all the time for the first month
you know. But I must leave the rest for next time. Ah sweetheart, it seemed impossible for anything else to bring us closer
than we were, but what a wonderful bond of union is this precious little life! *Our* baby *your* baby! I love it twice as well because
it is yours, and I *love* you, oh! *I love you infinitely*, my husband.
You too make *me* happy even in our separation. I lie & think
about you & the baby all day long & dream happy dreams & in

the morning watch the clock for Uncle W[arren Brown]. & my letter, my daily bread. I was so glad to get the letter from Boston—how eagerly I shall follow your movements. Am *so* glad about the nice letter from Heath, & that everything is so satisfactory about the libraries &c. But they say I must stop, please excuse *desperate* haste.

I love *love love*, my darling, my life, my own precious husband.
Your little wife   Eileen

ALS (WC, NjP).

Two Letters to Ellen Axson Wilson

Boston, April 25, 1886. 12:53 P. M.

Oh, my love, my darling, how shall I tell you what I felt last night when I opened an envelope and found *your* handwriting inside! I laughed and cried at the same time in reading those precious words—and, after reading them went to bed in a sort of ecstacy. I had just come back from Cambridge, from dining with Mr. Houghton; I was tired and sleepy, and thought nothing would be so sweet as to go to bed: but when the clerk handed me my mail with my room-key and I found your precious note in it, I forgot all about bed, forgot that I was tired,—forgot everything but the supreme joy in my heart. My lovely little wife's own words about our baby! And so the baby is a beauty, is she, precious? I might have known it—*your* baby couldn't well manage to be anything else—and yet—for it's *my* baby, too—I—I—yes I have a funny secret, a rather droll confession, to divulge: aunt Lou had said nothing about the baby's *appearance* except that it had big blue eyes, though she had said that it was perfectly formed, beautifully developed, &c.,—and I was beginning to have a dim suspicion that our little daughter wasn't pretty—had received too much from her father in the way of looks, &c. But now I know differently. I have your testimony—and if it *is* interested, I'd take it against all the world. *Of course* the baby's a beauty—what a goose I was! I wasn't mourning over the suspicion: but I am all the more radiant in my fatherhood because the suspicion was unfounded. What a fellow I am: so oppressed by silence—so dependent upon speech from my loved ones! And your heart aches to see me, and to have me see the baby? You darling!—& don't you suppose that mine aches quite as much on just the same score. Oh—my little wife and my jewel of a little daughter! I'd give my life for you! Sweetheart, when the nurse isn't about, tell the baby about her papa—won't you? Tell her that he loves her—

as much as *you* do—and that, when he comes, he will carry her, and sing to her, and romp for her benefit, to her dear little heart's content—nay, even surfeit! Will you? And kiss her for me as often as you dare—and let her kiss you for me! For her lips came partly from me! Oh, my queen! how eagerly I shall wait for the letter you are to write to-morrow—you splendid well little girl! By the time it comes, the pencilling on this sweet note that came last night will have suffered something approaching obliteration from kissing.

Aunt Lou's—*dear* aunt Lou's—note that came in the same envelope would have made me radiant by itself. It necessarily suffers some by comparison with yours—the sweetness of everything *you* write is supreme: but it was *very* sweet and did me immense good! I *love, love, love, love* you, sweetheart!

But to resume my narrative. I went out to the Riverside Presses with Mr. Houghton yesterday afternoon at half past two. When we got out there, he turned me over to Mr. Mifflin,[1] who is in charge there—a brisk, clear-voiced, hearty, well-conditioned, rather young man (say seven and thirty). Mr. M. took me through the whole establishment in order, from where the type are set to where the completed books are mailed and shipped to dealers &c., and to the store-houses where the 'plates' of the books are stowed away in odd little square boxes marked with the name of the book. Of course it was all exceedingly interesting. If ever I have another book published I shall be able to follow it in imagination through all its stages. Mr. Houghton's carriage came for us a little after four o'clock and we rode about Cambridge, seeing the homes of all the literary celebrities &c. &c. Then came the meeting with a pleasant lady, Mrs. Houghton, and her three daughters. Mr. Scudder came in: we eat dinner amicably and chattily: we talked agreeably in the luxurious library after dinner; and then (10:30) I came to the hotel—to find my darling's sweet, sweet letter!

This morning I walked out Commonwealth Avenue, the great fashion street (at least *one* of the great) and attended service at Dr. Duryea's[2] church, hearing a delightful, eloquent, refreshing sermon from him. How much of my pleasure in the sermon was due to the taste left in my mouth by your letter, I could not calculate. This afternoon I am going to call on Mr. Bradford. Mr. Ross is away, in Europe.

Love to dear aunt Lou, sweet little sister (with kisses), cousin Loula & all: and for my matchless little wife and my incomparable little daughter the whole heart of

Your own   Woodrow.

[1] Houghton's partner, George H. Mifflin.
[2] The Rev. Dr. Joseph T. Duryea, pastor of the Central Congregational Church of Boston.

Boston, April 26 1886. 3:18, P. M.

My Eileen, my darling little wife,

I can complete my narrative now—for the next thing to do is to take the train at 6:30 this afternoon. Unless I get home (or, rather to Bryn Mawr—for it isn't 'home' so long as you are not there) to-morrow morning, and so give myself part of the day for resting, I can't have any sort of a lecture ready for Wednesday. Besides, I'm rather tired, and have accomplished about all that I came to accomplish. It would require something like a month, instead of another *day* simply, to go *thoroughly* through these wonderful libraries here.

I got out to Mr. Bradford's (No. 8 Prescott Str—do you remember?—the address we searched for once amongst the scraps in the scrap basket, after I had prematurely torn up the letter from G. B. jr.) about four o'clock and stayed till about 10 in the evening, taking tea with the enthusiastic reformer. We did not *sit* and talk all that time, but spent most of the daylight hours walking out to Mt. Auburn (the cemetery) and taking the fine view from the tower there. The ladies of the house are his sister and his cousin. His sister was very bright and chatty; his cousin was sleepy. We talked on all sorts of topics (necessarily, to fill up five or six hours); I instructed (?) him on some points of his hobby—as well as on others; and, altogether, I made the usual blunder of talking too much—more than my share.

This morning I went out to Cambridge & called on the ladies at Mr. Houghton's, on Mr. Houghton[1] & Mr. Scudder at the office, on Mr. Heath at his office, and on my new acquaintance, Mr. A. L. Lowell. The latter I found out; and when I came back to the hotel I found his card here—the second time he has called & missed me.

So now for Bryn Mawr, to meet my letters from Gainesville. Those letters are the chief (external) feature of my life nowadays —the words from and about my darling ones. You must hurry to write me yourself again just as soon as ever it's safe to do so —because this first note is fast wearing out under repeated perusals—and other things! Oh, how sweet, how unspeakably sweet that little note is! It is one of my treasures. It sent me to bed happy last night again—just as if it were newly come. As I have several times had occasion to remark, love is a wonderful, *wonderful* thing as it has visited us. And oh, my darling, what shall I say of my joy at the marvellous way in which you have come through the crisis of the baby's birth! My delight is beyond all words. What a splendid, perfect little woman you are physically, as well as every other way! My pride in you is almost as great as my delight in you. And my heart has been full to overflowing with thanksgiving to our heavenly Father for his unspeakable goodness to us! How gracious and loving He has been! What a sweet duty it will be to teach our little daughter to love him!

Sweetheart, I *love, love, love* you—and the baby, oh, how much! Love to aunt Lou and all   Your own   Woodrow

ALS (WC, NjP).
¹ Houghton gave Wilson a copy of Charles Egbert Craddock, *Down the Ravine,* just published by Houghton Mifflin. Inscribed by Wilson, "From Mr. Houghton, April 26/86," this volume is now in the possession of Robert Reidy Cullinane, Washington. Charles Egbert Craddock was the pen name of Mary Noailles Murfree.

From Melville R. Hopewell

Dear Sir,   Tekamah, Neb., Apl 26 1886
I note yours of 16th. I have leased for grazing purposes, 240 acres of your mothers land described as follows, subject to her approval.

W½ NE1/4 sec 4— ⎫
W½ SE1/4   "   "— ⎬ 21-11-E-
E½ SW1/4   "   "— ⎭
for season of 1886, for . . . . 35." "
I retain fee of   . . . . 5." "
_____

and hand you in N. Y. Dft. 30.00
less ex[change]—
I think it likely I will be able to lease another tract.
                    Truly Yours   M. R. Hopewell
Keep me posted as to your P. O address.

ALS (WP, DLC) with WWhw notation on env.: "Ans. Apr. '86."

From Ellen Axson Wilson

My own darling Woodrow   Gainesville April 26 [1886]
Your third letter from Boston is just at hand, to my great satisfaction. Am *so* glad that you are enjoying it all, that you find the people you meet so pleasant & that all goes so well with you,— you don't say though how you are feeling;—if the indigestion is cured. I *hope* so. What a pleasant episode that was with Mr. Lowell! And you havn't seen Mr. Bradford yet or Mr. Ross. You

havn't half time enough. How I *wish* you could stay three weeks! You will have to go again at Xmas!

All is still well with your *family*! I sat up yesterday—the 10th day—& today. I can't walk or stand yet, that is I can't take more than two or three steps,—but I can sit two hours or more without fatigue, & I will gain strength fast now. I havn't any pains or disorders of any sort; except the inevitable trouble with my breasts,—raw & tender nipples;—baby's meals involve a not very mild form of torture for me; but that is scarcely more to be avoided than the birth-pains, & they will toughen in the course of a few weeks. Then I have the very welcome trouble of an excessive flow of milk—that is more than baby can manage yet,—so that they have to be rubbed & "drawn" & fussed with generally.

Baby grows sweeter and brighter all the time. I gave her your letter & told her it was from her Papa, and she seized it eagerly & gave it a hearty *kiss*! Now don't pretend, sir, that she wanted to eat it!—though even if she had, that would have been the highest compliment she knew how to pay you. By the way, I believe you have your wish; it is the general verdict that she is very much like her mother. Dr. Baily, looking at her the third day, volunteered the remark "she has her mother's face; no doubt about that," & they all say she grows more like me daily. Cool—isn't it?—for me to repeat that, after telling you how lovely she is; but of course I expect her to be an *idealized* copy if she *must* be like me:—besides I was a pretty baby!

Tell me darling—"honour bright!"—were you very much disappointed that she wasn't a boy?

But I must stop or Aunt Lou will scold,—and I have hardly *begun*, & I have but a corner in which to try & say,—what I *never can tell* you,—how I *love love love* my own darling, how I live hour by hour, & keep happy & am growing well & strong on his love for me[.] Ah my love, my life, the best & truest husband & lover in the world! You don't know how completely I live in & for you. Good bye sweet-heart.   Your little wife   Eileen

Can you manage to read these scrawls?

ALS (WC, NjP).

To Ellen Axson Wilson

My own precious little wife,   Bryn Mawr, April 27/86
    Here I am again in our cosey little rooms—not at home, as I

said, but constantly *reminded* of home—that is, of *you*! And I found a *piece* of home here on my table when I arrived this morning—my darling's second letter. Oh, sweetheart, sweetheart, what a well of gladness there is for me in these precious letters of yours! And this description of the baby! How I have devoured it! The long and short of it is, that the little darling *looks like you* —and that was the top of my wish in the matter! *I am so glad.* Those dark eyes will not have blue in them long—but soon their own sweet mother's beautiful brown eyes will have found their image in them. And then, with my darling little wife and sweet little daughter 'two of a kind,' wont I be the happiest man in the world? God bless you, my darling, my darlings; And so you *do* love the baby twice as much because she's *mine* too—oh you delightful, lovely, matchless little wife, you—you are a very genius at making me happy! *Can't* you make the baby understand that it has a papa far away who loves it with all his heart? Oh, I *wish* you could! *Because I do.*

But, let me finish my narrative. I left Boston last night at 6:30, on a through sleeper for Phila., and, bridging over the interval with a *tolerably* good night's rest, reached Phila. at 6:50 this morning—Bryn Mawr at 7:44, in time for breakfast. Mr. Houghton supplied me with reading for the journey, Miss Murfree's "Down the Ravine"

I find that the trip (five days hotel, instead of seven as we calculated) cost me *forty* dollars only, instead of seventy—quite enough, but less than I expected.

When I got back this morning, I found a copy of Mr. Dabney's novel[1] on my table. I have read the Preface only, and the introductory chapter (some forty pages in all, which do not reach the story) and, so far, am *very much* taken with the book. The portions I have read remind me of Sterne, modernized, of course, so discursive, mellow, witty are they. Whether the story will be of the same kind I cannot tell. If it comes up to the promise of these first pages, I will send them on to you at once that you may enjoy it. Ah, sweetheart, I *love, love, love* you—my precious, precious little wife! Kiss sister Maggie. Love to aunt Lou, and all.

Your own   Woodrow.

ALS (WC, NjP).

1 Virginius Dabney, *The Story of Don Miff, as Told by his Friend John Bouche Whacker. A Symphony of Life* (Philadelphia, 1886). See R. H. Dabney to WW, Feb. 1, 1886, ALS (WP, DLC), and R. H. Dabney to WW, Feb. 18, 1886, ALS (WP, DLC), enclosing a printed circular describing "A Southern Novel" which Virginius Dabney was to publish in April 1886.

Two Letters from Ellen Axson Wilson

Gainsville April 27 [1886]
No letter from my sweet-heart today, so that I must e'en console myself with reading over the old ones & writing to him. I
suppose there is some delay in the Sunday mails like that which
kept you in suspense so long last week. I was *so* sorry for that, by
the way, and also that Aunt Lou was not able to write you oftener
afterwards. But her cook had to be dismissed suddenly for steal-
ing the Monday after I came, & she had a raw hand in her place
& was kept very busy. Then later she was taken with a severe attack of rheumatism & was not able to write. I asked Loula to send
you a card every day,—hope they reached you regularly after the
first day. Auntie is much better now & sends you much love. How
very fortunate I was to get Mrs. Shepard! I don't know what we
all would have done last week if we had had a stupid negro in her
place. She is a remarkably good nurse, so Dr. Baily says; he has
the greatest confidence in her,—has been trying to engage her by
the year to nurse his patients here & there. Then she is very
cheerful & pleasant in her manner, I like her very much. Truly
God has provided tenderly for me in every respect. If I had been
taken sick the 6th of May I couldn't have got her, for she has an
engagement for the middle of the month. By the way, she never
sent the message about her health being so poor that we must
not depend on her; she never heard of me 'till the day Baby was
born. The cook whom Auntie sent for her, concocted the message
herself, without going near her, because she wanted me to have
a coloured nurse. She was afraid, she said, that a white woman
would be too proud to do everything and would make extra work
for her!
Baby is quite well & growing fast; she sends her love to her
Papa & a kiss planted just in the middle of the little circle. I wish it
could retain the flavour of her lips for I assure you they are *very*
sweet. I am a good deal stronger than I was even yesterday—sat
up three hours & walked a little. It is *such* a pleasure to be out of
bed; I always hated to lie in bed & do nothing more than anything

in the world. So you see what strange power you have, that merely *thinking* of you was enough to make even *that* comparatively
pleasant. Yet I could'nt *help* longing for you, darling, every moment,—thinking how rested & peaceful I would feel if I could only
see you sitting there at the table writing; and then when you
were *not* writing but close, close beside me! Ah darling,—Aunt
Lou says I am the most *"patient* patient" she ever saw, but there
would be small call for *patience* if *you* were here. The long hours
would be only too short with you to love me, talk to me, read to
me. But I hav'nt felt like complaining for a moment. My heart
has been so full to overflowing with gratitude that there has been
no *room* in it for complaint. Truly He hath crowned us with lov-
ing-kindness and tender mercies.

But I *must* close. Am wanting eagerly to hear more about your
visit. Goodbye my darling, I love you, *I love you, I love you.*

                    Your own little wife   Eileen

My own darling Woodrow,   [Gainesville, Ga., c. April 28, 1886]
Your sweet letters—those of Sunday & Monday—reached me
just before dinner, & I have just finished reading them for the
dozenth time or more. After that it is'nt necessary for me to say
that I am feeling very well & bright today. Ah sweetheart, why
can't I tell you with what a flood of happiness all these dear
words of love fill my heart! Why can't I tell you all you are to
me! But *you* know,—you know without the need of telling what is
in your little wife's heart. Ah yes, love, as we know it, *is* a
wonderful thing; it is wonderful that anything so sweet & perfect can *be* in a fallen world. God has given us His *fullest* blessing. How can I ever thank & love Him enough for it & all?

I have been sitting up almost all day & walking some, am gaining strength very rapidly; in fact *I* am not really weak at all; it
is only local soreness & weakness that prevents my walking as
much as I choose. I am to go to the table next Sunday. Baby
seems very comfortable & happy today. She was quite fretful,
restless & *nervous* yesterday, & scarcely slept any the night before, so that last night I became convinced that she was sick &
was very miserable about her;—ended by having a good cry when
nobody was looking. I suppose mothers get hardened to hearing
a baby cry; it farely tears my heart now. Aunt Lou after examining her declared that it was what the old women call "hives,"
a mild eruption that usually attacks them some time during the
first month. So they gave her a tea to "bring it out on her"; she
slept splendidly, and this morning, there was a slight breaking

out on her back & she is as peaceful as possible. I send you a little lock of her hair: is'nt it pretty? it is quite thick behind & in front there is enough to part & brush. She has pretty delicate long eyelashes too, a possession of which many young babies can't boast. You poor dear fellow! I am so glad your mind is relieved & you know that the baby is pretty. Of course some crusty old bachelor might see nothing in her but a little red mite, but by every standard of young babyhood she is peerless & promises great things in future. You should hear the universal admiration she excites. In short I again assure you, you have very good reason to be proud of your little daughter. Everything about her is pretty except the *crooked toe*! for she has it,—"sure enough,"—just like mine.

Please pardon these scrawls, darling: it is really the best I can do, for I strained my right wrist when the baby came, & it is still perfectly stiff, which makes me very awkward at writing. I can't manage a pen at all.

Give my love to Mrs. C., Mrs. Rhoads & any other friends[.] Goodbye dearest. I love you *I love you I love you*, my own darling,—I am with all my heart

Your little wife   Eileen

ALS (WC, NjP).

To Ellen Axson Wilson

Bryn Mawr, April 28/86

My own Eileen, my precious, darling little wife,

The ball has opened. My first lecture of this last term[1] (on the very deep topic, 'The Ethnical and Geographical Character of the Empire'—no less a theme) was delivered this morning—not without a sense of having been quite far away from thoughts upon the character of the Roman empire for a week or so—and, consequently, not without some difficulty, some stiffness of joint,—but delivered. And now for the home stretch—the six weeks that cruelly stand between me and my dear ones—my precious wife and baby! All this lecturing and all this preparation for examinations will seem as nothing—when they are over and past. By the way, my written examinations are fixed for the 21st. and 22nd. of May—my oral (before the 'Board of University Studies') for the 29, the next Saturday. I am looking forward to them just now with a queer stoical sort of indifference. That will probably wear off, *in due time*.

Another piece of news is, that the cottage is certainly to be rented.[2] I dread the moving and packing more than the examinations! I'd rather take a degree than be turned out of house and home.

I am reading Mr. Dabney's book with continued interest—am now well into the story. His conversations are bright and witty, his situations good, his innumerable small touches better, his Sterne excursions best. His 'grandfather' is almost as good as 'uncle Toby.' Indeed he shows in one or two places that he has been directly, perhaps consciously, affected by Sterne: and, barring occasional offences against good taste, his style, half pathetic, half humorous, is not inferior to Sterne's, though not nearly so well sustained. Altogether, I'm in sympathy with author and story so far—'The Story of Don Miff.'

But there is a sort of romance running in musical cadences through my heart all the while nowadays which makes me perhaps a poor judge of other people's stories. It pours its colour out upon all pictures alike, making them glow with a life not their own[.] *My* love story is so complete—how can I criticise any body else's? There's laughter and joy and beauty everywhere for me, because—well, you know why. If not, kiss the baby, and she will tell you! Love to aunt Lou & all.   Your own   Woodrow.

ALS (WC, NjP).
   [1] Wilson was not referring to an academic term but rather to the last weeks of the second semester. The college had just finished its spring vacation of a week.
   [2] The implication is that the college was renting the entire "Betweenery" to temporary occupants for the coming summer while the faculty tenants were away.

Notes for a Lecture on Roman History

Apr. 29/86

Provincial Administration under the Empire.

1. *The Governors*: Under the Empire the provinces were divided into 2 classes: the imperial provinces and the senatorial provinces. The principle upon which the division rested was a military principle. Those provinces which did not touch upon dangerous frontiers and which were regarded as securely pacific —Sicily and Spain, for example—were senatorial provinces and their administration given over almost entirely to the Senate. Those provinces, on the other hand, which were open to invasion or in which the Roman was not certain of securing ready submission to his rule were made imperial provinces and their administration given over almost entirely to the emperor.

Provincial Administration under the Empire.

1. *The Governors:*

2. *Other Provincial Officers:*

3. *The Senate:*

Wilson's shorthand notes for a lecture on Roman history

To the senatorial provinces, governors, consuls or praetors, were sent annually as in the days of the Republic; but their position and power in their provinces was very different from what it would have been under the Republic. The republican governors had been both civil and military commanders; the governors of the senatorial provinces were given no armies to command (were not given the *imperium* in short) and so had not that power of life and death which invariably went along with the *imperium* and which often had been so terrible an instrument in the hands of the old republican governors. The governors of the senatorial provinces were given no armies because no armies were needed, on the very principle of the provincial division. Theirs were the peaceful and orderly provinces: hence they were only civil magistrates, and their administration was generally mild and just.

The rule in the imperial provinces was military rule. The governor was a *legate* appointed by the emperor and acting in theory as the lieutenant of the emperor. His command did not terminate with the need but continued at the pleasure of the emperor, lasting almost always as long as three years, and often running for ten. Their provinces, chosen as the sites of disturbance, were often theaters for men of action. And men chosen for these posts seem generally to have been men of proved character and tried skill. The provincial legates have been called the "glory of the Empire." Their administration, though stern and decisive, was generally just, as being conducted under the eye of the emperor.

2. *Other Provincial Officers*: When, upon some exigency, troops were needed in the senatorial provinces, the emperor appointed a *legate*, who did not supersede but was assigned with the governor. The command of such a legate sometimes continued longer than that of the governor with whom he was assigned. It always happened, therefore, that the legate received more than his share of the homage of the provincials; and it often happened that his power quite overshadowed that of the governor. He was independent of the governor and his power, as military commander, was such that, beside it, the governor's power seemed almost nominal.

The financial management in the provinces was almost always given, under the Empire, to a *procurator* appointed by the emperor. His duties were substantially those performed by the provincial *quaestors* of the Republic. Appointed, as he was, by the emperor, he too was practically independent of the governor, and in case of a contest between the two, the governor was almost sure to come out second best. Governors were advised to let procurators and their business severely alone, by those who wanted to give the governors good advice.

3. *The Senate*: The Senate was, at least under the earlier emperors, the chief administrative council of the system, not in its old position of freedom and command, but in a new position entirely subservient to the emperor. Their freest action lay in the choice of the governors of the provinces. In everything else they simply served the administrative purposes of the emperor. Even in the choosing of the governors, as we have seen, they often did scarcely more than choose honorary posts: for, when any particular governing was to be done in the provinces, it was generally done by other officers appointed by the emperor. Still the Senate was kept very busy with the details of administrative oversight.

It was, besides, the court before which impeached governors were tried. These trials constituted its most important function. And impeachments before the Senate of the Empire were not farces like trials before the equestrian courts of the Republic. The senators were no more independent in their judgment, indeed, than the equestrians were formerly; they took their cue from the emperor. But the emperor was generally bent upon seeing the provinces well administered; and in ordinary times every delinquent or oppressive governor could count with confidence upon the severest punishment.

4. *The Emperor*: The emperor was, of course, the head and heart of the system. He had pro-consular powers throughout the Empire, which rendered the governors of the senatorial provinces scarcely less his lieutenants than were the legates. The administrative policy of the Senate was his policy; its judgment upon acts of the governors, his judgment. The better emperors spent much of their reigns in visiting the different districts of the Empire: so that provincial organization and administration was constantly receiving further touches from their hands. The machinery of imperial rule was to compel a province to run smoothly[,] that is[,] when the emperors slept or were drunk; when they were awake and earnest, and demanded obeisance, it was a facile instrument through which to rule.

Transcript of WWsh in notebook described at Feb. 9, 1886.

To Ellen Axson Wilson

My own precious little wife,   Bryn Mawr, Pa., Apr. 29/86
    Your third letter (that of Monday) came last night. Oh, you *wonderful*, well little mother! What a little paragon you are, my

Eileen. Is there *anything* that you can't do better than any other beauty that ever lived? It is *so* sweet of you, darling, to give me these particulars about yourself and the baby: they are *just* what I want. I am hungry for *every kind* of particular, big and little, about my matchless little '*family*.' I was just getting a list of questions ready, including one about whether you had milk enough for the baby. I am *so* glad that you have! No wonder the little Miss is growing bigger and sweeter and well-er every day. She is drawing her food from the sweetest, *wellest* mother that ever baby had—and the best and most inspiring. *I* have been better—in mind, in heart, in body—*every* way—since I have been one with that same splendid little mother, drawing my *spiritual* life from her. How much more should one expect of a little body who draws her *physical* life from her as well! And it is such an inexpressibly sweet thought to me that my love, by making that precious little mother —my darling little wife—happy, contributes to keep that precious little baby—my darling little daughter—well! Oh, my darling, my darling, I am so happy in you and my baby!

'And was I—"honour bright"—very much disappointed that she wasn't a boy?' No ma'am! 'Honour bright'—I was not. At first— at the very first—I was a little disappointed. I found that I *had*, after all, been hoping a little that it would be a boy. But, my darling, that regret did not last 24 hours. It passed away like a mere 'passing thought' and now I can say *with all my heart* that I am glad. She is like you—and nothing could make me happier than to have a daughter like you. Are you satisfied?

I've been neglecting to send you all sorts of messages—from all sorts of people. Of course Mrs. Coale and everyone here who has spoken to me of you has sent warmest love and congratulations. I wrote to sisters at once and they send as much love and gladness as you could wish. I've not heard from home yet.

Oh, sweetheart, my precious, precious little wife, I love you; I love you! Kiss, and kiss, and kiss the baby for me. Kiss sister Maggie. Love to aunt Lou and all   Your own   Woodrow.

ALS (WP, DLC).

From Ellen Axson Wilson

My own darling Woodrow   Gainsville, April 29/86.

Your sweet letter from home is just received,—for *my home is* at Bryn Mawr now. So you got back early Tuesday morning. I suppose it was best, but am sorry you couldn't have had the seven days. That would have been all too short. But as it was, you did have a nice trip; did you not? I am *so* glad you went.

Many thanks for the "Atlantic" & for forwarding Mr. Trinkoysen's cards.

Have you heard from Father & Mother since Baby came? I got Loula to write notes to them & "sisters" the day after. She received a sweet little note from Father, and I a nice letter from Sister Marion. Have also heard from Beth & Rose & Stockton.[1] The latter is extremely proud of his niece. He sent her a lovely little gold pin. I wish you *could* see Beth's letter to Aunt Lou. It is certainly *rich*; I never saw Auntie so amused. She tells her how to feed me & care for me in various ways, giving her minute directions about matters which everyone understands who has ever been in a sick room. It is a pity the dear girl will make herself so ridiculous; & it has grown on her in consequence of her good unselfish life too; she has always taken care of other people since she was a little child & she thinks she must take care of everyone.

I am still improving;—you should have seen the waiter of dinner that I disposed of a little while ago,—beefsteak, rice, asparagus on toast, and egg-bread, not to mention the milk & butter.

But I had to stop writing for some time to nurse the baby &c., & now the nurse says I must rest. So I must make haste to close & get this off. Baby is quite well today & sweeter than ever. You may be sure I *do* tell her about her dear father, darling! To have *such* a father as hers & not know it is a sort of ignorance that must be far removed from *bliss*; and to think that she will be two whole months old before she can see for herself! Ah why don't the days *fly* as I wish them to!

But two weeks have passed,—last night,—I always count time from Wed. nights now,—that is one fourth of the time. I must have patience—patience. The joy of the meeting will atone for all. And now, my love, my life, my dear, dear husband, I must say "goodbye." With a heart full to overflowing with love for my darling, I am   Your little Wife

ALS (WC, NjP).
[1] Elizabeth Adams Erwin to EAW, April 21, 1886, ALS (WP, DLC); Stockton Axson to EAW, April 19, 1886, ALS (WP, DLC). The letters from Marion W. Kennedy and Rosalie Anderson are missing.

To Ellen Axson Wilson

Bryn Mawr, 30 April, 1886

My own sweet, precious, *precious* little ~~little~~ wife (you are not so little as all that—I didn't mean the *second* one: if there had been an extra 'precious' or two it would have represented only an unconscious striving after the inexpressible truth.). There was a gentleman in this room this morning whose performances I wish you could have seen. His name shall be unmentioned. I'll let you *guess* who it was. He stood before the callendar there under the mantel-piece, and, looking at the date, Friday, Apr. 30, he exclaimed, 'Why my little daughter's two weeks old to-day! Oh, my little baby!' The words were very simple—but the tone in wh. they were uttered arrested my attention[.] I couldn't for the life of me *look* at him (though he evidently was not thinking of me, and wouldn't have noticed it if I had) but I am sure that there were glad tears in his eyes—his voice was that kind of a voice. And then afterwards he stood looking down as if looking down at a little child—with all his heart and all the gladness of his life in the look. He's a queer fellow! If you have guessed who he is, you have remembered that I caught him going through a somewhat similar performance down by that wee stream over there in the hollow. By the way, I found him standing over another little stream out in the country the other day. I could not hear what he was saying—but he was evidently talking *with some one in his heart*! Poor fellow! I'm glad for his sake that he has so much work to do!

I'm *so* sorry that one of my letters was late in reaching you, my sweetheart. I have posted everyone with my own hands—now that I'm back here, I will not trust Wm. with letters *to you*. I take them down to a particular mail myself everyday. Oh, my lovely one, there's a minor key in this sweet letter of yours to-day. You were *lonely* when you wrote it—in spite of your brave words! Listen, sweetheart: *I live on your happiness.* (You see, I *know* you now, my little wife, and can give you this motive for being happy) The only thing that makes this dreadful separation *bearable* for me is that you are happy all the same—in my love and our sweet baby's presence. Oh, how glad I am that baby came when she did (how good God is!) *She* is there to keep her mother company, and to fill that dear mother's heart with joy. For, you see, Miss, you constitute 2/3 of the family, you two—and you must keep each other happy, for the sake of the other 1/3.

But good-bye. I know that I can count on my darling! *Oh I love you, I love you, I love you*—I devoured the baby's kiss in the little circle! Love to all   Your own   Woodrow

ALS (WC, NjP).

From Ellen Axson Wilson

My own darling,   [Gainesville, Ga.,] April 30, 1886

The lid of one of my eyes is slightly inflamed today, seeming to threaten to stye, so they think it more prudent for me to rest them entirely. I must therefore write only a line to tell you that we are both quite well, & that I am very *very* much in love with my Woodrow. Do you ever feel impressed with the idea that there is a "harnt" in the same room with *you*! Because there *is*. I am with you in spirit all the time in that cosy little room of ours, sitting on my little stool at your feet or in the big chair close by. I *can't* keep away. Oh, darling, my darling, you are all the world to me,—you and the baby; you won't be jealous that I add *her* name! With a heart brim full of love,

Your little wife,   Eileen

ALS (WC, NjP).

To Ellen Axson Wilson

My own precious little wife,   Bryn Mawr, May 1, 1886

I enclose a draft on New York for $40.00. I would send more but for three facts, (1) that they are charging me $12.00 a week for these two rooms, which brings the payment now due, for the last five weeks, up to the usual sum ($64.00); (2) that the bill will come in presently for the books I ordered from England some weeks ago; and (3) that I shall have to go to Baltimore twice this month for my degree examinations. If $40.00 should not suffice my darling, I can *very easily* get more on an advance. You must not get it into your dear little head that I have not *kept* enough. I have some left over from last month, you know.

Is there prospect of your getting a good nurse, sweetheart, after Mrs. Shepard has to go? Couldn't cousin Minnie induce our old lame friend to come to you from Rome? I don't like the idea of your having to take anybody you don't *know*. Oh, how thankful I am that you got Mrs. S. God is indeed beyond measure gracious in his dealings with us!

How sweet it was in you, darling, to think of sending me that cute, beautiful lock of hair of the baby's! It is the loveliest colour I ever saw! And what a treasure the dear little strands are to my father's heart! At last I have seen a *part* of the baby, anyhow! Bless your heart, my dear, *dear* little wife. How it swells my heart to have you manifest your love for me by so many tokens of thought for my happiness. You are the truest, loveliest little wife and sweetheart that ever made a man wish himself nobler and better. Oh, my queen, my darling, my lovely, *lovely* little wife! How shall I ever repay you for the happiness that is flooding my life with light and filling it with rest and peace!

I am *so* sorry about the strained wrist, darling; don't *try* to write much; please—and when you do write never mind how you 'scrawl [.]' I can read it with the greatest ease—and every stroke of it seems to me prettier than any other handwriting I ever saw!

Oh, you dear, precious little mother! The tears came irrepressibly to my eyes as I read you [your] account of your distress at our little pets 'hives.' You poor, dear, loving little mother. I would give more than all I can think of for five minutes in which to hold you in my arms and kiss you—you and *our* baby. Oh, my little wife, those two words, 'our baby,' are the sweetest I ever read or heard. I repeat them aloud I don't know how many times a day.

Love to aunt Lou, little sister, and all. What does little sister think of the baby?   Your own   Woodrow.

ALS (WC, NjP).

From Ellen Axson Wilson

My own darling,   Gainsville May 1 [1886]
I am still deprived of the privilege of writing you a regular letter on account of my eye. It is about as it was yesterday—not at all bad but only demanding prudence. Otherwise I am quite well; even my wrist has limbered up! The dear little one is just as sweet and good as ever, and more so. Take good care of *your* self, darling, and make as good a record as mine as regards health. I dread these next six weeks for you more than a little,—the constant lecturing and reading. So you must make *two* trips to Balt. for the examinations! That seems a great pity; couldn't they arrange it better for you? I hope you take a great deal of exercise,—nice long walks in this beautiful spring weather. Do you cultivate the other men as you proposed? But I *must* not write today. Goodbye, my love, my dear, dear husband. I love you from my heart of hearts.
                              Your little wife   Eileen

ALS (WC, NjP).

To Ellen Axson Wilson

                              Bryn Mawr, 2 May, 1886
Do you know, my precious little wife and sweetheart, that you

are in danger of not fulfilling your *whole* duty in the matter of health bulletins? Now, "I am still improving" is a satisfactory enough expression in itself—and an additional reference to a waiter of solid viands suggests some *very* satisfactory particulars of the improvement mentioned. But, after all, it must, I think, be admitted that there are innumerable *degrees* of improvement—that there are even some degrees of it which are quite the reverse of satisfactory, so slow, partial, and undecided are they. And, as for the big dinner—you may have had an equally good appetite the day before—so that *that* does not furnish any criterion for the *rate* of improvement. I can imagine improvement, even improvement accompanied by the punishment of big dinners, which would not be encouraging: as, for instance, if it was very slight, the patient had lost sleep, or was as easily fatigued as ever, &c. &c. In brief—but allow me to make a short explanation of a thing or two bearing directly upon the making up of the bulletins in this particular case. Let us suppose a set of circumstances. Let us suppose a young husband and wife separated as we are, and under the same circumstances. Suppose that the young husband has what, for brevity's sake, we will call a very *tragic* disposition, and that there are two facts wh. stand out in his consciousness as if the universe, for him, contained no others, viz. (1) that he never was happy until he was married, having found in his young wife's love and companionship *complete* joy and content; and (2) that, unless he can have that dear wife restored to him, herself well and strong and happy, as when she was his newly-won bride, he can never be happy again:—suppose, in short, that she is, in a sense as deep as the tragedy of his own disposition, *all the world* to him. Suppose that all that keeps his loneliness from being intolerable while she is away from him is the fulness of the news of herself that he gets from her own dear hand, in the letters which keep him alive. *Suppose* a case like this: do you think that 'I am still improving' would satisfy *him*? Couldn't he imagine that it was just true enough to be written—to keep him from being anxious? Couldn't he—but you see what I mean. Now take *my* case—but—oh sweetheart, my darling, my *life—you see what I mean*!

So much for *one* sheet (it's Sunday: why *shouldn't* I write *two*, pray!). Now for the remark to which the preceding discussion naturally leads—which, in fact, it contains, unspoken, in every sentence (as any reader who knows the writer can, I dare say, readily detect)—namely, *I love you*. Ah, my darling, my darling, if you could but read my heart in the only half-articulate words of this letter—or in any letter that I write to *you*—you would know how much of my *life* is summed up in those three little syllables. All of my life that is not in them when I utter them to *you is* in them when you utter them to me! My body is here in Bryn Mawr— as I am sadly aware—and a fair-seeming ghost of my mind (its *professional* faculties, namely)—but my heart, all that is real of my *self*, is far away in Georgia, in a room I have never seen, with a sweet little mother and her precious baby: and I've found out, in the last two weeks and a half, that I can't do anything *normally* until my body is joined to my *self*. 'The last two weeks and a half'! Oh dear; whatever shall become of me!—*is that all*! I could swear that I've existed *a year* since the night I kissed my darling's hand at the car window! Dear me! what did poor wretches of young husband's do—I wonder—when there were no daily mails, and no steam expresses to carry them! What would *I* do if I could not tell my darling everyday how much I love her! Even this miserable, inadequate writing of it down—with never a kiss or a caress to go with it—with never a glimpse of the dear object of the love—is better than having one's heart break in silence —break *because* of silence. And, worse still, suppose one could not *get* daily words of sweetest, womanly love, written on sheets that had received everywhere the pressure of the dear hand whose touch has so often been to him like the touch of an angel!

Well, well!—how one's ideas will change! I used to think that when one got married he wouldn't write 'love letters' exactly to his wife: that his epistles to her, though deeply affectionate, wd. manifest their affection indirectly rather than demonstratively ('My dear wife: & etc.—all about family affairs.—Your affectionate husband.') Whereas, see what I have learned—that eight pages devoted exclusively to that business (tho. he had little scraps of news to tell her—as, for instance, that he is quite well) are by no means sufficient to contain the love—nay the *courting*—he would put into them! I have discovered that I am *more* irresistibly impelled to make love to my wife than I ever was to make love to my sweetheart,—and that there will be *more* romance and delight in going to her *next* June than there was in going to her *last* June—and the baby—oh! the baby!!

Love to all   Your own   Husband

ALS (WC, NjP).

From Ellen Axson Wilson

My own darling Woodrow, Gainsville, May 2/86

My eye is so much better today that it no longer seems necessary to put you off with short measure, provided I spare it in every other way. As Dr. Baily has gone to St. Louis to the convention & I couldn't consult him, & the little wash Aunt Lou gave me seemed to do no good, I wrote to Brother George yesterday for a prescription; the trouble is very slight but I want to be rid of it as soon as possible so that I can use my eyes as I choose. Otherwise I am quite well,—sat up all day yesterday, from nine till after tea, & promenaded the room a good half hour or more. I should have been out of the room before but for the very decided cool change in the weather.

The young woman whom Mrs. Shepard is to attend next passed by a few minutes ago on her way from the depot; she lives in Atlanta & is to be at her mother's *next door*. I am very much interested in the case, of course, as my hold upon Mrs. S. depends on her. As it is her first child too I am afraid she will follow my example & "go off half cocked." But as she doesn't *expect* it until the 26th I trust we are safe. Dear little Margaret is quite well and happy. I am *very* glad that you were not more deeply disappointed at little Woodrow's non-appearance! After all, I should not be surprised if the little maid should steal her way into your heart of hearts and find for herself the very tenderest spot of all; from which not even the boy, when he comes, will be able to oust her, —though of course he will excite more the paternal *pride* and *hope*. I confess that *I* think such a son as *you* would be the *greatest* of God's gifts—next to such a husband as you,—but a lovely little daughter is the sweetest of His gifts.

So they really are going to rent the house!—too bad! If I were *only* there to help you. I am distressed at your having all the trouble alone;—and alas, I am afraid it will keep you longer away from me. But you won't have to be examined after "school is out" (!), that is one comfort.

I did not tell you the news from Rome. All Papa's books were soaked by the flood & utterly ruined. *Is'nt* that a pity! I don't know where in the world Stockton had stored them. If they had *only* been left at the house! But it is no use grieving over spilt milk. A letter from Minnie[1] received a few hours after Baby's birth—written of course before—told me of it. Uncle Will lost heavily by the flood, & every one else in the town. It was a dreadful calamity. The water was *much* higher than it had ever been before;—six feet in the drug store;—our church was surrounded,—couldn't be reached at all. There was no gas and no water (!) for some days.

But I will close now in this corner, for if I *begin* another page I must *finish* it, & I ought not.

Give much love to Mrs. C. & other enquiring friends. I love you darling more—more than words can say, just as much as you wish me to. With all my heart　Your little wife　Eileen.

ALS (WC, NjP).
　[1] Mary E. Hoyt to EAW, April 12, 1886, ALS (WP, DLC).

To Ellen Axson Wilson

Bryn Mawr, 3 May, 1886

Oh, my sweet, *sweet* little wife, I am *so* sorry about the *eye*! What is the matter with it? The note that came this morning says that *still* you can't write 'on account of your eye,' and that "it is about as it was yesterday"—but how was it yesterday? I had heard nothing before of your eye having troubled you. Did you write a note the day before? If so, I have not received it. Oh, my darling, *please* take good care of those dear eyes. The eyes are specially liable to suffer after confinement, I understand, and I would not have those splendid eyes of yours suffer for the world. Somehow those wonderful brown beauties seem to me the part of you which specially belongs to me: they have contributed so much to my happiness. I have lived on the treasures of love which they, even more than your sweet tongue with its sweet love-eloquence, have revealed to me. Ah, those precious, *glorious* eyes! I can wish no greater good looks to the baby than the heritage of those eyes— except a heritage of the whole face that goes so beautifully with them—and she is sure of that!

Here's an extract, sweetheart, from dear mother's letter, re- ceived to-day:[1] "The thought of what *might* have been in that journey!—the fearful risk the sweet girl had run—quite unnerved me. . . . I cannot tell you how anxious I *have* been—and how thankful I now am. It was *so* kind in dear Ellie's cousin to write as she did—it was such a relief to us. And that extract from her Aunt's letter to you" [i.e. all that concerned you in dear Aunt Lou's letter written the day baby was born[2]], "given in your last, de- lighted us more than I can tell. You have reason to be *very* proud of your sweet and brave little wife. . . . I am now preparing your room—and it is funny to think how the idea of the sweet baby enters into all my arrangements. I have been reframing pictures to-day—and wondering if she will be old enough to enjoy some

particularly bright ones. . . . Oh, for the time to come when you
will come to us! I am hungry for you and yours." It must be as
soon as possible, darling—mustn't it?

You may be sure that I *am* taking good care of myself, darling
—for your sake. I don't think that the hard work of the six weeks
to come will do me any harm. It will be my *salvation*, on the contrary. I am not allowing myself to worry over it—I am going to
take plenty of exercise—and I'm quite sure I'll come out all right.
It is not at all as if the work were *composition*. I can't *write* now
without you. I am quite well—the stomach acting as well as could
be expected. Nothing can hurt me much except what *you* suffer.
You are my life, my all. Just so my darlings prosper, there'll be
no trouble about *me!* I love, *love, love* you, my precious, *precious*
little wife—my *darling* little daughter. Kisses for little sister; love
for all. Your own husband,   Your own Woodrow.

ALS (WP, DLC).
   [1] JWW to WW, April 30, 1886, ALS (WP, DLC); the ellipses in the extract
are WW's.
   [2] Louisa C. H. Brown to WW, April 16, 1886; WW's brackets.

From Ellen Axson Wilson

My own darling Woodrow,   Gainsville May 3/86
   Your sweet letter of the 1st with check enclosed is just at hand.
I am *so* much obliged to you, darling, but I *am* afraid you have
sent too much. I did not *need* all this, for you know I need not pay
the doctor's bill this month;—probably won't have a chance to do
so unless I ask him for it. Ought I to do that, by the way? I have so
little experience in doctor's bills that I don't know the proper thing
in such matters. I think it is a *shame* that they should charge you
$12.00 a week! Am astonished that they *could* do such a thing.
I didn't expect them to charge *any* more, & I couldn't have believed that they would add four dollars a week for nothing at all.
   I shan't need a nurse much while I am here; I want to try and
get Martha when we go to Rome, if we decide to stop there. There
is a certain "Aunt Olly" here, a "perfect treasure," whom Auntie
was very anxious for me to have, and we tried to secure her; but
it doesn't seem possible.
   Baby is quite well today, the "hives" don't seem to trouble her
now;—and she is "too sweet for anything." I am feeling *very* bright,
—have been visiting in Auntie's room,—have actually begun to
"primp" again, to "do" my hair &c., and of course that makes me
feel less invalidish. They say I look "as though I had never been

sick"; of course *that* is'nt so. I *am* pale & peaked, but not excessively so. After all it doesn't seem as though one night's suffering, when no severe illness follows, *ought* to pull one down much. And I *never* felt prostrated or even the least exhausted, not even when the baby had just arrived.

The little sister [Margaret Axson] has been rather jealous of the baby, she stands by looking very wistful when Auntie or Loula are "taking on" over the baby;—one day she asked very pathetically if she wasn't sweet too! But they have let her hold it several times of late, and that seems to have rendered her more kindly disposed towards it. Eddie is coming on Wed.! Isn't that nice? Presbytery meets here this week & Uncle Henry is going to bring E. over with him. Aunt Lou means to keep him until I go away if they will consent for him to leave his school. She is very anxious for Stockton to come up too, & I shouldn't be surprised if he can; for he wrote some time ago that the cotton season was nearly over and he had very little to do.[1] Would it not be delightful for me to have them *all* here together! And then when *you* come too, to cap the climax! I won't know what to do for joy. My darling you are "too clever by half" to detect my little moods of lonliness & homesickness, in spite of myself! I believe you do "know" me. But I promise to be a good girl—a *happy* girl. You *may* count on me, sweetheart. How *could your* wife be anything but happy at heart! Oh love, you are my very *life*; & there is no need to say how I love you   Your little wife   Eileen

ALS (WC, NjP).
[1] Stockton Axson, after withdrawing from Davidson College in June 1885, had been living with the Randolph Axsons in Savannah while working for his uncle's cotton brokerage firm of Warren and Axson, 54 Bay St., Savannah.

To Ellen Axson Wilson

My own darling Eileen   Bryn Mawr, 4 May, 1886

The missing note, about that dear eye which is misbehaving—so much to my sorrow and consternation—put in its appearance this morning. And how glad I am that that particular note was not lost! It's the sweetest tid-bit of a note that ever a sweet little woman wrote! Yes, ma'am: I *have* been impressed with the idea that there is a 'harnt' here in our little room with me time and time again during the last few days! (or, rather, the last few *months*—that *must* be the truth of the matter!) I almost *see* her here on the stool at my feet (by the way, I treat that stool very tenderly and affectionately nowadays!) or in the big chair just there. You would think I saw the sweet visitor if you could see me sitting here talking to her—talking and *looking* love at the places that I know as specially hers. I've taken to sitting in that big chair of late. It was not comfortable to me once; but now—well, some-how I *love* to sit in it now! Yes, my little sweetheart,—may-be you would be very jealous if you *could* hear what I say to this little 'harnt' that lives with me nowadays—would you? I confess that I pour out a whole heartful of love in what I say to her.—Oh, my little wife, bless, *bless* your heart! *I love you*! Do you really live all the day with your poor, far-away, lonely husband? I wish that this old pen of mine would—if for no more than a single moment —forget its inability to say aught that it would say—that I might find at least one phrase of love, of passionate devotion, that would make your heart thrill as mine does at the *slighest* word of love from you!

No, indeed, my darling, I'm not jealous that you should add the baby's name to mine in summing up your love—for I know that she is *added*, not subtracted, from the sum of your love for me. If *any*body—even my own precious little daughter, who is part of my *life*, were to turn the *ardour* of your love *from* me never so little, it would kill me, I verily believe! Whenever you think of the future of your sweetheart, please ma'am reflect on this wise: 'all the future of my dear husband—all that is to give it speed and strength and beauty—is sealed up here in my own heart. *I am* his destiny: my love can make it.' It need not frighten you, little woman—my little queen—that you hold my life in your hand—it doesn't frighten me: it fills me with the sweetest confidence that ever a man's heart held.

Ah, how I love to make love to you! Kiss our precious one *ever* so many times for her papa. Kiss little sister too: and give my love to Aunt Lou and all. For yourself keep *what you want* from
Your own   Woodrow.

ALS (WC, NjP).

From Ellen Axson Wilson

My own darling   Gainsville May 4/86
   Uncle Warren goes to the factory today & as our communica-tion with the post is rather uncertain during his absence, I must make haste to write before he leaves. Maggie is going with him, by the way, and is quite beside herself with delight at the prospect. They return tomorrow afternoon. I wish it were me—and *you*, a

thirteen mile ride in the lovely May weather would be *delicious*.

I have just had letters this morning from Cousin Hattie[,] Janie Porter & Brother George, the latter enclosing prescription.[1] My eyes are almost entirely well again however; still I am not sorry I sent for it; Aunt Lou had made me rather nervous telling me how often & how easily the eyes are permanently injured after confinement, & I did not want to take any risk. The letter from Cousin Hattie is *very* sweet. And she is going to send the baby her "baptismal robe & shirt." Isn't that charming? So I shan't make up mine with the lace,—but keep it for short dresses. She is very anxious for us to promise to go to Nashville, wants us to go as soon in the summer as possible,—asks if we can't come directly from Gainsville. The reason being that she "has an engagement later in the summer";—subsequently she explains the *nature* of the engagement! Poor girl! don't she have a life of it! The other one came last August, you know. Truly it is another case of "the baby, the little baby & the littlest baby of all"! What shall I write her as to our going to Nashville?

Baby is just as well & sweet & good as can be,—almost *too* good in fact, for she sleeps all day & gives me no chance to play with her. I have to content myself with watching her asleep. She is beginning to grow a little clearer as to her complexion now, & of course will become daily prettier in consequence. I am *delighted* that the Southern novel proves to be so good. I am looking forward eagerly to the pleasure of reading it. How I hope it will be well received by the public.

What do you think of the Jeff. Davis frenzy?[2] How do people speak [of] it North? How do the Northan papers treat the matter? Do you think it will do harm to the South, or the prospects for union & better government?

But I must stop or my letter will be left after all. Oh sweetheart, I *do love you*. I am just *wearying* for you. But the third week is nearly over. Time does move a *little*. I dwell so much on your coming, darling, dream of it so often, wondering if it will be in the morning or at night, letting my fancy play about the particulars of our meeting, that sometimes I feel my pulse beat as high[,] my heart throb as wildly as if that blessed time were already come. For a moment I seem to taste again the *full* joy of loving, not in memory or in anticipation but in very truth. For you know it isn't really *life* without you darling. I am conscious all the time that my life has come to a pause & I am only *waiting* for it to begin again. Believe me my love, my husband as ever

Your little wife   Eileen

ALS (WC, NjP).

    1 Harriet Hoyt Ewing to EAW, May 2, 1886, and George Howe, Jr., to EAW, May 2, 1886, both ALS (WP, DLC). The letter from Janie Porter Chandler is missing.

    2 Jefferson Davis emerged from retirement to be the guest of honor at the laying of the cornerstone of a monument to Confederate dead at the Capitol in Montgomery on April 29, 1886. Three days later he appeared in Atlanta at the unveiling of a statue to the late Senator Benjamin H. Hill; and on May 6 he visited Savannah for celebrations marking the centennial of the Chatham Artillery and honoring Nathaniel Greene, the Revolutionary hero. At each occasion, Davis spoke, usually temperately, but sometimes defiantly. All along his tour he was enthusiastically acclaimed by large crowds.

To Ellen Axson Wilson

My own precious little wife,   Bryn Mawr, May 5, 1886

Of course I can detect the mood that lurks in each of your letters. It is *very* sweet to have you *say* that you are 'feeling very bright'—for you are the most absolutely truthful little woman that ever spoke—but it is not at all necessary. There are a hundred announcements of the same thing between the lines—for a more transparent little woman (to those she loves) never lived. I can tell infallibly, upon closing one of your sweet letters, just the mood in which it was written: *But I don't want to tell that way.* I want you to follow this rule: to open your heart unreservedly to your husband *always*. Why, sweetheart, what's the good of me, if you don't? How do I differ from anyone else you love? It nearly breaks my heart to read one of those letters in which you try to *conceal* your loneliness or homesickness. I feel as if I must relieve my heart with a—or else *go and write on the Calligraph.* If you would only tell me just what's the matter—there have been several of those pathetic letters recently—you would both relieve your own dear heart and enable me to relieve mine, by showing me what line of love-making to take in order to drive the tears out of my darling's eyes. Oh, my little wife!—but you've promised to be a happy little woman, haven't you? And *to-day* Eddie comes to you! —oh, how glad I am! And if Stockton does come, that will complete my gladness. *Then* you must *forget* that you need *me*. You must be the happiest little sister and mother in the world, and— no, you mustn't *quite* forget me: I must keep *my* heart from breaking as well as yours! You must just make the time before my coming short by living in the dear brothers and in our darling baby—your adopted children and your own little treasure, *our* child! Let her *remind* you of me just now and then that this precious little 'harnt' may not desert me.

No, sweetheart, I don't think that you need *ask* the doctor for his bill. I will do that when I come, if he does not render it before.

Might you not write to cousin Minnie about securing Martha? Or would you rather trust to your own persuasion?

I am beyond measure distressed to hear of the results of the flood in Rome!

I am quite well, precious: and I *love you*, oh, *I love you*, my queen, my life, my Eileen. You and our darling are all the world to me!

Love to Eddie, & to *all*.   Your own   Woodrow

ALS (WC, NjP).

From Ellen Axson Wilson

My own darling   Gainsville May 5/86

Your delightful *double* letter,—your Sunday letter—came yesterday and I can't tell you how much I enjoyed it. Oh my love, do you think you have any idea how precious *all* your letters are to me—how these sweet love-words constitute the very breath of life for me? What would we do, indeed, without the daily mails! I don't see how the poor lovers in the olden time lived[.] But as they knew of nothing better perhaps they didn't feel the deprivation quite so much. I could *not* live without my letters, now. My note of Friday by-the-way, seems to have miscarried, the one in which I first mentioned my eye. It was only a slight inflamation of the lid, something like a stye; the ball was not at all affected. So you don't think my health bulletins full enough, dear? Why I have been thinking that my letters contained nothing else; have been ashamed of writing so much about myself; have had to tell myself over & over that you would wish such details, to remind myself how *very* anxious for them I should be if you were sick, to reconcile myself to writing so much on such a dull subject. I assure you, darling, my recovery has been very steady and wonderfully rapid. The daily "improvement" is of the most gratifying sort. And I promise faithfully to conceal nothing which concerns my health. To prove my good faith, I will tell you, as I had not intended doing since the trouble was so temporary, that I was not so well yesterday. It was the first time that there has been the *slightest pause* in the rapid improvement, and it was altogether my fault, You see our little lady takes her meals in quite an epicurean fashion. She wants to "sit long at table," (!) & have many courses. Sometimes she spends an hour & a half at it, indeed she has been known to take three hours. She takes a good many naps in the course of it, but if one tries to act under the impression that she has finished she wakes up and declares vigorously that she is just starving. So night before last, I was so overcome by sleep that before I knew it I dropped off in the midst of it & we both slept three hours, I with arm and shoulder uncovered & bosom partly exposed. So when I awoke it was with an acute pain in the latter, & severe headache—back & legs aching too, & so chilly that I could not keep my teeth from chattering. It seemed for a time as though I would at last be *sick,*—you know I haven't been yet. But they worked with the breast, poulticing it, &c., and got it *all right* again before night; and in the course of the day & (last) night I succeeded in throwing off the cold *entirely.* There isn't a trace of it left today; all the pain, feverishness & langour of yesterday have passed away; & I am feeling *quite* as well as I did the day before —that is *perfectly well!* What a long & unnecessary recital! But I want you to *feel* now, my darling, that you know *everything.* I have had so many visitors today that my letter has been postponed until late in the afternoon & now I must make haste to close. We are expecting Uncle H. & Eddie every minute. They come by private conveyance. Please excuse haste.

I love you, my darling husband, deeply truly, tenderly, passionately.   Your little wife   Eileen

ALS (WC, NjP).

To Ellen Axson Wilson

My darling, matchless little wife,   Bryn Mawr, 6 May, 1886

There is a passage in one of your most recent letters upon which I want to make a few remarks which may interest you. 'You would not be surprised if the little maid should steal her way into my heart of hearts and find for herself the very tenderest spot of all; from which not even the boy, when he comes, will be able to oust her.' Ah, little lady, do you imagine that *all* of that is *in the future?* Why, my little daughter *has* found a place in my heart of hearts from which *no*body shall ever oust her. It is singular how my love for the little maid grows and grows in spite of the fact that I have never seen her. Your descriptions of her have given me a very distinct image about which to group the events of my day-dreams; and, as I sit here and seem to see my little daughter grow up, to be first a merry romp of a girl, then a ripening Miss at school, and finally a lovely little woman who shall seem like her precious mother's younger self,—while I watch my daughter grow, I can see her drawing nearer and nearer to my side, content at last to sit long at the feet on which it used to be her—and may-be is still her little brother's—delight to *ride*, and listen with her sweet mother to all I have to say (sage or silly, profound or playful) about history, and governments, and laws;—I can feel the expansion of my heart under those blessed influences; and I *know* that no 'Woodrow'—especially if he be like me —can ever take the place of that dear girl as my child-companion and delight—especially if she be like you! Yes, my darling, my heart has explored a whole new world of love since that little maiden came—& not you yourself can love her more than I do, and shall. As for 'little Woodrow'—I can't imagine him yet—we'll discuss him when he comes.

And so you *do* look 'pale and peaked,' although you are so well? I am *so* sorry, my sweet one. I can't bear to think of my darling, my matchless little wife, as in *any* way *hurt* by her ordeal. Your image, even, has a sort of sacredness in my eyes, darling; and I can't bear to think that *I* have been the cause of robbing it, for ever so short a time, of even its colour. Please ma'am try to get p[l]ump and rosy by the time I come: be just as happy as the day is long, and you can effect it. If I were not responsible, it would not go so hard with me to think what you've been through—*but I am*!

I have just rec'd another invitation from Isham[1] to dine with him in New York! What a persistently kind fellow! What new form shall I find for the inevitable declination?

I love you, my sweetheart, *oh I love you*! Kisses for baby and little sister: love to aunt Lou and all.   Your own   Woodrow.

ALS (WC, NjP).
  [1] William B. Isham, Jr., who in 1884 had begun the practice of giving annual dinners for members of the Class of 1879 at his home in New York. See Alexander J. Kerr, "The Isham Dinners," *Fifty Years of the Class of 'Seventy-Nine, Princeton* (Princeton, N. J., 1931), pp. 199-206.

From Ellen Axson Wilson

My own darling,   Gainsville, May 6/86.

Uncle Henry and Eddie arrived safely last night; the dear little fellow has grown tremendously and is much improved apparently in health, has a good colour, &c. He is the same sweet, good, thoughtful, happy little fellow he always was, and you may be sure I am happy at the sight of him. Little Maggie is quite wild with delight over him. She is perfectly devoted to him. But the stammering!—oh the stammering! It was *dreadful* last night. It seems to be worse, however, when he is excited or embarrassed.

I watched him playing with Maggie–& the kittens–an hour or so this morning without detecting a trace of it. I am anxious to keep him here until I leave, and give those rules a thorough trial myself.

Thank you, darling, for that sweet extract from dear mother's letter. Even you don't know how deeply I appreciate such words, and *every* mark of affection from your–from *our* dear parents. Yes indeed we will go to them as soon as possible, dear, and that will be as soon as you wish; for my having taken time by the forelock as I did makes it possible much sooner than we anticipated. Just think that this is the day we expected the baby! And she is– to my extreme satisfaction–three weeks old! I am going to lose Mrs. Shepard on Monday, and I am as the French would say, *desolated* at the prospect. Her grandfather is very ill and wishes for her; so she thinks she must go. It seems a pity, as the old man is dying slowly of old age, and as he has several hundred other children, that she can't be spared a little longer. Due regard for my reputation for veracity impels me to pause as I reread that last sentence and solemnly assure you that it is *literally* true! He *has* several hundred children, even to the *fifth* generation. Mrs. S. herself has eighteen brothers & sisters.

I am as bright as a new pin today,–take my meals with the family & no longer make any pretence at being an invalid. Though they still won't let me put my head out of doors. It seems to me this excessive dread of fresh air and cold water in such cases *must* be a relic of the dark ages. But I ought to be thankful that I havn't been poisened [?] by being kept in a close, dark room,–a black hole,–as is the fate of so many poor women. Baby too is quite well today, and very good; she slept splendidly the last two nights, & it is unnecessary to add that I did too.

I had a nice letter from Cousin Allie,[1] in Detroit, yesterday. She has sent the baby an afghan, but it hasn't come yet. Isn't that nice?–*just* what I wanted! and Allie does such beautiful needlework.

So you *do* sometimes feel that your little wife is in her old place! –*darling!*–we are not very far apart after all. Why I can shut my eyes and almost believe that I am nestling close to the great, tender heart that loves me and that I love, oh! so infinitely. As my poet says

> "There is one with whom I dwell, whom I have loved
> With such communion that no place on earth
> Can ever be a solitude to me"–[2]

No, my husband, even such words as those in today's letter do not frighten me now as once they did I confess. For now I know what you want, not a—for *me*—unattainable excellence—not the sort of woman that I think ought to have been *created for you!*— but *love*—yes—*my* love. Oh, if I could but tell you *how* I love you, —how altogether lighter than vanity for me is everything else in this world as compared with your happiness & well-being. I would *die* to serve you, darling; with what perfect joy do I dedicate my life to that service.   Your little wife   Eileen

ALS (WC, NjP).

[1] Alice Hoyt Truehart, whose letter is missing.

[2] Adapted from Wordsworth's "There is an Eminence. . ." in *Poems on the Naming of Places.*

To Ellen Axson Wilson

My own lovely little wife,   Bryn Mawr, 7 May, 1886

Baby is three weeks old to-day, isn't she? The little monkey! I wonder if she don't know that she's a very 'previous' young person—only now due, and yet already three weeks on the scene! But oh, I am so glad *now* that she—came when she did! She has, as I can see more and more plainly in your letters every day, been such a help to my darling, driving off so much of loneliness and depression. How merciful our blessed Heavenly Father is to us!

I am *so* much obliged for this minute account of yourself in the letter that came this morning, my darling. You may be sure that you can *never* add a particular too much. It is an immense satisfaction to know that that very serious experience of catching cold is over with now without having left any lasting hurtful consequences; but even now it frightens me. And, my dear, *dear* little wife, I don't a bit like the facts which your recital incidentally reveals. I think that you are making a very serious mistake in letting the baby form such habits of nursing. It will presently be too late to break her of them. It must be very injurious both to you and to her to have her always at her meals. I don't know that I have the true medical view of the matter; but I do know that I have been very much distressed all morning about the matter— and that I shall be until some healthier, more natural rule is established. Surely both your health and hers depend upon regularity in such matters! It frightens me because I know that she is likely enough anyhow to get worthless digestive organs from me, poor little girl. You'll forgive my interference in such a matter, wont you, my darling, and, if I am wrong, tell me why I am? The least of the questions which affect you and the baby is to me of more moment than any question, even the biggest, that might affect anybody else in the world—or any*thing* else.

Oh, my *precious* little wife, you *musn't weary* for me! I[t] makes me *hate* my work here to think that it is the real cause of your sorrow. Why, my darling, isn't there a '*harnt*' with *you*, living all the day close by you and the baby? I have not dared, and I will not dare, to tell you how much I want to come to you: my whole heart's history of the past weeks is summed up in that wish! Don't dwell on my *coming*, sweetheart, but upon my *presence*. I am with you *all the time*, darling! Do you suppose, Miss, that I *live* up in these rooms all by myself the livelong day? Not a bit of it. *I'm never here*. It would break my heart to be a bachelor again— and so I don't run the risk of trying it. I *cant* live here. So I have deliberately separated my functions. I *work* here, but I *live* with you! Ah, sweetheart, if you could only know how almost *literally* that is true, you *could* dwell on my *presence*, and almost *forget* my *coming*, as I advise. You dear little wife, you! Do you suppose that I *could* live any way *now* but as your husband! You don't know—you evidently have no conception—how you capture a fellow, my little siren—and you do it *without singing*—by just making a song out of *life* with you! When once one gets within that wonderful influence of your love, there's no danger that he will ever be anything else but your lover. He may *do* a variety of things, but *that* is his life—loving you, *loving* you, *loving* you, until his whole life is one with yours. Kisses innumerable and *paternal* for our precious little darling, and love for aunt Lou and all.

Your own   Woodrow.

ALS (WC, NjP).

From Ellen Axson Wilson

My own darling,   Gainsville, May 7/86

You must not let yourself be disquieted over those "words" which you are so clever in detecting, dearest, and, sweet-heart, don't imagine either that I try to *conceal* anything, or that there is anything "the matter." When I tell my love that I am *wearying* for him I tell him *all*. I am not at all unhappy, but you know it *can't* be just as if you were with me. Would you wish it to be? You remember the dull weather we used to have sometimes last winter, & which, as you say, always weighs so heavily on your spirits. We were not unhappy because of it; *I* was not conscious of feeling depressed or blue; and yet when the sunshine came again we knew that our hearts were made more glad because of it: "for the light is sweet, and a pleasant thing it is for the eyes to behold the sun." And you are *my sun* sweet-heart. My sun, it is true, has power to cast it's beams across the space that divides us, I am still living in it's light. I could not live at all if it were withdrawn. But when my *summer* comes, the sunshine will feel warmer and brighter and my life will be fuller.

But oh, darling, you know how it is! I need not try to explain how I can be, and *am* happy in your absence and how I *must* be happier in your presence. And *our* little one *does* make the time pass more quickly. You never said a truer word, dear, than that all my love for her is *added* to the sum of my love for you. It would be hard to say that anything could make you dearer to me, —that I could love the father of my child more passionately and entirely than I have loved my husband. Somehow that would seem to be placing the child before the father. I am more sure that the reverse is true, that I love *her* more because she is my Woodrow's child. But most true it is that she is an *added* cause for love between us,—a wonderful new bond, closer than any other in some respects.

The little darling is as sweet as possible today; she took her first plunge bath this morning in the most heroic fashion. She is *very* well today,—last night she had a slight touch of colic, I suppose,—didn't cry much, but could not sleep;—slept one hour early in the evening and then entertained me until four this morning. Then she went to sleep and did not wake 'till twelve. Not as well regulated as she might be, eh? I am quite well with the exception of a *very* slight headache from loss of sleep. Aunt Lou, Eddie & all send love. I *love* you, Woodrow my darling, with my whole heart   Your own little   Eileen

ALS (WC, NjP).

To Ellen Axson Wilson

My own darling Eileen,   Bryn Mawr, 8 May, '86
As ill luck will have it, the mail into which I must get my letters to you every day, in order that they may reach you regularly, always at the same time of day, leaves here at 2:40; so that when, as to-day, I am a little belated in writing and do not begin till after lunch, I have to scribble at a great rate to get through in

time. You would be charmed to see the devotion with which I
brave all weathers to carry my letters to you to the Post Office
in season for that particular mail. When it's raining, I put on my
rubber boots, my rubber coat, and my old hat (you know my *only*
hat is *old!*) and set out, 'not giving a cent' what the elements may
be doing. Isn't that a picture of devotion! I tremble to ask the results. *Do* my letters always reach you by the same mail? If not,
all this desperate regularity on my part is in vain—and I shall
have to go down and strangle the postmaster!

Oh, my little sweetheart, you don't know with what a peculiar
feeling, compounded of love and worship, I prepare these letters
that *you* are to read. No matter how hastily I have to dash them
off, I have the same feeling, that all my heart is going into the
words, that it is not ordinary writing I'm doing, but writing into
which all that is best and strongest in me, all of me that is immortal, is somehow finding expression, *just because you are to
read it.* Writing to you is, for me, like looking you in the eyes. I
can't look you in the eyes and keep my heart out of the look: &
just so, I can't write to you and keep my heart out of the words.
You may, therefore, be always quite sure, my precious one, that,
no matter *what* the subject of the letter may *seem* to be—no matter how far towards the end business, or other topics, may push
the *expressions* of love,—love is really the burden of every sentence. It is as if I talked to you about other things holding you
in my arms, punctuating my sentences with kisses, and all the
time *acting* (save for my tongue) as if I were absorbed in making
love to you.

By-the-way, Miss, there's one advantage in being separated
from you just at this season(!) Making love to you (in *person*)
is my ideal of 'holiday,' and presently the holidays and making
love to you are to begin together! Think of that, my little queen!
Isn't that jolly? Will you solemnly promise to make love to *me*?
Kisses when and as they are due. Love to all.

Your own   Woodrow.

ALS (WC, NjP).

From Ellen Axson Wilson

My own darling,   Gainsville May 8/86
I wonder if the sweet little "Beauty," my childhood's favourite,
found that wonderful magic glass of her's most consoling or tantalizing!—the one, I mean, which showed her always what her
dear ones were doing and how they fared but which brought her

no nearer to them. It would be sweet to know every moment what
you are doing, what you are thinking, how you are feeling just
then and not two days after when the letter comes. I catch myself so very, very often longing for that knowledge. And yet what
should I do if I caught you at times looking sad or depressed or
lonely—if something in "the look of you" should make my foolish
little heart fancy that you needed *me*,—what should I do when my
mirror told me that you had a head-ache or the "blues"! Oh, I
should feel like a caged bird in very truth,—one of the wildest
sort—a stormy petral, I suppose. I should break my heart and
well-nigh kill myself in the vain longing to escape to you. And
yet how much I have wished all this sweet May morning that I
could just peep at you and know what you were about, and if you
were happy and feeling at peace with all the world, as one should
when that world is so bright and beautiful and sunshiny as it is
today. What are you doing I wonder,—reading for your ordeal,
writing lectures with imposing titles,—you havn't been telling me
of late what they are about, by the way. I *know* at least what you
were doing for a while,—perhaps in my own hour, after lunch.
And so the "Democracy"[1] can't go on for want of *me*! Just to
think of it! How important I ought to feel! I wonder what your
Boston friends would say to that. Be that as it may I must leave
the book out of any speculations as to what you are about, except
that you will be thinking about it perhaps as you take your long
walk this afternoon,—and perhaps you will spare time for one
little thought of me too—down by the brook!

But after all perhaps it would be more satisfactory to you if
instead of such guesses about you I told you what *I* have been
doing. I *have* done something new today, I have been out in the
beautiful sunshine & it has made me feel very bright & happy;
for the rest I have spent the day as usual, nursing baby, reading
a little, talking &c. Baby is very well today and so am I. She had
a good night was awake only two hours instead of seven or eight.
All send love. Goodbye, my darling, I love you with my heart of
hearts. I am as ever,   Your own little   Eileen

ALS (WC, NjP).
  [1] A reference to Wilson's statement in his letter of May 3, 1886, that he could
not write while separated from Ellen. She was referring to Wilson's plans for
further work on "The Modern Democratic State."

To Ellen Axson Wilson

My own darling little wife,   Bryn Mawr, 9 May, 1886
  I am in 'quite a state of mind' to-day! I have had no letter from

my darling since Friday morning, and to-day, being Sunday, I
can't even find out whether any has come yet or not! And the
last letter received told of my darling's *having been* sick the day
before! Of course there are a score unalarming reasons that I
can imagine to account for the delay; and I have not allowed myself to get into a panic yet. But the trouble is that, under the
circumstances, my imagination wont work in the reassuring direction, but must needs suggest all sorts of aid to anxiety! In
brief—if you are as much in love as I am, you will doubtless already have made the discovery for yourself,—it is monstrously
hard to be philosophical about such matters when one is in love.
I find that love has played the oddest pranks imaginable with my
methods of reasoning about some things. Under present circumstances, for example, all sorts of premisses lead *to the same conclusion*:—namely, that *something* is wrong with my loved ones.
Perhaps the lover's imagination is a very 'stuck-up' imagination.
Perhaps it thinks that while it's about foreboding it will be very
grandly thorough and forebode the greatest conceivable evils.
And you see, Miss, that just at this present juncture my imagination has not the least difficulty in selecting from amongst evils
that which would be the greatest. Although, as I explained yesterday, I have not *dared* since you left even to *play* at being a bachelor again, I have been close enough to that desolate condition to
get a vivid glimpse of what it used to be: and never before did
I see what it really was to live by myself in those old days which
now seem so happily far away. In a word—as you see I've been
trying to say for some lines back—I've been reckoning up, in a
tumultuous, heartful sort of way, the value of my little wife to
me. I can't *state* the result—there are no terms of value in which
it can be stated—but perhaps I can give you some idea of what
its proportions would be if it *were* stated. My little wife has taken
all real pain out of my life: her wonderful loving sympathy exalts
even my occasional moods of despondency into a sort of *hallowed*
sadness out of which I come stronger and better. She has given
to my ambitions a meaning, an assurance, and a purity which
they never had before: with her by my side, ardently devoted to
me and to my cause, understanding all my thoughts and all my
aims, I feel that I can make the utmost of every power I possess.
She has brought into my life the sunshine which was needed to
keep it from growing stale and and [*sic*] morbid; that has steadily
been bringing back into my spirits their old gladness and boyhood,
their old delight in play and joyous laughter:—that sweetest sunshine of deep womanly love, unfailing, gentle patience, even, hap-

py spirits, and spontaneous, girlish mirth, that is purest, swiftest tonic to a spirit prone to fret and apt to flag. She has given me that perfect *rest* of heart and mind, of whose existence I had never so much as dreamed before she came to me, which springs out of assured oneness of hope & sympathy—and which, for me, means life and success. Above all, she has given me *herself* to live for! Her arms are able to hold me up against the world; her eyes are able to charm away every carking care; her words are my solace and inspiration;—and all because *her love is my life.* If you can sum all these wonders up, you will have the value of my little wife to me.

I know that I have told you all this before, my darling; but I also know that you wont mind my saying it all again, to relieve my heart of some part of its pent-up yearning! And, besides, I have a special right to tell it all over again just *now.* During this separation of ours, sweetheart, I have had innumerable opportunities to stand, as it were, and look at my life with you almost as if I were a third person,—and yet with an infinitely deeper insight and more perfect perception than any third person could have—and I seem to myself to have seen as I never saw before the deepest meanings of the happiness that came to me on our marriage day. The needs of the moment, which are unfilled because you are absent, have helped my analysis to a keener appreciation than ever it reached before of the infinitely high and unspeakably sweet part played in my life by my Eileen, my queen, my blessed little wife! That ideal vacation at dear Arden, that trying stay at Haverford, the winter of love and work and anticipation here,—all seem to me now like an open book of hope assured. I pore over that dear record of sweet memories constantly nowadays with an ever increasing joy, and a more and more eager purpose to live worthy of the love you have given me. I would rather be worthy of my privileges as your husband than win a fame like Milton's. I would a thousand times rather repay you a tythe of the happiness you have brought me than make my name immortal *without* serving you as the chief mission of my life. Ah, my little wife, do you know how completely I am yours? Do you know that my whole self has passed over into my allegiance to you? Do you know *all* that I mean when I say that I am

Your own   Woodrow.

P.S. I think that the comments in one of the *Nations* I send, together with the extracts in the paper *"Public Opinion,"* which I send with them, will answer as completely as possible your question as to the impression created by the "Jeff. Davis frenzy." It will soon be entirely forgotten by everybody but the N. Y. *Tribune* and that tribe.[1]

Poor cousin Hattie, indeed! She does have a hard, a terribly hard, time of it. Please give her my love when you write—warm regards to Mr. E. (tho' he ought to be ashamed of himself.).

Innumerable kisses to our darling—many for little sister. Love for Aunt Lou and all   Lovingly,   Woodrow.

ALS (WC, NjP).

[1] Wilson's enclosures, which are missing, undoubtedly consisted of "Jefferson Davis and the Lost Cause," *Public Opinion*, I (May 8, 1886), 61-66—a collection of extracts from editorial comment in ninety-six newspapers on the reception accorded Davis in Montgomery and Atlanta—and the New York *Nation*, XLII (May 6, 1886), which on page 372 printed two short editorials on the ceremony in Montgomery. Among the extracts in *Public Opinion* was one from the New York *Tribune*, April 30, 1886, describing Davis as an "unrepentant old villain and Union-hater" who should have been hanged in 1865.

From Ellen Axson Wilson

My own darling,   Gainsville May 9/86

Everybody is away at church except Mrs. & Miss Wilson & their nurse, so I will take advantage of the quiet and write now, not waiting for Uncle Warren to bring your letter, as I like best to do. It is such a lovely morning that somehow it makes me wish even more than usual to see you, to have you here to enjoy it all with me,—the sweet Sabbath peace, the warm sunshine, the cool soft breeze, the garden full of sweet "clove" pinks & heartsease and other old-fashioned flowers, and above all the dear little one asleep here beside me. You don't know how lovely she looks asleep,—the dear little cherub! She is as sweet & well as possible today, and so am I,—well & *sweet both* I mean of course, and I won't be contradicted, sir! And I won't have you lamenting my pallour either, dear. I am not looking sick or badly at all,—and I can prove it in a moment by the simple fact that I have on at this moment my dove wrapper with the lace! And, you know, I couldn't be bribed to wear it if I were *very* pale or dingy! I am too much of a woman! That colour, you know, brings out all the yellow in flesh-colour and so is as strikingly unbecoming to a muddy complexion as it is strikingly becoming to a clear one. And the *idea* of your considering yourself "responsible" for any possible loss of bloom in me! You dear absurd boy! I assure you, sir, that even if I am, as Mrs. Cowles [Coale?] predicted, thin & pale for a long time—or forever—the "ordeal" will have no more to do with it than a tooth-ache several months—or several years—ago! It will, in fact, be caused by loss of sleep—by *broken* rest, which somehow always tells on me more than anything else. But I think that perhaps now when it is not an occasional but a constant thing I won't feel it so much,—at least not after a while,—that my physical being will gradually adjust itself to the new conditions. But of course for a time one who is accustomed to eight or nine solid hours of sleep must feel the difference between that and five or six broken hours. I suppose it is scarcely worth while to try to cross a bridge *six months* before we reach it; but my chief difficulty at present concerns *your* fate next winter. Do you think you can learn to sleep through a good deal of stirring around, & a *very* moderate amount of crying (she is a real good baby) as a great many husbands do? Because if you can't learn it & quickly too, we will have to put our wits to work & make *some* arrangement to ensure you peace [and] quiet,—you will have to be put out of the way, poor fellow—into the little hall room (!) or the study perhaps; but that is almost like being in the same room. Well we will see when the time comes. In the mean time I crave your forgiveness for this young usurper & tyrant; she would not deign to ask it for herself. My darling, my love, my dear, *dear* Woodrow, *I love you* with all my heart.

Your little wife   Eileen

ALS (WC, NjP) with WWhw notation on env.

To Ellen Axson Wilson

My precious, lovely little wife,   Bryn Mawr, 10 May, '86

I was thrown into a sort of ecstacy this morning by the two letters, of Thursday and Friday, that came to me at breakfast time. I wish that you could see how they have transformed me. I don't care much now whether these dull clouds get away from the face of the 'natural' sun or not. There is light and joy enough in my heart to supply half a dozen worlds with the noblest substitute for sunshine. For these are the most perfect love letters that were ever written—from the hand of the most *glorious* little wife that ever a chap had and did not deserve!

By the way, Miss, I want to dictate a theme for your next letter—don't you dare to decline it! It is, 'The sort of Woman that ought to have been created for Woodrow.' I want a very specific treatment on that subject. I know that you can express perfectly your views on that head, because anybody who can express love as perfectly as you have done in these two blessed letters, can write perfectly of *anything*. And I am intensely curious to get your ideas distinctly on the subject assigned, because I have just gotten hold of a perfect pen portrait of the woman who *was* created for me, and I am, naturally, *very* anxious to compare what you have to say with this wonderful picture. Don't fail me, do you hear? 'Tackle' this great theme the very next time you take up your pen. Let me see—it will be Friday next before I can get it. I shall expect it then.

Now that you are sitting up so constantly, you precious, well little woman, you, can't you draw me that sketch of our little Margaret? I am *so* eager for it—I *must* have just that *glimpse* of her—*if your eyes will permit.*

Oh, I wonder if I can't find *some* word that will tell my darling something of the infinite, joyous love that dances and laughs and hums mute melodies to itself in my heart to-day because of her, my glorious little wife! Why, my little queen, how eloquent you can get! These expressions of love that fill your letters are surely, in substance, the very sweetest, most beautiful poetry ever written! And, if poetry interprets nature, surely *this* does—not only your own nature, but mine too, and that of all true woman's love as well. Why can't I do the same for this love that fills my heart to bursting. My heart is big, I'm sure, but not half big enough to hold the love I bear for my Eileen—and yet I can't pour it out even into her ears. What shall I do? I am resolved what to do: I will never give up *trying* to tell her how much, how passionately, how infinitely I love her; and I will try harder and harder, with more and more *singleness* of devotion, to live for her happiness—and *so* prove my love. Oh, my little wife, my little wife—my darling!—my whole heart and life are yours.

Love and kisses unmeasured for *our* precious little daughter. Kisses for little sister. Love for Eddie, Aunt Lou, and all from
Your own   Woodrow.

ALS (WC, NjP).

From Ellen Axson Wilson

My own darling,   Gainsville May 10/86
Your sweet letter of Sat. has come duly to hand at the regular time. Yes, dearest, they always come by the same mail. When we hear the eleven o'clock train come in Mrs. Shepard never fails to say "there's your letter," and Uncle Warren never fails to bring it at one. *How good* you are to me, my darling! how kind & thoughtful in everything great and small. I am *sure* you are the best husband in the world, no trouble is too great that will make your little wife happy or save her a pang of disappointment. I

wish I could tell you how deeply she appreciates it all,—how her whole heart goes out to you at every such mark of tender love.

But I must try to answer your questions in yesterday's letter; —with regard to the nursing, I mean. (The idea of your begging pardon for "interfering" in matters concerning your own wife and baby! If you havn't the right, sir, who has?) After all I don't know what to say except to repeat what Aunt Lou said when I quoted you to her;—indeed we had already talked it over often, for it seemed very bad to me too. She says that what you say is perfectly true in theory but that we can't reduce it to practice with such a young baby. Later on we may, but now it could only be done at the expense of much hard crying, and that might injure her seriously. The truth is the little thing is, as they say, unusually "hearty," and I don't believe that while she is so young her strength will permit her to suck long enough at once to satisfy her very vigorous appetite. And she *isn't* "always at her meals"; when she does finally go to sleep she takes unusually long naps,—three hours as a rule. I assure you, it isn't half as bad as it might be. Said Auntie one morning after the baby had been awake almost all night, "you are unusually fortunate, I never saw a young baby give less trouble; a great many keep people awake like this *every* night." "Why," said I, ["]I don't see how the mothers ever get back their strength without any sleep, to speak of." "Oh no," she said calmly, "of course, they *don't* get back their strength." Think of that, sir, and be thankful! I get several hours of *good* sleep every night and I *have* gotten back my strength.

Mrs. S. left this morning. We miss her very much & I am afraid my being without anyone will give Auntie more work than I ought to allow her to do. But I have derived much pleasure today from taking care of her myself. Mrs. S. however is coming back on Wed. to finish out her month, if she can leave her Grandfather. But there is Baby, awake, & though Auntie is on the scene she will hardly satisfy her, so I must close abruptly, for it is almost dusk & I will have no opportunity to resume. Goodbye 'till to-morrow. *Won't* I make love to you in our holiday time! and oh *how* I love you now.   Your little wife   Eileen

I didn't remember to thank you for the package of envelopes which I have just begun to use.

ALS (WC, NjP).

From Marion Wilson Kennedy

My dearest Woodrow— Little Rock, 5/11/86.

I have just taken advantage of my first opportunity to write again to dear Ellie. Every time I look at our little girlie, I think of yours, and almost as often wish I could see the whole "*family*" for a little while. I could not find words too strong to express my appreciation of your last letter, Woodrow. It was exactly what I have wanted so badly, and was beginning to fear I would have to wait and see for myself, if I ever obtained it at all. I found I had almost no questions to ask Ellie when I wrote, as you have answered them as fully as possible. You are a wonderfully good brother, anyhow, Woodrow. I have so often mentally compared your uniformly kind and gallant treatment of me with the descriptions other sisters gave of their brothers, and it always ended in a sense of *proud satisfaction* with my brother. . . .

Ross send warmest love, in which most heartily joins,

Your loving sister, Marion.

ALS (WP, DLC).

To Ellen Axson Wilson

My own darling, Bryn Mawr, 11 May, '86

I was long ago acquainted with the saw, 'boasting goes before a fall'; but I have only just now learned how *immediately* the fall follows. You doubtless remember that I said the other day that I could tell *infallibly* in what mood your letters were each of them written. Well that declaration was hardly written and despatched than there came (last night) a letter in which, unless she had said, with her own truthful pen, that she was in high spirits after her first stroll in the sunlight, I could not for the life of me have read my lady's mood! I read the letter again and again, and was completely baffled. On that point it was inscrutable. Plainly I never saw my darling in that mood—for I can't recognize it at all. Maybe it's a mood that does not grow in my presence—an absence mood—in which the spirits are light but somehow have no *spring* in them: they will not *bound*. I will not boast any more, but will set myself to learn more. But how I'm dribbling, without coming to the point! The point is this, that I am disturbed by any failure on my part to follow my precious little wife through all her moods, because I feel that, unless I can do that, I will not know how to write *my* letters. My study is to make my sweetheart happy: that is my *life*; unless I can do that I dont care to do anything. And I want my letters to be suited, by perfect sympathy, to my little queen's heart-wants. Not that I expect the moods of her letters to last until my answers can reach her. I want to reveal some phase of my love for her that will fit each mood, so that she shall always have some food of gladness. *That's* the point. My love is *for her* and I am eager that there should be no moment of her life in which she does not *feel* that love as a strength and solace—as going out towards her as entirely, as sympathetically, as ardently in *that* mood as in all others; as something that *absolutely* identifies me with her, in a sympathy so close that nothing but *perfect love* could produce it. But, after all, you know that, don't you, sweetheart? Haven't you seen me trying to *live* that thought into your heart for the last eleven months?

Oh, my sweet little lady, what thoughts of you fill all my days, how passionately in love with you I am! You and our precious little daughter are the loved centre of all my emotions. I have almost gotten rid of myself: all my actions are labelled 'Eileen's and the Baby's.'

I am *so* much grieved to hear of Eddie's continued *stuttering*. I *hope you* can effect something. Give my love to the dear little fellow—and to little sister and Aunt Lou and all

Your own   Woodrow.

ALS (WC, NjP).

From Ellen Axson Wilson

My own darling   Gainsville May 11/86

I have just discovered that Auntie is going to "society" after dinner and that her sister-in-law is to spend the afternoon with me, so as I suppose it would not be polite to write then, I must now at the last moment scribble off a hasty note.

First—before I forget again—a word about the visit to Cousin Hattie. I quite agree with you that we don't want to stay there any length of time. You know we decided at Beth's that a visit ought to be either *very* short or long enough for one to become domesticated—to fit into the family life. If, as I am told, we pass through Nashville on our way to Clarksville I suppose it would hardly do for us to decline the invitation altogether; but I should think two or three days would be *quite* enough. I know that it is very important both for the sake of your work and your *rest* that you should get where you will feel free and settled and at home as soon as possible, and I don't propose that you shall be forced to fritter away half the summer among my relatives, *whatever* they say about it. Am sorry we must go to Rome, but it seems necessary to spend a few days there to see about the books and things,—to gather up the fragments that remain. Uncle Henry and his family are *very* anxious for us to make them a visit, but I told them you couldn't possibly spare the time, and that I felt too inexperienced and too anxious about the baby to pick her up while she is so young and take a journey all by myself, without even a nurse. They—that is the women—seem so offended at my refusal that Aunt Lou thinks of going over with me for a few days the first of next month; or perhaps sending Loula. Both Aunt Emmie and Fannie were deeply offended with me for not going there two years ago, instead of to Wilmington, I suppose! I *was* to have gone you know, but was taken sick & spent the time alloted to them here in bed. They seem never to have gotten over the "slight" and Fannie, who has been here ever since I came, has been making herself very disagreeable about it. Uncle Henry left Eddie, to my great delight. He is to go to school here as soon as his books come that he may not get behind his class. He has become very ambitious, it seems; & is at the head of his class in everything.

But there! It is time for me to close & I have had room for nothing but one stupid matter. But remember that "no matter how far toward the end business, or other topics, may push the *expressions* of love,—love is really the burden of every sentence." I am *so glad* that you understand & appreciate that fact, my darling; and you may be sure that *I* do too. Every sentence of *my* letters too is "written, as it were, in your arms and punctuated with kisses." Baby is quite well & had a *splendid* night—the best yet; I am also perfectly well. Sweet-heart, do you know that there is someone in Georgia who loves you to distraction—who is *perfectly devoted* to you? And her [name] is Eileen,

Your own little wife

Please excuse this abominable pen.

ALS (WC, NjP).

To Ellen Axson Wilson

My own precious little wife,   Bryn Mawr, 12 May, 1886

The idea of my being demoralized by a letter of yours! And yet it is even so:—by this letter, rec'd yesterday, which confesses that your rest is broken *every night*, and that the prospect is that you will be kept thin and pale in consequence! Oh, my darling, my darling! Of course I ought to have known that it was to be so, and

I suppose that I *did*; but I did not *realize* that my darling was to be teased thus out of her health. No, we will not cross now a bridge which is six months ahead, and I'm sure I don't care a picayune *how* much sleep *I* lose. If sleep were not necessary to keep me effective to work for you and baby, I should be more than willing to lose *all* mine if by so doing I could give you yours. It's devoutly to be hoped that the baby can be induced to sleep the nights through before she is six months old; but, in any case, you need not mind my fate in the matter. There's one comfort—at least one *half* comfort—this fate need not attend you all your life—it need not attend you *any* more after this. I would give half of all I expect to win in the world, and *more* than that, for a son worthy of you and of our hopes; but I will not break my precious little wife's health to gratify any wish or hope, however long and dearly cherished, that I ever had. If I love her enough to over-balance with my love my settled nature of self-indulgence—as I hope and believe that I do—I can live for her hereafter in this respect as in all others. Oh, my darling, my darling—why did you ever get married? You are too exquisite a little woman to be any man's *slave*!

But what am I saying? Am I forgetting the creed I have held all my life long, that a woman is glorified and made perfect by marriage and motherhood? No, I am not forgetting; and I know that no man ever wanted children more than I have wanted and do want them. But then my little wife! She is the crown and joy of my life! It is for her that I live. She is before *everything*. How can *I* waste her health for *any* purpose, be it the highest and purest and holiest in the world? Oh I pray God I may be taught what is right! I wish that not *all* things seemed to add to the tragedy of life: but that is about the same as wishing that I had less heart—and I don't wish that. I can think of myself having pale cheeks and wearied senses with perfect equanimity; but I can't think of my darling borne down by burdens with anything but a broken heart.

Don't imagine this letter a product of the "blues," sweetheart. I am not a bit 'blue' to-day; but I *am anxious* and I am—*sorry*, oh, *so* sorry! Kiss the dear little mischief-maker for me ever so many times—I can't help loving her passionately for all she treats her mother so ill. Kisses too for little sister. Love for Eddie, Aunt Lou, and all   Your own   Woodrow.

ALS (WC, NjP).

From Ellen Axson Wilson

Gainsville May 12/86

Oh my darling, my darling, what can I say to you in answer to the *precious* letter received yesterday! What a mockery it seems, this trying to translate into words *any* strong emotion, and especially to tell you through such a medium the joy which fills my heart almost to bursting as I read these wonderful words. Indeed, I doubt if I could express to you in *any* way all that letter has made me feel,—the exaltation of spirit, the sort of *glorified* state in which it has left me. If I were with you *perhaps* I could make you understand—ah! if I could but try! These happy tears which I cannot keep out of my eyes as I read those precious words or think of them would tell you somewhat. This letter shall be one of my chief treasures, darling, as long as I live. Time and again in the old days I picked out some letter of yours as my special treasure; but ah how much dearer is this than any of those! for they *promised* that I should be certain things to you, upon which all my heart was set,—but this tells me that I *have* been all that and more. *Can* it be that it is all *true*, darling, *every one* of these sweet words? Ah, love is verily a wonderful, wonderful thing since by merely *loving* I have acquired such supernatural power,—for I am sure I never came by it in the *ordinary* course of nature.

It is true, as you say, darling, you *have* "told me all this before," and you can never never tell me too often for it is the sweetest music that lips ever uttered. But to *write* it all after a quiet, calm review of all our days together seems *different*, somehow. For might it not be that *saying* such words to your little wife, holding her in your arms the while and looking in her eyes,—knowing too her great love for you and her great longing to make you happy,—your heart is so filled with your true love for her that there is no room *then* for other desires,—the unsatisfied needs of your nature can not for the time make themselves felt?

To be sure this idea never occurred to me before, and I have always rested in fullest content upon your *verbal* assurances that your wife had made life sweeter for you; but I am hunting about now for some explanation of the fact that this written testimony has moved me so deeply. Alas! it is time for me to close now, and I have *so* much to say to you, darling!—but then I *can't* say it, so after all, why try? I can never tell you with what thoughts and feelings I too have been living over since we parted this beautiful, blissful year. It is my *deliberate* belief, love, that no one else in the world is as happy as I am, and have been since the day I was wed; that scarcely anyone else could be made to believe such perfect happiness *possible*. *I* could not believe it one year ago, even with *your* love to help me. It is like the joys of Heaven which the strongest imagination is powerless to reveal to us;—until we attain unto them they are altogether hidden from us. But you, darling, have made an earthly paradise for me.

Your little wife   Eileen

ALS (WC, NjP).

To Horace Elisha Scudder

My dear Mr. Scudder,   Bryn Mawr, Pa., May [12], 1886

I write this letter for the purpose of laying before you a literary scheme which I have in mind, and upon which I very much want to get your advice; but I must begin with two requests upon which I wish the chief emphasis of my letter to lie, namely, first that you will not regard the letter as in any degree prompted by my knowledge of your connection with a publishing house, and, second, that you will feel at perfect liberty to give your opinion or not, as you may choose, upon its contents. I was about to add that I should esteem it the best possible proof of your belief in my sincerity should you *not* reply. But I am very anxious to get an answer, and so will not, upon reflection, cut myself altogether off from the chance in any such Hibernian (?) fashion.

I have for some time been planning, on lines which seem to be the 'lines of least resistance' in my mental physics, some 'Studies in Politics' (say—for I have not *begun* with a label) to be hung upon such topics as these: I. The nature, structure, ends, and functions of the modern democratic state. This I have worked out to some extent of *mss.*, and to a still larger extent of tentative thought and investigation.[1] My object in treating it would be a very ambitious one: no less than to answer Sir Henry Maine's "Popular Government"[2] by treating modern democratic tendencies from a much more truly historical point of view than he has taken; keeping very close to the concrete examples of popular govt. by means of careful comparative constitutional study,—careful but not narrow; aiming to reckon with all the actual forces of thought and machinery in modern popular governments—especially our own, of course,—in as broad and philosophical a way as I could steadily command, and to do for such political facts something better than I did for the existing facts of our constitutional system in "Congressional Government," though in the same spirit.

II. *Political Morality*. Seeing that the state is a moral person (*vide* Mulford),[3] the democratic state is, in view of the foregoing discussion, a moral person with a very peculiar, delicate constitution. What is moral in popular politics in view of that constitution? What is the healthful operation of such a state? What is the proper point of view for responsible interpretation of written fundamental law, the 'liberal' which reads into that law whatever the times call for, the logical (like that taken in the *Political Science Quarterly* by Prof. Burgess)[4] which regards such law as having little coercive moral power in itself and as being, in some cases, a mere perversion of a rational sequence of events, or that which regards more carefully the growth of institutions in and through the developing thought and character of the people, the continuity of tradition, &c. In a word what are the moralities, what is the proper legal conscience, of a life of self-government?

III *Political Progress*. What, in view of the family history and the consequent inherited nature of popular government, and in view of the moralities of self-government, *is* political progress, what glimpses do we get from such studies of its *law*, and how can its conditions be supplied?

IV. *Political Expediency*. A big subject, and as important as big, hitherto largely neglected, save from the boss's point of view. It would be possible under this topic, to give a vivified statement of (if I remember aright) Austin's[5] conception of law as resting upon expediency in the broadest sense of the term; to discuss with some conclusiveness the legitimate range of compromise; and to give a more or less satisfactory answer to the question, What, in view of what we know of the moral growth of communities and of the law of political progress, is political expediency?

V. *Political Prejudice*. The part played by prejudice in political development—its *good* offices as well as its bad. How far are these crystals of experience to be crushed, how far respected as true jewels of conservatism worthy of a comely setting?

VI *Practical Politics*, as it is, and as it looks in the light of the foregoing discussions.

By this time you have doubtless quite lost your breath. It is a *vast* subject (I hope that you will not find it *necessary* to laugh at me because of its size as compared with mine) and in my dreams with reference to its treatment and development, I had not thought to compact all its parts from the start as chapters of a single book, but to develop it, in the course of as many years as might be necessary, in the form of monographs (say, like Fiske's "Idea of God")[6] which might eventually be revised and

winnowed, and all that was best in them put into a single volume
—my world into which these separate stars had tumbled.

If you should care to express your opinion as to the feasibility
and worth of such a work as I have indicated, and as to the wisdom of its being undertaken, with whatever seriousness and
enthusiasm, by a young man of my calibre, I should be deeply indebted for such an expression given with the utmost plainness.

Of course the work would go on very slowly. I am teaching
history and political economy—and they fill my time so that all
work in my own special, chosen field is necessarily overwhelmingly handicapped. Until I can get a chair in which my professional
and original work can go hand in hand the case must continue
the same: and, since there are only one or two such chairs in the
country, and none of them with the least thought of becoming
vacant for me, I must calculate on such a continuance.

As a spur to the most solid sort of constitutional and political
study in preparation for the work of which I have written, I have
agreed to write for D. C. Heath a college text-book on 'Government,' which will treat of the origin, functions, &c. of government
in connection with a comparative study of modern constitutions.[7]

This is my first essay in asking literary counsel of a friend. I
don't know why I have presumed. Although you have shown no
more interest in me, I suppose, than you would show in any young
man of sober and creditable literary ambitions, I have somehow
gotten it into my head that you will know better than most men
how to understand and forgive an impertinence like this.

Please present my regards to Mr. Houghton. I shall always
remember his generous hospitality with very keen pleasure.

Very sincerely Yours,   Woodrow Wilson

ALS (Scudder Papers, MH).

[1] See the Editorial Note, "Wilson's First Treatise on Democratic Government,"
and "The Modern Democratic State," printed at Dec. 1, 1885.

[2] This interesting comment raises the crucial question of precisely when
Wilson read Maine's *Popular Government*, for the reading of this book seems to
have been the catalyst for Wilson's revision and enlargement of the plan for a
grand study of modern democracy, the embryo of which is to be found in "The
Modern Democratic State." *Popular Government* was published in London by
John Murray in 1885 and in New York by Henry Holt in 1886. On the flyleaf of
his copy of the New York edition (in the Wilson Library, DLC), Wilson wrote
his autograph and the date "Jan. 26, 1886." His reading date, "Jany 27, 1886,"
on the last page of the book shows when he completed his first reading.

[3] Wilson's notes on and extensive extracts from Elisha Mulford's *The Nation*
are in the first of the two envelopes of research notes and memoranda described
in n. 4 of the Editorial Note, "Wilson's First Treatise on Democratic Government."

[4] John W. Burgess, "The American Commonwealth: Changes in Its Relation
to the Nation," *Political Science Quarterly*, I (March 1886), 9-35.

[5] John Austin, distinguished English jurist.

6 John Fiske, *The Idea of God as Affected by Modern Knowledge* (Boston, 1886).

7 See the Editorial Note, "Wilson's Plan for a Textbook in Civil Government."

To Ellen Axson Wilson

My own precious little wife,   Bryn Mawr, 13 May, 1886

I have, for the first time in many weeks, a piece of news to tell, small and of a very mild nature, but still news. I last night despatched a long letter (12 pages) to Mr. Horace Scudder in Boston, laying before him with considerable fulness my literary scheme, as to Democracy and the rest, and asking his opinion and advice upon it! A very new and novel rôle for me! I never did such a thing before in my life—and probably never shall again. I don't know what put it into my head, but I have been drawn very strongly towards Mr. Scudder and crave his literary friendship. If, as I hope, he will be inclined to respond, I feel that my gain will be great. He has a keen literary instinct and a catholic literary sympathy which would make his counsels very valuable.

This letter will reach my darling on her *birthday*: but I am not going to write her her birthday letter to-day: that shall be written on Saturday—there's no inspiration in the *13th*. But I can refer you to my next Saturday's letter and, meantime, send you a heartful of love and congratulations. When I racked my brains to think what my present to my darling should be, I found, to my dismay, that I did not know what you wanted for the *baby* (I wish that you could have seen me walking bashfully and helplessly through the infants' department at Wanamaker's inspecting the goods there!); but I recollected how you used to carry your sewing things about in the sewing machine drawer, and so I sent you a work-box—not the sort I wanted, but the best I could find in Philadelphia. If you would rather have a work-basket, you shall have one so soon as ever we get back here next winter. I got the box as something which could be *packed*.

Alas, alas! this last letter of yours completes my despair about your prospects for rest! "Oh no; of course mother's *don't* get back their strength"! Thank Heaven husbands at any rate have it in their power to determine whether their wives shall *be* mothers or not! I am a poor, weak sort of a creature; but I suppose I *can* sacrifice myself for love's sake! But I've said enough on that head: I ought to be pouring out into *this* letter my admiration for my splendid little wife that she should have gotten back as much of her strength as she has under such adverse circumstances. Oh, my love, you are a *perfect* little mother, as you have been a perfect sweetheart and wife! I love you, I *adore* you! You are my queen, my heart's whole strength and delight—my Eileen.

Kisses overwhelming for our precious baby; kisses for Maggie; love for Eddie, Aunt Lou, and all.   Your own   Woodrow.

Sweetheart you *must* not go without a nurse. Did I not send you money enough? I can send you more.

ALS (WC, NjP).

From Ellen Axson Wilson

My own darling Woodrow,   Gainesville May 13/86
I have been having a comical experience, yet a very common one with me, since the arrival of your sweet letter of the 11th. I have been sitting for a half hour or so making a vain though desperate effort to recall the contents of that enigmatical letter. I suppose your memory serves you the same trick sometimes with regard to my epistles; it is because our letters "lap over" each other, I imagine, that I so often get "mixed" and can't decide what or which is being answered. Am sorry I can't read the riddle for you, my dear, for I don't aspire to be "inscrutable" to *you*. But stay!—you do give me a clue by which perhaps I may recall the "mood" if not the letter;—it was the first day that I went out of doors. I do recall something about that;—and if I said I was in "*high* spirits" I did not choose the right word, but I *was* happy in the "Il Penserosa" fashion perhaps, but that is a very real and sweet form of happiness, after all. There is a quiet, dreamy, peacefullness that is very apt to steal over one sitting all alone in the soft sunshine of a still summer day; and I remember sitting so, and brooding with a sort of happy sadness over "the tender grace of the days that are gone." Yet after all it *is* an "*absence* mood," for how can I think of my absent darling, & of those happy days together—without something of *wistfullness* which I surely never felt in your *presence*. It is a wistfulness however all untouched by pain, for those sweet days are not gone to return no more. If I had reduced the feeling to words it would perhaps have been merely this, that life is short and youth still shorter and yet my love and I are spending a fair May morning apart,—indeed a whole month of such mornings. And, to be sure, one doesn't deserve any great commiseration whose *only* cause for sadness is so fanciful as that.

I havn't forgotten. Was interrupted here by the baby and have been busy with her ever since, until now, ten at night. She has had a little touch of colic today & has been very wakeful & fretful; and now that I am her only (regular) nurse, I have little time for anything else. Think I will have to give up writing anything much but health bulletins &c. for the present. As it is I can't keep my wits about me to know what I am saying amid such constant interruptions. I am sure the last few letters must have baffled you by reason of this incoherency.

I am sorry I could not "have out my say" today, darling, because I had much on my heart to write in answer to that *sweet sweet* letter received yesterday and because too this will probably reach you on my birthday. But even if I had the words—I have not the opportunity now to say what I would, for I really ought not to write at all at night. So, darling, I can only, in the shortest, simplest words, pledge you anew my love and fealty, my *whole self*, my *whole life*. The *last* birthday, however old and grey-haired it may find me, will find no change in that love—no *loss* even of it's poetry, but only the *gain* of innumerable sweet and precious memories of life together. Woodrow, my love, my pride, my joy, my dear husband *I love you* truly, deeply, tenderly, passionately, and I will love you so all the days of the years of my life. "And if God will, I shall but love thee better after death."

Your little wife   Eileen

I am *quite* well & the baby isn't *sick*, don't be at all anxious about her.

ALS (WC, NjP).

To Ellen Axson Wilson

My own, splendid little darling,   Bryn Mawr, May 14, '86.

I think that, if I could have an opportunity to continue our correspondence a few months longer than it is destined to last this time (which Heaven forbid!) I could learn enough of your sweet disposition to discover fully my duties as your correspondent! So "Fanny has been there ever since you came," has she, and has been 'making herself very disagreeable' on some points? And *I*, not knowing that you were able, even under such adverse circumstances, to declare yourself happy have been lapsing from my privilege, of writing you letters which would fill your days with sunshine, so far as I was able to illuminate them, and have been giving vent to my *distress* on certain points. What an exceedingly cheerful time you must have been having: that sharp, reasonless tongue at one ear and my distresses at the other. Forgive me this time, my precious little heroine, and I'll never do so again! And *your* letters, all the while, as bright and delightful as possible— only 'business,' prosaic settlement of plans, bringing out the truth of your situation! Oh! my brave, splendid darling! 'You're a brick!' that's the long and short of it—and, with me, that expression means *everything* in such a connection. I hope, for my sake and for hers, as well as (most of all) for yours, Fannie will not be in Gainesville when *I* come. The idea of her having been hateful to you (kissing our baby—*my* baby—too, the while, of course!) will make me likely to say something to her more conclusive of all intercourse than anything she ever heard before that was at the same time not at all insulting. Oh, my sweetheart, I'm *so* sorry! Oh that I could always be by to defend you, with a tongue that I'm glad to make *ruthless* in the defence of those I love!

But hurrah! it's less than a month now—it's just four weeks from to-morrow (your birth-day) before the night train lets me out (Providence permitting) at Gainesville, to take my wife and baby in my arms, and forget that anything ever went wrong with me! The examinations for entrance in history are set for the morning of June 12, from 9 to 11. I will have my trunk packed before they begin, will look over the papers that day (if there be a hundred of them!) and will be off that very night. It's just as well that my appointments keep me here so late. I shall need that much time to pack things here after getting through at Baltimore.

And then, sweetheart, we will carry out the program you propose. We will spend a few days in Rome, a few days in Nashville, and then be off for home, to love each other, to be loved by those we love, to watch our darling grow, to work together, to play together, to make up in a thousand ways for these two months of dreadful separation: to be *married* once more in heart and life! Oh think of it, sweetheart!

Kisses such as only *you* know how to deliver for our sweet one. A kiss for little sister; love to Ed., aunt Lou, and all *but Fannie*.

Your own   Woodrow.

Sweetheart, you *must* have a nurse, if there's one to be had. Keep Mrs. S. until the 26th if you can.

ALS (WC, NjP)

From Melville R. Hopewell

Dear Sir   Tekamah, Neb., May 14 1886

Herewith find	Dft	11.90
	ex	.10
	our fees	2.00
	Total	14.00

for lease of grass for 86, on E½ SW1/4 10-21-11-E- to J. M. Gorey.

In answer to your question as to whether Grazing benefits land or otherwise, will say, that if the land is fed over by a very large number of cattle, they will eventually tramp out & kill the grass, and weeds will come up instead. This to a certain extent is already true of the land in 4 & 9. It is impossible to keep stock from grazing on this land & in my opinion it is better to sell the exclusive privilege when it can be done.

Yours Truly,   M. R. Hopewell

ALS (WP, DLC) with WWhw notation on env.: "Ans."

From Ellen Axson Wilson

My own darling,   Gainsville May 14/86

I must try to write you before dinner today (though it is almost dinner-time now,) for I find that there is no chance at all afterwards now that baby has given up sleeping in the afternoon. She slept well last night and has been *so* sweet this morning,—smiling at us all in the most delightful fashion. I am perfectly well too, a little languid and "tired" perhaps by reason of the intense heat, but so is everyone else. The hot spell overtook us so suddenly that *no* one can help feeling rather collapsed.

Alas, alas, a great misfortune has befallen me! I am in a state of perfect despair! "For why?" I have "nothing to wear[.]" I have just been trying on my dresses and not one of them will meet across the bust by several inches!—and no seams to speak of! Isn't it *dreadful*? I am at my wit's end just now, though I suppose that when I bring my *whole* mind to bear upon it I will eventually find some way out of the dilemma, but am afraid they will always have a cobbled up appearance. Truly, a woman's figure is subject to many up and downs.

I had a nice letter from Sister Marion yesterday which I will enclose for your pleasure; indeed I may as well send *both* of her letters,[1]–they are always so charming. She seems rather congratulatory than not over baby's sex; does she not? I fancy a good many parents would echo her sentiments with regard to girls being more "comfortable" than boys. Who is it who says that "we like girls for what they *are* and boys for what they *promise* to be"? Though I pronounce that a base slander, and I have seen a good deal of boys.

We heard from Mrs. Shepherd last night; her grandfather died yesterday morning & she says she will come back tomorrow if we wish. Aunt Lou thinks I had better keep her another week if possible, as she doesn't consider me strong enough yet to nurse the baby all day. We tried to get a cheaper nurse but couldn't succeed. But I had rather have Mrs. S. one more week for her (Auntie's) sake,–to save her loss of sleep. She isn't strong enough to stand it, but she *won't* consent to my taking entire charge of baby at night yet.

When have you seen Uncle Tom? Auntie got a note from him the other day asking how I was. Do you go in on Sunday or how do you spend the day? And how are your lectures & other work going on? What are you doing in *particular*? It seems so strange now, darling, only to know only in a *general* way what your occupations are. Knowledge of your work in it's every detail, thought about it, intense interest in every step of it's progress, has grown to be so large a part of my life. You don't know how I miss it darling. Yes, it *is* well that baby came when she did for my substitute for that occupation is to *study* her, to watch for every faintest sign of growth & development, to note the subtle change that each day makes.

But I have scarcely left room to say I love you Woodrow, my darling. I am with *all my heart*   Your own   Eileen

ALS (WC, NjP).
1 Both enclosures are missing.

To Ellen Axson Wilson

My own peerless little wife,   Bryn Mawr, 15 May, 1886.

It would seem, from the sweet, sweet letter I received yesterday from my darling, that the letter I intended to write to-day was written last Sunday: for that letter has moved my little wife just as I would have this one move her, by the truth and power of its love. Since I know that our hearts are *one*, I can't wonder, sweetheart, that that letter brought happy tears to your eyes: it brought them to *mine* as I wrote and as I read it—just because every word was sober, earnest, sweetest truth.

But, after all, though I have the same things to say over again to-day, you have said that you can never hear them too often, and I have, perhaps, some new thoughts to add to-day. I can't think about to-day without contrasting it with your *last* birthday and wondering, with wonder and joy unspeakable, at the changes that have been wrought in your life—and wrought *through me*. *There's* the new point of view. Last Sunday's letter was, in a certain sense, selfish: its thought was all of what *I* had won; the irresistible thought of to-day is of *your* part in the contract—of what you may have won or lost. Your birth-days all of them bring substantially the same message to me: I don't know it for the first time, I am only surer than ever, that you *could not* have been born any other time but in the heart of May, when the year is full of its sweetest promise. When you were born, darling, a spring-time was prepared for my heart which should set in so soon as you should begin to love me, and should last so long as your love for me should last. Just to think, sweetheart, that I have never yet been with you on your birth-day, and that on this one of all others I can't be with you to tell you what I feel—telling it in that position which we have devised for the telling of sweet secrets! But there *is* the advantage, which you have discovered so sweetly, in "writing it all" in that calm deliberation which deprives it of all touch of mere impulse. Take, then, last Sunday's letter as part of this, my sweetheart, and listen to what I have to say about you in a slightly different aspect: It would be hard to conceive of a greater change than has taken place in your life since last May. Then you were absolutely free, in everything but heart—with your own living to make, it's true, but with a sure means of making it; now you are a wife with a dear baby in your arms, no longer free at all, but with your fortunes indissolubly bound up with the fortunes of a man with no *sure* means of bettering his narrow circumstances! Yes, I know!—but I am purposely stating the mere worldly side of the matter, in order to point a moral—in order to weigh the compensations. I am responsible for all this, and the only compensation I have to offer is *my love*; you have accepted that love as an abundant return for what you have given me, because you have thought it the whole treasure of my heart; and my joy is in the knowledge that my love for you *is* perfect, *is* the whole treasure of my heart. I *know* that, if you can be satisfied by love, I can satisfy you! *That's* the thought that I would send you on this birth-day of yours, sweetheart, my little wife: *I love you.* I know now how truly I can say that I have found my way into your sweet, loving, glorious heart—and that I can satisfy that heart simply by following the strongest impulses and principles of my nature. Oh, how *supreme-ly happy* that knowledge makes me! If I can sit calmly down and, after a deliberate review of the blessed year that has passed, declare, with the whole truth of my life in the words, that my little wife has been everything to me that my heart desired, *how much more* can I say that I *love* that little wife! I love her with a passion of deep joy and devotion whose depths even I have never been able to sound. Ah, my queen, if such compensation can make you rich, you are richer than any woman that ever wore any *other* sort of crown. Do you remember, Miss, that you have sometimes declared my eyes beautiful, when they were full of love for you? (I can believe that they are beautiful then, if ever; for then they contain all that is purest and highest in my life!) Well, if you would imagine the crown which signifies you my queen, imagine a crown set richly with jewels of that lustre made *infinitely perfect.* And oh! my love for you has so many *sides*! It has its side of *pride,* which glories in your loveliness (you must let me use the words, darling, that express my thought—I want every part of it to go into words that can find words to go into.) It has its side of *ambition,* spurring me to prove myself worthy of you; its side of gaiety, replacing the old, sombre perseverance of my life with a joy and zest in living; its side of infinite tenderness which suffuses all my relations in this sweet wedded life with lights of the softest beauty; its side of strength and helpfulness turned towards every part of my life. Oh, the joy and the privilege of loving you, my Eileen! And you have brought me a little daughter, a precious baby, to give my heart a new experience in loving. As if it were not enough for me to love you, you give me someone compounded of our two selves to love—your own sweet image wrought over again for my delight. Oh, little lady, what a blessed day is this! How I thrive under its gifts! How I love my darling wife! I live, and rejoice, and hope because I am your husband,

Your own   Woodrow.

ALS (WC, NjP).

From Ellen Axson Wilson

Gainsville May 15/1886

Oh my darling, my dear husband, I am *so* sorry about the letter that has distressed you so!—and I only wanted to reassure you about the effects of my sickness! Yet I *did promise* to tell you everything, and I suppose I ought not to repent having kept a promise. On the whole, I don't approve of such promises; it is *dreadful* to have to tell you every little trifle when I am not with you to laugh you out of taking it too "tragically." Yet the letter has made me glad as well as sorry,—how can I help being glad at heart of such wonderful, over-whelming evidence of true, *perfect* love. Oh darling, I am the richest, happiest woman in the world to have such a lover,—such a husband!

Surely, no one was ever so loved before! Who else was ever ready to make such sacrifices merely to save his wife a little fatigue,—to avoid what most men would consider so entirely a matter of course and not worth a second thought! But you forget, sir, to enquire whether *I* am ready to make the same sacrifice, for the sake of a little rest and rosy cheeks! And I assure you I am *not* ready! Don't you suppose, sir, that I too have my heart set on a son "worthy of you and of our hopes"? and that "if (some) sleep were not necessary to keep me effective" for serving my husband and baby I should be more than willing to lose *all* mine in such a cause? What dreadful heresy is this about marriage! Fie, sir! you deserve a good scolding, but as you show some signs of repentance later on, I will be merciful and spare you. If I were too exquisite a creature to be a happy wife and mother I would have died in the budding beauty of young maiden-hood (!) and been laid away "under the violets," and had ever so much poetry written about me in the local papers explaining that I was too good and lovely for this world! But you see I missed the chance for that sort of apotheosis;—and I am sure my own husband at least might pay me the compliment of considering me too ex-quisite a creature to be a "horrid old maid"!

I assure you, darling, the case isn't half as bad as your anxious love makes you think. I will *soon* grow accustomed to it; I don't mind it now nearly as much as I did. And I will soon learn the mother's habit (which Mama had to perfection,) of making the most of every available moment, dropping to sleep just when I will and at a moment's notice. Now, of course, the frequent inter-ruptions sometimes make me wakeful and so I lose valuable time. Then when baby gets older I may be able to train her;—and if I can't I shall make a conscientious effort to "make up" the time somehow or other;—to secure at least seven hours in the twenty-four. For instance last night baby, after being awake all the afternoon, "dropped off" at tea-time; so as I knew she would sleep all the evening and be wakeful at night, I followed her lead and went to bed too at eight o'clock. So you see, though she was awake from ten to one and then roused at half past five "for good," I still *almost* secured my seven hours. And I can afford to sacrifice my evenings for a while in the good cause. Oh I assure you, I hav'nt the slightest idea of losing my health and strength, and if I lose a little *good looks* that doesn't make any difference —or *hardly any* (!) to me, provided *somebody* will promise to love me, in spite of it just as much as ever! No, darling, my health is more precious to me than ever it was before because I perceive that unless I am well and strong my child cannot thrive nor my husband be happy.

> "If I be dear to someone else
> Then I should be to myself more dear.
> Shall I not take care of all that I think,
> Yea, even of wretched meat and drink,
> If I be dear,
> If I be dear to someone else?"[1]

Mrs Shepherd says I am the ["]sweetest patient she ever had," because I am so wonderfully *docile* you see. I do exactly as I am bid, even when it seems to me utterly unreasonable,—as for instance the order that I am not to put my foot out of doors until the baby is a month old because it involves my going down a *single step*! And I submit to all such things *consciously* for *you*, my darling;—because I don't know anything about what precautions *are* necessary and I don't want to run the *slightest* risk of giving you an invalid wife. In truth one could not be farther removed from invalidism! I am as sound as a nut; I doubt if any woman in civilized lands is better able, physically, to take upon herself the sweet cares of motherhood. If you expect to see hollow cheeks and prominent cheek-bones when you come you will be sadly disappointed; I am scarcely thinner than when we were married. And I think I am getting a little colour; I am very pale in the morning, but I believe I improve in looks as the days advances. *Well*! this *is* a long sermon, with a sorry text! But I wanted to *exhaust* this subject, and have done with it once for all. And now "time's up" & I *must* stop. Darling, I *wish* I could show you all that is in my heart this bright birth-day. *Oh, I am so glad I was born.* If I were from the Orient I would wax eloquent in pouring forth blessings upon "the day I was born." I would produce a long poem on the subject full of startling and flowery imagery; and even then I could not unburden my heart of the joy and love with which it is overflowing today. Goodbye my love;

I am sorry that I must wait another year for my first birth-day kiss—but never mind! June kisses are just as sweet.

Your own little wife   Eileen

ALS (WC, NjP).

[1] From Tennyson's "Maud."

To Ellen Axson Wilson

My own precious little wife,   Bryn Mawr, 16 May, '86.

Our little daughter is one month old to-day. Just to think of it! What a luckless chap I am to be condemned to be a father two months and not see my child! I've often imagined, in reading of cases, in stories, of fathers who had children they had never seen, how they must feel: now I *know*. But I don't mean to complain. I am so blessed beyond all my fellows in everything else that concerns my little family, that I certainly have no right to a single word of complaint. But, darling, there is one thing I must insist upon: *you must have a nurse. Why* are you baby's "only (regular) nurse"? Are you waiting for Mrs. Shepard to return, or have you too little money? I can send you more money, if necessary: for you must have a nurse, to relieve you at least of the drudgery of nursing, if you can get anybody at all tolerable. You can surely have a girl to wait on you, even if you can't get, for so short a service, a woman of some experience. Offer good wages, the best or more than the best, and surely you can get what service you need. Of course I don't want you to give the baby over to the care of anybody—I shall never want you to do that—but I do want you to have, I do insist upon your having, regular and constant help in nursing.

How earnestly I did wish, my darling, that you were with me to share my pleasure at the Greek play last Friday night! You remember—don't you—that there was to be such a play, given by the students of the University of Pa.? Well, it came off on Friday night, with wonderful, I might, perhaps, say, with *perfect*, success. It was a comedy by Aristophanes, 'The Acharnians.' One of the *Nations* I sent you the other day contained an excellent analysis and description of it.[1] I read that, and then heard Dr. Shorey[2] translate it (excellently well, too) to his classes. I had, besides, the use of a libretto containing both the original and a translation at the play (it sounded very odd, by-the-way, as you may imagine, to hear the boys in the lobby crying out 'Book of the play: words both in *Greek* and English'!) so that I followed the performance very easily and pleasantly. And I enjoyed it immensely. I can now *imagine* that part of a Greek festival: for these fellows really did it all *very* well, and the play was mounted splendidly. About twenty or thirty were there from Bryn Mawr—in excellent seats in the very centre of the pit. I imagine that the audience—which was immense—was the most distinguished that Phila. ever saw. There were prominent scholars from all directions: Boston, New York, Baltimore:—a congregation of 'all the talents.' But, oh, the *solemnity* of that audience, in the presence of a 'roaring farce'! I never saw such a sober, hard-worked looking crowd; and I never heard applause break out with such manifest relief at anything whose meaning was evident to the *eye*, or at the end of the fine choruses. It was all a delicious study. And yet I believe that most of the audience were really interested. After all, there were very few *scholars* present who could follow the Greek without a libretto—to whom the *spoken* language was like their old friends, the words in their books. The scholars themselves did not seem to find many of Aristophanes' jokes very laughable. Certainly I was as solemn as anybody:—but I had a good time all the same.

Do you know, Miss, that it's church time, and that I'm writing to you instead of going to church! But don't think that I've turned heathen. My Sunday programme has been this, ever since I got back from Boston. I spend the morning writing. At 2:44 I go into town, walk down to the Post Office to mail my letter (for it would not get off in time for its usual train if mailed *here* on Sunday) and then go to four o'clock service at Chambers' Church,[3] going home with uncle Tom and aunt Sadie afterwards and coming out home on the last train in the evening, the 10:15. The last two Sundays, Ed. Cooper, aunt Sadie's brother, has been there. A very clever, well-read, loud-laughing fellow he is! He is so intensely Southern in every respect that I conceived at once a distinct liking for him—and yet his very *Southernness* has given me rather mixed feelings in his presence. Why do I notice it—why does some of it grate on my sensibilities—why does it seem to me so much like a reminiscence, if it be not because I have myself become *Northernized*? I don't want to believe that—the only remarks of yours that have ever hurt me have been those in which you suggested that you believed that—and I don't believe it. It's not what is Southern, but what is *provincial,* in Ed. Cooper that I now find myself unable to sympathize with. His *Southern* traits move me strangely. They almost bring wistful *tears* to my eyes. Darling, *I love the South*—don't you believe that I do?

And, oh, I long unspeakably to be in a certain part of the South just now! The longing grows upon me day by day: till I'm almost ready *to run away* and go where my heart is! Oh, my little wife, and my sweet, cherub baby! It wont be always that I'm separated from you. I'm coming *soon*, in less than four weeks, and *wont* I make up for lost time then—wont I be the happiest man in all Christendom!

Love to all.   Your own   Woodrow.

ALS (WC, NjP).
  [1] It was the New York *Nation*, XLII (May 6, 1886), with the account, "The Acharnians," on pp. 379-81.
  [2] Paul Shorey, then Associate in Greek and Latin at Bryn Mawr.
  [3] Chambers Presbyterian Church, of which Hoyt was pastor.

Two Letters from Ellen Axson Wilson

My own darling Woodrow   Gainsville, May 16/86

I am so very, *very* much obliged to you for the *beautiful* gift received last night. It is *so* lovely! You evidently haven't forgotten my "penchant" for crimson plush,—but then when did you ever forget *anything* that would contribute to my pleasure,—you *darling*! I certainly never expected to possess anything so sumptuous in the way of a work-box; it is almost too beautiful to soil with use. It nearly took my breath away when I opened the box last night. I feared I I [*sic*] should have to wait for it 'till Monday; but at tea-time it occurred to me to ask Uncle Warren if they delivered express packages here. He said "no," & asked if I was expecting one. And then, without my know[l]edge, the good soul went down and brought it to me, after I had gone to bed.

This is a *very* interesting piece of news in yesterday's letter. It is an excellent idea and I trust it will result profitably and pleasantly for you. I should be so glad if you could find a literary friend just to your mind, and I have been delighted that you had the opportunity to make and cultivate so pleasant and congenial an acquaintance as Mr. Scudder. So I wish the letter all success. Did you "send me enough money" indeed! You sent me a great deal more than enough, dearest, as I before complained to you. I have paid Mrs. Shepherd up to last Tuesday $19.25, and except the wash-woman there has been little other expense so far, only small "incidentals." Mrs. S's charge was $1.00 for the first ten days, 75 cts for the next week, & 60 ct for succeeding weeks. I am glad to learn from Aunt Lou that the doctor's charge is, she thinks, not more than $10.00 or $15.00.

There is some prospect that I may get "Aunt Olly" after all. I will know this week. I should be "set up" from all accounts, if I succeed in securing her. Aunt Lou says she is in all respects the best and most desirable servant she ever saw.

Had a letter from Stockton last night,—full of the centennial and "Jeff.["] Davis and Gov. McDaniels daughter[1] (!) whom he had the pleasure of escorting to the reception. They have had a whole week of noise & excitement there. Stock's chief pleasure in it seemed to arise from the fact that his hero, Col. Olmstead, had the place of greatest honour.

By-the-way wasn't that a good phrase quoted from the Troy paper—"that Confederate *wake* down in Alabama"—it described the "occasion" so exactly.[2]

To my great disappointment Stock says he can't get off before I leave G. so I shall miss him altogether this summer. Isn't it *too bad*? I don't know when I am ever to see him again. But I am hurried today & must close now, sweetheart. The baby isn't quite well,—is very restless & needs me. Don't be alarmed; it is a *very* slight trouble, she only needed, & has had, a little dose of oil.

Just think how old the little lady is growing—a month old to-day! Once more darling I thank you for the beautiful present, and once more let me tell you my dear, dear husband that I love with my heart of hearts. I love you just as much as you want me to.   Your little wife   Eileen

[1] Davis made two speeches in Savannah on May 6, and during the evening of that day he attended a banquet given in his honor by Governor Henry D. McDaniel. Davis was lionized as a hero in Savannah, as he had been in earlier appearances in Montgomery and Atlanta. See EAW to WW, May 4, 1886, n. 1, and Stockton Axson to EAW, May 8, 1886, ALS (WP, DLC).
[2] From the Troy, N.Y., *Telegram*, quoted in *Public Opinion*, 1 (May 8, 1886), 66. Wilson had enclosed a portion of this copy of *Public Opinion* in his letter to EAW of May 9, 1886.

My own darling,   Gainsville, May 17/86

So the 13th of June is to be the day of days! Oh dear! how far away that seems! Still it is a comfort to have the day appointed, to know definitely how large a stock of patience I must lay in. And I will try and be good & not murmur because it is three or four days longer than I *hoped*, for after all I knew I couldn't *count* on your getting off by the 8th or 9th. I wish this four weeks were as short as the last four weeks before I left Bryn Mawr. But alas, it isn't for parted lovers that "time gallops withal." What *shall* I do to hasten those lagging footsteps! I should almost like to fall asleep and wake only on the morning of the 13th of June. But then,

"in a wakeful doze I'd sorrow,
For the hand, the lips, the eyes,
For the meeting of the morrow,—
The delight of happy laughter,
The delight of low replies."[1]

And after all, it is foolish and weak to frame such wishes even as a passing thought. I have'nt forgotten and I won't forget the nobler ways in which, as our favourite love-poem tells us, we may—

"charm the interval that lowers
Between this time and that sweet day of grace"[2]

And so your first trip to Baltimore is to be this Sat.! How are you feeling about it now? I hope you are not dreading it any more than you did; and I *do so* hope it won't be very disagreeable or wearing to you. *How* glad I will be when it is all over and off your mind forever. My love and best wishes attend you my darling on the journey.

You must not imagine, sweet-heart, that there was anything in my "situation" as affected by poor Fannie that even *threatened* my happiness for a moment. Oh no, my peace of mind isn't to be disturbed by such things as *that*. It all went in at one ear and out at the other, and it's power to annoy me lasted no longer. But if you don't speedily take back some things in this letter I *will* be *distressed* in good earnest, and I won't scruple to tell you so, sir! I mean all that about telling me your "distresses," your regret at having done so and your promise not to do it again. How *dare* you say such things to me sir, after all your remarks of late about it's being my duty to tell you every thing,—to reveal my very moods! Surely, I need not enlarge on this point; it is only necessary to recall your own letters to your mind to convict you of your inconsistency—nay, of your heinous transgression,—and to bring you to the proper state of mind, viz., that of deepest contrition. Really darling, I shall be more unhappy than I can say if you keep your troubles and cares—or "moods"—from me. And *you have been doing it*;—confess now. I have been suspecting you; for I know that with those examinations impending, the trying work that they involve, the hard class work of this last term, the lonliness (what conceit! I hear you murmur) the spring weather,—say—&c. &c. you *hav'nt* always felt as bright as these sweet letters would make me believe. Now, will you promise faithfully to do better in the future? As for the distresses that you *did* mention,—they all con-

cerned *me*, and as I told you before they made me very very sorry
—and no less happy. I would not have you distressed for such
causes, darling, but since you were I would not for a great deal
have missed knowing it. It afforded me such sweet precious wonderful proof of your love. It left my heart full almost to bursting
with the joy & the wonder of it. Oh Woodrow, my darling, my
husband I love you *I love you*. God grant I may be worthy of you,—
may bring you happiness as deep and full and perfect as that I
owe to you!   Your little wife   Eileen

To think I should forget to say how baby is today! But that is the
strongest evidence that she is much better,—*well*, in fact.

ALS (WC, NjP).
  ¹ From Tennyson's "Maud."
  ² From Frances Anne Kemble's "Absence."

To Ellen Axson Wilson

My own darling,   Bryn Mawr, 17 May, 1886.
    I can't tell you how distressed I am by this continued news of
no nurse. You must have one, if a *decent* one is to be obtained for
love or money. I am terribly in earnest about this matter, sweetheart, and if you don't heed what I say, it will be infinitely the
worse for—*me*! If you want to help me, you must have a nurse.
The idea!—doing without a nurse within the first month! Of course
you are not strong enough! It's little less than suicidal. Get a helpful nurse *at any price*, if one can be *had* at any price—even if you
have to send to Atlanta and pay twice as much as you pay Mrs.
Shepard—I will send money enough. For *pity's* [sake] do this, darling, if from no other motive! I can't stand this anxiety—it will
make me ill! Don't think that I'm uttering a syllable of blame, my
precious one: I know that you've tried to get a nurse "cheaper
than Mrs. S."—but that wont do. *Get any you can.*
    Poor little girl: that *is* a quandary about your dresses not fitting
your new figure. If you need any additional material, darling,
send me samples, if possible, and I will try to match them in
Phila. Cant you get some one to do your sewing for you? I dread
your doing that sort of work *now*. You have but just emerged
from the *most* dangerous period, and any imprudence now will
be just so much contributed to your—and, perhaps even more to
my—future misery.
    Will you think this an *outrageously* quarrelsome letter if I add
to the passage at its opening that I have a 'crow to pick' with you
(you know my scoldings are plays which always have love for

their motive and kisses for their plot.) Please ma'am don't enclose *anybody's* letters in yours. Send them separately, if you will, but don't enclose them—to think that I have a *long* letter from my queen, and then to find that the bulk of the envelope is made up by—*any*body else's words, involves a disappointment too keen to be thrust gratuitously upon any fellow not a criminal. My love for you is my absorbing passion—I open each of your letters with an eager heart-hunger which no number of written messages can *satisfy*, but which every word of yours helps to assuage. Every sweet cadence of love in these precious letters of yours—and my heart can often detect such cadences even in passages which are not formally love passages—is just so much added to my present power to live, to bear up against my present loneliness. Oh, if you could but see my heart, my Eileen, and *see* how I love you, you could understand the passionateness of my feelings as to everything wh. concerns you or my sweet baby. My love, my sweetheart, my wife, my queen, my Eileen, my *all*!! I love you, oh, I *love* you with every power of my nature. For me life is to be

Your own Woodrow.

Love to all. Dear Aunt Lou! How I love her for her goodness to you!

ALS (WC, NjP).

From Ellen Axson Wilson

Gainsville May 18/86

How can I thank you my darling for the sweet, sweet birthday letter, the delightful continuation of last Sunday's precious message of love! Never, I am sure, were such love-letters as yours! Why can't I too write such? Why can't I find words that will really express my ideas and unburden my heart? I think it must be because you are a *genius*. Keats' love-letters are sweeter than a common mortals though the latter may be as deeply in love! But don't forget, dear, that though I can't put as much *in* my letters as you, there is quite as much *behind* them. I have as great a *genius* for *loving* as you though I havn't your genius for *expression*. What would I not give for the power to tell you what *I* think of the changes which this year has wrought for me through *you*! But at the very thought of it such a flood of joy and love, of wonder, and gratitude—to *you* and to the Giver of all good—comes surging over me that that [*sic*] there seems left me no power of speech. "Silence is the perfectest herald of joy; I were but little happy if I could say how much[.]" A glorified saint, darling, could as easily

measure her gain in leaving her low estate as I could measure the
joy which this year—which your love—has brought to me.

Yes, it would be hard to conceive of a greater change than that
which has taken place for me since last May; and yet let me try
to do it,—let me imagine myself placed just as I was last May
only without your love and its sweet attendant hopes, let me
think of myself as indeed "free" (!) in heart as well as in hand.
My heart stands still at thought of its own wretchedness and desolation in such case; and yet, darling, that is the *real* measure of
my gain. It is from *that* I was saved by you;—and not even you, no
one but a true *woman* can know how unspeakably sad, and empty,
and dreary such a life would have been, however fair a face it
might have presented to the world. Thank God you saved me
from even a *taste* of it. I have not to *recall* but only to *imagine* it;
—for when the old life with it's sweet natural ties of love and duty
was slipping away, the new life had *already* begun. The great
heart and the strong hand were already beneath me to support
me through all the storm and stress of life. Oh, love, would that
I could tell you all that you have been and are to me! *Can* you
think there is any question of weighing *gain* against *loss*? Don't
you *know* that it has been all, *all* gain for me? I wish there *had*
been sacrifices for me to make—great and terrible ones, that I
might prove by such means how I prize your love. But there is no
sacrifice *possible* because you give me with *yourself everything*.
You satisfy every possible need of my nature; my heart and mind
are both filled. You have given me someone—the *right* one—to love
and trust and believe in perfectly, to look up to and honour entirely. You have given me the numberless sweet joys that come
from daily intercourse in the perfect intimacy of love with an
entirely congenial nature, a nature with which I feel that I am in
every thought and feeling and desire *one*, which I can follow in
every mood, grave and gay, with a sympathy which it is always a
delight to me to give because it is always natural, spontaneous,
not to be with-held. And then, darling, how you satisfy *my* pride
and ambition. You don't know how I *glory* in your splendid gifts,
your noble, beautiful character, that rare charm of manner and
"presence,"—indeed *every*thing about you. And as for ambitions,—
mine are destined to be much more fully satisfied than ever yours
will be, because, you see, *I* am so fully satisfied with what you do,
while I suppose it is the nature of things that you never will be.
By the same rule how much greater is my delight in your triumphs
than it could ever have been in any little success of my own. Oh,
it is a great thing to be the wife of such a man! How much greater

to become one with him and follow him in his noble progress than to move on and on in one's own little narrow orbit!—for with the enlargement of that orbit the universe itself seems somehow to grow greater, and life to be infinitely grander and more precious and better worth the living. Ah, darling, I am indeed a *queen*, crowned by a true king among men! And I hav'nt mentioned the last great gain—the *baby*—which I owe to you, which sweeter still, we owe to each other. What a wonderful unexplored country of delight is that into which she is leading us together. Thank God that this best of birthdays finds me a happy wife with a dear baby in my arms[.] Always & altogether,

Your own little Eileen

ALS (WC, NjP).

To Ellen Axson Wilson

Bryn Mawr, 18 May, 1886.

My own precious, delightful little wife,

If I were not compelled by nature and by force of love to be absolutely sincere in all that I say to you, I might be tempted to pretend all sorts of anxieties and resolves as to your health and welfare in the hope of drawing from you such replies as that received last night! One would think, in listening to the sweet eloquence of this precious letter, that you were not only just as well and 'spry' at the present moment, *the* month but barely over, as if you had never had a baby & had never gone through any of the fatigues and trials preparatory to having a baby—and that, more than that, you were eager to emulate cousin Hattie in your career as mother! You sweet, precious thing! All this delightful argument has proved to me—what I did not need proof of, but what I would like to hear proved *this* way a score of times over again—that you were *made* to be those greatest of womanly things, a wife and a mother; and I believe that it is true also that "no woman in civilized lands is better able, physically, to take upon herself the sweet cares of motherhood." But you dear, precious, loving darling! you don't suppose, do you, that I needed proof of your whole-hearted willingness to bear children to me? I've never had a moment's doubt about my little wife's *joy* in being everything that a wife should be. She's the most perfect little *woman* that ever man purified himself by loving. But I was thinking *altogether* of my responsibilities in the matter: and I confess I feel them very keenly, notwithstanding this wonderful, loving argument, which makes me love its writer, if possible, more than

ever! Oh, you dear, *dear* little wife! Was ever a man loved so perfectly, *so to his own mind*, as I am! This letter shall certainly be
put aside as one of *my* special treasures! Do you suppose, Miss,
that anything I might choose to do for you would be a *'sacrifice'*?
I thought that I had instructed you better in the use of words.
Nothing that I can legitimately feel that I am doing *for you* has
a single *symptom* of sacrifice in it! You need not suppose, my
queen, however flattering the thought may be, that I am capable
to making even the slightest sacrifice for you! Not a bit of it! Just
give me leave to think that what I am doing is for you—for *you*,
my lovely, peerless little darling—and I'm the happiest, most self-
indulged man in the world! My love for you is my *self*: when I
indulge it, I indulge myself! *Now*, I venture to claim that that is
as conclusive as anything in *your* letter. Bless your heart—you
don't know me yet!

Don't you *dare* to lose your good looks, Miss! Shall I assure you
that I'll love you all the same in any case? No, I won't: for you
know as well as I do, that I love your good looks only as open
proofs of your good *health: I love you*! Your letter has made me
so happy, sweetheart! Now I *know* what good care you are taking
of yourself, *for my sake*, you sweet thing. Kiss my baby ever so
many times. Kiss little sister, too. Love to Ed. and aunt Lou, and
all.   Your own   Woodrow.

I'm *so* glad you like the work-box, pet: and I *hope* you *can* get
"Aunt Olly"—that would complete my *satisfaction*.

ALS (WC, NjP).

From Ellen Axson Wilson

My own darling,   Gainsville May 19/86
My time has been so taken up today with the baby, people
"dropping in," &c. &c., that it is now almost night and I am afraid
I shall have to put you off with short measure. Somehow I have
very hard times trying to get my letters written. I can scarcely
write more than a few lines at a time, and of course hurriedly at
that, so that I scarcely know what I am saying. I hope when you
sit down to them, you arm yourself with "a great patience" and a
readiness to overlook *everything*. I thought I had long ago entirely
lost all sense of shame at the sort of epistles I send you, but I
confess I have again felt a touch of it over some of these disjointed, incoherent scrawls, which I am sure must violate every
rule of grammar and orthography to say nothing of the rare union
of other defects. If I could look them over I might make them a
little more *intelligible*, but *often* I havn't the time,—as was the

case yesterday:—indeed that document *barely* escaped *burning*—only I know you would rather have the most absurd hotch-potch than no word at all from us. But a truce to excuses,—I throw myself on your charity, which I know is able to cover a multitude of *my* sins.

I havn't forgotten the sketch of the baby, darling; I have been intending to do it every day for some time; and will just as soon as I can.

As for the *other* request, for the pen-picture of the wife you *ought* to have had—I must beg off from that for the present. I havn't the time for such an undertaking now. It needs to be meditated upon longer beforehand. Besides, I think *you* could paint it better than I; for she should be *your* ideal of a perfect woman—not *mine*. Though to be sure I have some qualifications for the task, since our ideals are rather apt to be the same, and I am sufficiently intimate with you to know something of your tastes. Still I must postpone this important subject for a more convenient season.

I mustn't forget to tell you what a pretty present baby had yesterday,—a beautiful crocheted sacque and the daintiest of little hoods, from Cousin Mamie McWhorter, Mama's dear friend at Athens. A sweet note too saying how glad she was I had named it for Mama. And I didn't even know she had heard I had a baby!

The *morning* train for some unknown reason, has not come in *yet*, and I am, of course, still waiting as patiently as may be for my letter. But the delightful one of yesterday came safely to hand. Am *so* glad you enjoyed the Greek so thoroughly, and that you spend your Sundays at Uncle T's. I was *hoping* that you did. I suppose this letter will reach Bryn Mawr just as you are leaving for Balt or perhaps after your departure. My love and best wishes go with you, my darling. My loving thoughts will attend you through it all. In fact *I myself* am going with you, for are not my heart & my thoughts the largest part of me. Sweet-heart, I love you, *I love you*, I am entirely *devoted to you*

Your own little wife   Eileen

ALS (WC, NjP).

To Ellen Axson Wilson

My own, peerless Eileen,   Bryn Mawr, 19 May, '86.

I have not been telling you the particulars of what I am doing nowadays because there are really no *particulars* to give. I finished *writing* my lectures last week and since Saturday, having at last manufactured a pause for the purpose, have been making hasty reviews of Eng. and American constitutional history. I am to be examined on those topics next Friday, the 21st. My examination in Political Economy will be postponed, if I wish (and I do) until the following Friday, the 28th, the oral following on the next day, the 29th. That will be a much more convenient distribution of the work than the one at first proposed. Next week, therefore, you may imagine my class reading their reports on Mommsen, and me reading Freeman's 'General Sketch' for the oral examination, and looking up 'points' here, there, and everywhere for Dr. Ely's tests.

I am *so* glad, my sweet little counsellor, that you approve my having written as I did to Mr. Scudder. I have received no answer as yet: he is either cogitating deeply on my project, or is going to take as sincere (which it certainly was) my request that he should feel in no way bound to reply, if he did not feel altogether inclined to give his opinion and advice. I am very curious—and a bit anxious—to see what he will say. The size of my *scheme* as compared with *my* apparent size will perhaps startle him as much as it would seem to have startled dear father—who, you remember, gave never a hint of *his* opinion about the matter, leaving my letter on the subject unanswered, and covering his retreat by a full opinion of commendation of the plan for the *text-book*. If my own father can have no opinion that he likes to express about the wisdom or folly of this proposed 'life-work,' what will poor Mr. Scudder do, or say? Somehow I have considerable confidence in my powers as regards this particular undertaking; but I can't a bit blame these gentlemen if they have *not*. It has occurred to me, 'Why did I ask advice seeing that I am determined to carry out my plans in any event?' The only answer I can give is, because I want counsel which will throw some light on the larger details of the vast subject. What does Mr. Scudder think of the *inside* of the scheme, so to speak?

But this is not what I intended to write about! I did not intend the love of this letter to be left *so long* to implication. I don't get half so much pleasure myself out of writing to my darling as I might, if I don't devote *most* of the space to making love to her. Wont you be afraid to see me (three weeks from next Saturday) since you must know that I'll be so hungry for the *full* privileges of love-making that I'll be ready to eat you up. Oh, how *infinitely* I love you, my queen, my little wife: and I love the baby too, a little!

Love to all.   Your own   Woodrow.

ALS (WC, NjP).

From Melville R. Hopewell

Dear Sir   Tekamah, Neb., May 20 1886
I send you copy of suppleme[n]t of Weekly, Burtonian giving
notice of Fishcreek Ditch assessments for widening & deepening
Ditch. The same as now constructed not being suffic[ie]nt to carry
off the water.

You will notice such of your lands as are included in the notice.
I cannot advise you now as to whether, in my opinion, your land
will be benefitted to the amount of the assessment. The Enjineer
and Commissioners evidently think it will. If you have any suggestions to make or wish to contest the assessments, we will carry
out your wishes as well as we can.

Yours &c   M. R. Hopewell

ALS (WP, DLC) with WWhw notation on env.: "Ans. May 24/86."

To Ellen Axson Wilson

My own precious little wife,   Bryn Mawr, 20 May, '86.
And so you suspect me of concealing my moods, do you, and
would have me make a clean breast of it in confession? Well,
I *can't* confess: for the simple reason that I can say neither 'yes'
nor 'no' to the impeachment. Of course this time of separation
from my darling—from all that I live for or joy in—has for me
been full of the keenest heart pains and the blankest, dreariest
loneliness that a man could possibly suffer in the presence of
hope, and I have constantly to fight against heart-breaking moods.
But, my precious one, I could not put such moods into my letters
to you, for they *disappear*, through the subtle agency of some
sweet influence, when I sit down to write to you. *Then* my love
transforms my spirits. My pains are cured even by *this* communion with you. While I am speaking to *you* I am filled with a
glow of love and happiness which enables me to rise from my
writing a happier, better man for the rest of the day! Oh, sweetheart, you don't know how I love you: I *can't* carry a downhearted
mood far into a letter to you. The only unjoyous thing that can
find place there is my passionate anxiety about you and baby.
And, besides, little lady, I don't *give way* to my distress at any
time. I can say for myself that I am too much of a man for that.
I have to struggle against it *all the time*, but that prevents its taking me off my guard. I yield much more readily to the transient
'blues' that come upon me when you are by (selfish fellow that
I am!): the remedy is so infinitely sweet!

See the delightful conclusion of the matter, then! You exercise that sweetest function of comfort even at this distance. I have but to come to you *there* to remove even the *strain* of threatened low spirits. Ah, my queen, next to your letter to me, I am dependent on my letters to you—you blessed little woman, you! You would not have me recount all my narrow escapes from breakdown of courage at a moment when the very act of writing to you is freshening my courage for the next twenty-four hours, and so, by dwelling on my distresses, cheat myself of the comfort of the letter? If I were, *per force*, to work the mood into my letter, against all the natural laws of the moment, I should do myself great harm—and should have to write another letter, later in the day, to work myself back into a normal condition.

Isn't that a triumphant defence? Every word of it is sincere and true. *I am concealing nothing.* I do find our separation terrible—and that constantly—but I do *not* give way *at any time* to actual low spirits; and one of my chief weapons of self-defence is my daily letter of love and *non-self* to you! When I come you shall have the full pathology of the case—then I can analyze it in perfect safety—in your arms. I dare not dwell upon it now, and I do not—and am happy, in consequence! I turn to my love for you for rest and strength and courage—and I never fail to find them there. You may be sure that the mood you find in my letters is the predominant mood of my life—that *you are in these dreary days to make them tolerable*, in view of their speedy ending. Are you satisfied? I *have* made a clean breast of it—and the moral is, *love, love, love* for my darling, my queen, my Eileen, my peerless little wife! Oh, sweetheart, sweetheart, *you are my life*! and I am *altogether*   Your own   Woodrow
Witness how my spirits have risen in the composition of this letter!

P.S. I go to Balto. at 4:02 this afternoon. I will write from there after my examination in History to-morrow.

The enclosed scrap is from the Boston letter to the N. Y. *Evening Post* of Tuesday.[1]

Kisses uncounted for my blessed little daughter; kisses for Maggie; love for Eddie, aunt Lou, *and all.*

My heart is yours and *I* am   Yours   W.

ALS (WC, NjP).
[1] An announcement of Wilson's proposed textbook in government. It is printed in the Editorial Note, "Wilson's Plan for a Textbook in Civil Government."

From Ellen Axson Wilson

My own darling,   Gainsville, May 20/86

I hope you are not having as hard a time as I am, trying to "possess my soul in patience" during this cutting off of communication;—for I presume that dreadful "wash-out above Charlotte" is serving you just as it has me. No letter yesterday or today! If it is the same tomorrow I will be ready to tear my hair in desperation. Yet of course it is a comfort to know that it *is* a "wash-out,"—not to be panic-stricken about you,—and I must console myself with that thought. And I needed your letter more than usual today too, because I have "been and gone and made" myself miserable about the baby! To be sure there is *no* cause for *anxiety*, —so don't you *dare* to be anxious!—but I am too young a mother yet to take little things coolly, no matter how often I am told that "young babies *must* have little ailments now and then, it is *always* so." The trouble is costiveness; she has been so for more than a week now; we give her a dose of oil and think for a day that she is *well*, but as soon as the effect wears off the trouble returns. It makes her restless—rather colicy—in the afternoons and, worse still, seems to keep her from growing fast as she did at first. But Dr. Baily gave us some powders for her yesterday and I hope it will be all right in a day or so. It is really a *very slight* trouble, so *please* don't be worried. I *wish* I hadn't to trouble you when you are so far away with all these *little* things.

I wish you could see her now holding a "sugar-bag" in her mouth,—it looks so funny! We are trying to break her, with the aid of them, of nursing so long,—and she holds them in her own mouth as well as anybody could. Mrs S. says she never saw a young baby have "such good use of itself"; she can turn herself completely over, hold up her head like a soldier, and do just what she pleases with her hands;—most of them, you know, can't *begin* to find their own mouths. I wish you could have seen her the other day. They were giving her some "tea" and she seemed to enjoy it exceedingly; but every time they took the spoon away to replenish it she would yell,—evidently not understanding why it didn't flow in a continuous stream like her milk. At last she seemed to make up her mind that she had stood that nonsense long enough; so she deliberately seized the spoon with both hands and held it firmly to her mouth with a satisfied *grunt*, as if to say "*there! now*, I'd like to see you stop me until I get enough!" And I *assure* you we could scarcely get it away from her, she is so *remarkably* strong!

By the way, I didn't tell you that I had begun to cultivate her taste for *poetry*! But she doesn't seem to appreciate it much *yet*; she rudely interrupted me at the most thrilling passage with the information that she wanted something to eat! You see, I was looking over Wordsworth last Sunday and I came across a poem entitled "Address to my infant daughter on being reminded that she was a month old on that day,—Sept. 16." So I immediately proceeded to "address" her.

But it is almost night again and I must close at once, for I *must* write to Cousin Mamie before dark. My love, my joy, my pride, my own Woodrow, I *love you* with all my heart. I am always and altogether   Your own little wife   Eileen

ALS (WC, NjP).

To Ellen Axson Wilson

My own precious little wife,   Balto., May 21, 1886.

I have been so little my own master to-day that I will have to put you off with a wee note. I am through with my written examination in History, however, and passed rather more easily than I expected—though by no means brilliantly—about in accordance with the standard of five days' preparation. It's a great relief—my spirits are considerably easier. I have seen many friends; have been very cordially received; and *love you* oh, with all my heart. Hurrah for the finished examination! Love to all
                    Your own   Woodrow.
Two weeks and six days after you receive this you will be in my arms, darling—you and my precious baby!

ALS (WC, NjP).

From Ellen Axson Wilson

My own darling Woodrow,   Gainsville May 21/86.

No letter again today! Isn't it a *shame*? I am just as cross as I can be with those railroad people! How many days does it take people in N. Carolina to ride *ten miles*? What is to prevent their transferring the mail-bags,—hauling them across the washed out region? But I suppose I won't make anything by grumbling. I *wonder* if you are being served in the same way; fortunately you are to be in Balti. two days and of course expected to do without letters while there.

How I wonder what you are about just now!—if you are in the midst of your ordeal. Probably you have hardly begun yet. Poor boy! I am *so* sorry for you!—and *won't* I be glad when it is all over!

Baby had a good night and seems a great deal better today, though of course it is too soon yet to be sure. She has been sleeping peacefully most of the morning,—is out walking in the garden now. We have a small household today. Uncle Warren and Eddie went to the factory yesterday, to return tomorrow, & Aunt Lou and Maggie are dining with Loula. So I have just finished eating dinner in solitary state, the rest of the family—Charlie & Mrs. Shepherd—having eaten before, while I nursed the baby.

I wish you could have seen Maggie as she went away, she looks *so* pretty in her little hood & "Mother Hubbard." She is a *lovely* little thing,—so sweet and bright and "cute";—but unfortunately so *very* shy with strangers that it won't be possible for you to make her acquaintance during your short stay. It is only recently that I have been able to get anything out of her. She would come to me from the first, nestle up to me, stroke my hand and my hair in her pretty way, but not a word would she say. Yet she told Auntie, only two or three days after I came, that she loved me "better than *any*body." I must tell you about her prayer,—after "Our Father" & "Now I lay me," she always ends with a short prayer of her own,—"God bless me and make me a good girl, and bless my sister and brother. Amen." "*Which* brother and sister? Maggie" Auntie often asks her, and she always says "Sister Ellie-ooo and Ber Woorow"! "Very well; but now why don't you pray for your *other* brothers and sisters and your friends?" But she never will!

I had a nice letter from Sister Annie yesterday, from which I learn that Father is in Columbia.[1] She says Mother is far from strong. I *do hope* our being there—such a crowd (!) of us,—so long, won't wear on her—making her house-keeping labours heavier. Do you think there is any danger? Of course it will do her good in other respects. Sister A. says Father is very anxious to have us go, to cheer her up. That she hasn't been quite herself since the death of Uncle Thomas. Sister says nothing about Father's knee.[2] I was anxious to know Bro. George's verdict. Have you heard? Good-bye, my darling, my own true love. Oh, my dear husband, I love you *I love you* more than tongue can tell. My heart fairly *aches* to see you,—to be able once more to *tell* you that *I love you*.   Your little wife,   Eileen

ALS (WC, NjP)

[1] Annie Wilson Howe to EAW, May 17, 1886, ALS (WP, DLC).

[2] Dr. Wilson had stopped in Columbia on his way to General Assembly in Augusta in order to have his ailing knee treated by Dr. George Howe, Jr. See JWW to WW, March 11, 1886, and JWW to WW, Feb. 17, 1886, ALS (WP, DLC).

To Ellen Axson Wilson

My own sweet Eileen,   Balto., 22 May, 1886.

Here I am in the Balto. station waiting for my train. By an exceedingly original method of misreading my schedule, I concluded that my train, which leaves at little after *ten*, left a little after *nine*; so I have an hour to wait—and am comforting myself in the best manner possible, by writing to you. I am beyond measure impatient to get back *to your letters*; they make Bryn Mawr seem something like home—as much like home as possible under the circumstances.

Of course I'm very tired to-day. After writing all yesterday morning, and running about all the afternoon, I am entitled to feel a little dull now;—and one consequence is, of course, that I am not so well satisfied as I was yesterday even with the way I passed the examination paper. But, after all, I guess it's quite safe to say that I *got through*—and nothing but pride would demand more. For all my running around, I have not seen many people —not half so many as I wanted to see—not Hiram, for instance, though I saw the rest of the Woods family.

Oh, how full my thoughts are to-day, darling, of the fact that, God willing, I shall three weeks from to-day be well on my way towards t[w]o sweet ones—towards my home, close to your heart! When you receive this letter it will be but *two* weeks and five days —think of that, sweetheart! Isn't that glorious! Oh, how it will rest and *expand* me to take my little wife in my arms once more— and how strange and sweet the delight of seeing my precious *baby*! There is one *disadvantage* (!), Eileen, my queen, in the time's growing so short. While it was long I could hold my heart in strong repression; but now it beats so violently at the sweet thoughts that crowd in upon it that I can hardly hold it to its duty of steady, manly patience. Still there's a joy in this tumult of heart which I would not for the world exchange for the dull, resolute waiting of two or three weeks ago! My heart *must* have a *little* play, now that this sort of play is growing less and less dangerous very rapidly. I can indulge it now with a few dreams of how and what I shall do when I get to Gainesville, how I will deport (!) myself towards that lovely, peerless little wife of mine, who promises to be so glad to see me, and towards that so precious little daughter, who will not be a *bit* glad to see me, but whom I will *worship*—with as little awkwardness as possible! I suppose one need not mind being a *clumsy* father the *first time* he is a father; but you've had (you will have had) two months practice in being a *mother* and you must teach me how to behave. Ah, how I shall delight in practicing! My own, your own—*our* own—sweet baby; and *my* own matchless Eileen, my *glorious* little wife! I have such a new sensation when I travel nowadays, sweetheart. I am filled with the sweet wonder *of being dear to you*, of being followed everywhere by your loving, and as it were *guardian*, thoughts. It gives me a strange new *elation* and self-confidence. 'My darling *believes* in me heart and soul,' is my thought, 'and I must make the most of myself—the most of what is *good* in me—for her sake.' So *literally* is your love my strength and inspiration!

I wonder, darling, my little wife, if we can't manage *never* to separate again? Let's try with all our might—wont you? But *this* will soon be over! With examinations off my mind and my little *family* in my arms, what can ever damp my spirit, again!—Much love to all   Your own   Woodrow.

ALS (WC, NjP).

From Ellen Axson Wilson

My own darling husband,   Gainsville May 22/86

At last I am happy again,—my letters have come—three of them, the one that was properly due today being still missing. Oh *how* glad I was to get them and *how sweet* they are, and how I have pored over them reading and re-reading and reading again (as if I didn't *always* do that!) But really I was almost famished; I havn't been so long without hearing from you since—since when? —not since I was here last, at least. The very *scolding* of which you remember, sir[,] your Monday letter was full!—was honey-sweet to me. In fact, there was more than one reason why some of it was sweet. Of course it was *delicious* flattery to be told that you so greatly prefer *my* scrawls to Sister Marion's charming letters! *My darling!* I promise not to disappoint you again in that way, since it *is* a disappointment.

About the nurse question too I promise to do just as you say,— not to send to Atlanta &c. &c!, but to be sure and have *someone*. I still have Mrs. S. because after all you said I didn't (&, *don't!*) dare give her up until I found someone else, but it goes exceedingly against the grain to pay fifty cents a day so long. I *never* saw a place where it was so hard to find servants! Then Aunt Olly kept me waiting on her so long and losing time,—and I havn't got her after all. You see, I was about to engage her, in advance, when I first came, but her son was suddenly taken with fever in Atlanta and she had to go and nurse him; and I gave her up. Then her son died and she came back and sent me word that she would like to come when I was ready for her. But she did'nt make her appearance, and now she sends me word that she is very unwell & she is afraid her health won't allow her to take the place! So I am disappointed again; but I have heard of another that I hope I can get early next week.

Baby seems—and looks *much* better today; she had a splendid day yesterday but a very bad night;—today however she seems quite *well*;—it was simply colic last night.

I am glad your Balt. schedule is arranged so much more to your satisfaction. Hope you will spend your Saturdays and Sundays in Balt. for a change,—won't you? I had such an absurd dream about those examinations the other night; first we had a long talk about them before you started to Balt. Then the baby waked me,—and after I went to sleep I began again. You had come back from Balti. then and were telling me about it. (I was in Bryn Mawr.) I asked what the questions were, and you told me the first one was,—"What is the population of Cal. and what are it's principal products?" Then we had such a laugh over the absurdity of the question;—after which you told me to look in some book—the *geography* I suppose—and see if you had answered correctly. I proceeded to do so, and thus failed to learn the rest of the questions. A *great* pity! wasn't it? I might have sent you the whole list and then you could have made sure of the answers before you started!

By the way, all this reminds me of Mr. Shinn. I have been so occupied with other affairs that I havn't once thought of him before,—but it is odd—isn't it?—that he never wrote us a word about our *poem*. I dare say it wasn't "subtil" enough for the "Overland"![1]

Oh I have no doubt you will hear from Mr. Scudder in time: one naturally waits awhile—for reflection!—before replying to a letter that requires a *long* answer. And the *idea* of thinking that Father's silence on the subject was due to disapproval! I can't believe you *really* think so though. No, he is such a poor correspondent,—waits so long before answering a letter,—that when he did write, your letter was mislaid, other things engrossed his attention, and that subject was lost sight of—great as it is. He knows as well as I do how fully your powers are equal to the undertaking. I am so glad, though, that you are not going to let your own opinion on the subject, or your plans, be unduly influenced by anyone else. I'd like to see the subject that is bigger than *you*,— my *splendid* darling!

Oh! I forgot to say, as I *meant* to very *emphatically*, that I *don't* believe you have become "Northanized." *You* know—don't you darling?—that I didn't believe it when I said it, and that I wouldn't for the world have said it even in fun if I had thought it would hurt you. Of course you are not a "Southerner" either in the old sense; you are an American citizen—of Southern birth. I *do* believe you love the South, darling,—that she hasn't a truer son, that you will be, and are, an infinitely better, more helpful son to her than any of those who cling so desperately to the past and the old prejudices. I believe you are her *greatest* son in this generation and also the one who will have greatest claim on her gratitude. But you *are* free from "provincialisms" of *any* sort;—that expresses the whole state of the case. Oh, I am so glad you havn't any of those prejudices! What a clog they would be at once to your usefulness and your own success in life. I am glad to find since coming South that I have gotten rid of them to a greater extent than I thought. You know I am always trying to shake them off but I scarcely knew to what extent I had succeeded because of my occasional *relap[s]es!* For at the North, something *will* happen now and again to produce in me a strong revulsion of feeling. And of course those prejudices exist for me now—when they exist at all—altogether as *feelings,* not as *opinions.* Oh, dear, see how long I have rambled on & now I find but a corner left in which to tell you *I love you.* But then we have told each other that we can *find* the love all through our letters whatever the subject. You *must* find it in mine for it is the life and breath of every syllable. Darling I *do* love you with *my whole heart*

Your little wife   Eileen

ALS (WC, NjP).

  [1] It is missing from the Wilson papers and was evidently never published.

To Ellen Axson Wilson

My own precious little wife,   Bryn Mawr, 23 May '86.

  Please put '*via Philadelphia*' on your letters hereafter. I came back yesterday to experience the bitter disappointment of finding *no letter at all* from my darling, though two were overdue. During the day one came in from the *west,* from Harrisburg, just as I was about to go down to telegraph to know whether anything was the matter. The Post Office men at Gainesville must have suddenly lost their heads altogether: for the immediate predecessor of this much belated letter that came from the west has not put in its appearance at all, though it was due here on last Thursday; and the mail that usually brings your letters failed me again last night: so that the net result is one letter in four days! If that one stray letter had not come bearing post marks which suggested a possible explanation of the non-appearance of any others, I don't know what would have become of me in my disappointment and anxiety. Please ma'am, therefore, put 'via Philadelphia' as plainly as possible somewhere on the envelopes you send. After all this regularity of delivery, I can't imagine what can have gotten into the men at the Gainesville office to be so elaborately stupid!

I found myself excessively tired when I got back yesterday, and the warm weather which has just set in vigorously upon us here is not calculated to restore one's vigor very rapidly. But I am considerably rested this morning, after a thorough night's rest. I am still too tired to feel quite like going in to uncle Tom's this afternoon: but I may feel more like the trip when the time comes to take it; and there is always that great argument for it, that it is only by going into town that I can get your letter off at the usual time.

I am very sorry that the conditions of your life just now are such as this last letter depicts them. If you are so taken up with the baby and with 'droppers-in' that you cannot find time to write even a few lines without interruption, it is evident that your days supply you with absolutely no chance to rest, and that the scant allowance you get at night is *all* that you get. If I find you altogether broken down when I come, I shall be broken hearted but not a bit surprised. Poor little girl! I wish I knew how to go off somewhere and have a good *cry*! I *beg*, sweetheart, that you will not *try* to write letters to me under such circumstances. I shall not enjoy them when I know that they are just so much added to your worries & so much subtracted from your strength. Get some postal cards, and either fill them out with a brief health bulletin every day, or get someone ('poor Fannie,' perhaps?) to fill them out for you. I will not consent to have you 'going' all day. If you have time for a letter, *take it all for rest*—and be quite sure that in doing so you are giving me the most acceptable service of your love. The best thing you can do for me is to take care of yourself. And remember that Clarksville is a *very* hot place. You will need all the strength you can get to stand the summer there. I don't know that we *can* stay there the whole season through. Perhaps neither you nor the baby can stand it. I imagine that the climate is not unlike that of Rome. Please tell me in every bulletin how you feel, *and how you look*. Have you a nurse yet to succeed Mrs. Shepard, or is she with you still?

As I went over the route between Phila. and Baltimore Thursday afternoon and yesterday morning, darling, I had such sad and yet sweet reminiscences of our little journey to Washington together that sad, sad Wednesday night. As the train sped on and on my thoughts went as fast through all the experiences of that ride. It brought tears to my eyes to think of the depth of tears that was in my little wife's eyes that night, and my tears only came the stronger—though from a different source—as I thought of that sweet speech, that sweet, *sweet* speech, of my darling's, which so thrilled me with a strange sort of pathetic joy at the time, 'that, after long searching in vain, she had at last found something pleasant to think about, which was that I would love her as much while she was away as I did when I was by her side.' Oh, precious sweetheart, what a lovely, womanly, wifely thought that was as you brought it out, your sweet eyes brimming with a tender joy which carried exquisite comfort to my heart! Nobody but my Eileen could have said such a thing in such a way—*nobody* but my peerless little wife, whose subtle charms hurry my heart through a round of gladness, admiration, and love such as surely no other heart ever experienced before.

You dear, impracticable little woman! I sketch my ideal woman! Don't you see *why* the thing is impossible? It is impossible simply because, as I have found out by repeated experiments, I cannot make you comprehend *your own loveliness*. *You* are my ideal woman—protest as you may about what you don't understand, your own qualities. *I* am the *infallible* authority on this point, as you will readily understand. I know what I love; I know what qualities in those I love make me most happy; I know my heart-history; and, through this knowledge, I *know* that my Eileen is the ideal wife of my dreams. It is no longer an experiment: it is an *experience*, this married life of mine; and I know that the only dissatisfactions of my life now are rooted in *myself*, and in separation from you—that in you I *have* my heart's *whole wish*!

Kisses innumerable for baby: love for all.

Your own   Woodrow.

ALS (WC, NjP).

From Ellen Axson Wilson

My own darling,   Gainsville, May 23/86
    Those wicked, cruel railroad people have again kept my letters back! I have none today, and there should have been two. I believe they know how sweet and precious they are and are loth

to give them up. I can sympathize with those missionaries who for a year had been without letters from home, & when the mail-bags finally came the natives refused to give them up: for perceiving the great eagerness of the owners to get hold of them, they concluded that it was some rare delicacy for the table;—everything that was not good to *eat* being, in their estimation, good for nothing. So they proceed to boil and eat all of that precious freight before the very eyes of the tantalized English. However I have just had the wished-for opportunity to give one of the railroad men a piece of my mind, and of course I feel better for it. It was one of Uncle Warren's country cousins who dined with us. By the way, I am afraid he considers me a very gay and frivolous person, and I am sure there was nothing in my behaviour to warrent such an opinion. He offered me the [Atlanta] "Constitution" to read with the remark that he always like to see the Sunday paper, there was so much interesting *society* news in it! Now he greatly belies his appearance if the society columns are really his favourites, and I seriously suspect him of attempting to adapt his conversation to my capacity! However I was glad to get the paper for I am watching with some amused interest the terrible conflict that is now rending Georgia in twain viz. that between Gordon and Bacon.[1]

By the way, some of my friends need to be taken in training by you! Here is Janie Porter talking arrant "treason" a-pro-pos of the Jeff. Davis celebration, and Minnie mourning, lamenting and grumbling over the non-passage of the Blair bill,—"which would get them out of all their troubles." It seems the town is so impoverished by the flood, that it was obliged to close the schools a month sooner than usual.

Baby is *certainly* all right again. She looks better than she has done at all today; she had a splendid night and has been a perfect little cherub all day. She and I are having a nice quiet Sunday afternoon alone, Mrs. S having gone home and all the rest being asleep in their rooms. I am spending it very happily and peacefully looking at the baby and thinking about *you.* Oh darling, just to think that three weeks from today we will be *together!*—only two more Sundays apart! The time *is* passing, we *are* making progress. I begin to see daylight ahead, to *feel* that there will be an *end* by and by.

I wonder what we will be doing at this time three weeks from today. How my heart dances to think of it. I can scarcely keep my feet from dancing too. If I am so happy at the mere thought of my future happiness what *will* become of me when that future becomes the present! Oh darling, *my* darling *I love you*, you are my joy, my pride my life—*everything* to me

Your own little wife   Eileen

ALS (WC, NjP).

¹ General Gordon and Augustus Octavius Bacon were rivals for the Democratic gubernatorial nomination in Georgia in 1886. There were numerous charges of corruption against Gordon, but he won the nomination in the state convention and went on to election. Bacon, a member of the Georgia legislature for a number of years, served in the United States Senate from 1894 until his death in 1914.

To Ellen Axson Wilson

My own precious little wife,   Bryn Mawr, 24 May '86.

You are in nothing more successful than in disproving your own ideas about yourself. The latest instance is this wonderful letter in answer to the one I wrote on your birth-day. You begin by deploring your inability to tell me how much you love me, and then immediately proceed to give to the loving thoughts of your heart what seems to me the most perfect expression that could be given to a woman's love. You may not have *my* "genius for expression," but you have your own, which is far better! Your letters are beginning to arrive again now, but with no sort of observance of the proper order of chronological succession. So far as the dates show, this very letter which seems to me such a *gem* of love-making is the one of which you said on the following day that it narrowly escaped burning! Oh, my queen, *don't* feel that way! If *this* letter is "incoherent," please be incoherent as often as you can after the same delightful fashion. If you make love this way when you are hurried, you can delight me out of all self-possession whenever you may choose to take your time to it. Why, my darling's heart comes out in this letter in a way that not all the art and "genius for expression" in the world could excel. It *is* my peerless little wife's *self*. I have read it and read it and read it again, have lingered over it and talked love to it as I would dwell upon and woo a perfect picture of you, if I had one! My precious, my *lovely* little wife! *Do* you love me so much! Oh, I love *you*, darling—and I shall strive more and more to make my whole life an *expression*, a more and more *perfect* expression, of my love. You shall receive over and over again the gift of my love, of myself, as if by a *new* consecration of my life to you—to your happiness! My pride, my Eileen—my precious, precious little wife! Please ma'am write me as many of these "inadequate," "incoherent" love-letters as you can! They give me new life; make me forget loneliness—everything but my unspeakable joy in you; fill me with *the glory of being your husband* (that's the only way I can express it!) till my heart is near to breaking with fulness of supreme happiness! My darling! If I have brought happiness to you, I am of all men most blessed!

And so it was "a wash-out above Charlotte," and not the stupidity of P. O. officials that has been disordering our correspondence —and I was too hasty as usual in my conclusions! Oh, I am *so* sorry that *you* had to suffer the same things that I did in consequence of the interruptions! My poor little sweetheart! And baby unwell too, the while! My heart overflows with sympathy and love, my precious! I *hope* all is well now. Kiss my sweet one ever so many times for me. Kiss little sister too, and give my love to Eddie, Aunt Lou, and all   Your own   Woodrow.

ALS (WC, NjP).

From Ellen Axson Wilson

My own darling,   Gainsville May 24/86
Hurrah for the finished examination, indeed! Accept my heartfelt congratulations, sir! I am *so* glad it is over; and so glad to think that in only four more days you will be through with examinations *forever*. I always had a perfect horror of them myself and my sympathy for you in these times of trial is proportionally deep. You have never said whether you were going to stay over Sunday in Balt., so that I could not locate you, in my mind, yesterday;—didnt know whether to think of you as singing hymns with the Woods or exercising your conversational powers with Aunt Sadie and her brother. Naughty boy! Don't you know I am never easy in mind unless I know where you are?—am so afflicted with jealous fears and suspicions (!) you see! I hope, and take for granted, that unless you were obliged to spend the Saturday in preparation for Dr. Ely and "the board" you staid over in Balt. You wrote me on Thursday the 20th; did you not? The letter is still missing,—I hope it isn't lost. The one due today of course hasn't come yet either. But I am so glad of the news in the note that *did* come that I will try and be content until tomorrow.

I have a nurse at last,—have just engaged her but she can't come 'till Monday. If nothing happens—and our neighbour seems to be holding out bravely—Mrs. S. will stay until Sat. morning. Oh, the *expense* of it!—all *your* fault, sir!—for I am so well now that I could have done without a nurse, this week, *easily*. The nurse is named Adaline. She lived with Aunt Lou for a long time as cook, nursing Maggie "in between times";—of course that is a great advantage as Auntie knows her well and recommends her highly;—says she is honest amiable and very capable & industrious, above all *very* fond of children and good to them. Maggie is devoted to her. She is a young woman,—quite nice looking, remarkably trim and neat—in fact she belongs to the *aristocracy*! Indeed her greatest fault seems to be that she is too fond of *society*! But she won't be in Clarksville long enough to form a very long visiting list.

Loula & "Cousin Jim" have decided to go to Maysville with me. They too have been promising to go and it will be pleasanter for us to do as Fannie urged,—all go together. We will probably go a week from Sat., though we havn't decided.

By-the-way I should have gratified you by informing you sooner that Fannie left Friday before last!

Two weeks and *two* days after you receive *this* I will be in your arms darling, and will put your baby in your arms. Oh how delightful to check off the days, thus, and see them diminish *appreciably*! Baby is *quite* well and growing fast again, one can see the improvement plainly from day to day. She went visiting this morning. Aunt Lou took her over next door to give "Dell" "a pattern to go by," she said! Dell is the lady from Atlanta. With just as much love as you want—more than you can possibly dispose of

Your own little wife   Eileen

ALS (WC, NjP).

To Ellen Axson Wilson

Bryn Mawr, 25 May '86.

Alas, alas, my darling, my letters from you still continue to straggle in from the west: does that mean that *you* are still receiving *none at all*? Oh, I *hope* not. It breaks my heart to think of your suffering so for want of these letters I write daily—that I am deprived of even this poor means of contributing to your happiness! I dare not *telegraph* to reassure you: a telegram after the long suspense would frighten you more before you opened it than it would comfort you when you read its message. My poor little sweetheart! Well, you'll have a jolly time reading the whole budget of belated letters when it does come in! You can treat them as a new volume from my pen, my *mss.* 'History of a Week'—or anything else that you may choose to call it.

I have not been feeling very well yesterday and to-day, because of persistent misbehaviour on the part of my bowels—caused, I suspect, by the wet, changeable weather we have been having the last two or three weeks. I have stayed away from my classes to-day, to be extra prudent, and have spent the morning reading political economy for next Friday—a useful combination of purposes! Don't be at all alarmed about me. There's no cause to be. I just need to be careful with these treacherous digestive organs of mine.

I am just now deploring my position as an *examiner*. Not only have I to grind out questions for 'finals' and for 'entrance' here, but I have just sent in two papers, one on Greek history and one on the "Protestant Revolution," to a girls' school in Philadelphia, which wishes to train up its pupils for Bryn Mawr, and to which, because of its 'standing,' we cannot politicly refuse examiners. I am to receive $10.00 for the service, I believe—that service to include, alas! the reading and grading of the answers! I'll be at my wit's end for questions one of these fine days soon!

Sweetheart, do you know whom I love? *I love you*. And do you know whom else I love? I love my little daughter. Ah, what a big part love plays in my life nowadays! It is the whole *motive power* of it. When I'm tired, I have only to think of the rest—the precious, delightful rest—that is now almost at hand. When I am discouraged, I have but to remember *who* believes in me. When I am lonely, I have but to think of the precious, loving 'presence' that is here at my side—my little wife's longing, caressing thoughts of me. Political economy gallops amain when I think how she is putting the whole heart of her sweet, perfect sympathy into this ordeal I am undergoing. Nothing can go much amiss so long as I can be thus conscious of this glorious strength of loving and being loved by my queen, my Eileen. Ah, little lady, *I love you, I love you, I love you*! My life, my all is yours and *I* am

Your own   Woodrow.

Love to aunt Lou and all.

ALS (WP, DLC).

From Ellen Axson Wilson

My own darling,   Gainsville May 25/86.

Your sweet letter from the Baltimore station was safely received today. So you did not remain over in Balt.! I suppose you *will* feel more in the humour for that next week when it is all over.

I am afraid I shall be obliged to write a mere hurried note to-day for it is beginning to grow dark now; all sorts of things have combined to prevent my writing today,—that is *this afternoon*. I waited till after dinner to write in order to get your letter. Most of the morning I spent very quietly, amusing myself in my favourite way, viz. sitting under the trees in the swing alternately swinging vigorously and reading *German* this morning. The weather has grown *delightful* again, and baby and I are out of doors a great deal. She enjoys it extremely. She is *very* well,—improving rapidly everyone says; and *so* sweet that I can scarcely keep from "squeezing her to death." Yes, it will be rare fun to see you when you first begin to "handle" her! Did you ever have anything to do with a real young baby? Uncle Henry couldn't be induced to touch her—said he was afraid she would "break to pieces." I was amused at Eddie; he came to me afterwards and with the most serious manner asked, "Sister, do young babies ever *really* break to pieces?" By the way, I must tell you his latest speech. He was reading "Gulliver" to me a little while ago for *practice*, and when he had finished he exclaimed, looking over the book, "*my! sixty*-one pages of 'the life of Swift'! *What* a *long* life he must have had!"

I am rather more encouraged now in my efforts for Eddie's cure. I think he is really improving. Until recently it seemed as though I could never accomplish *anything* because of his extreme sensitiveness on the subject. He *tried* to do as I told him, but he couldn't read three words without 'choking up.' You may imagine the general effect when crying was added to the stammering;—it seemed utterly hopeless. I tried every sort of delicate management but all to no effect. At last I bethought me of *bribes*; & offered him five cents a day for two hours practice;—and found it a far more effective cure for sensitiveness (if not for stammering) than all my "tact"!

I am *so* glad, darling, that you can feel that I attend you, in thought at least, as you travel, because I *am* always in heart and imagination at your side,—in all your "in-comings and out-goings." That was what I meant yesterday when I said I wasn't "easy" unless I knew where you were. I feel *lost*, as it were, and you know what a dreary feeling that is;—my "occupation's gone." Oh how delightful it will be once more to know where you are, simply because I know where I am myself! Yes we *will* try never to separate again, try with all our *might*—that is for any length of time. I propose to send you to Boston as often as possible, and to as many Alumni dinners &c. as I can coax you into attending. But I *must* say 'good-night[.]' I love you, *I love you* darling, and indeed I *do* believe in you *heart and soul*.

                              Your own little   Eileen

I suppose 'the world' would consider lovers very absurd and un-reasonable folk;—I am mourning over that lost letter of the 20th as deeply as if it were the only one you had ever written me! Don't you think you could recall it and write it all over again for me?—the *sweet* part at least!

ALS (WC, NjP).

To Ellen Axson Wilson

My peerless little wife,   Bryn Mawr, 26 May, '86.

I am infinitely relieved to learn that *some* of my letters at least have reached you. Knowing what the delays cost *me* at this end of the line, I was growing *very* anxious about what they might cost you at the other end. Mine have begun to come *straight* now; I do *hope* yours have too!

You mischief, you! to draw me on so to tell you again what I think of you and your letters—or do you really *mean* that you are surprised that I like *your* letters *infinitely* better than those of sis-ter Marion or *any*body else? If you do mean it, you are the most completely unreconstructed young woman I know of—still believ-ing that our marriage constitution is a compact and not an abso-lute *oneness*, and still doubting the principle upon which I have so constantly dwelt in expounding that constitution, namely, that in the opinion of *this* part of the union (*viz.* myself) you are the loveliest woman and the most consummate letter-writer that ever lived! There now, madam; I hope that you feel sufficiently re-buked for your rank heresy. And I'm not *half* trying to emphasize my opinion either! I still strongly suspect that you are only trying to draw me out for your own private delectation; and, rather than encourage any such subterfuges, I refrain.

I am feeling much better today. I went to see Dr. Savery[1] yes-terday afternoon, and you will, I am sure, be delighted to learn that he *laughed* at me—at my anxious detailing of symptoms—and sent me away with some innocuous pills and the intimated opin-ion that it was simply a cold passing through my bowels. I have not taken the pills: but both my mind and my bowels are re-lieved.

What a sweet discourse that was of yours about the baby and her splendid infantile skill in the 'use of herself.' You can't write me too much of that sort: I think so much and so longingly about our precious little one, and have so few particulars to think about. Oh, you sweet little mother, you! I seem to love our little baby now with a sort of double, two-sided love—a love which goes out directly to her as my little daughter, and a love which flows to her *through* my love for *you*—and your love for her. That's triple, isn't it? I love her because she is mine, because she is yours, and because you love her. Any one of these phases of my love is strong and complete enough, I suspect, to serve as the ordinary paternal feeling—but combined they constitute a *passion*!

Nay, madam, 'tis not so much—it's only *two* weeks and three days—when this reaches you, it will be only two weeks and *one* day—before we are together! Isn't that *glorious*? You splendid, brave little woman! how heroically you have waited! I'm *so* proud of you—and oh, I love you to distraction. I'm sure that even yet I've never known happiness—delight—such as I shall know when next I hold you in my arms! Love to aunt Lou and all

Your own   Woodrow.

ALS (WP, DLC).
1 Dr. William Savery of Bryn Mawr.

From Ellen Axson Wilson

Gainsville May 26 1886

I am *so* sorry for you, my poor darling, in your disappointment and perplexity about the letters! I can well be sorry for you since I know so well how it is myself. I was half hoping that as there are more roads and trains North than South, your letters would "go straight";—and they did make better time than mine. The one due you on Thursday I presume shared the fate of *yours* written on that day. I couldn't help laughing though in spite of my sympathy at the vials of wrath poured out on the unoffending head of the poor post-master here!—and probably the railroad men on whom I chose to wreck my vengeance were just as little to blame. Our railroad friend of Sunday said that all letters must take the East Tenn. route for the present. I concluded that of course you would hear of the "washouts" as soon as I;—ten miles of the track is gone above Charlotte, beside numerous other breaks.

I am *so* sorry, my darling, that the heat is wearing on you so! I *hope* it won't last. It seems to be on the whole an unusually cool spring. We had a few very hot days, but now it is delightful again.

I am feeling spendidly and "looking well" too. Don't worry about me, sweetheart! To think how *very* well I am getting on in *every* respect, and yet my darling wants to go away and take "a good cry" over me! It is too bad,—it makes *me* want to cry. How *can* I be so stupid as to write things that will worry you needlessly! But *I* saw nothing in the slightest degree disturbing in the conditions of things depicted in that letter. There are some days, you know, in every woman's experience that seem to be completely lost by reason of visitors and other unforseen interruptions; but I don't have many visitors here as a rule. Then for about ten days, you know, the baby, while not exactly sick was not exactly well either. She was very restless and took only short naps through the day. There was quite enough time for resting, but of course it was only a few minutes *at a time*. But she is well again now and sleeps almost as she did at first,—two or three hours at a time; and I have abundant opportunities for both rest and exercise, and for writing to my darling too;—and a little besides for exercising my ingenuity upon those dresses! I shan't hurt myself sewing, darling. There isn't a great deal of work & Loula is going to help me. I shan't use the machine at all,—unless I make Eddie turn it. Thank you dear for offering to match them; but it won't be necessary.

What a very *very* foolish boy you are about that wife of yours, sir! But I have long ago found out the folly of protesting, so I will say no more. And you are just as *splendid* as you are foolish —there! I couldn't express it any more strongly. You are *my* ideal *man*, my ideal husband. "It is no longer an experiment but an *experience*, this married life of mine, and I know that the only dissatisfactions of my life are rooted in *myself* and in separation from you." I *must* steal your words sometimes. They are so sweet and so exactly what I want to say to *you*. Oh *how* true it is that you ["]hurry *my* heart through such a round of gladness admiration and love as surely no heart ever experienced before." Surely no one before was ever so happy as

Your little wife   Eileen

ALS (WC, NjP).

To Ellen Axson Wilson

My own Eileen, my darling,   Bryn Mawr, 27 May, '86.
    Here it is Thursday again, and I am about to repeat last week's

programme. I shall leave here at 4.02 this afternoon; reach Baltimore a little before seven; get up to No. 8 McCulloh[1] in season to get some supper; spend the evening reading till early bed-time; go through Dr. Ely's mill to-morrow between ten and one or two o'clock; spend to-morrow afternoon reading; go to bed early; go through the *oral* mill at noon on Saturday (if you get this at one on Saturday, I shall by that time probably be all through); and then—I don't know yet whether I shall stay in Balto. over Sunday or come back and "exercise my conversational powers with Aunt Sadie," as I did last time; but probably I shall come back, to save expenses. There's no saying 'for certain,' however: I'll feel mightily like going on some sort of a spree if I scrape through my examinations all right! I'll try to rejoice *mildly*, but rejoice I *must*. It will be an *immense* load off my mind to secure that petty title!

Though we continue to have the most trying wet and cold weather, as changeable as April and almost as disagreeable as March, I continue to improve in health. So soon as the present strain is removed, I shall be easily all right again—I'm sick of this grind, that's all that's the matter with me!

I am to go to the Garrett's[2] to a reception next Thursday evening. Both Mrs. Garrett and Mrs. Haines have repeatedly sent the most cordial messages to me for you and have made the most genuinely interested enquiries about you and the baby: and, in inviting me this time, Mrs. Garrett made a very sweet expression of her wish that you were here to go too, and of her desire to welcome you and "bonny Margaret" next year. Shall I not give her a special message of love from you when I see her?

It's *real* good news, darling, that you have secured a satisfactory nurse for the summer! It lifts a big load of anxiety off my heart. And hurrah for my precious little Margaret, being such a dear *well* little girl and making her thrice precious mother so happy thereby! Oh, my sweet baby! How I love her! If "Dely" *does* manage to pattern after the copy shown her, it will be the eighth wonder of the world. *No*body could in the nature of things have a baby comparable with yours!

Sweetheart, when you get this I will be but *two* weeks off—two weeks and *no* days, but just a few hours! Oh, the time *is* passing away—and I am drawing nearer to my glorious little wife and sweetheart and my lovely little baby! It makes me unspeakably happy to think such thoughts and to *give myself up* entirely to being   Your own   Woodrow.

When you bid Mrs. Shepard good-bye, give her my warmest regards and thanks.

ALS (WC, NjP).

¹ The address of Mary Jane Ashton's boardinghouse, where Wilson had roomed while a student at the Johns Hopkins and to which he would return during future stays in Baltimore.

² Probably the John Biddle Garretts of Bryn Mawr. Garrett was a trustee of Bryn Mawr College.

Two Letters from Ellen Axson Wilson

My own darling,   Gainsville May 27 1886

I believe I have said several times lately that I would have to write a *short* letter and ended by sending one of the usual length; in fact I find it next to impossible to leave any corner of a sheet uncovered when writing to you. But I *must* try to curtail my letter this time because it is *night*, and I have promised *myself* to rest my eyes at night until baby is two months old;—not that there is *anything* the matter with them. It is only a precaution, due to the many warnings I have received.

I havn't been able to write before because I have been *frolicing* all day! That seems a poor excuse for neglecting or putting off my darling's claims, but I knew he would prefer to have it so if I was to get any good out of it,—as I *have* done. Mrs. Shepherd carried me out riding this morning as soon as we could get off. She "hitched up" herself & drove like "an old campaigner"; it is an accomplishment which I am sorry I did not discover earlier for the horse and buggy stand here idle all the time for want of someone to drive,—is never used except when Uncle Warren goes to the factory. We stopped for a few minutes at Loula's and she persuaded us to come back with the baby and spend the day. So we went, and had a very pleasant day, the baby behaving like a little angel. We took another short drive in the afternoon to give the baby a little airing. It is the first time I have been outside the gate since I came, six weeks today;—the change did both baby and myself good,—made us feel brighter, though baby *was* cross after our return, and prevented my writing before dark.

I met Uncle Warren on my way to Loula's and received your letter of the 25th; so they have begun to come up to time again.

Oh, I am *so* distressed darling to think of your being sick and I so far away,—not able to do anything for you. No, I won't let myself be unreasonably alarmed, but I can't help being greatly disturbed knowing how "treacherous" those digestive organs are, and how *very* badly it is probably making you feel. I am so, *so* sorry, my darling! How eagerly I shall wait for tomorrow's letter to learn how you are!

Just to think that when this reaches you those miserable examinations will be all over and you will be a Ph.D. (that is if you are not too unwell to go.) I am sure you won't feel a whit happier or more relieved when it is over than I. I feel something as I did ten (?) years ago when that terrible logic examination hung over my head;—it is with a vast difference though, for I am so absolutely sure that *this* examination will be *well* passed.

Oh darling is it *really* true that my sympathy is a help to you in your work, that my faith in you comforts you when discouraged[,] that my love rests you when weary? Oh I am *so glad, so glad*! It is impossible to tell you with what joy such words thrill me. My darling, my own husband, it is impossible to say how completely my heart and soul, my whole self, my whole life are devoted to you & your service. Yet it seems to me that I *do so* little of all I wish to do. So imagine if you can my joy to find that little enough to make you happy. Believe me darling always & altogether   Your little   Eileen

P. S. This letter is very much 'curtailed'!—is it not? But the time spent on it was so short, that I hav'nt *quite* broken that "promise["] to myself!

My own darling,   Gainsville May 28/86
   This is indeed good news that comes to me in today's letter,—that you are "much better,"—"feeling relieved." I am *so* glad you went to Dr. Savery, and *more* than glad that he laughed! That laugh found its echo away down here in Georgia; in a laugh of pure relief. Oh, I hope you are quite well by this time! Take good care of yourself, darling, but I *know* you are doing that, for my sake. I can't say how glad I am that this spring session is almost over; I have been so anxious about you all the season, remembering last spring, and the unusual load of work and worry you have had upon you of late. I have been *so* glad to find you keeping up as well as you have;—taking for granted that you hav'nt been concealing your bad feelings—which you couldn't do, you know, without breaking your promise. We are both very well,—baby has been unusually quiet and good the last two days and has slept well at night. She is out walking now with Mrs. Shepherd. She seems to enjoy being out immensely—looks about her at everything in such a wide-eyed wondering way. She is "just *too* lovely"! I always loved babies dearly and thought them sweet, but I had no idea they were *so* sweet as this baby, or so interesting! I catch myself so often thinking in a dreamy sort of way about

Mama when she was a young mother,—wondering if she felt all that I do now about *me*,—her little firstborn daughter. My motherhood seems to make me feel more closely drawn to her than ever before. And oh, how it makes me long for her,—to be with her if only for a *little* while!—to have her see the baby! But it is only one other great longing added to the old one always so strong within me,—that she might have known *you*. But I must not talk so—in a letter. It might trouble you, making you think that I am sad. But *you* know that I am not sad, darling, but oh so very, very happy! *Your* wife—the mother of *your* first-born[—]is happier today than she was even in her sunny childhood, in her own sweet mother's arms. You are *everything* to me, love. You *fill* all my heart. Your love makes unhappiness, unrest of heart, *im*possible to me.

I had a pleasant letter from Stockton last night with a new photograph of him—miserably poor. I had written begging him to meet us in Rome since he could not come to Gainsville. But he says it is impossible [to] get off as early as June. So my last hope of seeing him this summer is gone. Have just had a delightful and characteristic letter from Minnie, too, which I would send for your entertainment, but for your prohibition![1]

We had another pleasant ride today, Mrs. S. the two children & myself.

Went out to New Holland spring.

Give my love to Mrs. Coale the Rhoads &c. Aunt Lou is constantly sending love to you. Take that message always for granted. With a heart full and brimming over with love for my darling I am as   Your own little wife   Eileen

ALS (WC, NjP).
[1] These letters from Stockton Axson and Mary E. Hoyt are missing.

To Ellen Axson Wilson

Balto., May 28, 1886.

Have been working all afternoon and so left no time to write. Got through this morning about as well as I had expected. Pretty tired and anxious now, but quite myself. Will write to-morrow more fully, in the afternoon. I shall return to B. M. to-morrow, as I should otherwise have to travel on Sunday. I have a slight cold, but not enough to make any real difference. May say I am quite well. As ever   Yours   W.

API (WP, DLC).

To Ellen Axson Wilson

My own precious little wife,   Balto., 29 May, 1886.

Hurrah—a thousand times hurrah—*I'm through, I'm through*
—the degree is actually secured! Oh, the relief of it! I have a rat-
tling headache just at this moment, but it isn't a headache that
means I am at all unwell—it's only the result of the nervousness
accompanying & preceding that *oral*: I don't care a snap of my
finger for it—I'd pay twenty such headaches for such a relief! I
got through the dreaded ordeal much better than I had expected
to—was as nervous as possible and displayed considerable ignorance on some points, but was given an exceedingly fair set of
questions and answered most of them as well as the circumstances allowed.

And now I can dream away all the day, with a clear conscience,
about my darling little wife and my precious little daughter—and
I *will* do so—as nearly 'to my heart's content' as separation will
permit. Two weeks from to-day—*one* week and five days from the
time you receive this, darling! I don't mind a bit the work I shall
have to do at Bryn Mawr moving our things upstairs—everything
will go easily after this—there'll only be such work as will speed
the hours. Oh what unspeakable joys the hours are bringing
me! My little wife in my arms—my little baby in the arms of *both*
of us at once! I care not how the rest of the world treats me if I
but be in *that* position, and feel that my dear ones are *happy*. Oh,
my sweetheart, I love you, I love you, I love you!

I'm going back to B. M. this afternoon—it's time to get ready
for my train, and I'm extremely tired, so I'll say good-bye and
write a Sunday letter to-morrow with the lightest of light hearts.

My darling, my queen, my Eileen, my little wife, with all my
heart I am   Your own   Woodrow
Love to all.

ALS (WC, NjP)

From Ellen Axson Wilson

Gainsville May 29/86

Oh my darling only to think that it is *just* two weeks—*no* day &
no hours over! Two weeks from this very moment I will be in
your arms, or at any rate I will be waiting with feelings that beg-
ger description—waiting and listening every moment for the train.
And to think that tomorrow morning,—no,—*tonight* when I wake I
can say "he is coming *next* week"! Oh I hope my heart won't burst

with the joy of mere anticipation before the wished-for moment comes!

How much I have to make me happy tonight!—first this thought of your coming so soon and then the knowledge that the examinations are *all over*! I congratulate you from the bottom of my heart, darling,—*Dr*. Wilson, I should say! When do they confer the degree, by the way? Immediately after the "oral mill"? I am *sure* that you will feel better now, physically as well as mentally. It will be a shame if you don't stay over in Balt. *Of course* you need to go on a spree now, and an evening or so with those jolly Woods will afford you much more thorough relaxation than anything at Bryn Mawr,—even including the reception at the Garretts. Give much love for me to all the ladies of the family and tell them how sorry *I* am that you are there alone. Tell them I am very eager to introduce to them the little Margaret.

But I *really* am going to write a short letter tonight, because it is growing late. This has been one of baby's restless colicy days and I have had no time to write before. And of course, Mrs. Shepherd being gone, I am more tired than after other similar days. Dear good soul! How we miss her; and she seemed about as sorry to leave,—went off crying. I am just as well as can be—am both looking and feeling well, and so is the baby. (Does that suggest Dode's "I am"?) She *will* have a little colic off & on, but colic don't "count." I love you sweetheart deeply, truly, tenderly, passionately. I am forever   Your own little wife   Eileen

Uncle Warren says there will be another derangement of the mails this coming week. So don't be troubled if your letters are delayed,—forewarned is forearmed. There will be *no* trains on the Air Line Tuesday, they are going to change the guage from "broad" to "standard"; and they are going to do it over the whole length of the road in *one day*.[1]

Many thanks for the envelopes, dear, received tonight. But why so many? Thank Heaven, I don't need them! I have but eleven more letters to write,—and six envelopes on hand. We will have to turn these over to Mother, they will last her "till we leave Bryn Mawr for good"!

Isn't it queer that I *can't* summon resolution enough to leave a sheet unfilled!

ALS (WC, NjP).

[1] Sunday, May 30, 1886, was the day on which most southern railroads altered the gauge of their tracks by three inches to conform to the "standard" gauge used by northern lines. The "Air Line" (the Atlanta and Charlotte Air-Line Railway) may have waited until June 1 to avoid profaning the Sabbath, as some other roads did.

To Ellen Axson Wilson

My own peerless darling,   Bryn Mawr, 30 May, 1886.
I am in the lightest-hearted love-making mood this bright morning that I have known since you went away, and, if you were but here at my knee, pressed close to my heart, so that I could tell your eyes and your lips how I love you, surely I could add *words* which would for once make the confession complete! Don't you think, my sweetheart, that it is a perfect proof of the absolute completeness of your reign in my heart that when I am tired or downhearted or sick there is perfect cure for me in your love, and that when I am gayest all my high spirits are transfigured into love for you? Whatever my mood, it somehow leads me into deeper love for you! Take the present case. The successful conclusion of my examinations in Baltimore, with all that that success secures, has lifted a great weight off my mind and raised my spirits just as high as they could conceivably go in your absence. What is the result? I find it impossible to translate my feelings otherwise than *that I love you.* Ever since I woke up this morning, rested and happy, I have been doing nothing but indulge in ecstasies of thought about you. You are the centre of my life and no fulness of that life can find expression but in love for you! That's the delight of it all! I won the degree *for you.* I don't care for it for myself. I *did* rejoice in writing to dear mother to-day that I was Ph.D. I saved the news as a surprise; and I know how it will gratify the dear home folks. *That* would have been well worth while anyhow! But *I won the degree for you. I* could live on $1,500 a year very easily: and I hope that my fortunes will grow with my reputation (though that is problematical) But my spur in the struggle of preparation I have just been through was to please *you,* and to make *you* more comfortable. In so far as the degree has a commercial value, it was earned for you; in so far as it has a sentimental value, it was won for you! If there's any triumph, it is *yours.* You see *here's* one key to my happiness in such matters, darling: I know that you would be glad, with the inimitable gladness of love, to live with me on 'nothing a year' —on any pittance that would keep us from starvation; I know that you set no store at all by my *income,* so I have but enough to keep *me* from anxiety and fit for work, and it is that knowledge which makes it so keen and pure a satisfaction to me to be able to do anything to preserve you from the cares and discomforts of too narrow circumstances. Just because you *don't* require it, I delight to supply fuller means of easy support. But, after all, it was, so

to speak, *only in my own mind* that I won the degree for your sake in *this* sense: I knew that *you* were not thinking of it in that light, and that your pleasure in my success would come from a very different source. I won it, therefore, to make you happy: and it is because I am sure that that success will make you happy, that I am so happy myself! Oh, Eileen, my queen, *I live for you in everything.* You have made me the happiest man in the wide world. Your love for me is a bottomless well of joy for me—and my love for you, an exhaustless source of strength.

My inclination to organize a '*spree*' after the examination was over yesterday took the form finally of a ride in the "limited express" to Philadelphia. It made the journey very much easier and pleasanter. You may be interested to know that the reading I did, in Frederic Harrison,[1] on the way was largely a sham because of my interest in the young lady in the next seat, for whom I did various little services, such as hanging up her 'things,' picking up her dainty smelling-bottle, and the like, receiving in payment very charming smiles and thanks. She was *very* pretty—but her mother was along! I *had*, therefore, to read my book *some.* You see, Miss, I did not know, before you taught me, what infinite sweetness there is in a woman; and, though I know that no woman has any charm that will compare with the least of my Eileen's, you have dangerously inclined my imagination to clothe every lady-like little beauty that I meet with attributes that engage, for the time at least, my affections. You will further observe, however, that by the very terms of this confession jealousy on your part is excluded. To be attracted by said beauties is, under such circumstances, just another way of loving you. You supply the personality which they serve to suggest. Ah, if you only *knew*, sweetheart, how much I love you! I made a discovery this morning. I found that I had a picture of you. In my sorrow at your absence, I had been forgetting all this while that I had one—indeed, after having had *you*, no photograph of you seemed to me *anything* until now that I have gotten so *desperate* because of my longings for you that anything that in any way suggests to me your self is unspeakably dear to me. You would have imagined me a devout person at a shrine had you seen me before that little bracket over there in the corner a little while ago. The little treasure in my watch has been a comfort to me all along—it seems doubly you: but I had forgotten about that sweet photograph in the corner. I went back to it this morning with all my old delight in it, and talked resistless love to it—and kissed it—only less joyfully than I would woo and kiss you—you *precious* darling, my pet, my sweetheart, my queen, my life, my matchless little wife! I love, *love, love* you, darling! Kisses uncounted for my precious baby. Kiss little sister for me and give my love to Eddie, aunt Lou & all.   Your own   Woodrow.

I hope you will enjoy going to Maysville. Take *all* care of yourself, my treasure. The nurse goes too, doesn't she?

ALS (WC, NjP).
   [1] Author of many works of literary criticism and history. Wilson was probably reading Harrison's *Order and Progress* (London, 1875).

From Ellen Axson Wilson

My own darling,   Gainsville, May 30/86
   The long lost letter of the 20th actually came to hand this morning, to my great satisfaction. Why, I wouldn't for *any*thing have lost *this* letter darling!—this sweet "defence" of yourself against the charge of concealing your 'moods.' Yes, I admit the defence is triumphant, though it's success is due chiefly to it's skill in winning the sympathy of the judge. Oh, you *darling*! No wonder you say that you wish I could "see your heart," for every fresh glimpse I get of it makes me love you more than ever before,—if that be possible.
   If I had known how delightful the missing letter was I should have lamented it's loss even more than I did. I had been consoling myself with the thought that since it was sent on Thursday, the day of your departure for Balt., you probably had time to write but little,—chiefly details of your plans; which of course I had learned anyhow after they were carried out!
   I began this early in the evening, dear, but baby interrupted me, and now I think I had better close with a few words as it is nearing eleven,—especially as she isn't asleep yet. She has been a perfect cherub all day,—but very naughty too for she would not sleep at all and still less would she lie still without sleeping, though as long as I held her she was contentment itself. Of course, I hav'nt had a moment for writing. Last night was my first of undivided responsibility and it passed off splendidly, she slept better than she has ever done, straight through from eleven to five,—worn out I suppose with restlessness yesterday.
   Uncle W. brought me your card when he came from church tonight. Oh my darling, it makes my heart ache to think of you "tired & anxious"! How *unspeakably* it makes me long to be with you. But thank Heaven it is over at last.

Please excuse haste. We are both quite well. With a heart full to overflowing with love I am as ever

Your little wife   Eileen

ALS (WC, NjP).

To Ellen Axson Wilson

My own precious darling,   Bryn Mawr, 31 May, 86.

Following up the discovery of yesterday, I am writing with your picture right before me here on the table—not that I need inspiration of this artificial sort in writing to you: the *thought* of you is enough, as I have confessed before, to draw me out of any mood into one of pure love and joy—and that is surely only another way of describing inspiration. But this sweet photograph *is* an immense *comfort* to me. It gladdens my *eyes* as much as the act of writing to you gladdens my heart.

Do you know, sweetheart, that, Providence permitting, you will receive only *nine* letters after this one from me before you receive me myself—that on the tenth day after you receive this *I* will come? A week from day after tomorrow I shall write my last letter to you before leaving for my home, my precious little wife's arms! Oh, how I love to count the days, now that they are getting few in number. Those dreadful two months are *almost gone*—oh, how happy, how happy I shall be when they are altogether gone.

So you've been taking rides with Mrs. Shepherd, have you? That's *good*—I'm so glad that you've had the chance. How fortunate it is that "Dely" has held out so long, so that you have been able to keep Mrs. S! I'm much obliged to "Dely."

I found Mrs. Trueheart at uncle Tom's yesterday. She has been staying lately at Mrs. Seaman's in New York, and says that they were very much surprised and pleased to hear that you have a little daughter, & sent you their love and congratulations. "You know," added cousin Allie, "there's a young man boarding there who was *dreadfully* smitten with Ellie; and he made very particular inquiries about her—wanted to know what sort of a man she had married." The Englishman—ah the Englishman! Poor fellow—if he deserves pity, certainly *I* ought to be sorry for him! Mrs. T. will go to Mrs. Ewing about the first of July—meantime oscillating between Phila. and N. Y. 'She had received *such* a sweet letter from Ellie'—I can well imagine—Ellie *can* write sweet letters when she tries—though *how* sweet only one person in the world knows! As for him, he *lives* on the sweetness of her letters! 'Is it *really* true that your sympathy is a help to me in my work, that your faith in me comforts me when discouraged, that your love rests me when weary?' Oh, my precious darling—*isn't it*! That's the whole meaning of my life nowadays—it is the *whole* truth of my heart's experience. I could not have gotten through these last few weeks *at all* if it had not been! My precious, *precious* little wife, if my inadequate confessions of this blessed truth make your heart thrill, what would it not experience if it could see my heart? Kiss, kiss, kiss my little baby for me—I love her with all my heart! As for you, I am

Your own Woodrow.

ALS (WC, NjP).

From Ellen Axson Wilson

My own darling,   Gainsville May 31/86

Saturday's note was received this evening telling me, what I knew right well already, that the examinations *all* passed off successfully. Oh I *can't tell* you how glad I am, and relieved that the strain is off of you,—of course I can't be *relieved*—but only *delighted*, at the result since there was never any doubt about that. I am *sure* that in spite of the head-ache you will be a great deal better now. "Hurrah!" sure enough, and once again *hurrah*! I am sorry to say that it is again *night* and getting late so that I must again be brief; I had plenty of time too for writing today, but I was so anxious to get your letter first that I waited for it, putting off writing, until I lost my opportunity. Baby is very well today though as wakeful as ever; but her new nurse has had her out of doors a great deal and she is always happy in the open air. She had another splendid night—slept straight on from half past twelve 'till morning. *I* am feeling as bright as a new pin;—took quite a long walk today, not about the garden as I have been doing but through the town. I must gradually become accustomed to wearing 'dresses and things' again before you come and we start on our travels. They are a great trial though—are *clothes*! I think of going in for the dress reform!

What do you think Eddie said just now! He asked who was going to baptise the baby, and I said "Father." After a moment of profound thought he asked, "Sister, what relation is he to *me*? is he *my* father too?["] I said laughing that they were not related at all, whereupon he declared that he thought it *very* curious that people should be related to me and not to him. But I really *must* not write a letter tonight;—tomorrow I shall get regulated again and write in the morning. Tomorrow! the first of June! Oh, how I shall welcome it! I wonder if you know, darling, how rapidly and steadily my spirits are rising now from day to day. What a different state of mind it is from the patient, or at times *impatient* endurance of a few weeks ago. Oh how much I have to make me happy these days—and *always*! But now every day brings fresh cause for happiness. Today with its happy note from you has certainly brought joy with it.

Darling I love you. I am yours, *all* yours, heart and soul
Your own little wife,   Eileen

ALS (WC, NjP).

Wilson Reviews His Course Work at Bryn Mawr

[c. *June 1, 1886*]

. *History*. The instruction in History was given by class exercises and by lectures upon special topics, illustrative of important epochs or of political principles. The study of Ancient History comprised that of Greece and Rome, conducted simultaneously, until that of the former merged in that of the latter. The teaching of Modern History included an outline of European History from the fall of the Western Empire to the establishment of the Empire of Charles the Great.

The attention of students was directed to the influence of leading historical characters upon contemporary events, and the students prepared biographical notices of them, which were read to the class and commented upon by the professor. Instruction was provided for the Fellow in History, who is now continuing her studies in Zurich.

Printed in *Bryn Mawr College. The President's Report to the Board of Trustees, for the Year 1885-86* (Philadelphia, 1886), p. 9.

To Ellen Axson Wilson

My own darling little wife,   Bryn Mawr, 1 June, '86.

So you think that twenty odd envelopes will last dear mother in writing to me until we 'leave Bryn Mawr for good'? That interests me immensely! Where are we going, pray? Have you discovered a haven of cheapness in which the profits from the textbook are to support us? I am eager to know your plans, you dear, confident, little woman, you. Maybe you have discovered a lucrative field for literature in new Georgia (?) The absolute assurance with which you speak prompts me to expect some great discovery. Oh, you dear, *dear* little girl!—if I can be but half as successful as you expect me to be, I shall soon be a great man. Was ever any one so delightfully believed in as I am! My darling! I wish I could tell you how much I love you and believe in you in return.

The suggestion of the sweet letter received last night has added much to my good spirits. It *is 'next week'* that I am coming. I had not thought of that delightful formula: I had simply been counting the days. 'Next week' conceals the uncomfortable fact that it is to be the very last day of the week that finds me with you—and permits one to think the days scarcely any longer worth counting! Oh, sweetheart, Eileen, my little wife, as I think of being with you, it seems to me that it will be as if I had never been with you before—a fresh discovery of all the infinite comforts and delights of your love and presence,—only I *have* been with you & know what I shall find—can foretaste the sweet things to come. And it *will* be knowing in some sort a new Eileen, who is not only my precious, peerless little wife and queen but also the mother of my baby—made all the more beautiful and sacred in my eyes by the fact of her motherhood. Ah, how I love to think of you as a *mother*, darling! How sweet it will be to see you caring for your baby and mine! How hard I shall try to be a father worthy of such a mother-mate! I seem to feel a great flood of new love for you surge through my heart whenever your letters bring me some note of your new heart-experience because of the baby's coming. I cannot tell you, darling, how sweet seemed to me those confessions of yours about how your memory of and love for mama have been renewed by your own motherhood. My *lovely* pet. You are such a *real*, natural, perfect little woman, such a genuine *lover*. No wonder I was instinctively made to feel, from the first time I met you, that I would give my life for your love! That love has increased a thousand-fold the worth of my life. I am what I am, and will be what I hope to be because you have taken me as   Your own   Woodrow.
Love to aunt L. & all.

ALS (WC, NjP).

From Ellen Axson Wilson

My own darling,   Gainsville June 1/86
This is the day appointed for changing the "guage," so I am without a letter. How very long and blank that circumstance seems to make the day! Still I am bearing it very well; my hap-

piness at present is too deep to be *greatly* disturbed even by that untoward event. I have only to let my thoughts dwell the more on that quickly nearing time when I will have no need of letters. Oh my love, my love! my heart *aches* for gladness at the thought of your coming! May our God who has in all things so richly blessed us, add the crowning blessing of bringing you to me in health and safety! I am sometimes actually *frightened* darling at the intensity of my love for you. It seems to me I *could* not bear it if any evil of *any* kind should befall you. It would be *so* much easier to die myself than to see you ill or in trouble. But I won't think such thoughts. "Our times are in His hands," and we know that our Father never tries His children above what they are able to bear. I am *sure* that His blessing is with us in our love, and after all such love is a tower of strength in itself. However much it increases our power to *suffer* in the same proportion it increases our power to *bear*. A love like ours, imperishable, unchangeable even in death, cannot but bless with true happiness even in the darkest hour.

Baby is perfectly lovely today—seems to be trying herself. She had the most *wonderful* night on record,—actually slept without stirring from half past *ten* to *seven*! Isn't that almost incredible? Aunt Lou says she begins to think she is sleeping better because undisturbed by Mrs. Shepherd's cough, but I suppose it is principally because she sleeps so little in the day. They say babies grow faster when asleep than at any other time, so at this rate she ought to make rapid progress. Her little face & body were always plump, but her limbs were thin; like those of all young babies,—except *possibly* the twelve pound boys we hear of. They are filling out to the general satisfaction, but I am in a *desperate hurry* to see them *real* fat and firm. Not that I care to see my dear little girlie—my dainty wee thing, a great gross baby. If she were a boy I might aspire to see her a "big bouncing fellow."

Both she and I are especially well today. I am also "looking well,"—am getting back some colour. I *hope* your head-ache is quite gone now and your recovery in every other respect complete. Was *so* sorry that I couldn't hear from that head-ache today.

Are *all* the college catalogues for next year printed? Won't Dr. Rhoads be able in some way to insert your degree and your new rank in the faculty? Should think he would be very anxious to do the former since he "sets so much store by" degrees!

Goodbye darling. I *love* you, *love* you, *love* you, now and forever   Your own   Eileen

ALS (WC, NjP).

To Ellen Axson Wilson

My own darling,   Bryn Mawr, 2 June, '86.

What do you think? I found just now an *unopened* letter of yours on my table. It had evidently been there several days—since May 28. What do you think of that? 'Is *that* the way I treat your letters—leave them unopened for five or six days?' The 28 was Friday; I was in Baltimore, 'taking' Dr. Ely's examination. When I got back Saturday evening, I ran upstairs to see what mail had come in my absence—and there it was lying in a little pile on the corner of my table—but only *one* letter from you. I mourned over the loss of the one that had been due on Friday for some days, but finally reconciled myself to the inevitable consequences of a wash-out. Just now I was looking over the little stack of unanswered letters that stands by the row of books at the other side of the table, when I came across one of yours. 'Hello—here's one of my darling's letters; *it* ought not to be there: I'll put it away.' But first, of course, I had to re-read it. Lo and behold it wasn't opened! Mary[1] had 'straightened up' my table and put it in the pile with the old letters! You may imagine how eagerly I tore it open and read it! I was like a boy who discovers uneaten and forgotten sweetmeats in his pocket. There was a coincidence in the 'find' too. The letter that came this morning, and which I had just re-read before making my 'find,' contained rejoicings over the final arrival of my delayed and wandering letter of May 20th, and this newly discovered letter of yours, wh. had to all intents and purposes been lost, contained the only extended antecedent reference to the loss of my letter of the 20th aforesaid.

I too am glad that that particular letter of mine reached you. I wanted you to hear my defence against the charge of concealing my 'moods'—and I was wondering why you had made no reference to it, because I had forgotten the *date* of the letter that contained it. And oh, I am *so* glad that this letter of yours did not remain 'lost' on my table here. It contains one pricelessly precious passage—a glimpse of my little queen "sitting under the trees in the swing alternately swinging vigorously and reading," of my precious little family "out of doors a great deal." It is the first sight of you that I have had that gives my imagination real hold of the scenes towards which my heart turns at all times all the day long, and I shall treasure it accordingly. Oh, my sweet, sweet pet! My heart longs *unspeakably* to be with you! *Next week* I am coming! Then you may expect to greet the happiest man, the proudest husband, the most enthusiastic father that ever you saw or heard about. I love you, darling—*I love you*. I am quite well and in excellent, easy-going spirits.

Your own   Woodrow.

Love to all.

ALS (WC, NjP).
1 The Wilsons' servant, Mary Freeman of Rosemont, Pa.

From Ellen Axson Wilson

My own darling,   Gainsville June 2/86

I thought this morning that I was already as happy as I *could* be apart from you but I find that I was mistaken, for these two *delightful, perfect* letters have just doubled my happiness, because they have added the full sum of *your* happiness to mine,— of that "light-hearted mood" which I know because you tell me of it but still more because it breathes in every line of these sweet letters. *I too* am in the lightest-hearted mood, darling! I should like to dance or sing or do something else *very* startling—for me— to give my spirits vent. Yes sweetheart it is perfect proof of your love that your heart should turn at once to your little wife in every mood,—in trouble and joy alike. *I* have often tried in vain to decide whether I wanted you most when happy, to share it with you, or when troubled, because I *need* you;—but whatever the mood it takes me *straight* to you. Every thought and feeling begins and ends in you. You are my *life* darling, I could easier cease to breathe than leave you out of any part of it.

Yes, darling *that* I am[—]happy over your success,—glad that you have the reward of merit that you so richly deserve. True I know the degree is but a decoration—a ribband,—the *merit* was all there before; and no number of degrees could indicate to the public how transcendent is that merit. "The rank is but the guinea stamp. The man's the gold for a' that." I am *always* rejoicing with a joy past telling in all your rare gifts, darling. Oh, I *glory* in you! I never dare tell you in *full* my opinion of you lest so much praise to your face should offend your taste. But my *constant* delight in your powers doesn't prevent my feeling a quick fresh thrill of pleasure at every and any fresh *recognition* of them—at every new honour paid you. Truly I—and all whose sweet privilege it is to love you—have the pleasure of feeling that sort of 'thrill' very often. You seem to be running a race against time to see what you *can* do! You are certainly a rapid young man. Just think of it! In two short years all sorts of university honours,—fellowships, degrees—distinctions of every kind. Then a great book written, published,—a splendid reputation won, with all the various tributes to your powers which follow naturally therefrom!—a list far too numerous to *begin* upon. Oh you don't permit your companions on this life journey of yours to lack for pleasurable excitement! especially that companion whom love keeps closest at your side, and allows to know and share *all*. Ah darling, you *ought* to be happy—one of the happiest of mortals! How could one help it who all his life long has been giving such *perfect* happiness —nothing but happiness—to others by everything he *is* and everything he *does*?

Yes, darling, I am sure you *do* know that the question of income doesn't enter into my thoughts on such subjects. *I* should [be] quite happy and content with an attic and a crust and *you*. I should be ideally happy in that "piny-woods" cabin (!)—always supposing *you* were happy,—"free from anxiety and fit for work." But now I think of it, I *am* very glad of the degree "in this light" also, for it *will* make you more free,—*quite* free—from anxiety and therefore in better working condition. It will make you more *light*-hearted; and I imagine that everything, even wood-cutting, goes better with a light heart than a heavy. I am *sure* book-writing does.

It is only fair that the degree which my darling won for *my* sake I should value for *his*,—though I also prize it *because* it was for my sake, as I do *every* proof of your wonderful love,—my own *darling*!

We are both *very* well today. Baby had a good night and a splendid day. Aunt Lou sends much love; and I send just as much as you want   As *ever* your own little wife   Eileen

ALS (WC, NjP).

To Ellen Axson Wilson

My own precious little wife,   Bryn Mawr, 3 June '86.

It makes me so glad to think of you as being "as bright as a pin," taking long walks out-of-doors, and the like. It seems such tangible proof of your growing strength—and my happiness depends on your growing strength. And then to see your *spirits* rising too—just because the time for my coming is drawing near —oh, what a help and joy it all is to me!

You will be glad to know that I have already finished the heaviest part of the moving that is to be done for the summer.

Yesterday was rainy and disagreeable—as fully half of our spring days here have been—with an East wind blowing that made me feel like no *other* sort of work, so I 'pitched in' in the afternoon and carried the two open bookcases with their contents upstairs —with Benjamin's help. I shall leave the closed book-case where it is, tacking some sightly cloth behind the door-glasses and locking the doors. To move it would involve taking it to pieces and putting it together again—and that's a little too much. The packing will now be an easy matter, to be accomplished by unlaborious stages. It was the moving of the books that I dreaded.

I have become an outrageous loafer these last few days. Since those harassing examinations have been lifted off my mind, and no strain left to keep me up to a tense pitch of exertion, I have seemed incapable of any steady work. My class are reviewing the text-book, and I am 'taking it easy,' notwithstanding an hour's struggle every morning with Miss Bancroft. I am, so to say, letting myself down into a vacation state of mind. To-morrow comes my last class exercise (think of that) and then, next week, come two examinations, a 'final' on Wednesday afternoon, three to six, and an 'entrance' on Friday morning, eleven to one. In between times, packing and happy anticipatory dreams!

Does the shortening of the time make you impatient of writing letters, as it makes me? The delights of an infinitely sweeter and altogether satisfying intercourse being just at hand, the poor baldness of *this* way of making love to you is the more painfully emphasized. But I'm not going to abuse it. It has been for so many weary weeks my chief solace, next to receiving your precious letters, that I'm not "going back on it" now that it is about to be superceded by something with the delights of which *nothing* can compare. It's my solace still, for all it is so far short of being a complete compensation for talk with a little beauty in my arms, giving love for love. Don't you think that that is at least *one* of the chief pleasures of being together, sweetheart,—that we can love each other in the same vein at the same time? Oh, how infinitely, how variously, how absorbingly I love you, my Eileen! I am altogether and always   Your own   Woodrow.
Love to all.

ALS (WC, NjP).

From Ellen Axson Wilson

My own darling   Gainsville May [June] 3/86
    Baby has just gotten settled after her bath and I shall try and

write the first thing, so that I won't be so hurried or interrupted. She had a good night again, and is *lovely* this morning;—has been smiling and cooing in a ravishing manner for an admiring audience of three grown people and five children. She is getting to look at one so intelligently now. Her eyes are *beautiful*! They are such a lovely colour,—a deep dark blue; I am *sure* when you see them you will [be] more than anxious to have them retain that colour. She is *very* well this morning[,] hasn't had a touch of colic now for three days. I am also *very* well;—have had several good nights and it has made me feel brighter; and I also get out every day. Mrs. Shepherd came and took me to drive again yesterday, and I enjoyed it very much. A pro-pos of your order always to say how I "*look*"! I met Dr. Baily while driving and he seemed genuinely delighted at my appearance—"never saw me looking better." Loula, too, informed me the other day that I "looked just as though nothing had happened!" Is that satisfactory, sir? Our good friend Mrs. Shepherd finds it hard to be away from us, she says;—she came day before yesterday a long hot mile and more to see us, and then again yesterday, though her daughter is quite sick. She is very sincerely attached to us I think;—as she said very often she never met a stranger that she loved so much;— only I "don't seem like a stranger[.]" She "feels like she has known me for years." And I certainly share her attachment; she [is] indeed a good, brave woman for whom I feel a strong respect as well as affection:—and she is the most faithful of nurses.

This whole house is a nursery now,—six children,—five babies, —in it! Mrs. Minor Brown, Uncle Warren's daughter-in-law, has been here for the last three days on a visit to the dentist,—and she has her three babies with her. We have been having lively times, as they are not nearly so well regulated as Maggie. Auntie privately confided to me that the noise and confusion had gone to her head she thought, "it was fairly spinning around." As they went out of the room last night, all of them dragging at her and all clamouring for something, Auntie looked at me and said laughing "Behold your own future!" What do you think of that for a threat? However she isn't a professional fortune-teller like my New York friend;—in whom, by-the-way, I have lost confidence, for you remember that according to her baby was to be a *boy*.

I really am impressed by the fact that in one respect at least I am a *model* wife, in that I can with perfect equanimity—without a twinge of jealousy[—] hear my husband coolly confess that his "affections were engaged" by a "little beauty" on the cars!—and then narrate his assiduous efforts to engage *her* affections. But I mean to set a good example in that respect to certain people who need it—or rather who *did* need it—as it is too late now for you to profit by an example. It only remains to show you how you ought to *have* behaved,—when for example I frankly showed my interest in entertaining young clergymen! And now I think of it I *did* set you an example at the time, for didn't you rave over the Misses Bingham and Miss Hall and I don't know who beside? And did I allow the fact to disturb *my* peace of mind? No sir! *Never!* I was only sorry for the poor girls because they stood in such danger of a broken heart.

I hope darling that you are still improving physically, that the headaches and all bad symptoms are entirely gone, and that the next great task—the packing, won't *quite* wear you out. Oh if I were only there to help! *Isn't* it a good thing that the degree is off your mind,—that you don't have to stop for it on your way south, as we at first thought. When you come, dear, will you please bring me a little more camphor-ice (!) a tooth-brush like the last—they wear *so* much better than any others—and a box of *charcoal* for sketching. I don't think I remembered to look in the washstand drawers for the remnant that I had. It *may* be there and it *may* be enough. It comes in thin flat boxes holding fifty very slender sticks—price about 50 cts. The coarse for outlining (which I don't want) is in deeper boxes and thicker sticks. You can find it at Janentzky's. But I *must* stop and try to write to some other people today. My time for doing it is growing so short. We will run over to Maysville on Monday. I love you, I *love* you my husband my Woodrow my own darling. I cannot measure the depth of the love I have given you except it be by the capacity of that great heart of yours to hold it. I will give you all the love you want.   Your own little wife   Eileen

ALS (WC, NjP).

To Ellen Axson Wilson

My own darling,   Bryn Mawr, 4 June, '86.
I have just returned from my last class exercise. Think of that! How much nearer it seems to bring me to you! I shall proba-bly have to go on, an hour a day, with Miss Bancroft next week, but that does not mean any work outside of that one hour, and will, I think, by giving me something to do, save me the im-

patient feeling which would inevitably come with unoccupied days *on which I could not go to you.* True, I'll have packing to do, and I shall probably spread it over several days; but if I knew that I could go to you as soon as I finished my packing, it wouldn't take me many hours to finish! I could be off *to-night!* One week from to-night I *will* be off—Oh, isn't that just too good to be true!

I received a very sweet letter from Jessie this morning[1]—and a pretty, embroidered, lined, and scented blanket for baby, which I am to bring to you. She did not know your address. Here's a passage from the letter: "And cousin Woodrow you must see that Ellie Lou does not exert herself too much, or she will sow the seeds of invalidism that will make you both miserable in years to come. When I was in Rome I heard that she had gotten up already, and it made me feel dreadfully sorry to hear it. I write you this for I am afraid she, like every young mother, through ignorance, may injure herself for life." Rather a remarkable statement, that 'every young mother injures herself for life'! I smile, and think of Beth; but, as my letters will prove, I can't help saying 'amen' to the advice conveyed. She says that 'we have started out to raise a family about as quickly as they did'! But you shall read the whole letter when I come. 'When I come'! How many things of all sorts I have been putting off till that sweet time—principally *love-making!* You may not think, Miss, from the character and contents of some of my letters, that such a postponement has been very evident in this correspondence; but it has been very evident to me. I confess that I have made love *as hard as I could* in my letters—to the very top of my power of putting such feelings into *words.* But the mere words are not half of love-making, are they? I can't find the light and sweetness and power in my eyes that your love puts into them—and I'm sure that my voice has never yet learned to lend itself perfectly to the expression of any emotion—but, for all that, my words of love seem to me almost impotent unless I can *say* them with my lips and interpret them with my eyes—not to mention that sweet love-making in which there are no words spoken at all. But *I'm com-ing*—and then we'll *see* if it isn't better! Kiss my precious baby ever so many times for her father. A kiss for little sister; love for Eddie, aunt Lou, and all. You are my sweetheart, precious, my queen, my life—and I am *all*   Your own   Woodrow.

I enjoyed the affair at the Garretts' very much indeed last night. I shall *myself* be the sixth letter after this!

ALS (WC, NjP).
[1] Jessie Bones Brower to WW, June 2, 1886, ALS (WP, DLC).

From Ellen Axson Wilson

My own darling   Gainsville May [June] 4/86

I have been so busy today with sewing and other little things necessary to be done before going to Maysville, that night has come again and found your letter unwritten; for just as I was about to write this afternoon two ladies called and I lost my last chance. I will try to make up for short measure tomo—no, Sunday for I shall be very busy tomorrow too. You see, they all advised me to sew only a very little until the baby was six weeks old, so this week I have been extremely busy trying to arrange something to wear, and to make Eddie a little more respectable. Aunt Emmie, you know, has her hands drawn with rheumatism so that she can't sew, and the condition of Eddie's wardrobe is therefore deplorable. He is actually in *rags*—and as for buttons, he has forgotten what they look like, poor little fellow! And poor me! who must witness it, *I* mind it a good deal more than he does.

Loula was not able to get off on Sat. so we are going on Monday, coming back Friday morning. Minnie[1] comes up from Athens the same day. I had good news from Sav. today; Stockton is coming after all, for a flying visit, three or four days. He will come next week. I wrote begging him to come the last of the week so as to see as much of you as possible. I am so anxious for you to know each other better. When he wrote he was not sure just when he could get off.

We are both perfectly well[.] No baby could do better than she is doing now, not a trace of colic, costiveness, or anything else undesirable.

But it is quite late and I *must* close; please excuse haste. I havn't even time for more than a short love-message tonight, so I will just think an extra number of love thoughts instead. I *must* have some relief for my feelings. Oh darling, my love, my joy, my pride, *do* you think it possible for you to conceive how much I love you? how entirely I am   Your own   Eileen

ALS (WC, NjP).
[1] Ellen's first cousin, Minnie Brown.

To Ellen Axson Wilson

My own precious little wife,   Bryn Mawr, 5 June, '86.

What a wonderful love-letter this is that came this morning—the one of Wednesday, provoked by the light-hearted mood of the letters I wrote just after returning from Baltimore! Oh, you delightful little woman—with what supreme sweetness you **can love!**

Fortunately (or is it *un*fortunately?) I view my own achievements so far as irredeemably common-place; so that there is little or no danger of this too generous praise of yours turning my head at all. It all comes to me just as another way of saying the words that are the symbol of the strength and joy of my life—that tell me that I have won your whole heart. Ah, my perfect little charmer, you have left out from your enumeration of my titles to admiration the single thing concerning wh. my pride is without alloy: I won *you* for my bride, my precious wife, my all-sufficing, sweet companion! No man ever did more than that—no man ever more completely—surely no man ever *so* completely—made his heart's and his mind's—his *spirit's*—fortune at a single stroke. You were everything to me from the first; but you have been drawing closer and still closer to me ever since that sweet marriage day, till *now* I know no words in which to measure the full round of my supreme content and happiness. I have often told you, sweetheart, that you have realized for me my ideal of a sweet, perfect wife, but I don't believe that I have ever told you just *how* you have done so in some minor points. The imaginary, ideal woman whom I used to fancy I would like to marry had some characteristics which you have not, and you have proved to me that in those points I was mistaken—you have shown me how any qualities but just those that you have, and in just the combination in which you have them, would have jarred upon my peculiar sensibilities. In other words, although you have but confirmed my ideal in all essentials, you have altered and *perfected* it in some details—revealing to me *all* of my own heart in such matters. Oh, how awkward and slow I am in saying all this! But *you* can read my meaning, darling. It is, that you have taught me the small things of perfect love, as well as the great, by making me love as I love my life—*more* than I love my life—every motion of my darling's life—every impulse of her heart, every phase of her thought, every glance of her eye. All my *self* is married to her—to my sweet, my matchless Eileen!

Sweetheart, I have an ocular device for appreciating the shortening of the time of our separation. I keep the necessary number of envelopes addressed to you on the table here before me and watch the little pile dwindle day by day. To-day there will be but four left!

Oh, my wife and my little baby, *I love you.* I am coming to tell you how much.   Your own   Woodrow.
Love to aunt Lou and all.

ALS (WC, NjP).

From Ellen Axson Wilson

My own darling,   Gainsville, May [June] 5/86

I have been, as I predicted, very busy again today,—barely finished my "stint" by dark,—so I shall be obliged to put you off with
short measure *once* more—especially as I must write to Stockton
too tonight about doing some shopping for Eddie. But the short
letters don't matter so much now that the time is short too. Yes
indeed, love, I *do* share that feeling of impatience with letter-
writing which you describe. The bondage to pen and ink like every
other sort becomes harder as the time of release draws nearer.
One learns a sort of dull patience when serving out a *long* sentence. Then it is *so* true that not the most frequent exchange of
letters can take the place of "being together" for enabling us "to
love in the same vein at the same time." No "communion of spirit" in this world at least is perfect which is not shared by lip and
eye. For with their help understanding and sympathy pass and
repass with the speed of light;—then indeed do

> "Our hearts ever answer in tune and in time, love,
> As octave to octave and rhyme unto rhyme, love"—

And oh, the *happiness* to think that I can make such comparisons
now without endangering my peace of mind! Such thoughts
would only have made me desperate six weeks ago, but now ah,
joy of joys! they but add to my happiness, for that fullness of
content is but *one week* away! One week from this moment I
will be in my darling's arms. I will be *at home.* I must wake at
twelve tonight, if baby doesn't rouse me that I may say as soon as
possible "it is *this* week!" But I *must* say good-bye till tomorrow.
I am still perfectly well—the baby ditto. In fact neither of us
could be weller. And *one* of us could not love you, darling, more
than she does nor be more entirely   Your own   Eileen

Will you please bring me, dear, some *darning cotton*? two small
balls or "hanks" of blue two of brown and *four* of black—as Auntie
wants two. I wonder if they have silk darning *cotton*—so to speak!
I should very much like a little ball of it for my *black* silk stock-
ings. You may *ask* for it but don't *hunt* for it, for I can go on darning with sewing silk as I have always done. Now I think of it,
four or five skeins of black silk *flawse* (!) would do nicely.

ALS (WC, NjP).

From Horace Elisha Scudder

My dear Mr. Wilson   Cambridge, Mass 6 June 1886

This letter, I suspect, will be a surprise to you, for you must have made up your mind by this time that I had taken you at your retracted word, and intended to show by my silence how highly I valued your confidence in me.[1] Well, my silence may count for something, for if your letter had been an ordinary incident in my daily life I should have answered it promptly, and dismissed the matter. Whereas, it was a rare and exceedingly interesting event to me and I have postponed answering it until I could find some leisure for a more or less adequate reply.

I sometimes receive a letter expressive of interest in some piece of work which I have done, and I value such indications of friendship highly, but I confess to finding a very subtle pleasure in being treated to a disclosure of a friend's plans for his own work. I only wish that I had you this quiet Sunday afternoon on my piazza where we could talk freely upon subjects which I have much at heart, but which you have really more at mind than I. Where are you going to be this summer? I wish you could plan to spend a few days with me at our sea-side quarters. We go to a house which we hire at Little Boar's Head on the New Hampshire coast. I am obliged to spend from Monday morning to Wednesday evening at the office in Boston but the rest of the week I expect to be with my family, bathing, loafing and working. Come and share with me the first two of these occupations!

Your scheme is so comprehensive that I can only now make very partial observations on it. In its scope it seems to imply nothing less than an organon, and as such it has peculiar interest for me. I have had floating before me for some time the conception of a history of the United States upon lines which I partially disclosed in my school history.[2] Now I am convinced that no one can write our history adequately who has not grasped with some firmness the notion of organic growth. It is in the apparent absence of any conception of this that [John Bach] McMaster's work seems to me a somewhat idle and curious collection of phenomena. What I am feeling after with reference to historic composition will no doubt be illuminated by such work as you propose for yourself, and my want is that of many men—students and others —who do not contemplate writing an historical treatise, yet do require in their thought and in their work a clear, constructive statement of the principles which underlie our national development.

There is only one caution which I would offer. I do not understand you to intend either in form or in special spirit a reply to Maine or to Burgess, but what you say leads me to fear lest you may be too much influenced in your construction by the wish to answer these writers. I think all polemical matter in such cases should be in footnotes; that one's own constructive thought should be the final statement and other men's theories or views be divergent from it. Such work as Sir Henry Maine's may well suggest the need of another treatment, and may affect the process of one's argument, but an answer is never so effective as an independent assertion. I hope the final form in which you cast your thought will be so positive and so constructive as to lift the whole discussion above the field of controversy.

I have been thinking about the tentative publication. There are certain advantages in so doing. One tries on one's thought and sometimes elicits further discussion, and if one is sure upon the main lines of his thought, he may be able thereby to strengthen afterward minor considerations. On the other hand there is a weakness in the effect produced by a book when it has already appeared piece meal in magazines and journals. I do not like to advise you in such a matter, but I should *think* that the delivery of your thought in the form of college lectures if your chair permits this, would answer the purpose of defining and clearing your mental operation, and leave you free to say your whole say in a book at last. I question somewhat the wisdom of publishing monographs and finally combining them into a whole. Better the patient waiting upon one's thought and the deliberate presentation of a completed work than the occasional delivery of a portion here and a portion there, with the almost necessary repetition which this involves.

I say this with reference to your book. I would not say it with reference to every book, even of its kind. The magazines do much to familiarize people with currents of thought, but after all they tend to prevent monumental works, and to engender a species of literary haste and impatience. I would far rather see from you occasional magazine articles upon outlying topics, while the book was slowly taking form to appear at last not as a republication of fragmentary papers, even remoulded, but as a solid structure.

I do not know that I am answering any of your questions, but I have written out of a strong interest and have not been anxious to say what you might like to hear. Let me ask you, by the way, if you have ever looked at a volume of Bampton Lectures on The World as a Subject of Redemption by Canon Fremantle?[3] I think

I have the title right. The book would set you to thinking and enrich your thought, I suspect, in the field which you have chosen.

This letter has been written with many interruptions, and may read accordingly, but I have delayed answering your welcome letter so long that I must not hold this for another possible stretch of leisure.

Do let me hear from you when you will, and especially give me the hope of seeing you this summer.

Yours very truly   H. E. Scudder

ALS (WP, DLC) with WWhw notation "Ans. July 10/86."
  [1] He referred to WW to H. E. Scudder, May 12, 1886.
  [2] *A History of the United States of America* (Boston, 1884).
  [3] William Henry Fremantle, *The World as the Subject of Redemption* (London, 1885).

To Ellen Axson Wilson

My own darling,   Bryn Mawr, 6 June, '86.

What you tell me about her makes me like Mrs. Shepherd immensely. *Any*body who had been long with you would love you, if they had any heart to love with; but Mrs. S. *shows* it so genuinely. She is evidently made of true womanly stuff. You precious little woman, you—how fatal it is for everybody that comes into contact with you! Their hearts are not safe for a moment. You are a perfect *love-centre*, towards which people of all degrees are drawn—from Englishmen down to—Shepherds. The fact that you yourself do not know this explains the fundamental and persistent error of a certain part of your philosophy—the part, namely, which treats of the difference between my being jealous and your *not* being jealous, at a certain interesting period of our lives. *I* am no love-centre; but *you are*: there's the whole difference. Nobody but your own dear, eccentric little self ever thought seriously of falling in love with me; *every*body of both sexes falls in love with you, as if by a law of nature. At one time I suspected that you took this view of the case, as regards me. I used to write rhapsodies about the Bingham's, Miss Hall, and other pretty, commonplace young women with the deliberate purpose of seeing whether or not you would manifest any symptom of jealousy. Never a bit! And the fact that you did not was susceptible of more than one explanation. One possible explanation, you will perceive, was of a nature to contribute to my jealousy of any one whom I might imagine more *naturally* lovable than myself! If you *had* been jealous, it would have proved that you knew neither yourself nor me. You see how complicated the whole matter was.

No, if Aunt Lou says that a crowd of little ones pulling at her skirts is a type of your future, she is not a reliable prophetess. That's a matter which depends, not upon chance, but upon me, and—but I have already recorded my thoughts and purposes on that head.

Oh, sweetheart, I can't tell you how it delights me to know that you are so well, and are *looking* so well. My dear, splendid little wife! I'm just as proud of you as I can be. Will it help you to keep well this week to know that I am coming at the end of it —to make my heart glad with the sight of the bloom on my darling's cheek? Oh, it will make me so happy to see you not only a mother but a perfectly well, radiant little mother! You don't know, Eileen, my queen, how the excitement of the prospect of seeing you has risen with the incoming of this week—the prospect of seeing you and *my baby*! In spite of the reality and joy of the new love that has sprung up in my heart since baby came, I find it impossible—will you laugh at the confession, I wonder—to divest my thoughts of my little daughter of a certain odd sense of *unreality*. In other words—living off here in lonely bachelorhood—I cannot *fully* realize *yet* that I am a father! Your references to the baby in your letters—growing more and more the familiar, matter-of-course references of one who is quite used to having a baby— fill me sometimes, for a passing moment, with a queer feeling of *strangeness* to the life upon which you have entered. My dear one, my precious little wife, whose life during those past sweet months that we were together was absolutely one with mine, has gone on ahead of me into a life I *know* nothing of—that's the thought. It is almost as if you had left me behind, however much against your will. You are two months ahead of me in parentage; and I already begin to foretaste the strangeness of seeing baby, and trying to feel that she is mine! You will have to teach me that she is not a little stranger—that she has *all along* been mine! I am so glad that she is not old enough yet to shrink from strangers: it would hurt me dreadfully to be a stranger to my own little daughter!—I suppose that the whole of my feeling is summed up in the *wonder* which one must naturally feel about anybody whom he loves, and loves more and more, with an ever growing tenderness, day by day and yet has never seen. Then, too, the situation is not without its element of *awe* for me—may our gracious God grant me patience, tenderness, and wisdom such as a father should have! I am not fit for such responsibilities; but I can and must strive to grow fit!

So you go to Maysville to-morrow? My heart shall follow you

thither, darling, praying for your safety and happiness, wondering about your experiences, longing for the week to pass and bring you to my arms.

I go into town again this afternoon, as usual. It will probably be my good-bye visit to uncle Tom's. It has been very pleasant to go in and dine with him as I have done, and it is only for reasons with which he has nothing to do that I am glad to count this the *last* of these visits,—the last before I turn my face *home*wards, to *you*. I rejoice in recognizing *any*thing as the last before *that*— my joy shall be almost full when I count the last *day*—it will be altogether full when I count the last *moment*! This dreadful separation has tried my strength of spirit to the utmost—and now that it is almost over I begin to realize what its ending will be for me. It will be freedom and life once more! It will be rest and strength.

I shall make the little purchases you name to-morrow, when I am going in with a list of my own. Are you sure there's nothing else you want?

I love you, my darling, more than tongue can tell.

Your own   Woodrow.

ALS (WC, NjP).

From Ellen Axson Wilson

My own darling,   Gainsville May [June] 6/86

Your letter giving an account of the one from Jessie and the pretty present is just at hand. I am *very* much obliged for the latter; please tell her so for me and I will write later, after I see it. So Jessie too adopts the motherly tone towards me!—began it, as I now remember, before we were married! I believe girls when they marry, no longer recognize their old birthday, but begin to count their age from their marriage-day. All my married friends evidently consider themselves my elders by just the difference in the dates of our marriages. I must begin to send letters full of wise counsel to Rose!

I am truly delighted that the packing is progressing so easily,— the hardest part all done. Oh what a load is off my mind to think that you are actually *through*—with lectures and lessons at least and almost through with *every*thing! I feel and I hope *you* feel as light-hearted over it as I "used to" do when school "let out" for vacation. But then I have so many reasons for being light-hearted now that it is hard to say always which is in the ascendency,—though there is no doubt on that score *today*, the one all-absorbing, joy-inspiring thought is that "it is *this* week,"—only five days more! Oh darling, darling I could almost cry for joy at that thought. *Next Sunday* we will be together,—those five days would seem a great deal longer if Sunday were one of them.

But besides all the various causes for rejoicing which *you* afford me, I am *especially* happy over the baby these last few days. She seems to have taken "such a fine start,"—is doing so much better than for some two weeks before, seems so entirely relieved of the colic and the costiveness which until this week seemed so hard to control. I began to fear that the milk disagreed with her, and of course was very much worried. Did I tell you that we are feeding her a little now?—twice a day,—morning and evening. I, alas! no longer have enough;—she requires a great deal more, and I had such a dreadful time with my breasts for a month or more that I give a great deal less. They say that now they are well and I am taking more exercise I may have more again. But I should always be afraid to trust to it entirely— she is such a *very* hearty child. I should always be haunted with the idea that I was starving her to death; as Auntie says so many young mothers do. She is firmly convinced that she really killed her child that way. She says the feeding of children is her "hobby." That most women,—or *ladies* at least, alas for the distinction! —are obliged to feed their babies some, and most of those that don't *ought to*. In fact I have heard so much on that subject, that from being very miserable at the necessity I have come to feel it a great comfort to be able sometimes to *know* from the evidence of my own *eyes* that baby has had enough, and not merely to *infer* so from certain indications. Indeed *I* want to stuff her at all hours so as to be *sure* she don't "starve." I am quite pleased with my new nurse, by-the-way. She is very capable, amiable and kind, seems to love children dearly. I must not forget to add that I had another wonderful night last night; baby slept from ten to *six*! I used to say she was a very good baby as babies go, but now I declare her a perfect cherub. I think she will at least *pretend* to be glad to see you, she can give you some very sweet smiles of welcome at any rate; & I will give you *one* or *two* to supplement them. Oh my darling *won't* I make love to you! I thought in the old days that I was as happy as I *could* be when you were 'coming,' but now all those experiences pale by comparison with *this*!—now my heart is like to break with gladness. Ah, Woodrow darling, I am glad I did not love you then as I do now. How *could* I have borne the separation. One day I will look back on these two months and they will seem like a strange

bad dream, and I will wonder how I bore it. But I have had that wondering thought about every trouble I ever had after it had passed;—as before it came I would have thought that I *could* not bear it. There is no promise which we can more clearly see fulfilled than that which tells us that "as thy day is so shall thy strength be." And there is scarcely any blessing greater than our inability to look beyond the day,—to know what the future need will be. But oh, let us pray that the future will not bring us much of separation to bear,—that if possible we may never again be two whole months apart. I am my darling forever, heart and soul,
                                   Your own little wife,   Eileen

ALS (WP, DLC).

To Ellen Axson Wilson

My own darling,   Bryn Mawr, 7 June 1886.
    I was kept over the hour by 'Bancy'[1] this morning; this is my shopping day—so that I must go into town as early as possible; the usual half-hour has slipped away in shaving &c., and the aggregate result is that I will have to be very brief this morning in order to catch even the 11:48.
    I went to town yesterday according to program, but found 'Aunt Sadie' tolerably disagreeable. Cooper[2] has had the whooping cough for some time and she has contracted a sympathetic 'bark' which has not aided in keeping her temper in an equable poise. She knew absolutely everything about every topic that was broached; and I came away more disgusted and tired than ever by her shallow wit and surface information. Uncle Tom is either very blind or of a heavenly temperament, to stand as he does the *kind* of disagreement with which she treats some of his opinions —not frank but full of a poorly disguised acid of antagonism. It would ruin me within a twelvemonth to live with such a woman, with just sense and brilliancy enough to baffle you with the regret that she hasn't something to give them weight and dignity—some insight—some heart—some *real thought*. It's a sort of blank cartridge mind—full of the noise of effective discourse, but never sending a shot to the heart of anything!
    I am feeling quite well—though a wee bit languid because of the rather heavy weather we are having.
    I am *so* sorry, darling, *so* sorry to hear of your sewing so hard! No excuse for short letters, short of sickness, could make me more uneasy that [than] that does! Please, *please* get a sempstress, if one is to be had!

I am delighted to hear that Stockton is coming after all—and I sincerely hope that he *can* stay long enough to see me.

I love you, darling, with all my heart. Thoughts of you shall go with me every where to-day and shall make me happy—as happy as happy can be!   Your own   Woodrow
Love to all.

ALS (WC, NjP).
1 Miss Bancroft.
2 Cooper Hoyt, son of Thomas A. and Sadie Cooper Hoyt.

Two Letters from Ellen Axson Wilson

My own darling,   Gainsville May [June] 7/86
We are still in Gainsville, you perceive. It rained all last night and had not cleared off this morning so that we were afraid to start with the baby. But this after-noon it is very bright, so we will probably go in the morning, that is if the trains on this road will condescend to run. Something seems to be always wrong with this poor unfortunate road; there was an accident on it yesterday and no train and no *mail* today. But if it will only come through safely and on time Saturday, I will forgive it all past delinquencies.

Don't imagine that the thing I enclose is really a *likeness* of baby, it is hardly a suggestion, except of the *shape* of the head and face. It looks—for *one* thing—too old and large. I send it merely because I can't be easy in my mind, somehow, unless I at least "go through the motions" of fulfilling every promise I am rash enough to make. I have been trying hard to find opportunity to do a better one, but it seemed impossible; whenever I begin she is sure to stir; and besides I have been so busy of late. Havn't time to finish this now, even if it were worth it. Baby is just as well as ever, had a good night again. I am also feeling splendidly, though needing to get out again,—as I shall this afternoon. You have gotten me in such training that I miss exercise much much more than I used to. It has been raining now for several days. Last night we had an *earth-quake*,—the first one in my experience —an[d] I didn't *experience* it, for I knew nothing about it! But it gave us quite a nice little shaking according to Aunt Lou.

So Miss Bancroft holds on to the last, does she? Is she as exasperating as ever? Are you to have the other old lady[1] next year? On the whole, I don't know but what I shall be glad if you do! When I consider how susceptible you are to the charms of of [sic] pretty girls on the *cars* I am almost afraid to have you closeted for an hour a day with one! I shall feel disposed to join the class myself!

Oh dear, just to think that but for a few hours work—two examinations—you might have been with me a whole week sooner! It is very hard;—however this is no time for complaints, the time of rejoicing is too near; and when you come the joy will be great enough to make up for everything. Oh love, my heart is *so* full,—too full almost for words. I only want to sit and dream of you and of it all. When writing now I am constantly catching myself sitting with pen suspended and thoughts all with *you*, but far, far away from the *letter to you*. Evidently the writing,—though not the *receiving* of letters has almost fulfilled its mission for this time.

Oh darling, darling, I am so happy at the thought of seeing you, so eager for the time to come, so impatient of the writing that altogether it is almost more than I can bear. I need Grandfather to preach me a sermon on "calmness[.]" I will at least try not to let myself be *killed* by excess of love and joy. But that is *all* I can do. Woodrow, *I love you.* I am forever,

> Your own little,   Eileen

I suppose of course, dear, you called on the Millers; did you not? Never having heard you say, I thought perhaps I had better remind you, in case you had forgotten.

ALS (WP, DLC). Enc.: EAW's sketch of Margaret Wilson.
1 Ellen probably referred to Lucy Maynard Salmon, born in 1853, who was the History Fellow at Bryn Mawr in 1886-87.

My own darling,   Gainsville, June 7 1886
I am so afraid I shan't have an opportunity for writing tomorrow in the hurry of getting off and the confusion of reaching a new place, that I will write a little tonight instead. Though I am hoping that it will be raining again tomorrow,—it looks very threatening now. I should be delighted to escape going altogether.

My letter was received safely tonight,—the road having been patched up again. Such a sweet precious letter as it is! It is a fact that never ceases to be as wonderful to me as it is sweet,—that fact of your love for me and *content* with me. And the crowning joy is that I can listen to such words now with no fears or doubts for the future,—with never a shadow across the sunshine with which your love surrounds me. For I am sure now that my darling can't be under any delusion with regard to me; after a year spent in the sweet intimacy of marriage. He *must* know me, and knowing, he still loves me. If he can be happy with me for one year surely he can through the years to come. Aye, happier,

I hope. I believe that is the law of a true marriage always; the sympathy, the dependence, the love are ever growing. Surely living with you,–living in your thoughts so constantly I shall bye-and-bye be more truly your *help-meet*–your companion. I shall be ever taking from you,–learning of you–and my dearest wish will be in *some* form to render it back again. I should never have dared to marry you, darling, if I had not thought that I could *grow*. I *must* grow it seems to me with such a master. It is–in a slightly different form–the old argument to which in past times I returned again and again to still my doubting heart,–"since I have the average amount of intelligence, surely my great love will do the rest. It will make me quick to see all his needs, and teach me how to satisfy them,–all those that wifely love and sympathy and devotion *can* satisfy." I cannot tell you, love, with what surpassing joy I dedicate myself–heart and soul and mind to your service,–how *entirely* I love you, nor what happiness I find in loving–and in being loved. I cannot think that in all the world there is another such happy wife and mother. No. I must modify that statement. The happiest mother in the world is without doubt *yours*. She is most truely blessed among women. And since you are beyond all other men unselfish it *must* be that you are also happy, because you are the source of such wonderful, perfect happiness in others. Whatever *you* think of yourself and your achievements, darling, you know at least that you give joy of the rarest, purest, most perfect sort to all who love you. That is *one* achievement which you *can't* ignore or underestimate. And however little satisfaction you derive from your other triumphs, *this* one I trust you will enjoy with all your heart. With all *my* heart   Your own little wife   Eileen.

ALS (WC, NjP).

From Daniel Collamore Heath

Dear Prof. Wilson:–   Boston, June 8, 1886.

The enclosed letter from W. C. P. Breckenbridge of Ky.[1] to whom I wrote some time since for an elementary book on the subject, may be of interest to you. You may return it if you please.

Do you object to our putting the book under the general heading that we have used?

Very truly yours,   D. C. Heath & Co.

TL (WP, DLC) with WWhw notation on env.: "Ans. July 14, 1886"; also WWhw notes on verso of the letter and a memorandum about receipt from his parents on July 27, 1886, of $175.00 in two drafts on the American Exchange National Bank of New York.

To Ellen Axson Wilson

My own precious Eileen,   Bryn Mawr, 8 June, 1886.

It's really a shame that I should have to cut these *last* letters short! But again the hurry of last things to be done has made it necessary—and perhaps, after all, it is true lover's art to have it so. Short letters will leave my sweet mistress unsatisfied and all the more eager to have me instead. And, besides, it isn't the *length* of a letter that *tells* but the character of its message. If I could but have the gift of love-speech for which I have so often vainly wished, a single page would suffice me to say what my darling would hear me say—and *all* that she would hear me say. I would translate my love for her and my surpassing joy at the prospect of seeing her so soon into words which would make her sweet heart thrill, if ever words did. My life is brightening wonderfully as it approaches *her* once more! My thoughts revolve about her with a sweet speed of hope and joy that is delicious. Oh, if I only knew a *song* to put my love into! *That* would be the only true language for my present mood. I am *rejoicing* in all this hurried work that is closing the term—it does not *tire* or *worry* me in the least, because it all ends *in you*, my queen, my darling, my matchless little wife. When you are once more safely in my arms, I shall be *perfectly happy. I love you*—that is the whole of my life—that and the sweet fact that *you love me*, that I am

Your own   Woodrow.

ALS (WC, NjP).

Three Letters from Ellen Axson Wilson

[Gainesville, Ga.,] June 8th [1886]

Again we have failed to get off. Decided first not to attempt it because early in the morning it was misting, and later discovered that there was *no train* today! Will try again tomorrow and if we again fail will give up the trip. I am almost afraid to go now lest something should happen to detain me there beyond Friday night. The morning train leaves Maysville before day,—too early to start with the baby. If it *should* be storming so that I can't leave I will send a telegram to meet you at Lulu on Sat. night. Then you can leave the train there and come *directly* to Maysville. But of course

I shall in all probability be back in Gainsville—if I leave it at all. We are both perfectly well, and I am just as much in love as ever.

Your own   Eileen

I enclose a description of our next journey together.

ALS (WC, NjP). Enc. missing.

My own darling,   Gainsville June 8/86

Again I will write a few lines in advance, lest the confusion of the morrow prevent. But it must be a *very* few lines for it grows late now, and I must, if I get off, rise very early in the morning. But I hope a short message will make no difference to you by the time this reaches you, that you will be thinking too much about *seeing* me to care greatly for merely *hearing* from me. Oh, my love, I pray God you may have a safe journey and a pleasant [one], that you may be just as *happy* as I was *sad* when I passed that way, and that your happiness at the end of your journey may match with your *welcome*. Do you know that Mrs. Sanford, Auntie's sister-in-law, said this afternoon that she thought you were very fortunate to be *just* coming *now*,—that you miss all the troubles inevitable at such times and have all the joy. You arrive on the scene just as baby is emerging from the first troubled period of babyhood to where it is smooth sailing; and also just as she is ceasing to be merely a little animal and becoming more like "folks,"—growing perceptibly sweeter every day. I think she is in great measure right. And though I know that your sweet unselfishness, darling, would make you only the more anxious to be with me, *because* of these little cares and troubles which surround the business of getting a little mortal fairly started on it's life journey, I have often been very very glad that you could not be involved in them, *especially* because of all your other cares and occupations which *you* could not postpone,—as a mother can and *must*,—devoting herself entirely to the little new life. Ah yes, love, however hard it has been, I am glad, *most* glad I came, I am sure that God's hand was in it all from first to last,—that he answered our earnest prayers for direction, and ordered all things well. I believe that, unless you had been sustained by *love* alone, you would have been quite broken down had you had the care of wife and baby allways on your mind in addition to the lectures and examinations.

Mrs. S. also said that it was part of your good fortune that you were absent all the while that I was weak and pale and more or less sick,—that you will see me again only when I am as well and bright and fresh-looking as ever. But I know that my true lover who loves me so purely and unselfishly does not echo the first part of that proposition, so neither do *I* dare do so.

And now "good-bye" my love until we meet;—though even now we *are together*, and I shall come with you all the way. Ah, if my power equalled my love what a guardian angel I should be to you! But there is One who loves you even more than I;—to His *all-* powerful love I commit my treasure. With what redoubled earnestness will my prayers ascend until He in mercy brings you to me safe and well! I *love you* my darling, with a perfect love, and I am *forever*　　　　Your own little wife,　Eileen.

ALS (WC, NjP).

[Gainesville, Ga.] June 9th [1886]

The weather is brighter this morning and we are actually off,— just about starting. Both quite well. Hurriedly but lovingly.

Your own Eileen.

ALS, written on EAW to WW, June 7, 1886, second letter.

From Richard Heath Dabney

My dear Tom:　　　　　　　　Richmond. June 19th, 1886.

Allow me to congratulate you most heartily (though, I confess, somewhat tardily), on your new dignity of fatherhood! I was delighted to hear of your being a papa, and that both mother & daughter were doing so well.[1] May all three of you live long & prosper! I suppose you feel very ancient now. At all events, it makes me feel so myself to think of such a very ass, so illimitable an idiot's being a sire. You have gotten far, far ahead of me; and, with such a handicap, I know not when I can hope to catch up with you.

After congratulating you on so important an event, I feel as if it were almost superfluous to offer congratulations on your having taken Ph.D. For, after all, such a "label" looks very dwarfish & insignificant by the side of the much larger label that you already possess—& that too, not bestowed by the Hopkins or any other institution—the label, namely, of "Author of *Congressional Government.*" However, as you say, the caudal appendage bestowed by the Hopkins may quicken to some extent your promotion in the way of salary etc.; and, if so, it was worth the trouble you took to get it.

Many thanks for the kind criticism you gave in your letter of

Don Miff, as well as for that which you wrote for the Wilmington paper.[2] I should like very much to see the latter, but don't know what the name of the paper is. Could you let me know when you write again? I might then write to the editor & ask him to send me a copy.

I have been elected prof. of History in the Indiana Univ., and have strong reason to believe, from what Jordan has said, that it was your recommendation, more than anything else, that secured my election. Please accept, therefore, my sincerest thanks for the great service you have rendered me.

In some respects the place is quite a desirable one. For instance, I shall have entire control over my department, except that it is prescribed that I devote such & such a number of hours a week to such & such classes. I am somewhat afraid, however, that I am not going to give very thorough satisfaction, & that I may be "bounced" at the end of one year. For Jordan evidently saw something about me, when I went out there, that he didn't like; and, in fact, he again offered the place to a Dr. Albert Shaw (a Hopkins man) after seeing me. Shaw declined it, however, as he was getting a larger salary as editor of some Western paper. Altogether, the Hoosiers have treated me in a manner which we Southerners, with our effete notions of honor & straightforwardness, would call anything but high-toned. It would make too long a story to tell you all the details; but I will just mention that, while Jordan had all along led me to believe that my salary would be $1500, in case of my election, he sent me a telegram after the Trustees had met, saying that they could give me only a thousand the first year. The other five hundred went to the ejected professor whose place I am to take, & who was not informed that he was to be ejected until Commencement day. That is to say: I had to suffer because the authorities of the place were not square & candid enough to tell the man in time for him to have a chance to get another place, although it was perfectly well known to them months before that he would not be retained.

Jordan requested in his telegram that I should telegraph whether I accepted or not. I accepted, but told him that I did so with reluctance, & requested that, in case he decided to eject me next year, he would inform me of the fact before the last day of the session. He says in reply that my salary would not have been cut down but for the fact that the univ. lost $10000 of its income this year through a legal quibble. This seems like a partial excuse; but, as I have heard from another & reliable source that the $10000 will almost certainly [be] recovered in the autumn, I am afraid I have to deal with a rather shady set. If I could now get any other place, I should resign this one; but places are scarce, & I thought I had better hold on to the bird in the hand while I had him. I should have had a good chance of getting a place at W. & L. if any had been established; but the trustees were unwilling to incur the expense just now. . . .

I came down to Richmond ten days ago to act as groomsman at the wedding of my Cousin Virginia Bagby (daughter of Dr. B.) & shall be here till nearly July 1st, after which I shall be in Middleburg, Loudoun Co., Va. With best regards & best wishes to Mrs & Miss Wilson, I remain, as ever,

Your sincere friend   R. H. Dabney.

ALS (WP, DLC) with WWhw notation on env.: "Ans. Nov. 7/86."
  ¹ This letter from Wilson to Dabney is missing.
  ² WW to R. H. Dabney, Nov. 7, 1886, reveals that Wilson did indeed write a "notice" of *Don Miff* and send it to Theodore B. Kingsbury, editor of the Wilmington, N. C., *Morning Star*. In this letter to Dabney, Wilson said that Kingsbury had not even acknowledged receipt of the review, and that he, Wilson, did not know whether it had ever been printed. All evidence indicates that it was not. Kingsbury, in the *Morning Star*, June 15, 1886, said that he could not review *Don Miff* because he had not read it, but that he would reprint an appropriate review if one appeared elsewhere. He printed one by William Preston Johnston, President of Tulane University, on June 20, 1886.

To Thomas Randolph Ball[1]

Dear Mr. Ball,   Clarksville, Tenn., 10 July, 1886.
    Your card of June 23, addressed to Wilmington, N. C., has reached me here. Yes, indeed, I would like to have my diploma. I enclose the necessary 30 cents. My address will be as above for the summer.
    With kindest regards, and thanking you very much for your kindness in communicating with me in this matter, about which I was on the point of writing you, I am

Yours sincerely,   Woodrow Wilson

ALS (MdBJ)
  ¹ Clerk of The Johns Hopkins University, 1878-89; Registrar, 1889-1923.

To Horace Elisha Scudder

Dear Mr. Scudder,   Clarksville, Tenn., July 10, 1886.
    I cannot express too warmly my obligations to you for your kind and suggestive letter. It reached me in Bryn Mawr just as I was, so to speak, in the midst of leaving—performing the last duties for the dying session of the college; and since I got away I have been almost constantly on the wing, having only just now

settled down after a great deal of preliminary fluttering. Mrs. Wilson had preceded me by a couple of months or more in coming South, and was waiting for me with a little daughter whom I had not seen. You will understand, therefore, why I did not reply at once to your cordial and exceedingly gratifying invitation—which was as tempting as it was gratifying—to join you at the sea-side. I fear that, under any circumstances, I should have been obliged to decline—much as such a visit would contribute to my enjoyment and advantage every way; but, under the circumstances I have mentioned, it was impossible for me to turn either thoughts or steps in any direction but that which I took so soon as ever I was free to leave my college duties.

After making a considerable circuit of visits with my little family among relatives, I am at last stationary for the summer—so far as I see—at my father's home here in Clarksville, Tenn.—a brisk little tobacco market which cheerfully and hopefully pays its own way in everything else, but whose weekly paper is in favour of the 'Blair Bill.'[1]

Each time that I read your delightful letter I find my acquiescence in its welcome advice more complete. Its suggestion with reference to the exclusion of controversial matter from what I purpose writing I accepted from the first, on the principle on which advice is generally accepted:—that it fell in entirely with my own views. On the question of the mode of first publication—in monographs or as a whole—I followed, on the first reading, what is also a very common course: I admitted the wisdom of your counsel, but I demurred to its acceptance on other grounds —on *personal* grounds. I was inclined to put myself before the work I proposed doing in this matter—especially since I had persuaded myself that, by advancing my own interests, I should advance the interests of my work. I had thought that, by issuing the various parts of the work separately, and in a somewhat fuller form—fuller, i.e., as regards discussion and illustration—than I should wish them to be when combined at last, I might possibly make, during the progress of the work, reputation enough for myself as a thorough worker and thoughtful writer to attract the attention of university trustees and increase my chances of securing a special chair of political science such as would afford the best opportunities for the comp[l]etion of my work and its final re-writing as a whole. Without the advantages of such a special chair, the work must continue to be done 'out of hours,' and will, I fear, suffer much in consequence. I am a slow writer, and so long as the regular duties of my chair constitute a distraction from my original work, I must produce with painful slowness and perhaps with more than the inevitable amount of imperfection, because of the absence of all proper conditions for concentrated and continuous thought. Looked at from this point of view, the question as to mode of first publication really seemed to be a question as to the possibility of completing my scheme at all or not—and the monographic plan seemed, after all, a plan for the benefit of the work as a whole.

But, as I have said, my own thoughts have been yielding to yours on this point, as on others. No part of the work can be made so satisfactory disjoined from the other parts as it would be standing in all its connections—and the finished work might suffer from the impression of incompleteness—of *scrappiness*—made by the separately published parts. I must trust to more occasional writings to win favour with college authorities while my book is a-making.

I am much obliged for your mention of Canon Freemantle's Bampton Lectures. I shall certainly obtain and read them. I had not known of the book; and I am conscious that my thought needs enriching on that side.

Now that I am assured of your interest in what I am doing, I will venture to add a few words as to the way in which I am trying to study government. Dr. Mulford furnishes me with inspiration and philosophy, but the 'historical school' furnishes me with *method*. I want to come at the true conception of the nature of the modern democratic state by way of an accurate exposition of the history of democratic development. I want to keep safely within sober induction from concrete examples of political organization and of realized political thought. I would read the heart of political *practice*, letting political theory wait on that practice and carry weight only in proportion to its nearness to what has been actually accomplished. I would trace the genesis and development of modern democratic institutions—which, so far, seem to me expressions of the adult age of the state, the organic people come to its self-possessed majority and no longer in need of the guardianship of king or aristocracy or priesthood—as Maine has traced the genesis and development of modern legal systems.

Just as most economists have, until very lately, deduced their whole science from certain hypothetical states of fact and an analysis of certain fictitious kinds of men, so most writers on politics have—like Hobbes, Locke, Rousseau, *et id omne genus*—evolved government out of a primitive condition of mankind for the actual existence of which they could adduce no sort of evidence. They adopted the method common among many novelists of a certain class—of creating collections of dissected qualities and then bringing about situations in which those qualities could put on the similitude of real persons: a method opposite to the dramatic, Shaksperean method—of setting forth words and actions, and *so* letting character emerge. As we can know persons only from what they say and do, and the manner of their acting and speaking, so we can know governments only from what *they* say and do and the manner of their speech and action. But in governments and persons alike we can look beneath the surface, if we have discernment enough, and so discover more of *character* than any amount of *a priori* speculation can reveal. I have not hit upon a very happy analogy; but you will catch my thought. It is, that the true philosophy of government can be extracted only from the true history of government.

This is simply saying that I would apply the now common inductive method to the study of democratic government—to the study of the genesis and development of *our* democratic government in particular—; but I want to say more than that. I want that method to carry me further than it carries most of those who employ it. Men study the material universe so; and stop short at the differentiated *forms* of matter and life. Aristotle studied politics so; but did not get further than the outward differences of institutions—did not press on beyond logical distinctions to discover the spiritual oneness of government, the life that lives *within* it. The ideal thing to do would be to penetrate to its *essential character* by way of a thorough knowledge of all its outward manifestations of character.

But the number of pages to which even these vague general statements have led me demonstrates for the nth time the impossibility of saying anything specific, in a letter, about the big subject I have taken in hand. I wish the more than [that] I could do what you so unselfishly offer me the opportunity to do: *talk* it over with you. *Then* I might go at least a little way *inside* the subject I so love to explore, but whose outside only I have been able to touch here.

Thanking you again most cordially for your generous interest in my plans, and for the interesting and valuable advice contained in your letter, as well as for your invitation, I am

Yours most sincerely,   Woodrow Wilson

ALS (WC, NjP).
1 The paper was the *Tobacco Leaf*.

Two Letters from Daniel Collamore Heath

Dear Prof. Wilson: Boston, July 19, 1886

Yours of the 14th inst. is received. Our catalogue has been so delayed that the answer happened to be in time for our purpose, so your apologies are all unnecessary. We did wonder, however, why we did not hear from you, but concluded you had gone to Europe.

We will get the list of books and send you as soon as possible. If you would like to have us send a part of them as they come in before waiting for the whole list, please drop us a postal to that effect. It is possible we can aid you in getting lists of books on your subject from the Atheneum and the Boston Public Library if you do not find your list. It suits me all the better to have your book progress slowly and surely so that when it is done it will be safer to the publisher as well as more creditable to the author. I believe your plan of having it "grow" is by all means the right one. We have had many calls for a new book for the lower grades in Civil Government, similar for instance to the enclosed which comes in the same mail as your letter.[1] Will you kindly return it, and give us if you can the name of a good man to prepare an elementary book, or would you like to prepare an elementary one after making the larger one?

We took your note on the announcement to mean that you wished us to leave out any description of yourself further than that you were the author of Congretional [sic] Government rather than a description of the book, so we leave a description of the book in and change the other as you suggested.

I trust that the little Wilson is better, and that you are now having a pleasant vacation.

Very truly yours,   D. C. Heath & Co.

TL (WP, DLC) with WWhw notation on env.: "Ans. July 23/86."
  [1] It was a letter from J. A. M. McDowell, superintendent of the Millersburg, Ohio, Public School. Wilson returned the letter but made a digest of it: "Mem. for text-book in *Civil Government*," WWhw MS. (WP, DLC).

Dear Prof. Wilson: Boston, July 27, 1886.

Yours of the 22d received. If you are willing to forego copyright on the books until a sufficient number have been sold to remunerate the publisher for actual cost for preparing the work for the press, or still better if you would own the plates yourself, we giving you 15% copyright until you got back your money with interest, and thereafter the usual 10%, we shall be glad to undertake both of the books. We send you one of our copyright forms that you may see that this is the arrangement we usually make. Of course when the author owns the plates we should wish to pay copyright from the very first. If you will kindly return the form we send you with your wish as to the arrangement on both books we will try and meet you, and will announce the small book together with the other giving no description of the other, simply saying it is for the lower grades of schools.

We send the Bagehot and Dowes' book. Macy's we shall be able to send in a few days.[1] It is not yet published. A few of the other books we have already obtained and will forward to you charging you exactly what they do us with the postage added. We could obtain none of the French and German books, and are therefore obliged to import them which will take some little time of course. Very truly yours, D. C. Heath & Co.

TL (WP, DLC).
[1] Walter Bagehot, *Physics and Politics* (New York, 1884); Anna Laurens Dawes, *How We Are Governed: An Explanation of the Constitution and Government of the United States* (Boston, 1885); and Jesse Macy, *Our Government: How It Grew, What It Does, and How It Does It* (Boston, 1886).

To Daniel Collamore Heath

Dear Mr. Heath: Clarksville, Tenn., 31 July, 1886
I have received your letter of the 27th and have carefully considered its contents. I cannot take upon myself any of the expense of preparing the contemplated text books for the present; and if you think such an arrangement desirable with reference to the elementary book, I will be quite willing of course to let the suggestion of your letter of the 19th, that I should undertake it, be as if it had not been made—and no harm done. I still feel that I should very much like to prepare such a book, regarding it, as I do, as work thoroughly worth doing, and doing well; but I could not afford to engage to do it unless assured of its publication at the best market rates for such work.

I know nothing of the rates at which authors are paid for text-book work, and I am therefore not in position to suggest terms. I know only that for what I have already published I received terms considerably more liberal than those mentioned in either of the 2 alternate arrangements outlined in your letter. I had expected to postpone our money arrangements as to the work on which I am now engaged for you until you should have seen my complete manuscript; and, so far as I now see, I should prefer to do so. After you have seen the book you can tell me upon what terms you may think it worth while to publish it. I have no doubt we could drive a bargain then—and I should of course accept your assurances as to what the best market rates for such work are.

As to the elementary textbook, I leave my connection with that entirely to your choice, in view of what I have said.

I have received Stimson's 'Statute Law,' Bagehot's 'Physics and Politics,' Coulanges' 'Ancient City,'[1] and Miss Dawes' textbook. Please accept my thanks for your promptness in sending them. I was afraid the French and German books could not be got on this side and had therefore prepared my patience for their importation; but I hope the main part will be prompt.

Very sincerely yours   Woodrow Wilson

Transcript of WWshL (draft) (WP, DLC).
[1] Wilson's copy of Numa Denis Fustel de Coulanges, *The Ancient City* (Boston and New York, 1882), in the Wilson Library, DLC, has Wilson's reading date, "8/25/86," on the last page of the book. Frederic J. Stimson, *American Statute Law* (Boston, 1886), and Walter Bagehot, *Physics and Politics* (New York, 1884), are also in the Wilson Library.

From Daniel Collamore Heath

Dear Prof. Wilson: Boston, August 5, 188[6]

Yours of the 31st received. We had already electrotyped and gone to press with the catalogue including both of your books, feeling sure that we could agree on terms even though you might not like accepting what seemed to us to be fair, and what at least three-fourths of our authors have done; quite a number preferring to own their own plates on the basis named to you, and some of the others preferring to give the books to us on this basis rather than to others on a more favorable ground, and still others because we would publish only on this condition. You must not forget that school book publishers do not pay nearly as large copyright as the publishers of miscellaneous books, and when you consider that at least four-fifths of all of the money received for books is put into agency work, which the miscellaneous publisher does not use, you will understand one reason why we cannot pay large copyrights. You have doubtless been told too of strong competition which obliges the school book publisher not only to put his books down to a low price but to take old books in exchange, and even to give new books in order to get them into the schools. Then at least a thousand copies, or the first edition, must be given away to teachers as samples. Because therefore such a large proportion of receipts must be used in putting the books on the market we can afford to pay only about half as much as the publisher of miscellaneous books can afford to pay. By the way, I have a page torn from the Publishers Weekly that I enclose you that may give you some further information in the matter. Please return it to me, and oblige. But do not forget that while we pay a much less copyright you will in the end get a much larger amount of money from us for the same book than you could get from a publisher who does not make a specialty of school books, and does not use the ordinary methods of putting them on the market. By our methods we can sell at least five times as many books as the other publisher, and therefore we pay you two and one-half times as much copyright even though the amount on one book is only half as large, but we offer you on one book the ordinary copyright of 10% or 15% in case you own your plates, and until you have got back the money invested in plates, and thereafter the usual 10%, but you will always own your plates, and in case of the failure of the publisher they would go to you as your property rather than to the melting pot or auction room.

If you prefer to leave the arrangement about the books until after they are in manuscript that will satisfy us just as well, though we should not of course wish to give them a wide advertisement in the meantime for the benefit of some other publisher. If for instance we should give you the same copyright on your book that Ginn & Co. pay Macy, though we havn't the slightest idea what that is, we presume that would be satisfactory to you, and we would certainly be willing to do that. We leave it to you therefore to decide whether the whole arrangement had better rest just where it is until the books are quite ready, or whether we shall now make an agreement that will be mutually satisfactory.

We will send a copy of Mr. Macy's book the first of next week.
Very truly yours,   D. C. Heath & Co.
P.S. Mr. Heath has just been called away by sickness of his father and forgotten to hand us the page from Publisher's Weekly of which he speaks. On his return we will ask him to forward to you.
DCH & Co [per] K

TLS (WP, DLC) with WWhw notation on env.: "Ans. Aug. 10/86."

Outline of an Elementary Text

The American State.   [c. Aug. 8, 1886]
  I.   *The Government of the United States*
       A general description in attractive, figurative, illustrative terms, such as to enlist attention and interest.

II. *Primitive Society*
  Contrasted with civilization; definition of civilization; means of transition from primitive society to civilization.

III. *Primitive Germanic Society.*
  The McDonough boys: how they illustrate primitive Germanic ints.
  Connexions between latter and English insts, and with our own insts., at least in New England.

IV. *Beginnings of English Government in America.*
  How America came to be settled by the English.
  Differences between different settlements.
  Likenesses do. do. do.
   All English
   How English govt. differed from the govt. of other countries.

V. *Colonies and States*
  Their development and several peculiarities.

VI. *The States and the Union.*
  Growth of the Union into its present solidarity.
  Division of functions
   Idea of checks and balances, and how far operative. Advantages—disadvantages.
   Constitutions: what they are, how made, changed, etc.
  Types of organization among the states
   Though there are three types of organization, there is only one set of functions: the several organizations mean, simply, several ways of doing the same set of things.

VII. *What Government Has to Do*
  What society is, and the relations it bears to govt.
  The several kinds of govt. that try to do govt's work.
  Ours the most complex system.

VIII. *State Functions*
  Their great number, size, importance
  Instrumentalities: (See VI, 2; and Macy, Raleigh).
  Incorporation
  Organization of towns, counties, school districts, etc.

IX. *National Functions*
  The forces of harmony, general defence, general facilitation, etc.

Means: money (banks); Post-office; R.R. Commission;
Army; Navy; Indian affairs; etc.
Revenue: Tariff.

X. *Present Difficulties of Government*
Economic society: what it is.
What it does
Its history
Its methods and conditions
Its relations to government.

XI. *History of Parties in the United States.*
Not now organized to meet the special difficulties
mentioned under X.
Three periods:
1. European-colonial,
2. Sectional,
3. American: feeling after a policy to suit new economic conditions.
Faults remaining, etc., etc.

WWT MS. (WP, DLC).

Fragment of a First Chapter of an Elementary Text

[c. August 8, 1886]

Our govt. ought to be one of the most interesting in the world
it has so many parts so nicely fitted into one another and all working
so curiously together; and, to anyone who knows an interesting
thing when he sees it, it is one of the most interesting governments
in the world. One might compare it to a vast house in which
there are a great many rooms, each serving a special purpose,
and all full of an activity the greatest that ever a people showed
in managing their affairs. In the big central rooms of the house
the work which is meant for the whole nation is done; in the
other rooms, great and small, the work of the States is done. The
important thing to notice is, that it is all one house. Different
things are done in the different rooms, and for different people;
only the big rooms in the centre of the vast building see things
done which are meant for everybody: but all is done under one
roof.

Our govt. is one govt., but it has many parts. There is the state
part, in which you hear of a governor, a lieutenant-governor, and
a legislature sitting at the state capital; and there is the great
national part with its president and vice-president and Congress.
Each one of us lives both in a state, of course, under state officers,

and in the U. S. under national officers. But the state and national govts. are not separate govts; they are parts of the one large plan of political management. They fit into each other, the one doing what the others do not do.

An American boy ought to know a great deal about his govt., because if he would only keep his eyes open he could see so much of it right around him. His father and his grown-up brother, and all the other full-age men who are his friends and neighbours help almost every year to elect men who are to manage the govt.; and he himself probably knows some of the men who have been elected and who manage the parts of the govt. which are nearest his home. Perhaps he knows the Sheriff or some of the other men who are always in and around the town-hall. These are the men who have been made parts of the govt. by being elected. If the American boy don't know anything about the govt. it is because he does not ask anybody to tell him about it. The pieces of it are everywhere to be seen. The post-office is a part of govt.—a part of the national govt.; the court-house is a part of the State govt.

First, there is, in most parts of the country, the township with its meeting every year in the town-hall, where all the men who can vote get together and talk over the things to be done for the district in which they live; about the school houses that are to be built or repaired, the roads that must be made or put in good condition, the best way to keep the live-stock from straying and doing damage, and everything of that sort which is important to the people of the neighbourhood. If they determine to do anything that will cost money, they also talk over and settle the taxes to be paid by the people of the township, that is, by themselves and their neighbours, to meet the expense. Then, too, officers are elected to carry out all the schemes that are decided upon by the town-meeting.

It is not all parts of the country that have townships. The people of the southern states do not make much use of this rather small piece of govt. Their smallest arrangement for carrying on their affairs is the County.

Then there is the school-district, with its school-houses, its school-directors, its superintendent, and its busy teachers. Sometimes the school-district is as big as the township; sometimes the township is divided up into several school-districts, which thus become, as it were, pieces of the township. Where there are no townships, but only Counties as the smallest parts of the govt., the school-district is a piece of a County.

The County is the part of the govt. which takes care of the long roads which run from township to township. It builds poor-houses and takes care of the poor when the townships of which the county is made up feel that they cannot afford to have each its separate poor-house, superintendent of the poor, &c. The County, too, is the district in which court is held to try criminals and decide cases of debt and the like when one man sues another. The Sheriff is a county officer. He acts as the agent of the court in keeping prisoners, arresting men suspected of crime, taking property which the court decides ought to be sold for debt, &c. The county has its court-house, where the court sits and where the office of the county-clerk, who keeps the courts books and papers, and the office of the Sheriff are to be found.

The people of the County, as well as the people of the township, elect their own officers, and, though they do not have county-meetings, their opinions count for a great deal in determining how county affairs are to be managed. They will not elect a second time officers who do what they do not like.

The township, the school-district, and the County are not separate govts. they fit into each other as parts, some large, some small, of one great organization which we call the state. It is the state which determines what things the school-districts, the townships, and the counties shall be allowed to do for themselves. This the state does partly by laws made by the state legislature sitting at the state-capital, and partly by its "Constitution," which is a great law passed by the people of the state which shows what officers the people have voted that the state shall have, what sort of townships and counties the state shall be divided into, what sort of courts it shall have, and what powers the state legislature and the different officers shall have.

The state in its turn is a member of the government of the United States, the great national government whose capital is at Washington. Under this government the states join to do certain things which are for the interest of the people of the whole country, and which could not be well done if each state tried to attend to them for itself. The president and vice-president of the United States govt. are elected by the people of the whole country; its other officers, like the postmasters, &c, are appointed by the president; and its legislators are sent up from the states.

WWhw and WWT MS. (WP, DLC).

To Daniel Collamore Heath

Dear Mr. Heath,   Clarksville, Tenn., 10 August, 1886

I have rec'd your letter of the 5th. Its fuller explanation of the conditions under which text-book publishing is conducted places the propositions as to terms contained in your previous letter in a somewhat different light—to my hitherto uninstructed eye. I understood from the first, of course, the advantage there would be in owning the plates. I declined to invest any money, not because I did not care to own the plates, but because *I have no money to invest*—the best & most conclusive of reasons. The other arrangement—of letting you have the books on the understanding that I was to receive 10% after you have been reimbursed to the amount of the cost of the plates—was the only one of the two alternative arrangements mentioned in your letter that I could in the nature of the case agree to. I knew too little, however, of the terms usually offered to authors of text-books to be able to judge as to the advisability of acceding to that.

I am not at all disposed to be shy or hard to please in coming to an agreement with you: I am only anxious not to act in the dark—to be sure that I am not working at a disadvantage as compared with others in turning aside from even more important literary plans to prepare these books. And, as I said, I am quite willing to accept fully your assurances on that point.

It wd. aid me in forming an opinion if you wd be kind enough to let me know about how many copies of (say) such a book as Stanley Hall's Methods of Teaching and Studying History[1] would have to be sold before you would have covered by its sale the cost of the plates and begun to pay copyright? Does such an arrangement mean that you must first be reimbursed the cost of the plates out of *net* profits?

I see of course that you could not both advertize the books and postpone our bargain. I did not know that it was yr. plan to advertise them before their completion, further than to announce them in yr. catalogue. Since it is I am ready to come to an understanding at once; and if you will let me know the particulars of the best terms you can offer in view of the fact that I have no money to invest[,] I have no doubt that we can agree speedily.

Very sincerely Yours   W.W.

ALI (draft) (WP, DLC). Att.: D. C. Heath to WW, Aug. 5, 1886.
[1] Wilson's copy of G. Stanley Hall, *Methods of Teaching History* (Boston, 1885), is in the Wilson Library, DLC, and has Wilson's autograph and the WWhw date "1885" on the front flyleaf.

From Ellen Axson Wilson

My own darling,   Clarksville, Aug 13/86

I hope by this time (3 P.M.) your tedious journey is over and you are safe with Sister Marion. I trust you reached her well and not *quite* worn out. We are all well and in good enough spirits—considering our *loss*! Josie was rather blue this morning over the meeting last night.[1] They "went back on" him as he says at every point,—particularly in the matter of the circulars which they voted he had no right to send without their *special* consent,—though he *is* "the committee" and authorized to act for them. In short they made idiots of themselves and Josie has written his resignation as secretary. But he is in good spirits again now for Mr. Brandon (?) Sec. of the fair Ass. is his enthusiastic ally, and he says they two alone are going to make a great success of it and show the club "what fools they have been."

Baby is quite well and as sweet and good as possible, except that she is, as Adeline says, "so biggity"; she had one good cry this morning for your *finger*. But she had a good night's sleep, and so did I,—*one* portion of it *very* good for I dreamed of *you*,—dreamed that it was all a mistake,—you hadn't gone away! I *thought* you were gone at first, but coming suddenly into the room,—it was our sitting-room at Bryn Mawr, and I entered at the hall door—I saw you stooping before the big book case. And then I was in your arms and *so* happy that I awoke,—and found it all a dream. Oh dear! it is *only* for a week! It ought not to be so *very* hard; ought it? But then some weeks are so much longer than other weeks, and though you *will* be back soon "that makes it no less true that you are absent *now*." My darling, my darling! I love you so that even a short absence from you is harder to bear than many another thing which on the face of it would seem to make much greater demands on my fortitude. But don't think, sir, that I am making myself unhappy about it;—not a bit of it! I am going to have just as good a time as *you*, and I am sure as things are with you at present that is saying a good deal. I can't help envying you;—tell dear sister Marion I did long to go with you. Give a heart full of love for me to her and all the rest. Kisses for dear little Jessie—and the boys too if they will submit.

Mother[2] sends love to all & says she misses you muchly,—and I wont say *how I* miss you sweetheart.

Your own little wife   Eileen

ALS (WP, DLC) with WWhw train schedule on env.
[1] Of the Bicycle Club of Clarksville. See WW to EAW, Aug. 15, 1886.

[2] Dr. Wilson had left Clarksville for his annual vacation in the North. See JRW to WW, Aug. 9, 1886, from Saratoga Springs, ALS (WP, DLC).

Two Letters to Ellen Axson Wilson

Little Rock, Ark., 13 August, '86.
My precious, *precious* little wife,

I arrived safe and sound to-day at about one o'clock, and find them all quite well. As for myself, I am not so tired as I expected to be—though tired enough of course—and am just as well as when I left. These dear obstreperous children[1] have not contributed much towards resting me by their tumbling and frolicing over my knees and about my neck; but I am glad to be 'hail fellow well met' with them all the same. I will tell you about them to the best of my ability in my next, to-morrow.

I am not going to tell you how sore my heart is over the parting which was necessary in order to this meeting—I don't mean to spoil the pleasure of seeing dear sister and bro. Ross and their little family by letting my mind dwell on that; but I *can* let my mind dwell on *you*, my matchless little wife—my darling, my queen—and so *add* to my present satisfaction. I don't have to nerve my heart to a *long* waiting this time—so I can indulge myself in thoughts of you just as much as I please. Did ever man have *such* a wife to think about!—*to return to*! I am going to *play* that she is beside me to-night (as I have already been playing to-*day*) and swell my heart and my pride by telling her my whole thought about her. I love you darling! All my best thoughts live with you—my whole life is with you—you carry my strength and all that is best of me about with you. I am an exile: but I am a happy exile, because *I am coming back* to the sweetest, lovliest wife the sweetest, lovliest woman in the world.

All join in warmest love to all—I am not half as welcome as I would have been had I brought some of the rest of you along! Give 'Dode' and precious mother such messages from me as you know my heart would dictate. I *love* them. Kiss my blessed baby for me—and remember that you are all in all to

Your own   Woodrow

ALS (WC, NjP).
[1] The Kennedy children were Joseph Leland, born February 8, 1875; William Blake, born April 8, 1877; Wilson Woodrow, born in 1879; Jessie, born June 1, 1882; and one child who died in infancy, whose name is unknown.

My precious darling,   Little Rock, Ark., 14 Aug., 1886.

In order to be *comparatively* cool while writing I have determined to try the experiment of composing my letter out here on the front piazza where brother Ross and sister Marion are sitting and where little Jessie is playing—with that irresistible tendency to come to me on all sorts of pretexts which very young ladies seem all to feel. I haven't that power of abstracting my attention from all disturbing sights and sounds which you possess; so I will have to give over all attempt to write about anything that might require new combinations of thought, I suppose, and confine myself to those thoughts which with me are, so to say, automatic and instinctive—thoughts of you—thoughts filling up every measure of love and of delight. I am no longer afraid nowadays that you will grow tired of hearing my accustomed confessions of love for my darling. When I write over again the now familiar and habitual phrases, it is an addition to my delight in you that these old phrases are never old or stale for you—that they still carry their first fulness of meaning, and even more than their first fulness of meaning—a new, *richer* fulness—eloquent of sweet *married* days, of which those first love messages knew nothing. It is because of these blessed married days that I know how my oldest phrases will be rec'd: the unspeakable beauty they will bring into the most beautiful eyes in the world— the wonderful radiance they will bring into the loveliest face in the world—the delight of love confidence that it will bring into the sweetest, wifeliest heart in the world. Oh, my darling, my darling, what an unfailing delight and strength you are to me— what confidence for the future is bound up in the sweet memories of the past—of that past which is ours, and only ours. Sometimes I think that baby is a very fortunate little mortal, to have been born into a share of such happy lives as ours. Surely it will be our own fault if we don't make her happy as I am—and as you are, my queen. We'll do our best—wont we, precious?

Have you thought about me, little lady, much since I left? I wonder! Oh, if I didn't *know*, what a wretched fellow I would be! My little wife does think about me and with all the love of her heart—that precious*est* heart that ever sweet woman had. I don't deserve a bit of it—but it fills my life with the sweetest joy that ever filled man's life.

I promised to tell you something about this little family of children in this letter—didn't I? Well, none of them have made much impression upon me except Woodrow and Jessie—the other two are simply bigger than they were. Woodrow is so big a boy, and little Jessie I never saw before. W. has a very interesting face —the most so in the lot—full of brow, and calculating in eye. I expect most of him. He is the most self-contained of the children. Little Jessie is just like the bigger boys in character, though with her sex's greater affectionateness. She has a face rather sweeter —fuller of meaning—than her picture shows;—but she is not so interesting as Woodrow. He will *last* best. Tell 'Dode' that Josie is a really expert bicyclist, mounting and dismounting by the pedal with considerable ease and confidence.

Tell Mama and 'Dode' that I love them with all my heart.

I am well and nearly rested—and next week I'm going to follow all my thoughts—to you, my queen, my joy, my precious, matchless Eileen. A score of kisses for baby

Your own   Woodrow.

ALS (WP, DLC).

From Ellen Axson Wilson

My own darling,   [Clarksville, Tenn., c. Aug. 15, 1886]

I am writing with baby in my lap so you will have to excuse everything. Am so sorry that I can't write a letter today, but you know I am nurse this afternoon, and a *busy* one since it is so hot baby can't sleep. Would have written this morning but was busy with her much of the time & after I finished I managed to take a little nap, which as we had a sleepless night was somewhat needed. The little monkey didn't go to sleep 'till towards three & then woke five or six times before morning. She was not sick at all—didn't cry; it was simply the intense heat. She seems very well today. And I am perfectly well,—had such good sleep the night before that I could afford to sit up last night.

Your sweet *sweet* letter came last night after all. My *darling*! you don't [know] how precious every word in your letters is to me. You don't know how I love you. But baby is protesting against this, so I must close in haste   Your own little wife   Eileen

Mother is very well & sends love to all.

ALS (WC, NjP).

Two Letters to Ellen Axson Wilson

My own darling,   Little Rock, Ark., 15 Aug., 1886

Your first letter reached me this morning. It should have come yesterday afternoon; but some delay on the road kept it back. I hope that mine have gone straighter through. The news of the Bicycle Club's treatment of 'Dode' has filled me with feelings which I need not describe. There is but one thing for him to do, in self-respect, and that is, to resign his membership of the Club, —not simply his office in it. He cannot keep his connexion with those fellows and his self-respect too. I can't express my indignation at the affair. The miserable hounds! I'd rather have 'Dode' a member of a negro organization than have him associate with these fellows any longer! The negroes would not pretend to gentility: these fellows do. Out on the miserable ingrates! But, let's change the subject.

It makes me *so* happy to know that you and the baby are both so well—but you did not say that *you* were *well*, did you?—but only that you *slept* well. How is the bowel trouble, darling? How are *you* feeling?

I heard bro. Ross preach this morning, and enjoyed the sermon very much. His delivery has too much emphasis in it—too many words come under the hammer of his tongue; but the substance of his sermon was excellent and I liked ever so much worshipping in the neat little church. I will hear him again to-night, of course.

It goes without the saying that I am enjoying my stay here, but I must confess to being made very nervous by the children during most part of the day—the fretting, the mischief, and their check by a nervous, spasmodic discipline are not calculated to seem pleasing to a writer on government. I long to take these youngsters in hand; for they are fine children in the rough. But I don't let more distress and worry get hold of me than just so much as can't be kept off—and I can say with all sincerity that I am enjoying myself—all the more since that sweet letter came this morning—my queen's sweet message of love! I know that you miss me, darling—I know that you love me—but oh, how sweet it is to have you say so! It seems to make my knowledge more sure: it certainly does make it more joyful. Say it, please ma'am, as often as you can! My little sweetheart! My love, my queen! How profoundly I love you! You are my wife indeed, my darling—the wife of my heart and mind as well as of my busom! If there is joy for you in the thought that you have linked me to you with bonds which make me—my love, and all that I am—*yours* and only yours 'for good and all'—yours inseparably and inalienably—you may have the *fulness* of the joy of that thought. *It is true*—literally and in all its remotest consequences. I love you; I love you; I love you!—and I love the baby as much as you do.

Sister and bro. Ross send lots of love to dear mother, 'Dode,' your own sweet self, and the baby—and *I*? I love and miss you all as much as your hearts c'd. wish.   Your own   Woodrow

P.S. I am quite well.

My own darling,   Little Rock, Ark., 16 Aug., 1886.
    That you *are* a good girl, to take your walks in my absence! Do you go by yourself, you darling? Ah, what would I not give to go with you—to take a stroll this afternoon with the lovliest little woman in all the world—my queen, my peerless little wife! Oh, I love, *love, love* you, Eileen! What a sweet dream that was you dreamed of me, you little bewitcher—that in which you found me not gone away after all and ran into my arms. Oh but you are a charming little woman—you were made to make some man love you to distraction; and that man is *me*!
    You must know, Miss, that the envelope wh. is to contain this letter was addressed by Mrs. Kennedy in order to save me the trip upstairs to the ink: for I am on the sick list for the time being, with a 'misery in my midst,' given me, doubtless, by some eccentricity in the cooking here—for of eccentricities in the cooking of this family there are many and various. It's nothing at all serious, my little lady, so that look need not come into your sweet eyes. It's just about as severe as you described yourself as having last week. It's just bad enough to make Jamaica ginger opportune and sitting still grateful as well as advisable. I'll be all right against the next time for writing. It doesn't dampen my spirits in the least to have only so much misery, so long as I have your letters to read and live with.
    Thank you, sweetheart, for your report as to book from D. C. H., and the letter from H. M. & Co.[1] I am glad that they 'take the liberty' of not charging the volume to me. They are certainly exceedingly courteous in these matters, making it a pleasure to deal with them.
    I have made no new acquaintances here as yet—except in my own peculiar gossippy way,—I know *about* a great many people: notably about a certain Judge Rose (now taking his vacation in the Sandwich Islands, for lack of any other new place to visit) who has a library of over three thousand volumes, of which he *prints* a catalogue—for his own and his friends' use.[2] This library serves sister Marion instead of a public library, seeing that the Roses are great friends of hers—Mrs. Rose making all sister Marion's preserves for her every summer with her own hands—but I musn't *begin* to gossip—where would—could—I end? I don't know

that I care to make any new acquaintances, since I have not Cobden's talent for making use to [of] strangers as pumps.

I read the first chapter of the text-book to sister Marion and bro. Ross this morning—and also part of P. o. P.[3] to sister. They seemed much edified. I mustn't read this stuff myself much more at present—lest I should burn it up, and have it *all* to write over again. It isn't so bad, I suppose, *absolutely*—but *comparatively*— compared with what I would have it—it is *all wretched*. If the public should think otherwise, I shall write the public down an ass.

I'm afraid I can't bring sister M. back with me—but she wants to come—and she and all send lots of love to you all.

When is dear father to arrive?

I love dear mother with all my heart, 'Dode' with all my heart— the baby as my precious little daughter and you as my pride, my queen, my all.   Your own   Woodrow.

ALS (WP, DLC).
    [1] Perhaps Ellen wrote this report on an additional page and enclosed it in her letter to Woodrow of Aug. 13, 1886; it is now missing. The letter from Houghton Mifflin was Houghton, Mifflin & Company to WW, Aug. 10, 1886, HwL (WP, DLC), saying that the firm would give a free copy of *Congressional Government* to Miss H. J. Cooke and "take the liberty" of charging it, not to Wilson, but to the advertising account.
    [2] Uriah Milton Rose, who practiced law in Little Rock from 1860 to 1913, wrote legal books and articles, and eventually collected a library of some 8,000 volumes.
    [3] "The Philosophy of Politics," the name Wilson was now using for "The Modern Democratic State."

From Ellen Axson Wilson

My own darling,   Clarksville, Aug 16/86
    As Josie is writing in the little hall room and I don't know where to find any other ink I will, if you will excuse me, write with pencil.

We are all quite well today; mother still seems to be improving, is very bright and cheerful in spite of the fact that she is a good deal worried about various discoveries concerning the cook's thieving propensities. We had a splendid night, I slept eight hours,— and baby is very well and good today in spite of the heat. Your sweet letter came duly to hand last night and was welcomed, every word of it—just as you *knew* it would be welcomed, my darling. Never, never can those sweet love-words do other than delight me, bring me an ever increasing delight—a fuller richer meaning. Every one of these sweet married days adds just so much to the meaning, to the *weight* of such words, and adds something to "the delight of love confidence" in your little wife's heart. Every day that passes brings with it fresh testimony to the wonderful perfectness, fulness and stability of the happiness which you have given me my love. Oh, darling, can it be possible that I have made you as happy as you have made me? It seems incredible—far too good to be true. Ah if I were only such a wife as I want to be—such an one as you deserve[,] my heart would be like to break for gladness! I pray God to make me every day more truly a "delight and strength" to you, more worthy to be your wife. Yes I think baby *is* a fortunate little mortal to be born into such happy lives as ours; and I mean it shall be *her* fault if she isn't as happy;—no, not *as* happy; that is impossible until she grows up and finds a husband just like *you*. No child that ever lived was as happy as I. The talk about the superlative happiness of children is all nonsense. But we will do our best to make her as happy a *child* as ever lived. And I think we will succeed, for she *must* have a happy disposition; how could she help it when I was so supremely happy before she came?

I was much interested in your account of little Woodrow. How old is he, by the way? We could not decide here. I wish I could see them all. You must tell them they have an Aunt Ellie and that they must love her if they can. Mother & Dode and *Ellie* send love to all. With a heart full and brimming over with love for you Woodrow my *darling* I am

Your own little wife   Eileen

No more mail for you.

ALS (WC, NjP).

To Ellen Axson Wilson

My own precious darling,   Little Rock, Ark., 17 Aug., 1886.

I am feeling better to-day, though not completely myself again —indeed how *could* one be completely himself in weather such as this? The sky has been like brass here for the past three days, and the thermometer has ranged between 96° and 99° during the whole time. If it were not for a pretty steady breeze that has fanned us the while, I don't know what we should do: we should probably suffocate! I devoutly hope that you have not been having weather of the same kind in Clarksville!

I have not seen quite as much as usual of sister Marion and bro. Ross to-day. The latter has been most of the time with his dentist, having a set of teeth fitted; the former has been taken away from me by the fact that she is just now entirely without a servant. She has been even more unfortunate about servants than dear mother has been; but she is able to bear the consequences; dear mother is not. Sister is *quite* strong and well, and the work doesn't hurt her at all—especially since she has very much more easily satisfied ideas of household order than dear mother has. She had a cook when I came, an 'uppish' Virginia negro (man); but he grew mutinous on Saturday and was summarily bounced.

I have not done much reading yet in the book I brought: my stomach trouble came at just the same time with an opportunity for reading. In the absence of physical capacity for *work*, I *dawdled* this morning over Drummond's "Natural Law in the Spiritual World"[1]—and that proved interesting enough to help me a *little* in bearing the disappointment of getting no letter from you this morning. I suppose Sunday made some sort of difference in the mails, and that I will get the missing letter this afternoon. Oh, what would I do without a letter from my darling—her loving words and news of herself from her own hand are my *life* when I am away from you. Eileen, my queen, my love, my matchless sweetheart, my life, *I love you,* I *love, love, love, love, love, love* you!!   Your own   Woodrow
Unbounded love to dear mother and 'Dode.'

ALS (WC, NjP).
[1] Henry Drummond, *Natural Law in the Spiritual World* (New York, 1884).

From Ellen Axson Wilson

My own darling Woodrow,   Clarksville Aug 17/86
As Josie is again busy with his extensive correspondence I must again beg you to excuse pencil.

I have just had delightful news from Nashville. Cousin Hattie has a beautiful little daughter, brown-eyed & black-haired. They have named it Lily. She had a "severe trial" but there were no after troubles and both she and baby are "doing splendidly." The baby is a week old today. *Isn't* this good news! Oh, I am *so* relieved.

Our baby is doing *well* if not "splendidly" too. Adeline took her to a new place to be weighed this morning and she weighs with her dress on 12 3/4 lbs. Isn't that good? I think it *is* doing "splendidly" considering the weather, for it is a gain of half her own weight within a month. She slept finely again last night,—for a wonder, seeing how she suffers from the heat; she is as cross as a cat all day. The ther. is 95° in our room at night. What a hot

journey home you will have! I dread the thought of it;—and won't
Father have a pleasant time. He reaches home Thursday night,
perhaps the same time with yourself; I have been hoping you
would let us know which night to expect you. If you leave on
Thursday I presume you will miss this letter. I hope you will miss
it, *so*; I am *sure* you must have been there more than a week already! At least you have been away from here more than a week.
How glad I am that the time is at the worst more than half over!
"There's nae luck about the house when my gudeman's awa." Ah
darling with what bonds you have linked *me* to *you*! I am *yours*
and only yours,—yours heart and soul and mind, *forever*. I can
never tell you what fulness of joy there is for me in that double
thought that you are mine and I am yours, always and altogether.

Josie seems to have quite gotten over the treatment of his club,
seems rather to like being able to do more entirely as he pleases
about the races.

I am sorry, dear, for the nervousness and the cause of it.

No more mail for you. I had a paper from Concord N. H. announcing the death of my dear old friend Mrs. Gilbert. She has
been very feeble for a long time so that it was not unexpected.

Goodbye darling until we meet again. I love you *I love you*
with my very heart of hearts.

　　　　　　　　　　　　Your own little wife　Eileen

ALS (WC, NjP).

To Ellen Axson Wilson

My own precious darling,　　Little Rock, Ark., 18 August 1886.

I was disconsolate yesterday: but two letters came to-day to
comfort me—the note written in face of baby's protests on Sunday
afternoon and the letter of Monday. My sweet pet! What gems
your little epistles of love are—how full of your own inimitable personality! They are worth their weight in gold as mere models of
perfect self-revelation;—as love letters no gold can measure their
value *to me*! You dear, splendid little woman! You need have no
more fears about your not being as good a wife as I deserve: if
you continue to love me as much as you do now, and to *wish* to
be a perfect wife, as you do now, *you will be*. And, oh, my lovely
sweetheart, if love can repay you, you shall be as richly repaid
as ever your heart can wish—I will love you always as I do now—
and will give my love leave, and room, to grow as it is growing
now, until you will have to enlarge *your* heart, by loving, to receive it!

I am *so* glad to know that Saturday night was an exception and that the other nights you and my precious little one have had such splendid sleep. You are *bricks*, both of you! As for myself, I have slept splendidly every night, despite the intense heat, and have now only a pang or two left of the trouble in my midst—and they only slight and occasional. I may pronounce myself *well*.

I have been sampling a book or two in my line from Judge Rose's library. I will tell you about them when I come—not much to tell—very slight books.

I finished reading the *mss.* of my text-book aloud to the folks here to-day. They don't make much comment—but they are evidently lenient and appreciative.

I have not quite fixed upon a time for leaving—but you may expect me either Friday night or Sat. morning—probably Friday night: and *then*, my darling will you come into the arms of

Your own   Woodrow?

Unbounded love from all to all. I am *so* happy and grateful [to] know that dear mother is so well!

ALS (WC, NjP).

From Daniel Collamore Heath

Dear prof. Wilson:—   Boston, August 18, 1886.

Yours of the 10th received. It is the custom, as you know, of English publishers to exempt a book from copyright until their investment has been returned to them; and that is fair as oftentimes a book will sell hardly more than enough to give the publisher back his money without any remuneration for time, labor, advertising, etc. It is getting to be more and more common in this country. It would surprise you to learn how many books daily coming to our notice are paid for by the authors or editors. Still I do not once anticipate your owning the plates except upon the terms I proposed, which are liberal, and which are the same as we give to about one-half of the authors upon our list: that is, one-half of them own their own plates on that basis. You ask how many copies of Hall's Methods of Teaching and Studying History would have to be sold before we would have covered by its sale the cost of plates. We think it would not be less than fifteen hundred copies, nor more than two thousand, though in the case of that book its expense has been much larger than it ought to have been. If the author's copy is well prepared so that not many changes have to be made after type is set the expense can be kept down to $1.25 or $1.50 a page. We allow 10% of the cost of type setting for changes. We do not mean that the cost of the plates must come back to us out of *net* profits, simply out of *gross profits*. For instance a book of which we make the wholesale price $1.00 would cost us 25 cents. We would sell it for 20% less than $1.00, and the difference between 25 and 80 cents is the gross profit, and it is *this* that we credit to the book on such an account as the one you spoke of. We do not count out time, clerk hire, advertising, or any other expense except the actual cost of paper, printing, and binding. As to advertising the books, we do not propose to advertise them much except by letter, in addition to the announcement we make in our catalogue; but *that* advertisement will go to fifteen thousand people, and will amount to considerable advertising. We shall write from time to time a good many letters concerning it to prepare the way for it, and shall be getting from time to time hints as to how the book may be made most salable, all of which we shall communicate to you. We should not want to take all this trouble if we were not to publish the book. I think if we could make an agreement with you such as the one written into the contract form sent with this, it would be fair to both of us. If it is not fair to you I should certainly wish to change it in any way that would be necessary in order to make it so. If, therefore, you write in such changes as you think ought to be made, and return it to me I will consider them, and if I can agree to them will draw up two forms for signature.

The enclosed letter just received may interest you. The postal will show you that one of the books we ordered for you can not be obtained. Do not hesitate to call upon us for any favors in this or any direction in connection with your work that are in our power to bestow.   Very truly yours,   D. C. Heath & Co.

TL (WP, DLC). Enc.: D. H. Hamilton Adams & Co. of London to D. C. Heath & Co., Aug. 5, 1886, APS (WP, DLC), saying that E. A. Freeman's *Federal Government* was out of print. The other enclosures referred to are missing.

From Raymond Landon Bridgman

My dear sir,   Boston, Mass., Aug. 26. 1886.

I inclose you a list of writers and subjects in my "National Problems" series, with numbers showing the weekly order of articles from the beginning. No. 37 will be sent out next week for publication Sept. 6 (7th in New England) in papers in the arrangement. It has been found advisable to shorten the articles to an average of 1500 words each and the state of the enterprise this summer has permitted me to pay but $15 per article.

Would you like to write for me at this time your proposed article on a new national party?[1] By the time it would appear the congressional conventions would be well in progress and it would be as timely as at any juncture before the next presidential election. I have letters out for an article to be received by the morning of Sept. 7 at the latest, but no answers are in yet. Would you like to write for that date, provided I do not hear from any other one before hearing from you?

Very truly yours,   R. L. Bridgman.

ALS (WP, DLC) with WWhw notations on env.: "But why extend the perplexing recital?" and "Ans. Aug. 31/86." Enc.: printed and hw list of authors and subjects.
[1] Wilson responded with "Wanted,—A Party," printed at Sept. 1, 1886.

First Thoughts for a Political Essay

[c. Sept. 1, 1886]

Our debt to the English:

Traditions ⎫
Capacity ⎬ of self-government.
Forms   ⎭

What we did *not* derive from them:
Written constitution.
Separation of Powers and consequent power of S. Court.
Indirect democracy of the Senate.
The disservice which the Eng. seem about to do us by their admiration of Senate, Courts, and written constitution[1]
Checks and guarantees well enough—to be thankful for—they are the stationary, the *stable*, the large structural features of the system.
But the question is as to the *action* of the govt., the *accomplishments* of the system. Apparently we dare not *test* our balances. Sir H. Maine compares our const. to a *reservoir*: in it the waters are *still*: they drive no wheels of policy.
Iniative [*Initiative*] is the key to the *work-room* of every const. It conditions both the action of the govt—whose *consistency* and *continuity* of policy depend upon it—and the formation of public opinion.
With whom does initiative rest under our Const?
With *Congress*. What is Congress? It is a body whose organization makes it disintegrate—only the nation in miniature.

Effects: (A) On the Executive

(1) Must stand or fall on *nominations* merely.

(2) It leaves him the initiative in treaty-making without any real hold upon that policy-making which renders such initiative significant.

(B) On Legislation

(C) On the political life of the country[.] Renders it difficult for the country (1) To *have* any well-defined purpose (2) To *effect* that purpose when it is formed—because of the country's lack of leaders and the State's lack of a *nerve-centre*.

With us leaders are *whipped* forward—they do not lead—their force is not *in* them but *behind* them.

E.G. Civil-service reform. Does the c. want it? It elected a reform Pres.; but was he not nominated simply because he was available, i.e. acceptable to a certain *minority* which seem likely to hold the balance of power in certain quarters? I believe the people *do* want reform; but how is one to tell? The politicians whom the people elect do not—Congress has been *pushed* the whole distance it has gone.

Leadership.—*integration* is what we need. For 'measures not men' ought to be substituted 'measures to *make* men, and then men who mean measures.'

The principle in accord with which leadership lives—for it *does* live on even amidst the most adverse circumstances—is the principle upon wh. *kingship* rests. *Leadership* is *kingship*—the best *elective* kingship.[2] The instinct of trust and allegiance is ineradicable: and how sacredly should we cherish it! for it is *the* social bond. Respect for law—a mere habit—*holds* men together—is a *drill*; trust in a fellow-man *unites* them—is an *inspiration*.

See how men insist upon attaching themselves to leaders: under *our* system because of his personal attractions,—to a Blaine; under a system permitting legislative leadership, because of the *cause* he represents,—to a Pendleton or a Hawley.[3]

Witness the civil leadership of such men as Jackson and Grant: a leadership wholly natural under a system wh. gives men no means but *war* of identifying themselves with the success of a cause (the South too preferred her '*brigadiers*' for political leaders); but a leadership wholly detrimental to *govt*.

Lincoln, on the other hand, serves as an example of a leader rightly chosen and nobly sustained. It happened that in such a crisis the *Presidency was* a chair of leadership.

Diagnosis of *mugwumpery*: mugwumps look for a *man,* not for a party. Would it not be better if, in finding a man they became a party,—by winning, not a representative merely, but a *leader* as well?

WWhw MS. (WP, DLC).
   1 Wilson was referring, among other works, to Sir Henry Maine's recently published *Popular Government.*
   2 Wilson picked this term up from the last chapter of *Popular Government.*
   3 Senator George Hunt Pendleton of Ohio, author of the Civil Service Reform Act of 1883, and Senator Joseph Roswell Hawley of Connecticut, defender of "sound" money and of the sanctity of the federal debt.

First Draft of a Political Essay[1]

[c. Sept. 1, 1886]

Prospects for a New National Party.

It is evident that identities are just now painfully confused in the relations of our national parties. The President is being attacked by many who were expected to support him, and supported by some who were expected to attack him. Taking the situation as a whole, it is really quite puzzling to know where to find party men when they are wanted for what have long been accounted habitual party uses.

The hope most frequently and naturally suggested by this posture of affairs is that a fresh division of parties will soon take place and new parties of principle supercede the existing parties of tradition. All observers are agreed that, looked at from a party point of view, the present period is transitional, and therefore singularly critical. Old party ties have been loosened, old party distinctions thrown much out of course. In sections of the country where thought is most active voters of the best class are find-

   1 Wilson wrote this essay in response to a request from Raymond L. Bridgman for an article for newspaper syndication. (See R. L. Bridgman to WW, Jan. 11 and Aug. 26, 1886.) Wilson wrote out a complete draft in longhand and then began a revised version on his Caligraph. After completing a little more than a third of the second draft, he realized that it was too long and discursive for a newspaper article and laid his revision aside without bothering to correct his typographical errors. He then prepared the briefer version, "Wanted,—A Party," printed as the next document.
   The text of "Prospects for a New National Party" is that of Wilson's revised typed version as far as it went, plus the balance from his handwritten draft. The bar on p. 334 indicates the dividing line between the two versions. All footnotes are the Editors'.

ing it impossible to be steadily either Democrats or Republicans. In other sections the disintegration of parties seems to be prevented by the force of habit or the tenacity of prejudice, rather than by the permanence of principle. Principle, indeed, has long had very little to do with the coherence of our national parties. The cement has been supplied by the memory of past events. Republican supremacy was, for perhaps half its period, an achievement of effective reminiscence. The Republican party kept itself in office by constantly reminding the country of what it had done for the Union, and of what the Democrats had tried to do against the Union. Its services had been great, and it lived a life of unstinted reward. It was pensioned with power.

But, in the course of nature, the real pensioners were not long in dying off. The men who had in proper person brought about the war and then won it and saved the Union were soon, most of them, dead and buried; and the people began to question the claim of their successors to this extraordinary form of pension. At the same time a new generations of Democrats also came upon the national stage who were found to be quite out of reach of the taunt or suspicion of disloyalty. Under such circumstances, it became yearly harder and harder to conduct national affairs with reference altogether to the past. The Union had been saved, and that was an inestimably blessing; but its past salvation could not be made to take the place of its continuous good government, which was to be its future salvation.

Reaction began to set in st[r]ongly in 1876. In that year the House of Representatives became overwhelmingly Democratic and a Democratic candidate for the Presidency was accorded a decided majority of the popular vote. Moderate discretion on the part of the new majority in the use of their legislative power promised to reverse the virtual attainder under which their party had suffered. The fortunes of politics were beginning to depend on the future, instead of on the past. Only the election of a Democratic President was lacking to complete the reestablishment of normal conditions of party warfare. That lack has now been supplied by the election of Mr. Cleveland. Whether his administration be good, bad, or indifferent, it will have accomplished a great result, if only it be not unpatriotic. The first thing to be desired is a choice of parties. That we may now have.

But it is this rehabilitation of free choice which is confusing party lines. So long as the test of politics was a past issue it was easy enough to draw distinct lines of party demarcation. Everybody who felt identified in sympathy or interest with the accomplished policy of the Republican party was a Republican; everyone else was a Democrat. So soon, however, as party affiliations were made to depend on future courses of action, this natural arrangement was completely upset. Not every one who treasures the traditions of Republican achievement in the past is to be counted on to accept the purposes of Republican managers for the future. Thinking men in possession of their right minds must have reasonable hopes as well as reverent memories.

To look closely at our two parties is to discover the potent operation of this principle at the present moment. The reform sentiment which brought about Mr. Cleveland's election was clearly not of party making. It was the result of a movement of opinion in the nation which took place quite outside party lines. Leading men in both parties were among its promoters, and both parties in Congress participated in passing the [Pendleton] Act which is its present legal recognition. That Act was proposed to a Republican Senate by a Democratic Senator; was passed by that Senate and by a Democratic House; and was signed by a Republican President. But Mr. Cleveland was made President chiefly, if not solely, because he was an avowed and practiced civil-service reformer. Here, consequently, lies the most prominent cause of party confusion. As a civil-service reformer the President has neither the Democratic nor the Republican party at his back. A united following, if he had any such, would draw its members from both parties and could use the name of neither. It would be a new party.

Upon all other questions Mr. Cleveland calls himself plainly a Democrat. But in calling himself a Democrat he evidently avows nothin[g] as to his attitude with reference to the greatest national questions of the day. He is opposed to the further coinage of silver; but Mr. Beck has been a leading Democrat much longer than Mr. Cleveland has, and Mr. Beck vehemently favours the coinage of silver, and in doing so unquestionably represents a very influential section of his party in Congress—as well as a numerically weighty body of Republicans.[2] If, again, Mr. Cleveland speaks the mind of Democrats on the tariff, he does so because that mind in [is] divided. His declarations on that head look two ways, and so do the utterances of his party. If we are to judge by the voting on the Morrison bill last winter, most of the Democrats and a few Republicans are in favour of a reduction

[2] James Burnie Beck, at this time a Democratic senator from Kentucky.

of duties;[3] but a powerful minority of Democrats, led by Mr. [Samuel J.] Randall, one of the strongest of party leaders, is immovably opposed to such a reduction. Lines run between man and man on the silver and tariff questions, as well as upon questions of administrative reform, would cut both parties in twain. When Mr. Cleveland names himself a Democrat, therefore, he means nothing as to his opinions on the principal issues of the day. His position with regard to them is a personal, not a party, one. He means that he is a Democrat by personal association, not by controlling conviction. He acts with all Democrats at the polls; he thinks with only some of them.

In brief, the artificial, memorial union of parties is fast being radically disturbed, and the disintegrate character of our politics promises to assert itself more confusingly than ever before. So long as the population of the Union was made up of a few simple and well-understood elements, so long, too, as both our population and our territory were compacted upon our eastern seaboard and there were foreign difficulties to be faced with united front, parties had a ready and normal growth. Such substantially were the conditions of our national politics for thirty years after the adoption of the Constitution. Such were the conditions which fostered Federalists and Antifederalists, Democratic-Republicans and Whigs. With the emergence of the Whigs, however, new interests began to make themselves prominent. Amidst new and vast movements of a mightily growing population the greatest constitutional struggle of our history opened. That struggle created an omnipotent compulsion towards party union. So long as the chief concerns of national politics centered in a few clearly seen, ever pressing, and ever menacing constitutional questions, there were definite, single purposes to cement party alliances and stiffen party discipline. Such were the conditions which continued to dominate up to and through the civil war. Such were the conditions under which a residuum of Democratic-Republicans became Democrats, under which the Whig line ran out and the Republican line was established.

As I have said, memories of these old issues have supplied until the present day the formal distinctions between parties. But, now that these memories are ceasing to be effective, there

<hr>

3 William R. Morrison, Democrat from Illinois, introduced in the House of Representatives on February 16, 1886, a bill "to reduce tariff taxes" (H.R. 5576). It put certain goods on the free list and reduced the duties on other products. On June 17, 1886, the House, by a vote of 157 to 140, rejected a motion by Morrison to consider the bill.

are no bonds of union left to our emasculated party associations. Republicans and Democrats are alike bankrupt in distinctive principles. There are no two simple forces in the nation's thought to serve as pillars for the two party structures. The threatened result is a thorough distintegration beneath the crust of party name—with what effect upon that crust may be imagined.

It is out of these apparent certainties that the question springs, Shall we not have new political parties? If the conditions of our politics permitted, we assuredly should have; as it is, we may have. A fortuitous concourse of individual atoms into party form is always possible. How fortuitous such a concourse must of necessity be two typical illustrations will suffice to show.

In that very amusing book, the "Souvenirs of a Diplomat,"[4] last year issued in translation from one of our American presses, M. de Bacourt thus complains of the difficulties of his duties in Washington: "I was obliged to visit Congress yesterday to talk over with several members business matters in which my Legation was interested, for here diplomatic affairs are not treated as everywhere else, where we communicate with the Minister of Foreign Affairs and arrange the matter with him alone. On the contrary, here the Minister submits the questions to the President, who decides whether to admit them. When he decides in the affirmative, he sends them to the Senate and to the House of Representatives, whence they are sent to the different committees whose business it is to examine and report on them. The chairman or president of the committee then reports to the House, who then vote for or against it. The result of this is that the diplomatic agent is obliged first to see the Secretary of State and explain the affair to him, then the chairman to interest him in the question and to persuade him to consider it favourably, and then to see each of the most important members of Congress and try to convince them. The delays are interminable. There are three affairs which have been hanging on for years, and I am anxious to have them settles [settled] during the present session." (p. 189.) A year later he writes: "I have been to see Mrs. Kennedy and Mrs. Winthrop. Their husbands are members of the House of Representatives, and on the committee having charge of commercial affairs, in which I am interested. . . . They say that these gentlemen are very particular about visits from foreign Ministers to their wives. I have also been to see the

---

[4] Adolphe Fourier de Bacourt, *Souvenirs of a Diplomat. Private Letters from America During the Administrations of Presidents Van Buren, Harrison, and Tyler* (New York, 1885).

Secretary of the Treasury about commercial affairs, with which I am constantly occupied. Congress seems at last disposed to discuss this question. I have taken great pains about it; but so far everything has been against me." (pp. 281-2) A few months afterwards, he has this experience to relate: "The President of the Committee on Ways and Means of the House of Representatives, of whom I asked a few moments' interview, much to my surprise appointed this meeting at eight o'clock in the morning. I was there punctually, but to my greater astonishment as I thought I should find him alone, he was surrounded by nine members of his committee, not one of whom I knew, and I was obliged to discuss with these nine fellows the most delicate questions relating to my mission. I was examined and cross-examined. I am ignorant of what impression I made upon these individuals." (p. 290).

This is certainly a very clumsy way of managing negotiations with foreign governments. Diplomatic agents in Washington are doubtless as much baffled and disgusted with such methods in 1886 as poor, mannerly M. de Bacourt was in 1842, and they are much to be pitied. But we have always sedulously avoided giving foreign ministers in Washington much to do; so that their embarrassments are serious only to them. The serious fact for us is, that our domestic affairs are managed in just the same multiplex, hide-and-seek fashion. The public is quite as easily thwarted and eluded amidst the mazes of Executive suggestion and Congressional oversight as diplomatists are. To effect anything, the public, like the diplomatist, must attempt the rôle of the lobbyist, button-hole members of this, that, or the other committee, and reason with individual Congressmen about the propriety of proposed legislation. Unless the public had so bestirred itself on the silver coinage question, for instance, the President's forcible recommendations in his message would not necessarily have brought on even a discussion of the question in Congress. It is only because members have been button-holed on all sides concerning the matter that "Congress seems at last disposed to discuss this question."

It is the absence from our system of any single person or small body of persons who can get things considered promptly and finally by Congress that leads to the disintegration of parties. There are no authoritative proposals of policy made in pursuance of consistent plans by a few leaders upon which parties can take issue, and so understand why they are parties at all. Policy is prepared in small bits by the committees, and since these bits

vary infinitely in character and importance, it is impossible that
the same sets of men should either favour or oppose any considerable number of them. These are II the circumstances which
make any concourse of individuals into such party form as will
outlast half a dozen Congressional votes in the highest degree
fortuitous. The old crusts of party name have hardened under
the heats of other days, and there seems to be no centred forces
just now that can form new crusts.

For the sake of further illustration, one has but to contrast
the course of any public agitation of a considerable public question that has taken place in this country with the course of a
similar agitation under such a system as that of Great Britain
abroad. It is most serviceable to take English politics for the uses
of such a contrast because they are familiar to us, and because
any other European popular system that we might take would be
but an imperfect copy of English institutions. The two greatest
agitations of public opinion in our history have been that upon
the question of slavery and that upon the reform of the civil
service. Probably the greatest analogous agitation of public
opinion in Great Britain was that which was directed against the
Corn Laws. At any rate, the great movements of thought upon
parliamentary reform presented no more typical forms of popular
canvass and appeal. Contrast the conditions of such agitation in
the two countries.

In the British system there is a common nucleus and source
for all governmental action. That nucleus is the Ministry of the
Crown. It constitutes the sensitive nerve centre of the constitution. From it the whole body politic receives impulse and direction. Upon it all the forces of public opinion act. Its functions
as the great single initiative and executive committee of the
House of Commons give integrate character to English public
action. It is the duty and the personal interest of this Ministry
to catch and effectuate what is sane and permanent in the public
purpose; and to do so, if possible, before agitation frets itself into
discontent or turbulence. Of course I am speaking now only of
the unideal province of a Ministry. It is its ideal province to
occupy the higher planes of statesmanship and lead the people
through such steps of conservative progress as shall bear the
tests of the longer processes of national growth, without too much
concern for the momentary popularity of their course. Their
policy must bear no taint of time-serving or of weak concession
to crude prejudices. Some of the greater figures of English history
have through a fine genius for bold conception and for captivating

popular allegiance proved themselves capable, as human capacity goes, of this high conduct. But it may be confessed without a touch of misanthropy or of disbelief in popular government that the ordinary statesman of ordinary periods can do little better than anticipate the common thought and give it its best and most reasonable expression in creating statute or rectifying reform.

The British agitator recognizes in the Cabinet the constitutional gauge of the heats and forces most active in the public thought and also the instrumentality through which all legislative, judicial, or administrative reform must be effected. He first tries to concentrate public attention upon the subject he has most at heart. All the voices of platform or press that can be made available are used for the purpose. Thought once aroused, the next step is, to harmonize, organize, unit[e] it upon a single purpose. Then it is that men begin to be elected to Parliament who represent the aims of the agitation. Through them effort first focuses itself upon the Ministry. They propose legislation, and, from the vantage ground of parliamentary debate reach the ears of many classes in the nation who never attended any of their monster meetings 'out-of-doors' and never read any of their appeals in the newspapers. If the movement which they represent have that vitality which justice and truth alone can give it, their ranks in Parliament are slowly recruited and their numbers begin to tell upon ministerial policy. They become an element which must be reckoned with. The ministerial gauge begins to register certain imperative influences in the opinion of the nation.

Such movements do not always have to wait for success till they have made sure of a majority in Parliament which can make and unmake Ministries. The Cabinet is the servant of the majority, but it is never quite its creature. Cabinets are, from the nature and necessities of the case, composed of the picked men and led by the picked debaters of their party. They are themselves the chief creators of opinion in the nation, the chief pilots of opinion in the House of Commons. They are men trained by careers formed at the hustings, in Parliament, and in executive office, and they have acquired superior quickness often in detecting the stronger forces of public thought. They may be converted to new doctrines oftentimes before all of their party is ready to follow them. Nowadays, at least, it is not uncommon to see in Cabinet seats a Chamberlain or a Dilke whom their own party call Radicals. Cabinets sometimes lead in directions in which once they were reluctant to be driven.

Such was the case when the Corn Laws were repealed. Sir

Robert Peel broke with his party to give the country that free trade which he had for long years stubbornly fought in the proposals of Villiars and Cobden and Bright. Indeed, in sketching in the abstract the natural course of agitations in England, I have been but describing without names or dates the actual fortunes of the Anti-Corn-Law cause. It gained first the ear of the people, then the ear of the people's representatives in Parliament, and then the ear of the Parliament's representatives, the Cabinet. But it it [sic] is not the first steps of its progress that render it significant by way of illustration here. The significant fact is that in getting a voice in Parliament its influence reached 'the govt.' In many other countries it might have won thousands of adherents in the nation and scores of spokesmen in the popular legislative body; but only in a state governed by a ministry responsible to the popular chamber could they by successes on the platform and at the polls bring all the forces of their cause to bear directly upon the creative powers of the government, and, by enlisting responsible party leaders in their interest, gain inviolable pledges for the security of their successes. Only under such circumstances could they get a permanent hold on the future policy of the country. When the coöperation of a Cabinet is won, the whole future becomes definite. In the persons of the Cabinet a party is won. The cause has become a party cause. The reputations of a great party's leaders have become identified with it. Neither that party nor its leaders can go back without loss of prestige.

It is concentration in the leading actions of a responsible executive ministry which gives what I have called an 'integrate' character to politics under such a system. In conferring with the Foreign Minister in England, M. de Bacourt would also have conferred with the committeeman who could best bring the matter before Parl. Cabinet minister and legislative leader would in that case have been one and the same person[.] It is the absence of any similar union and concentration of leadership and responsibility in our system which gives its disintegrate character to our politics. As I have said, either the anti-slavery or the civil-service ref. movements will serve as an ill[ustration]. But, rather than stop to reckon all the historic and factional forces which contributed to bring the slavery question to a burning focus, despite all the scattering and diverting influences of our politics, it is better to confine attention for the present purposes of illustration to the nearer and calmer and more normal agitation for the reform of the civil service. The abuses against which that agitation was directed are full fifty years old, and the sentiments

upon which the partial success of that agitation has been built
are as old as the abuses. The spoils system is not older than
strenuous opposition to it. And that first opposition to it came
from the highest quarters—from Congress itself, and from the
Senate, in whose hands lay the remedy. No one has since their
day more forcibly described, more clearly diagnosed, or more
sufficiently denounced the detestable practices to which Jackson
gave universality than did Jackson's own giant opponents,
Webster and Calhoun. What has been written in our own day
against such corruptions of the civil service, potent as it has been
in effecting reform, sounds almost weak in comparison with the
splendid arraignment of those initial abuses which prepared the
later rottenness of the system. And yet that overwhelming condemnation hurled, from the halls of Cong. itself, at corruption
in its infancy by the greatest men in the nation failed of effect.
The agitation for civil service reform began in the federal legislature itself at a time when the question of slavery had not yet
made all other questions necessarily secondary and it was still
possible for other things to enlist political feeling and purpose.
But Jackson was no responsible minister. He was a four-years
King. The thunders of the Opposition did not for a moment shake
his purpose. His popular opposition to the Bank was more to the
people than his alleged scandalous abuse of the appointing power.
His dominant personality covered all his own offences and, at
the same time, by assuming all responsibility, shiel[d]ed his party
from blame. His second term over, he retired into private life,
and there was no one left within reach of political punishment
who could fairly be charged with having originated the abuse.
For his successors, however, his policy became a precedent, for
which they, in their turn, were not responsible, and so the heresy
swung on of its own weight, nobody anywhere clearly charge-
able with its maintenance.

After the clearing of the atmosphere effected by the war, the
work of opposition to the spoils system had to be begun all over
again. And it had, of course, to begin outside Congress. There
were no longer any leaders within who could be counted on to
appeal to the country as Webster and Calhoun had done. Men
had to be put into Congress by action on public opinion through
the usual processes of popular agitation. But again the influence
of the representatives of the reform in Congress was almost
nullified by the broadcast way in which it had to be used. Attacking the abuse in Congress was scarcely more effective than
attacking it from the stump or in the press. There was nobody

there to attack on account of it. It was not Congress who made
appointments, or anybody in Congress, but some gentlemen at
the other end of Washington whose reputations and tenure of
office were hardly more affected by speeches made by a few
members in Congress than by speeches made by equally influential persons elsewhere. The only course left open to the agitators
was to convert so large a number of the people to their view and
to make continuously so great a noise in the world of print about
the corruption of the civil service that Congress, like any other
associated body of citizens, would be sure to know that a noticeable movement of thought upon the subject was taking place
and so be disposed to consider, and, if the movement became
formidable, approve measures of reform.

Naturally enough, the Executive was before Congress in feeling
the force of the demand for a correction of abuses. A single
person placed in a conspicuous position of trust is always more
apt to be sensitive to such demands, for the sake of his own fame
if for no higher reason, than three hundred men no one of whom
is responsible for what the other two hundred and ninety-nine may
do, and and [*sic*] every one of whom may always hide his single
self behind party excuses. President Grant invited the coöperation of Congress in the institution of competitive examinations;
but the leaven of the reform had not yet worked upon enough of
the atoms of that body to dispose it to a policy which promised
to rob it of much easily covered corrupt influence, and the good
intentions of the President failed to receive encouragement at
the capitol.

I have already recited the manner of the passage of the
Pendleton bill. The individualistic elements in our politics had
full play. No party principles, but only personal consciences or
fears, secured the enactment of the law. And now that the reform
has been begun, who is to be responsible for its completion?
There is no national party pledged to its continuance by any
pledges that can be readily enforced, but only *one man* with no
organized party at his back. There is a strong, nay an imperative,
sentiment of reform abroad in the nation; and, so long as that
sentiment creates in states like Massachusetts and New York
formidable masses of independent voters which can determine
the balance of power between the national parties, neither party
will lightly venture to outrage reform principles. Then, too, both
parties, doubtless, will presently have gone too far, under the
threat of public opinion, to dare openly to go back. But, in the
meantime, all the nation knows that politicians of all creeds and

traditions are lukewarm in the cause, and that even yet no one coherent group of them have staked their political fortunes upon the triumph of the reform. We have parties, but we cannot use them as parties for even the most important political purposes. Agitation of the question of reform has gained with us what successful agitation gains in England, so far as like successes are possible here; but that is not very far. The Executive has been won—as the executive Ministry would be won there. A representative of civil service reform is chief magistrate of the nation—as he would be Prime Minister there under like circumstances. But, whatever his official dignity and power, the President is still only one unit in a system of units. He is not a party leader. He does not control a legislative majority. He stands alone. If he were to die now, the reform would be again almost where it was before he was elected. When he goes out of office, another individual will have to be chosen to take his place and continue his principles in the public administration: and a fortuitous concourse of individuals will again have to be depended on to secure legislative support. There will be much advantage, of course, in having a President pledged to reform, because he is bound to that course, if bound at all, only by the unwritten law of public opinion, not by the written law of the Constitution. But there can be no final security for the cause until Congress is bound by the strongest thong of politics, definite party responsibility, to adhere to the right course. At present, though the House is nominally of the President's own party, who can be sure what Congress may not do when once public opinion for a moment sleeps? It is only general pressure from without, not party faith within, that holds.

It is such a loose, purposeless structure of parties that gives rise to that feeling of uneasiness and insecurity as to the possible course of legislation which we have so often seen manifested of late years upon the assembling of Congress. Outside of Congress the working of parties is often sufficiently coherent and satisfactory; inside of Congress it is always quite incoherent and unsatisfactory. I mean that the leaders of opinion 'out of doors' are often able to make their influence widely felt, through the press and other agencies, and it is often possible to perceive the existence of a wide agreement of thought as to such questions, for instance, as that of the coinage of silver or the right basis for a bankrupt law; but that such waves of opinion, though they rise to almost tidal height, seem to break at the doors of Congress. Opinion, united amongst constituents, breaks up into a score of discordant elements amongst representatives. It is not only those

Congressmen who represent divided constituencies who are in doubt as to what ought to be done: they have at least the excuse of provident caution. Even men who represent communities where not a doubt exists in any respectable quarter as to what legislation is desirable suffer in Congress a queer paralysis of judgment and purpose which can be accounted for only by supposing that their detached position there, where every man is his own leader, frightens them. Each would feel easier if he could be either a leader or a follower,—anywhere in an organized majority or in a concerted opposition. A caucus always gives him sinew, whether he agrees with its determination or not; but there is not always agreement enough amongst a nominal party to make caucus action possible. Even that force cannot always integrate our parties.

There can be no doubt, I suppose, that it is such party situations that disgust earnest, patriotic people with politics, and especially with parties. The very structure of our govt. compels Congressmen to thrust forward thus individual motive and judgment, and yet we condemn them as self-seekers because they obey the compulsion. We complain that each man seeks to promote only his own 'pet schemes,' and never shows himself capable of 'rising above party,' when the fact of the matter is that their is no other 'scheme' for him to promote, no real party for him to rise above. He does not find him [his] nominal party, Democratic or Republican, united upon any principle or course of action. He finds it existing for no legislative purpose, but only for campaign purposes. Inside Congress, and for Congressional uses, it can hardly be called a party at all.

This would seem to explain the evident fact upon which I have already dwelt at some length, that the reasons of union with our present national parties concern the past instead of the future. Their organization is personal, individualistic, not corpo‑rate. It is like the friendship of college chums, a thing of early association; not like the union of men of similar opinions for the accomplishment of a common object. Its ends consequently must be personal because its action is individual: there are no definite ends of policy possible.

Parties so situated are not to be envied. Any one in their ranks who has a loud enough voice can misrepre[se]nt and embarrass them. Where no one is leader all are leaders. All speakers are spokesmen. Corporate parties cannot exist without well-recognized leadership. With them there is none of the worry and humiliation of disclaiming self-constituted spokesmen. There is no occasion to say hastily and deprecatingly 'This fellow does not represent us.' Everybody knows who speaks with party authority. With disintegrate parties, on the contrary, who are not leaders? The antithesis is between a few coöperative purposes and a thousand cross purposes; between party plans and partisans' plans; between common ends and individual ends; between combined forces which can be reckoned with, and scattered, guerilla forces which cannot be reckoned with.

The President of the U. S. and the Speaker of the House of Representatives are in a sense elected party representatives, and, once every two years, the legislative policy of the country promises to take shape through the power of the Speaker to appoint the Standing Committees of the House. Mr. Tilden recognized this fact when he chose the opening of the present Cong. as the best time at which to give some public advice to the Democrats about the coast defences. He addressed an open letter to Mr. Carlisle, the ex-Speaker, who was sure of re-election. It was necessary thus to anticipate the organization of the House in presenting views upon such a question to the powerful functionary who appoints the Committee having such questions in charge. His, just at the moment when he was about to appoint, was the one formative power in the House. A committee favourable to the policy proposed would make its adoption possible; a committee indifferent or unfavourable would render it impossible. This segment of the disjointed House must be adjusted with these special ends in view, or the whole matter will necessarily go by the board.

We have carried individual initiative from the sphere of commerce and private enterprise, where it belongs and is beneficent, up into the sphere of government and public enterprise, where it does not belong and is disabling. In the life of the individual liberty and strength consist in guaranteed individuality: in the life of the state, in facilitated union. The state must have an individuality and oneness of its own which is not simply the aggregate or compromise resultant of the individualities of all concerned in its govt. In private life man's nobility consists in the privilege to be himself; in public life, in the observance of his duty to subordinate himself to the common good. The individualism of commerce or of invention makes politics selfish and mean, petty and weak.

At the same time, there is a very great sphere for personal individuality in the higher forms of political combination. Combined effort makes room for recognized and trusted leadership, and through such leadership, when once it is open to be won, the stronger minds of a nation eagerly seek a chance to impress their individuality upon state action. By disintegrating our politics by the institution of all sorts of equalities and cross-balances of authority in Cong. and out of it, we sacrifice the individuality of leadership, which ennobles men, to the individuality of competition and antagonism which makes them petty and base. We prefer selfish dissociation to public-spirited association. It is the old anti-federal principle over again, though this time it is operating not amongst the States but amongst the coördinate branches of the national government, and amongst the Standing Committees, the coordinate branches of Congress.

Such are the laws of our politics which condition the formation of a new national party. If I were warranted in thinking that my voice might be heard amidst the multitudinous voices of the public thought, I should say and say again, to the limit of my privilege, that the first united effort of opinion should be directed towards creating the conditions prerequisite to the existence of open, healthy, public spirited party government. This can be done only by creating in Congress some small group of leaders, whether that group be composed of members of the Cabinet, or of a single Standing Committee made up entirely from the party having the majority, who shall formulate policy and gather into a head the responsibility which now wanders amongst two score Committees till it is lost. If once Congress were thus enabled clearly to know its own mind and to organize its majorities and minorities fearlessly in the face of the nation, the further step of bringing it into cooperation with the executive would be feasible and the much to be wished for time of manageable party govt. would be in full view.

WWT and WWhw MSS. (WP, DLC).

A Newspaper Article

[c. Sept. 1, 1886]
Wanted,—A Party.

A man must nowadays either belong to a party through mere force of habit, or else be puzzled to know what party he belongs to. Party platforms furnish no sort of chart by which he can shape his political course. Unless they are carefully labelled, he cannot tell which party speaks through them, for they all say much the same thing. If voters chose their party instead of happening into it, they would probably choose by the aid of two questions, namely, first, "What policy do we favor?" and, second, "Which party advocates that policy?" Perhaps it is fortunate, therefore, that so many drift to the ballot-box and so few choose; for, otherwise, multitudes would lose their votes before answering the second of these questions. They would practically disfranchise themselves if they waited to answer it. The professions of existing parties do not furnish any satisfactory reply to it; still less do their actions. Does any one favor civil service reform? The present act establishing competitive examinations and a commission was proposed by a democratic senator to a republican senate, was passed by that body and a democratic house, and signed by a republican president. The senator [George H. Pendleton] who proposed it was afterward cast aside by his constituency because of his reform sentiments. His measure is now administered, with full sympathy for its purposes, by a democratic president elected because of his record on this question; but it is covertly attacked in a democratic house, and openly sneered at in a republican senate; and the democratic chairman of the house committee on civil service reform [William Ruffin Cox] fails of a renomination in North Carolina because of his fine reform work on that committee. Which party, then, advocates civil service reform?

Or turn to the question of federal aid to education in the states. Does some voter favor such aid? It was proposed in the senate by a republican,[1] fathered in the house by a democrat, carried in the senate by a complex mixture of republican and democratic votes, and smothered in the house by no one knows whom. Is it the democrats or the republicans that would have national aid to education in the states?

Or, again, is it the tariff that is crucial? Does some new manufacturer in the South want the import duties kept up? Let him examine the record of proceedings in congress. Democratic revenue reformers are kept from even so much as introducing a bill by the opposition of democratic protectionists, and republicans assist both sides. Is the protectionist voter to be a democrat or a republican?

Is the silver question to be made a test? Each party is on both sides. Or labor problems? Which party is on any side with regard to that, except the side of profession which will catch the laborer's vote?

But why extend the perplexing recital? It is sadly confounding

[1] In the much-controverted Blair bill, referred to in earlier volumes in this series.

to think about so much confusion. And, be it observed, I am not speaking of these things in ridicule of our national parties, or in disgust with our national politics, nor yet in despair of our national institutions. I am simply gathering facts to serve as food for reflection, and in order to state what my own reflections upon them have been. My chief reflection has been, not that our national parties are in a state of disintegration; that is not a reflection. It is a mere patent fact. But that such a course of things is tending, so to say, to *individualize* our politics is a reflection, and one which seems worth exploring somewhat at large.

First, let me explain what I mean by the individualizing of our politics. I mean simply that the voter who exercises any choice at all, is being obliged to choose *men*, particular individuals, to tie to, instead of parties. Of course the conscientious voter always chose between men, between candidates, in voting; but formerly he could choose them as representing parties. Now he must choose them instead of parties. The feeling is: "No party means what it says; some men do seem to mean what they say; we will tie to them when we can." The last presidential election of course furnishes the most striking illustration of the operation of this feeling. The mugwump is the man who has cast loose from parties, which don't mean what they say, and offers to follow men who do speak with a purpose. Mr Cleveland is a democrat. But he was not elected because he was a democrat, but because the civil service of the country needed reforming, and he evidently meant to reform it, if given a chance. A man of that sort in the presidential chair would be worth any number of party platforms; a great number of discriminating voters accordingly followed him in preference to any party,—"irrespective of party," to use the orthodox phrase.

Mr. Cleveland's case was only a conspicuous one, however; it was not isolated. There is a yearly increasing number of mayors, governors, and congressmen holding their offices because of personal qualities or opinions pleasing to constituencies who do not stop to ask, in choosing them, whether the parties they formally represent possess like qualities or opinions.

Various reasons, historical and others, might be offered to explain this interesting but necessarily transitional state of affairs; as, for instance, that the republican party has outlived the purposes for which it was organized, and that the democratic party has ceased to be opposed to it in most matters, except in a Pickwickian sense. The republican party rendered the country some inestimable services, and the country, in natural gratitude, pensioned it with a quarter of a century of power. Meantime, the democratic party kicked its heels with what philosophy it could command on the cold outside of the offices, comforting itself with dignified repetitions of certain old and important constitutional principles which had all of a sudden apparently lost their old power as charms to conjure with. But the republican pension has run out now. It could not reasonably be claimed for a second generation. The pensioners, too, got intolerable as they grew old. We, accordingly, have a president who is a democrat in favor of civil service reform, and a congress which is nothing in particular and in favor of nothing unanimously, save large expenditures of money. The old parties, to put it in the vernacular, have "played out," and we are choosing here a man and there a man who means what he says, while waiting for a party which shall mean what *it* says.

The new parties which are hoped for in the future do not form readily or quickly for the same reason that the old parties have not adapted themselves to changed circumstances. Our system of government has supplied no official place, no place of actual authority, for leaders of parties. A party, consequently, must be a merely fortuitous concourse of atoms; and we must wait on the atoms. Even after it is formed, any party of ours must keep together rather by grace and enthusiasm than by vital organization. There is no ruling station in the government for its leaders. It must follow them rather for what they eloquently profess than for anything that they can actually do. The most leader-like post in politics is the speakership of the house of representatives, which is the most unsuitable place possible for a party captain. If we did not have a natural talent for forming parties, and it were not the fashion in all popular governments to have parties, it is to be seriously doubted whether we would not approximate that "natural society," of which some philosophers and some anarchists have dreamed, in which everybody would act for himself and nobody act, except accidentally, or through chance amiability, in concert with his neighbors.

There is, however, another and a better reason why we always have parties, and that is, that we have a splendid habit of all believing in certain great principles of human liberty and self-government, without being tamely all of one mind about the way in which those principles ought to be applied in particular cases. No time was ever bigger than this with unsolved problems as to the best ways in which to make liberty real and government helpful. Labor questions, financial questions, administrative questions must all tax the best thought of the country from this time on, until some clear purpose of reform, of financial reconstruction, or of governmental betterment is conceived by some group of men who mean what they say, who all mean the same thing, and who know how to say it, begin to speak their purpose, so that the nation will wake as at a new voice—a voice which calls with authority to duty and to action. Then a new party will be formed—and another party opposed to it. All that is wanting is a new, genuine and really meant purpose held by a few strong men of principle and boldness. That is a big "all," and it is still conspicuously wanting.

But the generations that really loved the old and now disintegrated parties is fast passing away. It is largely the new generation that wonders that any one ever doubted that the war was over—even sometimes wonders what the war was all about—that is compelling a clearing away of the worn-out formulas of the old dispensation and a hastening of something not stated to determine their politics. With the growth of this new generation we shall unquestionably witness the growth of new parties.

Printed in the *Boston Times*, Sept. 26, 1886; editorial headings and by-line omitted.

From Melville R. Hopewell

Dear Sir   Tekamah, Neb., Sept 2 1886

I have just returned from a month's trip to Pacific coast, and find your letter of 26 ult. at hand. In reply, will say, that the project of deepening the Ditch, was not carried out, owing to objections by a number of land owners, so that the tax, as advertised will not be called for.[1]

It is an unfavorble time to sell this land now. 1st for the reason that the past two or three seasons have been unusually wet ones, rendering all bottom lands, practically valueless, for agricultural purposes. 2nd close times have depreciated the value, of lands generally. I will make an effort to get, an offer for some of your lands, and if I can get what I consider a fair offer will let you know.

I suppose usual terms say, ¼ cash, bal in 4 or 5 annual payments, secured by mortgage on the land would be satisfactory?
                              Yours truly,   M. R. Hopewell

ALS (WP, DLC) with WWhw figures on env.
[1] See M. R. Hopewell to WW, May 20, 1886.

From Lucy Maynard Salmon

Dear Sir,   Syracuse, N. Y. Sept. 3, 1886.

I have intended all summer to write you in regard to the work in history at Bryn Mawr next year. I should be glad to know at your convenience what work will be expected of me and also whether I can take up something in the line of political economy in connection with history. Possibly my desultory summer reading may be made to take a more definite form during the intervening month.   Respectfully,   Lucy M. Salmon

ALS (WP, DLC) with WWhw notations on env.: "Ans. Sept 8/86" and "136 East Genesee St."

Two Letters from Raymond Landon Bridgman

My dear sir,   Boston, Mass., Sept. 4, 1886.

I shall be glad to receive your article, but before your note came Mr. Sidney Dickinson promised me one for Sept. 7. So yours will be used the week following. It will be set up here and mailed for publication Sept. 20 in the papers in the arrangement (the 21st in New England) and will appear in the [Boston] Sunday Times of the Sunday following. It is my practice to send several copies of the Times to the writer, and the check, immediately after publication in this paper.

With thanks for your accommodation,

R. L. Bridgman.

My dear Sir,   Boston, Mass., Sept. 6. 1886.

Thank you for the article received this morning. It will be used as I wrote you in my letter of last week. It may make some of the party papers squirm, but I hope they will survive.

Very truly yours,   R. L. Bridgman.

ALS (WP, DLC) with WWhw notation on env. of first letter: "Ans. Sept. 8/86."

To Lucy Maynard Salmon

Miss Salmon,   Clarksville, Tenn., 8 Sept., 1886.

Your letter of Sept. 3, forwarded from Bryn Mawr, has just reached me here. I can give no definite answers to your questions until I have an opportunity of talking with you very fully as to your plans. We have not yet made out any fixed schemes for graduate studies at Bryn Mawr; for we have neither teachers nor graduate students enough to warrant separate & formal lecture courses for advanced workers. My plan last year was to give personal direction and as full criticism and aid as possible to Miss [Jane] Bancroft's original work. In short, I guided and assisted her constantly in ways which I thought led most directly to success in the sort of teaching she expected to do. I think this much the best, most stimulating method of instruction. I should prefer, therefore, to have an interview with you before fixing finally upon any course. I can then learn also your wishes as to adding political economy to our study in history. Possibly such an addition might be made without overloading the year's work.

Very truly Yours,   Woodrow Wilson

ALS (NPV).

From James E. Rhoads

Dear Friend,   Bryn Mawr, near Philadelphia, 9 Mo. 8 1886

As the students find the written examination papers inconvenient, we think it best to have those for the autumn examinations printed. Will you kindly send us the history papers at your earliest convenience, that they may be printed in time.

Yours cordially,   James E. Rhoads, per Secretary

HwL (WP, DLC) with WWhw notation on env.: "Ans. Sep. 13/86." Att.: WWhw list of questions for Bryn Mawr entrance examination in history.

From Marion Wilson Kennedy

My very dear brother: Little Rock, Sept. 8th [1886]

The book has just arrived safely, and I know you will be waiting impatiently to hear of it—so hasten to inform you, though that is nearly all I have to say at this time.[1] Ross[2] will be in Clarksville next week, probably, and can give you all the news.

I am so glad you found Ellie and the baby well. You did not say whether Ellie was glad to see you! Just think of my suspense! Kiss her and the dear baby many times for me, please—and thank her once more for sparing you to me for a week—which we all here enjoyed *hugely*.[3] . . .

Tell us any particulars you may know about the Earthquake in Columbia.[4] Is Annie there, or at Glenn Springs?[5] We have felt very anxious to hear something from them and from Uncle James' family.[6] When will you, *with your family*, leave for Bryn Mawr?[7] Have you ordered the Trycycicle yet? Don't forget to send us photograph of yourself, dear Ellie and baby at the earliest possible moment. You might have been generous enough to leave yours with us. . . .   Lovingly your sister,   Marion

ALS (WP, DLC).
    [1] A mysterious reference.
    [2] A. Ross Kennedy, her husband.
    [3] She refers here to Wilson's recent visit with the Kennedys in Little Rock, about which see WW to EAW, Aug. 13, 14, 15, 16, 17, and 18, 1886.
    [4] A severe earthquake struck Charleston, South Carolina, on August 31, 1886, but apparently was not felt in Columbia.
    [5] Annie Wilson Howe, then vacationing in Glenn Springs, South Carolina. See George Howe, Jr., to WW, Sept. 7, 1886, ALS (WP, DLC).
    [6] That is, the family of James W. Bones.
    [7] Woodrow and Ellen stayed in Clarksville as late as September 16. Hiram Woods to WW, Sept. 13, 1886, ALS (WP, DLC) with WWhw notation on env.: "Ans. Sept. 16/86," forwarded from Bryn Mawr, was received in Clarksville on September 16.

EDITORIAL NOTE

WILSON'S TEACHING AT BRYN MAWR, 1886-87

Wilson laid out his revised plan for a two-year course of study for history and political science majors at Bryn Mawr College in the copy that he supplied for the college catalogue for 1886-87.[1] In addition, in the documents printed in this volume at November 27, 1886, and June 1, 1887, Wilson gave detailed reviews of his classroom work and described his weekly "news-meetings" with students, which he seems to have begun in the autumn of 1886.[2] This note provides a guide to the additional documentary materials relating to Wilson's course work during his second year at Bryn Mawr.

Wilson's course program for 1886-87 was as follows:

Autumn Semester
(a) English history, given three times a week to twelve students.
(b) Special topics in American history, given twice a week to twelve students.
Spring Semester
(a) French history, given three times a week to thirteen students.
(b) The Italian Renaissance and German Reformation, given twice a week to fifteen students.[3]

All of Wilson's notes for his lectures in English and French history seem to have survived.[4] They give ample evidence of his coverage and level of treatment, and it is perhaps enough to say that the notes consist mainly of chronological and topical outlines based upon the standard authorities of that day.

    [1] Printed at Feb. 1, 1886.
    [2] For another description of these "news-meetings," see Mary Tremain to R. S. Baker, Jan. 1, 1926, RSB Coll., DLC.
    [3] Based in part on the Bryn Mawr "Register of Students, Vol. I" (bound ledger book, PBm) and Wilson's own list of students for 1886-87 in the pocket notebook described at Sept. 21, 1885.
    [4] The English history lecture notes are described at Oct. 4, 1886; the French history lecture notes, at Feb. 1, 1887.

Wilson's notes for lectures on American history also seem to be complete.[5] These notes, unlike those for Wilson's lectures on English and French history, are of some significance for historiography. For one thing, the notes for lectures on American history indicate that Wilson may have been a pioneer in developing the interpretation that emphasized the economic and social causes of the Civil War. These notes also reveal in embryo the ideas and interpretations that Wilson later put into *Division and Reunion,* published in 1893.

The notes for Wilson's lectures on the Italian Renaissance and German Reformation, all of which appear to be extant, consist mainly of chronological and topical outlines.[6] Even their brief contents, however, indicate a strong Protestant and Calvinistic interpretation. They also provide evidence of Wilson's interest in Italian art.

Wilson's only graduate student during 1886-87 was Lucy Maynard Salmon, the Fellow in History during that year. Wilson gave no graduate courses but met Miss Salmon for two hours on three afternoons a week. Miss Salmon later recalled that these conferences were "absolutely informal" and that conversation ranged over the whole field of American constitutional history and problems. In addition, Wilson helped Miss Salmon to review economics by reading to her the notes that he had taken in Dr. Ely's courses at the Johns Hopkins.[7]

The reader is referred to the *caveat* in the last paragraph of the Editorial Note, "Wilson's Teaching at Bryn Mawr, 1885-86."

[5] Described at Oct. 4, 1886.
[6] Described at Feb. 1, 1887.
[7] Lucy M. Salmon to R. S. Baker, Jan. 6 and 15, 1926, RSB Coll., DLC.

Notes for Lectures on English History

[c. Oct. 4, 1886-c. Jan. 31, 1887]

Contents:

(1) Notes for lectures on special topics in English history, mainly in WWsh, listed in WW's order: *"The Empire," "The Expansion of England," "Ireland since the Union," "Ireland before the Union," "The Peerage," "Curia Regis," "The Cabinet," "Periods of English Church History," "The Church: The Question of Disestablishment," "The Union with Scotland," "The Government of Great Britain," "Colonial Government," "Public Education,"* and *"England's Foreign Relations."*

(2) WWhw and WWsh outlines and bibliographical notes.

Loose sheets (WP, DLC).

Notes for Lectures on American History

[c. Oct. 4, 1886-c. Jan. 31, 1887]

Contents:

(1) Notes for lectures on special topics in American history, mainly in WWsh, listed in WW's order: *"America To-day (1886)," "America To-day (continued)," "The United States To-day. The Governments," "The Causes of the Civil War"* (transcript printed at Oct. 18, 1886),

"The Doctrine of State Sovereignty and the War" (transcript printed at Oct. 20, 1886), *"The Westward Migration and the West of To-day," "Texas and the Mexican War," "Andrew Jackson," "The Bank of the U.S. in Politics," "The Cherokee Case," "The Monroe Doctrine," "The War of 1812," "History of Parties," "Union, 1765-1789," "The Union: 1787-1789," "Causes of the Revolution,"* and *"Periods of American History."*

(2) Additional notes and outlines, mainly in WWhw, for what were apparently lectures on the Missouri Compromise, the Independent Treasury, African slavery in the South, the abolitionist movement, and the Kansas-Nebraska Act, some of which may have been prepared for a course in American history at Wesleyan University in 1889-90.

Loose sheets (WP, DLC).

From Charles Kendall Adams

President's Rooms, Cornell University,
My dear Professor Wilson: Ithaca, N. Y., Oct. 13th 1886

We have recently organized a Historical and Political Science Association, and I hope we shall be able in the course of the year to have a few addresses before the Association, and I write you for the purpose of ascertaining whether you have not some address on an administrative subject or a topic in comparative political methods that would be advantageous to our students. I ask you this for the double purpose of giving you an opportunity of seeing our University and of having a talk with you in regard to some of our plans for the future. My first thought was to visit you, and if it is impossible for you to come here before very long, say within 3 or 4 weeks, I may think it desirable to pay you a visit some time in the course of the next week. I shall be in your vicinity, and I could, if necessary, visit you probably on Thursday. Have the kindness to let me know without delay whether you could not give us an evening within the time above indicated. We should expect to pay your expenses. I regret that there is no fund with which I could pay more.

Very respectfully Yours,   C. K. Adams   [per] G

HwL (WP, DLC).

From Janet Woodrow Wilson

My darling Son—   Clarksville, Tenn. Oct. 17th '86.

We were so glad to get yours announcing your safe arrival at Bryn Mawr. My reply should have been more prompt, but I have been far from well. We were so sorry to hear of the discomforts of your journey, but took comfort in the reflection that they were all over at the time of your writing. I will not try to tell you how we missed you all—the precious baby above all. I could not help saying aloud from day to day—over and over again—"I wish I had the precious baby in my arms." I cannot tell you how I long for the sweet darling! I wonder how long it may be before I see her again! And when I do see her, she will shrink from me as from a stranger! Are you quite rid of your cold? And have you gotten comfortably fixed in your little rooms? If you are too busy to write & tell me *all* about yourselves, beg Ellie to write. We are so glad to know that you have secured a good nurse, for so much of dear baby's comfort & happiness depends upon that—to say nothing of yours & Ellie's.

I have moved our bed-room up to the study—and have moved the study into your room. We find the new arrangement very comfortable every way. The study makes a beautiful bedroom—the bedroom a cosy study—and then we are all together—which is a great thing for me, you know. . . .

The two Josephs are well—No. 1 busy from morning to night preparing for his classes, No 2 studying diligently. . . . We all love you with all our hearts—and long to hear from you—and all about each one of you as often as possible. With love unbounded from us each one to you three,   Mother

ALS (WP, DLC).

Notes for Two Lectures on American History

[c. Oct. 18, 1886]

VI

The Causes of the Civil War.

The differences which existed between the North and South were profound social and industrial differences; and these differences had existed ever since far back in colonial days. The South was engaged almost exclusively in agriculture, and work done in her fields was done by slaves. Such a system resulted in large plantations, in only moderate effort and no diligence on the part of the laborers, in the degradation of all labor that was not slave labor, and consequently a fixing upon the South [of] a single occupation. The North came to have many avenues of activity; the South continued to have but one, and differences between the 2 sections became daily more and more emphasized.

United States

VI

The Causes of the Civil War

[shorthand notes — includes dates: 1824; 1828; 1832; 1832; 1830; 1830, and markers A, B]

Wilson's shorthand notes for a lecture on American history

These differences very early showed themselves in political rivalry. This rivalry centered, for the most part about 2 questions: those of the tariff and admission of new states to the Union. A. Tariff: Southern members of Congress had supported the earliest tariff measures but it very soon became evident to the Southern leaders that tariffs, though beneficial to the North, where manufactures could grow, were not beneficial, but only expensive to the South, where only agriculture could be developed: they felt that the South was being made to pay for Northern prosperity. The contest may be said to have fairly begun about the tariff of 1824; it grew hot over the tariff of 1828; and the tariff of 1832 led to the assertion of the right of nullification on the part of South Carolina and almost to civil war—issuing in the compromise by which it was agreed that the tariff should by degrees be lifted.

It is not without significance that these controversies culminated in 1832. The year of 1830 is the greatest turning point in the history of the country. Up to that time the North and South had been drawing apart from each other economically and hence socially only by slow degrees; after 1830 they drew away from each other with startling rapidity. It was then that railroads began to grow and the West consequently began to be peopled and developed; it was then that new inventions improved steam navigation and so commerce received a new impetus; it was then, in brief, that the country began to put on those aspects which we know today. This emphasized all the differences between the North and the South: and the South became all the more reluctant to pay tariff duties to serve the interests of the North.

(B) The other point of antagonism was the admission of new states to the Union. Recognizing the fact of their diverse interests, the object of the 2 sections was to preserve the balance of power between them in Congress. During the first quarter of a century of the existence of the Federal Government, the South had practical control in politics; but this era of control began to break down. It could be maintained only by the creation of new states like her own in industrial and social condition: only by increasing natural leaders; only by creating for every free state that was admitted a slave state to offset it. Such was the significance of the Missouri question (1821), of the struggle over the admission of Texas (1845), of the Kansas-Nebraska trouble (1854). And this difficulty too began to hasten towards an issue in 1830. With the growth of the railroads and growth that accompanies the extension of railroads the migrations to the West of course greatly increased and territories became more and more rapidly prepared for admission into the Union. The whole of the Northwest was drawn into balance against the South. The results were, the breach of the Missouri compromise, the Dred-Scott case, the triumph of the Republican Party, and war.

What, then, were the causes of the war?

The fundamental cause was the radical differences about a condition between the 2 sections, which by 1861 had become painfully marked; and the efficient cause of those differences was slavery. A balance of political power between the sections could no longer be preserved; the free states of the Northwest had made the struggle of the South for political equality hopeless and desperate; the only course remaining was surrender or war; the choice was for war. The abolition of slavery has made the repetition of such a struggle impossible by making the 2 sections alike. It was slavery that made them unlike; it was their unlikeness that made them antagonistic.

[c. Oct. 20, 1886]

VII

The Doctrine of State Sovereignty and the War.

The doctrine of state sovereignty played so important a part in the argumentative side of the war that it would almost seem that war was waged as an assertion of state sovereignty. But that doctrine was not in reality of the essence of the struggle: it was only its formal basis. The real cause of the war was the irreconcilable diversities of political and social interests between the North and South caused by their radical unlikeness—an unlikeness which had been brought about largely by slavery. Had any other 2 sections of the country been thus permanently unlike the doctrine of state sovereignty would have found champions in the weaker of them as the formal basis for strife just as it found champions in the South.

This will appear from the following consideration: the question as to the causes of the Civil War is not why did *a* civil war take place in this country between 2 sections of the Union; but why did this particular Civil War take place and why were the parties to it these 2 particular sections, the North and the South?

The doctrine of state sovereignty had been asserted in all sections of the country at one time or another. It was strongly pronounced by the legislatures of Virginia and Kentucky in protest against the Alien and Sedition Acts of 1789; New-England talked of acting upon it in 1808 to rid herself of the burdens of the Embargo Act, and in 1812 to escape the inconvenience of the war with England; Pennsylvania arrayed her militia against the authority of the United States in 1809; Georgia successfully resisted the authority of the Federal Government in the case of the Cherokees in 1832; South Carolina unsuccessfully withstood it in the same year on the tariff question. So late as 1859 the legislature of Wisconsin declared the right of the state to judge infractions of the Constitution and to bid positive defiance to Federal laws which they deemed unconstitutional. But only in 1861 in the instance of South Carolina and the states which followed her into secession was the assertion of this doctrine followed up by action and war. This was not a doctrine peculiar to the South; it had many champions in the North; and when the North championed it the South had denied it. How did it happen that a doctrine which had been the refuge of every section when in trouble was at last fought about by these 2 particular sections, the North and the South? Because in every other case the causes of irritation had been temporary: in this case they were permanent. The North and South had been unlike ever since colonial days: the unlikeness and consequent diversity of interest culminated in 1861, the aggrieved section (the worsted section) fell back, as she had for many years been preparing to do, upon the doctrine of state sovereignty, the common refuge under such circumstances, and war came. Had the difficulties which had in other cases led to the assertion of this same doctrine come to a head, they too might have led to war. In such case the doctrine of state sovereignty would no more have been the cause of the war than it was in 1861. Wars are seldom fought about abstract theories. Such theories as that of state sovereignty are generally made to do service for uncertain antagonism; but the antagonism causes the war, not the theory. The North and South fought because their differences and antagonisms had become intolerable and state sovereignty was made the formal basis of the war just as it would have been made between any other 2 sections had intolerable differences existed between them.

Transcripts of WWsh in the second body of lecture notes described at Oct. 4, 1886.

Two Letters from Charles Kendall Adams

Dear Professor Wilson: Ithaca, N. Y., Oct 22 1886.

Thanks for your letter of acceptance. I cannot quite yet fix upon a date for the paper or lecture, but I think that Wednesday Nov. 3 will probably be the date. I will inform you definitely so soon as the time can be determined. We shall give you a hearing of perhaps a hundred & fifty listeners.

Hastily yours   C K Adams

My dear Sir: Ithaca, N. Y., Oct 28 1886.

Can you give us the evening of Wednesday, Nov. 3d for your lecture? Please give me the title, that I may have it properly announced.[1]   Hastily yours   C. K. Adams

ALS (WP, DLC) with WWhw notation on env. of second letter: "Ans. 10/30/86."
[1] Wilson's lecture was entitled "The Study of Administration."

EDITORIAL NOTE

WILSON'S "THE STUDY OF ADMINISTRATION"

As the letters from President Charles Kendall Adams of Cornell University have just shown, Wilson seized the invitation to speak before the Historical and Political Science Association of that institution. The documentary record also makes it plain that he decided at once that this invitation to speak before a scholarly group provided an appropriate occasion to expound the views on administration that had been crystallizing in his mind for more than a year.

There was no need for Wilson to do any new research for the kind of paper that he had in mind, for he had already done what he thought was the basic reading and research while writing "The Modern Democratic State."[1] Moreover, in mid-November 1885 he had also put his ideas on administration into embryonic form in a brief essay, "The Art of Governing," which he had never published.[2]

With "The Art of Governing" as a beginning, Wilson drew up an outline[3] and then wrote out a first draft of his new paper, "The Study of Administration." He was in fact able to use about two thirds of the pages of the first draft of "The Art of Governing" in preparing his expanded paper.[4] After much revision of this draft, Wilson typed a copy on his Caligraph, completing it on about November 1, 1886.

[1] See the Editorial Note, "Wilson's First Treatise on Democratic Government"; "Memoranda for 'The Modern Democratic State,'" Dec. 1, 1885; and "The Modern Democratic State," printed at Dec. 1, 1885.
[2] See the Editorial Note, "Wilson's First Writings on Administration," and "Notes on Administration" and "The Art of Governing," both printed at Nov. 15, 1885.
[3] Three WWhw loose pages (WP, DLC) with heading: "*Analysis: A. Political Admin. . . .*"
[4] This first draft of "The Study of Administration" is a WWhw MS. (WP, DLC).

　　The records of the Cornell Historical and Political Science Association have not survived—if, indeed, any were ever kept. However, a news story from Ithaca, printed in the New York *Evening Post* on November 4, 1886, gives us the essential information about Wilson's lecture:

　　"Before the Historical and Political Science Association on the evening of November 3 Prof. Woodrow Wilson read a very able paper on 'The Study of Administration.' Prof. Wilson outlined the history of the study, showed how it was a comparatively new development in political science, very cogently presented the necessity and value of such study, and indicated the methods by means of which it ought to be carried on."

　　Edwin R. A. Seligman of Columbia College, one of the editors of the new *Political Science Quarterly*, had earlier asked Wilson for a contribution.[5] Seeing the notice of Wilson's address at Cornell in the *Evening Post*, Seligman wrote him on November 9, 1886, asking for a copy for possible publication in the *Political Science Quarterly*. Wilson complied on November 11 by sending Seligman the typed copy that he had used for delivery at Cornell. Seligman, in a letter that has been lost, said that he liked the paper very much and wanted to publish it as it was. Wilson thereupon wrote to Seligman on December 6, asking him to return the manuscript for revision of one passage "which might convey a false impression when read." This passage consisted of the last two paragraphs in the second section of the essay. Wilson had written the following in his typed draft of the lecture:

　　"I know that there are a great many thoughtful people who are ready to see in a corps of civil servants prepared by a special schooling and drilled after appointment into a perfected organization the elements which may combine to make an offensive official class, a distinct, semi-corporate body with sympathies divorced from those of the progressive, free-spirited people whom they would serve, and hearts narrowed to the compass of a bigotted officialism. Certainly such a class would be altogether harmful and hateful in the United States. Any measures calculated to produce it would for us be measures of reaction and folly. But to fear the creation of a dominant, illiberal officialism as the result of the studies I have proposed is altogether to miss the principle upon which I wish most to insist. That principle is that the official organism to be born of such study shall be at all points sensitive to public opinion. A body of thoroughly trained officials serving during good behaviour we must have in any case: that is an unmistakable business necessity. The apprehension that such a body of officials will be anything un-American clears away the moment it is asked. What is to constitute 'good behaviour'? I say the question itself dispels all fear because its answer goes with it, as light with the sun. Steady, hearty allegiance to the policy of the government will constitute good behaviour. And that policy will have no taint of officialism in it. It will not be the creation of permanent officials, but of chiefs whose responsibility to public opinion shall be direct and inevitable. I have never heard that those who did service

[5] E. R. A. Seligman to WW, March 6 and 19, 1886.

under one who really served the people were apt to arrogate to themselves exclusive privileges or a domineering air.

"Those who fear the growth of an undemocratic professional officialism in this country are frightening themselves with bugbears which no one who does not live under a highly centralized government ought to allow to haunt him. In urging a perfected organization of public administration I have said not a word in favour of making all administration centre in Washington. I have spoken of giving new life to local organisms, of reorganizing decentralization. The end which I have proposed for administrative study in America is the discovery of the best means of constituting a civil service cultured and self-sufficient enough to act with sense and vigour and yet so connected with popular thought by means of elections and constant public counsel as to find arbitrariness out of the question."[6]

After substituting new pages for the above passage, Wilson returned the manuscript to Seligman. The paper was published in the *Political Science Quarterly* in the July 1887 issue. Wilson's typescript has apparently been lost.

[6] Four loose pages of Wilson's typescript (WP, DLC).

An Essay

[c. Nov. 1, 1886]

The Study of Administration.

I suppose that no practical science is ever studied where there is no need to know it. The very fact, therefore, that the eminently practical science of administration is finding its way into college courses in this country would prove that this country needs to know more about administration, were such proof of the fact required to make out a case. It need not be said, however, that we do not look into college programmes for proof of this fact. It is a thing almost taken for granted among us, that the present movement called civil service reform must, after the accomplishment of its first purpose, expand into efforts to improve, not the *personnel* only, but also the organization and methods of our government offices: because it is plain that their organization and methods need improvement only less than their *personnel*. It is the object of administrative study to discover, first, what government can properly and successfully do, and, secondly, how it can do these proper things with the utmost possible efficiency and at the least possible cost either of money or of energy. On both these points there is obviously much need of light among us; and only careful study can supply that light.

Before entering on that study, however, it is needful:

I. To take some account of what others have done in the same line; that is to say, of the history of the study.

II. To ascertain just what is its subject-matter.

III. To determine just what are the best methods by which to develop it, and the most clarifying political conceptions to carry with us into it.

Unless we know and settle these things, we shall set out without chart or compass.

I.

The science of administration is the latest fruit of that study of the science of politics which was begun some twenty-two hundred years ago. It is a birth of our own century, almost of our own generation.

Why was it so late in coming? Why did it wait till this too busy century of ours to demand attention for itself? Administration is the most obvious part of government; it is government in action; it is the executive, the operative, the most visible side of government, and is of course as old as government itself. It is government in action, and one might very naturally expect to find that government in action had arrested the attention and provoked the scrutiny of writers of politics very early in the history of systematic thought.

But such was not the case. No one wrote systematically of administration as a branch of the science of government until the present century had passed its first youth and had begun to put forth its characteristic flower of systematic knowledge. Up to our own day all the political writers whom we now read had thought, argued, dogmatized only about the *constitution* of government; about the nature of the state, the essence and seat of sovereignty, popular power and kingly prerogative; about the greatest meanings lying at the heart of government, and the high ends set before the purpose of government by man's nature and man's aims. The central field of controversy was that great field of theory in which monarchy rode tilt against democracy, in which oligarchy would have built for itself strongholds of privilege, and in which tyranny sought opportunity to make good its claim to receive submission from all competitors. Amidst this high warfare of principles, administration could command no pause for its own consideration. The question was always: Who shall make law, and what shall that law be? The other question, how law should be administered with enlightenment, with equity, with speed, and without friction, was put aside as "practical detail" which clerks could arrange after doctors had agreed upon principles.

That political philosophy took this direction was of course no accident, no chance preference or perverse whim of political philosophers. The philosophy of any time is, as Hegel says, "nothing but the spirit of that time expressed in abstract thought"; and political philosophy, like philosophy of every other kind, has only held up the mirror to contemporary affairs. The trouble in early times was almost altogether about the constitution of government; and consequently that was what engrossed men's thoughts. There was little or no trouble about administration,—at least little that was heeded by administrators. The functions of government were simple, because life itself was simple. Government went about imperatively and compelled men, without thought of consulting their wishes. There was no complex system of public revenues and public debts to puzzle financiers; there were, consequently, no financiers to be puzzled. No one who possessed power was long at a loss how to use it. The great and only question was: Who shall possess it? Populations were of manageable numbers; property was of simple sorts. There were plenty of farms, but no stocks and bonds: more cattle than vested interests.

I have said that all this was true of "early times"; but it was substantially true also of comparatively late times. One does not have to look back of the last century for the beginnings of the present complexities of trade and perplexities of commercial speculation, nor for the portentous birth of national debts. Good Queen Bess, doubtless, thought that the monopolies of the sixteenth century were hard enough to handle without burning her hands; but they are not remembered in the presence of the giant monopolies of the nineteenth century. When Blackstone lamented that corporations had no bodies to be kicked and no souls to be damned, he was anticipating the proper time for such regrets by full a century. The perennial discords between master and workmen which now so often disturb industrial society began before the Black Death and the Statute of Laborers; but never before our own day did they assume such ominous proportions as they wear now. In brief, if difficulties of governmental action are to be seen gathering in other centuries, they are to be seen culminating in our own.

This is the reason why administrative tasks have nowadays

to be so studiously and systematically adjusted to carefully tested standards of policy, the reason why we are having now what we never had before, a science of administration. The weightier debates of constitutional principle are even yet by no means concluded; but they are no longer of more immediate practical moment than questions of administration. It is getting to be harder to *run* a constitution than to frame one.

Here is Mr. Bagehot's graphic, whimsical way of depicting the difference between the old and the new in administration:

> In early times, when a despot wishes to govern a distant province, he sends down a satrap on a grand horse, and other people on little horses; and very little is heard of the satrap again unless he send back some of the little people to tell what he has been doing. No great labour of superintendence is possible. Common rumour and casual report are the sources of intelligence. If it seems certain that the province is in a bad state, satrap No. 1 is recalled, and satrap No. 2 sent out in his stead. In civilized countries the process is different. You erect a bureau in the province you want to govern; you make it write letters and copy letters; it sends home eight reports *per diem* to the head bureau in St. Petersburg. Nobody does a sum in the province without some one doing the same sum in the capital, to "check" him, and see that he does it correctly. The consequence of this is, to throw on the heads of departments an amount of reading and labour which can only be accomplished by the greatest natural aptitude, the most efficient training, the most firm and regular industry.[1]

There is scarcely a single duty of government which was once simple which is not now complex; government once had but a few masters; it now has scores of masters. Majorities formerly only underwent government; they now conduct government. Where government once might follow the whims of a court, it must now follow the views of a nation.

And those views are steadily widening to new conceptions of state duty; so that, at the same time that the functions of government are every day becoming more complex and difficult, they are also vastly multiplying in number. Administration is everywhere putting its hands to new undertakings. The utility, cheapness, and success of the government's postal service, for instance, point towards the early establishment of governmental control of the telegraph system. Or, even if our government is not to follow the lead of the governments of Europe in buying or building both telegraph and railroad lines, no one can doubt that

[1] Essay on Sir William Pitt. [All footnotes WW's. They have been numbered.]

in some way it must make itself master of masterful corporations. The creation of national commissioners of railroads, in addition to the older state commissions, involves a very important and delicate extension of administrative functions. Whatever hold of authority state or federal governments are to take upon corporations, there must follow cares and responsibilities which will require not a little wisdom, knowledge, and experience. Such things must be studied in order to be well done. And these, as I have said, are only a few of the doors which are being opened to offices of government. The idea of the state and the consequent ideal of its duty are undergoing noteworthy change; and "the idea of the state is the conscience of administration." Seeing every day new things which the state ought to do, the next thing is to see clearly how it ought to do them.

This is why there should be a science of administration which shall seek to straighten the paths of government, to make its business less unbusinesslike, to strengthen and purify its organization, and to crown its duties with dutifulness. This is one reason why there is such a science.

But where has this science grown up? Surely not on this side the sea. Not much impartial scientific method is to be discerned in our administrative practices. The poisonous atmosphere of city government, the crooked secrets of state administration, the confusion, sinecurism, and corruption ever and again discovered in the bureaux at Washington forbid us to believe that any clear conceptions of what constitutes good administration are as yet very widely current in the United States. No; American writers have hitherto taken no very important part in the advancement of this science. It has found its doctors in Europe. It is not of our making; it is a foreign science, speaking very little of the language of English or American principle. It employs only foreign tongues; it utters none but what are to our minds alien ideas. Its aims, its examples, its conditions, are almost exclusively grounded in the histories of foreign races, in the precedents of foreign systems, in the lessons of foreign revolutions. It has been developed by French and German professors, and is consequently in all parts adapted to the needs of a compact state, and made to fit highly centralized forms of government; whereas, to answer our purposes, it must be adapted, not to a simple and compact, but to a complex and multiform state, and made to fit highly decentralized forms of government. If we would employ it, we must Americanize it, and that not formally, in language merely, but radically, in thought, principle, and aim as well. It must learn our constitutions by heart; must get the bureaucratic fever out of its veins; must inhale much free American air.

If an explanation be sought why a science manifestly so susceptible of being made useful to all governments alike should have received attention first in Europe, where government has long been a monopoly, rather than in England or the United States, where government has long been a common franchise, the reason will doubtless be found to be twofold: first, that in Europe, just because government was independent of popular assent, there was more governing to be done; and, second, that the desire to keep government a monopoly made the monopolists interested in discovering the least irritating means of governing. They were, besides, few enough to adopt means promptly.

It will be instructive to look into this matter a little more closely. In speaking of European governments I do not, of course, include England. She has not refused to change with the times. She has simply tempered the severity of the transition from a polity of aristocratic privilege to a system of democratic power by slow measures of constitutional reform which, without preventing revolution, has confined it to paths of peace. But the countries of the continent for a long time desperately struggled against all change, and would have diverted revolution by softening the asperities of absolute government. They sought so to perfect their machinery as to destroy all wearing friction, so to sweeten their methods with consideration for the interests of the governed as to placate all hindering hatred, and so assiduously and opportunely to offer their aid to all classes of undertakings as to render themselves indispensable to the industrious. They did at last give the people constitutions and the franchise; but even after that they obtained leave to continue despotic by becoming paternal. They made themselves too efficient to be dispensed with, too smoothly operative to be noticed, too enlightened to be inconsiderately questioned, too benevolent to be suspected, too powerful to be coped with. All this has required study; and they have closely studied it.

On this side the sea we, the while, had known no great difficulties of government. With a new country, in which there was room and remunerative employment for everybody, with liberal principles of government and unlimited skill in practical politics, we were long exempted from the need of being anxiously careful about plans and methods of administration. We have naturally been slow to see the use or significance of those many volumes of learned research and painstaking examination into the ways and means of conducting government which the presses of Europe have been sending to our libraries. Like a lusty child, government with us has expanded in nature and grown great in stature, but has also become awkward in movement. The vigor and increase of its life has been altogether out of proportion to its skill in living. It has gained strength, but it has not acquired deportment. Great, therefore, as has been our advantage over the countries of Europe in point of ease and health of constitutional development, now that the time for more careful administrative adjustments and larger administrative knowledge has come to us, we are at a signal disadvantage as compared with the transatlantic nations; and this for reasons which I shall try to make clear.

Judging by the constitutional histories of the chief nations of the modern world, there may be said to be three periods of growth through which government has passed in all the most highly developed of existing systems, and through which it promises to pass in all the rest. The first of these periods is that of absolute rulers, and of an administrative system adapted to absolute rule; the second is that in which constitutions are framed to do away with absolute rulers and substitute popular control, and in which administration is neglected for these higher concerns; and the third is that in which the sovereign people undertake to develop administration under this new constitution which has brought them into power.

Those governments are now in the lead in administrative practice which had rulers still absolute but also enlightened when those modern days of political illumination came in which it was made evident to all but the blind that governors are properly only the servants of the governed. In such governments administration has been organized to subserve the general weal with the simplicity and effectiveness vouchsafed only to the undertakings of a single will.

Such was the case in Prussia, for instance, where administration has been most studied and most nearly perfected. Frederic the Great, stern and masterful as was his rule, still sincerely professed to regard himself as only the chief servant of the state, to consider his great office a public trust; and it was he who, building upon the foundations laid by his father, began to organize the public service of Prussia as in very earnest a service of the public. His no less absolute successor, Frederic William III, under the inspiration of Stein, again, in his turn, advanced the work still further, planning many of the broader structural features which give firmness and form to Prussian administration to-day. Almost the whole of the admirable system has been developed by kingly initiative.

Of similar origin was the practice, if not the plan, of modern French administration, with its symmetrical divisions of territory and its orderly gradations of office. The days of the Revolution—of the Constituent Assembly—were days of constitution-*writing*, but they can hardly be called days of constitution-*making*. The Revolution heralded a period of constitutional development,—the entrance of France upon the second of those periods which I have enumerated,—but it did not itself inaugurate such a period. It interrupted and unsettled absolutism, but did not destroy it. Napoleon succeeded the monarchs of France, to exercise a power as unrestricted as they had ever possessed.

The recasting of French administration by Napoleon is, therefore, my second example of the perfecting of civil machinery by the single will of an absolute ruler before the dawn of a constitutional era. No corporate, popular will could ever have effected arrangements such as those which Napoleon commanded. Arrangements so simple at the expense of local prejudice, so logical in their indifference to popular choice, might be decreed by a Constituent Assembly, but could be established only by the unlimited authority of a despot. The system of the year VIII was ruthlessly thorough and heartlessly perfect. It was, besides, in large part, a return to the despotism that had been overthrown.

Among those nations, on the other hand, which entered upon a season of constitution-making and popular reform before administration had received the impress of liberal principle, administrative improvement has been tardy and half-done. Once a nation has embarked in the business of manufacturing constitutions, it finds it exceedingly difficult to close out that business and open for the public a bureau of skilled, economical administration. There seems to be no end to the tinkering of constitutions. Your ordinary constitution will last you hardly ten years without repairs or additions; and the time for administrative detail comes late.

Here, of course, our examples are England and our own country. In the days of the Angevin kings, before constitutional life had taken root in the Great Charter, legal and administrative reforms began to proceed with sense and vigor under the impulse of Henry II's shrewd, busy, pushing, indomitable spirit and purpose; and kingly initiative seemed destined in England, as elsewhere, to shape governmental growth at its will. But impulsive, errant Richard and weak, despicable John were not the men to carry out such schemes as their father's. Administrative development gave place in their reigns to constitutional struggles; and Parliament became king before any English monarch had had the practical genius or the enlightened conscience to devise just and lasting forms for the civil service of the state.

The English race, consequently, has long and successfully studied the art of curbing executive power to the constant neglect of the art of perfecting executive methods. It has exercised itself much more in controlling than in energizing government. It has been more concerned to render government just and moderate than to make it facile, well-ordered, and effective. English and American political history has been a history, not of administrative development, but of legislative oversight,—not of progress in governmental organization, but of advance in law-making and political criticism. Consequently, we have reached a time when administrative study and creation are imperatively necessary to the well-being of our governments saddled with the habits of a long period of constitution-making. That period has practically closed, so far as the establishment of essential principles is concerned, but we cannot shake off its atmosphere. We go on criticizing when we ought to be creating. We have reached the third of the periods I have mentioned,—the period, namely, when the people have to develop administration in accordance with the constitutions they won for themselves in a previous period of struggle with absolute power; but we are not prepared for the tasks of the new period.

Such an explanation seems to afford the only escape from blank astonishment at the fact that, in spite of our vast advantages in point of political liberty, and above all in point of practical political skill and sagacity, so many nations are ahead of us in administrative organization and administrative skill. Why, for instance, have we but just begun purifying a civil service which was rotten full fifty years ago? To say that slavery diverted us is but to repeat what I have said—that flaws in our constitution delayed us.

Of course all reasonable preference would declare for this English and American course of politics rather than for that of any European country. We should not like to have had Prussia's history for the sake of having Prussia's administrative skill; and Prussia's particular system of administration would quite suffocate us. It is better to be untrained and free than to be servile and systematic. Still there is no denying that it would be better yet to be both free in spirit and proficient in practice. It is this even more reasonable preference which impels us to discover what there may be to hinder or delay us in naturalizing this much-to-be-desired science of administration.

What, then, is there to prevent?

Well, principally, popular sovereignty. It is harder for democracy to organize administration than for monarchy. The very completeness of our most cherished political successes in the past embarrasses us. We have enthroned public opinion; and it is forbidden us to hope during its reign for any quick schooling of the sovereign in executive expertness or in the conditions of perfect functional balance in government. The very fact that we have realized popular rule in its fulness has made the task of *organizing* that rule just so much the more difficult. In order to make any advance at all we must instruct and persuade a multitudinous monarch called public opinion,—a much less feasible undertaking than to influence a single monarch called a king. An individual sovereign will adopt a simple plan and carry it out directly: he will have but one opinion, and he will embody that one opinion in one command. But this other sovereign, the people, will have a score of differing opinions. They can agree upon nothing simple: advance must be made through compromise, by a compounding of differences, by a trimming of plans and a suppression of too straightforward principles. There will be a succession of resolves running through a course of years, a dropping fire of commands running through a whole gamut of modifications.

In government, as in virtue, the hardest of hard things is to make progress. Formerly the reason for this was that the single person who was sovereign was generally either selfish, ignorant, timid, or a fool,—albeit there was now and again one who was wise. Nowadays the reason is that the many, the people, who are sovereign have no single ear which one can approach, and are selfish, ignorant, timid, stubborn, or foolish with the selfishnesses, the ignorances, the stubbornnesses, the timidities, or the follies of several thousand persons,—albeit there are hundreds who are wise. Once the advantage of the reformer was that the sovereign's mind had a definite locality, that it was contained in one man's head, and that consequently it could be gotten at; though it was his disadvantage that that mind learned only reluctantly or only in small quantities, or was under the influence of some one who let it learn only the wrong things. Now, on the contrary, the reformer is bewildered by the fact that the sovereign's mind has no definite locality, but is contained in a voting majority of several million heads; and embarrassed by the fact that the mind of this sovereign also is under the influence of favorites, who are none the less favorites in a good old-fashioned sense of the word because they are not persons but preconceived opinions; *i.e.*, prejudices which are not to be reasoned with because they are not the children of reason.

Wherever regard for public opinion is a first principle of government, practical reform must be slow and all reform must be full of compromises. For wherever public opinion exists it must rule. This is now an axiom half the world over, and will presently come to be believed even in Russia. Whoever would effect a change in a modern constitutional government must first educate his fellow-citizens to want *some* change. That done, he must persuade them to want the particular change he wants. He must first make public opinion willing to listen and then see to it that it listen to the right things. He must stir it up to search for an opinion, and then manage to put the right opinion in its way.

The first step is not less difficult than the second. With opinions, possession is more than nine points of the law. It is next to impossible to dislodge them. Institutions which one generation regards as only a makeshift approximation to the realization of a principle, the next generation honors as the nearest possible approximation to that principle, and the next worships as the principle itself. It takes scarcely three generations for the apotheosis. The grandson accepts his grandfather's hesitating experiment as an integral part of the fixed constitution of nature.

Even if we had clear insight into all the political past, and could form out of perfectly instructed heads a few steady, infallible, placidly wise maxims of government into which all sound political doctrine would be ultimately resolvable, *would the country act on them?* That is the question. The bulk of mankind is rigidly unphilosophical, and nowadays the bulk of mankind votes. A truth must become not only plain but also commonplace before it will be seen by the people who go to their work very early in the morning; and not to act upon it must involve great and pinching inconveniences before these same people will make up their minds to act upon it.

And where is this unphilosophical bulk of mankind more multifarious in its composition than in the United States? To know the public mind of this country, one must know the mind, not of Americans of the older stocks only, but also of Irishmen, of Germans, of negroes. In order to get a footing for new doctrine, one must influence minds cast in every mould of race, minds inheriting every bias of environment, warped by the histories of a score of different nations, warmed or chilled, closed or expanded by almost every climate of the globe.

So much, then, for the history of the study of administration, and the peculiarly difficult conditions under which, entering upon it when we do, we must undertake it. What, now, is the subject-matter of this study, and what are its characteristic objects?

II.

The field of administration is a field of business. It is removed from the hurry and strife of politics; it at most points stands apart even from the debatable ground of constitutional study. It is a part of political life only as the methods of the counting-house are a part of the life of society; only as machinery is part of the manufactured product. But it is, at the same time, raised very far above the dull level of mere technical detail by the fact that through its greater principles it is directly connected with the lasting maxims of political wisdom, the permanent truths of political progress.

The object of administrative study is to rescue executive methods from the confusion and costliness of empirical experiment and set them upon foundations laid deep in stable principle.

It is for this reason that we must regard civil-service reform in its present stages as but a prelude to a fuller administrative reform. We are now rectifying methods of appointment; we must go on to adjust executive functions more fitly and to prescribe better methods of executive organization and action. Civil-service reform is thus but a moral preparation for what is to follow. It is clearing the moral atmosphere of official life by establishing the sanctity of public office as a public trust, and, by making the service unpartisan, it is opening the way for making it businesslike. By sweetening its motives it is rendering it capable of improving its methods of work.

Let me expand a little what I have said of the province of administration. Most important to be observed is the truth already so much and so fortunately insisted upon by our civil-service reformers; namely, that administration lies outside the proper sphere of *politics*. Administrative questions are not political questions. Although politics sets the tasks for administration, it should not be suffered to manipulate its offices.

This is distinction of high authority; eminent German writers insist upon it as of course. Bluntschli,[2] for instance, bids us separate administration alike from politics and from law. Politics, he says, is state activity "in things great and universal," while "administration, on the other hand," is "the activity of the state in individual and small things. Politics is thus the special province of the statesman, administration of the technical official." "Policy does nothing without the aid of administration"; but administration is not therefore politics. But we do not require German authority for this position; this discrimination between administration and politics is now, happily, too obvious to need further discussion.

There is another distinction which must be worked into all our conclusions, which, though but another side of that between administration and politics, is not quite so easy to keep sight of: I mean the distinction between *constitutional* and administrative questions, between those governmental adjustments which are essential to constitutional principle and those which are merely instrumental to the possibly changing purposes of a wisely adapting convenience.

One cannot easily make clear to every one just where administration resides in the various departments of any practicable government without entering upon particulars so numerous as to confuse and distinctions so minute as to distract. No lines of demarcation, setting apart administrative from non-administrative functions, can be run between this and that department of government without being run up hill and down dale, over dizzy heights of distinction and through dense jungles of statutory enactment, hither and thither around "ifs" and "buts," "whens" and "howevers," until they become altogether lost to the common eye not accustomed to this sort of surveying, and consequently not acquainted with the use of the theodolite of logical discernment. A great deal of administration goes about *incognito* to most of the world, being confounded now with political "management," and again with constitutional principle.

Perhaps this ease of confusion may explain such utterances as that of Niebuhr's: "Liberty," he says, "depends incomparably more upon administration than upon constitution." At first sight this appears to be largely true. Apparently facility in the actual exercise of liberty does depend more upon administrative

[2] Politik, S. 467.

arrangements than upon constitutional guarantees; although constitutional guarantees alone secure the existence of liberty. But—upon second thought—is even so much as this true? Liberty no more consists in easy functional movement than intelligence consists in the ease and vigor with which the limbs of a strong man move. The principles that rule within the man, or the constitution, are the vital springs of liberty or servitude. Because independence and subjection are without chains, are lightened by every easy-working device of considerate, paternal government, they are not thereby transformed into liberty. Liberty cannot live apart from constitutional principle; and no administration, however perfect and liberal its methods, can give men more than a poor counterfeit of liberty if it rest upon illiberal principles of government.

A clear view of the difference between the province of constitutional law and the province of administrative function ought to leave no room for misconception; and it is possible to name some roughly definite criteria upon which such a view can be built. Public administration is detailed and systematic execution of public law. Every particular application of general law is an act of administration. The assessment and raising of taxes, for instance, the hanging of a criminal, the transportation and delivery of the mails, the equipment and recruiting of the army and navy, *etc.*, are all obviously acts of administration; but the general laws which direct these things to be done are as obviously outside of and above administration. The broad plans of governmental action are not administrative; the detailed execution of such plans is administrative. Constitutions, therefore, properly concern themselves only with those instrumentalities of government which are to control general law. Our federal constitution observes this principle in saying nothing of even the greatest of the purely executive offices, and speaking only of that President of the Union who was to share the legislative and policy-making functions of government, only of those judges of highest jurisdiction who were to interpret and guard its principles, and not of those who were merely to give utterance to them.

This is not quite the distinction between Will and answering Deed, because the administrator should have and does have a will of his own in the choice of means for accomplishing his work. He is not and ought not to be a mere passive instrument. The distinction is between general plans and special means.

There is, indeed, one point at which administrative studies trench on constitutional ground—or at least upon what seems constitutional ground. The study of administration, philosophically viewed, is closely connected with the study of the proper distribution of constitutional authority. To be efficient it must discover the simplest arrangements by which responsibility can be unmistakably fixed upon officials; the best way of dividing authority without hampering it, and responsibility without obscuring it. And this question of the distribution of authority, when taken into the sphere of the higher, the originating functions of government, is obviously a central constitutional question. If administrative study can discover the best principles upon which to base such distribution, it will have done constitutional study an invaluable service. Montesquieu did not, I am convinced, say the last word on this head.

To discover the best principle for the distribution of authority is of greater importance, possibly, under a democratic system, where officials serve many masters, than under others where they serve but a few. All sovereigns are suspicious of their servants, and the sovereign people is no exception to the rule; but how is its suspicion to be allayed by *knowledge*? If that suspicion could but be clarified into wise vigilance, it would be altogether salutary; if that vigilance could be aided by the unmistakable placing of responsibility, it would be altogether beneficent. Suspicion in itself is never healthful either in the private or in the public mind. *Trust is strength* in all relations of life; and, as it is the office of the constitutional reformer to create conditions of trustfulness, so it is the office of the administrative organizer to fit administration with conditions of clear-cut responsibility which shall insure trustworthiness.

And let me say that large powers and unhampered discretion seem to me the indispensable conditions of responsibility. Public attention must be easily directed, in each case of good or bad administration, to just the man deserving of praise or blame. There is no danger in power, if only it be not irresponsible. If it be divided, dealt out in shares to many, it is obscured; and if it be obscured, it is made irresponsible. But if it be centred in heads of the service and in heads of branches of the service, it is easily watched and brought to book. If to keep his office a man must achieve open and honest success, and if at the same time he feels himself intrusted with large freedom of discretion, the greater his power the less likely is he to abuse it, the more is he nerved and sobered and elevated by it. The less his power, the more safely obscure and unnoticed does he feel his position to be, and the more readily does he relapse into remissness.

Just here we manifestly emerge upon the field of that still larger question,—the proper relations between public opinion and administration.

To whom is official trustworthiness to be disclosed, and by whom is it to be rewarded? Is the official to look to the public for his meed of praise and his push of promotion, or only to his superior in office? Are the people to be called in to settle administrative discipline as they are called in to settle constitutional principles? These questions evidently find their root in what is undoubtedly the fundamental problem of this whole study. That problem is: What part shall public opinion take in the conduct of administration?

The right answer seems to be, that public opinion shall play the part of authoritative critic.

But the *method* by which its authority shall be made to tell? Our peculiar American difficulty in organizing administration is not the danger of losing liberty, but the danger of not being able or willing to separate its essentials from its accidents. Our success is made doubtful by that besetting error of ours, the error of trying to do too much by vote. Self-government does not consist in having a hand in everything, any more than housekeeping consists necessarily in cooking dinner with one's own hands. The cook must be trusted with a large discretion as to the management of the fires and the ovens.

In those countries in which public opinion has yet to be instructed in its privileges, yet to be accustomed to having its own way, this question as to the province of public opinion is much more readily soluble than in this country, where public opinion is wide awake and quite intent upon having its own way anyhow. It is pathetic to see a whole book written by a German professor of political science for the purpose of saying to his countrymen, "Please try to have an opinion about national affairs"; but a public which is so modest may at least be expected to be very docile and acquiescent in learning what things it has *not* a right to think and speak about imperatively. It may be sluggish, but it will not be meddlesome. It will submit to be instructed before it tries to instruct. Its political education will come before its political activity. In trying to instruct our own public opinion, we are dealing with a pupil apt to think itself quite sufficiently instructed beforehand.

The problem is to make public opinion efficient without suffering it to be meddlesome. Directly exercised, in the oversight of the daily details and in the choice of the daily means of government, public criticism is of course a clumsy nuisance, a rustic handling delicate machinery. But as superintending the greater forces of formative policy alike in politics and administration, public criticism is altogether safe and beneficent, altogether indispensable. Let administrative study find the best means for giving public criticism this control and for shutting it out from all other interference.

But is the whole duty of administrative study done when it has taught the people what sort of administration to desire and demand, and how to get what they demand? Ought it not to go on to drill candidates for the public service?

There is an admirable movement towards universal political education now afoot in this country. The time will soon come when no college of respectability can afford to do without a well-filled chair of political science. But the education thus imparted will go but a certain length. It will multiply the number of intelligent critics of government, but it will create no competent body of administrators. It will prepare the way for the development of a sure-footed understanding of the general principles of government, but it will not necessarily foster skill in conducting government. It is an education which will equip legislators, perhaps, but not executive officials. If we are to improve public opinion, which is the motive power of government, we must prepare better officials as the *apparatus* of government. If we are to put in new boilers and to mend the fires which drive our governmental machinery, we must not leave the old wheels and joints and valves and bands to creak and buzz and clatter on as best they may at bidding of the new force. We must put in new running parts wherever there is the least lack of strength or adjustment. It will be necessary to organize democracy by sending up to the competitive examinations for the civil service men definitely prepared for standing liberal tests as to technical knowledge. A technically schooled civil service will presently have become indispensable.

I know that a corps of civil servants prepared by a special schooling and drilled, after appointment, into a perfected organization, with appropriate hierarchy and characteristic discipline, seems to a great many very thoughtful persons to contain elements which might combine to make an offensive official class,—a distinct, semi-corporate body with sympathies divorced from those of a progressive, free-spirited people, and with hearts narrowed to the meanness of a bigoted officialism. Certainly such a class would be altogether hateful and harmful in the United

States. Any measures calculated to produce it would for us be measures of reaction and of folly.

But to fear the creation of a domineering, illiberal officialism as a result of the studies I am here proposing is to miss altogether the principle upon which I wish most to insist. That principle is, that administration in the United States must be at all points sensitive to public opinion. A body of thoroughly trained officials serving during good behavior we must have in any case: that is a plain business necessity. But the apprehension that such a body will be anything un-American clears away the moment it is asked, What is to constitute good behavior? For that question obviously carries its own answer on its face. Steady, hearty allegiance to the policy of the government they serve will constitute good behavior. That *policy* will have no taint of officialism about it. It will not be the creation of permanent officials, but of statesmen whose responsibility to public opinion will be direct and inevitable. Bureaucracy can exist only where the whole service of the state is removed from the common political life of the people, its chiefs as well as its rank and file. Its motives, its objects, its policy, its standards, must be bureaucratic. It would be difficult to point out any examples of impudent exclusiveness and arbitrariness on the part of officials doing service under a chief of department who really served the people, as all our chiefs of departments must be made to do. It would be easy, on the other hand, to adduce other instances like that of the influence of Stein in Prussia, where the leadership of one statesman imbued with true public spirit transformed arrogant and perfunctory bureaux into public-spirited instruments of just government.

The ideal for us is a civil service cultured and self-sufficient enough to act with sense and vigor, and yet so intimately connected with the popular thought, by means of elections and constant public counsel, as to find arbitrariness of class spirit quite out of the question.

III.

Having thus viewed in some sort the subject-matter and the objects of this study of administration, what are we to conclude as to the methods best suited to it—the points of view most advantageous for it?

Government is so near us, so much a thing of our daily familiar handling, that we can with difficulty see the need of any philosophical study of it, or the exact point of such study, should it be undertaken. We have been on our feet too long to study now the art of walking. We are a practical people, made so apt, so adept in self-government by centuries of experimental drill that we are scarcely any longer capable of perceiving the awkwardness of the particular system we may be using, just because it is so easy for us to use any system. We do not study the art of governing: we govern. But mere unschooled genius for affairs will not save us from sad blunders in administration. Though democrats by long inheritance and repeated choice, we are still rather crude democrats. Old as democracy is, its organization on a basis of modern ideas and conditions is still an unaccomplished work. The democratic state has yet to be equipped for carrying those enormous burdens of administration which the needs of this industrial and trading age are so fast accumulating. Without comparative studies in government we cannot rid ourselves of the misconception that administration stands upon an essentially different basis in a democratic state from that on which it stands in a non-democratic state.

After such study we could grant democracy the sufficient honor of ultimately determining by debate all essential questions affecting the public weal, of basing all structures of policy upon the major will; but we would have found but one rule of good administration for all governments alike. So far as administrative functions are concerned, all governments have a strong structural likeness; more than that, if they are to be uniformly useful and efficient, they *must* have a strong structural likeness. A free man has the same bodily organs, the same executive parts, as the slave, however different may be his motives, his services, his energies. Monarchies and democracies, radically different as they are in other respects, have in reality much the same business to look to.

It is abundantly safe nowadays to insist upon this actual likeness of all governments, because these are days when abuses of power are easily exposed and arrested, in countries like our own, by a bold, alert, inquisitive, detective public thought and a sturdy popular self-dependence such as never existed before. We are slow to appreciate this; but it is easy to appreciate it. Try to imagine personal government in the United States. It is like trying to imagine a national worship of Zeus. Our imaginations are too modern for the feat.

But, besides being safe, it is necessary to see that for all governments alike the legitimate ends of administration are the same, in order not to be frightened at the idea of looking into foreign systems of administration for instruction and suggestion; in order to get rid of the apprehension that we might perchance blindly borrow something incompatible with our principles. That man is blindly astray who denounces attempts to transplant foreign systems into this country. It is impossible: they simply would not grow here. But why should we not use such parts of foreign contrivances as we want, if they be in any way service-able? We are in no danger of using them in a foreign way. We borrowed rice, but we do not eat it with chopsticks. We borrowed our whole political language from England, but we leave the words "king" and "lords" out of it. What did we ever originate, except the action of the federal government upon individuals and some of the functions of the federal supreme court?

We can borrow the science of administration with safety and profit if only we read all fundamental differences of condition into its essential tenets. We have only to filter it through our constitutions, only to put it over a slow fire of criticism and distil away its foreign gases.

I know that there is a sneaking fear in some conscientiously patriotic minds that studies of European systems might signalize some foreign methods as better than some American methods; and the fear is easily to be understood. But it would scarcely be avowed in just any company.

It is the more necessary to insist upon thus putting away all prejudices against looking anywhere in the world but at home for suggestions in this study, because nowhere else in the whole field of politics, it would seem, can we make use of the historical, comparative method more safely than in this province of admin-istration. Perhaps the more novel the forms we study the better. We shall the sooner learn the peculiarities of our own methods. We can never learn either our own weaknesses or our own virtues by comparing ourselves with ourselves. We are too used to the appearance and procedure of our own system to see its true significance. Perhaps even the English system is too much like our own to be used to the most profit in illustration. It is best on the whole to get entirely away from our own atmosphere and to be most careful in examining such systems as those of France and Germany. Seeing our own institutions through such *media*, we see ourselves as foreigners might see us were they to look at us without preconceptions. Of ourselves, so long as we know only ourselves, we know nothing.

Let it be noted that it is the distinction, already drawn,

between administration and politics which makes the comparative method so safe in the field of administration. When we study the administrative systems of France and Germany, knowing that we are not in search of *political* principles, we need not care a peppercorn for the constitutional or political reasons which Frenchmen or Germans give for their practices when explaining them to us. If I see a murderous fellow sharpening a knife cleverly, I can borrow his way of sharpening the knife without borrowing his probable intention to commit murder with it; and so, if I see a monarchist dyed in the wool managing a public bureau well, I can learn his business methods without changing one of my republican spots. He may serve his king; I will continue to serve the people; but I should like to serve my sovereign as well as he serves his. By keeping this distinction in view,—that is, by studying administration as a means of putting our own politics into convenient practice, as a means of making what is democratically politic towards all administratively possible towards each,—we are on perfectly safe ground, and can learn without error what foreign systems have to teach us. We thus devise an adjusting weight for our comparative method of study. We can thus scrutinize the anatomy of foreign governments without fear of getting any of their diseases into our veins; dissect alien systems without apprehension of blood-poisoning.

Our own politics must be the touchstone for all theories. The principles on which to base a science of administration for America must be principles which have democratic policy very much at heart. And, to suit American habit, all general theories must, as theories, keep modestly in the background, not in open argument only, but even in our own minds,—lest opinions satisfactory only to the standards of the library should be dogmatically used, as if they must be quite as satisfactory to the standards of practical politics as well. Doctrinaire devices must be postponed to tested practices. Arrangements not only sanctioned by conclusive experience elsewhere but also congenial to American habit must be preferred without hesitation to theoretical perfection. In a word, steady, practical statesmanship must come first, closet doctrine second. The cosmopolitan what-to-do must always be commanded by the American how-to-do-it.

Our duty is, to supply the best possible life to a *federal* organization, to systems within systems; to make town, city, county, state, and federal governments live with a like strength and an equally assured healthfulness, keeping each unquestionably its own master and yet making all interdependent and co-operative, combining independence with mutual helpfulness. The task is great and important enough to attract the best minds.

This interlacing of local self-government with federal self-government is quite a modern conception. It is not like the arrangements of imperial federation in Germany. There local government is not yet, fully, local *self*-government. The bureaucrat is everywhere busy. His efficiency springs out of *esprit de corps*, out of care to make ingratiating obeisance to the authority of a superior, or, at best, out of the soil of a sensitive conscience. He serves, not the public, but an irresponsible minister. The question for us is, how shall our series of governments within governments be so administered that it shall always be to the interest of the public officer to serve, not his superior alone but the community also, with the best efforts of his talents and the soberest service of his conscience? How shall such service be made to his commonest interest by contributing abundantly to his sustenance, to his dearest interest by furthering his ambition, and to his highest interest by advancing his honor and establishing his character? And how shall this be done alike for the local part and for the national whole?

If we solve this problem we shall again pilot the world. There is a tendency—is there not?—a tendency as yet dim, but already steadily impulsive and clearly destined to prevail, towards, first the confederation of parts of empires like the British, and finally of great states themselves. Instead of centralization of power, there is to be wide union with tolerated divisions of prerogative. This is a tendency towards the American type—of governments joined with governments for the pursuit of common purposes, in honorary equality and honorable subordination. Like principles of civil liberty are everywhere fostering like methods of government; and if comparative studies of the ways and means of government should enable us to offer suggestions which will practicably combine openness and vigor in the administration of such governments with ready docility to all serious, well-sustained public criticism, they will have approved themselves worthy to be ranked among the highest and most fruitful of the great departments of political study. That they will issue in such suggestions I confidently hope.

WOODROW WILSON.

Printed in the *Political Science Quarterly*, II (July 1887), 197-222.

From Herbert Baxter Adams

My dear Dr. Wilson: Baltimore, Nov. 3, 1886

I am preparing an educational report on the study of history in the United States and I wish to introduce a chapter upon "History in Colleges for Women."

Will you kindly prepare for me a descriptive statement of your courses of instruction, requirements for entrance and graduation, text-books, library advantages, seminary work, topics investigated, &c. &c?[1]

Is there any plate or photograph showing the interior of the Bryn Mawr library or your *historical "environment"*? I am going to make a strong point of this in my illustrations. If Bryn Mawr has such a plate, will you ask Miss Thomas to lend it to the Bureau of Education through me for use at the Government printing-office in January? 25,000 copies of my report (250 pages) are to be struck off and it will be quite worth the while of Bryn Mawr to be properly represented. If you will examine the report by my friend Dr. Hartwell on Physical Training in American Colleges, you will see what kind of pictorial effects I am seeking.[2] But I want *interiors*, not exteriors.

Very truly yours, H. B. Adams

TLS (WP, DLC).
[1] Wilson's description is printed at Nov. 27, 1886.
[2] United States Bureau of Education, Circular of Information Number 5, 1885, *Physical Training in American Colleges and Universities,* by Edward M. Hartwell (Washington, 1886).

From Richard Heath Dabney

My dear Tom: Bloomington, Ind., Nov. 6th 1886.

I am too much pressed for time to do anything more than to thank you for your article in the Boston *Times* on the decay of the old parties & the necessity of new ones in the near future, and to tell you in a very few words how I am getting along out here.

I need hardly say that I enjoyed the article, and that I agree with you entirely—or almost entirely. I am anxious to see the war issues dropped entirely and the old parties dissolved, but the Republicans must lay down their arms first. They must cease to wave the bloody shirt & to damn the South before I will vote for a Republican for President. So long as they continue to call the Southern people "traitors" & the like, so long do I wish to see the

South "solid," no matter what becomes of civil service reform, the labor question, the tariff question, the silver question, or what not. . . .

I suppose you are now at work again at Bryn Mawr with your time well occupied. I am settled down here in Bloomington, which I like as well as I expected, but which is by no means the garden spot of the world. In fact the Hoosiers, if I dare say so, are *not* the salt of the earth. Hoosierdom is preëminently the land of the free & the home of the brave, where all men are born free & equal—especially equal in their scorn for all soap except for that variety which is synonymous with "boodle." As the noble Hoosier has an inalienable right to sell his vote, this species of "soap" is plentifully used—about $5000 being used (so I hear) in this county on the late election-day. Both parties employed the "soap" with equal ardor—the "coon" vote being mainly purchased by the Dimmycrats.

Some of the members of the faculty here are nice men, but if there is a gentleman (in the Virginian sense) in the "city" of Bloomington outside of the faculty, I have thus far failed to discover him among the 3400 inhabitants.

I am interested in my work, but it is tremendously hard, & I have no time as yet for anything except the preparation of my class-work.   Ever your friend   R. H. Dabney.

ALS (WP, DLC).

From Daniel Greenleaf Thompson

The Nineteenth Century Club.
My dear Sir: New York Nov. 7. 1886
Hon. Justin McCarthy is to lecture before this Club,[1] Saturday evening Dec. 18th 1886 upon "The English Parliament." It will give the lecture committee great pleasure to be able to announce that you will discuss this lecture. It is usual to have at least two to participate in the discussion, but upon this occasion, it seems to us that if you will consent to take part it would be more interesting to give you the entire field. With a comparison between the English Parliament and the American Congress we should be sure of a very instructive discussion. If your engagements will allow of your acceptance of this invitation, I shall be glad if you will let me know by an early mail.[2]

Very truly yours,
Daniel G. Thompson   (Actg. Pres.)

ALS (WP, DLC) with WWhw notation on env.: "Ans. Nov. 9/86."
¹ The Nineteenth Century Club was founded in 1883 by Courtlandt Palmer of New York, a freethinker and heir to a large fortune. The object of the club, as a contemporary put it, was "to discuss topics relating to politics, industry, science, art, philosophy and religion, in the hope and belief that by interchange and comparison of conflicting opinions, a basis of agreement on important questions may sometime be evolved." Both men and women were eligible for membership. The Nineteenth Century Club held two annual business meetings and not less than six general meetings during the winter season. As the same contemporary explained, "The method followed at the meetings of the Club is to have a paper or a disquisition by some well-known man, and the subject is then discussed, for and against, by two representative speakers." *Club Men of New York, 1898-99* (New York, 1898), pp. 38-39. Palmer died in 1888, but the club survived at least until 1902. See *Courtlandt Palmer: Tributes Offered by Members of the Nineteenth Century Club to Its Founder & First President* (New York, 1889).
² For an account of Wilson's participation, see JRW to WW, Jan. 12, 1887, n. 1.

To Richard Heath Dabney

My dear Heath,   Bryn Mawr, Pa., 7 Nov., 1886.

Various things have conspired to prevent my writing since your heartily welcome letter of the early part of the summer¹ reached me in Tenn., not the least of which has been *lack of heart*. The account you gave of the treatment you—and others— had received at the hands of the Bloomington people filled me with an astonishment and a chagrin which until now I have been unable to express, but which till now I have not been able to write *without* expressing. I felt that *I* had gotten you into unpleasant quarters; and I did not have the heart to write to you till you sh. have been in Bloomington long enough to find out at least how tolerable the berth would be. In his correspondence with me [President David Starr] Jordan was so thoroughly pleasant and apparently so entirely straightforward, that I did not once dream of what you found revealed in him in your dealings with him. I was thoroughly disgusted and indignant when I read your letter—and the disgust and indignation continue till the present moment unabated. I sincerely hope, my dear fellow, that the reality is not so bad as the prospect threatened when you wrote—though what I heard the other day at Cornell doesn't aid my hope at all. I went up there last week to read a paper before the University Historical and Political Science Association; and, after the meeting, I was taken off by a φψ to meet some of the fraternity boys at a house they have just put up for themselves near the Univ. grounds. One of the men I met, (yclept Robinson,² I believe) was at Indiana Univ. last year, I found, and I asked him some questions about the state of affairs, previous to this year, in the history department—inasmuch as I have a friend now connected with that department in whom I am considerably interested. He said, amongst many things that were irrelevant to my purpose, this, which was extremely relevant, that your predecessor, Newkirk[3] (?) had been turned out 'because he too often spoke before he thought' and, thus speaking, had let drop 'Calhoun views' on the Constitution. In a word, you have gotten into a chair whose incumbent is expected to present, not the scientific truth with reference to our Constitutional history, whether that truth be on the side of Webster or of Calhoun in the great historical argument, but *'Yankee sentiments'*—sentiments agreeable to that eminent body of scholars, the Grand Army of the Republic. It's a shame; but I hope that the reality isn't half as bad as these bits of rumour. The shabbiness of the transactions connected with Newkirk's dismissal and your appointment can't be explained away; but the place may not be as uncomfortable as such preliminaries would indicate. It was such a genuine delight to me to be able to advance your candidacy that it would be *too* bad to find now that your success was not a *satisfaction* to you after all. Write me all about it, 'thou very ass,' at once, if you would comfort me.

That Wilmington editor treated me most cavalierly.[4] He did not answer my letter accompanying the notice I had written of 'Don Miff'; I have not been able to obtain a copy of the paper containing said notice (supposing it was published); the returns upon the venture, in a word, have been *nil*. The fellow's a boor! I knew that he was before; but I spoke him so fair in my letter that I hoped he would play gentleman for once. Not he! But, I'm glad to know that, however futile *my* efforts in its behalf may have been, 'Don Miff' has been, marketably as well as by merit, a decided success—three editions within about as many months: and I suppose more since? Hurrah, the taste of the 'reading public' isn't quite corrupted after all. *Some* members of it know a good thing when they see it yet.

I worked hard most of the summer—*all* of it after the receipt of your letter: first with a sick baby, and afterwards with a big subject—the treatise on Government which I am preparing for D. C. Heath & Co.[5] I told you of the undertaking, didn't I?—the origin and early history of govt viewed historically, of course, and *not a la* Rousseau, Locke, *et al*; the govts of Greece and Rome and of the Middle Ages, treated in the same spirit; comparative studies in the public law of the present, our own and the Eng. constitutions standing centrally and most prominent, of course; and, in the light of such studies, considerations on the functions and ends of govt. and on law (customary, statutory, &c.). A big task—especially in view of the condensation *and* clearness necessary to a book intended to be small enough and plain enough to be used as a college text-book; but a task full of delight and profit for me, and thoroughly well worth doing, because our language, so far as I know, affords no such work.

Speaking of this work,—which is just now imperatively interrupted by class duties, and must probably wait to be done in vacations,—leads me to ask your counsel on what is to me a matter of the very greatest moment. I'll set it forth as plainly and briefly as I can. In my special work in comparative Politics—indeed in *all* my work—as I need hardly tell you, I have to use *German* a great deal: I ought to use it a great deal more than I do. But, such are my engagements, and such is my position in other respects, I cannot find, either in term time or out of it, time or opportunity to learn the language well enough to be emancipated from the constant use of the dictionary in reading it. That's one side of my statement; now for the other. These studies in public law and the history of govt. for which Heath & Co. are waiting ought to be finished,—such is *my* interest as well as the publishers'—before the time at which vacations now promise to finish them. Besides, I have another scheme on hand, for what Mr. Scudder of Cambridge (Mass.) calls a *Novum Organon* on Politics[6] (I will lay the plan before you later if you are interested) for the preparation of which, not only a ready knowledge of German, but considerable leisure to know, better than I can possibly know it from any outlook available in Bryn Mawr, *the modern world*. That is the other side of my statement. Put together, the two pieces make this whole: I am just now pressingly in need of two things, German and a little leisure for wide observation of men and things. This is the best time to learn German because my acquiring faculties are still young; and this is the most desirable time at which to have leisure because my susceptibility to impressions from men and things is as yet unblunted.

Such being the case, my dear fellow, I want from you both counsel and information. Would you advise me to cut loose from employment and go abroad for one or two years? And could you estimate for me the cost of living in Berlin for a man, wife, and child who would not care a peppercorn for style, but who would require for a while, perhaps, a nurse, and always *comfort*? My plan would be to spend most of my time in Berlin, because that is the centre of German affairs, but not all of it; and not to connect myself regularly with any Univ., but to be a sort of detached student, writing, observing, digging at German, but attending regular courses only sometimes and perhaps. If prices be such as I hope they are, we might afford to stay in Europe for a couple of years. Meantime, I have gotten a start in German; and by next June can have gotten a better one.

What do you say, Heath? Would you advise it? I want to know your opinion, and your *whole* opinion. The leisure and the German would be invaluable to me: can I risk getting employment again when I return? Is the benefit to be expected greater or less than the risk which is inevitable? If you will answer me candidly as to your thought on these heads you will have revealed your dear, genuine old self once more to

Your sincere friend,   Woodrow Wilson

P.S. Mrs. Wilson sends warm regards.   W.W.
What is [Charles W.] Kent's address?

ALS (Wilson-Dabney Correspondence, ViU).
    [1] R. H. Dabney to WW, June 19, 1886.
    [2] William Houts Robinson, Jr., at this time a member of the junior class at Cornell.
    [3] John Gray Newkirk, Professor of History and Political Science at Indiana University, c. 1880-86.
    [4] The "Wilmington editor" was Theodore B. Kingsbury, editor of the Wilmington, N. C., *Morning Star,* to whom Wilson had submitted a review of the book, *Don Miff,* by Richard Heath Dabney's father, Virginius. See R. H. Dabney to WW, June 19, 1886, n. 2.
    [5] Wilson was referring to *The State.* See the Editorial Note, "Wilson's Plan for a Textbook in Civil Government."
    [6] Scudder had used the term "organon" in his letter to Wilson of June 6, 1886. Perhaps Wilson added the "novum."

From Edwin Robert Anderson Seligman

My dear Sir,   New York, Nov 9 1886
    Our attention has been called to an address of yours before the Cornell Polit. Science Association on the study of administration. If you think it at all suitable for the Political Science Quarterly, we should very much like to have you send it on for publication in the March or June number of the Quarterly.

The Quarterly has had a success—both financial & in point of subscribers here & abroad—far exceeding our anticipations,— & I have no doubt but that an article by you would attract attention.

Yrs very sincerely   Edwin R A Seligman

ALS (WP, DLC) with WWhw notation on env.: "Ans Nov. 11/86."

From Daniel Greenleaf Thompson

My dear Sir: New York. Nov. 10, 1886.

Your favor of yesterday is at hand. I am very glad to hear from you that you will be able to discuss Mr. McCarthy's lecture. Since writing you, Mr. Simon Sterne,[1] whom I expected to discuss Hon. Edward Atkinson's lecture has asked me to be allowed to speak on Mr. McCarthy's evening. Mr. Sterne is the author of a work on "Representative Government" and is a man we would be glad to hear upon the "English Parliament." I told him what I had written you and he said he did not think you would object to dividing the time with him. I should be glad to oblige Mr. Sterne and unless Mr. McCarthy talks too long, there will be no difficulty about it. I should be glad to know if this will be agreeable to you. I have written McCarthy to ascertain the length of his lecture. He is rather of a hard man to reach just now, inasmuch as he is upon a lecturing tour and you may have to exercise a little patience in regard to the abstract. I will do the best I can, however.

It is *usual* for the debaters to speak without MSS, using notes, however if they wish. Still there is no law about it. We have had remarks from a number of ladies and they all, I believe, read what they had to say. But of course the theory of a discussion of some other speaker's paper rather precludes the supposition of a formal preparation beforehand. . . .

Very truly yours, Daniel G. Thompson

ALS (WP, DLC) with WWhw notation on env.: "Ans. Nov. 11/86."
[1] A New York lawyer who had earlier corresponded with Wilson about *Congressional Government* and his own book, *Representative Government*. See WW to ELA, March 8, 1885, n. 1, Vol. 4.

To Edwin Robert Anderson Seligman

My dear Sir: Bryn Mawr, Pa., 11 Nov., 1886.

I am very much obliged indeed for your kind suggestion concerning my paper on the study of administration. I did not prepare it with any thought of publication, but only as a semi-popular introduction to administrative studies, treating of the history of the Science of Administration, of the conditions of the study, and of the needs for it in this country: the methods proper to it &c. In other words, it goes critically round about the study, considering it from various outside points of view, rather than entering it and handling its proper topics.

I have, however, no objection to publishing it, if it will at all suit your *Quarterly*: and I wish to leave that question *entirely* to you. I send the paper; but I wish to be taken *literally*—as meaning what I say in just the way I say it—when I suggest that, if you return it, so far from hurting my feelings in the least, you will only be confirming me in the thought that it is too *slight*—will only be paying me the compliment of agreeing with me.

Trusting to your kindness to consider *my* interests in this matter by considering the interests of the *Quarterly*,

Very sincerely Yours,   Woodrow Wilson

ALS (Seligman Papers, NNC).

From Daniel Greenleaf Thompson

My dear Sir: New York Nov. 12 1886

Your favor of yesterday is at hand. We could not think of letting you off, in favor of anybody. Mr. McCarthy has written me, approving of the plan of discussion and saying that he will conform his time to it. I think, therefore, we will say one hour for him, half an hour for you and about the same or a little less for Mr. Sterne. That will be about as usual. I thought probably Mr. McCarthy would want an hour and a half, in which event one debater would be enough. We always have two where the lecture is only an hour.

Very truly yours,   Daniel G. Thompson

ALS (WP, DLC).

To Charles Andrew Talcott

My dear Charlie,   Bryn Mawr, Pa., 14 Nov., 1886.

It takes special strength of fortitude to write to an old and dear friend after having left his last letter unanswered for fifteen months:[1] after all, it's only the fact that the neglected person *is* an old and tried friend that gives one the nerve to do such a thing. One can entertain at least a small hope of forgiveness. And I'm going to put on a bold front, and tell you, to begin with, that my *heart* hasn't felt guilty as towards you during the interval; for it has known how warm it was keeping its old-time love for the great 'Jones'; and, if I could bring my witnesses into court, I could prove myself guiltless in every other aspect of the case,—save in the one particular of demonstration of friendship by letter. I never had time and mind so thoroughly engrossed as

James E. Rhoads, first president of Bryn Mawr College

Merion Hall and Taylor Hall, Bryn Mawr College, when Wilson taught there

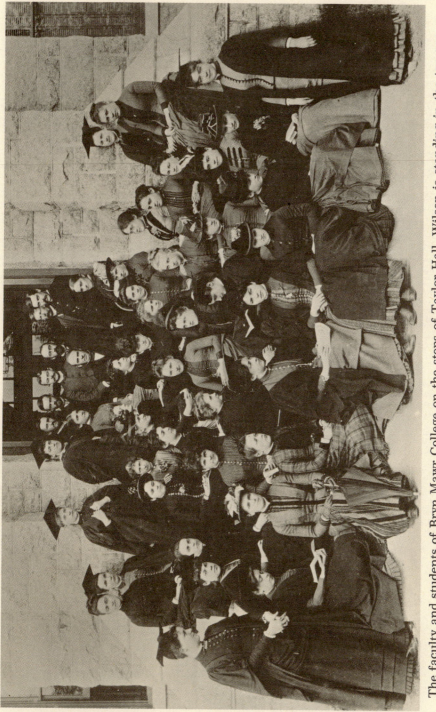

The faculty and students of Bryn Mawr College on the steps of Taylor Hall. Wilson is standing in the top row at the extreme right. President Rhoads is seated in the center of the doorway, with Dean Martha Carey Thomas on the left

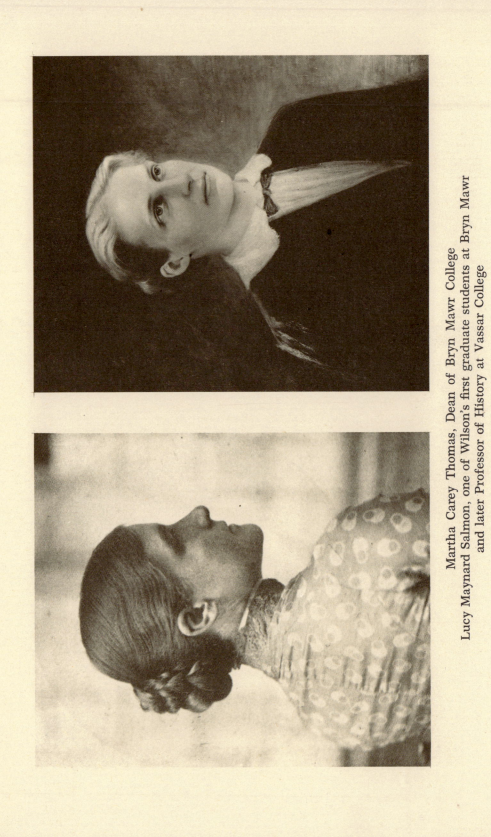

Martha Carey Thomas, Dean of Bryn Mawr College

Lucy Maynard Salmon, one of Wilson's first graduate students at Bryn Mawr and later Professor of History at Vassar College

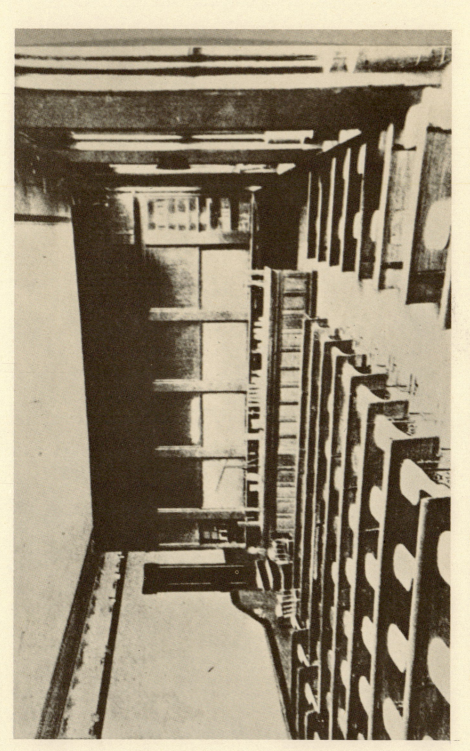

The room in Hopkins Hall, The Johns Hopkins University, where Wilson delivered his lectures

Woodrow Wilson during the Bryn-Mawr period

Joseph Ruggles Wilson about 1888

The statue of President James McCosh by Augustus Saint-Gaudens
presented to the College of New Jersey by the Class of '79

during the past year. After my winter had been hurried away in the unaccustomed, and therefore arduous, duties of the classroom, my summer vacation was swallowed up by work on a text-book on *Government* which I have been rash enough to undertake for D. C. Heath & Co. of Boston. But Mrs. Wilson could tell you how, meanwhile, my thoughts have constantly reverted to our old compact, of life-long coöperation, made at college, and to my old faith, embodied in that contract, that we could keep our friendship fresh, not a mere thing of memory and of boyish association, but a thing of ever renewed vigour and steady growth, by substituting a common cause, a common purpose of public service, for the actual social companionship which we cannot have.[2] And, now that I have at last a little leisure for writing to you, I am going back to make some more observations and confessions to you on that old text. If you are tired of the text, I trust to your honesty to say so. Your saying so will not check any of the old love; it will only make me feel a whit lonelier in the lines of work I have chosen. For in the thinking and writing I am trying to do, I constantly feel the disadvantages of the *closet*. I want to keep close to the *practical* and the *practicable* in politics; my ambition is to add something to the *statesmanship* of the country, if that something be only thought, and not the old achievement of which I used to dream when I hoped that I might enter practical politics. I seek therefore, in the acquaintances I make, not other 'professors,' not other *book*-politicians, but men who have direct touch of the world; in order that I may study *affairs*, rather than doctrine. But the 'practical men' I meet have not broad horizons; *they* are *not* students of affairs; they learn what they know rather by friction than by rational observation; they are at the opposite extreme from the men of books, who are all horizon—and the one extreme is as fatal to balanced thought as the other. Now you, Charlie, are both *in* affairs and studuous of them; if ever I met a fellow with whose ways of thinking I could sympathize, and from whom, consequently, I could receive aid and comfort, thou art the man,— *and I need you.* If you need me in any degree, the old compact between us is, therefore, *ipso facto* renewed.

I believe, Charlie, that if a band of young fellows (say ten or twelve) could get together (and by 'getting together' I mean getting their *opinions* together, whether by circular correspondence or other means) upon a common platform, and, having gotten together on good solid planks with reference to the questions of the immediate future, should raise a united voice in such periodicals, great or small, as they could gain access to, gradually working their way out, by means of a real understanding of the questions they handled, to a position of prominence and acknowledged authority in the public prints, and so in the public mind, a long step would have been taken towards the formation of such a new political sentiment and party as the country stands in such pressing need of,—and I am ambitious that we should have a hand in forming such a group. All the country needs is a new and sincere body of thought in politics, coherently, distinctly, and boldly uttered by men who are sure of their ground. The power of men like Henry George seems to me to mean that; and why should not men who have sane purposes avail themselves of this thirst & enthusiasm for better, higher, more hopeful purpose in politics than either of the present, moribund parties can give?

Now, that's the key-thought of my proposition for a partnership. If your interest and wishes run with me, we'll talk of it further and at length. Meantime believe me, exactly as of old,
                    Your sincere friend   Woodrow Wilson
Mrs. W. sends her regards

ALS (WC, NjP).
    1 C. A. Talcott to WW, Aug. 3, 1885.
    2 WW to ELA, Oct. 30, 1883, Vol. 2, describes Wilson's "compact" with Talcott, made during their undergraduate days at Princeton.

From Joseph Ruggles Wilson

My precious Son: Clarksville, Tenn., Nov. 15, 1886
    The weightily important letter to which this must be a reply, I have retained silently in hand so long as I dared. For its contents are such as could not be responded to off-hand; and yet my response ought I feel to be as prompt as *possible*. Much anxious thought has yr. European-trip suggestion given to me, and I think to your mother also. I imagined, however, that between the lines there might be read a more or less vague expression of your own decision in the premises. You cannot but have seen what I have long suspected, that superior situations in superior institutions are more or less regularly reserved for those scholars who have been "abroad[.]" And your visit to "Cornell" has served to confirm this view. For my own part, I by no means am disposed to indorse this growing prejudice—for prejudice it is. Yet in *your* case—with the specialty you have taken to your embrace, and its peculiar demands both for technical accuracy and for breadth of literary horizon—I can readily see a

propriety (possibly a necessity laid upon you) in your doing as circumstances seem now to indicate. My advice does, therefore, on the whole accord with your own inclination. Indeed, dearest son, I am afraid that a knowledge of your *wish* is always likely to be the measure of my *wisdom,* in respect to matters which affect your personal welfare: so that should you desire to visit the moon I would assuredly counsel you to go! You are my alter ego: what pleases you equally pleases me.

But, notwithstanding the fact that it must prove not a little to my distress to have to think of you as for a time beyond my reach—a great ocean and many months between us—still my judgment, looking at the matter with as dry a vision as I am able, is this: you had better arrange to study eighteen months or two years on the Continent of Europe. I do honestly believe that it will be of large advantage to you everyway, especially as a final, a sealing, preparative for such a professorship as you shall then have a right to claim:—and this, not because it is a conciliative falling in with a prejudice, but altogether because the existing attitude of your better earthly prospects appears to require the seeming sacrifice. Your dear Ellie's generous proposal making the way clear[1]—so far as can now be foreseen—I would sail as early in July next as you may possibly arrange for:—and may God bless her and you in carrying your forming purpose to the desired end!

Would it not be well for you to write to Dr. Adams, of Cornell, to tell him what is in your mind, and to ascertain whether there would likely be an opening in his faculty upon your return. At any rate, he and other of your influential friends ought to be placed in possession of your desire to secure such a chair as your studies are rapidly fitting you to occupy with honor. Might you not, also, secure a position as correspondent for some journal during your absence, which, if it should have no higher end, would at least keep you in the public eye?

Your dear mother agrees with me in what I say touching the advisability of the course you have outlined.

We are in our usual health, and in the experience of our usual love for you all.

Affectionately, *affectionately*   Your Father & Friend.

P.S. omitted. ALS (WP, DLC) with WWhw notation: "Three Creeds 7 Sacraments," and WWhw sums on env.

¹ It is very probable that Ellen had offered to pay the expenses of a European trip out of her share of her father's estate. She wrote to her brother Stockton Axson on about November 13, 1886, asking him to talk to their Uncle Randolph Axson, one of their father's executors, about the estate and to find out how

much she might expect to receive. Stockton Axson to EAW, Nov. 16 and Dec. 11, 1886, and Randolph Axson to EAW, Nov. 19, 1886, all ALS (WP, DLC), are the replies to Ellen's inquiry. It should be added that Wilson planned to take Ellen and their baby with him.

To Robert Bridges

My dear Bobby,   Bryn Mawr, Pa., 18 Nov., 1886.

I[t] costs me a great deal to say that I can't meet you in Princeton on Thanksgiving Day; but I can't.[1] I just *must* use every holiday,—every half-holiday even,—to advance my work on the text-book I am writing for Heath: which will grow slowly enough, do what I may. I believe I should 'cut' and go anyhow were it not for the fact that I expect to look you up in New York before Christmas. I am to discuss before the Nineteenth Century Club on the evening of December 18 the lecture which Justin McCarthy is to deliver to them then (by the way, did *you* have any hand in my being invited to do so?), and I hope to stay in New York part of the next day, Sunday, to see you, if that will be convenient for you. I have in mind just now some matters of great moment to myself about which I am anxious to consult you. Prepare, therefore, to be very unselfish on that day, to make room for my selfishness in talking a great deal about my own concerns.

I have rec'd the copies of the 'Post' you have sent me. I was immensely satisfied to see my Boston *Times* piece quoted;[2] and both Mrs. Wilson and I were extremely interested in that remarkable coincidence between the theory of your Christmas story and the fact about the Rochester crime, as noticed in the *Commercial-Advertiser*. I believe that every man who essays to write stories— i. e. to portray life—ought to have the *detective* somewhere in him,—the ability to read the mysteries of motive which go to make up life.

My class duties are driving me at an uncommonly rapid pace; but I am well, and as content as one can be who is in a boarding-house & has at every meal to hear nonsense rattle down from the empty pate to the clattering tongue of a fool or two.

Mrs. W. joins me in warmest regards. My love to any of the boys you may see at Princeton on the 25th

　　As ever,
　　　　Your affectionate friend,   Woodrow Wilson

ALS (WC, NjP).
　1 Wilson was replying to a recent letter from Bridges, which is missing, urging him to attend the Princeton-Yale football game in Princeton on Thanksgiving Day.
　2 A sarcastic reference to Francis Parkman to "Dear Sir," Oct. 25, 1886, printed in the New York *Evening Post*, Oct. 27, 1886, which seems to have been a summary of Wilson's "Wanted,—A Party," which had appeared in the *Boston Times*, Sept. 26, 1886.

From Joseph R. Wilson, Jr.

My dearest brother: Clarksville, Tenn., Nov. 21/'86.

I want to tell you about the fright we had last Friday aft.
Father and I were sitting in the dining room after dinner, mother
having gone up stairs to lie down as she had been suffering with
her head most of the day. In a little while we heard a noise as
of something falling, then a *thud*. I ran out into the hall and
found dear mother lying on the floor at the bottom of the steps,
she evidently having fallen *most* if not *all* of the way down stairs.
I want to ask you before I say any more not to be anxious,
because mother was not seriously, though painfully, hurt. I
called father, and we took mother up stairs and put her on the
sofa in the study. There was a very large bump on her forehead
and her nose was larger than usual. I applied cold water and
arnica, which reduced the swelling. We found that no bones
were broken, which comforted us very much. Mother's head
(especially her face), neck, and back are very sore. The blood
has settled around her eyes, and she looks as if she had been in
a big fight. Although she sustained some painful bruises, she is
not injured *internally at all* and no bones were broken. Friday
night she suffered considerable pain, but was much better yesterday. She stayed in bed all day yesterday, but got up to dinner
today, and says she feels much better. I cant understand how
she escaped without a broken limb, or *some* bone broken. I think
it was a miricle. It is surprising, also, that she did not *feel* the
jar more. Mother says her pains are gradually leaving her,
although she is sore of course. . . .

This letter, most of it at least, has been written in the dark,
hence the blots &c. Mother joins me in unbounded love to sister
Ellie,"Mag" and your dear self.

Your aff. brother   Joseph.

I have told you everything I know about mother's fall, keeping
nothing from you.

ALS (WP, DLC).

From Herbert Baxter Adams

Johns Hopkins University,
Dear Dr. Wilson: Baltimore, Nov. 25, 1886.

From a conversation which I had with President Adams at
Ithaca last September and from facts which I have recently

heard, I judge that you are likely to receive some overtures from Cornell University with respect to a position in the new departments of law and administration in that institution. You will remember that last June I said something to you in regard to the desirability of your communicating to our Baltimore Seminary the fruits of your present administrative studies, to which idea you responded. It has since occurred to me, in view of the above facts, that possibly some arrangement might be made whereby you could, with decided advantage to yourself, professionally and economically, remain at Bryn Mawr, which, by reason of its climate and municipal connections, is a vastly better place of residence than Ithaca. If you get an offer from Cornell, could you not so modify your present relations to Bryn Mawr as to permit you to lecture for a portion of the year in Baltimore? An assistant like Miss [Lucy M.] Salmon could easily relieve you of much class-work. I am not authorized to make you any proposition, but I should like to be clear in my mind as to your attitude toward such an arrangement.

Very cordially yours,　H. B. Adams

TLS (WP, DLC) with WWhw notation on env.: "Both ans. Nov. 27/86."

EDITORIAL NOTE

WILSON'S "OF THE STUDY OF POLITICS"

The date assigned to "Of the Study of Politics," printed below—November 25, 1886—is somewhat conjectural, for Wilson did not keep notes for or a manuscript copy of the essay.[1] However, certain clues in the text indicate that it was the "very solid little piece of work" to which Wilson referred in his letter to Robert Bridges of November 28, 1886.

For one thing, Wilson's mention of the Dilke affair would have been a natural sort of reference to an event that had attracted so much notoriety only a few months earlier. Stronger evidence that the composition of the essay occurred in late November 1886 was Wilson's frequent mention of the need for the scholar of politics to study government in the field. His letters at this time are filled with this same observation.

The theme of "Of the Study of Politics" is the same as that of Wilson's address to the Princeton alumni of New York of March 23, 1886, printed at that date in this volume. It is possible that Wilson pulled the manuscript of that address from his files and rewrote it at one sitting, making only the copy, which he sent to the *Princeton Review*.

---

[1] Except, perhaps, a single loose WWhw page in WP, DLC, with the title "*An Ideal Way of Teaching Politics*," which may have been the first page of the first draft of this essay.

An Essay

[*c. Nov. 25, 1886*]

Of the Study of Politics.

It has long been an open secret that there is war amongst the political economists. John Stuart Mill no longer receives universal homage, but has to bear much irreverent criticism; even Adam Smith might be seriously cavilled at were not the habit of praise grown too old in his case. He is still "the father of political economy"; but, like other fathers of his day, he seems to us decidedly old-fashioned. The fact is, that these older writers, who professed to point out the laws of human business, are accused of leaving out of view a full half of human nature; in insisting that men love gain, they are said to have quite forgotten that men sometimes love each other—that they are not only prehensile, but also a great many other things less aggressive and less selfish.

Those who make these charges want to leave nothing human out of their reckonings; they want to know "all the facts," and are ready, if necessary, to reduce every generalization of the older writers to the state—the wholly *exceptional* state—of a rule in German grammar. Their protest is significant, their purpose heroic, beyond a doubt; and what interesting questions are not raised by their programme! How is the world to contain the writings, statistical, historical, critical, which must be accumulated ere this enormous diagnosis of trade and manufacture shall be completed in its details; and after it shall have been completed in detail who is to be born great enough in genius and patience to reduce the mass to a system comprehensible by ordinary mortals? Moreover, who is going surety that these new economists will not be dreadful defaulters before they get through handling these immense assets of human nature, which Mill confessed himself unable to handle without wrecking his bookkeeping? Are they assured of the eventual collaboration of some Shakspere who will set before the world all the standard types of economic character? Let it be said that the world hopes so. Even those who cannot answer the questions I have broached ought to bid these sturdy workers "God speed!"

The most interesting reflection suggested by the situation is, that political economists are being harassed by the same discipline of experience that, one day or another, sobers all constructors of systems. They cannot build in the air and then escape chagrin because men only gaze at their structures, and will not live in them. Closet students of politics are constantly having new drill in the same lesson: the world is an inexorable schoolmaster in these courses; it will have none of any thought which does not recognize *it*. Sometimes theorists like Rousseau, being near enough the truth to deceive even those who know something of it, are so unfortunate as to induce men to rear fabrics of government after their aërial patterns out of earth's stuffs, with the result of bringing every affair of weight crashing about their ears, to the shaking of the world. But there are not many such coincidences as Rousseau and his times, happily; and other closet politicians, more commonly cast and more ordinarily placed than he, have had no such painful successes.

There is every reason to believe that in countries where men vote as well as write books, political writers, at any rate, give an honest recognition of act to these facts. They do not vote their opinions, they vote their party tickets; and they are the better citizens by far for doing so. Inside their libraries they go with their masters in thought—mayhap go great lengths with Adolph Wagner, or hold stiffly back, "man *versus* the state," with Spenser —outside their libraries they "go with their party." In a word, like sensible men, they frankly recognize the difference between what is possible in thought and what is practicable in action.

But the trouble is, that when they turn from voting to writing they call many of their abstract reflections on government studies of *politics*, and thereby lose the benefit of some very wholesome aids to just thought. Even when they draw near the actual life of living governments, as they frequently do, and read and compare statutes and constitutions, they stop short of asking and ascertaining what the men of the street think and say of institutions and laws; what little, as well as what big, influences brought particular laws into existence; how much of each law actually lives in the regulation of public function or private activity, and how much of it has degenerated into "dead letter"; in brief, just what things it is—what methods, what habits, what human characteristics and social conditions—that make the appearance of politics outside the library so different from its appearance inside that sanctum; what it is that constitutes "practical politics" a peculiar province. And yet these are the questions most necessary to be answered in order to reach the heart of their study.

Every one who has read great treatises on government which were not merely speculative must have been struck by their exhaustive knowledge of statutes, of judicial precedents, and of

legal and constitutional history, and equally by their tacit ignorance of anything more than this gaunt skeleton of institutions.
Their best pages are often those on which a modest asterisk, an
unobtrusive numeral, or a tiny dagger sticking high in the stately
text, carries the eye down to a foot-note, packed close in small
print, in which some hint is let drop of the fact that institutions
have a *daily* as well as an epochal life, from which the student
might "learn something to his advantage."

The inherent weakness of such a system is shown by the readiness with which it is discredited when once a better one is put
beside it. What modern writer on political institutions has not
felt, either directly or indirectly, the influence of De Tocqueville
and Bagehot? Both these inimitable writers were men of extraordinary genius, and, whatever they might have written about,
their writings would have been admiringly preserved, if only for
the wonder of their luminous qualities. But their political works
live, not only as models of effective style, but also as standards
of stimulating wisdom; because Bagehot and De Tocqueville were
not merely students, but also *men of the world*, for whom the
only acceptable philosophy of politics was a generalization from
actual daily observation of men and things. They could see institutions writ small in the most trivial turns of politics, and read
constitutions more clearly in a biography than in a statute-book.
They were men who, had they written history, would have written the history of peoples, and not of courts or parliaments
merely. Their methods have, therefore, because of their essential
sanity, gone far toward discrediting all others; they have leav-
ened the whole mass of political literature. Was it not Bagehot,
for instance, who made it necessary for Professor Dicey to entitle
his recent admirable work *The Law of the Constitution*, that no
one might think he mistook it for the *Life* of the Constitution?

Who has not wished that Burke had fused the permanent
thoughts of his splendid sentences of wisdom together into a
noble whole—an incomparable treatise whereby every mind that
loved liberty might be strengthened and fertilized? He had handled affairs, and could pluck out the heart of their mystery with
a skill unrivalled; he spoke no word of mere hearsay or speculation. He, it would seem, better than any other, could have shown
writers on politics the difference between knowledge and insight,
between an acquaintance with public law and mastery of the
principles of government.

Not that all "practical politicians" would be the best instructors
in the deep—though they might be in the hidden—things of poli-

tics. Far from it. They are too thickly crowded by daily detail to see permanent outlines, too pushed about by a thousand little influences to detect accurately the force or the direction of the big and lasting influences. They "cannot see the forest for the trees." They are no more fitted to be instructors *because* they are practical politicians than lawyers are fitted to fill law-school chairs because they are active practitioners. They must be something else besides to qualify them for the high function of teaching—and must be that something else in so masterful a wise that no distraction of active politics can for a moment withdraw their vision from the great and continuous principles of their calling.

The active statesman is often an incomparable teacher, however, when he is himself least conscious that he is a teacher at all—when he has no thought of being didactic, but has a whole soul full of the purpose of leading his fellow-countrymen to do those things which he conceives to be right. Read the purposes of men like Patrick Henry and Henry Clay and Abraham Lincoln, men untutored of the schools—read their words of leadership, and say whether there be anything wiser than their home-made wisdom.

It is such reflections as these—whether my examples be well chosen or not—which seem to me to lead directly to the right principle of study for every one who would go beyond the law and know the life of States. Not every State lets statutes die by mere disuse, as Scotland once did; and if you are going to read constitutions with only lawyers for your guides, be they never so learned, you must risk knowing only the anatomy of institutions and never learning anything of their biology.

"Men of letters and of thought," says Mr. Sidney Colvin, where one would least expect to find such a remark—in a *Life of Walter Savage Landor*—

> Men of letters and of thought are habitually too much given to declaiming at their ease against the delinquencies of men of action and affairs. The inevitable friction of practical politics generates heat enough already, and the office of the thinker and critic should be to supply not heat, but light. The difficulties which attend his own unmolested task, the task of seeking after and proclaiming salutary truths, should teach him to make allowance for the still more urgent difficulties which beset the politician—the man obliged, amidst the clash of interests and temptations, to practise from hand to mouth, and at his peril, the most uncertain and at the same time the most indispensable of the experimental arts.

Excellent! But why stop there? Must the man of letters and of thought observe the friction of politics only to make due allowance for the practical politician, only to keep his own placid conclusions free from any taint of scorn or cavil at men whose lives are thrown amidst affairs to endure the buffetings of interests and resist the tugs of temptation? Is not a just understanding of the conditions of practical politics also an indispensable prerequisite to the discovery and audible proclamation of his "salutary truths"? No truth which does not on all its sides touch human life can ever reach the heart of politics; and men of "unmolested tasks," of mere library calm, simply cannot think the thoughts which will tell amidst the noise of affairs. An alert and sympathetic perception of the infinite shifts of circumstance and play of motive which control the actual conduct of government ought to permeate the thinking, as well as check the criticisms, of writers on politics.

In a word, ought not "man of the world" and "man of books" to be merged in each other in the student of politics? Was not John Stuart Mill the better student for having served the East India Company and sat in the House of Commons? Are not Professor Bryce and Mr. John Morley more to be trusted in their books because they have proved themselves worthy to be trusted in the Cabinet?

The success of great popular preachers contains a lesson for students of politics who would themselves convert men to a saving doctrine. The preacher has, indeed, an incalculable advantage over the student of politics in having as his text-book that Bible which speaks of the human heart with a Maker's knowledge of the thing he has made; by knowing his book he knows the deep things of daily life. But the great preacher reaches the heart of his hearers, not by knowledge, but by sympathy—by showing himself a brother-man to his fellow-men. And this is just the principle which the student of politics must heed. He must frequent the street, the counting-house, the drawing-room, the club house, the administrative offices, the halls—yes, and the lobbies—of legislatures. He must cross-examine the experience of government officials; he must hear the din of conventions, and see their intrigues; he must often witness the scenes of election day. He must know how men who are not students regard Government and its affairs; he will get many valuable suggestions from such men on occasion; better than that, he will learn the available approaches to such men's thoughts. Government is meant for the good of ordinary people, and it is for ordinary people that the student should elucidate its problems; let him be anxious to keep within earshot of such.

This is not to commend the writer on politics to narrow "practical" views and petty comment; it is not to ask him to find a philosophy of government which will fit the understanding and please the taste of the "ward politician"; it is only to ask him to keep his generalizations firmly bottomed on fact and experience. His philosophy will not overshoot the hearts of men because it is feathered with high thought, unless it be deliberately shot in air. Thoughts do not fail of acceptance because they are not commonplace enough, but because they are not true enough; and in the sort of writing about which we are here speaking, truth is a thing which can be detected better by the man who knows life than by the man who knows only logic. You cannot lift truth so high that men cannot reach it; the only caution to be observed is, that you do not ask them to climb where they cannot climb without leaving *terra firma*.

Nor is the student, who naturally and properly loves books, to leave books and sit all his time in wiseacre observation amidst busy men. His books are his balance—or, rather, his ballast. And of course the men of his own day are not the only men from whom he can learn politics. Government is as old as man; men have always been politicians; the men of to-day are only politicians of a particular school; the past furnishes examples of politicians of every other school, and there is as much to be learned about government from them as from their successors.

Carlyle had the sort of eye for which one should pray when seeking to find men alive and things actual in the records left of them. Who has not profited by his humorous familiarity with the foibles and personal habits of the men who lived about the court of the Hohenzollerns? Who has not learned more than any other man could have told him of Prussian administration under its first great organizer by looking with Carlyle into the sociable informalities of Frederick William's "tobacco parliament"? Carlyle knew these men well enough to joke with and rail at them. He twitted them with their family secrets, and, knowing what clay they were of, was not awed by their state ceremonials. Yet he saw them, as he himself bitterly complains, only through the medium of crabbed documents and dry-as-dust books, with no seer like himself to help him in his interpretations. It was hard straining of the eyes to see so far back through the dense and murky atmosphere of formal record and set history; but he saw, nevertheless, because he did not need to be *told* all in order to know all; the dryest of historians could hardly avoid dropping some hint which would suffice Carlyle more than would tomes of "profane history."

If you know what you are looking for and are not expecting to find it advertised in the newspapers, but lying somewhere beneath the surface of things, the dullest fool may often help you to its discovery. It needs a good nose to do the thing, but look how excellent is the game to which a casual scent may bring you in such a domain as the study of politics. There are whole worlds of fact waiting to be discovered *by inference*. Do not expect to find the life of constitutions painted in the great "standard authorities," but, following with becoming patience their legal anatomy of institutions, watch their slightest movement toward an illustrative foot-note, and try to find under that the scent you are in quest of. If they cite an instance, seek the recital of the same case elsewhere, where it is told with a different purpose; if it promise well there, hunt it further still, and make sure you catch every glimpse it affords of men's actual dealings with Government. If your text mention names of consequence, seek them out in biographies, and scan there the personal relations of men with affairs for hints of the methods by which governments are operated from day to day. You will not need any incentive to read all their gossip, in letters and journals, and so see governors as men; but do more; endure official interviews and sessions of Parliament with them; collate their private letters and their public despatches—there's no telling when or where you will strike fresh trails of the game you seek. Interview judges off the bench, courtiers away from court, officers off duty. Go to France and live next door a prefect in the provinces; go to London and try to find out how things of weight are talked about in the smoking-room of the House of Commons.

Such excursions must, of course, lead the student far afield; he will often get quite out of sight from his starting-point, the "standard authority"; but he will not, on that account, be lost. The fact is, that all literature teems with suggestions on this topic of politics. Just as the chance news item, the unstudied traveller's reminiscence, the passing social or financial scandal,[1] and every hint of any present contact of men with law or authority, illumines directly, or by inference, the institutions of our own day, similar random rays thrown across the pages of old books by the

[1] Did not the Dilke trial, in London, for instance, help us to understand at least one influence that may sometimes make a lawyer Home Secretary? [All footnotes WW's. They have been numbered.]

unpremeditated words of writers quite guiltless of such instructive intent may light up, for those who are alert to see such things, the most intimate secrets of state. If it be beyond hoping for to find a *whole* Greville for every age of government, there may be found Grevillian scraps, at least, in the literature of almost every time. From men as far back and as well remembered as Cicero, down to men as recent and as easily forgotten as several who might be named, politicians have loved to explain to posterity the part they took in conspicuous affairs; and that portion of posterity which studies politics by inference ought to be profoundly thankful to them for yielding to the taste.

Approach the life of states by such avenues, and you will be convinced of the organic nature of political society. View society from what point you will, you will always catch sight of some part of government; man is so truly a "political animal" that you cannot examine him at all without seeing the points—points of his very structure—whereat he touches and depends upon, or upholds, the State.

In 1850, while Governor-General of Canada, Lord Elgin writes to Lord Grey:

> Our Reciprocity measure was pressed by us in Washington last session, just as a railway bill, in 1845 or 1846, would have been passed in Parliament. There was no Government to deal with, . . . it was all a matter of canvassing this member of Congress or the other.[2]

How? "No Government to deal with"? Here's a central truth to be found in none of the "standard authorities," and yet to be seen by a practised diplomatist all the way from Canada. About the same date M. Bacourt came to this country to represent the French Government and be made wretched by the crude deportment of the Americans. His chief concern was to get away to some country where people were less unconventionally at their ease in drawing-rooms; but he turned, when necessary, to the business of his legation; and whenever he did so he found that "here diplomatic affairs are not treated as everywhere else, where we communicate with the Minister of Foreign Affairs and arrange the matter with him alone." He must "arrange" the matter with several committees of Congress. He must go to see Mrs. Kennedy and Mrs. Winthrop, whose "husbands are members of the House of Representatives, and on the committee having charge of commercial affairs, in which" he "is interested," for "they say that these gentlemen are very particular about visits

2 *Letters and Journals of Lord Elgin*, p. 121.

from foreign ministers to their wives."³ Just Lord Elgin's testimony. Again the "standard authorities" are added to, and that in a quarter where we would least expect to find them supplemented. We need despair of no source.

These are only near and easily recognized illustrations of the errant mode of study I am expounding and advocating. Other systems, besides our own, receive similar chance illumination in the odd corners of all sorts of books. Now and again you strike mines like the *Mémoires* of Madame de Rémusat, the *Letters* of Walpole, or the *Diary* of a Pepys or an Evelyn; at other periods you must be content to find only slender veins of the ore of familiar observation and intimate knowledge of affairs for which you are delving; but your search will seldom be altogether futile. Some new-opened archive office may offer *cahiers*, such as revealed to De Tocqueville, more than all other records, the *ancien régime*. Some elder Hamerton may tell you of the significant things to be seen "round his house." All correspondence and autobiography will repay perusal, even when not so soaked in affairs as the letters of Cromwell, or so reminiscent of politics as the *Memoirs of Samuel Romilly*.

Politics is the life of the State, and nothing which illustrates that life—nothing which reveals any habit contracted by man as a political animal—comes amiss in the study of politics. Public law is the formal basis of the political life of society, but it is not always an expression of its vital principle. We are inclined, oftentimes, to take laws and constitutions too seriously, to put implicit faith in their professions without examining their conduct. Do they affect to advance liberty, for instance? We ought to go, in person or in imagination, amongst the people whom they command, and see for ourselves whether those people enjoy liberty. With reference to laws and constitutions of our own day we can learn such things best by supplementing books and study by travel and observation. The best-taught class in modern public law would be a travelling class. Other times than our own we must perforce be content to see through other men's eyes.

In other words, statute-books and legal commentaries are all very well in the study of politics, if only you quite thoroughly understand that they furnish only the crude body colors for your picture of the State's life, upon which all your finer luminous and atmospheric effects are afterward to be worked. It is high time to recognize the fact that politics can be effectually expounded only by means of the highest literary methods. Only master

³ *Souvenirs of a Diplomat*, pp. 189, 281.

workers in language and in the grouping and interpretation of heterogeneous materials can achieve the highest success in making real *in words* the complex life of states. If I might act as the interpreter of the new-school economists of whom I have already spoken, I trust with due reverence, I should say that this is the thought which, despite their too frequent practical contempt for artistic literary form, is possessing them. John Stuart Mill and Ricardo made a sort of logic of political economy; in order to simplify their processes, they deliberately stripped man of all motives save self-interest alone, and the result was evidently "*doctrinaire*"–was not a picture of life, but a theorem of trade. Hence "the most dismal of all sciences"; hence Sidney Smith's exhortation to his friend not to touch the hard, unnatural thing. The new-school economists revolt, and say they want "a more scientific method"; what they really want is a higher literary method. They want to take account of how a man's wife affects his trade, how his children stiffen his prudence, how his prejudices condition his enterprise, how his lack of imagination limits his market, how strongly love of home holds him back from the good wages that might be had by emigration, how despotically the opinion of his neighbors forbids his insisting upon a cash business, how his position in local society prescribes the commodities he is *not* to deal in; in brief, how men actually do labor, plan, and get gain. They are, therefore, portentously busy amassing particulars about the occupations, the habits, the earnings, the whole economic life of all classes and conditions of men. But these things are only the raw material of poetry and the literary art; and without the intervention of literary art must remain raw materials. To make anything of them, the economist must become a literary artist and bring his discoveries home to our imaginations—make these innumerable details of his pour in a concentrated fire upon the centre-citadels of men's understandings. A single step or two would then bring him within full sight of the longed-for time when political economy is to dominate legislation.

It has fallen out that, by turning its thoughts toward becoming a science, politics, like political economy, has joined its literature to those books of *natural* science which boast a brief authority, and then make way for what is "latest." Unless it be of the constitution of those rare books which mark an epoch in scientific thought, a "scientific work" may not expect to outlive the prevailing fashion in ladies' wraps. But books on politics are in the wrong company when they associate with works among which so high a rate of mortality obtains. The "science" proper to them, as distinguished from that which is proper to the company they now affect, is a science whose very expositions are as deathless as itself. It is the science of the life of man in society. Nothing which elucidates that life ought to be reckoned foreign to its art; and no true picture of that life can ever perish out of literature. Ripe scholarship in history and jurisprudence is not more indispensable to the student of politics than are a constructive imagination and a poet's eye for the detail of human incident. The heart of his task is insight and interpretation; no literary power that he can bring to bear upon it will be greater than he needs. Arthur Young's way of observing, Bagehot's way of writing, and Burke's way of philosophizing would make an ideal combination for the work he has to do. His materials are often of the most illusive sort, the problems which he has to solve are always of the most confounding magnitude and variety.

It is easy for him to say, for instance, that the political institutions of one country will not suit another country; but how infinitely difficult is it to answer the monosyllables How? and Why? To reply to the Why he must make out all the contrasts in the histories of the two countries; but it depends entirely upon what sort of eye he has whether those contrasts will contain for him vital causes of the effect he is seeking to expound. He may let some anecdote escape him which gleams with the very spark needed to light up his exposition. In looking for grave political facts only, he may overlook some apparently trivial outlying detail which contains the very secret he would guess. He may neglect to notice what men are most talked about by the people; whose photographs are most frequently to be seen on the walls of peasant cottages, what books are oftenest on their shelves. Intent upon intrigue and legislation, he may pass over with only a laugh some piquant gossip about legislator or courtier without the least suspicion that it epitomizes a whole scheme of government. He may admire self-government so much as to forget that it is a very coarse, homely thing when alive, and so may really never know anything valuable about it. The man who thinks the polls disagreeable, uninteresting places has no business taking up a pen to write about government. The man who despises the sheriff because he is coarse and uncouth, and who studies the sheriff's functions only from the drawing-room or the library, will realize the life of government no better than he realizes the vanity of "good manners."

If politics were to be studied as a great department of human conduct, not to be understood by a scholar who is not also a man of the world, its literature might be made as imperishable as that of the imagination. There might then enter into it that individuality which is immortality. That personal equation which constitutes the power of all books which have aught of power in them would then rescue books on politics from the dismal category of "treatises," and exalt them to the patriciate of literature. The needed reaction against the still "orthodox" methods of discoursing upon laws and constitutions, like that already set afoot against the "orthodox" political economists, should be a "literary movement"—a movement from formalism to life. In order really to know anything about government, you must *see it alive;* and the object of the writer on politics should be nothing less than this, to paint government to the life—to make it live again upon his page.

WOODROW WILSON.

Printed in the *New Princeton Review,* III (March 1887), 188-99.

To Herbert Baxter Adams

Dear Dr. Adams,   Bryn Mawr, Pa., 27 Nov., 1886.

I received your kind letter of Nov. 25 yesterday, and I hasten to reply. I had not forgotten my response to your suggestion that I should present in Balto. the results of my studies, now in progress, in comparative politics and administration; but, you remember, I coupled an 'if' with my assent: 'if I got my material into shape to be presented this winter,'—and there's the trouble. I worked diligently all summer, and I am taking advantage of every scrap of leisure afforded by my duties here to push my special studies, which just now, unfortunately, cannot be made to come in in class; but I have not yet gone over, with even a first survey, the whole field; and the habit of my mind is such that until I see my *whole* subject I can't write on a part of it anything that I would like to put forth in public as *results*. I am, therefore, so to say, *waiting on myself*, waiting on the slowness of my thought,—expecting the time when, all the ingredients of the *entire* substance of my studies being mixed in, the several portions of my treatment may crystalize symmetrically. I am writing, of course, when I can; but I have written nothing safe to be promulgated. I have only made sketches.

You will see, therefore, just how I must feel with reference to a possible invitation to lecture a portion of the year in Balto.,—

or all the year in Ithaca (I read a paper, *about* the study of administration, not long ago, to the Hist. Association of Cornell, by the way, which may have killed my chances there!) A division of my time between Bryn Mawr and Balto. would, however, commend itself most strongly to me, so far as I can see at present: and I see no reason to think that I would not, by the second half of the next University year at any rate, have something confident to say in a course of lectures on governmental methods. I think, too, that such an arrangement could be effected. The authorities here seem generously desirous to meet my wishes in most things.

What I have said is, I believe, the most definite thing I can say at present,—and is as definite as your question calls for. I have several schemes in head for next year; but none of them are final as yet; and any proposition from Balto. would be apt to give them pause.

ALS (H. B. Adams Papers, MdBJ). Letter incomplete. In the remainder, Wilson apparently replied to Adams's letter of November 3, 1886, and enclosed the description of his courses that follows.

Wilson's Description of His Courses at Bryn Mawr College

[c. Nov. 27, 1886]

The requirements for entrance are, the outlines of the histories of England and the United States, or the outlines of the histories of Greece and Rome. Students who expect to enter the classical courses are advised to offer Greek and Roman history; all others are advised to offer English and American history.

The major course in history runs through two years, five hours a week. One year is devoted to ancient history, the other to mediaeval and modern. Either year may be taken as a minor course.

No attempt is made to cover the field of general history. The histories of Greece and Rome are taken as representative of ancient history, those of France and England as representative of mediaeval and modern history, and it is the object of the instruction to make the students quite familiar with the development of these representative states. Constant text-book drill is combined with frequent lectures; and it is the aim of the lectures to open out the horizon necessary for a real understanding of the special tracts of history which are being traversed, by recounting the most important contemporary events in the histories of other countries, and by pointing out the chief and most memorable characteristics of the periods studied, as well as the philosophical connection of leading facts and tendencies. Lectures are also made use of to group and explain facts separated in the narrative of the text-book, and, in doing so, to keep the student mindful of the broad views of history to which the events in the lives of individual nations stand related. Recitations and lectures are supplemented by reports from members of the class on topics assigned (with bibliographical references) by the instructor.

The work in Greek and Roman history is so conducted that the two histories are carried forward simultaneously, alternating with each other week by week, in order that the histories of the two countries may run parallel up to the point where Greek history is merged in Roman by conquest, with a view to enable the student when reading or when hearing lectures to perceive for herself contrasts or likenesses. It is intended to follow a similar plan with French and English history hereafter.

In the course on Greek history lectures are given on such topics as the constitutional reforms of Solon and Clisthenes, the causes of the Persian invasion, the character and influence of the Confederacy of Delos, etc. As the history of the popular states of Greece turns largely upon the individual characters and influence of leading men, class reports concern principally the antecedents, lives, and work of the chief statesmen, dramatists, and orators.

The lectures on Roman history develop such topics as the sources of Roman history, the causes, means, ends, and effects of Roman conquest, Roman provincial administration, agrarian troubles and reforms, etc. Text-book drill is made more prominent in this course than in that on Greek history, because, the internal history of Rome hinging so largely, down to the time of the empire, on class struggles and consequent legal and constitutional reforms, it is thought that an adequate knowledge of the development of the state can be gotten in no other way.

The courses in ancient history are concluded and rounded out by lectures covering the period from the fall of the Western Empire to the establishment of the Empire of Charles the Great.

In the second year three hours a week are given to English and French history throughout both semesters; two hours a week are devoted to lectures on American history during the first semester; and the same amount of time to lectures on the Italian Renaissance and the German Reformation during the second semester.

In the course on English history text-book work is subordinate. The lecturers [lectures] aim for the most part to throw light on

the leading questions in the England of to-day. They treat, therefore, of the history of Ireland before and since the union with
England and of the circumstances attending the consummation
of that union; the history of the House of Lords, and of the
Peerage; the history of the English Church; the history of representation in Parliament; the tariff; colonial government; the
union with Scotland; the land laws and their effects on England
and on Ireland, and other like topics; and text-book work is
directed in these lines.

The history of the United States is also discussed in topical
lectures. Amongst the topics chosen are these: English colonial
policy; contrasts in colonial life, manners, and institutions; the
foundation of the colonies; England *vs.* France and Spain in
America; the Revolution and its causes; the Constitution; history
of political parties; the Monroe doctrine; President Jackson; the
national bank; the Mexican war; the westward migration; the
causes of the civil war; the results of the civil war.

Each year's work is prefaced by a few lectures on the philosophy of history and the objects and methods of historical study.

The text-books used are Smith's History of Greece, Leighton's
History of Rome, Green's Short History of the English People,
and the 'Student's' History of France.

Once a week a meeting of the class is held, at which the
instructor comments upon current events, *i. e.*, upon the important news of the week. Attendance at this meeting is entirely
voluntary.

Advanced lecture courses have not as yet been organized; but
advanced work of a very thorough sort has been done by the two
fellows in history, so far appointed, and by one other graduate
student. The instructor guides this work and exercises a constant
critical oversight of it. The topics taken up so far have been:
The growth of Federal prerogative traceable in the decisions of
the Supreme Court; the past and present colonial policy of Great
Britain (studied from the contemporaneous sources of each
period); Roman influences traceable in the institutions and laws
of modern Europe; race elements of the modern European
nations.

The library facilities here are limited, so far as the college's
own library is concerned, because that library is now only a year
and a half from its first purchase of books; but the libraries of
Philadelphia, which are easily available, are very full of excellent
materials on most topics in English and American history, and
very free use has been made of them for advanced work.

Printed in United States Bureau of Education, Circular of Information Number 2, 1887, *The Study of History in American Colleges and Universities,* by Herbert Baxter Adams (Washington, 1887), pp. 226-28. Wilson's text therein is printed within quotation marks. They have been deleted.

To Robert Bridges

My dear Bobby,   Bryn Mawr, Pa., 28 Nov., 1886.

The decision of the questions about which I threatened to consult you when I shall be in New York in December are pressing for settlement now a little more importunately than they were when I wrote to you last; so I am going to *open* the case to you to-day, and see what you may have to say.

All my plans for literary and professional work turn, as you know, as upon their pivot, upon an intimate acquaintance with the actual constitutions of the European states, not only as they live in books, but also as they live and move in practice. I must know not only comparative constitutional *law* but also comparative constitutional *life*. And this last I cannot know without seeing foreign systems and foreign people's as far as may be with my own eyes,—without coming into contact with the living organisms of their governments. What's more, I can't learn even what books have to tell me without coming into contact with the living organisms of the German and French *languages*. Here I have been wrestling with German for the past two years, and, do what I will, I cannot emancipate myself from the dictionary. In a word, I must go to Europe. Another imperative motive for going at once is, that the writing I am now doing is in immediate need of just such study as I can do only on that ground,—only in the homes of the systems I am writing about.

Accordingly, I am going, God willing, next summer. I shall have the means to stay one year, probably two; and that time would suffice in which to learn the language I most want to learn (German), as well as for much of the study I wish to do. But three years would round out the accomplishment of my purposes very much better: the longer I can stay the better. I have, therefore, been casting about in my mind for ways and means of adding at least a little to my small revenues while I am over there, and so spinning out my resources, that they may cover a rather longer period than they could unadded to. Of course you anticipate the appeal I am about to make to your kindness. Do you think that a fellow of my kind and calibre could make a few hundred dollars writing foreign letters to the newspapers?

I could not write news letters, of course. My only available line would be descriptions of legislative bodies and their practices; discussions, given in as light a touch as possible, of foreign governmental methods; letters about current foreign politics, and the like. Now is it likely that I could find two or three New York journals that would be ready to take such merchandize from me; and, if so, what would they be willing to pay for occasional articles of the kind? Further, would success be more probable if I waited and sent some samples of my work from abroad without previous arrangement: or should I try to effect a definite engagement before going? Again, which journals would be the most inclined to buy the wares I should have to offer?

I am ashamed to trouble you with all this, Bobby, the more because I know from of old how willing you are to spend and be spent for your friends,—and particularly for *this* friend, for whom you have done so much already. But I feel that I have reached a critical point in my career in making the decision I have made with reference to going abroad, and I am so anxious to make my trip count for as much as possible that I am rendered bold in asking aid. I know that I can trust your judgment; and I know that nobody can answer the questions I have put more adequately than you can.

My plan is, in fact, for just such a temporary retirement from professional work for purposes of literary study and construction as you will best be able to comprehend and to sympathize with: and I must make the retirement as long as may be. The work I expect it to yield will be of just the kind to get me the sort of place I want in my profession when I return to it. Tho' out of sight, I don't intend to be out of mind of college trustees and presidents.

What provoking hard luck about the Thanksgiving game![1] Were Charlie and Chang there with you.[2] I wished many a time during the day that I was; and, if it had not been that I did not dare to risk going with a heavy cold out on the open ball field in that bleak, dripping weather (that's the way it was here, at least) I believe I should have gone after all. As it was, I stayed at home, and did a very solid little piece of work, now salted down in my desk.

Answer this letter if you have time, Bobby, *if you haven't* wait until I come on, Dec. 18, if you will be in N.Y. then. I said, at the beginning of this letter, that my plans were pressing for final decision, because I am being pressed to make some promises about what I will do when I return which I can't either make or not make until I know how long I can stay abroad. But I *can* wait till Dec. 18.

Mrs. W. joins me in warmest regards. As ever,
Your affectionate friend,   Woodrow Wilson.

ALS (WC, NjP).
¹ The Princeton-Yale football game was played in Princeton on Thanksgiving Day, November 25, 1886, in a cold pouring rain. The game was called seventeen minutes short of full time and was, therefore, declared a draw or "no game."
² Charles A. Talcott and William B. Lee.

To John Barbee Minor

My dear Dr. Minor,   Bryn Mawr, Pa., 2 Dec., 1886.

My friend, Prof. E. J. James, of the University of Penn., is studying the history of educational foundations in this country, with the special object of discovering whence the founders of our earlier colleges and universities took their models.¹ He does not, of course, follow Dr. Holmes in his recent (poetical but apparently deliberate) ascription to Harvard of the credit of being mother to all the higher education of the country.² He finds Harvard's influence and example to have been of very little weight outside of New England. In Pennsylvania, for instance, as he tells me, the Scotch, and not the English, universities furnished the models of method, &c. He has been asking me what the European parentage of the University of Va. was,—what models (if any in particular) Mr. Jefferson had in his eye when he planned the work to be done at Charlottesville; and I have been unable to give him any satisfactory information, or to direct him to adequate (published) sources of information. I have so far been unable to find anything clearing up the point in Mr. Jefferson's published writings. I write, therefore, to ask your kind assistance. I trust that you will not allow me to encroach on your leisure; but, if you can do so without inconvenience, I should be deeply indebted if you would direct me to the proper sources of information on this interesting question.

I am pleased to find that a great many college people throughout the North are just now waking up to the fact that, in knowing nothing in particular about the University of Va., they have this long time past been neglecting to study one of the most singular, most successful, and most important institutions in the country,— and one in which many of the ideas they have fondly supposed original with themselves have been known and acted upon for more than half a century.

I am engaged very pleasantly at the new college here, and as my work progresses,—both my class work and my private study of political institutions,—I am increasingly thankful for the opportunities I enjoyed under you at the University. I have in consequence of my studies there a firmer foothold in English constitutional history than I could have otherwise obtained.

I sincerely trust that your health continues strong. Please give my warmest regards to your daughters, and believe me

Your grateful and affectionate pupil,   Woodrow Wilson.

ALS (Minor Papers, ViU).
[1] Edmund J. James apparently never published the results of this study.
[2] Oliver Wendell Holmes, "Poem for the Two Hundred and Fiftieth Anniversary of the Founding of Harvard College," *Atlantic Monthly*, LVIII (Dec. 1886), Supplement, 18-28.

From Joseph Ruggles Wilson

My precious Son: Clarksville, Decr 3rd 1886.

Yours of the 28th ult. has remained unanswered for two days, in order that the intelligence it conveys might simmer in our thoughts. It is certainly complimentary: the manifest reluctance of the Bryn Mawr authorities to face the possibility of your cutting from your present apron strings. But what you ought to do in view of the new complications—as are opened to sight in Dr. H. B. Adams flattering epistle,[1] and as appear mistily Cornellward—to say nothing of the proposition to allow yr. name to remain upon the list of Assistants during your absence—what precise line of conduct all this suggests is not easy to put into the words of an exhaustive proposition. It seems to be clear enough, however, that should you continue at Bryn M.—abandoning the European "invasion"—or should you resume at B. M. upon your return—the Baltimore chance ought to be made a practical certainty. Or, if during the winter a definite opening shall become manifest at Cornell, I would drop all at the end of your collegiate year, and go there at once; unless, indeed, the bosses at Ithaca would be willing to have you spend a year in Europe before entering upon the actual work of the proffered chair. Meanwhile, however, should nothing offer at Cornell, and you still shall conclude upon the transatlantic trip, I would yield—were I in your place—to the request of Dr. Rhoads to allow your name to remain upon the B. M. faculty-roll, with the understanding that it will be at your discretion whether or no to come back into your present berth:—and with the purpose on your part to look out for an election to the very professorship you desire, elsewhere. Having already a place—even though a nominal place—in a respectable institution, you will, I think, be in a better position to command the confidence of some other institution than if you were altogether vacant and a beginner de novo. Of course you will have written to Dr. *H. B.* Adams, informing him of your plans, hopes, &c. May it not be that at the end of one or two years, a regular professorship will be constituted for you at Johns Hopkins? At any rate, the added prestige of your preparing books will be very much to your advantage in the event of a rival candidacy there or at some other point of renown. On the whole, therefore, whilst I half tremble to reflect upon your giving up an existing certainty, leaving nothing but a *trust* in the future—yet this being in reality a trust in God which appears justified by providential circumstances—it may be best to cast yourself adrift from all visible, or half-visible prospects in the direction of your specialty, and, holding on to nothing save your nominal connection with B. Mawr, hope in the Heavenly Director for your welfare during your absence from the country and *afterwards*. Ask for His guidance, then, and wait upon His will. All that is *clear* to me, is, that your wisdom will be shown in not abandoning—*in toto*—the place you now occupy:—and, by February or March, new light may shine amid these perplexities.

Your dear Mother is getting on quite well, considering. Mercifully she was not killed, or helplessly maimed: and she is still permitted to "trot about" through her household cares, although her face is still black and yellow in spots of—rare beauty. She joins me in proud love for dear Ellie and yourself: as does sweet Dode² also.   Your devoted   Father.

ALS (WP, DLC).
¹ Woodrow Wilson, in his letter to his father of November 28, 1886, must have quoted from Dr. Adams's letter of November 25, 1886.
² Joseph R. Wilson, Jr.

From Robert Bridges

Dear Tommy: New York. Dec 3 1886

I had set aside last evening for writing letters, and hoped to have a leisurely talk with you, after making a short call, but was sadly interrupted; so that I must answer your letter briefly at this very annoying desk.

I broached your project to Mr. [Wendell Phillips] Garrison, and he told me to say that "he was very favorably disposed toward it" for the *Nation*. We at present have no German correspondent,

which would tend to make your letters more timely. Of course
he could not make a regular agreement, but I have little doubt
that your letters will find acceptance when offered. Mr. Garrison
is perfectly familiar with what you have accomplished, and as
he expressed it he "would feel safe in Mr. Wilson's hands."

Of course this may average ten or twelve letters a year which
should bring about $100.

I also spoke to Storey[1]—one of Harpers' editors, but he feared
there would be no chance in the weekly.

My idea would be that you should also seek a good Boston
engagement to which the *Atlantic Monthly* could readily help
you. There is also a very respectable syndicate in this city controlled by S. S. McClure which commands the very best talent
among fiction writers and might be induced to float an occasional
letter. I think they published a lot for Brander Matthews last
summer. We can talk this over when you reach New York. I see
no reason why you could not make $200 a year by judiciously
placed letters. It would be a great thing if you could form a connection with some English paper like the *Saturday Review* and
Contemporary. The latter pays 10 guineas per article. Then you
might work in occasional articles in the *Princeton Review*. (They
pay about $4[.]50 per page for editorials, and gave me $100.00
for the *political record*.[)] We can talk all these things over at
leisure when you come up here.

Of course all periodical work is precarious, and I don't want
to hold out any false hopes of great gain; but your writing should
command a good price anywhere, and at any time.

I heartily believe in your plan of European study, and am
tempted to cut and run with you. Still I know that my "Jeru-
salem" if anywhere is at my door.

I have many things to talk over with you, and am just now in
a kind of valley of desolation.

Your friend   BoBridges

ALS (WP, DLC) with WWhw notation on env.: "Ans. Dec. 5/86."
[1] The records do not reveal who this Storey might have been.

From Daniel Greenleaf Thompson

My dear Sir: New York Dec. 4. 1886.

I enclose a letter just received which explains itself. I doubt if
it be worth while to write to Mr. Max Milligan[1] but if you care
enough about it I will do so or you may write directly, as you
prefer. I don't think you will be troubled, if you have no abstract

in advance, for I imagine the lecture is rather descriptive than argumentative.

If you will kindly inform me where you will stop in New York I will have some one call for you and take you to the place of meeting. Tickets will be sent you and if you desire more, I will be happy to supply you.

Very truly yours,   Daniel G. Thompson

ALS (WP, DLC) with WWhw notation on env.: "Ans. Dec. 10/86."
  ¹ Milligan was probably Justin McCarthy's secretary and apparently had written to say that no advance copies of McCarthy's speech before the Nineteenth Century Club were available. Milligan's letter is missing.

To Robert Bridges

Dear Bobby,   Bryn Mawr, Pa., 5 Dec., 1886.

Thank you ever so much for your kind letter of Dec. 3. It contains just the sort of information and suggestion I was in need of,—and plenty of text for our coming conference. But its sentence about yourself distresses me not a little. I sincerely hope you were figurative in what you said,—except in your wish to go abroad with me. But, if anything serious is the matter, I need not tell you how sincerely my heart will engage in *our talk* about it. In haste and love   Yrs.   Woodrow Wilson

ALS (WC, NjP).

To Herbert Baxter Adams

Dear Dr. Adams,   Bryn Mawr, Pa., 5 Dec., 1886.

Thank you very much for your kind letter of Nov. 30.¹ Things are moving rather fast with me nowadays, and, although, as you say, there is no need for haste in my plans, so far as the development of my work is concerned, I feel that I should like to know what chances there are for the sort of work in comparative politics I want to do in order that I may see the whole field and so make no false move.

Amongst other things, I am thinking very seriously of going to Europe next summer to stay two, or it might be three, years and see the constitutions of the Continent *alive*. Of course, as you know, I have long *wanted* to go abroad; but it is only within the past few weeks that I have come within sight of probable means of realizing the wish. Now that new places such as I want are about opening to me,—now is the time to go, if by doing so I shall not be cutting myself off from advantageous engagements, but shall, as I believe, be only making myself surer of them, because better qualified for them. I *must* learn German as it cannot be learned from books, and I must see European politics and administration as no library can show them to me, even if these objects may be attained only piece-meal during successive *summers* spent abroad. It would be vastly better to give two or three unbroken years to the purpose; and that is what I am rapidly coming to the determination to do. As you know, what I 'go in for' is the *life*, not the texts, of constitutions, the practice not the laws of administrations: and I can get at these things only by cross-questioning systems at their homes. I have learned, for instance, all that is necessary to be known about what that autocratic person, the French *Prefect*, *may* do, and what the law has to say about his appointment:—*any*body can find such things out and make long-headed remarks about them. What I want to know is, what the Prefect *does* do and under what influences he is appointed. I must know the live prefect before I can feel that I know anything about French administration. And this will serve as an instance of what I am going to Europe to study. I can't believe that I am mistaken in thinking that such study would be the *making* of any courses I might afterwards be called on to deliver on comparative politics and administration. And, since positions such as I want are *ripening* rather than yet *ripe*, this seems the nick of time for my preparation. For, besides, *I* am riper than I was two or three years ago.

Very cordially Yrs.   Woodrow Wilson

I will get the photo. of the library for you the next time I go in to Phila.

ALS (H. B. Adams Papers, MdBJ).
   [1] H. B. Adams to WW, Nov. 30, 1886, is missing. All that remains in the Wilson Papers is the envelope with the WWhw notation: "Ans. Dec. 5/86."

From Robert Bridges

My dear Classmate: New York City, December 6th, 1886.
   The Executive Committee of '79 propose publishing a brief *Record* of the boys sometime in January, 1887. Will you kindly send to my address, at your earliest convenience, your present occupation and address, whether married or not; and if married since the last *Record*, to whom and when? Also any additions to your family, and any startling event in your career? If you know anything interesting about the boys, let us have it.

Very Truly,   Robert Bridges   for the Comm

Saw Prof Sloane[1] today; thinks he could use several articles from you while you are in Germany. Also glad to give your letters to [Richard Watson] Gilder, Editor of the *Century*.   BoB

TLS with Bridges' handwritten postscript (WP, DLC) with WWhw notation on env.: "Ans. Dec. 10/86."
    [1] William Milligan Sloane, Professor of History at Princeton, and editor of the *New Princeton Review*.

To Edwin Robert Anderson Seligman

My dear Sir: Bryn Mawr, Pa., 6 Dec., 1886.
    I am sincerely glad that you are pleased with the article on the 'Study of Administration,' and am quite content to have you use it without remuneration. I understood beforehand that you were not prepared to pay for contributions.
    When I sent the *mss.* on I hardly expected you to use it, and so did not rewrite one passage in it which might convey a false impression when read. It would save you expense,—would it not? —if I should recast it now, rather than after it is in proof. If, therefore, you will be kind enough to let me have the *mss.* again for a day or so, I could clear the passage I have in view of all ambiguity before it goes to the printer.[1]
                    Very sincerely Yours,   Woodrow Wilson

ALS (*Political Science Quarterly* Papers, NNC).
    [1] For a discussion of Wilson's recasting of this passage, see the Editorial Note, "Wilson's 'The Study of Administration.' "

Two Letters to Robert Bridges

My dear Bobby,   Bryn Mawr, Pa., 10 Dec., 1886.
    I took your invitation to stay with you next week so cordially and so spontaneously to heart that I did not have the manners to accept, or to say how much I appreciated your invitation: but I hope that you understood that the thanks were not *really* lacking.[1]
    Mr. Thompson, of the *Nineteenth Century Club*, writes to ask where I shall stop in New York. I have forgotten your residence address; so I wrote that I would ask you to drop him a card containing it. To save you time I enclose an addressed card on which your address is the *only* thing remaining to be put.
    I have a card of invitation for you of course for 'the occasion.' You will go with me; wont you?
    Thank you very much for the note, about Prof. Sloane and the

Century, added to your circular received the other day. You are a splendid friend, my dear fellow! As ever,

Affectionately Yours,   Woodrow Wilson

¹ Bridges' invitation had evidently been conveyed in a note or telegram to Wilson, now missing.

Dear Mr. Committeeman: [Dec. 10, 1886]

My present occupation is teaching History in the Bryn Mawr College for Women; my present address is, Bryn Mawr, Pa.; I am married, as related in the last Record; and I have to chronicle the birth of a daughter, Margaret Wilson, born April 16, 1886. I may add, as a matter of record, that I took the degree, Ph.D. at Johns Hopkins University on the 14th of June, 1886.

Fraternally Yours,   Woodrow Wilson, '79.

ALS (Meyer Coll., DLC). WW added the second letter at the bottom of the first.

From John Barbee Minor

My dear Mr Wilson,   University of Virginia, Dec. 13, 1886.

I invoke your indulgence for not giving a more immediate reply to yours of 2d inst. It is well nigh impossible to keep up with my correspondence, which is larger than one would be likely to anticipate, so that I am constrained to allow my many letters, asking opinions on legal topics, to go unanswered.

A "Sketch of the University,"¹ which at the instance of the Authorities, I prepared a year or two ago, may be of some interest to you, and of some help to Mr James in the task he has undertaken; and so I forward a copy to each of you, relying upon your good offices to explain to him how I happened so to presume. . . .

You need hardly have said that Mr James did not design to follow the example of Dr Holmes in indiscriminate laudation of particular local institutions. No one outside of N. England, could be suspected of such absurd extravagance. I thought the mutual admiration at Boston had gone to its extremest length before; but it is hard to imagine a limit when some provincial Cato

"Gives his little Senate laws,
And sits attentive to his own applause."

In this quarter, we never expect anything from N. England, but depreciation, and are therefore seldom disappointed; and are more indifferent than we should be to its insolent assumptions.

If I had time I would extract from an article of mine written 16 years ago some comments upon this gracious temper of our Northern countrymen, in connexion with an extraordinary attempt to appropriate the remarkable features of the University to swell the reputation of one of their colleges.[2] But I must reserve it until you do me the honor to make me a visit, which I hope you will soon think it incumbent on you to favor me with.

I am glad to find that your "Congressional Government" has gone to a second edition. Such success may well encourage you to persevere in analogous lines.

The rather despondent view of our institutions which you present, especially in the Introduction, is perhaps not too strongly put as a whole. The cowardice and selfishness of our public men generally, which is the immediate source of alarm, results doubtless from many causes, but I cannot help thinking chiefly from the late condition of the Civil Service, not yet effectually reformed, and from the defects in legislation which you have exposed, but which it will take long to reform. The profligacy and imbecility of the press is another source of peril, for which no cure, thus far, suggests itself.

I have nursed the hope that Mr Cleveland's apparent honesty and good sense would so warmly engage the confidence of the people, as to enable him not only to accomplish directly, much good by wise administration, but also to stand forth as an embodied assurance to our aspiring countrymen that virtue and sense were after all, the most certain guaranties of a grand success. Shall I hope vainly?

With many good wishes for your future usefulness and advancement, I am, dear Mr Wilson,

Your friend truly,   John B. Minor.

P.S. My daughters have one and all left us for a while, Miss Mary being at Norfolk, and Misses Mattie & Susie at Louisville. The latter two I hope to be able to re-claim before Christmas.

ALS (WP, DLC) with WWhw notation on env.: "Ans. Dec. 20/86."
   [1] *A Sketch of the University of Virginia* (Richmond, 1885).
   [2] Minor was possibly referring to his comments in "University of Virginia," Richmond *Old Dominion*, iv-v (March 1870-June 1871).

To Lucy Maynard Salmon

Dear Miss Salmon,   [Bryn Mawr, c. Dec. 16, 1886]

I find that I *will* have to be absent to-morrow morning; I shall, therefore, avail myself of your kindness in the matter of presiding over the quiz to-morrow from 9 to 10 A.M. Please propound the following questions:

Church of England.

1. Characterize the position and work of Wyclif.
2. Describe very briefly the five great religious revivals.
3. What is 'disestablishment,' and what partial measures have already been taken toward it?

Again thanking you very sincerely for your kindness in this matter,   Yours cordially,   Woodrow Wilson

ALS (NPV).

To Ellen Axson Wilson

My own darling,   N.Y., Friday morning Dec. 17, '86.

I *must* write you a few words this morning; so I have slipped in to the writing-room of the Astor House, and will make the best 'out' I can with hands only just warming after a long walk in this keen air.

I have bought my suit and overcoat, and I think they will both claim your approbation. I got the suit for $1.50 less than I expected to pay—the overcoat for just what I said. The latter is handsome *smooth* cloth, as you directed.

The meeting last night was quite a success.[1] Not as many men of my own class were there as I expected to see, but a great many old acquaintances put in an appearance and I had a very pleasant evening indeed.

Bobby is himself—more *himself*, I think than before, and I am enjoying my chats with him thoroughly.

But these are not the things I intended writing about—they can wait to be *talked* about: the thing that can't be delayed is the telling of my profound love for my peerless little wife. I am so lonely without her, and my heart turns so longingly back to her that this note had become a necessity so early as last night— it became a necessity the minute I passed out of sight of the window at which a little lady was standing. Ah, my Eileen, I love you, I love you, I love you—nothing can make my heart lose for a moment the sense of inspiration and strength and light- ness—the joy and bouyancy—the serious ardour which your love gives it. I am every moment and in all things

Your own   Woodrow

ALS (WP, DLC).

[1] This was a meeting at Delmonico's of the Princeton Alumni Association of New York and Vicinity. The members present voted unanimously to change the

name of their group to the Princeton Club of New York and to begin discussions
with other alumni associations of means of establishing better liaison with the
college's Board of Trustees (*New York Times*, Dec. 17, 1886). The Princeton
Club of New York did not acquire a building until 1899.

From Gamaliel Bradford

My dear Mr Wilson: Cambridge Dec 20 '86

I was much pleased to receive your letter of 10th & have only
delayed answering it till I could have an answer. Your conun-
drums are rather hard however & I have not found much.

La Rousse's Cyclopedia Art. [on the] Prefet tells what those
officials did under the empire.[1] There is an article in Fraser Vol.
86 Nov. 1872 'Six Months of Prefecture under Gambetta' which
tells something but it may be pure romance.[2] Hamerton in 'Round
My House' says something of the social relations of the Prefect.[3]
I thought there might be something in Grenville Murray, High
Life in France, but the book was unfortunately out at the Athenaeum.[4] There is here at the moment a M. Ribaud member of
the Corps Legislatif and Prof. in the Paris School of Political
Sciences. I called upon him and submitted your questions seri-
atim & give his replies, but he did not know of any book on the
subject

"The prefect has *now* no tremendous power & no veto. He is
the executor of the votes of the *conseil general*. If he does not
like them he can appeal to the minister of the interior, and if the
conseil is obstinate the matter goes to the *conseil d'etat*[.] The
conseil general meets twice a year, but have a committee or
commission departmentale who meet every month & keep a sharp
lookout on the prefect, carrying any complaints to the minister
of the interior, through their Senators & deputies. The wealthy
bourgeois are now generally against the Republic, & therefore
the prefects hold on public opinion is much less than formerly
and tends to decrease. In theory the minister appoints the prefects absolutely, but Senators & Reps exercise much influence &
can by combining secure the removal of an obnoxious prefect
which of course tends greatly to make him dependent and to
diminish his power. The *conseils* have power to appropriate
money to the extent of the taxes, and with the consent of the
ministry, through the prefect, of 'centimes additionels,' but cannot get into debt without a special act of the legislature[."]

Of course the general system has changed a great deal. Under
the empire the prefects had great power, and the central govt
interfered in everything, but the legislature is getting the upper

hand with a most promising tendency in the direction of our spoils system, and the condition of local self government must be silently changing very much from what it was twenty years ago.

I don't know as I have told you anything, but if you will put any farther definite questions I will try to answer them. My sister thanks you for your kind remembrance, and joins me in hoping that we may see you again in this part of the country[.] I hope also you are preparing another book and wish I had the courage to emulate you

Very sincerely yours   Gaml. Bradford

ALS (WP, DLC) with WWhw notation on env.: "Ans. Dec. 27, 1886."

¹ Pierre Larousse, *Grand Dictionnaire Universel* (17 vols., Paris, 1865-1900), XIII, 59-60.

² An Ex-Secretary, "Six Months of Prefecture under Gambetta," *Fraser's Magazine*, New Series, VI (Nov. 1872), 651-66.

³ Philip Gilbert Hamerton, *Round My House: Notes of Rural Life in France in Peace and War* (London, 1876).

⁴ Eustace Clare Grenville Murray, *High Life in France under the Republic* (London, 1884).

To John Barbee Minor

My dear Mr. Minor,   Bryn Mawr, Pa., 20 Dec., 1886.

An absence from home of several days has prevented my acknowledging sooner the receipt of your very kind letter of the 13th inst. I am most sincerely obliged to you for sparing me the time for so full and satisfactory an answer to my inquiries; and I am much indebted to you for the copy of your pamphlet on the Hist'y of the University which accompanied your letter. I shall take great pleasure in reading it; and I am sure that its contents, together with the hints given in your letter, will be of the greatest assistance to Prof. James.

I value very highly your remarks bearing upon the subject-matter of my 'Congressional Government.' I certainly join most heartily in your hope that Mr. Cleveland's example of courage and public principle will prove to our politicians the value, as means towards *success* as well as towards a good conscience and a good reputation, of virtue and sense; and I do not think the hope a vain one, if only Mr. Cleveland keep near enough the standard of most of his early acts. He seems to me to have made some sad mistakes within the past few weeks—mistakes which have put his influence for good in great peril: but I cannot believe that they were more than mistakes,—that they were deliberate departures from the principles he set out to establish.

With the warmest regards, and with renewed wishes for the continuance of your good health,—as well as renewed thanks for your great kindness,

Most sincerely Yours,   Woodrow Wilson

ALS (Minor Papers, ViU).

From Horace Elisha Scudder

My dear Wilson   Cambridge, Mass 30 Decbr. 1886

This is not a letter but only a friendly greeting at the close of the year. You brought me a good deal of pleasure in it by your letters and though I never answered your last[1] it was not for lack of interest, but because it came when I was obliged to give all my thought and time to the work which occupied me till late in the fall,—a new edition of Longfellow. It was not in itself all absorbing, but it came on top of abundant work and effectually quenched all aspirations for 'something more to do.'

I hope your scheme is rounding and filling itself out in your mind, and that you find yourself nearer practical issue. We wander through the woods in such matters a long time often before we come into the open field.

Can you tell me anything of the qualifications of E. J. James of the University of Penna to conduct a series analogous to Macmillan's English Citizen?[2] Has he staying powers? has he sound judgment? has he tact in dealing with men? I ask in confidence. He has proposed such a venture, and while I have a high impression of his attainments I know next to nothing of him personally, and personality counts for a good deal in such editorial work.

Mr. Gam Bradford spoke warmly of you to me the other day. You have good friends here and you must let us see you oftener.

I am ever,   Sincerely yours   H. E. Scudder

ALS (WP, DLC) with WWhw notation on env.: "Ans. upon receipt."
  [1] WW to H. E. Scudder, July 10, 1886.
  [2] For the English Citizen Series, see WW to R. Bridges, Oct. 28, 1882, n. 7, Vol. 2.

From Winthrop Saltonstall Scudder

Dear Sir: Cambridge. Dec. 31st., 1886.

I am connected with the firm of Houghton, Mifflin & Co. who publish your "Congressional Government," in which I have been much interested. I take the liberty of addressing you on the subject of this letter feeling sure that you will be interested in the question.

I live in Brookline, which has a population of 10,000, and a valuation of over 30 million. Our tax rate this year is $10.40, we disburse $600,000 annually, and enjoy all the conveniences of modern civilization.

However, we have had reason recently to realize evils which must come from large town meetings, where the demagogues or bosses can for their own ends influence or control the votes of the "great unwashed" by simply threatening them with loss of work.

No inducements or threats can either interest or bring out an equal number of well-to-do voters when occasion demands; although numerically they greatly out-number the "G.U." We have 1600 odd voters. Until we reach the 12,000 limit, we cannot, of course, have a city government, and even then we are not sure that a city government is desirable. In fact, the signs of the times seem to point to giving up the Common Council and retaining only the Upper Branch and Mayor. Waltham, as you probably know, is now trying this experiment, and it is also on trial I believe in other States. The objection to this, it seems to me, is that by delegating the conduct of the government to so few, another evil, one of the greatest curses of our political system is encouraged, viz., the apathy of the ordinary voter, who feels that by casting his vote once a year he washes his hands of all responsibility or interest in political affairs. When, however, some startling disclosure of fraud is made he is excited for a time, but soon falls back into his apathetic mood.

Is there any help for this? Is not a system which includes the largest number consistent with good government more desirable? You have heard doubtless of the "Quincy method," so called, originated by John Quincy Adams and his brother Charles Francis within a few years. The town of Quincy has 16,000 inhabitants, which of course entitles them to city government. They are still adhering however, to town government, with the following modification: The Moderator at the first annual meeting, at which no business is done but the election of Town Officers, appoints fifteen representative men who together with the Selectmen form a committee to digest the Selectmen's report, and present the result of their discussions in print to the Town a few days before the adjourned Town Meeting, at which the articles in the warrant are taken up for discussion.

This was tried in Brookline last year, and the result was most satisfactory. Although this Committee has no authority the result of their discussion presented in printed form was so satisfactory to the voters that much unnecessary and thoughtless discussion was avoided, and in three hours we were able to accomplish business which in former years had required three or four adjourned meetings[.] The Moderator in appointing the Committee of fifteen was careful to include the principal debaters, who had an opportunity of relieving their minds in committee, and what is more important, of having their objections answered reasonably. The greatest advantage, however, of the Committee work was, that questions were discussed, on their merits, no appeal to the Galleries being possible. Except in a few minor points the troublesome debaters did not "kick over the traces" in the Town Meeting, but adhered to the decision of the Committee.

Mr. Adams in speaking of the working of the Committee in Quincy as most satisfactory, acknowledged that there was still danger ahead owing to the unmanageable size of the Town Meeting, and was much pleased with the following suggestion which has occurred to some of us in Brookline, and on which I should be glad to have your opinion:

In order to preserve the form of the Town Meeting, and to prevent the mob element from entering into the discussion of affairs, also to include the largest possible number consistent with good government in the Town Meeting, we propose to have each of the five Districts into which the Town is divided (there being five Selectmen) represented by, say, fifty voters who shall constitute the Town Meeting, to be elected at the same time with other Town Officers, making a body of 250 or 300 voters. This number seems to be the limit of a legislative body in France, Germany, our own country and England, where, although the membership of the House of Commons is over 600, the number for whom seats are provided, and who transact the business, is not much over 300.

We propose to continue the form of Town government; giving the Selectmen no additional power, and perhaps increasing the salary of the Chairman to, say, $3000, and of the others to $2000; but keeping the veto power still in the hands of the voters (the 250).

There may be insuperable objections to this form of government which have occurred to you. If you can find time to reply to this letter by or before Monday next, you will greatly oblige
    Yours very respectfully,   Winthrop S. Scudder

Kindly address me at Brookline, Mass.

TLS (WP, DLC).

To Horace Elisha Scudder

My dear Mr. Scudder,   Bryn Mawr, Pa. 1 Jany, 1887.

I am sincerely obliged to you for your note of Dec. 30, which reached me this morning. It does me an immense amount of good to feel that I have won your friendship, and to receive such tokens of your interest in me and my work.

Term time is so full of varied duties and so broken up by all sorts of interruptions that I cannot do much work on large tasks which must be done connectedly; but, my thoughts being on the look-out for suggestions and materials, and knowing what they want, many parts of my scheme are falling into shape: in some directions at least the 'woods' seem to be thinning out towards the open. My plan is so very big that much of its territory has as yet no very distinct geography in my mind: but my heart's in the exploration, and I shall push it steadily.

Meantime, since I cannot work directly upon my *magnum opus*, I am half inclined to write, as bits of leisure may allow, on lighter, more literary themes, in order to loosen the joints of my style and vary the paces of my mind. Although I have *spoken* hitherto only on political subjects, knowing that in that direction, if in any, my special aptitudes lay, my taste for all sorts of themes that afford outlooks over men's life and thought has often tempted me to try my hand at other topics; and I have been deterred only by a strong sense of the importance of concentration. The question with me now is, how much concentration is compatible with breadth—and how far limitation of topic entails poverty of style. The style being the personality of the work, must not the style speak many interests and wide and various aptitudes if the work is to gain admission to patrician society in literature?

But this is taking advantage of your sympathy, and is not answering your questions about Prof. James.

I cannot say that I know Prof. James well; but I have met him several times, and my impressions of him are of the pleasantest kind. Both his appearance and his manner commend him: I should expect everybody who did not become jealous of his good looks to like him thoroughly. I cannot say anything about his lasting powers—except that his *health* is, I understand, preserved only by watchful care. If clear-headedness and calm balance in speech and argument are the constituent elements of sound judgment, he has that; and if thorough agreeableness in conversational argument betokens tact, he has that. I should say that his personality was altogether attractive. So far as I can judge after so brief an acquaintance, he has excellent qualifications for the editorial work of which you speak.

He was talking with me the other day about his desire to edit such a series, and, although I was much in the position of one who sees his own schemes stolen, I could not help seeing from what he said that he was the man for the work—provided only he knew how to choose his writers.

Again thanking you for your kind note, I am
            Sincerely Yours,   Woodrow Wilson

ALS (Scudder Papers, MH).

To Philip Gilbert Hamerton[1]

My dear Sir: [Bryn Mawr, c. Jan. 4, 1887]

I trust that my presumption writing to you may seem the less egregious in your eyes because I am prompted to it not by any motive which you would condemn, but only by a pressing mental need. I am just now engaged in studying the present Constitution of France: but the only books on the subject I can obtain or hear of contain only the dry legal bones of the constitution and help me scarcely at all to a realization of its *daily life*. My pressing need is to see the French Const. alive and if the sight may be obtained through books, I want to obtain it before visiting France.[2] My studies of our own pol. insts. and those of Eng has shown me the marked difference between the living organisms and their counterfeit presentments in the would-be expositions of them.

I want to know to know [sic] what sort of a person, and how practically powerful, the Prefect is; what influences control his app. by the Min. of the Int., what his relations are with the society of the prov. capital—and esp. with the Senators and Deputies from his prov.;—what sort of persons, and how, considered, the members of the *conseil general* are—what their executive committee actually accomplish, the voting habits and temper of the people &c.—in brief the life of local govt wh. cannot be learned in the statutes,—the operation of the statutes[.] And I have ventured to write to you, not of course, to ask you to enlighten me on these heads, but to ask you to point me to some sources of information upon these things—whether in magazines, in pamphlets, in novels, or in books written directly to the point,— should you happen to know of any such. What you yourself say incidentally in "Round My House" of the social position of the sub-prefect is just of the sort of comment I want.

            [Sincerely yours,   Woodrow Wilson]

WWhwL (draft) (WP, DLC).

[1] Readers familiar with earlier volumes in this series will recognize Hamerton as one of Wilson's favorite authors at least from 1879 onward. For example, Wilson used Hamerton's *Round My House: Notes of Rural Life in France in Peace and War* extensively in writing "Self-Government in France," printed in Vol. 1, pp. 515-39. Or again, the first book that Wilson gave to Ellen Axson was Hamerton's *The Graphic Arts.* See Vol. 2, p. 390, n. 1.

[2] Wilson abandoned his plans to go to Europe a few days later, when Ellen discovered that she had conceived.

From Winthrop Saltonstall Scudder

Dear Mr. Wilson: [Cambridge, Mass.] Jan. 11th., 1887.

Thank you for your very kind note in reply to mine so hastily written, and also for your expression of interest in the subject, and promise of writing out your ideas at length. There is no subject, it seems to me, of such importance at the present time in relation to the fundamental principle of government. It seems to me that the influence of the town meeting is more far reaching in its results than the unthinking man will acknowledge, and anything that can be done to preserve its central principles and graft them on to our absurdly undemocratic city governments will do more to purify politics, encourage good government, and stimulate the interest of young men in politics, than any one thing. I enclose a supplement to our Brookline paper, which will show you the result of the working of our committee of fifteen last year. I also enclose last week's paper in which is a summary of the discussion at the last meeting of our club.

Thanking you again for your hearty interest and response, I am   Yours very truly,   Winthrop S. Scudder

TLS (WP, DLC). Enc.: clipping from the Brookline, Mass., *Chronicle*, April 14, 1886.

From Elizabeth Adams Erwin

My dear Mr Wilson—   Morganton N. C. Jan 11th/87

Your letter recd. last night. I consulted Dr Moran this morning & he advises that you will have the enclosed prescription freshly filled, & try it thouroughly for a wk. If it fails then, consult a physician who makes women his special subject of study.[1] While in some cases there is no relief to be obtained, it is worth a hard fight[.] The little pills are to be taken about an hour after the capsules, if she suffers from that dreadful debility & pain in her back that is usually an accompaniment. I will mark the prescriptions, capsules 1, pills 2, so you can tell about them.

I certainly hope & pray she may experience *at least* some relief. As Dr. Moran says it is worth at least a thourough trial.

Dear Ellie I wonder if anywhere in the world there is another woman as sweet as patient as lovely. Not one word of repining, not one complaint in all her letter. If possible it would make us love her more than before. I will go up now, & get the prescriptions & enclose them in time for the mid-day mail, so that there may not be one moments unnecessary delay. Love & a kiss for dear little Margaret & for my precious friend. With warmest regards for yrself in which Mr. Erwin joins me, I am,

    Yours most sincerely   Lizzie Adams Erwin

ALS (WP, DLC).
  ¹ Ellen was already having a difficult time during the first stage of her pregnancy.

From Joseph Ruggles Wilson

My precious Son—   Clarksville, January 12th 1887.

I have thought of you so often and so much—and have in fancy conversed with you in hours so many—as to have blinded me to the fact that I had not *written* to you: not even when the New Year came in with its suggestions of good will. Pardon the seeming negligence—and now take for yourself and for Ellie (to say nothing of the amorphous lump known to a yet humble history as Margaret the Wonderful) all that can be said of the season's gratulations when most they thrill with honest love. Ah, however large the love that goes out of the hearts here to the responsive hearts there, there is always enough left to freight a Pennsylvania R. R. train.

The report which you gave us of your success at the Century Club added not to our love except to make it a still *prouder* experience. We had seen no notice of that night's story except a brief paragraph in "The World" which, after uttering ten or twelve lines touching Mr. McCarthy's address, added that it was "followed by a few remarks from Prof. Woodrow Wilson" and from somebody else whose name I have forgotten.¹ I suppose that this boasting journal had no reporter present, and got its information from some individual of the long-eared breed whose auditory nerve twanged only to the noted Irishman's sentences. I have wished that your own account of the scene, and especially of your share therein, had been fuller, by telling us what particular points you elaborated, how the audience at large seemed to be affected, and when in the course of your oration the applause was most emphatic. Yet, by leaving so much to our imagination, you well knew that we would fill the gaps with all the ecstasies of our own appreciation; and accordingly we clapped our hands and heeled the floor amazingly: with many an interjected 'God bless the noble boy' which it might have done your soul good to hear! . . .

As for myself, I am ding-donging theology and Greek exegesis into dull brains—and sighing over the poor prospects of the church's oncoming ministry. Surely God *does* make use of the weak things to confound the mighty!

Good-night, my beloved son. The other two join this third one in sending—well you know what—to dear Ellie and yourself.

Your affectionate & ever more affectionate   Father.

ALS (WP, DLC) with WWhw notation on env.: "Ans. Jany 23/87."
    ¹ Wilson's report of his "success" was apparently the only extensive one ever written, for his comments on Justin McCarthy's speech before the Nineteenth Century Club were largely or altogether ignored by the major New York dailies. The *New York Times,* December 19, 1886, printed extracts from McCarthy's speech but did not mention Wilson. Dr. Wilson's quotation from the New York *World,* December 19, 1886, should have read: "Mr. Simon Sterne and Prof. Woodrow Wilson followed Mr. McCarthy in brief remarks." The *New York Tribune,* December 19, 1886, had a fairly full account of McCarthy's speech but about Wilson and Sterne said only: "The discussion was continued afterward with speeches by Simon Sterne and Woodrow Wilson."

From the Minutes of the Executive Committee of the Board of Trustees of the Johns Hopkins University

Johns Hopkins University, Baltimore, Jan. 17, 1887

At the meeting of the Executive Committee on Saturday last, the following minute was adopted:

It was voted that the Committee will favor the engagement of Mr. Woodrow Wilson as Lecturer at $500. per annum for a period of three years, provided that arrangements satisfactory to the Committee can be made.

A true copy.   T. R. Ball

HwS copy (MdBJ) enclosed in Herbert B. Adams to WW, Jan. 18, 1887, which is missing.

To Herbert Baxter Adams

My dear Dr. Adams,   Bryn Mawr, Pa., 21 Jany., 1887.

Your letter of Jany. 18 came promptly to hand. I thank you very much for having urged the matter forward so promptly. Considering the travelling expenses I would be put to in going down to Baltimore every week for twelve or thirteen weeks, the offer is rather less than I expected: but I see the advantages which it offers, provided 'prospects' are beyond it. Before giving any definite judgment about it, however, I want to see whether or not we have in mind the same *subject-matter* for the lectures. I understand the field to be *comparative public law*: i. e. administration, but administration put in its proper *constitutional* relations and seen in its proper constitutional perspective: in a word, the way in which the functions of government are performed in the various states of most importance. Am I right there?

I am negotiating with the authorities here as to what modifications it will be possible to make in my work next year with a view to letting in work once a week at the Hopkins. I could not afford, pecuniarily, to give up any of my salary here for a diminution of class duties; and, on the other hand, I could not afford, mentally, too [sic] *add* lectures such as I should expect to write for the Hopkins to the sum of full duties here. The only chance lies in the direction of making room for the same course— in its rudiments at least—here;—or in getting an assistant. Of the latter I fear there is small chance till year after next. But of course I shall let you know results, and shall make up the elements for a decision in the matter as soon as possible. With sincere regard,

Very truly Yours,   Woodrow Wilson

ALS (H. B. Adams Papers, MdBJ).

To Lucy Maynard Salmon

Dear Miss Salmon,   Cottage No. 2 [Bryn Mawr], 22 Jany., 1887.

When my will comes to be contested, the counsel for the contestants will find in you a valuable witness in seeking to prove mental incapacity on the part of the testator!

I don't know what becomes of my mind on Fridays: I practically have none; and, if, as was the case yesterday, important business is forced upon my attention, I am left with less than none.

If you wish, I shall be really glad to meet you *this afternoon*, at three o'clock—especially if by meeting you I can aid your preparation for your Washington trip,—which I think will be of real advantage to you.

Please take this as I mean it,—cordially and sincerely. In brief, pay me the compliment of taking me at my word.

Very truly Yours,   Woodrow Wilson

ALS (NPV).

To Robert Bridges

My dear Bobby,   Bryn Mawr, Jany 23/87

I have not answered your note of Jany 4[1] before because Mrs. Wilson has been quite sick ever since it came, and I have not had the heart to write to anybody. She is considerably better now, however, and I can drop you a line or two.

I was deeply disappointed that the Scribner scheme fell through, I confess. It seemed to me an opening into the sort of thing you need, now that you've gotten all the nerve and skill and knowledge that a great newspaper office can give. But of course you can afford to wait, and your star is certainly rising. I am sincerely glad that your head is all right again. What you told me alarmed me just a little. All right again in your present grip, you can wait serenely for a new handle to offer itself:—and I shall wait, my dear Bobby, on developments in your fortunes with almost as much solicitude as you can feel yourself. I value your confidence, therefore, most deeply.

My own plans have undergone a radical change since I saw you. The state of Mrs. Wilson's health will prevent our going to Europe this year—and recent developments in my work seem to promise to delay our going for some years to come. I am promised an assistant here next year, so that I may confine myself for the most part to my own special field of political science: and I expect to add to my work here some lecturing at the Johns Hopkins. I am invited to deliver 25 lectures there (two a week, probably, for 13 weeks) on administration, or comparative public law—the functions and organs of govt.,—my favorite field, and hope to be able to do so with little or no extra work by delivering the same, or a similar, course here to a class of graduate students. Thirteen weeks is less than half a college year—and I have been wondering whether Princeton would not like to hear the same lectures during the other half year (Friday afternoons and Saturday mornings) at the same price—$500. What do you think? Are they not beginning to affect these 'lectureships' there? It would round out my scheme nicely. My contract with the J. H. U., as here, will be for 3 years—the least they will agree to.

With much love,

As ever Your aff. friend,   Woodrow Wilson

ALS (WC, NjP).
[1] It is missing.

From Richard Heath Dabney

My dear Tom: Bloomington, Ind., Jan. 25th 1887.

My conscience pricked me no little when your most welcome letter of the 21st inst. reached me yesterday.[1] For your November letter[2] was *not* lost on the way, but was received & read with the greatest interest, and certainly deserved a far prompter reply than it has met with. . . .

And now for the question of your going to Germany. It is a very hard question to answer, and I feel great hesitancy in expressing any opinion at all, since I know that whatever opinion I do express must be of exceedingly doubtful value. But still I will do what I can, and merely warn you to be very careful about the value you set upon the crude advice I have to give.

When I was in Germany, my expenses, exclusive of cost of ocean-passage, were *less* than four hundred and fifty dollars a year; and I lived well—though by no means in "style." That is to say, I avoided the "swell" localities of the cities I lived in, & especially those localities which are frequented by rich Americans & English. But in all three cities where I stayed for any time (Munich, Berlin & Heidelberg) I had a more commodious & better furnished room than I had ever had at home or than I have since had. For example, there was a comfortable sofa in every room I had, and in Berlin & Heidelberg I had handsome desks with pigeon-holes, drawers & doors. My food was abundant & wholesome, and was washed down with the foaming "Solace of Gambrinus" in whatever quantities that were dictated by the thirst of the moment. In regard to amusements, I saw more plays & heard more operas & concerts than ever before or since. Shakespeare is played, I believe, as much in Germany as in England & America combined, & I saw a large number of his plays, both tragedies & comedies, most excellently put upon the stage. I revelled in the music—Bilse's concerts in Berlin (like Theodore Thomas') costing only twelve cents (50 Pfennige) for *students*. Then, too, I did a good deal of travelling considering the smallness of the amount spent annually. I will leave out of consideration what I spent in Paris & London after I left Germany & was on my way home. But *during* the three years of my stay in Germany I took trips to Switzerland and Italy (Como, Milan, Lodi, Piacenza, Parma, Modena, Bologna, Florence & Rome) to Austria (Vienna & Salzburg with the surrounding country on a walking tour) & saw several cities in Germany besides the three in which I resided (e.g. Cologne Mayence [Mainz], Coblentz,

Augsburg, Nürnberg, Dresden, Bamberg.) When in Italy I drank wine at two meals a day, & in Munich I never swallowed one single drop of water, while in Berlin & Heidelberg I also touched this fluid but seldom, save for ablutionary purposes.

Now, when you consider all this, and reflect that *all* my expenses, both necessaries & luxuries, cost me less than $450 a year on the average during the three years, you will see, I think, that a fellow *can* live in Germany at very little expense & nevertheless have a first-rate time. . . .

And now for your second letter. To begin with, old fellow, let me express to you my hearty thanks for the kind & cordial proposal you make me. It is just like you to be always on the look-out for the interests of your friends; and the prospect of being associated with you in my work is one that tempts me mightily. Still, on the whole, I hardly think it would be wise for me to give up my position here (in case the trustees, which means Jordan, want me to stay), where I shall probably get $1500 next year, & where living is very cheap (my room costs $2.00 a week, & my board, which is as good as the town affords, $3.00 a week) for a salary of only $600 in a place where board is so much higher. For although Jordan is a snake-in-the-grass & a hypocrite of the rankest kind (as I am now still more convinced than before I came) it is not necessary for me to have very much to do with him; and although the average Hoosier is far from being a savoury animal, I am nevertheless of the opinion that this place is on the rise & is destined to become much more important than it is. Unless something better turns up, therefore, I think I had better stick to what I have got. . . . Well, as this is my last sheet of paper, I will wind up my epistle with sincere regards to Mrs Wilson & a kiss for the baby.

Ever your friend R. H. Dabney

P.S. The "Program" you mentioned hasn't arrived yet.

R. H. D.

ALS (WP, DLC).

1 It is missing. In it Wilson wrote about the possibility of an associateship at Bryn Mawr for Dabney at $600 a year.

2 WW to R. H. Dabney, Nov. 7, 1886.

From Herbert Baxter Adams

Dear Dr. Wilson: Baltimore, Jan. 25 1887

The mechanism of government is the idea. For short, men call it Administration or Comparative Administrative Law. I hope you will be able to arrange matters at Bryn Mawr. The combination strikes me as an *ideal* one for the next three years. You will need to spare yourself & advance gradually. 25 *dictetions* yearly will not be such heavy work as some institutions might require of you. While I would not dissuade you from accepting a full professorship in a real University or advise any measures to restrain you, I would simply remind you that *Phila. Balto. & Washington* afford the best vantage-ground in America for your studies & mine. I have a large idea in mind respecting a revival of Polit. Education in this country. That idea has just been approved by Secretary Lamar & will soon be published in an edition of 25,000 copies.[1] You had better camp near Washington.[2]

Very truly,   H. B. Adams

ALS (WP, DLC) with WWhw outline of course in administration on env.

[1] United States Bureau of Education, Circular of Information Number 1, 1887, *The College of William and Mary: A Contribution to the History of Higher Education, with Suggestions for Its National Promotion,* by Herbert Baxter Adams (Washington, 1887). In this circular, Adams reviewed the history of the College of William and Mary as a school for statesmen. He then went on to propose the establishment of a federal "civil academy," or institute of administration and public affairs, in Washington.

[2] Adams, in the circular just cited, also described the Johns Hopkins as the leading training school for administrators and public officials in the United States. The university, he added, enjoyed an ideal location for such service to the nation because it was situated between the North and South, had intimate connections with the West, and was close to Washington. What he had in mind, although he did not develop his plan in detail in this circular, was the establishment of a school of administration and public affairs at the Johns Hopkins which would have close relations with, if not in fact control, the "civil academy" in Washington. As the documents will soon reveal, Adams also planned for Wilson and Elgin R. L. Gould to head the Hopkins school of public affairs.

To Richard Heath Dabney

My dear Heath,   Bryn Mawr, 25 Jany., '87.

I am afraid that this letter will only cross your answer to my last, and so throw the correspondence into some confusion: but the sooner I put you into possession of all the facts the better—so I go ahead 'anyhow.' First of all, then, you can certainly get board here for $7 *per* week. Second, the Executive Committee of our Board of Trustees has definitely sanctioned the 'supposed case' put in my last letter and thus made it an official plan. The reason that they cannot offer more than $600 for next year is that they will have to organize at once a department of Physics and will have to expend some four or five thousand dollars in building the necessary room, obtaining apparatus, paying a teacher, &c. After next year they would, of course, hope to pay more—though, like the cautious Quakers they are, they never *promise anything,* but only *do* as they have the means. It amounts to the same thing in the end.

They adopt here the gradations of rank in the Faculty which are in vogue at the Johns Hopkins. There are first 'Associates,' engaged generally for any term from one to two years; 'Associate-Professors' (the rank to which I have now advanced) who are usually contracted with for three years; and 'Professors,' who hold during good behaviour. Your title would be 'Associate'; and, after all, for five hours work *per* week, $600 would be about in proportion to the salary usually given here for full work by an 'Associate.' It's little enough—especially as offered to a man who is already getting $400 more; but it is more than we are to get one or two other assistants for next year, who are men with the most thorough University equipment, but who are willing to take next to nothing (one of them $400, I believe) for the sake of obtaining congenial work *with prospects.*

The $7 *per* week board means just as good board as that which costs more—the only difference is a room in the third story instead of in the first or second: and the room seems to me as good as any. If Mrs. Wilson and I can manage to keep house next year we shall invite you—in case you decide to come—to take a *room* at our house at any rate, even if Mrs. Wilson should not be equal to taking you as a boarder.

Now, my dear fellow, I will not *advise* you to say 'I'll come,' because I could not for the life of me decide whether I was giving the advice selfishly or unselfishly. I may note a few considerations, however. I sh. say, in the first place, that the *prospects* for salary here would, on the whole, be quite as good as where you are. The conditions of work here are certainly very pleasant; and in history work—especially American history—the Phila. libraries are not inadequate,—are, indeed, very good. Then, too, this is "the East,"—which, from the student's and literary man's point of view, is a great advantage. One can lecture five hours a week and still have *some* time left for his own private enterprises of study. Altogether, I've come to the conclusion that I could hardly find a better place for work, until the special chair in *comparative politics* for which I am waiting turns up. "Professing" is not just the ideal life even for a student: but I suspect that there is as little vexatious friction about it here as anywhere. Since one must struggle with classes, he ought to be thankful for so comfortable a berth—where the classes are docile, intelligent, and willing,— where the administration is honest, straightforward, and liberal,—

and where there's sympathy to be found in one's work for the searching.

I wont say more till I here [sic] from you. Mrs. Wilson sends warm regards; with which is sent the love of
         Your affectionate friend,   Woodrow Wilson

ALS (Wilson-Dabney Correspondence, ViU).

From Richard Heath Dabney

My dear Tom: Bloomington, Indiana. Jan. 27th, 1887.

I have once more to thank you for a letter and for the thoughtful interest in my welfare which you have shown in obtaining the consent of the Executive Committee of the Board of Trustees to the proposal you made in your previous letter.

Before I make any answer to this official proposal of the Committee, let me tell you something which I didn't have time or space to tell you in the letter I wrote you the other day. I believe I *did* remark in a parenthetical way that I was exceeding weary of single misery—or words to that effect. But I didn't mention any definite plan of ridding myself of the said single misery. I *have* a plan, however, for all that. For, to tell you the truth, I am—engaged![1] . . .

Now, after reading this, you will understand better than before how it is that even the enticing inducement to be your fellow-worker is not quite sufficient to reconcile me to a salary of $600 with prospects of a thousand the ensuing year. To a fellow who is longing to get married, "prospects" are very poor encouragement. Possibly I may be over-cautious, but I don't think I could risk marriage on less than $1500 a year, even in a place where living is cheap. My sweetheart has nothing, and I have nothing but my salary; so that, if I am not to be compelled to defer my wedding to an indefinite period, it is very important for me to get at least a fairly good salary, even though I be obliged to be connected with a hypocrite like Jordan. Still, I should like you to let me know how long a time you would give me to decide on your proposition. Jordan appears to be satisfied with my work, & has told me as much, but he *may* be plotting to put me out for some reason unknown to me. Now, suppose such to be the case, & suppose furthermore that I fail to get the chair at the Univ. of Va. when the Board of Visitors meet there at the end of June. Would there still be a chance left for me at Bryn Mawr? Of course I don't want you to hold the place open for me any longer than you think expedient for the interests of the college, but I merely ask for information. It is after midnight, & so I will say good bye for the present.

Your sincere friend,   R. H. Dabney.

ALS (WP, DLC).
¹ To Mary A. Bentley of Richmond, Va.

To Robert Bridges

My dear Bobby,   Bryn Mawr, 30 Jany, '87.

Hurrah for the Scribner offer!¹ The very thing I was most wishing you could have: the very thing, it seems to me, most suitable to your present needs! I am sincerely and profoundly delighted, my dear fellow, and trust that you will very soon be fully installed. I shall be deeply interested to learn how the new harness feels at first. The only thing to be desired now is, that Burlingame² prove an agreeable, satisfactory 'chief.' You are certainly altogether to be envied, if he turn out to your taste: for your berth will then be of the sort I have always more than half wished for myself, as of all means of making a living the most dignified and improving, for a man of literary turn. The influence which one may exert upon the development of the literature of the country from such a post is certainly very great and extremely important. I can't help thinking that the part 'Harpers' and the 'Century' have been playing in that regard is an unworthy one on the whole. Aside from the fiction, the 'articles,' in 'Harpers' especially, are timely in the least elevated sense of that term. They are not such pieces as a man with serious literary ambitions, and with true views of what writing demands as an art, into which only the most earnest thought and the most chastened feeling ought to be allowed to enter, would care to put his name to. Of course to whet my ambition I should want a *Fortnightly*, a *Contemporary*, or a *Nineteenth Century*—in which one could *test* his thought before putting it into final shape: but meantime such a magazine as the 'Atlantic' is and 'Scribners' promises to be—shy of no contribution because it is not on the labour question, glad to publish anything, whatever the topic, if only it embody fresh thought and have the ring of true literary metal—does the greatest service to literature: and I envy the man who can contribute to such a policy.

My own plans have not fully crystalized yet: I shall write you when they are in final shape.

Mrs. Wilson sends warm regards and joins me in hearty congratulations on your deserved good fortune. With much love,
Your affectionate friend   Woodrow Wilson

P.S. I should think it extremely unlikely that Sloane would leave his delightful Princeton establishment, and all the rest, to go to Columbia; but, if he did resign, do you think I ought to try for the place? The work of the chair is largely routine undergraduate work in history: and what I am waiting for is a chance to give all my time to political science. If our plans here ripen, I shall be able to do that to a large extent here, and so shall, with one hand on the Hopkins, be enabled to wait for the University chair I want and need, making strides of preparation meanwhile. What do you think? If I could get such a call, it would give me a still further lift here; but ought I to seek it just as my work is turning to my own fields here? And not only here but at the Johns Hopkins also.

But more of these things another time.

Yours as ever,   W. W.

Thank you very much, Bobby, for the suggestion made to Dick Harlan.[3] You are the most *executive* man I know.

ALS (WC, NjP).
[1] Bridges had just been appointed assistant editor of the new *Scribner's Magazine*. His letter conveying the news is missing.
[2] Edward Livermore Burlingame, with Charles Scribner's Sons since 1879 and editor of *Scribner's Magazine*.
[3] Richard Davenport Harlan, Princeton, '81, pastor of the First Presbyterian Church of New York.

Notes for Lectures on French History

[c. Feb. 1-c. June 4, 1887]

Contents:
(1) Notes for lectures in French history, mainly in WWsh, listed according to WW's order: "*The Course of French History*," "*The Country and the People*," "*Germanic France*," "*The Northmen*," "*The Falling Apart or Feudalization of F.*," "*Rise of the Capets*," "*The Four Royal Houses*," "*The English in France. (I.)*," "*The Crusades*," "*Persecution of the Albigensians*," "*Louis IX*," "*The 'Estates,'*" "*The Religious Orders of Knighthood: the Templars in France*," "*Achievements of the House of Capet*," "*The English in France. (2)*," "*Hundred Years War: (1) English Successes*," "*Hundred Years War: (2) French Fortunes and the English Reverses*," "*Hundred Years War: Results in France Chas. VII and Louis XI*," "*Louis XI*," "*Charles VIII (1483-1498)*," "*Foreign Policy, 1498-1618*," "*The Huguenot Wars (1562-1610)*," "*1624. Richelieu 1642*," "*Louis XIV. 1643-1715*," "*Louis XV and Louis XVI*," "*Causes of the Revolution*," "*The Revolution*," "*Napoleon

and the Napoleonic Constitution," "From Napoleon to Napoleon III," "The Third Republic," "The Present Constitution of France ('87)," and "Résumé."

(2) Outlines and charts, mainly in WWhw, accompanying most notes for lectures.

Loose sheets (WP, DLC).

Notes for Lectures on the Renaissance and Reformation

[c. Feb. 1-c. June 4, 1887]

Contents:

(1) Notes for lectures in a course in the Italian Renaissance and German Reformation, mainly in WWsh, listed according to WW's order: *"Before the Renaissance," "The Preparation of Italy. (A) Political," "Machiavelli"* (transcript printed at Feb. 8, 1887), *"Italy's Intellectual Preparation for the R.," "The Revival of Learning," "Dante, Petrarch, Boccaccio," "Lorenzo de Medici; Poliziano," "1474. Ariosto. 1533," "Torquato Tasso. 1544-1595," "Art:—Painting and Sculpture," "Representative Painters [Giotto]," "Art: Representative Artists: Lionardo da Vinci," "Michael Angelo (1475-1564)," "The Venetian Painters," "Portugal and Spain—Discovery," "Renaissance—Reformation," "Luther and Zwingli"* (transcript printed at April 12, 1887), *"Calvin—Geneva, France* (transcript printed at April 14, 1887), *"The English Reformation: Colet, Erasmus, Th. Cromwell," "1618 The Thirty Years' War 1648,"* and *"Résumé."*

(2) Some outlines of lectures and bibliographical references, mainly in WWhw.

Loose sheets (WP, DLC).

Wilson's Copy for the Bryn Mawr Catalogue, 1887-88

[c. Feb. 1, 1887]

HISTORY.

The courses indicated suggest the topical plan of instruction which is to be followed. The histories of Greece and Rome are taken as representative of ancient history, those of France and England as representative of mediaeval and modern history; and in following these special lines the work of the classes will consist largely in the preparation by individuals of reports on specific topics and important episodes in the histories studied. These reports will be founded, not only upon the text-books used, but also upon all the standard authorities available.

Constant text-book drill will be combined with instruction by means of frequent lectures, whose object will be to give life to the narrative of the text-book used in recitation, by recounting the most important contemporary events in the history of other countries, and by pointing out the chief and most memorable characteristics of the periods studied, as well as the philosophical connection of leading facts and tendencies. The general purpose of the lectures will be to group and explain facts separated in the narrative, subordinating them to broader views of history.

The courses on the Italian Renaissance and the German Reformation will be lecture courses.

Each year's work will be introduced by a brief course of lectures on the philosophy of history and on methods of study.

First Year.
(Ancient History—Minor Course.)

Major Course.   I. History of Greece. *Five hours a week on alternate weeks during the first semester.*

In this course, lectures are given on such topics as the reforms of Solon and of Cleisthenes, the causes of the Persian invasion, the character and influence of the Confederacy of Delos. As the history of the popular states of Greece turns largely upon the individual characters and influence of leading men, class reports are required on the antecedents, lives, and work of the principal statesmen, dramatists, and orators.

II. History of Rome. *Five hours a week on alternate weeks during the first semester, and five hours weekly throughout most of the second semester.*

In this course the lectures deal with such topics as the sources of Roman history, the causes, means, and ends of Roman conquests, Roman provincial administration, agrarian troubles, the characters, aims, and reforms of the Gracchi.

In both courses, text-book drill is made prominent, but more especially in Roman history, because the internal history of Rome, down to the time of the empire, turns upon class struggles and consequent legal and constitutional reforms which can be mastered in no other way.

The plan of conducting work in both Greek and Roman history simultaneously, the two courses alternating with each other, week by week, is adopted in order that the histories of the two countries may run parallel up to the point where Greek history is merged into Roman by conquest, with a view to enable the student when hearing lectures to perceive for herself contrasts and likenesses.

III. European History from the fall of the Western Empire to the establishment of the Empire of Charles the Great. *Lectures five hours a week during the last weeks of the second semester.*

Second Year.
(*Modern History—Minor Course.*)

History of France. *Three times weekly, on alternate weeks throughout the year.*

History of England. *Three times weekly, on alternate weeks throughout the year.*

Italian Renaissance and German Reformation. *Twice weekly during the first semester.*

Lectures on special topics in American History. *Twice weekly during the second semester.*

The topics selected for the lectures on American history will be such as the following: the foundation of the colonies; the contest between England, Spain, and France for the possession of America; contrasts in colonial life and manners; the causes of the Revolution; the second war with Great Britain; the great westward migration; the Missouri compromise; the history of parties, with special reference to the rise and influence of the Federalist party.

Either year of the major course in history may be taken separately as a minor course.

Group. History and Political Science. Students that elect this group may take, as required studies, instead of one year of science and one year of history, one year of science and one year of French, German, Italian, or Spanish.

Two years of history may be taken without the course in political science, by electing one year of history as a minor course and a second year as a free elective.

POLITICAL SCIENCE.
First Year.
(*Minor Course.*)

Elements of Political Economy. (Text-book drill and lectures.) *Three times weekly throughout the year.* *Major Course.*

Origin and development of the State. (Fifteen lectures.) *Twice weekly during the first semester.*

Origin and development of law. (Ten lectures.) *Twice weekly during the first semester.*

History of Political Opinion. (Twenty-five lectures.) *Twice weekly during the second semester.*

Second Year.

(*Minor Course.*)

History of Political Institutions. (Lectures.) *Twice weekly throughout the year.*

English and American Constitutional History. (Lectures.) *Three times weekly during the first semester.*

American State Constitutions. (Fifteen lectures.) *Three times weekly during the second semester.*

European Political Revolutions. (Twenty lectures.) *Three times weekly during the second semester.*

ADVANCED COURSE IN HISTORY AND POLITICS.

The following advanced course in History and Politics will be offered by Dr. Woodrow Wilson, to graduate students, in the year 1887-88. It has been planned not only with reference to the needs of those who desire to prepare themselves to be teachers in these branches, but also as a useful preparatory course for students that are looking forward to special studies in law.

1st Semester.

The History, Functions, and Organs of Government. Fifty lectures. *Four times weekly.*

2nd Semester.

1. Nature and Influence of Roman Law. Ten lectures.
2. Comparative Constitutional History. Twenty-five lectures.
3. Growth of Modern Nationalities. Eight lectures.
4. History of Political Economy. Ten lectures. *Four times weekly.*

Throughout the year one hour a week will be given to the meetings of a Seminary at which reports will be read of graduate work done privately upon topics collateral with those of the lectures.

The modifications of the course in subsequent years will be announced at a later time.

Printed in *Bryn Mawr College. Program. 1887-88* (Philadelphia, 1887), pp. 33-36.

An Essay on Adam Smith

[*c. Feb. 1, 1887*]

An Old Master

Why is it that no one has ever written an essay on the art of academic lecturing and its many notable triumphs? In some

quarters new educational canons have spoken an emphatic condemnation of the college lecture, and it would seem to be high
time to consider its value, as illustrative of an art about to be
lost, if not as examplary of forces to be retained, even if modified.
Here are some of the questions which thrust themselves forward
in the topic: Are not our college class-rooms, in being robbed of
the old-time lecture, and getting instead a science-brief of *data*
and bibliography, being deprived also of that literary atmosphere
which once pervaded them? We are unquestionably gaining in
thoroughness; but are we gaining in thoughtfulness? We are
giving to many youths an insight, it may be profound, into specialties; but are we giving any of them a broad outlook?

There was too often a paralysis of dulness in the old lecture,
or, rather, in the old lecturer; and written lectures, like history
and fashion in dress, have an inveterate tendency to repeat themselves; but, on the contrary, there was often a wealth of power
in the studied discourse of strong men. Men bent upon instruct-
ing and inspiring—and there were many such—had to master that
central secret of literature and spoken utterance,—the secret of
style. Their only instrument of conquest was the sword of pene-
trating speech. Some of the subtlest and most lasting effects of
genuine oratory have gone forth from secluded lecture-desks into
the hearts of quiet groups of students; and it would seem to be
good policy to endure much indifferent lecturing—watchful
trustees might reduce it to a minimum—for the sake of leaving
places open for the men who have in them the inestimable force
of chastened eloquence. For one man who can impart an undying
impulse there are several score, presupposing the requisite training, who can impart a method; and here is the well-understood
ground for the cumulating disfavor of college lecturing and the
rapid substitution of "laboratory drill": but will not higher education be cut off from communion with the highest of all
forces—the force of personal inspiration in the field of great
themes of thought—if you interdict the literary method in the
class-room?

I am not inclined, however, to consume very many words in
insisting on this point, for I believe that educators are now dealing more frankly with themselves than ever before, and that so
obvious a point will by no means escape full recognition before
reforming methods of college and university instruction take
their final shape. But I also believe that it is very well to be
thinking about the matter meanwhile, in order that this force
may be getting ready to come fully militant into the final battle

for territory. The best way of compassing this end would seem to be the studying of the old masters of the art of learned discourse. With Lanfranc one could get the infinite charm of the old monastic school life; with Abelard, the undying excitement of philosophical and religious controversy; with Colet, the fire of reforming zeal; with Blackstone, the satisfactions of clarified learning. But Bec and Paris and Oxford have by no means monopolized the masters of this art, and I should prefer, for the nonce at least, to choose an exemplar from Scotland, and speak of Adam Smith. It will, no doubt, be possible to speak of him without going over again the well-worn ground of the topics usually associated with his great fame.

There is much, besides the contents of his published works, to draw to Adam Smith the attention of those who are attracted by individual power. Scotchmen have long been reputed strong in philosophic doctrine, and he was a Scot of the Scots. But, though Scotland is now renowned for her philosophy, that renown is not of immemorial origin; it was not till the last century was well advanced that she began to add great speculative thinkers to her great preachers. Adam Smith, consequently, stands nearly at the opening of the greatest of the intellectual eras of Scotland; and yet by none of the great Scotch names, which men have learned since his day, has his name been eclipsed. The charm about the man consists, for those who do not regard him with the special interest of the political economist, in his literary method, which exhibits his personality and makes his works thoroughly his own, rather than in any facts about his eminency among Scotchmen. You bring away from your reading of Adam Smith a distinct and attractive impression of the man himself, such as you can get from the writings of no other author in the same field, and such as makes you wish to know still more of him. What was he like, and what was his daily life?

Unhappily, we know very little of Adam Smith as a man, and it may be deplored, without injustice to a respected name, that we owe that little to Dugald Stewart—the worst, because the most self-conscious, of biographers, whose stilted periods sometimes run a page without advancing the sense a line, and whose style, both of thought and of expression, is excellent to be avoided. Even from Dugald Stewart, however, we get a picture of Adam Smith which must please everyone who loves simplicity and genuineness. He was not, perhaps, a companionable man; he was much too absent-minded to be companionable; but he was, in the highest sense, interesting. His absent-mindedness was of that sort which indicates fulness of mind—a mind content, much of the time, to live within itself, indulging in those delights of quiet contemplation which the riches of a full mind can always command. Often he would open to his companions his mind's fullest confidences, and, with a rare versatility, lavish upon topics the most varied and diverse a wealth of information and illustration, always to the wondering delight of all who heard him.

Those who met Adam Smith in intimate intercourse are said to have been struck chiefly by the gentleness and benignity of his manner—traits which would naturally strike one in a Scotchman, for men of that unbending race are not often distinguished by easiness of temper or suavity of manner, but are generally both *fortiter in re et fortiter in modo*. His gentleness was, possibly, only one phase of that timidity which is natural to absent-minded men, and which was always conspicuous in him. That timidity made it rare with him to talk much. When he did talk, as I have said, his hearers marvelled at the ingenuity of his reasoning, at the constructive power of his imagination, at the comprehensiveness of his memory, at the fertility of his resources; but his inclination was always to remain silent. He was not, however, disinclined to public discourse, and it is chiefly to his unusual gifts as a lecturer that he seems to have owed his advancement in the literary, or, rather, in the university, world.

Acting upon the advice of Lord Kames, an eminent barrister and a man of some standing in the history of philosophy, he volunteered a course of lectures in Edinburgh almost immediately upon his return from Oxford; and the success of this course was hardly assured before he was elected to the chair of Logic in the University of Glasgow. In the following year he had the honor of succeeding to the chair of Moral Philosophy, once occupied by the learned and ingenious Hutcheson. He seems to have been at once successful in raising his new chair to a position of the very highest consideration. His immediate predecessor had been one Thomas Craigie, who has left behind him so shadowy a reputation that it is doubtless safe to conclude that his department was, at his death, much in need of a fresh infusion of life. This it received from Adam Smith. The breadth and variety of the topics upon which he chose to lecture, and the felicity, strength, and vitality of the exposition he gave them (we are told by one who had sat under him), soon drew to Glasgow "a multitude of students from a great distance" to hear him. His mastery of the art of academic lecturing was presently an established fact. It appears clear to me that his success was due to two things: the broad outlook of his treatment and the fine art of his style. His chair was Moral Philosophy; and "moral philosophy" seems to have been the most inclusive of general terms in the university usage of Scotland at that day, and, indeed, for many years afterward. Apparently it embraced all philosophy that did not directly concern the phenomena of the physical world, and, accordingly, allowed its doctors to give very free play to their tastes in their choice of subjects. Adam Smith, in Glasgow, could draw within the big family of this large-hearted philosophy not only the science of mental phenomena, but also the whole of the history and organization of society; just as, years afterward, John Wilson, in Edinburgh, could insist upon the adoption of something very like *belles-lettres* into the same generous and unconventional family circle.

Adam Smith sought to cover the field he had chosen with a fourfold course of lectures. First, he unfolded the principles of natural theology; second, he illustrated the principles of ethics in a series of lectures, which were afterward embodied in his published work on the *Theory of Moral Sentiments*; third, he discoursed on that branch of morality which relates to the administration of justice; and, last, coming out upon that field with which his name is now identified, he examined those political regulations which are founded, not upon principles of justice, but upon considerations of expediency, and which are calculated to increase the riches, the power, and the prosperity of the state. His own notes of his lectures he himself destroyed when he felt death approaching, and we are left to conjecture what the main features of his treatment were, from the recorded recollections of his pupils and from those published works which remain as fragments of the great plan. These fragments consist of the *Theory of Moral Sentiments*, the *Wealth of Nations*, and *Considerations Concerning the First Formation of Languages*; besides which there are, to quote another's enumeration, "a very curious history of astronomy, left imperfect, and another fragment on the history of ancient physics, which is a kind of sequel to that part of the history of astronomy which relates to ancient astronomy; then a similar essay on the ancient logic and metaphysics; then another on the nature and development of the fine, or, as he calls them, the imitative, arts, painting, poetry, and music, in which was meant to have been included a history of the theatre—all forming part, his executors tell us, 'of a plan he had once formed for giving a connected history of the liberal and elegant arts' ";—part, that is (to continue the quotation from Mr. Bagehot), of the

"immense design of showing the origin and development of cultivation and law; or . . . of saying how, from being a savage, man
rose to be a Scotchman."

The wideness of view and amazing variety of illustration that
characterized his treatment, in developing the several parts of
this vast plan, can easily be inferred from an examination of the
Wealth of Nations. "The *Wealth of Nations,*" declares Mr. Buckle,
from whom, for obvious reasons, I prefer to quote, "displays a
breadth of treatment which those who cannot sympathize with,
are very likely to ridicule. The phenomena, not only of wealth,
but also of society in general, classified and arranged under their
various forms; the origin of the division of labor, and the consequences which that division has produced; the circumstances
which gave rise to the invention of money, and to the subsequent
changes in its value; the history of those changes traced in different ages, and the history of the relations which the precious
metals bear to each other; an examination of the connection
between wages and profits, and of the laws which govern the rise
and fall of both; another examination of the way in which these
are concerned, on the one hand with the rent of land, and, on
the other hand, with the price of commodities; an inquiry into
the reason why profits vary in different trades, and at different
times; a succinct but comprehensive view of the progress of
towns in Europe since the fall of the Roman Empire; the fluctua-
tions, during several centuries, in the prices of the food of the
people, and a statement of how it is, that, in different stages of
society, the relative cost of meat and of land varies; the history
of corporation laws and of municipal enactments, and their bearing on the four great classes of apprentices, manufacturers,
merchants, and landlords; an account of the immense power and
riches formerly enjoyed by the clergy, and of the manner in
which, as society advances, they gradually lose their exclusive
privileges; the nature of religious dissent, and the reason why the
clergy of the established Church can never contend with it on
terms of equality, and, therefore, call on the State to help them,
and wish to persecute when they cannot persuade; why some
sects profess more ascetic principles, and others more luxurious
ones; how it was, that, during the feudal times, the nobles
acquired their power, and how that power has, ever since, been
gradually diminishing; how the rights of territorial jurisdiction
originated, and how they died away; how the sovereigns of
Europe obtained their revenue, what the sources of it are, and
what classes are most heavily taxed in order to supply it; the

cause of certain virtues, such as hospitality, flourishing in barbarous ages, and decaying in civilized ones; the influence of inventions and discoveries in altering the distribution of power among the various classes of society; a bold and masterly sketch of the peculiar sort of advantages which Europe derived from the discovery of America and of the passage round the Cape; the origin of universities, their degeneracy from the original plan, the corruption which has gradually crept over them, and the reason why they are so unwilling to adopt improvements, and to keep pace with the wants of the age; a comparison between public and private education, and an estimate of their relative advantages; these, and a vast number of other subjects, respecting the structure and development of society, such as the feudal system, slavery, emancipation of serfs, origin of standing armies and of mercenary troops, effects produced by tithes, laws of primogeniture, sumptuary laws, international treaties concerning trade, rise of European banks, national debts, influence of dramatic representations over opinions, colonies, poor-laws,—all topics of a miscellaneous character, and many of them diverging from each other,—all are fused into one great system, and irradiated by the splendor of one great genius. Into that dense and disorderly mass, did Adam Smith introduce symmetry, method, and law." In fact, it is a book of digressions—digressions characterized by more order and method, but by little more compunction, than the wondrous digressions of Tristram Shandy.

It is interesting to note that even this vast miscellany of thought, the *Wealth of Nations*, systematized though it be, was not meant to stand alone as the exposition of a complete system; it was only a supplement to the *Theory of Moral Sentiments;* and the two together constituted only chapters in that vast book of thought which their author would have written. Adam Smith would have grouped all things that concern either the individual or the social life of man under the several greater principles of motive and action observable in human conduct. His method throughout is, therefore, necessarily abstract and deductive. In the *Wealth of Nations,* he ignores the operation of love, of benevolence, of sympathy, and of charity in filling life with kindly influences, and concentrates his attention exclusively upon the operation of self-interest and expediency; because he had reckoned with the first-named motives in the *Theory of Moral Sentiments,* and he would not confuse his view of the economic life of man by again lugging these in where selfishness was unquestionably the predominant force. "The philosopher," he held, "is the man of speculation, whose trade is not to do anything, but to observe everything"; and certainly he satisfied his own definition. He does observe everything; and he stores his volumes full with the sagest practical maxims, fit to have fallen from the lips of the shrewdest of those Glasgow merchants in whose society he learned so much of the uses of his theories. But it is noticeable that none of the carefully noted facts of experience, which play so prominent a part on the stage of his argument, speaks of any other principle than the simple and single one that is the pivot of the part of his philosophy with which he is at the moment dealing. In the *Wealth of Nations*, for example, every apparent induction leads to self-interest, and to self-interest alone. In Mr. Buckle's phrase, his facts are subsequent to his argument; they are not used for demonstration, but for illustration. His historical cases, his fine generalizations, everywhere broadening and strengthening his matter, are only instances of the operation of the single abstract principle meant to be set forth.

When he was considering that topic in his course which has not come down to us in any of the remaining fragments of his lectures,—the principles of justice, namely,—although still always mindful of its relative position in the general scheme of his abstract philosophy of society, his subject led him, we are told, to speak very much in the modern historical spirit. He followed upon this subject, says the pupil already quoted, "the plan which seems to have been suggested by Montesquieu; endeavoring to trace the gradual progress of jurisprudence, both public and private, from the rudest to the most refined ages, and to point out the effects of those arts which contribute to subsistence, and to the accumulation of property, in producing corresponding improvements or alterations in law and government." In following Montesquieu, he was, of course, following one of the forerunners of that great school of philosophical students of history, which has done so much in our own time to clear away the fogs that surround the earliest ages of mankind, and to establish something like the rudiments of a true philosophy of history. And this same spirit was hardly less discernible in those later lectures on the "political institutions relating to commerce, to finances, and to the ecclesiastical and military establishments," which formed the basis of the *Wealth of Nations*. Everywhere throughout his writings there is a pervasive sense of the realities of fact and circumstance; a luminous, bracing, work-a-day atmosphere. But the conclusions are, first of all, philosophical; only second-arily practical.

It has been necessary to go over this somewhat familiar ground with reference to the philosophical method of Adam Smith, in order to come at the proper point of view from which to consider his place among the old masters of academic lecturing. It has revealed the extent of his outlook. There yet remains something to be said of his literary method, so that we may discern the qualities of that style which, after proving so effectual in impart-ing power to his spoken discourses, has since, transferred to the printed page, preserved his fame so far beyond the lifetime of those who heard him.

Adam Smith took strong hold upon his hearers, as he still takes strong hold upon his readers, by force, partly, of his native sagacity, but by virtue, principally, of his consummate style. The success of his lectures was not altogether a triumph of nat-ural gifts; it was, in great part, a triumph of sedulously cultivated art. With the true instinct of the orator and teacher, Adam Smith saw—what every one must see who speaks not for the patient ear of the closeted student only, but also to the often shallow ear of the pupil in his class-room, and to the always callous ear of the great world outside, which must be tickled in order to be made attentive—that clearness, force, and beauty of style are absolutely necessary to one who would draw men to his way of thinking; nay, to any one who would induce the great mass of mankind to give so much as passing heed to what he has to say. He knew that wit was of no avail, without wit's proper words; sagacity mean, without sagacity's mellow measures of phrase. He be-stowed the most painstaking care, therefore, not only upon what he was to say, but also upon the way in which he was to say it. Dugald Stewart speaks of "that flowing and apparently artless style, which he had studiously cultivated, but which, after all his experience in composition, he adjusted, with extreme difficulty, to his own taste." The results were such as to offset entirely his rugged utterance and his awkward, angular action, and to enable the timid talker to exercise the spells of an orator. The charm of his discourses consisted in the power of statement which gave them life, in the clear and facile processes of proof which gave them speed, and in the vigorous, but chastened, imagination which lent them illumination. He constantly refreshed and rewarded his hearers, as he still constantly refreshes and rewards his readers, by bringing them to those clear streams of practical wisdom and happy illustration which everywhere irrigate his expositions. His counsel, even on the highest themes, was always undarkened. There were no clouds about his thoughts; the least of these could be seen without glasses through the lucid atmosphere of expression which surrounded them. He was a great thinker,—and that was much; but he also made men recognize him as a great thinker, because he was a great master of style,—which was more. He did not put his candle under a bushel, but on a candlestick.

In Doctor Barnard's verses, addressed to Sir Joshua Reynolds and his literary friends, Adam Smith is introduced as a peer amidst that brilliant company:

> If I have thoughts and can't express 'em,
> Gibbon shall teach me how to dress 'em
> In words select and terse;
> Jones teach me modesty and Greek,
> *Smith how to think*, Burke how to speak,
> And Beauclerc to converse.

It is this power of teaching other men how to think that has given to the works of Adam Smith an immortality of influence. In his first university chair, the chair of Logic, he had given scant time to the investigation of the formal laws of reasoning, and had insisted, by preference, upon the practical uses of discourse, as the living application of logic, treating of style, of the arts of persuasion and exposition; and here in his other chair, of Moral Philosophy, he was practically illustrating the vivifying power of the art he had formerly sought to expound to his pupils. "When the subject of his work," says Dugald Stewart, speaking of the *Theory of Moral Sentiments*, "—when the subject of his work leads him to address the imagination and the heart, the variety and felicity of his illustrations, the richness and fluency of his eloquence, and the skill with which he wins the attention and commands the passions of his hearers, leave him, among our English moralists, without a rival."

Such, then, were the matters which this great lecturer handled, and such was the form he gave them. Two personal characteristics of the man stand out in apparent contrast with what he accomplished: he is said to have been extremely unpractical in the management of his own affairs, and yet he fathered that science which tells how other people's affairs—how the world's affairs—are managed; he is known to have been shy and silent, and yet he was the most acceptable lecturer of his university.

But it is not uncommon for the man who is both profound and accurate in his observation of the universal and permanent forces operative in the life about him, to be almost altogether wanting in that sagacity concerning the local and temporary practical details upon which the hourly facilitation and comfort of his own life depend; nor need it surprise any one to find the man who sits shy and taciturn in private, stand out dominant and eloquent in public. "Commonly, indeed," as Mr. Bagehot has said, "the silent man, whose brain is loaded with unexpressed ideas, is more likely to be a successful public speaker than the brilliant talker who daily exhausts himself in sharp sayings." There are two distinct kinds of observation: that which makes a man alert and shrewd, cognizant of every trifle and quick with every trick of speech; and that which makes a man a philosopher, conscious of the steady set of affairs and ready in the use of all the substantial resources of wise thought. Commend me to the former for a chat; commend me to the latter for a book. The first will sparkle; the other burns a steady flame.

Here is the picture of this Old Master: a quiet, awkward, forceful Scotchman, whose philosophy has entered everywhere into the life of politics and become a world-force in thought; an impracticable Commissioner of Customs, who has left for the instruction of statesmen the best theory of taxation; an unbusiness-like professor, who established the science of business; a man of books, who is universally honored by men of action; plain, eccentric, learned, inspired. The things that strike us most about him are, his boldness of conception and wideness of outlook, his breadth and comprehensiveness of treatment, and his carefully clarified and beautified style. He was no specialist except *in the relations of things*. Of course, spreading his topics far and wide in the domain of history and philosophy, he was at many points superficial. He took most of his materials at second hand; and it has been said that he borrowed many of his ideas from the French. But no matter who mined the gold, he coined it; the image and superscription are his. Certain separate, isolated truths which served under him may have been doing individual, guerrilla warfare elsewhere for the advancement of science; he marshalled them into drilled hosts for the conquering of the nations. Adam Smith was, possibly, somewhat indebted to the Physiocrats, but all the world is indebted to Adam Smith. Education and the world of thought need men who, like Adam Smith, will dare to know a multitude of things. Without them and their bold synthetic methods, all knowledge and all thought would fall apart into a weak analysis. Their minds do not lack in thoroughness; their thoroughness simply lacks in minuteness. It is only in the utterances of such men that the mind finds such exhilaration and exaltation as come with the free air that blows over broad uplands. They excite you with views of the large aspects of thought; conduct you through the noblest scenery of the mind's domain; delight you with majesty of outline and sweep of prospect. In this day of narrow specialties, our thinking needs such men to fuse its parts, correlate its forces, and centre its results; and our thinking needs them in its college stage, in order that we may command horizons from our study-windows in after days.

The breadth and comprehensiveness of treatment characteristic of the utterances of such a teacher are inseparable attributes of his manner of thought. He has the artist's eye. For him things stand in picturesque relations; their great outlines fit into each other; the touch of his treatment is necessarily broad and strong. The same informing influence of artistic conception and combination gives to his style its luminous and yet transparent qualities. His sentences cannot retain the stiff joints of logic; it would be death to them to wear the chains of formal statement; they must take leave to deck themselves with eloquence. In a word, such men must write *literature*, or nothing. Their minds quiver with those broad sympathies which constitute the life of written speech. Their native catholicity makes all minds receive them as kinsmen. By reason of the very strength of their humanity, they are enabled to say things long waiting to be said, in such a way that all men may receive them. They hold commissions from the King of Speech. Such men will not, I am persuaded, always seek in vain invitations to those academic platforms which are their best coignes of vantage. But this is not just the time when they are most appreciated, or most freely encouraged to discover themselves; and it cannot be amiss to turn back to another order of things, and remind ourselves how a master of academic inspiration, possessing, in a great power to impart intellectual impulse, something higher than a trained capacity to communicate method, may sometimes be found even in a philosophical Scotchman.[1]

WOODROW WILSON.

Printed in the *New Princeton Review*, vi (Sept. 1888), 210-20.
[1] This essay was a revision of Wilson's lecture on Adam Smith delivered in Dr. Richard T. Ely's undergraduate course in political economy at the Johns Hopkins in January 1884. The Editorial Note, "Wilson's Lecture on Adam Smith," Vol. 2, discusses Wilson's research for and writing of this lecture and its relation to "An Old Master." A fragment of Wilson's lecture is printed at November 20, 1883, Vol. 2.

From Edward Livermore Burlingame

Dear Sir: [New York] Feb'y 3, [188]7

We have considered with a great deal of interest the paper you kindly sent us upon Adam Smith; and wish on account of the excellence of its treatment that we could think the subject would be of interest to a sufficiently large circle to warrant our choosing it among the large number of articles just now offered to us. Where we can use not more than a dozen papers or so in each number, however, you will readily understand that we must often give up things which have a positive interest for *us*, in favor of articles on more widely interesting subjects.

The manner of the article has, however, attracted us so much that we should be very glad if you felt willing at any time to allow us to examine other papers which you may have in hand.

We are,

Very truly yours,   Charles Scribner's Sons

LPC (Charles Scribner's Sons Archives, NjP).

From Charles Kendall Adams

My Dear Sir: Ithaca, N. Y., Feb. 3d 1887

Referring to your letter of January 29th, I would say that I think you would be exceedingly fortunate if you could get the assistance of Mr. Hodder[1] next year. I have supposed, however, that he expected to go abroad, and I should be surprised if he would be willing to take the place you name. Possibly, however, in view of the small number of hours, he might regard it as an opportunity for special study of a private kind. Mr. Hodder's accomplishments are unquestionable. He is scholarly in spirit, earnest in purpose, a steady and successful worker. I do not think his aptitudes as a teacher are quite equal to the extent of his knowledge, and yet he holds his class firmly to its work, and if there is any lack it is in the direction of a vivacious inspiration which I always like to see something of in a class room. During the past two years Mr. Hodder's health has not been perfectly sound; still it has not often interfered with the regularity of his work. But you cannot expect to get all of the accomplishments, and all the virtues at $600 a year. I have picked out Mr. Hodder as the best man I knew at $1000, and he has not disappointed me.

With pleasant recollections of your visit here, I am

Very truly yours,   C. K. Adams

HwL (WP, DLC) with WWsh and WWhw book references on env. and WWhw
notes on verso of letter.
    [1] Frank Heywood Hodder, Instructor and Assistant Professor of History and
Political Economy at Cornell, 1885-90.

From Richard Heath Dabney

My dear Tom: Bloomington, Ind. Feb. 3rd, 1887.
    You had better keep dark, I think, about my aspirations to the
chair of History at the Univ. of Va. From information lately
received I feel *almost* certain that Mr. Holmes[1] is to be retired
on half pay, but until it is *entirely* certain, I think it would be
improper for me, as a friend of his, to appear too openly as a
candidate. Hence, "mum is the word." . . .
    Mr. Gildersleeve & Mr. Price[2] will back me in my application
for the place; and I need hardly tell you how high a value I should
set upon your own recommendation. I have the highly flattering
letter which you wrote for me[3]—addressing it to nobody in particular, and will use it, with your permission, when the time
comes, unless you think that, in such an important matter, it
would be better to direct a special letter to the Board of Visitors
of the U. Va.
    I believe I told you that Mr. Holmes told my brother that he
wanted me to be his successor.
    No time for more now.
                    Sincerely your friend   R. H. Dabney.

ALS (WP, DLC) with WWsh notation on env.: "The history of France largely
but explanatory of the French Revolution."
    [1] George Frederick Holmes, author, first president of the University of Missis-
sippi, and Professor of History, Literature, and Political Economy at the University of Virginia from 1857 to 1897. Holmes was sixty-six when this letter was
written.
    [2] Basil L. Gildersleeve, then Professor of Greek at the Johns Hopkins, and
Thomas Randolph Price, then Professor of English at Columbia College. Both
Gildersleeve and Price had taught at the University of Virginia.
    [3] Printed as an Enclosure in R. H. Dabney to WW, March 25, 1887.

From Herbert Baxter Adams

Dear Mr Wilson: Baltimore, Feb. 6 1887
    What is the diplomatic situation? I have been expecting some
word from you for these many days. I see that you are advertised
among the prospective lecturers at Cornell University. From what
Pres. Adams said to me there last autumn, I presume you have
already received overtures of one sort or another from that institution. If you get a square offer, with a good salary, you will
doubtless think twice before declining it. I should hardly feel like

attempting to dissuade you from settling in a real University; but, in my judgment, the best point to make is *freedom to lecture* in Ithaca, Baltimore, or anywhere else, with Bryn Mawr for a home-base. You can force the appointment of an Assistant to do class-work; you can even force up your salary and professorial dignity. But I hope you will be quite frank with me as to the existing situation.

Very truly yours,   H. B. Adams

TLS (WP, DLC) with WWhw notations on env. Enc.: printed announcement of a forthcoming volume in The Johns Hopkins University series, *Baltimore and the Nineteenth of April, 1861,* by George William Brown.

To Herbert Baxter Adams

Dear Dr. Adams,   Bryn Mawr, Pa., 7 Feby., 1887.

Your letter of yesterday calls for an immediate reply. Surely it was not an official advertisement in which you saw my name among the prospective lecturers at Cornell; for not only is this the first I've heard of any such announcement, but no sort of overture of any official,—or, for the matter of that, *un*official—nature has been made to me concerning an engagement at Cornell. *All* that I know about the advertisement I learned from your letter, received this morning. It's certainly most extraordinary! Where did you see see [*sic*] the announcement?

I have not written to you before about the situation here, because nothing is yet *settled*, and I have wanted to delay writing to you till I could say something final. The strong probabilities are—indeed I may say that so much is certain—that I shall have an Assistant next year: but *what sort of an Assistant* is yet the unsettled point; and until I know that, I cannot tell how much *extra* work lecturing elsewhere will involve, or what outside engagements I can (mentally and physically) afford to make. I am hastening things to a conclusion as fast as possible: and you shall hear from me the moment such a conclusion is reached.

In the meantime you know the *whole* situation, so far as I myself know it; and I am every day giving some attention to a scheme and materials for the lectures I hope and expect to deliver at the Hopkins next year.

Very sincerely Yours,   Woodrow Wilson

ALS (H. B. Adams Papers, MdBJ).

Notes for a Classroom Lecture

[c. Feb. 8, 1887]

Renaissance

IV

Machiavelli

The political philosophy of Machiavelli may be taken as an epitome [of the] political state of Italy in that Age of Despots in which the Renaissance had its rise. Machiavelli (1469-1527) who first entered public life in the service of his native city of Florence during that brief period (1494-1512) of independence of the Medician tyranny which linked the 15th and 16th centuries. During the whole of this space of time he was a diligent and efficient servant of the republic, and her administration owed many beneficent features to his suggestions, though his chief services were not domestic but diplomatic. Driven from office by the return of the Medici in 1512 he spent the rest of his life in the composition of writings which were designed chiefly to break the exile of his retirement and win him a way back into political life, even, if necessary, at the expense of his former principles.

The first work written in his retirement was his "Prince" a treatise dedicated to Lorenzo de Medici and meant to give proof to that monarch of Machiavelli's willingness and ability to serve him in the consolidation and extension of his power, but also with a view to suggesting to that great prince the patriotic design of unifying Italy and thereby expelling all foreign powers from her territory. The book embodies "a theory of government in which the interests of the ruler are alone regarded, which assumes a separation between statecraft and morality, which recognizes force and fraud among the legitimate means of attaining high political ends, which makes success alone the test of conduct, and which presupposes the corruption, venality, and baseness of mankind at large."* In brief it is a cold and dispassionate analysis of the politics of that distracted age in dismembered Italy. It recognizes no morality but a sham morality meant for deceit, no honor even among thieves and of a thievish sort, no force but physical force, no intellectual power but cunning, no disgrace but failure, no crime but stupidity, and yet proposes to the tyrant whom its maxims were meant to court and assist the high end of establishing an orderly state, ruled for its own good, in which justice should be efficiently administered, in which beneficent peace should reign, and in which if not liberty

* Symonds: 'Age of Despots,' 335. [WW's note]

Renaissance

IV

Machiavelli

[shorthand notes] (1469
-1527). ... (1494-1572) ... 1512 ...

Wilson's shorthand notes for a lecture on the Renaissance

at least material prosperity should abundantly prevail. It embodies the political science of despotism of its day in brief frigid, conscienceless, scientific form.

Its theme is the efficient use of power: how kingdoms are to be acquired, free cities are to be governed as dependencies, how enemies are to be crushed and friends used. Its leading precept is that it is better to be feared than to be loved; but it will not do to be hated—for to be hated is insofar to be rendered weak: be bad therefore but seem good. Understand always that a spirit of liberty once aroused in a kingdom or city cannot be won over, it can be overcome only by being utterly stamped out. The only way to be rid of an opponent is entirely to extirpate him and his kin. Ruthless, but wary and cunning[.] Fraud, strategy, and violence are the only foundations for power.

Here is the mirror of the age's mind; Machiavelli did not invent iniquities, he simply put down and systematized what he saw about him.

Transcript of WWsh in the body of lecture notes described at Feb. 1, 1887.

From the Minutes of the Johns Hopkins Seminary of Historical and Political Science

Historical Library, Friday evening, Feb. 11, '87

The Seminary met at eight o'clock, Dr. Adams in the chair. . . .

Mr. [John Martin] Vincent read a review of De Laveleye's article on Democratic Government in the October number of the "Revue de Deux Monds."[1] The writer's arguments are based on Dr. Woodrow Wilson's monograph on Congressional Government, in the University Studies. The question turned upon the power of popular sentiment to influence Congress through a party medium. Dr. Wilson was present, and the discussion became general.

The Seminary adjourned at ten o'clock.

J. H. T. McPherson, Sec.

Bound minute book (MdBJ).
[1] Émile de Laveleye, "La Forme Nouvelle du Gouvernement aux États-Unis et en Suisse," *Revue des Deux Mondes*, 3rd Series, LXXVII (Oct. 1, 1886), 626-50.

To Richard Heath Dabney

My dear Heath,   Bryn Mawr, Pa., 17 Feby., 1887.

I need hardly tell you, 'in so many words,' that my interest in the contents of your last letters has been so great as almost to overcrow my great disappointment at losing all hope of having you with me next year. With the news of your engagement I was simply delighted: for it is evident, my dear fellow, from what you say that you have secured the girl you want, just the one you need and ought to have: and my own happy experience under similar circumstances prompts me to congratulate you with all my heart—and her: for I am convinced, after mature reflection, that she might do worse, whatever her own charms and deserts, than marry thee—even thee, thou very ass!

I am only less gratified to hear of your good chances for the chair at the University of Va. ('mum's the word'!), since they seem to be real chances. That would indeed be a real prize (though the chair *is* still burdened with English and Rhetoric, is it not?)[1] and I should rejoice to think of you back at the old place—I love it almost as much as you do—in the most influential faculty in the South. You would be very much to be envied: but *I* should not envy you because I *want* to see you at the top of things. I might envy another fellow, but not one of my own chums.

I put myself entirely in your hands with reference to a letter from me to be used in your candidacy, if you should want such a document. If you will send me the one you have, I will address it specifically to the Board of Visitors: or I will write another one to them, if you wish. You know the field best, and the best tactics, and I hope you will speak out in the matter.

The prospect now is for $850.00 for my assistant here next year—one thousand the year following (that's really the best our Trustees can do at present). I am afraid that the 'powers' would not wait till June to choose—indeed I am sure they would not: the field will be picked over before that; but it is possible that we may have to wait that long anyway: for the choice practically rests with me, and I am surprised to find, now that you are out of the question, how few men there are to choose from. I may not satisfy myself with anyone before June.

I enjoyed your *Courier* piece immensely—it's a rattler.[2]

With love as ever

Your sincere friend,   Woodrow Wilson

ALS (Wilson-Dabney Correspondence, ViU).

[1] Wilson was mistaken. Holmes's chair of history and literature was changed into a chair in history and political economy in 1882.

[2] It has been impossible to locate this item.

From Munroe Smith[1]

My dear Sir: Columbia College [New York] 1887 Feb. 19

I owe you an apology for not having informed you, before, that it has been found necessary to postpone the publication of your "Study of Administration" to the *June* number of the "Quarterly"

When I solicited the paper, there were two articles promised us on administrative subjects and it was my intention to use your article as a sort of introduction or preface—putting it at the top of the list, & following it up with the concrete discussion

Both these articles failed to come in on time; and it seemed best to us to adhere to the plan, but postpone its execution until June. As we have about twice as much matter on hand as we needed this was perfectly feasible. I hope you will not mind being put over, & will pardon me for not notifying you.

As to the titles of books on "The origin & history of law," I am a little puzzled to know just what you mean. There are plenty of books, & good ones, on the history of Roman Law & of German Law; and there are also books (but *not* good ones) on the History of English Law. As you do not specify *what law* you mean, I take it that you want books which treat of the evolution of law in general.

The work best known to English readers is, of course, *Maine's Ancient Law*. It is a brilliant book, but an exceedingly unsound & unsafe one.

The two best works I can think of at this moment are: (1) *Savigny's* Beruf unserer Zeit für Gesetzgebung und Rechtswissenschaft (1815)—which is translated into both French & English. This was primarily an argument against codifying German Law in 1815—but it contains chapters on the evolution of law which are to this day unsurpassed. (2) *Jhering's Geist des römischen Rechts*—translated into French under the title *Esprit du droit Romain*. This is the most suggestive, and in my opinion, the soundest, book ever written on the subject. It is primarily a discussion of the old Roman Law, but is really a work on the evolution of law in general.

Coulanges, Cité ancien should also be mentioned as a suggestive though one-sided book.

If I have misapprehended the drift of your question, pray let me know.

Yours truly   Munroe Smith

ALS (WP, DLC).

[1] (Edmund) Munroe Smith, born Brooklyn, N. Y., Dec. 8, 1854. A.B., Amherst

College, 1874; LL.B., Columbia Law School, 1877; studied at various German universities; Doctor of Civil and Canon Law, Göttingen, 1880. His entire teaching career was at Columbia: as instructor, 1880-83; Adjunct Professor of History and Political Science, 1883-91; Professor of Roman Law and Comparative Jurisprudence, 1891-1922; and Bryce Professor of European Legal History, 1922-24. Managing editor of the *Political Science Quarterly* from its beginning in 1886. President, American Political Science Association, 1917. Prolific writer in the field of legal history and jurisprudence. Died April 13, 1926.

From Talcott Williams

My dear Wilson: Philadelphia, Pa., February 21, 1887.
    Mason's translation of Von Holst's Constitution of the United States has just reached us. Would you like to do a review of this book, more in the nature of an interesting article than of a technical criticism, for The Press?[1]
    We pay for this work $10.00 a column. The review should be of about two columns or 3,000 words, and I should like to have it here by April 13. Kindly let me know whether you will take it up, and if so I will have the volume sent to you.
                    Yours very truly,   Talcott Williams

The review would want to tell something about Von Holst

TLS (WP, DLC).
    [1] The Philadelphia *Press*, of which Williams was the managing editor. Wilson responded with the review printed at April 17, 1887.

To Lucy Maynard Salmon

Miss Salmon,   [Bryn Mawr] Feby. 25 [1887]
    I am very sorry to say that I will have to ask you to excuse me from lecturing this afternoon on account of a severe headache.
                    Regretfully,   Woodrow Wilson

ALS (NPV).

From Munroe Smith

Dear Prof. Wilson: [New York] 1887 March 1
    The best source of information as to the literature of French legal history is given in Brunner's article on *Quellen des französischen Rechts* in Holtzendorff's *Rechts encyclopädie*. If this is not accessible to you, I will send you a list of books.
                    Yours very truly   Munroe Smith

ALS (WP, DLC) with WWhw notation on env.: "Ans."

From Robert Bridges

My dear Tommy: New York, March 2 1887

In talking over a lot of MSS. yesterday with Mr. Burlingame, he mentioned his regret that he had been obliged to decline your "Adam Smith" (before my arrival), and hoped that I would mention to you when the occasion offered that he was anxious to have you for a contributor. We especially need brief essays of about 3500 words (of which Perry's "Russian novels" in the Feb. Number is an inadequate specimen.) The idea is to have them different in form and character from anything to which the Magazine's or reviews have heretofore offered a welcome—not controversial, not didactic, not discursive—but, as I take it, a kind of modern echo of the Essays of "Elia" and the *Spectator*.

Mr. Burlingame said that the "Adam Smith" was too *special* in its treatment, but that a similar essay on a group of political writers would just suit our purpose. (Not having seen your essay,—I am not sure that I have caught his (E. L. B.'s) idea.[)]

I can assure you that there is a good chance for such material, and an opportunity for its early publication. We shall be obliged to build up a corps of contributors of this special kind of article, and I think it offers a great deal.

I have been here since Feb 23, and am so far delighted with my surroundings. The work has not proved wearing, and I already feel in better health and mental tone.

My kindest regards to Mrs. Wilson & the "bud."

In haste.   Your friend   R Bridges

ALS (WP, DLC) with WWhw notation on env.: "Ans. March 3/87."

To Robert Bridges

My dear Bobby,   Bryn Mawr, Pa., 3 March, 1887

It was a genuine pleasure to get your letter of yesterday with its news that you are fairly in your new work, that you are delighted with its conditions, and, above all, that you already feel the beneficial effect on your health of your emancipation from strain. Hurrah, hurrah! my dear fellow. I'm beyond measure glad. You are no longer part of a great inexorable machine (which, though noble after its sort, was terrible on a man with delicate sensibilities) but are in a position in which you can be thoroughly and healthily yourself. I believe in it:—it was just the thing your Good Genius was waiting to bring about, as it seems to me. I'm as glad as if it were myself!

I did'nt blame Mr. Burlingame in the least for returning my *ms.* I expected to see it come back. I had made my touch as light and attractive as I knew how, and cleared it of all technicalities,— had made it 'popular' as best I could; but the subject (I called it "An Old Master," but it was Adam Smith after all) *was* such as an editor of a *Maga.* naturally shies at, and I confidently expected it home again. But I hope that I shall be able to produce something to yr. taste before very long. A group of political writers *may* come suggestively together in my reading; but I'll be more likely to hit a vein like that in my 'Study of Politics' in the March "*Princeton.*" Is that at all near the pattern you mean?

Mrs. Wilson is much better than she has been, and sends warmest regards.

With love, as ever,

Your affectionate friend   Woodrow Wilson

ALS (WC, NjP).

From Herbert Baxter Adams

Dear Mr. Wilson: Baltimore, Mar. 7 1887

I should think four or five o'clock P.M. on Friday would be the best hour. There would be less danger of conflict with Hopkins Hall lectures if you could get here in time for the hour first named. You could undoubtedly defer your course until the second semester. [E. R. L.] Gould has promised to come over from Washington and give five or six lectures on Comparative Consular Systems. We shall have a School of Administration here before my Civil Academy idea takes deep root in Washington.[1] The report on that subject will soon be out, for I read the last proof last week.

President [Andrew D.] White of Cornell was here Saturday and Sunday, but has returned homeward. I judge there will be considerable difficulty in launching the new law school at Cornell. I am glad you have got Hodder.

I have lately had the presidency of a state university offered to me, but I am not prepared to go West or to sell out.[2]

Dr. Ely is all right again. He has just finished three articles on Corporations for Harper's Magazine.

Very truly,   H B Adams

Vincent has not yet sent his letter & meditates a revision![3]

TLS with hw postscript (WP, DLC) with WWsh paragraph for lecture on Dante, Petrarch, and Boccaccio on env.

¹ Wilson had attended the meeting of the Hopkins Seminary of Historical and Political Science on February 11, 1887, and Adams undoubtedly explained his plans for a school of public affairs at the Johns Hopkins and for a "civil academy" in Washington to Wilson at that time.

² A mysterious reference.

³ John Martin Vincent, then a graduate student at the Johns Hopkins, afterward Professor of European History at the same institution. Adams was probably referring to Vincent's revision of his plans for completing the requirements for the Ph.D.

From Joseph Ruggles Wilson

My dearest Woodrow—   Clarksville, March 12, 1887.

I am thankful to have received from your thoughtfulness the copy of the Princeton Rev. which contains your article upon the Study of Politics. In my judgment it is excellent both in matter and in the putting of it. You are acquiring—have indeed acquired —a rich racy style which (like all truly good things) is its own decoration, needing no help from rhetorical millinery. It was a positive pleasure to look through the transparent medium of your plate glass wording upon the very face of your easily-seen thought. I was constantly reminded of Bagehot, who was I think a model writer as well as an expert thinker. I am sure, too, that you have struck a vein of enquiry into the philosophy of politics, which must attract attention on the part of many who in this field of study care to arrive at truth, and who to reach it will employ the rare courage of trusting to their own eyesight instead of the spectacles which others have long used and blurred. Beaten paths are the best for easy travel but not for original discovery. I am very thankful that you possess a mind which, whilst it honestly appreciates what has been done by your forerunners, is not content to measure its tread by their footprints—but has a pathway of its own, where are new outlooks and rarer sceneries and fresh promises. In Theology I cannot but reverence the great names which illustrate its history; yet even I find it possible to improve now and then upon their doctrinal definitions and to discern in proof-texts either more or less than is in their exegesis. How much more ought it to be true in your case, and as to your line of study: you with your powers all in their spring-time, and possessing a truer perspicacity than that with which I was ever gifted! You are assuredly my second edition, "revised and improved," as to contents, and with a far superior letter-press and binding. How I bless God that it is even so, and that no law of His forbids the pride your father takes in his larger son. . . .

God bless the *three* children!

                         Your affectionate   Father.

ALS (WP, DLC) with WWhw notations and numbers on env.

To Francis Fisher Browne[1]

My dear Sir,   Bryn Mawr, Pa., 12 March, 1887.

I am very much tempted to undertake a review of "Franklin in France"[2] (I think, with you, that Greville's last volume calls for no more than a very brief notice);[3] but it is impossible that I should write anything of the kind now. I have promised to prepare a somewhat extended review of Mason's translation of Von Holst's monograph on our Constitution;[4] and that, in addition to other jobs already in hand, permanent and temporary, puts any further engagements out of the question.

I am very sorry; I shall hope to serve you at some other time.

Very truly Yrs.,   Woodrow Wilson

ALS (de Coppet Coll., NjP).

[1] Founder and editor of the Chicago *Dial* from 1880 to 1913.

[2] Edward Everett Hale and Edward Everett Hale, Jr., *Franklin in France. From Original Documents, Most of Which Are Now Published for the First Time* (2 vols., Boston, 1887-88).

[3] Wilson had reviewed the second volume of the Greville memoirs in the Chicago *Dial.* His review is printed at Feb. 1, 1886.

[4] His review is printed at April 17, 1887.

Agreement Between the Trustees of Bryn Mawr College and Woodrow Wilson, Ph.D.

Bryn Mawr, Pa. [March 14, 1887]

This agreement made the 14th day of March, 1887, between the Trustees of Bryn Mawr College and Woodrow Wilson Ph.D. witnesseth: That at a meeting of the said Trustees held March 11th 1887, they appointed Woodrow Wilson Ph.D. Associate Professor of History and Political Science for the term of three years from Sept 1st, 1887. On the part of the said Trustees it is agreed that they shall pay Woodrow Wilson at the rate of $2000.— per annum for each of the three years during which he shall be engaged in teaching at the College; that he shall have an assistant *as soon as practicable*;[1] and also shall have the privilege of delivering a course of twentyfive lectures yearly at the Johns Hopkins University at such times as shall not interfere with his regular duties at the College.

And Woodrow Wilson agrees that he will give instruction in his Department ten hours weekly, supervise the instruction in

History given by his Assistant, and direct the studies of a fellow in History.[2]

On behalf of the Trustees, James E. Rhoads
Woodrow Wilson

Hw contract (WP, DLC).
[1] Italicized words inserted above the line by Dr. Rhoads.
[2] This was a restatement of a resolution adopted by the Executive Committee of the Board of Trustees on January 21, 1887. "Minutes of the Executive Committee of the Board of Trustees of Bryn Mawr College," Jan. 10, 1884-March 9, 1894, bound ledger book (PBm).

From Richard Heath Dabney, with Enclosure

My dear Tom: Bloomington, Ind., March 25 1887.

Ever since the reception of your letter of the 17th ulto. I have been intending to write and thank you for your warm and cordial promise to aid me in my application for the chair that is *probably* to be vacated by Mr. Holmes in the summer. My delay has been caused by the fact that I have been still busier of late than usual, and have been worried by some matters that I shall not inflict upon you. However, now that another letter has come from you, I am determined to snatch time enough from my work to make at least a brief reply. . . .

And now, let me thank you most heartily for your promise to back me up for the place at the Univ. of Va. Of course, it is still uncertain whether there is to be any vacancy to be filled, and, I suppose, will remain uncertain until the end of June. Still, I have very strong reasons to believe that the vacancy will actually occur; and, altho' the thing seems almost too good for me to hope for, I really believe that my chances of election, in case there *is* a vacancy, are far from bad. I have excellent testimonials, and believe I can bring considerable influence to bear upon several members of the Board.

I enclose your own highly valued & valuable testimonial. It is a "daisy," and you will be putting me under still another obligation if you will address it to the Board of Visitors of the Univ. of Va., & send it back to me as soon as is convenient.[1]

Ever yr friend   R. H. Dabney.

[1] The presence of the enclosure in the Wilson Papers indicates that Wilson sent a new testimonial to the Board of Visitors of the University of Virginia and sent a copy of the new testimonial to Dabney.

To Whom It May Concern

Bryn Mawr, Pa. 22 Jany, '86.

A long and intimate acquaintance with Dr. R. H. Dabney warrants me in saying with confidence that he has a strength in study, in thought, and in the communication of thought which must qualify him for work of the highest order in the branches which he has chosen.

To this sum of my opinion as to his intellectual qualifications, I would add an expression of my conviction that Dr. Dabney's openness and geniality of character must make it very easy for him, in any station he may come to fill, to put himself in close sympathy with his pupils and to bind them to himself in a way which will make him most helpful to them.

Woodrow Wilson

ALS (WP, DLC).

To Herbert Baxter Adams

My dear Dr. Adams,   Bryn Mawr, Pa., 29 March, 1887.

I write to ask that you will be kind enough either to tell me yourself or to put me in the way of finding out something about the life and studies of Dr. v. Holst in this country, when 'getting up' our constitutional history, as well as about the rest of his career. I am about to write a review of Mason's translation of his monograph in Marquardsen's 'Handbuch,'[1] and the review must needs be interesting rather than learned or critical—about the book and its author rather than about the intimate points of its contents. You will greatly oblige me if you will put me in possession of materials for such uses which I may appropriate on short notice.

You have heard of no one yet who could serve us as an assistant in history? I was 'a little previous,' it turns out, in claiming to have secured Hodder. I could not get him after all; and now I am all at sea again—and, having accepted the lectureship with you, I am a little concerned lest I should miss getting an assistant altogether and be left with a quite overwhelming lot of work on my hands next year. It ought not to be hard to fill the place satisfactorily inasmuch as whoever took it would have the immediate prospect of having the whole of the history work handed over to him, with corresponding increase of pay, in case he did good service—and I suppose also the chance to have my place should I go elsewhere. At any rate I *wish* that the place *might* seem attractive to some such man as we need.

Very sincerely Yours,   Woodrow Wilson

P.S. I hope the B. & O. 'deal'[2] has brought in some wealth to the Univ. that may be made to work great advantage to the 'school of administration' wh. Gould and I are to inaugurate?[3]

Yrs.   W. W.

ALS (H. B. Adams Papers, MdBJ).
[1] For a description of this series, see n. 2 to the book review printed at April 17, 1887.
[2] See the New York *Nation*, XLIV (March 17, 1887), 218-19, for an account of the "B. & O. 'deal.'"
[3] For the subsequent development of this plan, see "A Plan for a School of Public Law," printed at May 22, 1888, and WW to D. C. Gilman, May 22, 1888, n. 1.

From Herbert Baxter Adams

Dear Mr. Wilson: Baltimore, Mar. 30, 1887

Here is an article about Von Holst which is based upon personal correspondence with the man himself. Please return it when convenient.[1]

You had better come over and look at [Philip Wheelock] Ayres, our Cornell man, who has attractive points. We could "doctor" him in a year or two. He has absorbed all that Cornell can give him and has been here two years. He is a fine fellow & a well-mannered Christian, full of enthusiasm, of good health and good works.

Nobody knows anything here about the B & O or its relation to our salaries!   Very truly   H. B. Adams

ALS (WP, DLC).
[1] Wilson did return the enclosure.

From Melville R. Hopewell

Dear Sir: Tekamah, Nebraska. Mch 31 1887

Yours of 18th inst at hand. In reply will say the taxes on your land this year for 1886 are   53.07

Our chge   1.
                                                        ———
Please remit $54.07

Think I can lease grass again on some of it, and think likely I

can make a sale of some. Will try it & send you any offers. I think
advisable to sell it.   Truly &c   M. R. Hopewell

ALS (WP, DLC) with WWhw notation on env.: "Ans." and WWhw room
measurements.

From Albert Bushnell Hart[1]

Dear Prof Wilson: Cambridge, Mass. April 1, 1887
    Your letter of the 24th has been received. After considering
and inquiring and talking with several possible candidates, there
are two young men whom I should like to suggest to you for the
position of Assistant.
    Mr. G. E. H. Weaver, a graduate of the College in 1884, has
been two years an instructor in Swarthmore College, and the past
year an instructor in history in Harvard College; his appointment
here is for one year only, and the work of the department has
been so rearranged as to provide for his course within the permanent staff; he will therefore not remain another year. The quality
of his work had, so far as I know, no influence on the rearrange-
ment, which was an act of general policy. Mr. Weaver is a very
steady faithful man, amiable and well-principled; he has no
striking originality and is not yet matured. I know very little
about his work as a teacher. He comes from Pennsylvania, and
you doubtless could learn much about him from people near at
hand. I have not talked with him about your proposition, but
know that he is on the look-out for employment. He is not a man
who stirs up students very much, but is careful and accurate.
    Mr. Edward Cummings, a graduate of 1883, and an A.M. of
1885 has been pursuing a variety of studies in Cambridge since
leaving college, in the law school, then the Divinity School, then
as a graduate student and instructor in English[.] His specialty
is History and Political Science[.] He (as well as Mr Weaver)
has taken our Roman History courses. I consider him a man of
considerable originality of mind, and of undoubted power. His
personal presence and influence are greater than those of Mr.
Weaver—and he seems to me to come nearer to what you have
in mind[.] He is a man who could not fail to be a moral and
intellectual power in any college with which he was connected.
He has had no experience in teaching history, but, I should say,
has a power of interesting in whatever he undertakes to present.
As between the two I should think him most likely to make his
mark as a student and teacher: he is a broad, well-read, well-
balanced and mature man. I have seen him, and he is disposed

to consider the matter very carefully; I told him that I would send you his name, and that you might correspond with him directly

Mr. Weaver's address is: *Hilton 23, Cambridge Mass*; Mr. Cummings' is: *Thayer 29, Cambridge Mass*. Either of these gentleman can refer you to the Dean of the College—the President is abroad.

Should you fail otherwise to secure some one, there are other graduate students here who might be approached.

Permit me to take this opportunity to thank you for your Congressional Government which I have found very suggestive, and which I constantly use in one of my courses. I have now a Graduate student who is making a systematic study of that field, and who has found the book very helpful.

It would give us pleasure at Harvard to know Prof Wilson in *propria persona* as well as through ink and paper. May we not hope to see you during the meeting of the American Historical Association in May?

If I can be of any service to you in securing your Assistant, or in any other way, I beg you will call upon me.

Sincerely yours   Albert Bushnell Hart

ALS (WP, DLC).

[1] Born Clarksville, Pa., July 1, 1854. A.B., Harvard, 1880; Ph.D., University of Freiburg, 1883. His entire teaching career was at Harvard University as instructor in history, 1883-87; assistant professor, 1887-97; Professor of History, 1897-1910; and Professor of Government, 1910-26. President, American Historical Association, 1909; President, American Political Science Association, 1912. Author or co-author and editor of many books. Editor of several series, including *Epochs of American History* (to which Wilson contributed a volume) and the *American Nation* series in twenty-eight volumes. Died June 16, 1943.

From Richard Hudson[1]

My dear Sir   Ann Arbor, Mich April 5, 1887

I found your letter awaiting me after a brief absence from the city. Otherwise you should have had a prompt reply. There is one man here whom I could recommend most highly, who would indeed, be, I should say, just the man for you but I doubt whether he would care to leave his present work. I have shown him your letter, told him he can get the strongest endorsement from everybody here and that if he wishes to be a candidate he must decide at once. If he concludes to seek the position I will write you at length   Very truly yours   R. Hudson.

ALS (WP, DLC) with WWhw sums on env.

[1] Assistant Professor of History, University of Michigan.

To Clarence Winthrop Bowen[1]

Dear Sir: Bryn Mawr, Pa., 6 April, 1887.

Enclosed you will find P.O. order for $3.00 in payment of my dues to the Am. Historical Association for the year ending Sept. 1st., 1887.

I am very sorry indeed that I have been obliged to delay payment so long.

Very truly Yours, Woodrow Wilson

ALS (American Historical Association Papers, DLC).
[1] Treasurer, American Historical Association, 1884-1917; publisher, the New York *Independent*, 1892-1912.

EDITORIAL NOTE
WILSON'S DESIRE FOR A "LITERARY LIFE"

"I have devoted myself to a literary life," Wilson wrote both to his wife on October 8, 1887, and in his confidential journal on October 20, 1888.

By a "literary life," he certainly did not mean a career as a political and biographical writer and essayist, for he had long been and was at this time deeply engaged in such activity. He also did not mean a career as a poet or writer of fiction. To be sure, he had earlier tried his hand at poetry,[1] but the fact that he wrote very little of it is some indication that he realized that he was not endowed with poetical talent. He also had earlier had some ambition to be a writer of fiction[2] and tried, perhaps in early 1887, to write a short story and a novel. However, both efforts were abortive.[3]

Wilson best revealed what he meant in 1887 by engaging in a "literary life" in "The Eclipse of Individuality," "The World and John Hart," and "The Author Himself," printed, respectively, at April 7, September 1, and December 7, 1887. Deeply troubled by what he thought were the trends in contemporary fiction toward too much sophistication and realism, he felt a strong urge to call writers back to old values, particularly moral values—in short, to be a literary critic.

The fate of his first essay, "The Eclipse of Individuality," is well charted in the letters in this volume, but it is interesting that Wilson seems to have been most impressed by the criticism of his father.[4] Though in great discouragement over his failure in this first attempt at literary criticism, Wilson recast "The Eclipse of Individuality" into fictional form in "The World and John Hart," revealing as well his perhaps unconscious longing for an idyllic life devoted to writing. When "The World and John Hart" met the fate of its predecessor— rejection—Wilson would not give up but instead made a third effort in "The Author Himself." This time, after two very unsuccessful tries,

[1] See the two poems printed in Vol. 2, pp. 91-94.
[2] See WW to ELA, Oct. 30, 1883, *ibid.*, pp. 501-502.
[3] "Margaret," a fragment, and the preface and outline of a novel, "The Life and Letters of John Briton," WWhw MSS. (WP, DLC).
[4] See JRW to WW, Sept. 12, 1887.

he achieved some authority in the *genre* of the literary essay. Ironically, he did not then submit "The Author Himself" for publication, perhaps because he was unsure of its quality and could not bear the prospect of another rejection.

Wilson's yearning for a "literary life" seems to have subsided after 1887, undoubtedly because he was deeply engrossed in the preparation of lectures, in teaching, and in writing *The State* and other books. He submitted "The Author Himself" to the *Atlantic Monthly* in 1891, but apparently only because he discovered the essay in his files and concluded after reading it again that it was better than he had thought when he wrote it. He later wrote and published additional essays in the same vein—"Mere Literature," 1893, "On an Author's Choice of Company," 1896, and "On Being Human," 1897. But these were occasional pieces, not the outpouring of a man who had devoted himself to a "literary life."

To Robert Bridges

Dear Bobby,   Bryn Mawr, Pa., 7 April, 1887.

I send with this an essay on the 'Eclipse of Individuality' for editorial consideration, and address it to you because I want to explain why I have written it under a *nomme de plume*. I have done so not because I was ashamed of it, but because it is a whimsical *obiter dictum* and contains (half playful) opinions on some heads which might make university trustees in some quarters think me a frivolous fellow not fond enough of the 'standard authorities' and not deep enough in scholarship (which would be the truth) to suit their sober purposes in recruiting a Faculty. I hope that the disguise will not make the piece less acceptable than it might otherwise have been.

As for the piece itself, I am not sure that I belong on such ground; but the thing is at least natural and spontaneous (in fact, whatever it may be in outward seeming) and its vein is one which I love to work when I have time—a day or two of vacation or the like—to turn away from my professional duties. I have made the treatment about the length you suggested: and, if Mr. Burlinghame likes it, I have some more of the same kind, I feel certain, where that came from.

I hope that you continue to enjoy your work—I am confident you *must*, for it's ideal, *for work*,—such a magazine and such a firm! My own work is getting on at its usual paces. I am kept from producing much besides daily lectures, but I'm convinced there's a good time coming when lectures shall be more or less 'in stock.'

Mrs. Wilson sends warmest regards and I am, with all the old love and new besides, as ever
Your affectionate friend   Woodrow Wilson

ALS (WC, NjP).

A Critical Essay

[c. April 7, 1887]

The Eclipse of Individuality
A One-sided Statement
by
Axson Mayte.

A man that God made is worth ten that books make
—New Proverb.

'It is hard nowadays to see men for the multitude of books; we are becoming such men as books describe by dint of looking at ourselves only from inside their covers; our libraries are over-awing our individuality; foot-notes and citations are ruling the market against native thought.' Such is the revolutionary doctrine which is tempting the belief of that large body of people who feel how opposite it is to the inborn disposition of the natural, carnal man to read and read and read all his days. What are we to say to such opinions? There is at least a ring of heartiness in them, which makes them *sound* almost true. If they be, we cannot run away from them, and might just as well stay and submit; if they be not, it is well to demolish them at once, before they collect further force and give us more inconvenience. Even if we are scholars,—and I and my readers are all of us scholars,—we might as well, in face of these dispositions of our fellow-men towards us, rehearse (to ourselves alone, in close conclave) the facts,—for I suppose there are some,—about modern scholarship (our own) and its tendencies.

It were best, perhaps, to state the other side first. Mr. Matthew Arnold has been at some pains to convince us that criticism, if its objects be true canons of taste and its spirit a spirit of appreci-ation, is worthy to have a place even beside diviner creation; and his argument has had its weight. Many persons of sense were already of his opinion; others were merely waiting to strike their colours to such sentences as his. But, then, creation too has its place after all: it will not do for all of us to be critics,—some of the world's forces would lapse thereby; and mere talk about other people's doings sometimes degenerates with a few of us into gossip,—does it not?—and there are deplorable 'literary notes' at the bottom of criticism as there is the history of literature at the top of it. It would be well to say something *for* others rather than all things *about* them. Anatomy is much; but at best it is secondary to birth.

And yet, if we live in libraries and experience only the power of print, will we not all be critics merely,—or, at any rate, critics first, and other things only by way of feeble corollary? The atmosphere of a library is capital if you go there to feed your own thoughts; but it will dim your eyesight and weaken your sinew if you frequent it only to exploit the thoughts of others. It's a matter of retaining your own individuality and making what you read subservient to your self.

Strangely enough, one's own individuality can be retained only in contact with other individualities,—not in contact with *types*, but with the ingredients of types, namely genuine individuals. It is having to make your place among men that makes you a man: it is having to compete with them that elevates you to command them: character is one of the things gained by practice. Now most books contain generalizations,—that is their business,—treating of men in the mass, as having this or that characteristic when taken 'by and large.' Constant contact with such books generalizes mankind to the vision, makes of it a dim total, a stalking, kaleidoscopic general principle, a lump human nature. There are books, indeed, rarest gems of the human spirit, which are either themselves the voices of individuals, like naïf personal memoirs or unstudied autobiographies, or the very mirrors of life itself, with all its multiform characters, all its infinite interplay of individual forces, like the plays of the greatest dramatists. But most books, we must admit, are not of these kinds; and may not one venture the statement that the individuality retained in the constant society of books of the usual kind, first mentioned, is a sort of impersonal, *book* individuality,—like that of Coleridge, or of Goethe, whose mind, while the whole ocean of European politics was running high before the great winds of national feeling, lay like a quiet pool apart, reflecting only the soft colours of a holiday sky; whereas the individuality retained in the company of the perfectest dramas and autobiographies is a genuine, human, first-person-singular, potent individuality,—like that of the elder Pitt or the living Gladstone?

To narrow the matter of our inquiry a little, we may allow to the adversary that histories have much to answer for in the way of dulling the personality of those who affect them: for histories

are of necessity epitomies, and, worse than that, they are epitomies in which the epitomizer does not appear, or appears only
very dimly. They are stories which are not told in the first
person,—or in any person in particular,—with a cautious imper-
sonality, indeed; and one somehow cannot but take them to
have more authority than the men who wrote them. When we
can see and know the man who tells a story we can make up our
minds readily enough as to how much credit we will give his
version: and we say afterwards only that 'So-and-so says so.' But
we read most histories, I suspect,—unless we be historians ourselves,—as if they had been produced by some elemental force,
quite independently of any personal intervention. It is like the
preconception we have concerning a paper found in the proceedings of some learned society[.] In brief, we are sometimes duped
much beyond the right of the author, as Mr. S——, with such and
such failings, to dupe us. He may have been too bashful to know
even his own sex, and yet we may have accepted his estimate of
some Queen Catherine whose real presence would have scared
him out of his wits. He may have been a Macaulay, who made
Whigs or Tories out of all his authorities and went about applying
to the opinions of men of all ages the plain square of Saxon
justice, and yet we may have followed him like sheep. He may
have been,—but enough! he may not have been the sort of man
to whom it was possible to know what he was talking about. We
meet neither him nor any other palpable individuality in his
book, and our own individuality is dulled by being drawn into
an unreal world.

Nor will mere historical truth in what we read obviate these
difficulties. It is not facts that make us, *but what we ourselves
do with facts* in our thought and conduct. We must seek ourselves among men, bathing our aptitudes in everyday circumstance, and using books merely to enrich our individual contributions to life and society. Life with books only is no *life* at all:—
it is mere cerebral involution.

Are not books which one can read without a single movement
of emotion dangerous books to which to entrust our minds,
though mayhap good enough books to dig in for sundry raw
materials? Are not anger, laughter, tears the elements of individuality,—and is not individuality eclipsed in absent-mindedness, in the turning away of the mind from its surroundings? Is
not the man absent when his mind is absent? Abstract reasoning
has no character in it: it may be done indifferently by a good
man or a bad man, by one who loves his fellow-men or by one

who hates them. It is a good thing to do; the world's thought needs it; but it quenches personality, and the unsophisticated, unconsciously recognizing this principle, make a favorite of a poet, but never of a mathematician. No book was ever immortal because it was correct; no book was ever hindered from becoming immortal because it was incorrect. Correctness is, questionless, a great virtue (men must love truth or else hate God); but, like the Law, it will not save: your personal meaning, your heart's contents, your self's value to men who would find a *fellow* of finest sympathetic stuff, must do that.

Once more to give a special application to our questionings. I am sorry to believe that the eclipse of individuality which is said to have taken place in some quarters is the result of the scientific spirit of the age. I say I am sorry to believe this, because I honour the scientist and see in him a genuine benefactor of myself and all the rest of the race. But I am bound to think him an extinguisher of personal traits who is levelling thought to a *formula* and making it daily harder for my uncle Toby to pity the fly as he would pity a fellow creature. Ignorance does not constitute individuality, but your own way of looking at things does: and, if you must always think of heat as a mode of motion, and never for a moment as having been born of the fire which Prometheus stole, you are robbed of all sympathy for some otherwise beautiful poetry, which might have enriched your imagination with those subtile elements which raise men above what is sordid and mean, the ideal, namely, and the heroic. If you cannot sympathize with men who do not think scientifically, you are reduced from a hearty manhood to a bleak mind-hood wherein your heart, which is yourself, is like to freeze to death. If you will but go a little farther with this reasoning than I can conduct you now, you cannot fail to discover that *imagination* plays a prominent rôle in the great drama, Individuality, and that, consequently, its withdrawal is the end of the piece.

Perhaps you will say, 'But must we not think correctly,—*is* not heat a mode of motion, and Prometheus a heathenish myth?' I believe so with all my heart,—but a plague on your exact reasoning! This that I have said is an illustration, and,—suppose I cannot think of any better?

Literature is personal, science and learning are impersonal: the one deals with the world that is in us, the others with that which is outside of us. And yet even some literature will need interrogation on this point. There is a 'fiction' of realism, for instance,—to come to the topic everybody is now debating,—of

which the critic says, Is it not fine work? Is it not the very picture
of nature? Yes, it would seem to be a very cunning reproduction
of certain parts of nature,—and in so far as it is faithful work it
is good work, excellent, indeed, of its kind,—nothing could be
better. But its kind? About that there are many questions asked
which we must in honesty answer, and whose answers will illustrate several things about literature in general which are much to
my present purpose. As thus: Why does fiction of this sort simply
amuse us; why does it not also move us? I feel quite safe in
asserting that it is not, as someone somewhere would have it,
because the heroes of these tales do not wear rapiers, and do
sometimes serve as street-car conductors. It is simply and quite
naturally because the author himself never warms towards
them as if they were indeed heroes: because the author is a sensitive plate and not a sympathetic person. He evidently does not
himself regard his chief male character as a hero,—and of course
we cannot without his assistance. He gives us, as it were, the
raw material for a moving tale of human life, but leaves it
raw material,—though laid out, indeed, in consummate perfection
of arrangement and described to us with faultless analysis,—and
never makes us conscious of a single throb of the interest he
himself may reasonably be suspected of having in his own creations. To be blunt, he is no artist. "Lorenzo," says Mr Symonds,
"was an analyst. He could not escape from that quality so useful
to the observer, *so fatal to artists*, if they cannot recompose the
data furnished by observation in a new subjective synthesis."
Let the artist write of the most trivial circumstances of humdrum
human experience, nay even of vulgar human experience, and
his product is the literature that moves; but let the man of photo-
graphic mind discourse even of the greatest motives and settings
of heroism, and his product is—the photography which pleases.
Someone who can ought to demonstrate to the world of readers
that even the best literature of photography is not the literature
of individuality, and therefore not the literature of immortality,
but must fade as the photograph does.

And here I am sorely tempted to enter on a long digression for
the purpose of expounding certain profound doctrines concerning
the essential differences and relations between the Romantic and
the Realistic. If I had space and a larger vocabulary, I would
insist that man is not a thing apart, but has infinitely deep and
varied sympathies binding him to the universe as to a parent and
nurse and life-long companion, and that the Romance which is
genuine, by which I would mean not merely fanciful, is nothing

else than the interpretation of man's life in its connections with all else that God has made; whereas Realism,—I would go on to show,—is mere dissection, mere analysis of man himself, the world of subtile forces in which man lives and moves and has his mental being, having no part or share in the story. In brief, having already shown that criticism is no tonic to individuality, I would conclude by finding no such tonic in Realism either; for I should have found that the realist was in fact a mere critic.

Perhaps I may be allowed to suppose for a moment that I really have advanced and successfully maintained the above weighty thesis, and to draw a conclusion from it,—or, if not, I will bring forward the conclusion anyhow, as an independent proposition capable of standing on its own legs. It may be reasoned thus: criticism generates self-consciousness, and self-consciousness is incompatible with individuality. An age of criticism, though very scientific, will be an age of self-consciousness, very stiff and unspontaneous. Individuality of the genuine sort is never self-conscious, but is always *naïve*. Self-consciousnesss means an acute sense of the compulsive force of other people's standards of thought or action, as is shown by the self-evident fact that it is produced by criticism. Criticism is an effort to force upon the criticised the critic's canons of taste or conduct. The man who suffers himself to become sensitive to criticism becomes self-conscious in all that he does; and self-consciousness is a surrender of individuality.

To return to our main topic, I am inclined to admit to the revolutionist non-reader that we can lose personality, and with personality force, in too constant contact with even the best personality that lives in books. We may sink our own natural activities in the more attractive activities of the poet or the romancist, and, instead of living a mental life of our own, live in him *by proxy*. And here I make bold to name a distinguished living author as an example of what may happen to even the very best minds in book atmospheres. Mr. Lang's 'Letters to Dead Authors' are charming, charming at every turn, but at every turn second-hand, absorptive, imitative,—even of the ghosts to whom he writes (strange manners!),—'Alexandrian,' my friend the Platonist calls them. They are extremely clever, but with a sort of librarian cleverness, the birth of criticism. Mr. Lang is accused of barely preventing the very clowns of his tales from quoting the classics.

Contrast masters like Burke, who have evidently touched all the sources of strength in literature, whose sentences are redolent with the rarest perfumes of the richest cultivated mental growths, whose power bespeaks the exercised muscles of the trained reader of men and events and books, and yet in whose writings, so vivid with their own individuality, you may hardly find a quotation. All that they have known and seen has been fused into their own personality and they have become types of constructive force. They do not look much through the long-used, blurred spectacles of other generations of observers, but through their own clear eyes, which have looked upon learning and found it a weapon, not a costume; a wine of strength, not a mere palateable cordial; a spur to new thought, not a seduction to rest content with old thought; a contribution to themselves, not an influence to level them with all about them; not a Delphic oracle, but a brotherly human voice.

And now, by the way, what *is* Individuality? That is a question which, possibly, we should postpone no longer; for we are arriving at the end of our one-sided talk, and it were well that a definition of the central word of our subject should not be altogether overlooked, or incontinently left out. What, then, is Individuality, and when may a man, read as every man should be in the masters of literature, be said to have retained his individuality, and when to have lost it? He may, it seems to me, be said to have kept his individuality in the midst of books when they have simply helped him to enrich the blood in his own veins, so that he contributes *himself*,—what everybody feels to be himself,—to every circle he joins, whether in print or in oral intercourse. Individuality, in contact with books as in contact with people, consists in absorbing everything instead of being absorbed by anything. It consists in not becoming *identified* with a Goethe, a Browning, or even a Shakspere, Society or literature. The service of the great no man would disparage, but the serf of the great no man would be. Brass reflects the sun's light and is ofttimes glorious to look upon; but brass is not on that account a sun or any source of light. Individuality is an unquenchable fire, sending forth its own light and stimulating warmth, greatly fed by the fuel of other men's thoughts, but devoting these to keeping bright its own vestal flame. Sometimes it scorches and consumes, like Carlyle; often it is only serene, like Isaak Walton, or genial, like Lamb; it is never cold,—like the analyst and the historical critic.

In literary production the effective sort of individuality is, doubtless, the *typical*,—the personality which, having absorbed and appropriated, sums up the permanent forces of the age.

Generally not the *first* man who gives expression to truths one day to be incorporated in all mental life gets the credit for it, but the man who comes later and, seeing them in fuller daylight, gives the *best* expression to them; the man who comes after the pioneer and constructs the broad, fair road on which all after generations are to travel towards knowledge. In brief, the personality,—or, what is the same thing, the *originality*,—which tells is that which gathers into itself the thought latent in the mind of its age and makes itself the full and living voice of that thought; is that which lays all predecessors and all contemporaries under contribution and gives back to its generation, in sum, its own thought—but with a new stamp upon it, and in a new synthesis instinct with the life of him who made it. This is dominant individuality. This is what the great lawmakers,—the Lycurguses, the Solons, the Alfreds, the Madisons, the Napoleons, the Benthams; the great philosophers,—the Aristotles, the Bacons, the Kants; the great artists,—the Pheidiases and Michael Angelos; the great artistic poets,—the Ariostos, Spencers, Tassos, and Chaucers; the great rulers,—the Caesars, Charlemagnes, and Bismarcks; the great religious reformers,—the Wyclifs, Luthers, and Wesleys,—all have done: they have gathered a thousand loose threads, none of their own making, into a single hand, and so then have woven a vestment for great minds.

The true, genuine, healthy individuality is that which is in perfect harmony and keeping with its surroundings. The individuality of the crank is a spurious individuality, in rebellion against its surroundings. True individuality is not rebellious; it leads, but it sympathizes and coöperates.

The sum of the whole matter, then, since we are putting but one side of the case, is this, that in much reading there is little strength: that strength comes from exercise, not from stuffing: that individuality,—which is self,—may become permanently eclipsed by being too long in conjunction with other men's thoughts; that a little reading wisely done waketh a man up, but much reading ceaselessly done putteth him forever to sleep,— 'perchance to dream,' but never to dream to any new purpose. In this age of book students, when students of affairs are reckoned 'by authority' mere tyros, all this is rank heresy; but then if there were no heresy what would there be for the champions of truth to do? and the ranker it is the more easily may it be smelled out.

WWhw MS. (WP, DLC).

From Herbert Baxter Adams

Dear Mr. Wilson: Baltimore, Apr 8 1887

Miss [Martha Carey] Thomas has been here and I was fortunately able to suggest to her a first rate man, one [Frederic] Bancroft, a Ph.D. of Columbia and for now two years a special student of history in Berlin, in Freiburg (with Von Holst) and in the École Libre of Paris, where he now is. He is a gentleman withal. I half fear that Von Holst has persuaded him to keep out of teaching for a year or two longer, but, at Miss Thomas' request, I have written to him inquiring whether he would undertake a small amount of work for a small amount of pay? I have urged him to do so. His plan has been to come to the Hopkins and write a book. If he is ready to open negotiations with Miss Thomas, you will be all right as regards an able assistant and will have a free hand for your special work. It seems to Pres. Gilman and me that the present arrangement is a very good one for three years. You will have a larger salary than you could otherwise make and you will be able to elaborate your work on comparative politics. You will have chances enough by and by for a first class academic position. Meantime the problem of harmonizing duty with inclination is fairly solved. It is a very difficult thing to combine the ideal and the real; but it seems to me that Bryn Mawr is about as near Paradise as a young man can expect to come in two years.

                                   Very cordially,   H. B. Adams.

TLS (WP, DLC) with WWhw sums on env.

From Joseph Ruggles Wilson

                                   Hotel Carrolina (So it is spelled)
My precious son   Durham, N.C. April 9/87.

Some time ago I wrote you that I had engaged myself to preach for a month or more (5 Sundays) beginning 1st Sabbath in April, in the occupancy of the pulpit here (vacated by the absence of its pastor who is visiting Palestine, &c). Well I came about a week ago; having meanwhile made a brief visit in Wilmington. Of course I think of you and yours constantly, but now all the more intensely because never was I placed in such solitude as I am now experiencing. The people of the church pay me no manner of attention—only one elder having called on me! And, in addressing them from the pulpit, I find only unresponsive hearers, while at the prayer meeting I conducted the other night, the air was chilled by their freezing manner. I know not what to make of it, and am disposed rather to smile had I any one to smile with! I dare not abruptly quit the field for my word is pledged. As I have intimated, I do not much care so far as personal feeling goes, but to find a Presbyterian church in such a condition!

This hotel where I am staying (they wanted to place me at a mean private boarding house!) is quite pretty and very comfortable, and I may stick it out by God's help. The novelty of the situation is a surprise, indeed; and I suppose I needed humbling!

Dont put yourself to the trouble of writing to me. I simply wished, in my extreme loneliness, to talk, if even for a few minutes only, with one who I have no doubt still loves me, and will say, ah me! in the way of sympathy[.] Love to dear Ellie & all, if they continue to remember me.

Your affectionate   Father

ALS (WP, DLC).

From James Burrill Angell

President's Office. University of Michigan.

Dear Sir Ann Arbor, April 9, 1887

The acceptance by Judge [Thomas M.] Cooley of a place on the Inter-State R. R. Commission will leave vacant the Chair of American History & Pol. Science.[1]

I should like to inquire whether you would be disposed to give any consideration to a proposition, if made, to succeed him. I have no authority at present to offer the place to any one. I need hardly say that the Chair occupied by Presidents [Andrew D.] White & [Charles K.] Adams & Judge Cooley furnishes, under our flexible elective system, boundless opportunities. We have about 700 students in the Collegiate Dept & 1572 in all.

I have to be in N. Y. on Wednesday at the Columbia College Centennial. If you are disposed to give consideration to this matter, and wish to confer with me, I will run down to Phila on Thursday morning & meet you there for an interview. I propose in that case that I leave N. Y. at 10 a. m. & that you meet me at the Broad St. Station on my arrival. If you consent to this arrangement, telegraph me not later than Wednesday morning at the Grand Hotel, Broadway & 31st. I expect to arrive in N. Y. Tuesday ev'g & I must go to Boston Thursday night.

The salary now is $2200, with a probability of going to $2500 this summer. That we think equal to about $3000 in the East.

Yours truly   James B. Angell

[P.S. on env.:] Perhaps you may receive this in time to write instead of telegraphing. A.

ALS (WP, DLC) with WWhw draft of telegram on env.
    ¹ The possibility of Wilson's appointment by the University of Michigan was first raised in C. K. Adams to WW, March 12, 1885, Vol. 4, and was frequently mentioned in the correspondence thereafter.

From Melville R. Hopewell

Dear Sir   Tekamah, Neb., Apl. 9th 1887
    We have leased grass on SE 1/4 SW 1/4 10-21-11-E. for year 1887, for   10.00

	our fee	2.00	
	Dft he[re]with less ex 8.00	10.00	

We have an offer of 10.00, per acre for it, but hardly know whether to advise sale at that price. This is one of the best 40. S. as I understand.   Yours Truly   M. R. Hopewell

ALS (WP, DLC).

To James Burrill Angell

                              [Bryn Mawr, Pa., c. April 12, 1887]
    Will meet you as you propose at Broad St. station on Thursday [April 14].¹

WWhw tel. on env. of J. B. Angell to WW, April 9, 1887.
    ¹ For the outcome of these negotiations, see WW to the President and Trustees of Bryn Mawr College, June 29, 1888.

From Melville R. Hopewell

Dear Sir,   Tekamah, Nebraska. Apl 14 1887
    I think I can sell 240. acres of your land at 9.00 per acre, and that is as much as I would want to give, if I were buying. Still I do not like to advise sale, have said to party, I would recommend sale at $10.00. He may conclude to give it. If he If he [sic] buys he will pay 1/3 or 1/2 cash.

Yours &c   M R Hopewell

ALS (WP, DLC).

Notes for Two Classroom Lectures

[c. April 12, 1887]

Renaissance

XIX

63.   47.

1483-1546   1484-1581

Luther   and   *Zwingli*

Luther came of a peasant family of Thuringia and had a bring-ing-up of the austerest kind at the hands of honest, upright, and religious but stern parents. From the repression of home discipline he passed to an equally repressive school experience and then entered upon the serious studies of life at the University of Erfurt. This discipline had rendered him morbid and timid but had not at all soured him or broken the native strength of his character which, all his life through, manifested that interesting mixture of buoyancy and somber consuming earnestness, that combination of playfulness and depth, said to be a Thuringian peculiarity. His training did incline him to be somewhat ascetic, however; and did issue in his choice, against his father's will, of the monkish profession.

He found little sympathy with real renunciation of the world in the church of his time: the church was then thoroughly secularized and committed to the doctrine of justification by works: and even that doctrine it had permitted to become so utterly degenerate as to be made to appear to furnish a foundation for scandalous sales of indulgences. As a monk Luther thoroughly detested the doctrine of works: no one ever sought more earnestly or more passionately to drive out sin by mortification of the flesh and by every device of penance. But in his own case he found that the remedy signally failed: his mind could find no peace through the torture of his body. His studies, not his vigils or fasting, brought him to the light: he discovered in Paul and Augustine the doctrine that gave him peace and hope, the doctrine of justification by faith.

He was thus brought into direct conflict with the reigning tenets of the church: indulgences were vain, all outward observance was vain, faith alone could procure salvation: immediately after his discovery he was called to do public preaching at Wittenburg: he preached his beliefs with the utmost boldness and the struggle began. In 1517 he published the theses against indulgences, in 1520 he burned a papal bull which excommunicated him, in 1521 he refused obedience to the Diet of Worms, in 1521-33 he gave to Germany the Bible in German with an invitation to every man to read and judge its contents for himself, thus giving Germany both a national tongue and a national religion.

Ulrich Zwingli, the leader of the Reformation in Switzerland, was in all points contrasted with Luther: his bringing-up was liberal and cheerful, his training had no touch of the monastery about it: he was a humanist theologian and advocate of radicalism with which Luther had no sympathy at all. Luther, even after his revolt from the church, was willing to let all of her old observances not contradicted by the scriptures remain: Zwingli would have nothing which did not find explicit sanction in the Bible. He not only threw off papal authority but reorganized the church upon a basis of congregational authority. Nor did he stop with religious reforms but went on to political, leading the party of democracy and dying upon the battlefield in the politico-religious contest between the orthodox and reformed cantons.

[c. April 14, 1887]

Renaissance
XX
Calvin—Geneva, France

John Calvin (1509 1564) was born in Noyon, Picardy, of well-to-do middle-class parents who gave him an excellent liberal education and imposed upon him none of the harsh discipline which so weighted Luther's youth. Like Luther, Calvin had been educated with a view to the study of jurisprudence, turned from it to the critical interest of the age, the study of theology. Luther's writings had a profound effect upon him and he followed the great German reformer in adopting the doctrines of Augustine and Huss: but in very many points he was entirely unlike Luther: inferior to him in sympathetic genius, he was superior to him in power of logical analysis, and superior to all predecessors and successors as an organizer of reform. He may be called the great reforming Christian *statesman*—and Providence put him in the best possible field for the exercise of his supreme gifts.

France in 1532, when Calvin first came publicly forward as a predestined reformer, was by no means so safe a place for dissent as Germany. It was the stronghold of ecclesiastical power and Calvin had, immediately upon the proclamation of his heresy, to flee the country. He went first to Basle where he pub-

Renaissance

XX

Calvin — Geneva, France

(shorthand notes)

Wilson's shorthand notes for a lecture on the Renaissance

lished in '35 his "Instruction of the Christian Religion,"[1] the literary foundation of his doctrines, and in its French translation one of the cornerstones of French literature. Thence he went to Geneva, then a place given over to political feuds and social corruption. From '35 to '38 Calvin played there the part of a Savonarola, castigating the vices of the people in sermons of such relentless severity that he was finally driven from the city in fear for his life. In '41, however, such had the disorders of the city become, by reason of the ecclesiastical and political feuds which constantly engaged it, that the citizens recalled Calvin and placed in his hands power of a dictator. From '41 to '64 he maintained there, under ordinances all of which were of his own making, that remarkable polity which was profoundly to affect Scotland, England, and France and which constitutes, even more than his doctrines, his claim to greatness and revolutionary influence. It was a government founded upon the authority of the congregation, centering in the church and the school, constituting as complete a fusion of church and state and as complete a subjection of the individual [to] humanity as ever existed in Greece and Rome. The minister of the gospel, acting as the agent and representative of the congregation, was the omnipotent ruler of all, and private life as well as public conduct was made to conform to standards of church discipline. This was the polity which represented the Reformation for France, Calvin's native land. The Huguenots were Calvinists: hence the natural impulse under which they undertook reconstruction of the political forms of life upon the basis of the democratic rule of the congregation. Their participation in politics was an almost necessary outcome of their adherence to the faith of the great Christian statesman of Geneva: their work promised to be a reconstruction of the society as his had been.

Transcripts of WWsh in body of lecture notes described at Feb. 1, 1887.
[1] Here Wilson was making his own translation of Calvin's title, *Institutio Religionis Christianae*, usually called *Institutes of the Christian Religion*.

A Book Review

[April 17, 1887]

"The Constitutional Law of the United States of America." 1 vol. 8vo. Translated by Alfred Bishop Mason from the German of Dr. H. von Holst. Authorized edition. Chicago: Callahan & Co. 1887.

"The more comprehensive and thorough one's knowledge is of

the conditions under which the United States have attained their present social and political status the more convinced will one become, despite all sharp criticism of individual instances, that a judgment of the whole phenomenon must be embodied in these words: No people of ancient or modern times has shown a greater genius for founding a state." Such are the words with which Dr. von Holst closes his latest exposition of our Constitution. And Dr. von Holst ought to know. He has not only mastered our Constitution['s] history through the medium of books with German thoroughness and learning, and so made himself a leading authority even on this side the sea; he has also learned what books could not teach him by having himself lived for five years in the United States. In short, Dr. von Holst was once an immigrant to this country. He came over with the full intention of identifying himself with us; and he paid our Constitution the compliment—the highest and most conclusive compliment that he could pay—of admiring it when he was himself subject to it.

Dr. von Holst was born of a German family in Livonia, Russia, and received both Russian and German training by attendance first upon lectures at the University of Dorpat, and then at the University of Heidelberg. He left Russia, as so many other Russians have done, because the amiable government of that country did not like men who did their own thinking, and came to the United States, as so many besides Russians have done, because the great Republic was willing that every man should do not only his own thinking, but also the thinking of as many others as needed to have their thinking done for them by somebody else. He was twenty-six when he reached this country in 1869, exiled because he had written a pamphlet which had political meaning, and prepared both by that circumstance and by his full university training to appreciate the freedom he found here. He spent the years of his residence in America with eyes and ears and heart wide open. He was a marked man of his kind, however, and was not suffered to make his home here as he had intended. He was called to be professor of history in the University of Strasburg in 1872, and in 1874 to his present chair, of modern history, at Freiburg, in Breisgau. He had remained long enough in America to see our Government alive, and he had seen it living in the midst of one of the test periods of its existence, the period of reconstruction.

It was with such preparation of personal contact with our institutions that Dr. von Holst undertook his now standard "Constitutional and Political History of the United States," the first volume of which appeared in 1873, while he was professor at Strasburg. He was equipped as few foreigners could hope to be for his task; and it must be said, if one is to speak the whole truth about this interesting man, that he himself is fully conscious of his peculiar fitness and capacity to expound our history and principles of government. In the foot notes to his pages he turns again and again to demolish, with the truly magnificent scorn and ferocity of superior knowledge, other German students who have ventured to write about our politics and constitutional history. "Since Schlief, *Die Verfossung den Nordamerikanischen Union,*" he says in one place, "is often cited by German authors, I think it my duty to show by example how little trustworthy a guide he is." (p. 23.) He, "for the most part, does not state, as he promises to do, what 'the actual constitutional law of the Union' is. Instead of this he states what, in his opinion, the Constitutional law should be, frequently what it should not be and only what it is in accordance with his erroneous view." (p. 49.) And so very often indeed. Herr Schlief is thrust quite out of the arena after a fashion of scant courtesy which must rejoice the hearts of all German professional gladiators.

This excess of belligerent spirit is, however, the result of genuine force in Dr. von Holst. He has won for himself a just title to exhibit this imperial bearing. Besides being masterful by nature he has made himself master by art, by a genius for taking pains, by accurate and indefatigable study. Those who have seen the man,[1] with his long, decisive jaw, his deep-set, glowing eyes and his firmly closing mouth, know how to read his books; and those who have followed him closely through his citations of authorities know how to respect his books, in spite of an occasional error.

Still, notwithstanding his long residence in the United States, his consequent sympathy with our ideas and his fully adequate acquaintance with all the standard authorities, Dr. von Holst writes like a Continental and not at all like an English or American jurist. The Continental jurist is absolute in his interpretation of law and fact, almost to the point of being what Dr. von Holst most contemptuously hates, namely, doctrinaire. The English or American jurist, on the other hand, is inclined to regard law and fact as having, no less than the animals the evolutionist talks

[1] Wilson saw von Holst when he lectured at the Johns Hopkins in October 1883. For Wilson's description, see WW to R. Bridges, Oct. 12, 1883, Vol. 2, p. 472.

about, an environment; to keep always in mind the cardinal circumstance that the constitutional history of his race has been a development from precedent to precedent—that is, from one understanding of the law to another understanding of it; and generally to deem English or American law to have been at any particular time just what the people at that time living under it supposed it to be. That is the way in which all our greatest expounders and statesmen have regarded the status of the united colonies before the formation of the present Constitution, and since the framing of that great instrument it, in its turn, has been held to contain from time to time just what the Supreme Court, its authoritative expounder, has found in it. This has always seemed to us the principle of interpretation most in keeping with our history and most consonant with the "genius" of our institutions.

This, however, is by no means the mode of reasoning to be met with in Dr. von Holst and the younger American writers who have followed his lead. They are very absolute. They say, "What are the facts of the case? Did any one of the colonies ever act as a completely sovereign state? No; the colonies were once sovereign states *in posse*, but never *in esse*. They chose to co-operate; therefore they coalesced without any choice in the matter. The Continental Congresses, having no distinct, but only a revolutionary or provisional, authority, had unlimited, that is to say sovereign, authority. From the first, therefore, we were a nation. The Confederation *was* a confederation; but only because of an unfortunate abdication of its authority on the part of the Continental Congress; presently there was a return to national integration and organization under the Constitution of 1787. The nationality of the preconstitutional stage was," they admit, "unconscious. The lapse into a merely federation form 'met with no opposition among the people. Its entire correspondence with their whole political thought and impulse was generally fully recognized, and another advance on the part of Congress would unquestionably have met with an opposition not to be overcome' (v. H., p. 10). But contemporary opinion, though the opinion of the whole people, is not admissible in evidence" with these writers; "only hard facts are to be heeded. Virginia and Massachusetts regarded themselves as sovereign states before agreeing to the Constitution of 1787, but they had never made war or contracted treaty obligations as such with foreign powers, and had, consequently, never been sovereign in deed. They had chosen to co-operate with the other colonies and so had lost their individuality as states and become commonwealths." This reading of events would probably not have been intelligible in the least degree to Hamilton, who wanted a consolidated power, or to Madison, who did not want one quite so much consolidated, or to Washington, who wanted only the wisest thing that could be managed under the circumstances; but this consideration does not at all alter the facts of the case. Sovereignty is indivisible; the colonies must have been sovereign entirely or not at all; they never assumed entire sovereign control of themselves; therefore, state sovereignty never was anything but a gratuitous impertinence, and the "limited sovereignty" of the gravest writers of the earlier time was sheer nonsense. "Story was unquestionably wrong" in many particulars.

Nobody is now likely to withstand the practical conclusions deducible from this reasoning. State sovereignty, though still, happily, alive and sufficiently vigorous in the shape of admittedly constitutional states-rights, is utterly dead as a question of politics, and no one has now the least hope or desire to see its resurrection. But it is as living as ever as a question of history; and it must be confessed that this broad-axe method of cutting all contemporary understanding away from the discussion of so vital a matter is not a little astounding and confusing, even to the student who wants to come to the same conclusions that these drastic jurists have reached. One begins to tremble lest this should prove to be a trick of materialistic philosophy to lure our souls to their destruction, for it shows that peoples go blindly to their fate and have no choice but to live under constitutions which contain they know not what.

But a discussion of such matters is several times too big for this review of a small book. We turn to the special features of the volume. This manual of our constitutional law, unlike Dr. von Holst's "Constitutional History," was not written for everybody, but only for a limited class—not for students who know much about the subject already, that is, but as a brief handbook for those who are unfamiliar with the subject and who seek only its presentation in general outline. It has been extracted, by the translator from a great encyclopaedic work such as Germans only, it would seem, can command the patience and the diligence (to say nothing of the learning) to produce, namely, the "Public [Constitutional] Law of the Present in Monographs," now being issued in Germany under the editorship of Professor H.

Marquardsen, of the University of Erlangen.[2] Much more space is devoted to the constitutional law of the German states in this work, of course, than to that of the other states of the world (which the Germans describe—with some idea, it would appear, of being themselves centrally situated—as "extra-German," *ausserdeutch*). The Continental states are all discussed by professors of their own universities; but England is assigned to a German for exposition (and not Professor Gneist,[3] either), and, of course, in the case of the United States the editor could turn to Dr. von Holst instead of translating a lucubration sent from across the Atlantic.

The monographs constituting this great work bear some general likeness to each other in respect of topical division and method of treatment, with the result of giving to Dr. von Holst's contribution on our constitutional law some features which seem quite novel to the student of the ordinary American manuals on the same subject. There is strict logical classification—which is good—and there is a relatively full treatment of the chief features of the law of the several states of the Union, as well as of that of the Union itself—which is even better—for, surely, despite the neglect commonly served it, the public law of the states is a part of the public law of the United States, and a very important part. The translator has withheld from the English reader the full advantage of the logical development of the subject by omitting the analytical table of contents which serves in the original as a most suggestive map of the whole matter of the book, and as a most useful object lesson in arrangement. The full significance of the author's admirable sketch of the law of the several states, however, remains, and is unquestionably greater than that of any other similar sketch yet attempted under such narrow limitations of space. It is brought within seventy-four octavo pages, and yet at very few points does it seem crowded. The author's view in this part of the work is much more general than where he speaks of the constitutional principles of the Federal Government, and it also constantly tends to be more historical; but it is never vague, because its brevity is not obtained so much by generalization as by selection. Only the general features charac-

[2] The *Handbuch des Oeffentlichen Rechts der Gegenwart* (4 vols. in many parts, Freiburg im B. and Tübingen, 1883-1906) was a massive collaborative work in political science and public law, which Wilson was to use extensively in writing *The State*. For extracts from various volumes with Wilson's marginal comments, see the Marginal Notes printed at Aug. 18, 1887; for comment on Wilson's use of the *Handbuch* in writing *The State*, see the Editorial Note, "Wilson's 'The State,' " Vol. 6.

[3] German jurist and liberal political leader.

teristic of our state governments are dwelt upon; and these are chosen with informed judgment; every paragraph has at once point and breadth of outlook.

An equal wideness of view is, indeed, maintained even in those portions of the work where a detailed consideration is given to the organization of the general government, with which Dr. von Holst is more familiar than with the state organizations, and in dealing with which he might be expected to be a little more narrowly technical. For in following Dr. von Holst we get rid of a couple of ideas apt not long since to creep into our consideration of almost every point concerning ourselves, namely, first, that ours is the only country in the world—or at least that, as compared with it, the European countries are decadent and "effete"; and, second, that we are what we are almost altogether by virtue of deliberate choice, and only very little because of any necessary historical development. The long processes of history by which other nations and systems were developed had their beginnings far back in systems which those other nations had no voice at all in choosing. We do not care to be so deeply indebted to a past which was not American, and are loath to assign our parentage to 'fathers' who were monarchical. Our idea has been that *we made* the United States, if not in 1776 or 1787, why then somewhere 'in colonial times' at any rate. Dr. von Holst did not rid us of these ideas; we got rid of them largely ourselves, a few years ago; but Dr. Von Holst quite confirms his readers in the rejection of such notions by writing as if the opposite notions were altogether matters of course—as indeed they are—and by studying our public law as if it were a historical growth—as of course it is—albeit a growth greatly advanced towards perfection by the sagacious husbandry of the great fathers of the Republic.

Two facts greatly impress Dr. von Holst, as they have impressed other students of our development, namely, the persistence of local self-government, and (what is, in part at least, only another side of the same thing) the eminently conservative habit of our democracy. Local self-government has survived in this country because our democracy has been conservative and has clung to the organization of government which it had when it first took settlement on American shores. The Anglo-Saxons took habits of local self-government with them to Britain, but the stress of later times broke the life of those habits, and ultimately something like centralization was effected under the Norman and his successors, only the seeds of local organization remaining, till they could spring up again. Here things fell out very differently. English government began its life in America in local centres, and it has never allowed that life to be radically changed, despite every step of co-operation, federation and union. The same thing that de Tocqueville noted Dr. von Holst finds the fact, that the central governments (those, that is, which are central as regards local government—the state governments) act generally, not through officers of their own, but through local officers, the elected servants of counties and townships. These men (sheriffs, treasurers, assessors, etc.) are not at all responsible to the governor for their execution of state business, but only to the criminal courts and to their own constituents. In brief, only the state governs the locality through general law, scarcely at all through direct administration. The relation of the local government to the central is, in practice, not a relation of subordination but a relation of confidence.

But this is not the only evidence of conservatism on the part of our democracy which discloses itself to a student like Dr. von Holst. It is conservative as opposed to *radical*; its conservatism, singularly enough, takes the shape of distrust of the democratic principle, the shape of a conviction that it is possible to have too much government by the people's representatives. The proof of this is the growing distrust of state legislatures so manifest in all recent changes in the constitutional laws of the states. The powers of our legislatures are being deliberately curtailed, their sessions made imperatively shorter and less frequent, even their honesty openly questioned. The general principle of constitutional revision would now seem to be: The less the people govern themselves the better—it is best, instead of trusting to yearly legislation, to have as much permanent law in the constitution as possible, to give wider functions to the courts and enlarged powers to the governor, leaving as little lawmaking to the people's representatives as may be. This is to question the *representative* action of democracy, at any rate, very seriously.

Contrary to reasonable expectation, the brief historical sketch of the "genesis" of the Constitution given by Dr. von Holst, our constitutional historian, at the opening of this work, is the least satisfactory section of the whole, more particularly as it was written for Continental readers, who may be supposed to have very little knowledge of the subject besides that here afforded them, rather than for American readers, who might in most cases be expected to be able to supplement the matter of the text. The statements made are so general as to be altogether vague. For instance, in regard to colonial union, Dr. von Holst says (p. 4) that "some" of the colonies "very early established closer ties with one another," for reasons which he goes on to state in very general terms to the length of half a page. Then the impression having been created that there were perhaps several attempts at partial union between several "some" of the colonies, he says: "The League of the United Colonies of New England—Massachusetts, Plymouth, Connecticut and New Haven—in 1643 against the Indians and the Dutch lost all significance with the occasion which had called it into life." This is the first and last mention of the League. Is the uninformed reader to understand that it was only one of several similar federations abortively born? Are these New England colonies the "some," and the only "some," that "early established closer ties with one another," or were there others? Dr. von Holst does not say. He knows the facts so well himself that he forgets the ignorance of others. It would be impossible from this sketch alone to get even a clear, general idea of the genesis of the union—the idea it leaves is only a hazy, general idea.

Dr. von Holst is very satisfactory in speaking of the co-ordination of the three branches of the Government—the legislative, the executive and the judiciary. He is quite clear upon the point that their co-ordination was not, and in the nature of the case could not be, their *equalization*, and that, consequently, Congress may be, whenever it chooses, practically the whole of the Government as regards the energetic part of governing, that is, the origination and direction of policies. "So far as the initiative is concerned," he declares, "the administration has no will of its own, but only an opinion" (p. 131). And certainly no one may gainsay him on that head. Dr. von Holst's treatment abounds in similar penetrative remarks, from which his style receives an occasional incisiveness which, as a general thing, it lacks; and these evidences of insight into the more intimate secrets of the system are the more satisfactory because they are associated with so broad and masterly an analysis and handling of his matter as a whole. He is able to group the features of the Federal Government under his general headings, "The Organization of the Federal Government," "The Functions of the Governmental Factors," etc., and under his less general captions, "Taxation, Finance and the Public Debt," "Commerce, Interstate and National," "Justice," "International Relations and Military Sovereignty," etc., in a way which of itself clears the subject of many intricacies, especially when one can follow the development of the topics in the analytical table of contents which the translator has left out.

Amongst the curiosities of constitutional law upon which Dr. von Holst has come in his studies is this in the Arkansas Constitution of 1868. That Constitution, whose framers would seem to have had enviably distinct views about the good of society, "commands the Legislature 'to tax all privileges, pursuits and occupations *that are of no real use to society*,' and forbids the taxation of all others." "How the laws of Arkansas have illustrated this remarkable provision in detail I am unable to say," adds our author with a smile.

It is very hard indeed to pardon the translator one liberty which he has taken with the original monograph: he has left out a considerable part of the list of authorities (the bibliography) which it contained. American students now appreciate at its full value bibliography of the careful sort characteristic of such work as Dr. von Holst gives out—it is indispensable to them. Mr. Mason could hardly have thought it superfluous to give the name of every book the author put on his list had he supposed himself to be translating for students; he must have thought that students would seek the work in the original, and that for the 'general reader' a part of the list would suffice. He can be hardly justified even in that conclusion. Let us suppose that his publisher compelled all possible abbreviation.

He at any rate deserves the thanks of the "general reader" for having made this admirable book available in English, for certainly no one who examines it carefully and follows its expositions to the end can fail to feel that Dr. von Holst has done us a very great service indeed in sending us this last treatise of his on so all-important a subject. If Dr. von Holst has had any ambition to serve the country he once thought of adopting as his own he has already doubly attained his object.

Printed in the Philadelphia *Press*, April 17, 1887; editorial headings omitted.

From Joseph Ruggles Wilson

Dearest Son,   Clarksville, Ap 29th 1887

We are becoming uneasy because of Bryn Mawr's silence.[1] We are of course sure that neither you nor dear Ellie is sick (very), or the well one w'd have written: but still our hearts yearn for a little word at intervals not so long. You are no doubt busy as you can be, and so possibly is Ellie; yet a *postal* (that last resort of the overwhelmed) would be better than nothing.

We are moving towards the end of the session in the even tenor of our ways (tenor not base!) and towards the sessions of the next Assembly.[2] Again the small men are sent (including Smoot[3] once more) and the whole thing will again be made into a devil's dish I greatly fear. They are after the *Clerks* now: Smoot's and Strickler's Presbyteries[4] overturing for a frequent election of these, &c &c. At the earliest decent moment I shall resign, never in this world to enter an Assembly upon any terms: and how glad I shall be to get rid of the entire concern! Your uncle James [Woodrow] will probably not be well enough to attend at St Louis—and it will be *just as well*—for he will thus escape much additional mortification.[5]

Your dear mother is far from strong—and I anticipate with eagerness her going to Columbia for George's advice.

Love, abundant, from her, from Dode, from me—to you both (or three)   Most affectionately   Your Father.

ALS (WP, DLC).
    [1] Actually, Woodrow Wilson had written on April 21. The letter was delayed in transit. See JWW to WW, April 31[30], 1887.
    [2] The General Assembly of the southern Presbyterian Church, which was to meet in St. Louis on May 19, 1887.
    [3] The Rev. Dr. Richmond Kelley Smoot, pastor of the Free (Presbyterian) Church, Austin, Texas, 1876-1905.
    [4] The Rev. Dr. Givens Brown Strickler, pastor of the Central Presbyterian Church, Atlanta, Georgia, 1883-96.
    [5] A reference to Dr. Woodrow's long fight with southern Presbyterian judicatories over the question of evolution. See WW to ELA, June 26, 1884, n. 1, Vol. 3, pp. 218-19.

From Janet Woodrow Wilson

My darling Son—   Clarksville, Tenn. April 31st [30th] [1887]
    Yours of April 21 was received yesterday. I dont propose to write you a letter today—but I suppose it is important to answer the business part of your letter at once. Your father thinks that the offer made for the land should be accepted—so, of course, you will act accordingly. I really dont know what is wisest—but am willing to abide by *his* decision. Of course I refer to the offer of $10.00 per acre—if it should come to that.

    I am so glad to hear of your pleasure at the prospect of a house of your own.[1] I can imagine what a comfort it will be to you—but, dear child, whatever can you want with *eleven* rooms! Why we have only *six*—and have abundance of room! Let me tell you—what I have learned from experience—it is a sad embarrassment to have *too many spare rooms*. But I dont believe such warnings can do any good—so I will forbear.

As your father has told you, I am far from well—and sometimes feel greatly discouraged—for I dont know what my two
"boys" will do, if I break down altogether. Still I try to hope for
much from my hoped for visit to Columbia. As soon as our plans
are definitely made you shall be informed. With love unbounded
from us all to you three dear ones.

Lovingly   Your Mother.

ALS (WP, DLC).
   1 Life in the Betweenery having become very difficult for the Wilsons, Woodrow Wilson was in process of renting the Baptist parsonage on Gulph Road, or
had already done so. For a detailed description, see Mary E. Hoyt, undated
memorandum in the RSB Coll., DLC.

To James Hamilton Woodrow

My dear Jimmie,   Bryn Mawr, Pa., 3 May, 1887.
   I am quite aware that, in the eye of *etiquette*, I have sinned in
not writing to you before about your marriage:[1] and I confess I
might have written when I ventured to send Miss Kate (as she
was then), in my own and Mrs. W's interest, an odd-looking
lamp,—as a *'remembrancer.'* But I hold that etiquette may be
dispensed with to a certain extent between cousins who are no
strangers to each other: and in this case I have the 'proud consciousness' that I know what I am about. In brief, as you are
aware, I've been married myself, and I know that *now* is the time
to congratulate you. Being now married yourself, you will, I am
confident, agree with me. In other words, instead of emptily
wishing you happiness beforehand, I want to tell you how glad I
am,—how glad *we* are,—that you are happy. This is the first
marriage I've heard of for a long time where I knew both
parties,—consequently I'm sure of my ground. When one knows
only one of the parties to such a contract, it's just as well to be
on the safe side and *wish* all sorts of beatitudes beforehand!
   With much love to you both from us both,
Your affectionate cousin,   Woodrow Wilson

ALS (in possession of James Woodrow).
   1 James Hamilton Woodrow and Katharine McGregor McMaster were married
on April 28, 1887, in the First Presbyterian Church of Columbia, S. C., by
Dr. James Woodrow.

To Andrew Dickson White

My dear Sir,   Bryn Mawr, Pa., 3 May, 1887.
   I take pleasure in forwarding to my uncle the letter and
pamphlet rec'd to-day. I am sorry to say that he is at present not

at all well, so that it may not be possible for him to reply at once, as he will no doubt wish to do. His address is, Rev. Dr. James Woodrow, *Columbia, South Carolina.*

Very truly Yours,   Woodrow Wilson

ALS (A. D. White Papers, NIC).

Mary Eloise Hoyt to Ellen Axson Wilson

Ellen, darling,   Rome [Ga.], May 4th 18[8]7

I always knew you were my good genius, but I never imagined that even you could plan out anything so beautiful.[1] It sounds like a bit of a fairy story, and you have made it all fit in so nicely. And let me tell you, darling, that more than all the wonderful advantages, even, and you know how I long to be educated, how even one year for study alone, even, would be a treasure, but more than the chances for study, and all that, I thank you for the sweet love that planned it all. I knew you loved me, dear, but I did not know you cared so much. And Cousin Woodrow, too, please thank him. I do not believe one man in a thousand would be so good to his own cousin even—much less his wife's. Even if things happen so that I can not come, I will thank you both as long as I live. And, dear, I do not believe I mind accepting it from you, in fact, I love to have you to thank for it. And you must consider that a wonder for I hate to live at home and not pay board. . . .

I have no idea that I can pass the examinations. I know they are terrible—you forgot to enclose the history paper—by the way—but I am going to do my best and you must not be disappointed if I fail—because it is what I expect to do. But it will break my heart to disappoint you, dear. You have always looked at me through golden glasses and I never could persuade you that I was a very, very ordinary girl, without much education, but pretty much heart. You must say, dearie, that you will not care very much if I fail and you will not let Cousin Woodrow think I am stupider than I am. . . . If I write a bit more I will be snappy to-morrow. Good-night and God bless you all, Ellen.

M. E. H.

ALI (WP, DLC).
[1] The Wilsons had invited her to live with them and complete her education at Bryn Mawr. Miss Hoyt was teaching school in Rome at this time.

From Edward Livermore Burlingame

Dear Sir: New York, May 6, 1887.

I have cordially appreciated your kindness in giving us another opportunity to see a paper of yours,[1] after my reluctant return of the article on Adam Smith with the objection which I am sure you fully understood. If I had not been absent and under an accumulation of work I should not have let so much delay occur in writing you as to the present manuscript. Its general drift I heartily like, and the whole paper is one which for its matter we should distinctly wish to have in the Magazine; but to speak frankly there is something in its *manner* which I should have been glad to have a little different for our purpose. As in all such cases it is difficult to express just what I mean without conveying more; but there is a suggestion of the colloquial and argumentative in the way the reader is addressed, which, while precisely in place if the paper were an essay in an editorial department, with a certain personality, somehow seems to take from the value of it when it is printed as the article of an evidently pseudonymous author. Taken in conjunction with that characteristic of the style, this feature of the pseudonym seems to me to become in itself an objection; and the two combine to keep the article out of either the one or the other of the classes to which it ought to belong. If I make myself clear you will see that I should frankly like to use it with some changes, and should be especially glad to have you among our contributors; but there is something in the present shape of the paper—as neither quite an argument nor a chat with the reader—which makes it seem a little nondescript and in short not quite fulfilling what I should like to do. I am   Very truly yours,   E. L. Burlingame

TLS (WP, DLC) with WWhw notation on env.: "Ans. May 7, '87."
   [1] "The Eclipse of Individuality," printed at April 7, 1887.

Randolph Axson to Ellen Axson Wilson

My dear Ellie   Savannah, Ga. May 9, 1887

Yours of the inst is to hand and carefully noted. I send you check on N York for $100.00. Dont spend *all* your money in furnishing your house. In regard to Mr Bones and the *rents*, he has paid you the same proportion that he has sent me for the other three children, which has been eighty two dollars and some cents apiece. The house rents for 250.00 per annum out of which, town & state & county taxes & insurance & water rents

&c have to be deducted. I think it would be a good idea to sell if a fair price could be had. Stockton writes that he has been sick since he went on to Gainesville. I doubt whether it would be best for him to return to Savannah, as the climate does not seem to agree with him. He had become extremely *nervous*. He told me you thought of taking Eddie to live with you when you returned next fall. Better talk the matter over with your Uncle & Aunt[1] this Summer, and have it *understood* so that no *feeling* in the case may ever arise. I hope Mr Wilson's prospects are *bright*, and that you will get along comfortably in your home. We expect to move to our new home in Aug't. Your Grandmother has not left her room for many months—remains about the same. The rest of us are all well. Send an acknowledgement of the receipts of this check. All unite with me in love to you and yours

Your aff Uncle   Randolph Axson

Mr Bones has sent me statements of Rents annually—showing how much he recd for rents & how much paid out for taxes &c— and what he has paid you up to 1st Jany last is right. He has sent me for the three children a few *cents* more for the proportion of each one. The *taxes insurance* water rent &c are very heavy.

ALS (WP, DLC).
    [1] Mr. and Mrs. Warren A. Brown of Gainesville, Ga.

To Herbert Baxter Adams

Dear Dr. Adams,   Bryn Mawr, Pa., 16 May, 1887.

I enclose the statement for which you ask.[1] I hope it will prove what you want.

A very unexpected resolution has been taken concerning the tutorship in history here. So few of the students now in college have offered ancient history (the course that would be given next year) that it has been determined to make them, and any new ones who may offer, wait a year, and *make no appointment* till the year '88-'89, when a larger salary can be given and a man such as we want probably secured.

I at last return the extract about von Holst which you were kind enough to lend me. Many thanks for it: it served my purpose excellently.

The William and Mary report came to hand, and I am delighted with 'the idea.'[2] It is brought out with great force (to which the official endorsement in the prefatory letter adds a valuable element) and ought to tell: would certainly tell if we had an integrate instead of a disintegrate govt: *may* tell anyhow. Fortune speed it!

Very truly Yours,   Woodrow Wilson

ALS (H. B. Adams Papers, MdBJ).

¹ Adams must have asked for a statement from Wilson about his plans for his lectures on administration at the Johns Hopkins in 1888. Adams's letter is missing.

² See H. B. Adams to WW, Jan. 25, 1887, n. 1.

From Edward Livermore Burlingame

My dear Sir: [New York] May 17, [188]7.

I did not mean to let your kind letter of the 7th go so long unanswered; but I have waited for an opportunity to look carefully again at the manuscript in connection with what you wrote.

I must say frankly that on doing so I have come to the conclusion which you feared was unavoidable,—that the *manner* of the piece is too integral a part of it to make it possible that the article should be worked over with entire satisfaction to both you and me. I can not but think it better, on the whole, though I come to this conclusion with reluctance, that this particular paper should go back to you for use elsewhere, than that you should take trouble with it which might result in nothing more than spoiling its present shape for you.

I know very well that letters such as this and my last can hardly fail to leave the impression of a rather indefinite and carping criticism, than to clearly explain to you my own point of view; but this is perhaps inevitable in letter-writing about matters so intangible as this.

I have no right to expect that my conclusion will not discourage you from some day letting us look at another paper; but I can sincerely say that I hope it may not.

Very truly yours,   E. L. Burlingame

LPC (Charles Scribner's Sons Archives, NjP).

From Martha Carey Thomas

My dear Dr Wilson,   [Bryn Mawr, c. May 17, 1887]

I suppose there was some misunderstanding about the entrance-examination in history[.] I understood Dr Keiser¹ to say that you would like to have been consulted in regard to the hour. If you will look at the program for 1886-87 you will find that the hour has not been changed since last year. What is a disadvantage in June is a corresponding advantage in September as the examiner does not need to return to Bryn Mawr in the early part of the week.[2] The order of the examinations remains the same from year to year (although the date changes one day) so that candidates may be able to calculate the times from one year to another. Hoping that the explanation is lucid

Yours very truly   M. Carey Thomas

ALS (WP, DLC).
[1] Edward H. Keiser, Associate Professor of Chemistry at Bryn Mawr.
[2] Entrance examinations in history at Bryn Mawr in 1887 were scheduled for Friday, June 10, and Saturday, October 1.

To Martha Carey Thomas

[Bryn Mawr] 17 May 1887

I am sorry that Dr Keiser thought it necessary to speak in my stead about the matter of the dates for the entrance examinations: I could probably have represented my position in the matter more exactly than he seems to have done. I had not failed to observe that the dates for the entrance examinations remained the same from year to year, and I of course perceive the advantage of their standing unchanged; I was simply at a loss to understand when and how the fixed schedule had been determined upon.

Were it possible for us to stay here till Monday, an examination on Friday would entail no very serious inconvenience; but the closing of the cottage on Saturday makes that impossible, and, since those of us who have long distances to go must start on Friday to reach our far-away destination before Sunday, it becomes an impossibility to read all the papers of a Friday examination before leaving. You of course appreciate the inconvenience of such a circumstance[.] If it cannot be avoided, however, it need not be discussed.

What I wanted to speak of principally, had I seen you myself, was what seemed to me a serious 'conflict.' Miss Cope, Miss Elder, and Miss Paxson[1] who failed in history on entering, are, I understood, to take their examinations in June. Two of them (all three perhaps) are in Biology which is set for the same hours. It wd. be quite irregular, as it seems to me, to postpone their making up of the condition much longer.

[Sincerely yours,   Woodrow Wilson]

WWhwL (draft) (WP, DLC).
[1] Julia Cope, Louise R. Elder, and Caroline Ely Paxson.

From Albert Shaw

My Dear Wilson: Minneapolis, Minn., May 23, 1887.

I am delighted to get your picture, which has just this moment come to hand. It makes you look a little pale and thin, and suggests a query as to your health; but the likeness is otherwise quite satisfactory, and will be prized.

You have not written to me for a long time, and I have had to depend upon indirect sources for information about you. In fact I have a sort of boycotted feeling. I haven't heard in a long time from Levermore, Yager, Shinn, Jameson, Scaife, Gould, Ramage or Dewey. Bemis has been out here recently, and I have seen Tolman and John Dewey within a year or so. But as for the rest I'm afraid I have passed pretty nearly out of remembrance. Holcomb[1] sent me his wedding cards, however, and your photograph is another welcome interruption of my solitude,—"Solitude" I mean, of course, as to J. H. U. friends; for this is anything but a lonesome neighborhood. There is a powerful fascination about the driving life and astonishing material developments of our best western cities;—and Minneapolis, let me say, is the very best one of the lot. It will take courage on my part to leave if duty and a proper ambition should call me to another place. The newspaper work has come to be a pretty tiresome grind; altho' I enter with enough heartiness into current and local life to find my work very tolerable. Now that you are an experienced professor, won't you write me frankly how the thing compares with more "practical" callings, and whether a step from my editor's chair[2] to a college place (for a good deal less salary) would be likely to make more of a man out of me and to prove itself satisfactory on the whole. Just your impression is what I want; of course it wouldn't be fair to ask you to give advice.

I am now in much better health than when in Baltimore, altho' I was nearly dead a year ago.

To change the subject, I was glad to see your article—both profound and bright—in the *New Princeton*.[3] Have you any big books on hand?

My energy spends itself, of course, in ephemeral work. I have a bit of comment on Northwestern legislation in the May number of the *"Contemporary Review,"* which the editor has seen fit to entitle "The American State and the American Man," doubtless having in mind Mr. Spencer's "The State versus the Man." The article was rather hastily put together, and I am not sure that it conveys my ideas very clearly. But it will at least inform the world that legislation is very chaotic in this part of the world. Hoping you may find time to write to me before your summer vacation ends, and particularly wishing that you might come out here for a vacation trip sometime, I am, as ever,

Yours sincerely   Albert Shaw

ALS (WP, DLC) with WWhw notation on env.: "Ans. May 29/87."
 ¹ These former fellow-students and associates at the Johns Hopkins were Charles H. Levermore, Arthur Yager, Charles H. Shinn, J. Franklin Jameson, Walter B. Scaife, Elgin R. L. Gould, Burr James Ramage, Davis R. Dewey, Edward W. Bemis, Albert H. Tolman, John Dewey, and William P. Holcomb.
 ² Shaw had advanced to the associate editorship of the *Minneapolis Daily Tribune*.
 ³ "Of the Study of Politics," printed at Nov. 25, 1886.

From Robert Ewing

My Dear Sir: Nashville, May 28th. 1887
    A thought occurs to me. I don't know whether its worth communicating to you or not, but I will do so, in the hope that it may *possibly* result in something and by further possibility bring you here.

    You remember, when you were with us,¹ I drove you by our Normal School Buildings² and explained to you briefly, how the school was maintained, viz—by the joint contributions of the Peabody Trust, the Nashville University and the State: the first contributing largely more than both of the others combined.

    The then Chancellor, E. S. Stearns has since died and the election of his successor is now about to occur.

    The place would be permanent and financially considered is worth a beautiful home and $3,000.00 a year, paid promptly.

    You are in every way well qualified to fill it.

    No one has been fixed upon. Do you want it?

    Are you willing to offer for it?

    Does it involve a sacrifice? Are your other engagements honorably *breakable*?

    Does a new field offer enough inducement?

    Write me if its worth while to pursue the matter and I will reply fully.

    Dr Curry, Minister to Spain³ and J. D. Porter Ass't Secy. of State have been mentioned, but I don't think either one is prepared to accept.

    Of course I don't say I can get it, but I will pull off my coat, if you respond favorably.

    See Mr Hoyt⁴

Yours   R. Ewing

TLS (WP, DLC).
¹ The Woodrow Wilsons visited the Robert Ewings in Nashville in June 1886 before going on to Clarksville.

² The Peabody Normal Institute, renamed the George Peabody College for Teachers in 1914.

³ Jabez Lamar Monroe Curry.

⁴ Added in longhand. Ewing was referring to the Rev. Thomas A. Hoyt.

To Robert Bridges

My dear Bobby,   Bryn Mawr, Pa., 29 May, 1887.

It must have seemed to you simple 'bad manners' that I did not answer at once your letter of the 25th,¹ asking me to go out on Long Island with you for to-day and to-morrow; but it was literally out of my power to do so. We have rented a cottage for next year and for the last 3 or 4 days every hour not spent in discharging class duty I have spent superintending and *doing* the work necessary to get it in shape for occupation. I haven't had a moment for thought of anything but my own household plans, and nights have found me hardly able even to *hold* a pen. It would indeed have been delightful to go with you on your 'days-off'—it would have rejoiced both soul and body; but all sorts of things, great and small, hold me fast here and I am obliged, physically at least, to confine myself to a very few square miles.

In spite of the disappointment it brought me, by showing me a delightful thing I could not do, I was sincerely glad to get your letter. It gave me the first authentic word I have had as to how you fare in your new berth: and I have long been hungry for news on that point. I am the gladder to get it because it's good news—of the 'contentment' I hoped the new employment would bring you. I say hurrah! with all my heart!

No, you did not mislead me as to the character of article that would be likely to suit the magazine: but I haven't time to *prepare* articles of any sort: i. e. to *study for* them[.] I must make up what I write for magazines of the thoughts which come to me through my necessary daily contact with men and books: thoughts wh. are none the less serious and none the less carefully worked out— when I come to write them—on that account: but not forming themselves at beck of my will into articles of any particular class. They are simply the *horizon* to my reading and study. If we had in this country a periodical of the aim of the 'Fortnightly,' say, my study could be made to contribute directly to it: but to all we have it contributes only indirectly.

Mrs. Wilson sends warmest regards. As ever
                    Yours affectionately   Woodrow Wilson

ALS (WC, NjP).
     1 It is missing.

To Albert Shaw

My dear Shaw: Bryn Mawr, Pa. 29 May, 1887.

If past daily thoughts could be gathered up and put in evidence, I could easily prove to you that you have as little passed
out of my remembrance as any of the others of the small number
of my valued friends. Alas, my dear fellow, if silence on my part
were to be construed as indifference in all cases, I'd have few
friends to value. Letter-writing is for me, somehow, a thing of
serious difficulty—letter-writing, such as I like to please friends
with. A mere perfunctory thing of a few lines—2 or 3 pages of
note paper—I can write anytime to anybody, of course; but it
pains me to send such to those to whom I'm not indifferent. A
good, honest, down-right letter, weighty with something really
said about things one genuinely thinks about seems to me, even
in these days of facile, frequent correspondence, the only sort of
message worth sending—well (to proceed *ad hominem*) worth
sending you. It's a wrong-headed doctrine, doubtless: for short
letters get written, long ones don't. But that's my thought, notwithstanding, and I'm always waiting for the time which never
comes, when I'll have 'time' to do the real genuine thing, which
requires pains and thought and the whole fibre of one's best
energy of both heart and mind. I don't write to some people
because I don't care to: I don't write to you because I do want to.
Dr. Albert Shaw will never lose his grip on one Woodrow Wilson
by any movement originating with the said W. W.,—that I'm
sure of!

Hurrah for 'Ikaria'![1] I won't pretend to have read it in this
form, but I am delighted with the fact of its *übersetzung.* You are
certainly to be congratulated: and—it may be impertinent intru-
sion on my part into another man's triumph, but I can't help it if
it is—I feel as if something propitious and 'setting-up' had happened to me! We are supplied with the Eng. magazines, unhappily, by the slow Leonard-Scott concern, and so have not yet
seen the *Contemporary* for May;[2] but I have read with extreme
satisfaction the *Academy's* verdict[3] that Mr. Shaw's paper was by
far the most interesting piece in the No.,—and I'm waiting to see
it myself with a great appetite for its contents. You are becoming
quite European!

I have been a professor long enough, I think, to give my

impression of the sort of place a professorship is likely to prove, on the whole, to a man who wants above all things the best life for his mind: certainly my impressions on that head are very distinct. I believe that a professorship is likely to prove very much more satisfactory to such a man than any of the 'practical' professions of which I know anything, because it will enable him to wait on the slowness of his complete thought. Rather, it will compel him so to wait. Unless his teaching lies directly and all along in the line of his special interests and studies, he will have, willy-nilly, to wait till he has gone over the whole course at least once before he can do anything systematic at his 'own' work (I have waited 2 yrs. and must wait 2 more); but meantime he's getting horizons and is being forced into all sorts of knowledge he might otherwise never have touched at all, greatly to the sacrifice of completeness. Even if his teaching does take him nowhere but where his special interests lead him, his class demand the rudiments and he must grind over them before he may pass on to do his own developing from them: and this necessity to wait seems to me greatly advantageous. I have chafed bitterly at what seemed the grind, the drudgery of these first yrs. of my teaching; I doubtless shall growl and fret again next year, and the year after. But I am conscious in saner moments that I'm benefitting by being thus held back from too hasty production. In the 'practical' professions—law, medicine, journalism, whatnot—a man must think from hand to mouth, and must put forth his thought piece-meal. You know how ardently I believe in the students keeping close to affairs, in contact with the thought of the unstudious, practical world; but the man of the practical professions is not in contact with this world: he's in it and of it, and can get no leisure and no distance for an adequate view of it. Above all his thought, no matter what his genius for thinking, can at no time be entire. Now, if a man who knows and values the 'practical' world will withdraw himself to a professor's chair— not to profess the higher mathematics but something that will raise and advance society—he may obtain just the aloofness of view he needs; and, if he be content to let himself settle solidly in the routine of his new post—let the time first arrive when, though still doing his work freshly, it will not exhaust or fatigue his originating faculties or steal all his reading and writing hours —he can at last, I believe and hope, come out upon firm opportunities for whole, sane, and beneficent thought. I speak earnestly, for my own mental future depends from this question. I have two considerable undertakings in mind (partly in hand)—

a textbook on govt. (comparative law and constitutions)[4] and (don't think me audacious) an extended study and analysis of Democracy,[5] which latter I hope to fill with the best thoughts of my lifetime:—but these must wait, wait, wait for their serious development. Meantime I feel that I am growing a little day by day: and having chosen my themes, I am growing towards them. Or, rather they are growing. Hence my hope—my enlarging confidence that someday I shall be able to say what I have to say, be it great or small as a contribution to the world's thought, as I could never have said it from the hurry and (mental) incompleteness of a 'practical' life. I am tempted to go on and unfold my great Democracy plans (into which all my previous schemes have merged drawn by a centripetal force unmistakably natural); but I must reserve that for another letter, contenting myself this time with a first draft of my impressions of a professor's life and may-be's.

As ever, yours affectionately   Woodrow Wilson

TCL (in possession of Virginia Shaw English).
[1] Albert Shaw, *Ikaria. Ein Beitrag zur Geschichte der Kommunismus*, trans. by M. Jacobi (Stuttgart, 1886).
[2] Albert Shaw, "The American State and the American Man," London *Contemporary Review*, LI (May 1887), 695-711.
[3] Perhaps a reference to Shaw's article in the London *Academy*, which has escaped the editorial eye.
[4] See the Editorial Note, "Wilson's Plan for a Textbook in Civil Government."
[5] See the Editorial Note, "Wilson's First Treatise on Democratic Government."

Wilson Reviews His Course Work at Bryn Mawr

[*c. June 1, 1887*]

History.—For special reasons the scheme of making the instruction in the history of France run parallel with that in the history of England throughout the year was changed. The history of England was completed in the first semester, and that of France taken up in the second. Advantage was taken of this change to make the method of instruction employed during the first semester somewhat different from that in the last. English history was taught backwards; a steady effort was made to render the lectures and all the class exercises a series of explanations of the conditions, geographical, social, and political, to be seen in the life of the English nation to-day, and all the chief and most pressing questions now agitating England were discussed as fully as possible. To such purposes voluntary "News-meetings," usually held one evening weekly throughout the year, were directly auxiliary. In these meetings the most important news of the day was considered, and the relations of passing events to their historic antecedents shown; the interest proved so great that the attendance much outgrew the limits of the class.

The History of the United States was also studied in the first semester, and the instruction was given almost wholly by lectures. In these consecutive narration was not attempted, but exposition of carefully chosen representative periods or events.

During the second semester an elaborate series of lectures was given in French history, and the history of the Renaissance and Reformation. In the first series of lectures the object held in view by the instructor was to make conspicuous the several steps in the growth and policy of the monarchy, the causes of the Revolution, the political development of the present century, and the constituent elements of modern France. Under the Renaissance, its causes were fully discussed, as also the political and intellectual preparation of Italy, the leading characteristics of the Renaissance as shown in the works of the chief writers and artists, the great sea discoveries which opened the western doors of Europe, and, in general, the beginnings of modern influences.

The Reformation was considered in its connection with the Renaissance; the lives of the principal reformers were dwelt upon; and the Lutheran, the Genevan, and the English Reformation movements were contrasted.

Printed in *Bryn Mawr College. The President's Report to the Board of Trustees for the Year 1886-87* (Philadelphia, 1887), pp. 18-19.

Announcement of a Graduate Program in Political Science

[c. June 1, 1887]

Bryn Mawr College.

Advanced Course in History and Politics.

By Woodrow Wilson, Ph.D., *Associate Professor of History and Political Science.*

Author of "Congressional Government."

The following advanced course in History and Politics is offered to graduate students for the year 1887-88. It has been planned not only with reference to the needs of those who desire to prepare themselves to be teachers in these branches, but also, as a useful preparatory course for students who are looking forward to special law studies.

First Semester:

    The History, Functions, and Organs of Government.

        Fifty Lectures. Four times a week.

Second Semester:

      1. Nature and Influence of Roman Law.
                    Ten Lectures.
      2. Comparative Constitutional History.
                    Twenty-five Lectures.
      3. Growth of Modern Nationalities.
                    Eight Lectures.
      4. History of Political Economy.
                    Ten Lectures.

        Four times weekly throughout the Semester.

Throughout the year one hour a week will be given to the meetings of a Seminary, at which reports will be read of graduate work done privately upon topics collateral to those of the lectures.

The modifications of this course for subsequent years will be announced at a later time.

    Students expecting to attend this course are requested to communicate with the Secretary, as early as may be convenient.

                Address, Bryn Mawr, Pa.

Printed announcement (WP, DLC); WWhw figures omitted.

From William Peterfield Trent[1]

My dear Wilson,   Richmond, Va., June 5th, 1887.

    I have for some time thought of writing to you,[2] but then concluded I had better wait until I heard definitely about the place, before I meddled with the matter—for I think such things had better settle themselves. Now that it is settled, I want to thank you heartily for thinking of me and for your trouble in the business. I should have liked the position—especially because I think being under you would have been a great help to me in my studies. As it is I shall go to the Johns Hopkins next fall and do my best there. . . . I am delighted to hear that you will lecture at the J. H. next year—I hope I shall prove an apt pupil—I am certain I shall be an appreciative one. By the way, Heath[3] is to be here for a month to see his fiancée. I shall try to fill up some of the chinks of his time. I hope that your own family (hard to think of it when poor I am a bachelor) is well. With many thanks for your kindness—I am

Ever your friend,   Wm. P. Trent

ALS (WP, DLC) with WWhw notation on env.: "Ans. June 25 1887."
  [1] Whom Wilson had known at the University of Virginia. Trent was born in Richmond, Va., Nov. 10. 1862. B.Litt., University of Virginia, 1883; A.M., same institution, 1884. Graduate student in history and political science, The Johns Hopkins University, 1887-88. Professor of English Language and Literature, University of the South, 1888-90; Professor of English Literature, Columbia University, 1900-27. Author of many books and articles. Co-editor, *The Cambridge History of American Literature.* Died Dec. 6, 1939.
  [2] Wilson seems to have asked Trent whether he would be interested in the assistantship at Bryn Mawr.
  [3] Richard Heath Dabney.

A Course Examination

Examination in French History

June 7, 1887.

1. Name the 3 greatest kings of France before Louis XIV and *discuss* their work and influence.
2. Account for the Crusades and state carefully and fully the chief effects, direct and indirect, upon Europe, more especially upon France.
3. Discuss the origin, growth, and character of the Feudal System, and contrast the political features of feudalism with those of the system of Louis XIV.
4. Discuss the Hundred Years War, and note particularly its influence upon the throne and upon nationality in England and France.
5. Detail the causes and chief steps of the Revolution.
6. Describe the present govt of France and give a brief critical a/c of its establishment.

WWhw MS. (WP, DLC) .

From Thomas Dixon, Jr.

Wake Forest College, Wake Forest, North Carolina,

Dear Wilson: June 7, 1887.

I to-day proposed your name to the Trustees of this institution for the degree of LL.D & I'm sure you will get it.[1] And you will be the only one too though several have been proposed I understand & some of them backed by the Gov. of N. C. too. Your work is in our library & your name was magical when I suggested it to the Faculty for approval. We've some Johns Hopkins men here as Professors now & of course they swear by you as well as I. Let me hear from you occasionally. My boy is 4 mos. old & I'm out here with my Darling girl & we're having a good time. You will be duly notified if thus honored as you will be.

Sincerely,   Thomas Dixon, jr.

ALS (WP, DLC) with WWhw notation on env.: "Ans June 25/87."
  1 Dixon at this time was pastor of the Raleigh, North Carolina, Baptist Tabernacle. He was not a member of the Board of Trustees of Wake Forest College and must have been attending the commencement exercises of the college.

From Joseph Ruggles Wilson, with Enclosure

Dearest Woodrow—   Clarksville, Tenn., June 11, 87

Enclosed, you will find a card addressed to me by the Rev. Dr. Pritchard[1] of Wilmington, the Baptist minister. The college— "Wake Forest"—which has conferred this LL.D is perhaps the very best in North Carolina apart from the University. Don't be vain, however! To think that I, the only Prof. of Theology in the land, have not such a title, and my boy has! Wear it long, my darling, and wear it shiningly

I have just returned from N. Carolina, after delivering the Baccalaureate at Chapel Hill. My sermon was greatly praised, and I came away thinking myself to be somebody! But the authorities never thought of an LL.D!

Can you or Ellie not find time to write even a postal? We are hungry for news from B. M.

Our commencement here passed off *very* well. Your Mother and Josie will go to Columbia in eight or ten days. I may follow soon after. She is quite feeble—and I imagine that George alone will be able to meet her case, if any physician can do so.

We all send quantities of love to you both—you *three*.

In haste and most lovingly   Your Father

ALS (WP, DLC).
  1 Former President of Wake Forest College and at this time a member of that institution's Board of Trustees.

ENCLOSURE

Thomas Henderson Pritchard to Joseph Ruggles Wilson

Honored Brother: [Wake Forest] June 8th 1887.

It gave me pleasure to-day to urge by voice and vote the conferring of the honorary degree of LL.D. upon your Son Woodrow

Wilson, as a member of the Board of Trustees of Wake Forest College. This was the only degree conferred this year.

Yours fraternally,   T. H. Pritchard

APS (WP, DLC).

From Melville R. Hopewell

Dear Sir   Tekamah, Neb., June 13 1887.

I have given to some parties the right to get what grass they can off your land in secs. 4 & 9, 21— 11— for this season, for $55.00 which they have paid. We retain $5.00 and send you N. Y. Dft. for $50.00 less ex.

The party who was thinking of buying some 400. acres, declines to give 9.00 per acre, but would give 8.00. If mine I would not like to sell at that price.

Very Truly Yours   M. R. Hopewell

ALS (WP, DLC) with WWhw notation on env.: "Ans. June 20/87."

From Robert Ewing

Dear Mr. Wilson,   Nashville, Tenn., June 14th. 1887

I received yours of the 1st. some days ago and would have answered it at once had I not expected to be in Philidelphia last week; but being disappointed in this, I now write to say that I have since the receipt of your letter talked fully with my colleague in office—Mr A. J. Porter,[1] who happens to be Chancellor Pro-tem.

This talk with him was rather discouraging for two reasons— first because he says that he thinks the Board in their contract with the gentleman to be elected will stipulate that he shall devote his entire time to the school: that it was rather a matter of complaint that the chancellor just dead did not do this, and secondly because he thinks it possible that the salary may be reduced to $2,500.00 per annum.

If this last is done, it will come about in this way.

The Normal College is somewhat of a joint affair.

The University Board contribute the Buildings and the interest on their fund.

The Peabody trust [contributes] a considerable sum of money annually and the State $10,000.00 per annum.

This aggregate sum maintains the institution.

Each board is represented. The State Board do not work in harmony with the other two.

They are inclined to inject politics into the working of the college and are also somewhat inconsiderate and dictatorial.

It is at their instance that the 30th. has been fixed for the filling of the vacancy.

To this Peabody trust (Gov. Winthrop)[2] and the University Building [Board] will not perhaps agree and may be will take a firm stand on this and other matters.

If there is a split, they will in all likelihood say to the State "take your $10,000.00 and depart."

If they lose this $10,000.00 the salary will perhaps be reduced to $2,500.00 and thus render the position less desirable.

I should rejoice to see you at the head in this new field. I think some day the Peabody trust will do much for it—if we don't absolutely drive them away, and the good you could do yourself and our people would be well nigh. incalculable—but even if this were so "I am almost persuaded" that your hearts idol ought not to be abandoned.

If you are in Boston this Summer, make yourself known to Gov. Winthrop—change the conversation from the weather to this subject and see how the thing looks.

Situated as well as you are, I am afraid to move very strongly.

Love to Ellie and baby

Yours,   R. Ewing

Excuse type-writer

TLS (WP, DLC) with WWhw notation on env.: "Ans. June 20/87."
1 A member of the Board of Public Works and Affairs of the City of Nashville, of which Ewing was the chairman.
2 Robert Charles Winthrop, former Speaker of the United States House of Representatives and United States Senator from Massachusetts, at this time chairman of the board of the Peabody Education Fund.

From Almont Barnes[1]

My dear Sir: New York, June 18th, 1887.

I have seldom read an article, upon any subject, more interesting to me than yours upon the Study of Administration, in the June "Quarterly."[2] This arises partly from the fact that during about eighteen years of service of the Government I have made our executive system a study, to some extent, with views not wholly defined always, but in striking harmony, after all, with those expressed in your very clear and able article, wherein you lead expression if not thought also upon this subject.

I know I need not ask pardon for what I may further say,

after several readings of the first paragraph of your article on page 213.[3]

I have studied particularly the distribution and arrangement of administrative business through the seven executive departments and the one so-called department (Agriculture), and my service under the War Department (army), State Department (as chief of bureau and consul), my dealings with other departments and duties as an officer of Congress for five years, have given me practical knowledge of considerable scope and variety. Your article indicates that you possess also an accurate knowledge of what the executive system is and how it moves, as well as how it ought to.

My observation of the departments, and some study of their history, have led me to certain conclusions which I think will interest you; and if they are correct I shall value your approval highly. I think there is a natural law which should govern the formation and operation of executive business as truly as it does the formation and operation of any natural object, or group of naturally related objects.

In relation to an administrative system and its parts I state the law thus:

The operations of administration must be in true relation to the objects of administration through perfection of the administrative organization. This, differently worded, would apply to the solar system, or the simplest natural creation.

A perfect department, or bureau, for administration, contains all and only the business of the government pertaining to it by character and the means required for its execution. This is only a definitive statement of the same law—a natural law of construction and operation.

Before thinking out these statements I had concluded that Perfect organization is necessary to a Government in all its departments, on one hand for the certainty, completeness, facility, and economy of the operations of the departments, and on the other as a measure of the normal power and efficiency of the executive government.

Over three years ago I applied these rules to the existing departments, and thus made a classification of the executive business. It resulted in changes, but in symmetry, and immediate economy of millions—on paper. I fear the "perfect day" is postponed by very strong selfish interests; but I hope with you it will come.

Very truly,   Almont Barnes.

ALS (WP, DLC) with WWhw notation on env.: "Ans. June 28/87."
    [1] A minor functionary in the federal service since 1868, particularly in the Department of Agriculture.
    [2] Printed at Nov. 1, 1886. In fact, the article appeared in the issue of July 1887.
    [3] He is referring to the paragraph in "The Study of Administration" that begins "There is, indeed, one point at which administrative studies trench on constitutional ground. . . ."

From William Hartwell Pace

Dr. Woodrow Wilson   Raleigh, N. C., June 20th 1887.
    As Secretary of the Board of Trustees of Wake Forest College it is my duty—and from what I hear of you I assure it is a great pleasure—to notify you that upon the recommendation of the Faculty of Wake Forest College the Trustees of said Institution did at their annual meeting on the 9th inst confer upon you Degree of LL.D.[1] Permit me to state that this is the only Honorary Degree conferred by the Bd. at their annual meeting in June.
            I am very Truly   W. H. Pace   Sec. &c

ALS (WP, DLC) with WWhw notation "Ans. June 25/87"; WWhw list of correspondents; and WWhw figures on env.
    [1] This honorary degree, Wilson's first, was conferred *in absentia*.

To Almont Barnes

My dear Sir,   Gainesville, Georgia, 28 June, 1887.
    Your very kind letter of June 18th, addressed to Bryn Mawr, has been forwarded to me here, at my summer address.[1]
    Allow me to thank you very warmly for its contents. I was afraid that my article in the 'Quarterly' was too broad, too general, too vague to strike to the heart of the interest felt in such subjects by those whose ear I most wish to catch. To have assurance, therefore, that it has arrested the attention of one so specially and adequately fitted to judge whether there was anything of point in it is indeed an encouragement. Your letter was the help I needed.
    I can give entire assent to the principles you formulate: unquestionably they are of the greatest importance. I think, however, that you will agree with me in saying that they reach but part of the way to complete truth in the matter of administration. Organization which consists in differentiation, in classification,—in getting all like functions within a single bureau, and excluding all others,—though indispensable and the *first* thing needed, must be completed, or rather supplemented, by *coördination*: by so harnessing the Departments and their bureaux *together* that they

shall perfectly coöperate in pulling the whole load of government. There must be a general plan, a common mind, in administration no less than in policy; and I suppose that one of the reasons why work and responsibility cannot be properly distributed under our present system is that the administration of the govt. is not,— except in the ineffectual (for such a purpose ineffectual) meetings of the 'Cabinet'—*a whole*. Not being a whole, it cannot well realize the lack of proper adjustment amongst its parts. Each division of it stands alone, and must bear as best it may its own awkwardness and confusion.

The European govts. are most of them quite different from our govt. in this respect. The whole administration, with them, generally comes together at the top in some Council of State or other body, composed not of politicians but of distinguished experts, as well as of the ministers of State, and to this body belongs a general supervision of administration and the privilege of discussing proposed legislation affecting administrative arrangements[.] Anomalies in the distribution of functions, confusions and conflicts in *accounting*, clumsiness of method, or errors of principle cannot long escape correction under such systematic and constant oversight—especially since this Council is commonly a court of appeal to whom individuals, inside or outside the service, may resort.

Our system, in short, is left *at loose ends* and until it has wholeness cannot have symmetry.

Pardon this effusion. My interest in the subject does not count pages.

Very truly Yrs.,　　Woodrow Wilson

ALS (photostat in Berg Coll., NN).
1 The Wilsons left Bryn Mawr for Gainesville as soon as Wilson had read the entrance examinations in history and at least before June 15, for letters received in Bryn Mawr on that date were forwarded to Gainesville. They went to Gainesville so that Ellen could be near her aunt, Louisa Brown, and again under the care of the obstetrician, Dr. J. W. Bailey, during the last stages of pregnancy and the birth of her second baby. The Wilsons roomed and boarded first with Mrs. S. A. Langston, whose table, according to Aunt Louisa, was "considered the best in G— by the boarding population," and later at the Piedmont Hotel, run by General James Longstreet. See Louisa C. H. Brown to EAW, May 19, 1887, ALS (WP, DLC), and receipts from the Piedmont Hotel dated Sept. 29 and Oct. 12, 1887, in WP, DLC.

From Joseph Ruggles Wilson

Dear Woodrow—　　　　　　　　Columbia, S. C., July 6, 1887
　I am expecting to make a call upon you and Ellie, about Saturday—arriving via Greenville, &c. I will stop at hotel.[1]

Love from all—J R W.

API (WP, DLC).
¹ Probably the Piedmont Hotel.

Two Letters from Ellen Axson Wilson

My own darling,   Gainesville, July 13/87.

Your most welcome letter reached me safely last night.¹ I am *so* sorry about the delay,—how *very* provoking!—what can make agents so stupid! I am glad however that you are able to take it so philosophically and to "settle down" in Seneca to your ordinary occupations so satisfactorily,—am equally glad that you find the hotel comfortable.

We are getting on very nicely indeed. I am *quite* over my "spell"—feel *just as well as usual.* Mrs. Baily² brought the medecine herself soon after you left, and two doses did the business. Margaret seems very well; there is no looseness about her bowels and no sign of blood, but there is still a good deal of the slime. But unless she gets worse I won't send for any more medicine, but wait for the instructions from Columbia. She has but two actions a day, and as well as I can tell for the queer colour they seem to be pretty well digested.

She—Margaret—has been lovely since you left,—actually affectionate, it looked almost as if she were trying to console me for your absence. I am bearing that same absence quite bravely I think. I sewed a good while yesterday but at last found that didnt do, so spent the rest of the day reading Shakspere; and by that means managed to fight the blues pretty successfully; I believe I read five plays through. Of course I was obliged to have the relief of "a good cry" just after you left, but I have been quite cheerful since. You see I am so *very* glad for your sake that you have gone, that—since two things can't be in the same place at the same time—there really isn't *room* for me to be *excessively* sorry even for my own sake.

I think it will do you *so* much good to have a complete change of scene for a time, to get away from this atmosphere of aching and grunting and other even less agreeable physical phenomena. And then I hope I am unselfish enough to be not only willing but glad to give you up to dear mother for a while—especially now when she is sick, and needs you more than ever. But oh my love—my life—nobody knows how happy I will be when "your time is up"! But it is nearly dinner time and I must stop, so that Mr. Wilkie³ may take this down for me. Do excuse this queer arrangement of pages; I turned two leaves at once, you see, and only found at the end that I was on another sheet. With much love to *all* the dear ones and an overflowing heart-full for you, my precious one—my own Woodrow,—I am as ever,

Your own   Eileen.

1 Wilson had just left Gainesville for a visit to his sister and brother-in-law, Dr. and Mrs. George Howe, Jr., in Columbia, S. C.
2 Wife of Dr. J. W. Bailey.
3 Probably another resident at Mrs. Langston's.

My darling Woodrow,   Gainesville July 14/87
I am glad to learn from your telegram that the serious undertaking of getting to Columbia is at last safely accomplished. How I hope you have reached there feeling as well as when you started! I am waiting eagerly now for my first letter from Columbia.

I am quite well, still, but this puzzling baby has again thrown me into consternation. She has been looking much better the last two days—shadows quite gone from under her eyes, and her action this morning was *perfectly* healthy so that I thought she was well; and suddenly two hours after she had another all mucus streaked with blood. How I wish I knew what these sudden changes meant! Why won't doctors talk—treat people like sensible beings! I think poor bewildered mothers—and others have a *right* to know something of the nature of the desease they are nursing & of the meaning of symptoms. If doctors would only condescend to tell them they would have what they are always wishing for, better, more intelligent nurses and patients. Stockton [Axson] came in just after she was taken worse, said he was worse too and had come down to find the doctor,—had found him on the square and he had promised to meet him here in a few minutes. So I thought that would just suit me as well as him. But after waiting all morning we have just seen him drive past to New Holland! Stockton has left in disgust, declaring that if there were only another *decent* doctor in town, he would certainly go to him, Dr. Baily neglects him so. I have already sent a note to his house but when he will get it is another matter. But enough of these greivances for the present. Baby has had but the one bad action this morning and still looks and feels quite well. Poor Stockton looks quite badly, and seems a good deal discouraged about his case.

But it is a few minutes of one, and I must close this charming (!) letter. Please forgive it this time, somehow I can't *help* saying just what I happen to be thinking to you darling. And I

know that just because it comforts *me* to pour it all out my dear
unselfish darling won't mind.

Oh sweetheart you are *so* good to me, such a *perfect husband!*,
and I love *love love* you,—ah *why* can't I tell you how much how
entirely I love you.

With a heart full of love to all, as ever

Your own,   Eileen.

ALS (WP, DLC).

To Ellen Axson Wilson[1]

My own darling,   Columbia, S. C., 15 July, 1887.

Your (first) letter reached me yesterday and did me almost as
much good as if I had had a look into your precious eyes. A word
direct from you, written on paper which has been close to you,
with a thought straight from the heart which is mine—the source
of all my best delights—is to me a sacred thing which I treasure
as one does the things that are most genuine, most enriching.
When I have left you, sweetheart, I feel as a general must who
has been forced away from his chosen base of operations. I
cannot concentrate my forces; I cannot make sure of my directions; my efforts run all 'abroad'; I can only scout. It isn't a mere
fancy, darling: the sensation is distinct: one condition of thought
seems lacking. It only shows how central a thing the heart is
with me. *Its* queen is *my* queen—when she's away the Kingdom
is anarchical—there's no provision in its constitution for a
regency.

It's *only* my heart that's giving me trouble just now. The rest
of me seems all right again. I spent a perfectly comfortable night
last night—except for the terrible heat and to-day begin on a
digestion-tonic with a sedate stomach. I can therefore spare time
to give you some instructions about the baby. Bro. G. thinks that
the fact that the blood in baby's actions is in *streaks*, not mixed
up, and that it comes, together with the mucous, only now and
then, indicates that the trouble may be with only the last eight
or ten inches of the bowel. He advises, therefore, that twice, or
at the most 3 times, a day you inject about ½ pint of water about
100° Fahrenheit—smallest nozzle, fountain syringe. It may 'come
away' immediately—even forcing itself out around the syringe.
Never mind that: put in some more. The object is to distend the
bowels at the same time that they are being cleansed, in order
that the water may reach every nook and corner. If this does not

correct the trouble within a reasonable time the trouble is probably deeper and must be reached from the other end. So much to start on.

I am anxious for the news to-day's letter will bring of my darling. Oh, I *hope* she is well! My darling! my matchless, precious little wife. All join in *big* love to you and our sweet pet.

Your own   Woodrow

ALS (WP, DLC).
1 This seems to be the only letter that survived from among those Wilson wrote to Ellen from Columbia.

Four Letters from Ellen Axson Wilson

My own darling,   Gainesville, July 15/87

Loula and the baby[1] have been making me a visit and now it is almost dinner time and I fear I have only time for a hasty greeting, and to say that I am still quite well and the baby much better. The trouble—the blood I mean—has again disappeared as suddenly as it came. As for me I really feel quite strong, which is rather surprising since we are having the hottest "spell of weather" of the season. I have been getting up rather early and taking a walk in the "back yard" before breakfast[.] I also promenade there diligently after sunset. The surroundings are not very inspiring but I suppose there is as much air and exercise to be had there as elsewhere.

I am sorry,—after yesterday,—to say any thing more today about *doctors*, but I am *so* anxious about Stockton that I really must. He has really decided to give up Dr. Baily, being aided and abetted in it by Aunt Lou, who proposes to cure him herself with that remedy he tried before, you remember,—salts and laudanun[.] Aunt Lou notwithstanding her devotion to Dr. B. declares that he is no good, in summer at least, for anything but serious cases; he has so many of those that he takes no interest in any others, seems quite unable to keep them on his mind. Certainly for two weeks he has done nothing for Stockton but forget him,—or when actually brought to bay to prescribe the same thing over and over though it hasn't had the slightest effect. Aunt Lou says this remedy was Papa's, which reassures me somewhat, for he generally knew what he was about in giving medecine, and he doubtless got it from some physician; but won't you please ask Brother George about it, and in short consult him as to the case? I know it is quite a liberty to take but I am *so* anxious I feel as though I *must*.

Everything is perfectly quiet with us here—there is really nothing to tell except the old old story that I love you my darling, my own Woodrow. I am with you in imagination *all the time*, I dream of you by day and by night. Oh sweetheart, you are my strength, my life, my *all*. I wonder if you know how entirely my life is bound up in yours. With warmest love to all

Your own   Eileen.

excuse haste

1 Loula Brown Evans and her baby, Hoyt Brown Evans, born March 12, 1887.

My own darling,   Gainesville July 16/87

I did not get my letter written this morning as usual but by sending it down early this afternoon by Maggie[1] it will doubtless reach you as promptly as the rest,—and by waiting I am able to answer at once you[r] first and second letters from Columbia. I was distressed to hear about the colic but equally glad to learn today that you are "all right again." *How* I hope you will improve rapidly notwithstanding "the terrible heat." I am still quite well and "spry"

Baby seems to *feel* all right too. But when your letter came at dinner time she had just had another action with traces of blood and I had just sent to the doctor for more medecine. I shan't give it to her however at present, but of course follow Bro. George's directions. I gave her the first enema just after dinner. The water came away again immediately accompanied by a considerable action, not bad-looking however—and two rather large *clots* of blood. It didn't seem to give her any pain;—such is my report so far.

There is really no news with us except that poor little Aileen[2] fell down the steps & knocked out one of her front teeth just now & that the parrot has learned to call "Margaret" and does it most constantly and shrilly to the great amusement of the household. Oh yes, you may be interested to know that I had a battle royal with a *bug* in the middle of the night who bit me badly on the cheek and then in spite of all my endeavours escaped! I have been looking for him ever since!

But I am afraid I must cut this short darling, for my back really *won't* let me sit up more than a moment or so at a time today, and I am in a great hurry to get this mailed.

Oh love, how can I thank you for the precious words in today's letter; how can I tell you how I shall treasure them, for they tell me that I am to you what, more than anything else in all the

world I wish to be. Ah darling if I could but find the words which
would tell you what you are to *me*!

With a heart-full of love to all, ever

Your own   Eileen

[1] Maggie Hulsey, a nurse attending Ellen, whom Wilson had apparently
employed before going to Columbia.

[2] Not a member of the family of Warren A. Brown; probably a Negro girl
whom Ellen had hired to look after Margaret Wilson.

My own darling,   Gainesville July 17/87

Your sweet letter written yesterday has just reached me. I can't
say how much I thank dear Bro. George for his kindness in
sending such full and satisfactory directions for Stockton. I feel
nearly as much relieved as if he were already well. Am in such a
hurry for him to get it that I shall send Maggie to intercept the
family as they come out of church. Baby is doing nicely I think;
I have applied the remedy twice since I last wrote, each time she
had a small action with very slight traces of blood—no more clots.
I am feeling quite well, my back even is better than usual today.
And how are you, darling? You say nothing about your own
health in this letter, but I won't take that as a bad sign because
you know you are pledged to perfect frankness on that subject.
But if it is very much hotter there than here I fear you can't be
feeling very bright[.] The heat here is very great but it is miti-
gated by a pleasant breeze of which I am getting the benefit.
Indeed but for flies in the daytime & *bugs* at night, I should be
quite comfortable as to my surroundings! I had three several
battles last night, all in the small hours! One was with one of
the monsters that "buzz and bump their head against the wall."
I smashed him, but that was only the beginning;—think of
pinching two immense inch-long fellows on the bed—on *me*! One
I hope was my enemy of the night before,—he looked just like
him—for I sent them both over to the majority. But as you may
imagine after that I saw bugs every where, kept waking with a
start fancying that I felt them crawling over me! See how inconvenient it is to be a *goose*! But you needn't laugh, sir, for they
really are *dangerous*(!) Isn't one whole side of my face inflamed
now,—thanks to the wretch! Oh, if this little monkey would only
sleep without a light!

By the way before I forget it I must must mention a note to
you from Mrs. Ansley[1] begging you to come and see her when in
Atlanta and saying "how much she loves you and yours." That is
all the mail except papers and Ed Browns[2] wedding cards.

Oh dear! how I wish I could send a real, long, old-time letter!–
spend all this quiet Sunday morning writing to my darling! But
nothing hurts my back—and front (!) and sides for that matter—
half so much; as soon as I begin I feel as though I *must* stop,
and I go to scribbling desperately to get even a short note written.
It seems I *never* can open my heart to my darling. But then
fortunately he knows already what is in that heart, how full to
overflowing it is with love for him, how truly his love is the very
breath of life to his little wife, and how all his sweet words of
love are treasured in her heart of hearts.

With warmest love to all   Your own   Eileen.

1 Of Decatur, Georgia, whom Wilson had known in Atlanta.
2 Edward T. Brown was married to Mary Celestine Mitchell of Norwalk, Ohio,
on July 12, 1887.

My own darling,   Gainesville July 18/87
Your letter written yesterday is just at hand; at eleven o'clock.
They come with delightful promptness now. I hope mine reach
you as quickly; when (if you know) is the best time of the day
for me to write and mail my letters to attain that result?

The "Howe treatment" is certainly a success; the baby seems
to be *well* again, her actions look perfectly healthy; but as this is
the first day that they have been entirely free from mucus I shall
keep up the treatment a little longer to be sure.

I think she is doing splendidly considering her teething and the
intense heat together—therm. 98 yesterday,—nights as well as
days hot,—therm. 90 after nine o'clock at night. Then she is cutting both her stomach and eye teeth, one stomach tooth is quite
through. And no sign of the little incisors between them and the
front pair! I wonder if she isn't going to have any there. Ask
Bro George if such is ever the case. I remember that Babyhood
spoke of certain teeth being sometimes missing but I can't recall
which.

I am still quite well,—my great and only trouble being to find
some way to "rest myself"! The bed is simply intolerable because
of the heat and when I sit up very long the pain in my back or
rather around my waist becomes equally intolerable; so I am like
a restless spirit forever in motion from the bed to the chair and
back again. Oh for a hammock in the room!

You will be glad to know that I have quite finished my *sewing*,
even to washing and doing over my old hat,—it looks charmingly
by-the-way. I shan't have another stitch to take this summer
except the weekly mending, or fancywork. I am anxious now to

get all my letters answered so as to have no arrears of work of any sort on my mind while I am sick. But that is *so* tiresome that it fatigues me even to think of it; I fear I shall make slow progress if any.

I still keep up my walks and I am very glad, dear, that by so doing I can please you. I went at it with twice my usual spirit and vigour yesterday and made it twice as long, inspired by your words! I am so delighted, dear, that you didnt have dysentery after all. But what was it then? simply the piles? and are you entirely relieved? is there no more blood? Do you think it possible that Stockton's trouble could be piles? He has never had them in his life. But on the day that Dr B. was to meet him here, and forgot, his object was to examine him on that point. I sent him word that Stock had waited for him here all the morning and would now like to see him at home, and he said he would go that afternoon, but he has never been yet. The whole thing was rather funny in its way. Poor Stock was evidently very much worried that morning, and on going away he explained that the doctor "thought perhaps something more was the matter with him than he at first supposed" and he was to have examined him that morning to see. I, much too anxious to be discreet, asked "what?" and he said looking very miserable, "hemorrhoids[.]" The terrible name had scared him half to death! I never saw such relief as he showed when he learned that was "only piles";— though alas they are bad enough.

But I have scribbled quite a long letter *considering*, & really must stop. Give my best love to all, beginning this time with dear Bro. George. Bless his heart! I *do love* him; I can't begin to say how much I thank him for all his goodness. It certainly is fortunate for *us all*, that you went to Columbia when you did.

But you don't say anything definite in this letter either about *your* health. I shall begin to scold, sir, if you don't do better. I must have *full particulars* in your next. Good-bye my love, my Woodrow, my dear dear husband; I love you, I love, *love*, *love* you my darling.   Your own   Eileen

ALS (WP, DLC).

From Thomas Dixon, Jr.

Raleigh Baptist Tabernacle, Raleigh, N. C.
My dear Wilson: July 18, 1887.
So busy I was at the time I rec'd your letter the only reply I could make was to send you a paper which I hope you rec'd.[1] You

see I'm in the ministry, been preaching just a year the 25th inst. My church is one of the most progressive bodies in the state, now has about 475 members & a good outlook[.] My congregations are large—they say equal to the combined congregations of all other churches in city which I think is an exageration however. My first pastorate was at Goldsboro & I've been here since first of May. I enjoy the work—it's a glorious one! & smile as I think of the vagaries of my boyhood. I think I'm the happiest man in the world—got the sweetest wife and baby I'm quite sure[.] . . . We are now very pleasantly situated here in a handsome little cottage with all modern conveniences & Raleigh now flourishes with 15000 inhabitants & gives us street cars, electric lights & water works, & all to-gether life is very agreeable. I am here at the Capital too in centre of old political associates & influence which gives me strength in my new field of work. I'm going to Balto. Sat. to fill my brother's pulpit two Sundays. Wish I had time to write more but I haven't. Let me hear from & tell me what you're doing & expect to do. My wife, who was educated at Bethlehem Pa, wants to go to see her old teachers & if we go north next winter hope we can see you at Bryn Mawr. Hoping to hear from you soon.

Sincerely,   Thomas Dixon, jr.

ALS (WP, DLC).
¹ See EAW to WW, July 20, 1887, second letter of that date.

Ten Letters from Ellen Axson Wilson

My darling Woodrow,   Gainesville July 19/87

Nobody has been to the office this morning so your letter is not yet at hand; I feel disposed to wait for it but fear I should have to wait to[o] long to get mine mailed in good time.

We are still getting on nicely; there is today however some mucus—no blood—in the baby's actions. Of course as long as that is the case I must go on with the treatment; must I not? She seems to feel *very* well, has a tremendous appetite, considering the heat,—takes her bottle full to the brim every time.

A card yesterday asks you if convenient "to return the book you have out to the Mutual Library"—the book in question being the "Revue des deux Mondes." There is no other mail for you of any sort. I have been having a real treat this morning reading my "Art Amateurs" which came last night. They are *delightful*, and have such numbers of fine supplements. Four came; the subscription dating from the first of April through the year. I am reminded, dear,—I don't know why—to ask about Wanamaker's bill for the baby's shirts. It was not paid; was it? Is the bill here,— where I can find it? I suppose it ought to be attended to. And since I happen to think of it I may as well remind you of the two letters you were to write for me,—to Haverford and to Mr. Estrada[.][1] If you havn't written them I will be very much obliged, darling, if you would when you get time.

What do you do with yourself all day? play billiards? write essays? read? What have you been reading? You left your "David Copperfield,["] and I took possession of it; have just finished it; have been crying over "little Emily," old Peggotty, the "child wife" &c. as heartily as if I had never done so before. Have been on the whole *almost* as well entertained as if it were Mr. Howell's thrilling and affecting narrative of Mr. Mavering's embarrass- ments and his fiancee's whims.[2] At any rate since the latter is inaccessible this month Dickens forms a tolerable substitute, out of date as he is. By-the-way—the "Overland" is very gloomy this month over the current tastes in literature. "School-girls used to be *allowed* to read Scott and Dickens as an exciting recreation; they are *persuaded* now to read them for self-improvement, and regard it as a laudable and severe mental exertion." "It is appall- ing to reflect on the loss of mental power it may imply!" &c. &c.[3] But I must think of closing. Give a heartfull of love to all the dear ones for me. Is dear mother still improving or is the heat pulling her down? I was *so* delighted at you account of her improvement in appearance. What would I not give for a peep at her and all of you! What would I not give to be even for a moment in my darling's arms *now—this minute*! Oh darling, my love, my life, you don't know how I miss you! But fortunately I *can't* be *really* separated from you. I am *always* with you in spirit. If I were not I should simply be dead, for to love you and to think of you is to *live*. With all my heart

Your own   Eileen

How hot *is* it in Columbia? therm here *101°* in the shade both yesterday & today!

ALS (WC, NjP).

[1] Rafael Estrada, of Grocers' Steam Sugar Refining Co. of Philadelphia, to whom the Wilsons had sublet the Baptist parsonage in Bryn Mawr for the summer.

[2] William Dean Howells' novel, *April Hopes*, was being serialized in *Harper's New Monthly Magazine*.

[3] "Etc." [a monthly column], *Overland Monthly*, 2nd Series, x (July 1887), 106.

My darling Woodrow,   Gainesville, July 20/87

Your letter of the 18th reached me last night. I can't help being distressed, dear, that you are making so little progress towards health, even if there *is* "no cause for anxiety."

How *very* glad I am that you are with Bro. George! I can at least have the satisfaction of knowing that everything possible is being done and done *promptly*.

You mustn't think of coming away until you are all right;— indeed I think you had much better make up your mind at once to stay a third week anyhow. I have been intending for several days to urge that upon you. I assure you, sir, that as for me I would *much* rather have you there than here! I am so much more content about you. This place is so wretchedly dull for you that it really makes me unhappy to think of *my* keeping you here nearly all the summer. I think it is your *duty* for the sake of your health, mental and physical, to stay as long as possible. Of course I miss you—as regards winding the *clock* for instance (!)—it is generally run down because I can give it but two or three turns,— but I am getting on nicely—becoming quite "used of" your absence! Don't you believe me? Now that the hot weather is probably over;—for I trust this delightful change has extended to Columbia,—you will doubtless improve faster, and it is more desirable than before that you should remain. Hasn't it been a terrible "spell"? Stockton told me this morning that he saw it was 106° in Columbia! Poor boy! no wonder you feel badly.

The change came just in good time for the baby. I *never* saw anyone so broken out with heat,—in spite of all I could do,— bathing her three times a day with milk, &c. &c. She bore it beautifully until night before last, and then she seemed to grow desperate, was *miserable* yesterday and in the afternoon was thrown into really a hot fever by the irritation. I was *extremely* uneasy about her:—when a splendid breeze suddenly sprang up and then a thunderstorm came and the *glorious* rain I could have fallen on my knees in thankfulness. Both last night and today were—are!—*delightful*, and baby seems pretty comfortable though of course the heat hasn't disappeared yet. Her bowels are *all right*. Stockton came this morning and took me to ride— havent seen or heard from him before since Sunday when he came down just after dinner to get his prescription filled. He says now he is *well*,—trouble apparently at an end,—that he feels like another creature. But he has promised to be very careful as it is a "kinder decievin' " desease. Of course he is enthusiastic in his gratitude to Bro George,—and well he may be. Please give him the reiterated thanks of us both.

But there—the clock strikes one, and I am not ready for dinner, so must add only a hasty "good-bye."

With much love to all the dear ones and a heart full, full to overflowing with true, tender, passionate love for my darling, I am as ever   His own   Eileen.

ALS (WP, DLC) with WWhw names and sums and WWsh draft of a portion of "Socialism and Democracy," printed at Aug. 22, 1887, on envelope.

My own darling,   Gainesville July 20/87

I did not think to ask you whether I should forward your mail or no, and now that a *letter* has really arrived I don't know what to do with it. It isn't one that requires immediate answer however, only a long, odd, pleasant letter from your friend "Dixon" telling about his home and church,—how he "has a larger congregation than all the other preachers in the city put together"! He also tells you about his courtship and his three rivals who were "a real host (?) of the Devil"! I think it's *"host."*[1] What a queer genius he must be! He thinks he will be north next winter and will bring his wife to see us at Bryn Mawr. I shall be glad to make his acquaintance.

The Atlantic came last night too. Don't you want me to forward it and the Nation &c.? If you follow my advice and prolong your stay you had better let me do so.

There also arrived at dinner-time some other mail matter from *Rosemont*, viz. your *article*,—and a rejection from that dull idiot, whom I do perfectly despise.[2] It seems to have been mailed in Boston on the 21st of June. There is no explanation of the delay in returning it. In fact the whole thing is a mystery; I can understand nothing about it except that Mr. Aldrich is—I must say it—an egregious ass. How can the man be so senseless as not to see that such essays as yours are just what his magazine needs above *all* things to raise its tone, to make it attractive to people of the truest, finest culture and refinement, to give it so to speak *distinction*; one such paper is worth a dozen—*hundreds*—of his foolish, vulgar stories? Or is it that he has felt the pulse of his public, and knows that there is no adequate audience for such things in this poor crude America. I have just re-read it all with more delight than ever. It is *delicious*, almost as bright as Mr. Birrell[3] and more thoughtful, eloquent, suggestive; while the style is simply *exquisite*. Oh "what fools these mortals be." But I suppose it won't help them or me to fall into a fury.

I forgot to say in mentioning your mail that there is also a paper from Mr. Dixon containing another account of the Wake Forest commencement, in which the Pres. of the Board of Trustees announces your degree. He stated that Prof. Wilson was but thirty years of age; "but that institution was going to give honors to men when they *deserved* them be they young or old;—it would no longer be guilty of reserving them for winding-sheets."

But I must close for the present; you perceive it is still the 20th[.] I am merely writing now because I *feel like* it. Will add a line in the morning to say how we are then. Baby is still a good deal worried with the heat—the eruption I mean,—even seems somewhat feverish again, which worries me greatly as I haven't an idea what to do for it; will you please send me directions as soon as possible.

Give much love to all the dear ones and keep for yourself love unspeakable from your little wife. Oh if I could only put my arms about you and *tell* you how I love you! It seems to me I never wanted to see you, to be close, close to you so much. "Oh that I had wings like a dove for then would I flee away and be at *rest*!" Or if I were but a disembodied spirit and could flit at will between here and there. But I feel too much like a disembodied spirit as it is; for haven't I been violently parted in twain, and isn't one half of me hundreds of miles away? And if spirits feel as homeless, as comfortless, as desolate as I do without you I will never wish to be one again. It is too unnatural a condition. Indeed it does help me to realize, not, it is true, the Christian conception of "the spirits of just men made perfect" who "do immediately pass into glory," but the old heathen idea, that colourless, dreary, homeless semi-existence in some vague, shadowy unreal place. Ah darling, you are as I have so often said my very *life*. I can never never tell you how I love you, honour, admire, *glory* in you; nor what a sweet, precious, beautiful thing life has become to me,—my own life—since it has been absorbed in yours, since I have begun to live in and through you. Ah what a blessed privilege it is to be *your* wife! Daily hourly, I am "lost in the *joy* and in the *wonder* of it[.]" "The happiest" woman "in the world must from the necessities of the case" be

Your little wife   Eileen.

I don't know what *has* got into me that I can't go straight ahead through a sheet of paper any longer. Either I am bewitched or this paper is.

July 21—

According to promise I add a line this morning to say how we are. I am still well. Baby had quite a hot fever yesterday afternoon, and I was of course very anxious for I didnt think the "heat" explanation would serve. I didn't know *what* to do,—hated so to go back to Dr. B. that I thought of telegraphing to you for directions. But I reflected that it was probably her teeth, & that Bro. George couldnt lance gums by telegraph. So I sent a note to Dr. Baily asking him to come over. He didn't come however. Baby refused to eat at bedtime or during the night and was very restless until twelve. Then she slept quietly until nearly five when she woke screaming—with hunger apparently. I fed her and she went quietly to sleep again. But in the meantime I had become extremely alarmed by the strange way in which she rolled her eyes up; I had heard that was a sign of brain troubles,—convulsions &c. So at half past five I got little Sallie to stay with the baby & I went for the Dr. He starts out so early that I was afraid of missing him if I waited. He came over soon after,—said the fever really was due to her teeth—the two eye-teeth which were *almost* through. So he lanced them and she seemed at once relieved. He said I need not be alarmed at the rolling of the eyes— it was probably due to some disturbance in her stomach. Started to give her some more "powders" but stopped when I told him that her bowels were in excellent condition. So he left no medecine at all; said if the fever returned this afternoon to let him know and he would give her a little aconite. Baby has been quite herself all the morning—no fever yet—12 a.m.—bowels still all right. I have been, at the doctors suggestion, putting Pond's Extract on the heat & it is getting much better

With a heart full of love   Your own   Eileen.

ALS (WC, NjP).
    1 She refers to an unpublished portion of T. Dixon, Jr., to WW, July 18, 1887.
    2 Thomas Bailey Aldrich, editor of the *Atlantic Monthly*. The rejected article was "The Eclipse of Individuality."
    3 Ellen was reading Augustine Birrell, *Obiter Dicta, Second Series* (New York, 1887), with the WWhw inscriptions on the title page and flyleaf, respectively: "*Ellen Axson Wilson* July, 1887." and "To a young lady with a rare zest for the juiciest fruits of literature—and whose enjoyments are to him as his own, from Woodrow Wilson." From the copy in possession of Robert Reidy Cullinane, Washington.

My own darling,   Gainesville, July 22/87.
    I fear I have but a moment or so for writing, for it is drawing near dinner time now and I am expecting the bride and groom every moment. So I won't try now to answer that sweet, *sweet* letter received yesterday and which has been like a song in my

heart ever since. I was *so* sorry, darling, to hear of your sickness and discomfort. How I *do* hope this is the beginning of the end! Surely Bro. George and the pleasant change in the weather will together prove too much for that obstinate malady. We are doing nicely. Baby seems all right again[.] She was just a *little* feverish yesterday, but Dr. Baily who was here this morning—to see someone else—said it was of no consequence, and she needed no medecine. So I hope that this crisis in the teething business is safely over. We are still have delightful weather.

But you will want to know about the bride and groom. It is Ed Brown and his wife of course. They came last night and leave today. The thoughtless boy only telegraphed to his mother from Atlanta at three o'clock yesterday afternoon that they were coming. But doubtless she was ready for them, for she has been working herself nearly to death—poor thing—for a week. Has seven great wedding cakes iced and dressed! She had a sort of family reception for them last night. As they didn't arrive until half past nine, it was rather hard on the poor girl I thought! I didnt envy her!—just after her long journey from the north. Stockton came down this morning to get them a carriage, and said they were coming here. But as the carriage couldn't be had until very late, I am afraid they won't accomplish it. Of course I am curious to see her. But I must stop so as not to be taken by surprise in case they do come.

With a heart-full of love to all the family and more than I can ever put into words for you my dear one, my Woodrow, my lover-husband, I am   Your own little wife   Eileen

ALS (WP, DLC).

My own darling,   Gainesville, July 23/87
Whether or no our experience on the 20th is a case for the Society for Psychical Research I cannot say, but it certainly was as Jessie would say "a singular coincidence." My experience was, minus the "apprehensions," exactly similar to yours, as is proved by the fact that for the first time in my life I was moved—aye *compelled*—to write you *two* letters on the same day. Such an overpowering flood-tide of love and tenderness kept rising—rising within me all day long that by night my heart was—as you describe it—like to break with its weight of love and longing. I even remember smiling at my "folly" to find that I—I too!—was stretching out my arms to you. So you may believe that your letter of the 21st was a delightful revelation to me, and I have been

in a most blissful state ever since owing to the peculiar vividness and reality it seemed to give to the great fact that *you love me.* You know darling that nothing in Heaven or earth is stronger than my faith in your love; it is what I *live* on; if it should fail— as it never can—I should surely die. But never before, I think have I *felt* it so deeply—have my pulses so thrilled with the exquisite delight of it. But there seems no end to the sweet surprises that grow out of being your love—your *wife.* One would think that two years would have inaugurated the reign of "calm wedded affection" of which we hear so much. And yet you are always do- ing or saying—not to speak of *being*[—]something to throw me into such a rapturous condition as is unparalleled in all the happy days of my most happy courtship and honeymoon. Yes dear, every joy of that time is mine still undimmed and in addition ah! how much deeper, more wonderful joy—that which springs from "the deep *confidence* and infinite *peace*" which you have taught me to feel in your love.

I think I may report baby & myself *both quite* well. She had no fever yesterday & is as bright as a button today. Thank you—and Bro. G.—very much for your last explanation regarding her symptoms. It is a *great* comfort to know that her little ups & downs—as I supposed them—are not necessarily threatened relapses but "a natural process."

With warmest love to all and as much as you want for your dear, dear self I am as ever

Your little wife   Eileen.

ALS (WC, NjP).

My own darling,   Gainesville, July 24/87.

Yours of the 22nd reached me last night. I wonder why it is that we must sometimes 'wait till a later mail" for our letters. I always mail mine at the same time and so I imagine do you. But every few days your letter comes by the night mail, and then I go to bed feeling *blank* and lonely;—to bed but not to sleep, only to listen for Mr. Wilkie's step without, to wait till it retreats to the back regions of the house and then to steal like a ghost into the dark hall and grope about the table for the mail. By-the-way, I havn't told you how I have reformed in my habits since you left. I rise at five every morning, (owing I must confess to the *flies*). But it is charming after I am really up and out. I walk in the garden—just outside the windows where I can hear the baby if she cries—and then swing in the hammock and read. I have appropriated the back piazza, to my use, because it is deserted by everyone else. So after tea I promenade it long and vigorously and then again enjoy the hammock and the cool air till nine o'clock, when I go to bed.

The dinner-bell rang yesterday while I was in full career and I was obliged to close so hurriedly that I hadn't even time to say anything about your terrible fright, which has been frightening me in retrospect ever since. Oh my darling, my darling what a narrow escape! What *might not* have happened! It makes me shiver to think of it even yet. Isn't there any way to *detach* the wires during a storm? It seems like *helping* the fearful force to enter the house—making a straight road for it. Mr. Stewart was telling at breakfast how their's was struck the other day and balls of fire as large as his fist rolled all about the room.

I am *so* happy darling that you are "much better":—glad too that you promise to stay at least until you are on firm ground again. As for your argument for not staying longer,—well, I admit it in perfect simplicity;—not to do so would be to doubt your love my darling. But I must insist that there are many strong arguments on the other side. If the surroundings here were attractive, if I were strong and well—in short if this were Arden, I would not be concerned for you because of the isolation. But what have we here?—a sordid little country-town, a dingy boarding-house, food that disagrees with you because badly prepared, a house full of intensely commonplace people—much worse than no people at all—and a wife always "ailing," too weak to go with you anywhere, too languid half the time even to talk to you much. Do those conditions furnish the sort of rest and recreation necessary to sooth and recuperate a hard-worked brain? And it seems so important for your work that your summer change *should* be to your advantage. You see my plea deserves some *attention*, at least, for I am putting it most honestly on the score of *necessity*— of *duty*—not mere "selfish pleasure." I know my darling how you love me but from one point of view that very love makes the situation so much the more doleful and therefore unwholesome for you, for it causes you to take all my aches and pains to heart, —to concern yourself about them in a way that they certainly don't deserve. And so in short my last word is a request that you reconsider the whole subject.

We are both quite well still, and are still having splendid weather, fine rains every afternoon and cool though bright mornings.

Sweetheart I wonder if you could guess how often I have read those "last two or three letters,"—if you know half how much I love you, how entirely, truly, devotedly I am

Your own   Eileen

ALS (WC, NjP).

My darling Woodrow,   Gainesville July 25 [1887]

I have promised Stockton, with whom I have just been driving —to write to Mr. Ewing for him this morning, and, I fear therefore I shall have to hurry through my letter to you lest my back, somewhat tired already from the drive, should give out. Stock went down to Atlanta the other day and saw most of the gentlemen to whom he had letters. They were all very pleasant, but had nothing for him at present, would let him know in the fall. So he begs me to write to Nashville for him. Bro. George certainly made an effectual cure in his case. The boy went down to Atlanta on the 21st[,] walked all day in the hot sun, and departing from the diet, eat "a big dinner" because he "was obliged to" and yet has had no relapse, as of course we all expected him to—has only had a severe cold. He said he felt that he *could* not put off his trip longer. By-the-way, Stockton seemed quite as much disappointed as I was at his not seeing Father[1] and talking that matter over with him, I advised him to write, but he said he could not take the liberty. Do you think Father would have time and would be willing to answer his letter if I should persuade him to write?

Baby is quite well still. I have a slight cold and sore throat today and am a little upset too in the old way, but am taking the powders again, having some left from last time, and will doubtless be all right in a few hours. I don't *feel* sick at all.

I am having such a battle "as never was" with baby about— *what* do you suppose?—drawing up her gown at night! Night after night she has been sleeping wretchedly,—would give a violent scream every ten or fifteen minutes through the night, rolling and kicking with all her might. For a long time I could not understand it. She was evidently not in pain; it was that sharp, sudden passionate cry we know so well,—the cry of anger; though generally she was crying in her sleep. I finally found by observation and experiment that it was owing altogether to having her feet confined. I let them go free for some nights while it was so warm and there wasn't a sound from her for twelve hours almost. But now the nights are cool again and I am afraid. What would you do? fight it out on the old line if it takes all summer? It don't seem to give her cold, even when the nights are cool but there must be some risk. She fights like a little tiger when I begin to draw the strings.

Do you think, dear you could get the address of "Good Housekeeping" at any news agency in Columbia? I know the price—$2.50 a year—but not the address. I think I *ought* to have something of that sort to study before I plunge into the mysteries of *northan* housekeeping; and there is a serial of special value for my purposes coming out in it now. On it's account I wish if possible to subscribe from the *first* of this year and I fear if I put off much longer I won't be able to get the back numbers.

But there! I have been betrayed into writing quite a letter after all, and fear I am not going to keep my promise to Stockton.

But "oh, that sweet, sweet letter that came yesterday"! I *must* thank you for it before I stop. My darling seems to be trying of late to fairly intoxicate me with love and gladness. How can I ever put into words the happiness I feel to know that my love is worth so much to you; that it is to you a source of blessing and strength and gladness. Surely such words from *you* are the sweetest tongue ever uttered. You know *I* don't think much of that wife of yours. I am very sad sometimes to think how little she can do for you. But all the help that woman's love and faith and perfect devotion can give are yours to command my darling now and always from   Your little wife   Eileen

Oh no, I "keep dark" about Bro. George.

ALS (WC, NjP).
1 Apparently Stockton had been out of Gainesville when Dr. Wilson visited Woodrow and Ellen on about July 9.

My own darling Woodrow,   Gainesville July 26/87
I have just been driving again with Stockton, who took me quite a long distance to see a fine view, so that I am again hurried in writing, for I was obliged to rest a little after getting back and now it is almost dinner time.

This is indeed *splendid* news in yesterday's letter, viz., that you are both strong and *well*. How very *very* happy I am to hear it. And oh how I hope that other *is* no more than "a pin-prick[.]" I can't bear to think of your suffering anything like an *operation* and me so far away from you.[1] But still it is delightful that it isn't going to "lay you up" as we thought it would;—and *what* a relief it will be to have it done!

Baby is still well and I am all right again—that is my bowels and my throat are well and I have only a little cold in the head.

No, I did not see the bride after all—they were so hurried. But I believe they are expected again soon for a longer time. They were all delighted with her. They say the picture does her no sort of justice, that she is *very* pretty—slender and fair, with beautiful brown eyes and light brown hair, and *very* sweet, bright manners. According to the local papers in her town,—it is a small place with papers of the gushing sort,—she is all-accomplished—artist, musician, authoress, &c. &c. &c.

Stockton has just been telling me something that interested me greatly. It was about a letter of advice and counsel that Papa wrote him soon after he first left home to go to school in Sav.,—in the fall of 71.[2] In it he told him that he could give him no better example of what he wanted him to be,—"no better model to follow than the son of his friend Dr. J. R. Wilson,"—telling him then of certain characteristics of yours,—of certain things that your father had mentioned about you. And the last night Stockton was ever with Papa, here in Gainesville, he told him about our engagement, reminded him of the letter, said smiling that he little thought then that they would ever be so nearly related, and expressed his great pleasure in it all. Of course all this was very pleasant for me to hear;—not that it was anything *new* to me, to whom he so often expressed in glowing terms his opinion of you. But how sweet it is to me, darling, to think how he loved and honoured you, and to think too that it was to him even at the last a source of such happiness that I was *yours*! Ah, if dear Mama could only have known you too and shared his happiness, or rather shared *my* happiness in your love as only a mother could! Now that *your love* has put far away into the past those old days when every thought of her was pain, I often take such strange pleasure in only *imagining* myself telling her about it all—about you and the wonderful happiness your love has brought me,—or going home to her now with you and the little one. Ah we will all go home to her some day! With a heart full even to breaking with love for you, I am dearest

Your own little wife,   Eileen

ALS (WP, DLC) with WWhw tel. on env., printed at July 29, 1887.
 [1] See EAW to WW, July 27, 1887.
 [2] She obviously meant 81, as Stockton Axson was born on June 6, 1867.

My own darling,   Gainesville, July 27/87.

So the operation is really over—and the piles are really gone! I am *so* glad darling, and *so* sorry for you too, for I perceive it was a great deal more than "a pinprick." Oh, if I were only with you! I *can't* reconcile myself to the thought of your suffering away from me. And do you really think that a few hour's rest will insure a cure? We are both well today—my cold *almost* gone and otherwise I am all right. Am just back from another long drive with Stockton[.] With the driving and my promenading together I take a good deal of exercise now.

A pleasant note arrived from Mr. Estrada this morning stating that he had forwarded the book. Many thanks to you, dear, for writing. A note from Miss Salmon[1] says that she has sent you "the paper" by express. She also asks for "the exact title and name of the author of a work on Greek law and Govt. of which you spoke last spring." She thinks the name was "Sherman." Her address is 42 Madison St. Ann Arbor. Her paper has not come yet.

Adeline has returned to Gainesville, and came to see us yesterday. Her presence was first announced to me by the baby's yells. Adeline had snatched her out of the carriage and was laughing and shouting over her as if she were demented—and you can imagine how the baby was screaming! I had difficulty in rescuing her for Adeline was as determined to keep her as Baby was to get away. She is a good-hearted creature but I am thankful to have a more quiet one. Maggie is a great comfort. I also had a visit from Mrs. Shepherd[2] a day or so ago; says she has been trying to come every day since I arrived but has'nt had a free moment from nursing. Some other lady had spoken to her for the first of Sept. but fortunately I was ahead. If I am sick though the middle of August I shall have to make out with two weeks of nursing I suppose. But as this is Mrs. Williams first child she is more apt than I to take the middle of Aug.

Well, darling since you *won't* be convinced that you ought to stay away as long as possible—since you think you *can* be content here, I may confess how very glad I am for my own sake. Oh I do so *long* to see you!—and oh the emptiness of *my* days without you! But then the perfect joy that will be mine when once again I look into your dear eyes and am clasped in your arms! When the ache at my heart is too great I turn to that picture—dwell on it— *revel* in it—and so make comfort for myself. Darling I do love you—love you with *"all my might"* and will so love *forever*

Your little wife   Eileen.

Warmest love to all.

ALS (WP, DLC).
    [1] Her letter is missing, but see Wilson's reply printed at Aug. 10, 1887.
    [2] Who had nursed Ellen after Margaret's birth.

My own darling,   Gainesville July 28/87.

I wonder if you too are having such a tremendous "spell of weather"! If it were Rome I should be looking out for a flood, it has been pouring so steadily and so long. We are obliged to have lights on the table when we eat. We are both well however—that is Margaret is quite well; the change of weather—it is very chilly—has made my cold a little worse, but 'tis nothing to speak of,—only a little sore throat and hoarseness.

A letter arrived from Dr. Rhoads yesterday given [giving] the terms at those schools.[1] It is $180.00 at Haverford including dinner,—he don't say what, minus the dinner—car-fares $20.00 more, $200.00 in all! Isn't that *dreadful*? At the Phil. school, which he says is better, tuition is $125.00, dinner $45.00 car fare $34.00! So of course it is settled for the present that Eddie must study at home. And after "the present" if we remain there I am sure I don't know what is to be done. Am very much perplexed. If matters were different at Maysville I would feel that perhaps the whole matter of taking [him] with us ought to be reconsidered,—that perhaps I would be doing him a great wrong to take him where his expenses will be so heavy and the getting of an education surrounded with such difficulties. But it seems out of the question for him to stay there; I think I should rather have him grow up uneducated than unloved—and *worse*. I suppose at the *worst* he could study at home for two or three years and then go to some southern church school where there is no tuition and board next to nothing,—Fort Mill for instance. But the responsibility we are assuming is certainly more serious than I supposed. We must talk it all over, and you, dear, must say frankly and exactly what you think we ought to do. You need not trouble to *write* about it though since you are coming soon. I, of course, only introduced the subject "to relieve my mind"!

By the way did you see in the papers the singular thing that has happened at Bryn Mawr? A little boy killed himself on the grave of his pet dog? What a strange affair!

I am waiting with unusual eagerness today for my letter so as to hear how you are. How earnestly I hope, darling, that it is all right, and that the healing process is going on rapidly! Oh if I were *only* with you! It is almost *too* much for me to be away from you now. I don't see how I bear it at all. I *don't* bear it without such a heart-break as I never felt before, even when *I* was sickest last spring. Oh my darling I love you so tenderly and devotedly! How gladly I would die for you,—how entirely I live for you! May

God help me to live to some purpose for you,—to make the life which is all yours of some real worth to you! Oh if I could only be all that I want to be to you,—all that *your* wife should be! But I am a poor little creature, alas, and fail at all points, save only in perfect love and faith and devotion. There *no* one could give you as much as   Your own   Eileen

Warmest love to all.

ALS (WC, NjP).
¹ For her brother, Edward Axson, eleven years old, who was then living with their uncle, the Reverend Henry F. Hoyt, in Maysville, Georgia. Dr. Rhoads's letter is missing.

From Philip Gilbert Hamerton

Dear Sir—   [Autun, France, c. July 28, 1887]
   You once asked me [to] recommend a book to you about the history of French constitutions & civilisation.¹ I recommended one & now can recommend another [:] "Histoire de la Civilisation française" par Alfred Rambaud, Professeur à la Faculté des Lettres de Paris [1885-87] Two Volumes, published by Armand Colin & Co. 1 Rue de Mézières.
                    Sincerely yours,   P. G. Hamerton

APS (WP, DLC) with WWhw notation on recto: "Ans. 10 Aug. 1887." Postal damaged.
¹ WW to P. G. Hamerton, Jan. 4, 1887.

To Ellen Axson Wilson

[Columbia, S. C., c. July 29, 1887]
   Expect me this Saturday evening¹
                    W. W.

WWhw draft of telegram on verso of env. of EAW to WW, July 26, 1887 (WP, DLC).
¹ July 30.

From Ellen Axson Wilson

My own darling,   Gainesville, July 29/87.
   Your sweet letter which came duly to hand at dinner time yesterday relieved my mind very much as to the operation and it's results. I trust you will be quite well in a day or so, at this rate of progress:—and *won't* it be *splendid* to be rid of that torment! I am very sorry though to hear of the relapse in the other

direction. Poor darling! What a hard time you have had! How glad I am that Bro. George got hold of you when he did.

We are getting on nicely,—my cold I hope better,— baby *quite* well. Dear, you must not be anxious about me,—above all you must not leave before your health justifies you on my account. I assure you I am not unhappy or sad even. Of course I can't deny that your absence "makes a difference"! but I have so many sources of comfort, Love, in *thinking* about you, in reading your letters, in dwelling on your love that I won't *let* myself be sad. It would be too ungrateful. And besides I have been too glad for you to have the change. Then too I have been, most of the time since you left, stronger than before, and so able to keep quite busy in various ways, and of course there is always genuine enjoyment in that. As long as I am able to work or study,—or to be exact, as long as the pleasure isn't decidedly outweighed by the pain or fatigue of it I am sure to "get on" nicely. I must confess that I *did* have the blues a little yesterday. The weather was so outrageously bad,—and I was a little "under the weather" physically, besides. It was one of those days that makes one feel as though some misfortune is going [to] happen,—or if you are separated from those you love, that it has already happened. I thought the day would never end,—went to bed at half past seven, so as to curtail it—to get rid of myself and it. But though the weather is still about the same I feel somehow a good deal better today.

I had a letter from Beth yesterday urging us to come there—to her.[1] She has cool (!) downstairs rooms for us &c. &c. Should you like to go? Minnie Hoyt also wrote the other day begging us in her mother's name to come there,—says Rome is very healthy this season.[2] But of course that wouldn't do. And we seem to be doing very well here now. By-the-way, Beth recommends a queer remedy for back-ache—*home-made blackberry wine*! Doesn't *sound* very effective, does it? I suppose, by-the-way, that not even Bro. George can suggest any help for that, eh? For the little baby's sake even more than my own, I *would* like to have better health the last part of the time, since I am *obliged* to be so sick the first three months. Take it all in all the poor little fellow don't seem to have much chance. But perhaps as long as my appetite is so good it makes no difference to him what pains and aches I have! I sincerely hope so! But I must stop, for the clock strikes "one,"— the most welcome sound of the day for me, for it means that a letter will soon be here from my darling. Oh how I *love* him and his sweet letters. What joy it is too to be told that my love is to him a source of "courage and hope and help"! Ah dearest, my love will indeed be worth something to you if it brings you only *half* the happiness that *your love* pours into the heart of

Your little wife   Eileen.

ALS (WC, NjP).
  1 Elizabeth Adams Erwin, whose letter is missing.
  2 Mary E. Hoyt's letter is missing.

From Edward Ireland Renick

Dear Wilson,   Washington, D. C., Aug 2, 1887.

Speaking to Mr Sigourney Butler, Second Comptroller, this morning for the place made vacant by Oscar J. Harvey, the forger,[1] I learned that only a person of real character and genuine legal attainments would be chosen, if it took all summer. In giving him a synopsis of my career I mentioned our law firm in Atlanta & I discovered that he knew of you.

If not distasteful to you be so good as to write for me to be presented to him what you know of me as a lawyer and as a man. I hear that all the papers will be forwarded for Mr Cleveland's perusal as he regards the choosing of Harvey's successor a most important step.

Trusting that you & yours are all well & happy (we are) & that sometimes you will let me hear from you

I am as ever yours faithfully,   E. I. Renick

ALS (WP, DLC) with WWsh draft of letter printed at Aug. 10, 1887, on verso of letter and WWhw notation on env.: "Ans. Aug. 10/87."
  1 Oscar Jewell Harvey, a Treasury clerk convicted of forgery and recently sentenced to twelve years in prison. For a note about his appointment and crime, see the New York *Nation*, xlv (July 28, 1887), 61.

From John Franklin Jameson[1]

Dear Wilson: Amherst, Mass., Aug. 7, 1887.

I hoped before this to give you a fuller exposition of the scheme of which I once spoke to you, and in which I sincerely hope you will take a hand.[2]

My plan, (which please keep to yourself for the present), was for the publication, on March 4th or April 30th, 1889, of a commemorative volume of essays by graduates of our department,— say you, Shaw, Yager, Dewey, Levermore, and I and certain others,—upon subjects in the constitutional history of the United States during the formative period, 1775-1789. Almost all of us, though getting up a book is hard, can find time to write an essay. But an isolated essay seems to have little weight. If, however, several essays are combined, still more if they are on subjects in the same field of history, still more if they appear at a time which plainly connects them with that field, they have a momentum with the public.

But I think a still better result may be obtained. I think the book can be made to help in establishing a certain tendency in American historical work on the constitutional side. All sorts of labor have been put on the history of the formation and adoption of the documentary Constitution. But meanwhile little has been done to elucidate the origin and development of the elements not comprised therein and of the unwritten elements generally, and to develop the continuity of institutional life between the colonial and the subsequent period. I should hope that such a volume, conceiving as it would our constitutional history in this wider sense, would help to emphasize this need in our historical work.

You asked me to send you my list of subjects. I shall rather suggest some that have occurred to me, and leave every man to find, among them or elsewhere, a subject that suits him. I want each man's choice free; it will be better for the book that no one man shall choose subjects. All I care for is that they shall be within the constitutional field in that period, and well done.

Well, I think one man will write on the history of the suffrage during that period, to show how far the Revolution made for democracy. I myself shall probably write on the origin of the Articles of Confederation by imitation of the constitution of the United Provinces. Another man might, e.g., write on the influence of the state constitutions of the revolutionary period on the constitution of 1787; some other, on the use made of history by the founders of the constitution. There are several subjects connected with the executive departments. The effort ought to be made to go back of the acts of 1789, not to be content with referring the arrangements then made to the "creative fiat" of some one man, but really to investigate *origines*, e.g., to show how much the state colonial and state Treasury Boards and that of the Confederation contributed, how much Hamilton. So of other departments. The relations of the Old Congress to its ministers might be interesting, as bearing on the cabinet; so might the diplomatic functions and organs of the Old Congress. A subject has been suggested to me by Professor Morse,[3] which I should think might have special attractions for you, as a man of legal training; that is, the history of the process by which the colonial judiciaries adapted themselves to their new task as independent tribunals, expounders for sovereign states. But you will be able, much better than I, to pick out a subject which will interest you. I can only say that I hope very much that you will be one of our number; and that, if you consent, I shall be glad to assist you in respect to anything which may need to be looked up in Washington, to which I not infrequently resort. Philadelphia has of course very much in the pamphlet literature of the period; but if those in Boston can help you, I shall also be able to be of use there.

Now write soon and tell me that you will consent, and I shall be greatly pleased. Believe me

Very sincerely yours,   J. F. Jameson.

P.S. Please say nothing of this at present; I do not want it to get around just yet.[4]

ALS (WP, DLC) with WWhw notation on env.: "Ans. Aug 30/87."
  [1] At this time Jameson was an Associate in History at the Johns Hopkins.
  [2] Jameson had conceived his plan, which he explains in this letter, in 1886 and spoken to Wilson about it in Baltimore on February 11, 1887. See the entries in the Jameson diary for March 4 and December 1, 1886, and February 11, 1887, printed in Elizabeth Donnan and Leo F. Stock (eds.), *An Historian's World: Selections from the Correspondence of John Franklin Jameson* (Philadelphia, 1956), p. 42.
  [3] Anson Daniel Morse, Professor of History and Political Science, Amherst College.
  [4] Wilson had to withdraw from the collaboration on account of the pressure of other work. See WW to J. F. Jameson, Sept. 28, 1888, Vol. 6. The book was J. Franklin Jameson (ed.), *Essays in the Constitutional History of the United States in the Formative Period, 1775-1789* (Boston and New York, 1889).

To Lucy Maynard Salmon

My dear Miss Salmon,   Gainesville, Georgia, 10 Aug., 1887.

Your letter came while I was away from Gainesville; but now I am here again and the *ms.* is safe in my hands.[1] I shall read it with as much pleasure as care.

The book of which you speak is, "Antiquities of Greece: *The State*," by G. F. Schöman; translated by E. G. Hardy and J. S. Mann. London: Rivingtons.

I hope that the Ann Arbor library is rewarding your search better than the collections (according to size) in Phila. did, and that you are enjoying your summer thoroughly.

I sincerely trust that the university has not been seriously hampered by the Governor's outrageous *veto*.[2]

Very sincerely Yours,   Woodrow Wilson

ALS (NPV).
  [1] An essay, which Miss Salmon apparently never published.
  [2] A veto by Governor Cyrus Gray Luce of the appropriations bill for the University of Michigan. The veto message, dated June 6, 1887, is printed in *Journal of the Senate of the State of Michigan* (2 vols., Lansing, 1887), II, 1806-1807.

To Edward Ireland Renick

My dear Renick,   Gainesville, Georgia, 10 August, 1887.
   Your letter of Aug. 2 has been forwarded to me from Columbia.
I needn't say that I respond to its request with alacrity and pleasure. Rather than stop to write you a letter, I will send what I
have to say on at once.
   Keep a friendly eye open for any govt. position attainable by
me which you think would suit a man bent as I am and possessing my particular desires for inside views and experiences of
government.
   We are quite well—and delighted to hear that you are. You
need not despair of receiving a long letter from me 'one of these
days.' I have you much and often in mind, with all the old feelings of   Your sincere friend,   Woodrow Wilson

ALS (B. M. Baruch Papers, NjP).

To Sigourney Butler

                              [Gainesville, c. Aug. 10, 1887]
   I was associated with Mr. E. I. Renick for one year in the
intimacies of a partnership and I feel that I can therefore speak
of his character and attainments with confidence. His character
has doubtless spoken for itself in his present employment, as
that of a man of strictest integrity, sincerely and watchfully
interested in his work and steadily diligent in its execution. There
may, however, have been little scope for an adequate display of
his abilities. It gives me great pleasure to speak of them in the
highest terms.
   Mr. Renick seemed to me to have a mind of the clearest and
strongest sort—just the mind for a lawyer and man of business.
His knowledge is always of a clear-cut executive sort, at the same
time that it is broad, fully appreciative of the large relations of
principles, as well as quick to retain technical detail. Broad, clear
and thorough are the words I would select as descriptive of his
methods as a lawyer, for I know that he has the tastes of a
scholar as well as the aptitudes of a man of affairs.
                              [Woodrow Wilson]

Transcript of WWshL (draft) on verso of E. I. Renick to WW, Aug. 2, 1887.

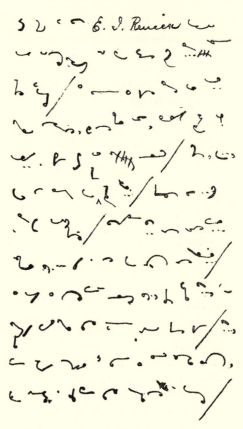

Wilson's shorthand draft of his letter
to Sigourney Butler

From Edward Ireland Renick

My dear Wilson: Washington, D. C., August 16, 1887.

Your very kind letter, with still kinder inclosure, came to hand in due time. You must be sure before hand of the strong gratitude it awakened. It was presented to Mr. Butler at once. I am told that all the papers have been called for by the President who intends to make the selection himself, so it will probably be some time before the matter shall be determined.

I have waited a few days hoping to have something definite to announce. My dear fellow, we have set our hearts on this— that you & Mrs Wilson &c—on your way north this autumn must stop with us. Mrs. Renick is already talking about the pleasure she expects from this and I can talk fully with you about "that Govt. place."

And then, is there not [E. M.] Gadsden, and [W. E.] Faison & I know not who else for you to see?

"It must be done." Let us hear that it will be done. We are keeping house very cosily. I am now in charge of the old Consular Division & getting on very pleasantly. Have you read Schurz's Henry Clay? It is the best American biography that I have read.

Thanks, again, for your prompt and very ardent support in the Treasury matter.

With kindest regards from us all to you & Mrs. Wilson
I remain,   as ever yours,   E. I. Renick

ALS (WP, DLC) with WWhw notation on env.: "Ans. Aug. 26/87."

Marginal Notes on Reading for *The State*[1]

[Aug. 18, 1887-1888]
Transcripts of WW
Shorthand Comments
[Aug. 18, 1887][2]

Hermann Schulze, *Das Staatsrecht des Königreichs Preussen*, in Heinrich Marquardsen, ed., *Handbuch des Oeffentlichen Rechts der Gegenwart* (4 vols., Freiburg im B. and Tübingen, 1883-1906), II.

From Chapter 11, "Innere Verwaltung," p. 113:
Die Verwaltung der auswärtigen Angelegenheiten steht jetzt im Wesentlichen dem deutschen Reiche zu und wird deshalb im Reichsstaatsrechte behandelt. . . . Dagegen fällt die gesammte innere Verwaltung ihrem Schwerpunkt nach dem Landesstaatsrecht zu. Wir verstehen darunter diejenige Staatsthätigkeit, welche für die Förderung der individuellen Interessen der Staatsangehörigen zu sorgen, die Bedingungen eines menschenwürdigen Daseins zu beschaffen hat. Sicherheit, Bildung, Wohlstand der menschlichen Gesellschaft sind ihre Ziele. Zwar hat auch das deutsche Reich die Förderung der Wohlfahrt des deutschen Volkes ausdrücklich unter seine Aufgaben aufgenommen und es ist nicht zu verkennen, dass die Reichsgewalt seit der Zeit ihres Bestehens Grosses und Wichtiges auf diesem Gebiet geleistet hat. Aber das Reich, als Bundesstaat, beschränkt sich in der Regel auf die Aufstellung allgemeiner Grund-

The whole point of view is that of consolidation—a Bundesstaat indeed.

[1] The following are representative illustrations of Wilson's reading in Heinrich Marquardsen (ed.), *Handbuch des Oeffentlichen Rechts der Gegenwart*, in preparation for writing *The State*. For comment on Wilson's use of these and additional sources, see the Editorial Note, "The State," Vol. 6.

[2] This reading date on p. 165 of Schulze is the only one in the books from which extracts are printed in this group.

sätze, während *es* der Verwaltung der Einzelstaaten die Ausführung *überlässt.* Dahin gehören
die meisten in A. 4 der R. V. "der Beaufsichtigung des Reiches und der Gesetzgebung desselben" unterliegenden Angelegenheiten. *Hier
erscheinen die Einzelstaaten, dem Reiche gegenüber, als Körper der Selbstverwaltung.* Auf
vielen andern Gebieten der innern Verwaltung
sind die Einzelstaaten ihrer eigenen Gesetzgebung unterworfen, sie geben sich selbst allein die
Normen, nach welchen sie die Verwaltung
führen. *Hier erscheinen sie als wahre Staaten,
die auch dem Reiche gegenüber noch ihre selbst-
ständige Rechtssphäre behaupten.* [All italics
WW's]

From Chapter 12, "Die Rechtskontrollen der
Verwaltung," p. 160:
   Vor die ordentlichen Gerichte gehören alle
bürgerlichen Rechtsstreitigkeiten. Gegenstand
und Zweck eines Processes lassen sich in Bizie-
hung auf die Kompetenzfrage zwischen ordentlichen und Verwaltungsgerichten nur nach dem
Inhalte und dem Antrage der Klage beurtheilen.
Das Wesen der Privatrechtsstreitigkeiten, welche
vor die Civilgerichte gehören, besteht darin, dass
mehrere, wenigstens zwei sich gleichstehende
Persönlichkeiten über Privatrechte streiten, d. h.
über Rechte, die sie fur sich, nicht als Genossen
des Staates oder einer öffentlichrechtlichen Korporation, als individuelle Einzelrechte in An-
spruch nehmen. . . . Dagegen gehören grundsätzlich nicht vor die ordentlichen Gerichte alle
Fälle, in welchen ein Einzelner, eine Gesellschaft
oder Korporation behaupten, durch die Massregel
einer Verwaltungsbehörde in Widerspruch mit
den Gesetzen in ihren subjektiven Rechten verletzt zu sein. Hier hört die Zuständigkeit der
ordentlichen Gerichte auf, welche nach unserer
heutigen deutschen Auffassung nicht über die
Ausübung staatlicher Hoheitsrechte zu entschei-
den berufen sind. *Hier* beginnt die Zuständigkeit
der Verwaltungsgerichte. [WW's italics]

That is, with the
use of the *Hoheits-
recht.*

Paul Laband, *Das Staatsrecht des Deutschen
Reiches,* Marquardsen, *Handbuch,* II.

From Chapter 2, "Die rechtliche Natur des
Reiches und sein Verhältniss zu den Gliedstaaten," p. 18:
   1. . . . Es ist eine unabweisbare Konsequenz
aus Art. 78, dass die gesammte Rechtssphäre der
Einzelstaaten zur Disposition des verfassungsmässig erklärten Willens des Reiches steht.
Durch diesen Satz aber ist die Souveränetät,
das ausschliessliche Selbstbestimmungsrecht, der

Einzelstaaten verneint und die Souveränetät des Reiches anerkannt.

2. Im Zusammenhange hiermit steht der im Art. 2 der R. V. ausgesprochene Grundsatz, dass die Reichsgesetze den Landesgesetzen vorgehen. Es ist dies eine logische Consequenz davon, dass das Reich die souveräne, d. i. höchste Gewalt besitzt, da das vom Reich erlassene Gesetz im Verhältniss zum Landesgesetz als der Befehl einer höheren Macht sich qualifizirt. Aber die verfassungsmässige Anerkennung dieses Satzes ist andererseits auch ein Symptom, aus welchem sich auf die Natur des Reiches und auf das durch dieselbe gegebene Verhältniss zwischen Reich und Einzelstaat ein Rückschluss gewinnen lässt.

Are the "supreme law" of the land.

From Chapter 2, p. 22:
Die Einzelstaaten empfinden auf allen Gebieten des staatlichen Lebens die höhere Macht, der sie unterworfen sind, da sie sich nur innerhalb des Raumes bewegen können, den die Reichsgesetzgebung ihnen frei lässt. Aber ein solcher Raum ist vorhanden; er ist durch das Reich begrenzt, aber nicht absorbirt. Allerdings hat das Reich nach Art. 78 der R. V. und kraft seiner Souveränetät ideell eine unbegrenzte Kompetenz; es kann die verfassungsmässig (im Art. 4) gestellte Grenze zwischen seiner Machtsphäre und der Machtsphäre der Einzelstaaten in der Form der Verfassungs-Aenderung einseitig, d. h. ohne Zustimmung der einzelnen Gliedstaaten, verändern; es kann also den Gliedstaaten die ihnen verbliebenen Hoheitsrechte entziehen. In einem gewissen Sinne kann man daher sagen, dass die Einzelstaaten ihre obrigkeitlichen Rechte nur durch die Duldung des Reiches, nur kraft seines Willens haben.

A very important difference between the united German states and the united American

From Chapter 2, p. 26:
Die Frage, um welche es sich handelt, ist daher lediglich die, ob die rechtmässige Vereinigung mehrerer Staaten zu Einem, sei es in Folge des gültigen Thronfolgerechts, sei es in Folge rechtsgültiger Staatsverträge, durch ein verfassungsänderndes Reichsgesetz genehmigt werden muss. Diese Frage würde zu bejahen sein, wenn die Reichsverfassung die Fortdauer derjenigen Staaten, welche bei der Reichsgründung vorhanden waren und noch jetzt bestehen, ausdrücklich oder stillschweigend anordnen würde. Einen solchen Rechtssatz enthält die Reichsverfassung aber nicht. Sie enthält zwar an 3 Stellen, in der Einleitung, im Art. 1 und Art. 6, *einen Katalog der Staaten*; aber an allen 3 Stellen hat diese Aufzählung nicht die Bedeutung einer selbständigen Rechtssatzung. In der Einleitung wird

What our own Constitution just escaped having.

lediglich erzählt, welche Staaten zur Reichs-
gründung sich vereinigt haben; im Art. 1 wird
der Umfang des Bundesgebietes dadurch defi-
nirt, dass die Staaten genannt werden, deren
Gebiete es umfasst; und im Art. 6 wird dem
Prinzip über die Vertheilung der Stimmen im
Bundesrath ein Register der in Folge dieses
Prinzips den einzelnen Staaten zustehenden
Stimmen beigefügt. Aus dem Wesen des Reiches
als Bundesstaat folgt aber ebenfalls nicht die
Unveränderlichkeit seines Mitglieder-Bestandes;
denn wenn auch zuzugeben ist, dass das
Deutsche Reich als Bundesstaat nicht gedacht
werden kann ohne autonome Staaten, so lässt
sich doch gewiss nicht behaupten, dass das
Deutsche Reich aufhören würde ein Bundes-
staat zu sein, wenn es statt aus 25 aus einigen
Gliedstaaten weniger oder mehr bestünde.
[WW's italics]

From Chapter 4, "Die Organisation des Reiches,"
p. 40:
Die Gesammtheit der deutschen Landesherren   An idea quite
nebst den Senaten der 3 freien Städte als Einheit foreign to our own
gedacht—tamquam unum corpus—ist der Träger federal Constitution
der Reichssouveränetät. Die Landesherren und so far as I know.
Senate üben diese Mitgliedschaftsrechte aber aus
durch Bevollmächtigte, ebenso wie im ehemaligen Deutschen Reiche die Stände nicht persön-
lich den Reichstag besuchten, sondern sich
durch Gesandte vertreten liessen. Die Versamm-
lung dieser Bevollmächtigten der Bundesglieder
ist der Bundesrath; der letztere vertritt daher
den Reichssouverän, d. i. die Gesammtheit der
verbündeten Regierungen; er ist dasjenige Organ
des Reiches, durch welches der souveräne Herr-
schaftswillen desselben zu Tage tritt. [WW's
italics]

From Chapter 4, p. 42:
Die Kompetenz des Bundesraths lässt sich   Not unlike the
nicht durch eine allgemeine Regel abgränzen.   Roman Senate in
Da der Beschluss des Bundesrathes den Willen   general features
der Gesammtheit der Bundesglieder, also des
Trägers der Reichssouveränetät, darstellt, so ist
die Kompetenz des Bundesrathes eine allgemeine, d. h. alle Bethätigungen und Aeusserun-
gen des staatlichen Willens des Reiches umfas-
send, welche nicht durch Bestimmungen der
Reichsgesetze anderen Organen, insbesondere
dem Kaiser und den Reichsbehörden, zugewiesen
sind. Keine Thätigkeit des Reiches ist dem
Bundesrath grundsätzlich entzogen; er ist Organ der Gesetzgebung, der Verwaltung, der
Rechtsprechung.

From Chapter 4, pp. 51-52:
Die Verhandlungen des Reichstages sind öffentlich. R. V. Art. 22 Abs. 1. Ein Ausschluss der Oeffentlichkeit durch Beschluss des Reichstages ist unzulässig; eine nicht öffentliche Sitzung hätte nur den Charakter einer Privat-Zusammenkunft von Reichstags-Mitgliedern; ein in einer solchen Sitzung gefasster Beschluss wäre kein "Reichstagsbeschluss" im Sinne der Verfassung, sondern ein Beschluss von Privatpersonen. Wahrheitsgetreue Berichte über Verhandlungen in den öffentlichen Sitzungen des Reichstages bleiben von jeder Verantwortlichkeit frei. R. V. Art. 22 Abs. 2. Strafges. B. §12.

> An excellent rule to apply to our own Senate.

From Chapter 4, p. 55:
Die Behörden lassen sich wissenschaftlich nach sehr verschiedenen Gesichtspunkten grupiren; für das Staatsrecht entscheidend ist die rechtliche Stellung derselben zu den Organen des Staates, d. h. die Verantwortlichkeit. Auch in der absoluten Monarchie giebt es Beamte, welche dem Monarchen für die Verwaltung der ihnen unterstellten Ressorts verantwortlich sind. . . . Im constitutionellen Staate erlangt diese Unterscheidung eine noch erhöhte Bedeutung, weil die Verantwortlichkeit nicht nur dem Monarchen, sondern auch der Volksvertretung gegenüber besteht (sogen. parlamentarische Verantwortlichkeit). Man pflegt diese Behörden mit selbständiger politischer Verantwortlichkeit als "Minister" zu bezeichnen; sie bilden eine Behördenkategorie für sich. Nach der Reichsverf. giebt es nur einen einzigen Beamten dieser Art, den Reichskanzler. Denn nach dem Art. 17 bedürfen alle Anordnungen und Verfügungen des Kaisers zu ihrer Gültigkeit der gegenzeichnung des Reichskanzlers, welcher dadurch die Verantwortlichkeit übernimmt. Hiernach ist der Reichskanzler der einzige und alleinige Minister des Kaisers; es giebt kein Ressort der Reichsverwaltung, dessen oberster Chef nicht der Reichskanzler wäre; der Reichskanzler hat unter allen Beamten des Reichs keinen Kollegen, sondern nur Gehülfen oder eventuell Stellvertreter (siehe unten S. 57).

> Responsibility (minister's responsibility) rests only with the imperial Chancellor.

From Chapter 4, p. 58:
Für die dem Bundeskanzler obliegenden Geschäfte ist durch den Präsidial-Erlass vom 12. August 1867 (B. GBl. S. 29) eine Behörde unter dem Namen "Bundeskanzler-Amt" errichtet worden, welche Anfangs 3 Abtheilungen umfasste (die sogen. Centralabtheilung, Post, Telegraphie). Ausserdem wurden die Preussischen Ministerien der auswärtigen Angelegenheiten und der Marineangelegenheiten auf den Bundesstat genommen und zu Bundesbehörden erklärt.

> Chancellorship was, then, originally, in theory at least, the only imperial office under the Emperor: the branches of

Durch die Fortschritte der Gesetzgebung und Verwaltung des Reiches hat sich diese einfache Behördenverfassung immer mehr entwickelt und es ist namentlich aus dem ehemaligen Reichskanzler-Amt eine ganze Reihe selbstständiger Centralverwaltungsbehörden des Reiches hervorgegangen.

the imperial office developed as branches of the chancellorship.

From Chapter 5, "Die Funktionen des Reiches," p. 102:

Die Reichsverf. hat im Eingange des Art. 4 diese Grundsätze anerkannt: "Der Beaufsichtigung Seitens des Reichs und der Gesetzgebung desselben unterliegen die nachstehenden Angelegenheiten." Es ist hierin die Kongruenz der Gesetzgebungs-Kompetenz und der Verwaltungs-Kompetenz des Reiches ausgesprochen und die Verwaltungsthätigkeit des Reichs ausdrücklich auf die Beaufsichtigung beschränkt. Hinsichtlich einzelner Angelegenheiten ist dann in den späteren Artikeln der Reichsverfassung oder in besonderen Reichsgesetzen dem Reiche auch die unmittelbare Geschäftsführung ganz oder theilweise übertragen worden. *Es sind dies Ausnahmen, während Art. 4 das allgemeine Prinzip aufstellt.* Ergänzt werden diese Regeln durch den Grundsatz, dass den, bei ihrem Eintritt in den Norddeuschen Bund und das Deutsche Reich souveränen, im Vollbesitze der staatlichen Gewalt befindlich gewesenen Staaten alle diejenigen Rechte verblieben sind, welche nicht durch die Verfassung oder durch verfassungsmässig erlassene Gesetze ihnen entzogen worden sind.

1. Die freie Verwaltung der Einzelstaaten. Alle Angelegenheiten, welche der Autonomie der Einzelstaaten unterliegen, bilden das Gebiet der vollen und freien Verwaltung derselben. Aber dieselbe ist keine souveräne und rechtlich unbeschränkte; denn abgesehen davon, dass ihr Gebiet reichsgesetzlich umschrieben ist und das Reich berechtigt ist, alle Uebergriffe in das der Reichskompetenz unterworfene Gebiet zurückzuweisen, so finden auf die Handlungen und Rechtsgeschäfte der Einzelstaaten auch vielfach die vom Reich erlassenen Vorschriften des Privatrechts, Strafrechts und Prozessrechts Anwendung.

2. Die beaufsichtigende Verwaltung des Reiches.

a) Auf denjenigen Gebieten, auf welchen das Reich zur Gesetzgebung befugt ist, hat das Reich nicht blos eine Aufsicht darüber zu führen, dass die vom Reich aufgestellten Rechtsregeln von den Regierungen der Einzelstaaten nicht verletzt werden, sondern es kann in Folge des formellen Gesetzesbegriffes auch die Thätigkeit der Einzelstaaten positiv bestimmen. Das Reichsgesetz

Very nearly the equivalent to the provisions of our own eleventh amendment.

Empire can command not only [what] must be done but also the way in which it shall be done.

kann nicht nur einen Rechtsbefehl, sondern auch einen Verwaltungsbefehl enthalten, d. h. den Einzelstaaten Handlungen anbefehlen. In sehr zahlreichen Gesetzen des Reiches ist dies geschehen und in allen diesen Fällen ist die Geschäftsführung der Einzelstaaten Vollziehung oder Ausführung des Reichsgesetzes.

From Chapter 6, "Die einzelnen Zweige der Verwaltung," p. 128:

Das umfangreiche Gebiet der inneren Verwaltung ist im Allgemeinen den Einzelstaaten verblieben. Zwar sind sehr bedeutende Theile desselben reichsgesetzlich geregelt, das Reich aber ist auf die nach Art. 17 der R. V. dem Kaiser zustehende Ueberwachung der Aufsführung der Reichsgesetze beschränkt. (Siehe oben S. 103.) Der Inhalt dieser Reichsgesetze bildet daher keinen Gegenstand des Reichsstaatsrechts und kann hier um so mehr übergangen werden, als die meisten dieser Gesetze ihre nothwendige Ergänzung in Landesgesetzen finden und nicht aus dem Zusammenhange mit denselben gelöst werden können.

> Empire sets the rules, the states administer them.

Alois von Orelli, *Das Staatsrecht der schweizerischen Eidgenossenschaft*, Marquardsen, IV.

From Chapter 2, "Das schweiz. Bundesstaatsrecht auf Grundlage der Bundesverfassung v. 1874," p. 27:

Die Bundesverfassung von 1848 und ebenso diejenige von 1874 gewähren den Kantonen ihr Gebiet, also ihren damaligen Territorialbestand. Ferner garantirt der Bund den Kantonen ihre Verfassungen. Die Bedeutung dieser Garantie wird in Art. 5 selbst näher dahin erläutert, dass sie umfasse die Freiheit, die Rechte des Volkes und die verfassungsmässigen Rechte der Bürger gleich den Rechten und Befugnissen, welche das Volk den Behörden übertragen hat.

> More explicit than our own Constitution.

Thomas Erskine Holland, *The Elements of Jurisprudence* (4th edn., 1888).[3] Pp. 40-41:

Although scarcely any traces remain in history of the transformation of a People into a State, it is impossible to affirm, with Savigny, that a People, which he calls 'an invisible natural whole,' never exists as such; never, that is to say, without 'its bodily form' the State. Aristotle speaks of the Arcadians as remaining an ἔθνος till, by the founding of Megalopolis, they become a πόλις. Nor can we follow Savigny in regarding the creation of the State as the highest function of Law. Morality may precede, but Law must follow, the organisation of a political society.

> Political society existed, of course, however before the creation of *modern forms* of the State, its local habitation, its official organization, etc.

[3] This volume is in the Firestone Library, Princeton University.

From Melville R. Hopewell

Dear Sir: Tekamah, Nebraska. Aug 18 1887
    Have sold the grass on NE 1/4 SW 1/4 10-21-11, for 5.00 net.
& hand you dft herewith for same less Ex. We have good crops
here & favorable prospects for farmers.
                          Very Truly Yours,   M. R. Hopewell

ALS (WP, DLC) with WWhw notation on env.: "Ans. 29 Aug/87."

Marginal Notes

Richard T. Ely, *The Labor Movement in*   Transcripts of
America (New York, 1886).   WW Shorthand
                                                         Comments
                                                      [Aug. 22, 1887][1]

P. 208:
    In the meantime, while waiting for a   What about the necessity
more fortunate basis on which to oper-   to would-be cooperators
ate, it is well to encourage every attempt   of the entrepreneur? Can
of working people and of others to co-   this man be obtained if
operate. It is a training, a sowing of   he may play only the
seed; and even now, under favorable   part of a salaried or equal-
circumstances, co-operation can accom-   profiting superintendent?
plish much good. We must not turn   And by what means is
aside from small economies, nor must   cooperation to supply a
we be so ready, as heretofore, to despise   substitute for the capital
the day of small things.   of the industry?

P. 247:
    One of the chief heroes of the Inter-   Eclipse of the moral
nationalists is Darwin, whose portrait is   individual is not a difficult
considered worthy to be associated with   conclusion for the shallow
that of their greatest leaders; while *all*   mind to draw from the
the more renowned natural scientists   writings of science.
[WW's italics] are admired, and their
writings studied with surprising diligence. Whatever else may fail in the
lists of books recommended by the
Anarchists for the education of their
followers, one may count for certainty
on finding a goodly number of works of
Darwin and Huxley; and no newspapers
in the United States have given so much
space to natural science and its great
lights as those published by the Chicago
Internationalists. Nearly all social demo-

1 WW's reading date on p. 332.

crats and anarchists are thorough-going Darwinians, and in this they seem inconsistent, for as Professor de Laveleye remarks, "It is impossible to understand by what strange blindness socialists adopt Darwinian theories, which condemn their claims of equality, while at the same time they reject Christianity, whence those claims have issued and whence their justification may be found."

P. 276:

An attempt is being made to win English-speaking followers [to socialism], and the National Executive Committee advertises six pamphlets and a series of socialistic tracts in the English language. An English organ is contemplated. Some progress has been made in winning English-speaking adherents to the party, and large success has met their efforts to diffuse their ideas among the laboring classes; but, as the *Sozialist* frankly acknowledges, *they are still a "German colony, a branch of the German social democracy."* Indeed, one bond of union holding them together is their interest and active participation in the election of members to the Imperial Parliament of Germany. [WW's italics]

This fact suggests thoughts as to the possible effects of state socialism. It may fairly be said that no modern state is more socialistic than Germany: it is at the same time as absolute in its power as any modern state which at all admits the principle of popular representation in its constitution—as absolute as every socialistic state must be. Does life under such a semi-socialistic state constitute an education in the doctrines of the socialistic labor party and of the internationalists?

An Essay

[c. Aug. 22, 1887]

Socialism and Democracy[1]

Is it possible that in practical America we are becoming sentimentalists? To judge by much of our periodical literature, one would think so. All resolution about great affairs seems now "sicklied o'er with a pale cast of thought." Our magazine writers smile sadly at the old-time optimism of their country; are themselves full of forebodings; expend much force and enthusiasm and strong (as well as weak) English style in disclosing social evils and economic bugbears; are moved by a fine sympathy for the unfortunate and a fine anger against those who bring wrong upon their fellows: but where amidst all these themes for the conscience is there a theme for the courage of the reader? Where are the brave plans of reform which should follow such prologues?

No man with a heart can withhold sympathy from the laborer whose strength is wasted and whose hope is thwarted in the service of the heartless and close-fisted; but, then, no man with a head ought to speak that sympathy in the public prints unless he have some manly, thought-out ways of betterment to propose. One wearies easily, it must be confessed, of woful-warnings; one sighs often for a little tonic of actual thinking grounded in sane, clear-sighted perception of what is possible to be done. Sentiment is not despicable—it may be elevating and noble, it may be inspiring, and in some mental fields it is self-sufficing— but when uttered concerning great social and political questions it needs the addition of practical, initiative sense to keep it sweet and to prevent its becoming insipid.

I point these remarks particularly at current discussions of socialism, and principally of 'state socialism,' which is almost the only form of socialism seriously discussed among us, out-side the Anti-Poverty Society. Is there not a plentiful lack of nerve and purpose in what we read and hear nowadays on this momentous topic. One might be excused for taking and keeping the impression that there can be no great need for haste in the settlement of the questions mooted in connexion with it, inasmuch as the debating of them has not yet passed beyond its rhetorical and pulpit stage. It is easy to make socialism, as theoretically developed by the greater and saner socialistic writers, intelligible not only, but even attractive, as a conception; it is easy also to render it a thing of fear to timorous minds, and to make many signs of the times bear menace of it; the only hard task is to give it validity and strength as a program in practical politics. Yet the whole interest of socialism for those whose thinking extends beyond the covers of books and the paragraphs of periodicals lies in what it will mean in practice. It is a question of practical politics, or else it is only a thesis for engaging discourse.

Even mere discoursers, one would think, would be attracted to treat of the practical means of realizing for society the principles of socialism, for much the most interesting and striking features of it emerge only when its actual applications to concrete affairs are examined. These actual applications of it are the part of it which is much the most worth talking about,—even for those whose only object is to talk effectively.

Roundly described, socialism is a proposition that every community, by means of whatever forms of organization may be most effective for the purpose, see to it for itself that each one of its members finds the employment for which he is best suited and is rewarded according to his diligence and merit, all proper surroundings of moral influence being secured to him by the public authority. 'State socialism' is willing to act through state authority as it is at present organized. It proposes that all idea of a limitation of public authority by individual rights be put out of view, and that the State consider itself bound to stop only at what is unwise or futile in its universal superintendence alike of individual and of public interests. The thesis of the state socialist is, that no line can be drawn between private and public affairs which the State may not cross at will; that omnipotence of legislation is the first postulate of all just political theory.

Applied in a democratic state, such doctrine sounds radical, but not revolutionary. It is only a acceptance of the extremest logical conclusions deducible from democratic principles long ago received as respectable. For it is very clear that in fundamental theory socialism and democracy are almost if not quite one and the same. They both rest at bottom upon the absolute right of the community to determine its own destiny and that of its members. Men as communities are supreme over men as individuals. Limits of wisdom and convenience to the public control there may be: limits of principle there are, upon strict analysis, none.

It is of capital importance to note this substantial correspondence of fundamental conception as between socialism and democracy: a whole system of practical politics may be erected upon it without further foundation. The germinal conceptions of democracy are as free from all thought of a limitation of the public authority as are the corresponding conceptions of socialism; the individual rights which the democracy of our own century has actually observed, were suggested to it by a political philosophy radically individualistic, but not necessarily democratic. Democracy is bound by no principle of its own nature to say itself nay as to the exercise of any power. Here, then, lies the point. The difference between democracy and socialism is not an essential difference, but only a practical difference—is a difference of *organization* and *policy*, not a difference of primary motive. Democracy has not undertaken the tasks which socialists clamour to have undertaken; but it refrains from them, not for lack of adequate principles or suitable motives, but for lack of adequate organization and suitable hardihood: because it cannot see its way clear to accomplishing them with credit. Moreover it may be said that democrats of to-day hold off from such undertakings because they are of to-day, and not of the days, which history very well remembers, when government had the temerity to try everything. The best thought of modern time having recognized a difference between social and political questions, democratic government, like all other governments, seeks to confine itself to those political concerns which have, in the eyes of the judicious, approved themselves appropriate to the sphere and capacity of public authority.

The socialist does not disregard the obvious lessons of history concerning overwrought government: at least he thinks he does not. He denies that he is urging the resumption of tasks which have been repeatedly shown to be impossible. He points to the incontrovertible fact that the economic and social conditions of life in our century are not only superficially but radically different from those of any other time whatever. Many affairs of life which were once easily to be handled by individuals have now become so entangled amongst the complexities of international trade relations, so confused by the multiplicity of news-voices, or so hoisted into the winds of speculation that only powerful combinations of wealth and influence can compass them. Corporations grow on every hand, and on every hand not only swallow and overawe individuals but also compete with governments. The contest is no longer between government and individuals; it is now between government and dangerous combinations and individuals. Here is a monstrously changed aspect of the social world. In face of such circumstances, must not government lay aside all timid scruple and boldly make itself an agency for social reform as well as for political control?

'Yes,' says the democrat, 'perhaps it must. You know it is my principle, no less than yours, that every man shall have an equal chance with every other man: if I saw my way to it as a practical politician, I should be willing to go farther and superintend every man's use of his chance. But the means? The question with me is not whether the community has power to act as it may please in these matters, but how it can act with practical advantage— a question of *policy*.'

A question of policy primarily, but also a question of organization, that is to say of *administration*.

WWhw MS. (WP, DLC).

[1] The catalyst of this essay was Wilson's reading of Ely's *Labor Movement in America.* Wilson wrote the first two paragraphs of his essay in shorthand on the envelope of EAW to WW, July 20, 1887. There is a brief shorthand outline of the essay in WP, DLC.

From James E. Rhoads

My Dear Doctor Wilson,   Bryn Mawr, Pa. 8 Mo. 25. 1887

We *can* spare $800. for an Assistant in History next year, if it be desirable to appoint one. I wrote to Mr Lunt[1] who has just spent two hours with me. He is a man of 24 years; about 5 ft. 9 in. height, of a dark complexion and strongly marked, but rather agreeable features. He has a due measure of self-reliance, and plain but courteous manners. He entered Harvard in 1882, and graduated in 1886. He took two years in Greek and Latin, reads French readily and German less readily; and has spoken both to a limited extent when on a bicycling tour last year. He has given considerable attention to the study of English. He is fluent in conversation, with a manly but rather nasal voice.

He has given special attention to American History and to Political Science. In the History of Greece & Rome he has taken the preparatory study required to enter Harvard in Leightin & Smith,[2] and such additional study of the history of those peoples as came in relation with his classical courses, but he has made no *special* study of ancient History. He would prefer not to attempt to teach ancient History and do so only with much reluctance.

In the History of the U. S. Mr Lunt has followed the courses of Mr Hart, made careful notes of his lectures, and read his references to a large extent. Here he feels at home and would be willing to teach.

In the History of Modern Europe, including England, he has taken the courses marked in the Harvard Catalogue sent by the same mail with this letter.[3]

He mentioned "Epochs of History," as one of the many books to which he was referred, and which he had read. He would be willing by the aid of his notes and reading to make out a course of lectures substantially identical with that marked "1" on page 108.[4] He has taken all the courses marked.

He has never lectured. As Instructor, students singly or in groups came to him for private aid in their study, additional to the lectures of Mr Hart, and exclusively in American History.

He would come for $800. and should know our decision by

Septr. 15th. I will inquire through his references as to his personal character.

If he had two years more of such training as is given at the J. H. U. or perhaps also at Harvard, he would be better prepared for our work.

If we take him it would be necessary for him to teach modern rather than ancient History, yet the regular course for next year would be ancient—not modern. No student that has applied to enter next year has as yet indicated a desire to study history. No graduate student in History has applied for next year. Except that Miss Mary Patterson wishes to take a course in *Modern* History in order to enable her to graduate next June, there is no apparent reason why we should have an assistant further than this, that it fills out our program and permits students who may enter without a choice as to the manner in which they will arrange their courses of study to take one in Modern History. Now if you think that under all those circumstances it is best to make Mr Lunt Asst, and have him ready to conduct a course in Modern History provided any students can be found for him after the college opens,[5] I will immediately take steps to have such an appointment made, if the Executive Committee are willing that it should be done, and I think they will act upon our deliberate judgment.

I am very truly yours,   James E Rhoads

Mr Lunt would decidedly prefer to accept a graduate scholarship & position as Instructor at Harvard for this year & come to us another year.

ALS (WP, DLC) with WWsh musings and WWhw notation on env.: "Ans. Aug. 29/87."

[1] Edward Clark Lunt, who apparently did not go into academic work.

[2] Robert Fowler Leighton, *A History of Rome* (New York, 1879), and William Smith, *A History of Greece from the Earliest Times to the Roman Conquest* (New York, 1854; many later editions).

[3] *Harvard University Catalogue, 1886-87* (Cambridge, Mass., 1886), pp. 108-109.

[4] "Course 1" was an introductory course on "Mediaeval and Modern European History."

[5] Although Wilson's reply is missing, it is clear from J. E. Rhoads to WW, Sept. 8, 1887, and WW to the President and Board of Trustees of Bryn Mawr College, June 29, 1888, that Wilson strongly recommended Lunt's appointment.

To John Bates Clark[1]

My dear Sir,   Gainesville, Georgia, 26 Aug., 1887

I trust that you will forgive me the liberty of a self-introduction for the purpose of thanking you for profit and pleasure derived from the perusal of your volume on the 'Philosophy of Wealth.' A constant pressure of college work prevented my reading the book in term time; but vacation has given me the leisure, and, having read the book, I feel under special obligations to its author. I feel that it has fertilized my own thought not only in the field of economics but also in the field of practical politics in which my special studies lie, and that, besides refreshing me with its original views and methods, it has cheered me not a little by its spirit,—its moderation and its Christianity. A sane, well-balanced sympathizer with organized labour is very dear to my esteem; and one who finds all the necessary stimulations of hope, not in chimeras or in hastened reformation, but in the slow processes of conservative endeavor is sure of my whole respect.

I shall, I am sure, return to your book again and again with undiminished pleasure and sympathy, and I hope I may be allowed to subscribe myself

Your sincere friend,   Woodrow Wilson

ALS (NNC).

[1] Born Providence, R. I., Jan. 26, 1847. A.B., 1872, A.M., 1878, and Ph.D., 1890, Amherst College; studied at the Universities of Heidelberg and Zürich, 1872-75. Professor of Political Economy and History, Carleton College, 1877-81; Professor of History and Political Science, Smith College, 1882-93; Professor of Political Economy, Amherst College, 1892-95; Professor of Political Economy, Columbia University, 1895-1923. Editor, *Political Science Quarterly*, 1895-1911. Director, Division of Economics and History, Carnegie Endowment for International Peace, 1911-23. Author of many articles and books, including *The Philosophy of Wealth. Economic Principles Newly Formulated* (Boston, 1886) and *The Distribution of Wealth; a Theory of Wages, Interest and Profits* (New York and London, 1899). Died March 21, 1938.

From Annie Wilson Howe

My precious Brother,   Columbia, S. C. Aug. 31st 1887

Dr. George unites with me in *warmest* congratulations to you and dear Ellie.[1] I would have written long before this but have been quite under the weather ever since Mother and Josie left us.

As to your razor-straps and cravat I am quite ashamed that they have not been sent to you. When Josie left I proposed that he take them in his satchel as he expected to see you as he passed through Gainesville. He said he would and I thought he had done so until last week when I found them put away in a drawer in his room. I will send them today. . . .

When do you leave Gainesville? With love to you both in which Dr. George joins me, I am,

Your devoted sister,   Annie.

Kiss the two babies & their dear Mother for me.

ALS (WP, DLC).

¹ Jessie Woodrow Wilson was born on August 28, 1887.

From Marion Wilson Kennedy

My dearest brother: Little Rock, Sept. 1st 87.

Your note, with its good news, was a very pleasant surprise to us, coming as it did the very day we reached home. We have been to Griffin Springs, about fifty miles north-east of this place, and the children and I spent six weeks of the "heated-term" there. Ross was with us parts of two weeks, and then went east for another two weeks. He visited Niagara, and New York, and saw as much as any man ever saw in so short a time. We spent last week in Batesville, and are now heartily enjoying being at home once more.

We are very glad for you and dear Ellie. I think it is so nice the children are both girls, as they can be such good play-fellows always, as Annie and I were, until *your* superior attractiveness drew my play-mate away. What is baby's name? And whom does she most resemble do "they say"? I want to hear all about her, the dear Mother and little Margaret. What does she think of the new-comer? Don't treat her as if she is quite a grown woman because she is the older of the two babies, please. Mother was always so careful about that, and so perfectly fair. Am I not good at giving gratuitous advice? . . .

Was sorry to hear that Mother is still not well, and Father suffering from a boil. Do you know what George Howe thinks of Mother's condition? How soon do you go to Bryn Mawr? Will Ellie go with you? Ross joins me in much love to *you all*. There are only two more of us than of you now, you know.

We are all well, except me, and I will be all right when I get rested, I hope. I weigh more than ever since leaving school, one hundred and twelve pounds, so you may know I am not ill at all.

My hand is very tired now, though, as this is my third letter; and I must write Annie a note, and Josie, too. Kiss the dear babies and their dear "Mama," and take their return kisses as all from

Your sister,   Marion.

ALS (WP, DLC) with WWhw list of authors and titles on verso of letter and WWsh and figures on env.

A Short Story[1]

[c. Sept. 1, 1887]

The World and John Hart
A Sketch in Outline

A blustering November Nor'-easter, driving before him keen arrows of chill rain, is an ugly customer, encounter him where you may; but in the streets of a city he is simply unendurable. Out of town, on some 'breezy upland,' or in some spacious valley flanked by placid hills, there is something to help you,—a bracing, athletic sense of battling with the elements,—the example of sturdy trees or patient fields,—traditions of rustic robustness,— some thought caught from the open country, which even in storm has its own fineness and inspiration. But in a city, with dripping walls and gutters about you and the ignoble mud of ugly drains splashing at your feet, this howling, pelting monster is only and wholly a nuisance, meeting you with his rude slap at every corner and chasing you with his intolerable bravado up every street. These are no circumstances under which to be gallant in face of the foe!

But John Hart was apparently not of this mind as he trudged sturdily through the streets of —— one November night in the midst of such a storm. He held his umbrella as if he could have held it against twenty such winds; his face beamed unsolicitous good-will upon all who passed him; and he quietly whistled as he went such bars as he could remember of a favorite comic opera. Once in a while, as he met the wind in turning a corner, the shrill notes of his whistling rose to a 'whew!' intonation; but that was his only outward recognition of Nature's ill temper.

Perhaps it was because he did not have very far to go, and had no errands to delay his reaching a warm fire and a good dinner. He stopped only once on the way; just after leaving his office he dropped a small package into a post mail-box. Then he swung on,—for he was big enough to go with a swing,—to the rythm of his whistling, which seemed to have begun long ago within the recesses of his office and not to have been made up at the outer door out of mere swagger in face of the storm. And yet it could not have been because he had not far to walk; for, when ten or fifteen minutes of his cheerful striding had brought him to the

---

[1] For some comment on this short story, see the Editorial Note, "Wilson's Desire for a 'Literary Life.'"

fire and the dinner, he had not reached just the sort of hearth that might be expected to make a man jolly.

No one who knew Miss Sarah Hart as well as her brother John knew her could have thought it much 'fun' to go home to her alone; and yet it was to her alone that John went home. There was no one else in his bachelor quarters. They two were, with the exception of a married sister, the sole surviving representatives of their branch of the Hart family; and they were quite used to sitting down *tête-à-tête* to breakfast and dinner every day. They were an odd pair,—worth knowing both of them, and more amusing to know together than apart: which is my special excuse for introducing them thus orphaned and *tête-à-tête* at their private dinner table.

Nature's first intention had been to make Miss Sarah Hart a large person: she had consequently planned her bony frame on a very liberal scale; but, on second thought, it had seemed hardly wise to waste too much flesh on the Hart family, and Miss Sarah was at the last moment cut off with a very scant covering for her frame, besides the indispensable muscles, and was left to grow up presenting many angles to the world. She at once thrust out an angle towards her brother:

"John," she said, in a voice which, like herself, was of large plan but meagre fibre, "John," she said, as she seated herself at the table, "I heard from Mary to-day."

Now Nature had planned John large and had carried out her plan generously. He presented to the world a full, manly, handsome person; and he replied to his sister in as gentle a tone as a very sonorous, masculine voice could command,

"Well, I hope they're all right?"

"No, of course they are not," she retorted, swallowing her soup with the stern steadiness with which, one may imagine, Socrates drank the hemlock,—hence her metaphor: "Mary is drinking to the full the cup of troubles which marriage always forces on a woman."

"Does she make a wry face over it in her letter?" queried John.

"No," sighed Miss Sarah, "she simply says that her oldest child has the measles and her next a dreadful eruption, and that she expects soon to have another!"

"Another eruption?" asked John.

"No; another baby."

"Oh!" said John; and he choked off the laugh that surged within him with a convulsively taken spoonful of soup, making as small pause as possible before saying,

"Whenever she writes to me, Mary seems to regard life as a good kind of holiday, anyhow."

He brought the remark out as if he were singing bass in an oratorio, probably by way of driving all the chuckle out of his voice.

Miss Sarah had not seen anything to laugh at: and her reply was to the effect (her voice had no echo of an oratorio in it) that both her brother and sister had entirely missed the point of life in having missed her conception of fate as a martinet. "Mary," she added, "is almost as irresponsibly content as the impossible women in your stories."

John's stories were few. It was his business to practice law; but it was his pleasure to write fiction; and these first ventures of his in that line had concerned men with muscle and women without nerves. He put a great deal of life and love into his characters, and to his editor and readers their life and love had seemed quite like the originals; but his sister Sarah read them differently.

"As for my women," said John (who as a matter of fact had no women, though he very ardently wanted one whom he knew) "as for my women, when a fellow's making people, why should'nt he make them to suit himself, with plenty of laugh and contentment in them? He need'nt force bad company on himself, need he?" And John smiled his placidest smile.

"Not if he thinks there's no moral purpose in writing," was the answering broadside, "and that it's a young lawyer's proper business to invent fictitious people instead of serving real ones."

You perceive, reader, Miss Sarah Hart was not really a disagreeable person: she only made herself disagreeable. And this she did out of a sense of duty. Her brother and she had enough to live on, with something handsome left over; for their father had not only made a great deal at the bar, but had left a snug sum of it to them. But then John had taken his father's profession, as a sort of intellectual inheritance, and was occupying his father's office, and Miss Sarah thought that he ought to be trying for more practice than he got, instead of 'making up' stories, as she put it: and he would be a very unconscientious person indeed who should say that she was wrong.

"A young lawyer's business is itself a largely fictitious thing," asserted the unruffled John, "and the air of his office seems to breed fiction. The people I bring into my office with my pen are not quite like those who come in in the flesh, but they have about as much business to offer me, and they are a much jollier lot."

John Hart was of that peculiar sort of sensitive composition which you have not perhaps often observed among your acquaintances, but which nevertheless exists, which reacts at once strongly and healthily from its surroundings. It may be defined as a sense of the balance of things. In proportion as his sister's sternness became her steady policy in conversation, he bent his thoughts upon creating all possible diversions of amusement, by way of keeping things in equilibrium. If you want to know what the impulse is, watch your own remarks when talking with some one who is inclined to take a very roseate view of fortune, and of the economic condition of the laborer. John had a nature which constituted a sort of commission to him from Fate, or some such person, to supply the compensations for which she is said by certain essayists to have provided.

And so it happened that dinner went well with John, in spite of the fact that his sister's conversation continued to hold its duteous way past every topic of admonition or anxiety which their family's moral diary afforded at the time. He offset her at every point with the easy success resulting from long practice; and then he went into the library, lit himself a pipe which kept his sister out of the room none the less effectually because it was not meant to do so, and, comfortably established at the big writing table in an old coat and an older pair of slippers, drew forth from a drawer some *mss.* and began to adorn it with numerous erasures and interlineations. Only a man of John's unhesitating digestion can or ought to revise a story immediately after eating a hearty dinner; but John could, and that was what he was doing now, with as innocent an air as if there were no one in the house who disapproved of such an occupation for him.

The fact was that Miss Sarah furnished the chief inspiration to her brother's work: she would have been beyond measure shocked had she known that she created the success which encouraged John to go on with his unlawyerly practices, and no one would have been more astonished than John, had he known it,—he would have known twice as much of himself as he did know—but, though neither of them suspected the fact, a fact it was. The whole thing was as simple as all psychological phenomena. John had a fine equipment for writing stories: a strong realistic imagination, an absorptive appreciation of the life which passed around him every day in the business and society of the city, and a sturdy, simple, perspicuous way of putting forth the fancies that were in him in words that were the express image of his thought; but the cardinal fact was his genius for reacting from his surroundings. He wrote sometimes a little in his office, but oftenest and most here in the library, after a dinner interview with his severe sister and while he was reacting from her. The result was matter which the editors and readers of a certain cheery metropolitan monthly greatly rejoiced to get. They had never met Miss Sarah Hart, but they got the benefit of her. These stories were sane and broad and humorous because she was austere. John found that somehow the generous motives of action suggested themselves to him always in the evenings in the library very much more than they did in his office during the day. He made his people have trouble, and there was a dash of tears in many a passage which the great hearty fellow wrote with brimming eyes. He knew quite well that things do not go ideally with anyone in this world: and he saw in sorrow one of the great presences of every household. He never gave out a picture all sunlight: but he used the shadows to heighten the lights and made it quite evident to everybody that he depended on the lights for the force of his composition. His sorrows never subdued or soured the characters who were central in his plots: discipline did not issue in dull, incessant care, or in anxious paralysis, but in its more perfect fruit of strength and dutifulness and glad devotion. His "impossible women" were content, not because their paths were strewed with thornless roses, but because love and womanliness enabled them to bear without repining every burden that was honestly come by. He wrote from a heart which found cheer amid the hardness of the way because of strong faith in the balanced rightness of the world. It was wonderful how serene and wholesome and stimulating the atmosphere of that library was, in spite of the tobacco smoke that loaded its currents. The world was, for John, like his own good stomach: it digested good and bad alike and got abounding health as a result.

This story that he was revising was full, it was evident, of rollicking good cheer and honest, downright fun; he was chuckling in unrestrained private merriment over its jokes even as he sharpened them with his pen: the keen point he was giving them was being given only to satisfy his delicate critical taste as a skilled workman—their substance was enough already to content his sense of humor deliciously. He presently got through with them, however, locked their *mss.* body away, and threw himself luxuriously into an easy chair before the fire with a book in his hand.

He read for some time; but the book seemed easy to get away from, and John was very soon looking over it into the fire. He wasn't a man to dream, so heartily ran his blood; and he did not dream now—he thought. Having thought a bit, without ruffling his strong, placid features, he looked at his watch: his watch seemed to counsel a look out of window to see how his friend the November storm fared: watch and winds together advised bed; and to bed he went, looking in on his way to his room upon the unjoyful needlework of Miss Sarah in the sitting-room, and saying to her, after his stout kiss had been planted on her forehead, that 'it was a jolly good night to sleep, and he thought he would go up and try it.' John was not simply the unimpassioned, matter-of-fact fine digester he looked: you did not need to read his stories, you had only to study his eyes a moment to discover depths of poetry and laughter in the man. He made for himself, wherever he happened to be, a sort of private world of manly sentiment: and he always wanted to say something affectionate to his sister when he told her good-night: the only trouble was, that, being a humorist, his eye was quick to see incongruities, and somehow it always seemed to that humorist eye of his (just in the corner of it, where humor shaded off into pathos) that it was more appropriate to speak to her—about something else. Still, when he had looked over his book into the fire as he sat in the library he had been thinking that affection was rather a natural inclination of his, and that he was not half sorry it was. Hence his look at his watch (it was not late) and at the skies outside. Hence also what happened afterwards.

II.

The next evening, being tired of the rather too often repeated non-society scene of tobacco and *mss.* in the library, John Hart put a new play on his stage. After dinner he dressed up,—no, not *up*, but *out*,—out of the office look his figure had worn even in face of his dining, and went forth to make a call. It was a call which John delighted to make, on a medium-sized, lovely, blue-eyed sunbeam of a girl with naïve delights in his favourite books and modes of thought: and yet when John entered the parlor where he was to see her he looked for all the world like a brother to his sister Sarah[.] Such was the odd nature of the strange fellow that his visage was now as stern as those melting gray eyes of his would permit. He had been in this cosey parlor a good many times before, and always he had borne himself in the same way towards his surroundings, as if he would under no circumstances break the solemn calm with a laugh—a demeanor which would have been very much admired at his own dinner table if he could only have managed it there, but which greatly puzzled this young lady upon whom he had called. The fact is, that this was a literary acquaintanceship. John did not publish his stories over his own name but over the name 'Henry Blount' and few of his friends knew that he wrote at all; but Miss Albright had found him out through an intimate friend of his, and of hers, who had been unable to foil her clever detective stratagems. John had forgiven the betrayal of confidence, since the discovery of himself by Miss Albright had led to his discovery of her. But imagine her surprise upon contrasting the man with the author. She had found him, not brisk, cheery, racy, like his stories, but sedate and grave; interesting indeed, but not entertaining; loyal to the standards of his tales, but a little inclined to qualify somewhat their attractive views of life; an admirable, even lovable, type of quiet, judicious manhood, strong in scholarship and catholic in taste, a man to engage your loyalty; but not at all the genial, playful giant of his stories, not a man to delight your holiday humors. The puzzle to Miss Albright was not so much in this singular contrast, however, as in the glimpses she caught, now and again, in John's conversation of the man she had imagined the author of her favorite current stories to be. Her own gay wit would sometimes surprise him into sallies that gleamed with the sunshiny wisdom or the stingless satire that stood out, for their illumination, in so many passages of his writings. Why was it hard to provoke him to these, which seemed so natural to him when he wrote? She could account for it only in her own whimsical fashion, by supposing that there was something in what she had heard about a certain *afflatus* which maintained authors at their inspired pitch, and that occasionally, by some lucky stroke of talk, she excited this mysterious influence to action. She liked John immensely; but she was a trifle piqued at finding a man she could not quite understand,—most men were so easy to understand, she thought.

When she came into the parlor on this particular evening, her pretty face according in every feature with the arch mischief in her eyes, she plied John with an immediate quizzing question.

"I suppose, Mr. Hart, that you haven't a single thing to say in defence of your not having been to see me for weeks and weeks?"

"Why no," said John, "I have only to ask for your condolence." He had been hastened by her onset into a playful venture at compliment, and Miss Edith was delighted.

"I don't pity you a bit," she said, "if you've been spending the time with some story characters of your own making: for you make them do famously well for good company." Miss Edith had carelessly sacrificed her strategic advantage, for John, she knew, never found an *afflatus* in a compliment. She hastened to regain her lost position by adding artlessly, "I've got a character I'm working up myself."

"Indeed," said John, "what character is that?"

"My own," declared the lady demurely; and her advantage was regained. John laughed outright,—and supplemented, "And you are making famously good company out of it."

She had brought a fresh breeze into the room which for a moment had quite blown away his sombre humor. But his surroundings presently recalled him to his gravity, and he asked, as if only completing his remark, "How has your reading in Marlowe gone recently? Do you still wish that you had contented yourself with Lamb's extracts?"

"No," she said, keeping her discomfiture out of all but the corners of her recently smiling mouth, where the smile still lingered, "but I think yet that one gets the best of him in Lamb, and that one might do better than explore all of him. I was very hungry for something else before I got through. What do you think makes an author easy to read?"

"I don't know that I could say without thinking the matter over a little," replied John slowly, regarding the lambent fire in her eyes with all calmness and deliberation the while. "Perhaps catholic sympathy and an artistic sense of proportion, a speedy, inartificial way of setting forth what he has to say; or perhaps genuine warmth and earnestness and a certain sterling character of thought—the qualities which make a person pleasant to know."

"You dont think, then, that the satirists are easy to read, the sharp, vindictive fellows who simply hit hard, whether it's fair or not? I acknowledge I take great delight in reading Swift and the rest sometimes: it's famously easy work. But maybe that isn't your experience: I can fancy that it wouldn't be."

"Why?," asked John promptly.

"Because the moral purpose of it isn't evident enough in it. You would not want follies whipped except for their own improvement,—which mere whipping isn't likely to effect."

"Well, I am willing to accept that criterion," declared John, with some fervour, "for don't you think that when we pull down wrong views of life we ought to build up right ones in their stead? I think that the men who simply go about flinging their wit at everything and anything which seems to them disagreeable or out of place are pests"—John did not think so ordinarily, but in this house he generally did, for some reason or other,—"It's irresponsible work they do: and the less merely satirical writing done the better. I don't see why it should be impossible, or even difficult, for any sane mind to see the relative proportions of things. We are very far from living in a Vanity Fair, from which goodness and fairness and soberness are excluded."

"We mustn't have a scruple more of frolic than of gravity, then, in what we think and do?," inquired Miss Edith.

"I don't know how near we can come to striking an exact balance," answered John with unrelaxed soberness; "but at any rate virtue of thought and of life seems to me well enough represented by a mean between two extremes."

"Dear me!" sighed the lady, "wouldn't I have a sad time trying to weigh out my pleasures against my responsibilities and disappointments! I can't for the life of me help being light-hearted for a great deal more than one half of the time. Ought I to try?"

"One doesn't have to be heavy-hearted to be serious and look life straight in the face," John explained.

"Not even if life has a *very* duteous face indeed?" urged Miss Edith. "And, if one's life has a very nice, good-natured face indeed, mayn't one smile at it as much as one pleases, so long as her smiles don't disturb other people?" And she ventured on a comical little smile, partly solemn, partly pleading, mostly mischievous, which did disturb John in certain regions of his being very much indeed.

"Why yes: I've no sort of objection to smiles," said John, very truthfully, "and some people seem to have been appointed to smile"—whereupon he ventured a reassuring smile himself,—"but then there are other people who are equally appointed to bear the burdens and execute the responsibilities, and so make good the balance, not of solemnity—there's nothing in that by itself—but of judgment, let us say."

And so this hearty fellow and delightful author, John, went on discoursing to this delightful, winsome girl, who delighted nobody more profoundly than she delighted him, and yet who was seldom able to draw from him anything more delightful to her blithe spirit than this serious sort of elevated talk about the great things that make for happiness. Another girl would have been repelled, perhaps, though it would have been hard for any one of either sex to be repelled by a man with eyes and voice and visage so notably honest and unusual; but Miss Albright was only attracted—though attracted in spite of her private, abstract standards as to male conduct in the presence of female companionship. There was something in John—not all of which was transferred to him by her imagination from his writings—which suggested an infinite fund of tenderness and good-fellowship concealed in deep fountains somewhere in him. After a while, on this occasion as on others, she was able to lead him into talk about people whom they both knew, and in such talk, though still serious, he was so sympathetic and so generous in all his judgments that she was delighted, and abandoned herself to playing with the topics of their conversation quite as the moment prompted, and as she could not help suspecting that John liked her to do.

And then, after saying 'that it was like a walk in fine spring air to come to see her,' John went away, leaving her with the queerest feeling of suspense in her gentle womanly heart, as if somehow her acquaintance with John was always broken off for a season just before it had become complete. As for John, he went home at an athletic speed, joked with his sister Sarah in a most unseemly manner (she thought) as he warmed his feet at the fire downstairs and bade her good-night, and went off to bed in a perfect gale of whistling, stopping only to jot down on a scrap of paper the outlines of a very humorous situation to be inserted in the unfinished story down in the library.

III.

Within eighteen months both John's pleasures and his responsibilities were very much increased. He was married, and Edith, instead of Miss Sarah, was mistress of his home. Miss Sarah had carried out a plan which she had long cherished by assuming the cares of matron of an orphan asylum which her favorite uncle had founded some years before in a quiet rural village not far from the city, and which only her duty to bachelor John had prevented her taking charge of from the first. Just as John was about to marry, the first matron opportunely resigned, and Miss Sarah, who was already a trustee, promptly took her place.

In the meantime John had published only the story we have seen him revise. The engrossments of engagements and marriage had proved very antagonistic to composition,—principally by keeping John free from all desire to write, or to do anything, beyond visiting Edith and attending to his business, except think.

After his marriage, however, his literary activity returned—to bring him a great surprise. He wrote his first post-matrimonial story with as much spontaneity and as much enjoyment of the work as had ever attended his composition, and he fancied that he was making a decided advance upon what he had done before. The story embodied a more satisfactory expression of his ideals than he had ever heretofore managed to frame; and he sent it off to his editor with a sort of enjoyable anticipation at that worthy man's gratification at his contributor's improvement. *But it was rejected,*—sent back within the week with the editor's regrets that it was in a vein which he was afraid the particular people who subscribed for his magazine would not appreciate. John was astounded. He carried the *mss.* to Edith, and said,

"What do you think, my dear, they've sent back the 'Minister's Experience,'—they don't want it!"

"What a shame!" Edith exclaimed, after the pause which was necessary to take in the full meaning of the news, "what for? Because one magazine can't stretch its standards over more than one kind of story, and this is a new sort that the editor is afraid of?"

"Why this is not so very different from what I've written before, is it?" said John, a little surprised.

"Yes, dear, it is very different," said Edith gently.

It was very different; so different that when John had read it to his devoted, glad-eyed little spouse from time to time as it developed under his hand, she had felt a strange vague sort of surprise at what she heard, not unmixed with a slight sense of apprehension. The story was excellent; it was even a little more than excellent: it was impressive, the style strong and masculine, the feeling deep and sincere, the situations dramatic, the plot complete and striking. All the old power was there,—but hardly a touch of the old humor. It was a sober, intense story, intent upon the deep things which mould human character and shape human destiny. It nowhere rang with any note of mirth, and some of its passages even made Edith feel sorely tempted to cry. She supposed it was only the versatility of her lord's genius which had effected this change, but she wondered once or twice whether she herself had anything to do with it. She had suspected before that John himself was not conscious that he was writing a new kind of story: and she was quite sure that it was no unhappiness on his part that had sobered his imaginative work. Never had husband been more evidently happy than was John: she had seen him once or twice with his sister Sarah when he was fairly gay in his fine high spirits, and seemed to be talking out of one of his first stories. But Edith of course remembered how she used to contrast his conversation with his writings, and now, since this new story had begun to grow in much the same lines as the old talks she had had with John, she put these two facts together in her thoughts, that those conversations had been with her and that this story was written with her. Was *she* the cause of the rejection of this story by the editor of *Piper's*?

"How is it different?" asked John, a new light beginning to dawn on him.

"Why, I hardly know how to describe it," Edith said, "I thought you were conscious of the difference yourself, and meant it to be different. It's much less humorous and playful than the stories you wrote before. They were splendid holiday tales, and this is so much more serious and passionate. Surely you knew that! I've all this time been admiring your ability to write equally well in two opposite veins;—and I'm sure that all you've got to do is to send the *mss.* to the *Old Dauphinville Review*, if you want it printed. They seem to want fiction of that serious, elevated sort."

John sat down, and looked in an odd, puzzled, quizzical way at the *mss.* in his hand. Then he looked at Edith with eyes that seemed to spy out a comedy somewhere. Presently he asked, with great deliberation and evident satisfaction,

"And so this is an entirely new sort of story for me to write, is it?"

"Yes," said Edith, watching him with rising laughter and delight in her eyes.

"It would seem odd to publish a story in anything but *Piper's*, wouldn't it? It would be breaking in upon the uniform edition of one's works at an advanced stage."

"Yes," agreed Edith, expectantly.

"And you think that this good, grave, high-pitched composition would look better on a solid page in big type than in double columns, where it would look more like a story which an editor's subscribers would appreciate?"

"Yes," said Edith, with a mischievous little nod.

"Humph!" said John, beginning to turn the pages of the *mss.* slowly and critically. "These fellows here in the second part *might* be a little more amusing, that's so. I wonder if something could not be done for this hypochondriac conversation here between Tweedledum and Tweedledee?" And he drew his chair meditatively towards a table where there was pen and ink.

"Oh, don't change it!" cried Edith, "you'll ruin it!"

"Will I?" said John, "that would be a pity. A laugh right in that particular place *might* mar the harmony of the old monochrome, I believe." Then, laying down his pen, leaning back in his chair, and looking Edith mock-anxiously full in the face, he asked, "What do you suppose was the matter with me when I wrote this thing?"

"I don't suppose that anything was the matter with you," said Edith, "unless I have bewitched you,"—with the glitter of tears in her eyes. Whereupon John forgot all about the story; and remembered it again, some hours later, only when Edith asked and obtained his consent to do it up and address it to the editor of the *Old Dauphinville*.

Her prediction proved correct. That *Review* did very readily accept the 'Minister's Experience,' and critics very generously applauded the new success of that very clever writer, Henry Blount, in the latest number of the *Old Dauphinville*. The editor of that magazine 'had been fortunate to secure a story from so able and promising an author; and the 'Minister's Experience' proved that Mr. Blount's long silence had not been without its rich fruit,' &c. But the odd thing, to John's and Edith's minds, was that for a long time,—that is, through three years and four stories, one of which was considerably longer and more elaborate than any he had written before—'Mr. Blount' continued to write for no one but the editor of the *Dauphinville*. Apparently the old vein had been worked out completely: only now and then would the former breezy gladness and blithe freedom of life steal into John's writings and touch a dramatic narrative with a gleam of the manner so pleasing to his first editor. His humor seemed to have transferred itself to Edith, as to a fitter vessel, John being left to enjoy and admire his charming little companion's inimitable imaginative wit, but to get on without any of that marketable gift himself. His former self lived in her, much more gracefully and delightfully than it had ever lived in him; and he turned to the exclusive cultivation of those other qualities of style and thought, still fitly retained by himself, which made his writings seem to many prophetic of work equal to George Eliot's in that great author's own field.

IV.

No man,—not even a man of John Hart's unfailing self-command, both mental and physical,—can go on forever writing short stories. The author habit is like the opium habit: big doses must follow small doses: the excess of the sustained novel must ensue upon the moderate indulgence of the brief sketch. And so it was with John Hart: he turned at length from editors to publishers

and ventured upon intricacy of plot and fulness of detail in his
story-telling.

Not, however, before many changes had come upon his life. A
competence secure and the literary life increasingly seductive, he
gave up, a few years after his marriage, the office in which he
had tried to keep in mind his father's reputation, and to nurse
the elements of his father's legal learning for the benefit of a few
clients, and betook himself to a suburban cottage and garden
which seemed to him a favourable place for the health and
growth both of his literary faculty and of the promising boy with
which Edith had presented him. But the new life was unexpectedly beset with distractions. Sister Mary sent a strapping youngster to him to be kept near the school advantages of the city:
and this youngster, full of the Hart vigour, was also full of minor
masculine predilections which gave Edith no end of trouble and
sadly marred the literary calm of John's chosen retreat. Then
sister Sarah was driven by stress of ill-health from the orphanage
and divided her invalidism into half-yearly periods which she
spent, turn and turn about, with Mary and John. At John's, where
she spent the winters, it was her pleasure to apply to Mary's
youngster the stern processes of an ineffectual oral discipline.
At Mary's, in the summer, only the superior plan of her sister's
domestic generalship prevented her keeping the whole family
under the shadow of her vigilant sober conscience. Edith was not
without defensive resources herself, but somehow these could
not avail to control George, Mary's rampant boy, and even seemed
to fail to shield John from direct witness of the strained relations
existing between the several members of his little household.

Written under such circumstances, John's novel was not an
unqualified success,—at least not in the eyes of the serious critics,
who wanted a work of art, throughout consistent with itself, and
found only a good story with a variegated plot, consistent with
nothing but John's self. One or two publishers refused the *mss.*
before it found itself in type and on young ladies' tables; and
John was not much surprised that his offspring met with these
initial difficulties: for he had found that he couldn't himself like
all its vagaries of plot and style. He had come near absolute disgust with it as he revised it,—if he had thought that he had a
great reputation to be careful of, he would not have published the
book at all. A short story can generally manage to get read by its
author in much the same mood in which he wrote it; at any rate
it is 'all of a piece,' because of its very shortness, and must make
a harmonious impression. But John could not always, when

revising the chapters of his novel, hit upon just the humour in which he had written them,—and to try to change them when in another mood was only to introduce discordant notes and put the whole chapter more hopelessly out of tune. He had to confine his attention to the grammar, and, believing the story sound on the whole, offer it for publication, with the brave indifference of the man whose income is independent of his literary fortunes.

That part of the public which was not composed of serious critics and which cared more for the entertaining than for the artistic elements in what they read, made the book a financial success by buying, liking, and talking about it: for it was as full of vim as was John himself, and as full of surprises as was John's life of domestic distractions—a story to enjoy and wonder at,— and be glad you had not written.

How much the serious critics,—who devoured the good things of the story but duteously wrote about the bad things,—how much they would have learned about the possible domestic history of literature, if they could only have known how that odd novel was written! Sister Sarah exasperated nephew George at the dinner table with well-meant admonitions about sma[c]king his lips and not coming into too immediate contact with his meat; Edith gently intervened and was cut off with a rebuff, for nothing like intervention could divert Miss Hart from the full performance of duty; and after the meal was over one of John's characters developed into the jovialest despiser of proprieties and conventions imaginable. Alas! this was the very fool, as it turned out, to whom the critics objected. They said he was forever popping in, to the upsetting and spoiling of the serious work of the otherwise promising plot. They had not seen John's dinner table with John's eyes.

George was away on a holiday at a school-fellow's across the country; sister Sarah had gone to see her orphans; Edith sat in the study all the evening, quietly sewing, to be turned to in all phases of thought or perplexity for sympathy or rest; and John wrote one of those paragraphs throbbing with eloquent religious thought which the critics said was set so queerly amidst love-making and jests.

A letter came from sister Mary urging Miss Hart to come to her sooner than usual in view of an expected sickness, and saying that an excellent private school was to be opened in her neighborhood to which George would of course be sent next year; and a death occurred in John's fiction which the critics said destroyed all reasonable hopes for the plot.

And so John worked out his first novel through episodes and to a conclusion which surprised no one more than himself. He never suspected that George or sister Sarah were in any way responsible for the too sudden and too various transitions of his story. He never thought critically about himself: it could never occur to him to analyze his own frames of mind. Thinking with him was a perfectly normal and spontaneous function and went into his writing unquestioned and fresh from its sources. He thought *out from himself*, not in upon himself. The result was that he could never hit upon a proper mental economy for himself, simply because he never meditated hitting upon such an economy. It would have been as impossible for him to think about his own thinking as it was for him to feel his own digesting. His mind never looked at itself: it only obeyed the *momentum* of his simple, straightforward, massive nature and quite unconsciously wove the strong fabric of his thought, which it deftly illuminated as it went with the quaint patterns of his fancy.

And so John never guessed why he had constructed this strange mosaic of moods and fancies; but Edith did. She more than suspected, she knew, that she had solved the mystery which had begun with the 'Minister's Experience' and its rejection by the magnate of *Piper's*. She knew now why, in the days before her marriage, John had seemed in her drawing room so different from the man she would have deemed competent to write stories that moved the blood to its quickest and most joyous movements. She knew that she had married the most sensitive, as well as the least morbid, of men. Best of all, she saw how she could realize her dearest ideals and be of infinite service to the man she loved.

That scapegrace of a novel had opened her eyes. As John had read chapter after chapter of it to her, while it was a-writing, he had unconsciously opened wider and wider before her the book of his own character. Herself in the midst of the same domestic scenes, she saw how domestic scenes and all his surroundings coloured John's moods, shaped his fancies, transfigured his thought, dictated his style, made his novel. Hand in hand with her discoveries went her resolves as to what she would do. By the time the story was published her plans were made. She would constitute herself dramatic manager for her husband; knowing his standards with reference to his work, she would create the proper conditions for homogeneous, artistically sound and whole production. She would make it her care to supply atmospheres for his mind, that it might register only harmonious effects. She would assume the rôle of business partner, watching the thought market, establishing proper conditions for manufacture, and erecting suitable machinery; while John furnished capital of thought and skill of execution.

Of course John had no conception of the designs of his little mate, any more than he had of the facts of disposition on which she was building; how could he? But the plan was put into execution .nevertheless, with immense advantage to his fame and untold additions to his pleasures. The critics were astonished at the variety and perfection of what came from the pen of the man at whose first romance they had felt in principle bound to look askance. They would have wondered less had they known John and seen Edith's management in the light of her own designs.

She led John to Lake George for a stay long enough to enable him to watch two changes of season pass over the beautiful water in its basin of wooded hills,—from the earliest Spring, through the season of tourists and hotelfuls of human curiosities, far into the bleak Autumn when visitors had ceased to thrust their vari[e]ties of type upon his thoughts and only a full resultant conception of life and human circumstance remained with him. He wrote the while a tale of sustained passion, swift plot, elevated moral such as made the critics rub their eyes, doff their caps, and pour the milk of human kindness into their ink-stands wherewith to write their notices of 'John Marston's Faith.'

Edith took her author to London for a Winter and made him give all his leisure to taking her among the poor of the great metropolis, that she might indulge her love for serving the homeless and destitute, at the same time that she learned conditions of abject misery such as the cities of her own land did not yet afford, but might some day, did not she and others learn betimes the best means of helpfulness and all sane plans of charity. The result was a novel from John which in light-hearted force went far beyond even the promise of his first bright stories, so mellow was its kindliness, so rich its hope, so joyful its progress, so sweet and wholesome its plot. One could not read it without being made better and stronger for having passed a time of delight in the company of men of spirit and honor and women inspired with love and helpfulness: for having come in contact with a life strong despite its faults, glad despite its sorrows.

Another year found John, still led by the gentle hand of his little manager, in the mining regions of the West, where he wrote of sedate burghers, wearing the full harness of law and civilization; another at the Hague, where he wrote of disordered passions and desperate fortunes.

In brief, the management was a signal success. Edith had discovered the receipt for making a consistent artist out of the splendid man given her to care for: and in love and tenderness she gave him not only a satisfying home wherever they sojourned, but at last a great reputation and the full honors of intellectual maturity and success.

Edward Coppleston

WWhw MS. (WP, DLC). There is a WWhw first draft of this story in WP, DLC.

From John Franklin Jameson

My dear Wilson: Amherst, Sept. 4, 1887.
I have received your letter of August 30th, and hasten to say that I shall be very glad to accept your proposition. Do what you can. Says Hosea Biglow:

> "I don't appruve o' givin' pledges;
> You'd ough' to leave a feller free,
> An' not go knockin' out the wedges,
> To ketch his fingers in the tree."[1]

I doubt not we shall in the end have something very good from you.   Sincerely yours,   J. F. Jameson

ALS (WP, DLC).
[1] James Russell Lowell, "A Letter from a Candidate for the Presidency . . . ," *The Biglow Papers*, First Series, No. VII.

From Joseph Ruggles Wilson

My dearest Woodrow—   Clarksville, Sep 6 87
I received from Saratoga on Saturday, the package containing yr MSS. for the Fortnightly Review—and this morning I forward the same to England.[1]
You do not need my assurances as to the excellency of this article. The thought is itself new; especially when regarded in those its practical bearings which you somewhat elaborate, or rather "point out." The style of composition is *first rate* with the one only drawback of being clothed in a mist to a certain extent: but it is a *mountain* mist, & so may be regarded as admirable.
We were all made glad by learning that dear Ellie had passed through her crisis so successfully. Present to her, with our love, our parental congratulations. I could have wished for the advent of a *boy*—but maybe next year will do better than this!
We are in our usual health—or half-health. Your dear mother

I feel concerned about—but am everyday hoping for her complete rehabilitation.

I can write no more now—as it makes me very nervous to pen even so short a letter as I am thus constrained to send to my precious son and friend.

All join me in love   Your ever affc   Father

ALS (WP, DLC).

[1] The article was "The Eclipse of Individuality." Wilson, in his letter to Bridges of May 29, 1887, had indicated that the idea of submitting the article to the *Fortnightly Review* had occurred to him. Perhaps Wilson had told his father about the article in Columbia, Dr. Wilson had asked to read it, and Woodrow Wilson had sent it to him with the request that he send it on to the *Fortnightly Review* after reading it, if Dr. Wilson thought that it was worth submitting.

From James W. Bones

Dear Woodrow   Rome Ga Sept 8/87

Yours of 2d has been received. We had heard already thru the Hoyts of the arrival of the little one & are now glad to learn that she & the dear mother are both doing so well.

In regard to the balance I owe your mother as Trustee of your Aunts Estate I regret very much that it cannot be paid at present. I have not been unmindful of the matter for the past two years, but my affairs have been in a very embarrassed condition for a long time & have now terminated very disastrously. The property of the estate, the mill & Helenhurst[1] are to be sold this winter under foreclosure of mortgage. The debts are large. Should the property realize more than the mortgage debts I will be able to pay the amount due your mother. Otherwise I see but little prospect of anything being done unless sometime in the future I may be able out of my poverty to do something. With the help of a friend I have been keeping the mill going in a small way for several months past so as to make a bare living. When it passes out of my hands as it will do this winter I will have to seek a clerical position of some kind, so as to make a living. Dear little Helen[2] is being lovingly cared for by Jessie.[3] Marion[4] is now organist of our church on a small salary & has obtained the position of assn't music teacher in the Rome Female College. She will have a small income from these two sources. The dear girl is very full of the idea of making her own living & is quite bright & happy. My dear old mother[5] has a small income of her own. You see from all this that it is likely to be a hard pull for us to get along. Failure has been stamped upon all my efforts so far in life. It is no doubt all for the best, & I try not [to] yield to feelings of despondency & gloom. I have done poorly by my dear children but they still love me & that is a comfort.

My mother suffers but little pain now but is still unable to walk.

With love from us all.   Your affec uncle   James

ALS (WP, DLC) with WWhw figures and notation on env.: "Ans. Sp 15/87."
¹ His home in Rome, Georgia.
² His youngest child, Helen Woodrow Bones.
³ Jessie Bones Brower, then living in Chicago.
⁴ His second daughter, Marion McGraw Bones.
⁵ Maria Bones.

From James E. Rhoads

My Dear Doctor Wilson,   Bryn Mawr, Pa. 9 Mo. 8 1887

Since my last letter to you, I have learned that Miss Mary Patterson even if a course in *Modern* History were offered could not graduate next year without attempting an almost impossible amount of work. Moreover she does not propose attending the lectures regularly, if offered the opportunity, but to be at them occasionally, learn their drift and "pass" the examination in virtue of having read a good deal of modern History. This does not afford any encouragement to have a course for her alone. If there be no course in History next year for undergraduates it will still be practicable for students entering this autumn to take a major course in history and graduate in four years; and any disadvantage that might arise to the History Dept. from the omission of lectures the coming year could be avoided by proper advice to students when they were choosing their majors.

Moreover the only assignable reason why Ancient History has not been more sought for by the students is that the first course was less interspersed with lectures than those attending thought would have been helpful. The course in Modern History was much liked by the class. There is the more reason that the next course in Ancient History should be the best practicable. Now Mr. Lunt was unwilling to attempt a course of instruction in Ancient History; and to have him do so and not succeed would be more prejudicial to the Dept. than to wait a year.

If we had a really able assistant, I wd be more disposed to favor an appointment, but as Mr Lunt is certainly weak on Ancient Histy., I think it better to make no appointment, secure a well trained man for 1888-89, pay him better and have the Dept. as strong as may be.¹

I feel assured that you need not and ought not to give your classes in Ancient History less "strong meat." A slight modification of the plan of 1885-86, throwing in more lectures to show to the students the relation and meaning of the facts they find in the text books, would be all that was necessary.

Drs Collitz[2] and Keiser arrived from Europe day before yesterday—very hale & full of spirits. Drs Wilson & Gregory[3] are here.

The time for opening seems very close at hand, and we shall be expecting the pleasure of greeting Mrs. Wilson and yourself soon. With kindest regards to her, I am

Yours very truly   James E Rhoads

ALS (WP, DLC).

[1] Wilson's reply to this letter is missing. However, WW to the President and Board of Trustees of Bryn Mawr College, June 29, 1888, makes it plain that Wilson returned an emphatic dissent to Rhoads's decision.

[2] Hermann Collitz, Associate Professor of German Literature and Language.

[3] Edmund B. Wilson, Professor of Biology, and Emily L. Gregory, Associate in Botany.

From Joseph Ruggles Wilson

My dearest Son—   Clarksville, Tenn., Septr 12, 1887

I am very sorry that my criticism of your MSS. has served to discourage you. And I hasten to say that this could not be the effect if I expressed myself clearly. I ought perhaps to have said that in writing the essay which I have just despatched upon its fortunes,[1] you did not always keep your subject *in view*: in view, I mean, not of yourself but of the reader who must now and then look to the *heading* to be sure of his whereabouts. Your published book does not so treat the interested student of its pages—nor do the chapters of yr new book which you so kindly read to me last summer (1886)[2] miss their always luminous mark. But in these productions the supposed reader has somehow been taken into your confidence, and you give to him the very same *inside* look of the subject which you have yourself—i.e., you seem to be *answering* his *questions* as you go along together, so that he is never long kept in the dark. I mean this—you often as much as say—without saying it in actual words. I think, therefore, that the partial obscurity of your briefer pieces, is due to their very brevity: and this because in part you have not room in which to *play* with your subject (as every racy writer ought to do)—and so in the confined space which is full of mental furniture, you knock over here a chair, there a table and kick up a sort of intellectual dust that obscures the light of one and another window that otherwise would pour in the full light of day;—and partly because you begin too far off from your principal topic, leaving it, after various turns of thought, to be caught up with only towards the last of a long run when you are a little out of breath.

If my analysis be correct, you have no occasion for discouragement surely. On the contrary you will observe that it is because you have too much wealth in use for the purpose in hand—and hence you have only to appear poorer in order to appear stronger —to cast away something and not to accumulate more. A man who has only a dollar to expend in the market may indeed find it more difficult to make up his mind what to buy than he who has a hundred dollars to waste—but when his mind is made up, he goes at his purchases with a finer directness than does his richer fellow who scatters his coin over the entire scene:—yet maybe his family fares none the better for the wide flings he makes. My precious son, you are this wealthy marketer. Your golden sentences touch at too many stalls, and fall too broadly upon the laughing pavements. In your review-articles you need to concentrate more upon the capital point you have set out to enlarge and illumine—making every output of statement, and flash of sentiment assist every other in their common and manifest consequence towards the appointed end. Thus, therefore, after *mastering* the case to be presented, you may begin where you will upon its literary outskirts and yet may be sure of its thorough elucidation, and even of its *cumulative* elucidation— just as would be the case were you called upon to publicly *speak* upon it before an appreciative audience—who, if you have promised to show them an elephant must always be brought nearer and nearer to the majestic creature until the whole vast fabric of him—from great trunk to little tail—greets the sight.

You can never, indeed, have too *much* to say—but you may easily have too *many things* to say:—and in multitude there is obscurity. You are not stingy enough, in your acts of creation. God's greatness in His works is seen not less I think in the parsimony with which he completes than in the opulence with which He decorates.

Discouraged, indeed! Don't entertain the feeling! Rather be stimulated. Perfection is within your reach if only you keep well to the road your already well-groomed steed which is too much disposed to go afield.

Tell me if I am understood, and point out where I am wrong— for wrong I may easily be—yet not in affirming that you have splendid talent and are achieving a splendid style of composition.

We are all delightedly grateful because of the name you and

dear Ellie have given to the new babe. We thank you both, from our inmost hearts where the little darling is wrapt within the same broad folds of love which enclose, in complete parental warmth, its beloved parents.

Your mother & I are getting better by slow but sure degrees.

Your affectionate   Friend and Father.

ALS (WP, DLC) with WWsh musings and WWhw notation on env.: "Ans. Sep. 15/87."
¹ See JRW to WW, Sept. 6, 1887.
² The beginning of Wilson's textbook on American government for high schools, printed at Aug. 8, 1886. For the background, see the Editorial Note, "Wilson's Plan for a Textbook in Civil Government."

Marginal Notes

A. V. Dicey, *Lectures Introductory to the Study of the Law of the Constitution* (2nd edn., London, 1886).

Transcripts of WW Shorthand Comments [c. Sept. 19, 1887]¹

P. 114:
Supreme legislative power is therefore under the Republic vested not in the ordinary Parliament of two Chambers, but in a "national assembly," or congress, composed of the Chamber of Deputies and the Senate sitting together.
The various constitutions, in short, of France, which are in this respect fair types of continental polities, exhibit, as compared with the expansiveness or "flexibility" of English institutions, that characteristic which may be conveniently described as "rigidity."

What legislative power has the national assembly except to make changes in the Constitution; that is insert body of definite provisions: supreme constituent power it has, but not "supreme legislative power."

Pp. 191-92:
For the third salient feature of French *droit administratif* is that it is administered by administrative Courts; at the head of which stands the Council of State. These so-called "Courts" have of comparatively recent times acquired to a certain extent a quasi-judicial character, and have adopted a quasi-judicial procedure. We must take care however not to be deceived by names. The administrative authorities which decide all disputes in regard to matters of administrative law (*contentieux administratif*) may be called "tribunals," and may adopt forms moulded on the procedure of a Court, but they all of them, from the Council of the Prefect (*conseil de préfecture*) up to the Council of State, bear the more or less definite impress of an official or governmental character; they are composed of *official persons,* [WW's italics] and, as is implied by the very

Her judges not "official" persons; how does an administrative judge receive [acquire] a sinister character from being "an official person"?

¹ This reading date appears at the end of the volume, on p. 402.

pleas advanced in defence of withdrawing questions of administrative law from the civil Courts,
look upon the disputes brought before them from
a governmental point of view, and decide them
in a spirit different from the feeling which influences the ordinary judges.

Pp. 198-99:

Persons in the employment of the
government, who form, be it observed, a
much larger and more important part
of the community than do the whole
body of the servants of the English
Crown, occupy in France a position in
some respects resembling that of soldiers
in England. For the breach of official
discipline they are, we may safely assume, readily punishable in one form or
another. But if like English soldiers they
are subject to official discipline, they
have what even soldiers in England do
not possess, a *very large amount* [WW's
italics] of protection against legal proceedings for wrongs done to private citizens. The party wronged by an official
must certainly seek relief, not from the
judges of the land, but from some official Court. Before such a body the question which will be mainly considered is
likely to be, not whether the complain-
ant has been injured, but whether the
defendant, say a policeman, has acted
in discharge of his duties and in *bonâ
fide* obedience to the commands of his
superiors. If the defendant has so acted
he will, we may almost certainly assume, be sure of acquittal, even though
his conduct may have involved a technical breach of law. On this assumption,
and on this assumption alone, we can
understand the constant and successful
efforts of the French administration to
withdraw from the cognizance of the
civil Courts the long list of actions
brought against officials by members of
the "unauthorized congregations" which
were dissolved under the celebrated decrees of 29th March, 1880.

It is entirely unreliable
to take anything like
this for granted without
any examination at all of
the spirit of the judges
of French administrative
courts or any particular
information as to whether
these judges are *otherwise*
actively engaged in exec-
utive official duties: an
official judge, if appointed
during good behavior, and
if not of the judicial
function, occupies to all
intents and purposes
exactly the same position
as a judge of the
ordinary courts.

P. 203:

But if a civil servant may with us escape legal
punishment for breach of his duties to the state,
the fact that he serves the Crown gives him in
general no protection against actions for wrongs
to private persons. *Bonâ fide* obedience to the
orders of superiors is not a defence available to
a subordinate who in the discharge of his func-

Inquiry should be
made as to how
far administrative
courts are *courts
of law.*

ions as a government officer has invaded the
egal rights of the humblest individual. Officials,
ike everybody else, are accountable for their
onduct to a Court of Law, and to a Court, be
t noted, where the verdict is given by a jury.

p. 217-18:

It ["the rule of law"] means, again, equality
efore the law, or the equal subjection of all
lasses to the ordinary law of the land adminis-
ered by the ordinary Law Courts; the "rule of
iw" in this sense excludes the idea of any
xemption of officials or others from the duty of
bedience to the law which governs other citi-
ens or from the jurisdiction of the ordinary
ibunals; there can be with us nothing really
orresponding to the "administrative law" (droit
dministratif) or the "administrative tribunals"
ribunaux administratifs) of France; the notion
hich lies at the bottom of the "administrative
w" known to foreign countries, that affairs or
isputes in which the government or its servants
re concerned are beyond the sphere of the civil
ourts and must be dealt with by special and
ore or less official bodies (tribunaux adminis-
atifs), is utterly unknown to the law of Eng-
nd, and indeed is fundamentally inconsistent
ith our traditions and customs.

The "rule of law," lastly, may be used as a
rmula for expressing the fact that with us the
w of the constitution, the rules which in for-
gn countries naturally form part of a consti-
tional code, are not the source but the
nsequence of the rights of individuals, as de-
ned and enforced by the Courts; that, in short,
e principles of private law have with us been
' the action of the Courts and Parliament so
tended as to determine the position of the
own and of its servants; thus the constitution
the result of the ordinary law of the land.

As to the *droit administratif*, the
author seems to me to labor under some
very serious confusions of thought.
A practice which would have been most
disastrous if established by the
Stuarts before the English legal habit
or constitutional principles were
thoroughly established, might be
adopted with perfect safety and great
advantage now. The dominion of the
ordinary law in France is managed in a
way quite out of keeping with English
ideas, though in accordance with French
habit and opinion on the subject. The
question is this simply: Is the principle of
dominion of the law a proper one, the
conditions being these: a special body
of the laws (in keeping of course with
the legal habits and ideas of the
nation), a special set of courts, a
special procedure meant to be speedy
but not on that account capricious or
informal, special judges appointed
during good behavior and possessing a
special knowledge of a special body of
the laws and special modes of procedure,
a special end in view: speedy justice
between citizen and officer
of the state?

280:

In France the idea has always flourished that
e government, whether Royal, Imperial, or
publican, possesses, as representing the state,
;hts and powers as against individuals superior
and independent of *the ordinary law of the
id.* [WW's italics] This is the real basis of that
ole theory of a *droit administratif* which it is
hard for Englishmen fully to understand.

A rather
misleading
expression as
applied to any
continental state.

P. 401:

The authority of the Courts of Law as understood in England can therefore hardly co-exist with the system of *droit administratif* as it prevails in France. We may perhaps even go so far as to say that English legalism is hardly consistent with the existence of an official body which bears any true resemblance to what foreigners call "the administration."

This will be our examination

Notes on Dicey (The Law of the Constitution)[2]

The *proclamation* or *Decree* as a means of subordinate (l[egal] and administrative) legislation. Principles set forth by [the] legislature, applications made by the executive. Thi[s] arrangement obtains in all (?) European constitutions[.] Analogy in the legislating function of the Roman *Praetor*. As well as in the modern judge-made l[aw].

Topic for centennial volume:[3] *Origins of the Right of our Courts to pass upon the Constitutionality of Laws,*—make them "for legal purposes void." The influence of [the] fact that our constitutions are written and *originated* [in] *royal charters*. The rights of the colonial courts (un[der] Privy Council) to decide upon the constitutionality of colonial laws (either formally or in effect)? Similar po[wer] of modern British colonial courts. Consequent (histo[ri]cally) unsovereign and subordinate character of o[ur] "law-making bodies." What, then, is the position, in ou[r] system of the Courts? (See Dicey, 151-153.)

[2] These notes, written in WWhw except for the title of Dicey's volume, are on a loose page tucked into the book. For some reason, the right hand margin of the page was cut off.

[3] Wilson was referring to the volume mentioned in J. F. Jameson to WW, Aug. 7, 1887.

From Joseph Ruggles Wilson

My dearest Woodrow—   Clarksville, Thursday Sepr 22, 87

I am sorrier than you can be that I am unable to send you more than half of the little sum for which you ask. But this is all that I *dare* abstract from the sum of ready cash in my possession. My comfort is that it will do you *some* good at any rate.

I am grieved that you have to resort to *borrowing* in order to eke out a living. Yet you no doubt understand your own interest best. A rapidly growing family *is* expensive, however—and it will take you some time to learn the secret of cutting yr. cloth according to pattern.

I feel pained, dearest dear, that you have had matter for special worry during the summer—and that you are not in a fair trim for class-work. Still I have great hope that you will maintain yr vigor better than you now expect.

I write hurriedly—but out of a heart full of love[.] Your dear mother is somewhat better.

All send love unmeasured to dear Ellie & yourself

Your ever affc   Father

Please advise me of receipt of this driblet

ALS (WP, DLC) with WWhw sums on env.

From Ellen Axson Wilson

My darling,   [Gainesville] Thursday afternoon [Sept. 29, 1887]

Grandfather has gone over to Aunt Lou's and I take the opportunity to drop you a line. How glad I am that you saw him for a moment, but oh! *how* sorry that he didn't come a day sooner! It is *too* tantalizing that you should *just* miss him, and I should just *barely* fail of accomplishing what I had so set my heart upon,—viz. having the baby baptized by him! Certainly "a miss is a great deal *worse* than a mile[.]" Stockton thinks I ought to have him baptize her anyhow; but I *can't* have it done without you;—and yet how can I let slip the only opportunity I shall have to obtain this service from the dear Grandfather. What *shall* I do! It is one of those cases where either decision seems equally and *entirely impossible.* I must let you decide it for me;—and won't you please do so at once, dear, and write me by the next mail, so that I may get your letter before he leaves? He will stay until Tuesday.

We are, of course, enjoying his visit exceedingly. He is in everything his dear old self,—calm and cheerful as usual; but I notice that his thoughts turn constantly back to Grandmother.[1] He loves to talk of her. He says he would have given anything for a picture of her as she lay in death. There was such a wonderful change in her face, she looked as young as when he married her and her expression was most beautiful. I always supposed she had *no* special disease, but it seems the Dr. pronounced it softening of the brain.

We—the babies and I—are doing finely. Jessie had a hard but short cry when she finished her bottle, then went to sleep, and slept 'till *quarter of three*, nursed and is now asleep again,—without *any* cry. Margaret seems favourably impressed by her great-Grandfather, didn't yell at him, but sat quietly on my knee and studied him and finally condescended to play with his watch and chain.

But I have several things to do and must close. How glad I will be when I can begin to look for a letter!

God bless you, darling, and keep you safe and well, and bring me to you *soon*. I love you—*love you*, dear, with all my heart.

Your little wife,   Eileen.

By the way, we spoke of your seeing Uncle Tom with regard to Minnie,[2] but decided on nothing. Will you go or not? Do just as *you* think best about it, dear.

ALS (WP, DLC).
  [1] Mrs. I. S. K. Axson died on September 22, 1887. See I. S. K. Axson to Louisa C. H. Brown, Sept. 22, 1887, ALS (WP, DLC).
  [2] That is, the Rev. Thomas A. Hoyt of Philadelphia, about the possibility of Minnie Hoyt living with him if she attended Bryn Mawr College. See WW to EAW, Oct. 3, 1887.

To Ellen Axson Wilson

My own darling,   Bryn Mawr, 30 Sept., '87

Was there ever a more forlorn place for a lone widower than this? Murky, drizzling weather *plus* loneliness threatens to be almost too much for me in a place where (at present) dwells not a single person for whom I care a peppercorn! But I don't blame the weather, no, indeed, not I,—I am too magnanimous and fair! It would have been much the same after 26 hours of travelling whatever was happening at the signal bureaux. I'm miserable for lack of you, *and rest*. Don't flatter yourself, however, Miss: I'm not so *very* miserable! I am just miserable enough thoroughly to admire and enjoy myself, for having such complete emotions. I am quite in possession of all my faculties, especially of the faculty (which I may *sometimes* call mine) of 'keeping my head.'

The cottage[1] is *full*, not a corner for me, so I am at the hotel[2] till to-morrow, when I shall move over home[3] or go in and beg lodging with uncle Tom—how does that latter strike you? At any rate, you must think of me as comfortably fixed. I promise to take care to be comfortable.

I met Mary [Freeman] a few minutes ago. She is all right,—expecting to come to us. She has not found a cook for us yet (the *cooks* object that it is "too lonely" at the parsonage!) but she is still hopefully looking for one. I was mighty glad to see her—I like her much better than any one else here.

What a delight, my darling, to see Grandfather, wasn't it? It sent me off with something like a light heart to meet him at the station, because I knew how it would gladden you to see him. And he can baptize the baby—can't he—or is my presence technically indispensable? If not, it must by all means be done, darling. No other such chance may ever offer.

I dare not tell you how much I love you, sweetheart—I might break down were I to get on that topic. Suffice it to say that you are my idol, and that I am, oh *so* intensely and wholly,

Your own   Woodrow

ALS (WP, DLC).

[1] He was probably referring to the "Betweenery," where the Wilsons had lived from the autumn of 1885 to the spring of 1887.

[2] The Bryn Mawr Hotel.

[3] That is, the Baptist parsonage on Gulph Road, which the Wilsons were renting.

Two Letters from Ellen Axson Wilson

My own darling,   Gainesville Sept 30/87

One day and nearly another gone! Only two more left before I start! Isn't that good? And it is the *worst* day viz. the *first* that has gone! But I have stood that first day, and what is more the first *night* bravely and shan't dread those to come so much. The babies both slept finely and are as sweet as can be today. I am perfectly well and strong, and the weather is glorious. I had a delightful ride with Stockton this morning, and am enjoying dear Grandfather's visit extremely;—so you see all goes well and you must be quite happy about us. I am very busy though,—have ever so much sewing to do and only little snatches of time in which to do it, so I must try to do as you said and write short notes,— if I can get my own consent.

Speaking of letters, I have just been reading some that Grandfather brought me, among others such a beautiful one from Dr. Palmer, so different and so much better than most letters of condolence. There was also a most peculiar one from Mrs. Green.[1]

Poor Grandfather is in great trouble over the sad state of his church. Even his heavenly calm can't save him here. Dr. Bacon has literally ruined it already.[2] It is in a most deplorable condition, almost ready to divide. Indeed it is to be hoped they will do so, that is their only salvation. How easy it is for a church to get into trouble and how hard to get out.

But I *must* stop. I love you, sweetheart with all my heart and mind, deeply tenderly, passionately. I am always and altogether

Your own little   Eileen

¹ The Rev. Dr. Benjamin M. Palmer of New Orleans and Aminta Green of Baltimore. Their letters are missing.

² In December 1885, Dr. Axson, feeling the burdens of his office on account of his advanced age, requested the Session of the Independent Presbyterian Church of Savannah to call a minister to serve with him. The congregation, replying that only death could separate them from their beloved pastor, made Axson pastor emeritus, urged him to live in the manse for the rest of his life, awarded him a pension of $1,500 a year, and stipulated that he should preach at morning services every third Sunday in the month.

The congregation then called, on a trial basis, the Rev. Dr. Leonard Woolsey Bacon of the Woodland Presbyterian Church in Philadelphia. Dr. Bacon had previously been a Congregationalist minister in Norwich, Connecticut. Beginning his ministry at the Independent Church in November 1886, Dr. Bacon was never notably successful in Savannah. He particularly exacerbated feelings by preaching a sermon on July 3, 1887, in which he said that God had raised up Lincoln and Grant for the deliverance of His people. The congregation was hopelessly divided when the time came to consider extending a regular call. The final vote in congregational meeting was 119 in favor of calling Bacon and 185 against calling him. He preached his final sermon in the Independent Presbyterian Church on November 27, 1887, and then moved back to Norwich. The Rev. Allen F. DeCamp served as temporary supply until February 1889, when the congregation called the Rev. J. Frederick Dripps of Philadelphia. See Stockton Axson to EAW, April 20, 1887, ALS (WP, DLC), and Lowry Axley, *Holding Aloft the Torch: A History of the Independent Presbyterian Church of Savannah, Georgia* (Savannah, 1958), pp. 95, 125-27.

My own darling,   Gainesville, Oct 1/87

The telegram came last night and was more than welcome.¹ What blessings they are!—sometimes. And tomorrow I may begin to look for a *letter*—speed the hours, say I! We are all still well and doing well,—had another very good night. The weather is glorious and I send the baby out for an hour or more. I went out myself this morning, to Aunt Lou's for the exercise and to see about Eddie's clothes. I enjoyed getting out again very much. Loula is busy moving today and Stockton is helping her so I have not seen him. That is all the news I believe except that baby and I are still keeping up the fight, with victory still on my side. It is rather a costly victory though, a few more such will ruin me! I have but just now gained one.

The mutterings of the storm are still to be faintly heard. In the meantime I have been trying to read the article on the "Ecole des Beaux-Arts"² (I am quite incapable of doing anything else than *try* to read during the ordeal). It may have been that I was influenced by the circumstances but it seems to me the article in question was the poorest thing I ever read,—the most mixed as regards it's use of words. I really wanted to learn all the facts it contained about the school, but I could scarcely manage to endure it. What *do* these editors mean by publishing so much wretched English! Havn't they any sense of responsibility for the contents of their magazine? But it is late & I must make haste to close. I love you,—*love you*, dear, just as much as you want me to. My heart is with you all day long, my thoughts are following you, or trying to follow, in all that you do—in your "out-goings & in-comings, your down-sittings & up-risings." In short I am always and altogether,   Your own little wife,   Eileen

ALS (WC, NjP).
¹ Announcing his safe arrival in Bryn Mawr. The telegram is missing.
² An obscure reference.

Randolph Axson to Ellen Axson Wilson

My dear Ellie   Savannah, Ga., Oct'r 1st 1887
    Yours of the 29th is just to hand, and carefully noted.

    I send you for Eddie $100.00. I should think it would be best to get only such things that he actually needs *now* (Let Stock take him to one of the stores in Gainesville and fit him out) and after you return North, you could doubtless do much better for him in the way of clothing, shoes &c. Your Aunt Lou, yourself and Mr Wilson know the situation much better than I do, and can form a much better judgement than I can as to the best course to be pursued. From all that Stockton has written, and hints thrown out in your letter, it looks as if he was not wanted at your Uncle Henry's, although his wife¹ wrote me that she thought it was a great mistake to take him away. I believe he will be far happier with you than elsewhere.

    His income will not amount to more than $175.00 annually, possibly $200.00 if we get the rents from the house regularly. So you and Mr Wilson will just have to arrange for him as best you can. I hope he will be a comfort to you in your home. We all want to see your babies very much. You certainly have your hands full. How will you get back to Philadelphia without Mr Wilsons help?

    All join me in love to you all.
                    Your aff Uncle   Randolph Axson

Send me a receipt for 100.00 for Eddies account.

ALS (WP, DLC).
¹ Emily Roberts Hoyt, Ellen's Aunt Emma.

From Ellen Axson Wilson

My own darling,   [Gainesville] Sunday [Oct. 2, 1887]
It is now nearly seven o'clock and I havn't had a solitary moment in which to write, and if I don't mail this at once it won't go tonight, and the baby is screaming, and we are all *quite well*, and I love you dearly, dearly and am as ever
Your own Eileen!

ALS (WP, DLC).

To Ellen Axson Wilson

My own precious little wife,   Bryn Mawr, 2 Oct., 1887
You know what sort of a day yesterday must have been with me, and can guess, therefore, how it was that I was prevented from writing. Examination from 9-11; reading papers[1] (about 22 of them) from 11-4; after that a lot of small pieces of business, copying my report of examination &c; and finally a long, fruitless search after lodgings.

Both table and rooms are full at Cottage No. 2; Mr. Estrada and family will not be out of the house till Wednesday ('were expecting to hear from me; didn't know with whom to leave the keys; Monday is wash-day, &c &c.') so that after much hurried searching—much after the anxious manner of Miss [Emily L.] Gregory last June—I am still at the Hotel. I know of a place now, however,—the house at which Miss Gregory aforesaid boarded during the summer—where I shall, I am confident, be able to get comfortable quarters for the next few days. I shall probably move over there to-day.

Meantime the weather has cleared and become deliciously bright and cool and bracing—and with it the mental weather has vastly improved. It is slightly distracting to have no *permanent* abiding place and to be separated from my books: but that will be for only a day or two longer now, and I can no doubt stand the present arrangements well enough. How fortunate that you did not come with me!

Nothing has been said about the great assistant question as yet—the office authorities are busy letting in students who are heavily conditioned—but I imagine they have found my manner considerably changed and that some sort of a reckoning may be expected soon—the sooner the better! I regard the whole situation with the calmness of a philosopher now, and hope that I shall find it easy to be circumspect.

I answered your question about the baptism in my first letter, fortunately, my darling. *By all means* have it done.

Ah, sweetheart, how this place will be changed when you come —the light of my eyes—my matchless little wife and companion— my strength—my treasure—my all—my Eileen! Oh, darling, I *love, love, love love* you!   Your own   Woodrow

Love to all. I shall go in to see uncle Tom to-day, I think.

ALS (WP, DLC).
  [1] Entrance examinations in history.

From Ellen Axson Wilson

My own darling,   Gainesville, Oct. 3/87
     Randolph Longstreet[1] has just come back with the mail, and alas! without my letter, so I suppose I shall be left lamenting 'till tomorrow;—mails are very provoking things. So are *males* too sometimes,—Mr. Wade, for instance, who brought up the mail yesterday morning. When nearly here he met Grandfather and Stockton on their way to church and gives *them* my letter, which Stock. coolly takes and carries off to church. Immediately after[ward] Mr. Wade tells me here on the piazza about it, and I am left to count the minutes 'till the others return!
     I am *so* sorry for you, darling, for the dreary lonely time you are having, for the dismal weather and all. Especially am I sorry that you can't get in at the cottage. I do wish you *would* go to Uncle Tom's,—hope that you have gone already. I am sure they would be glad to have you, and that would be a real pleasant arrangement. There is *one* pleasant thing in the situation,—that Mary is ready and waiting;—and so the cooks think it lonely too "down our way"! Strange that we are the only ones who seem to appreciate the beauty of that situation. Perhaps they are afraid of the grave-yard. By-the-way if we get hard up this month we can borrow from *Eddie* instead of some one else. He is quite a capitalist at present. Uncle Randolph has sent me a hundred dollars for him. And he says his income is $175.00 a year. I wrote to him about Eddie's education and an answer came on which I will report tomorrow;—really havn't time today.
     Well, I actually did have the baby baptized yesterday! When *you* agreed with everyone here that it "ought to be done" I con- cluded that you must be right. But it was a hard trial to have it done without you; it seemed so unnatural,—hardly *right*. Grand- father said it *was* decidedly irregular, but he thought it might be

done under the circumstances; that as we have your consent, I could represent you. So we all went over to Aunt Lou's at three o'clock and had it done there. Though the service was quite long baby behaved beautifully—thanks to my *finger* in her mouth. How I wish you could have heard his remarks and prayer! I never heard anything so sweet, so beautiful and impressive. I always thought Grandfather excelled anyone I ever heard in all such services.

Goodbye, my darling, I *hope* things look brighter at Bryn Mawr by this time. Ah, how I *wish* I could be with you there *right now*, and how I love *love love* you, dear! Believe me sweetheart always and altogether,   Your own Eileen

We are all well and doing nicely both night and day. The baby's bowels remain the same. I saw Dr. B. in the hall just now and told him, & he is going to leave some powders for me at the drug store. He said *I* was looking *remarkably* well, seemed quite impressed by it. I really think I *have* improved even since you left.

ALS (WP, DLC).
[1] General Longstreet's son, Fitz Randolph.

EDITORIAL NOTE
WILSON'S TEACHING AT BRYN MAWR AND THE
JOHNS HOPKINS, 1887-88

The academic year 1887-88 was one of the busiest years of Wilson's life as a teacher. It was also one of the most important—a turning point in his professional career.

To undergraduates at Bryn Mawr, Wilson offered two courses that ran throughout the year: political economy, which he gave three times a week to eight students; and politics, which he gave twice a week to ten students. Wilson described these courses in the document "Wilson Reviews His Course Work at Bryn Mawr," printed at June 1, 1888.

For the course in political economy, Wilson prepared notes for only eight lectures, which surveyed the history of economic thought from ancient times to Wilson's own day.[1] He seems to have devoted the balance of his course to the textbook drill and class reports that he mentioned in the year-end review cited above.

Wilson's notes for his undergraduate course in politics are complete.[2] They follow exactly the outline of the course given in his year-end review, and Wilson used them, along with his earlier lectures on Greek and Roman history,[3] very extensively while writing *The State*.

[1] See the first body of notes described below.
[2] See the second body of notes described below. See also the course examination printed at Feb. 9, 1888.
[3] Printed at Oct. 15, 1885, and described at Feb. 9, 1886.

The year 1887-88 saw Wilson inaugurating his first full-fledged graduate program at Bryn Mawr. An announcement of it is printed at June 1, 1887. The following extract from the record of the History Fellow in 1887-88, Cora Agnes Benneson, gives another recapitulation:

Work done in Bryn Mawr College in 1887-88.
Followed Dr. Wilson's graduate course in Politics given in Program for 1887-88. . . .
The graduate courses of Dr. W. Wilson in History and Politics were,
For the 1st Semester—
The History, Functions and Organs of Government, fifty lectures.

Four times weekly.

For the 2nd Semester:
I.   The Nature and Influence of Roman Law, ten lectures.
II. Comparative Constitutional History, twenty-five lectures.
III. The Growth of Modern Nationalities, eight lectures.
IV. The History of Political Economy, ten lectures.

Four times weekly.

Throughout the year one hour weekly was given to Seminary work, and reports were read upon work done privately upon topics related to the lectures. Much private reading and collection of information from the libraries in the city were carried on.[4]

In his first-semester graduate course on government, Wilson almost certainly did not prepare separate lectures for his two graduate students—Miss Benneson and another whose name is unknown—but probably used some of the lecture notes that he had already prepared for his undergraduate course in politics. In any event, no separate notes for the graduate course have survived. Wilson's notes for his second-semester lectures on Roman law, comparative constitutional history, and the growth of modern nationalities are also missing. For his lectures on the history of political economy, he apparently prepared only the outline described at February 1, 1888.

The letters between Wilson and Herbert Baxter Adams and other items in this volume fully document another important development in Wilson's professional career—the beginning of his long association with The Johns Hopkins University as a lecturer on administration. Wilson described his plan for a three-year cycle and the objectives of his lectures in 1888 in the lecture printed at February 17, 1888. (As documents in Volume 6 will reveal, he soon discovered that the ground that he had staked out was too extensive, and he revised his three-year plan in 1890.) Wilson also described the twenty-five lectures that he gave in the first series between February 17 and May 19, 1888, in the document "Wilson Reviews His Lectures at the Johns Hopkins," printed at June 1, 1888. The Editorial Notes in Volume 6, "Wilson's Courses at Wesleyan and the Johns Hopkins, 1888-89," "Wilson's Teaching at Wesleyan University and the Johns Hopkins, 1889-90," and "Wilson's Lectures on Administration at the Johns

4 Bryn Mawr College Student Records (PBm).

Hopkins, 1890," provide a guide to the materials relating to the second and third series.

Of Wilson's lectures at the Hopkins in 1888 only the opening lecture, printed at February 17, 1888; the two lectures on the functions of government, printed at February 18 and 24, 1888; and the notes for two introductory lectures on administration, printed at February 24 and 25, 1888, are all that seem to have survived. However, Wilson undoubtedly used some of the notes for his politics lectures at Bryn Mawr as a basis for the balance of the Hopkins lectures.

Wilson also gave two lectures in a public series on "Certain Social Problems Relating to Modern Cities," in which Carroll D. Wright, Richard T. Ely, and others participated. Wilson's lectures (or drafts and notes) are printed at the dates on which he delivered them, March 2 and 16, 1888.

The reader is referred to the *caveat* in the last paragraph of the Editorial Note, "Wilson's Teaching at Bryn Mawr, 1885-86."

Classroom Lecture Notes

[c. Oct. 3-19, 1887]

Inscribed (WWhw) on first page: *"History of Political Economy"*
Contents:

WWhw and WWT notes for eight lectures on the history of political economy and economic thought, with bibliographical citations. Notations on versos that Wilson used these lectures in 1888, 1889, 1890, and 1891.

Loose sheets (WP, DLC).

Classroom Lecture Notes

[c. Oct. 3, 1887-c. May 31, 1888]

Inscribed (WWhw) on inside front cover: "Woodrow Wilson"
Contents:

(a) WWsh lecture notes with WWhw titles, as follows, with composition dates when given: "I. *The State.* (*origin*)"; "II *The Ancient City.* (*organization*)," Oct. 13, 1887; "III. *The Ancient State* (*Ideas*)," Oct. 14, 1887; "IV *The Imperial State*"; "V. *The Medieval State* (*Territorial Sovereignty*)"; "VI *First Form of Modern State.* (*The possessing King*)"; "VII. *Second Form of Modern State.* (*the ruling People*)"; VIII "*The Dependent* (*Colonial*) *State and Its Law*"; IX. "*The Federal State.*" "*The Governments of the United States. Elements of Historical and Practical Politics.* X. I. *The Double Government.* II. *Double Citizenship*"; "XI. III. *The States and the Nation*"; XII-XLIII untitled; "XLIV. *Local Government*"; XLV-LII untitled; and WWsh and WWhw note at end of Lecture LII: "Course finished May 31, 1888." Transcript of Wilson's more or less considerable revision of Lectures X-XXIV and part of Lecture XXV printed at May 1, 1889, Vol. 6.

(b) WWhw outlines accompanying many WWsh notes for lectures.

(c) (on back flyleaf) WWhw list of lectures for the Johns Hopkins in 1888.

Notebook (WP, DLC).

To Ellen Axson Wilson

My own darling,　　　　　　　　　　Bryn Mawr, 3 Oct., 1887

Here I am at last semi-permanently lodged at Evans's "Summit Grove House," where Miss Gregory was during the summer,— really a very pleasant, cheerful, comfortful place. It is cheaper here by the week ($10.00) than by the day ($2.00); I think therefore, that I shall stay my week out at least, using my study only in our house till time to open for you: oh, what a glad day it will be when you come, my loved one! When my queen is here my mind will be at rest—and so will the rest of me! I delivered my first lecture this morning, with as much confidence and ease as if I had spent all summer, instead of only some half an hour, a-preparing it. To-morrow morning I shall have to deliver another one of the same sort: after that, to my books and formal preparation. I don't yet see exactly how I can work in my text-book[1] as lectures, but the thing must be managed some-how.

I was *so* distressed, my pet, at the omission of that day in my letter-writing: for that reason I put a "special delivery" stamp on the letter of yesterday, so that it might, perchance, be delivered to you a *little sooner* than it otherwise would have been. I fear, however, that the scheme will operate only in the way of making an interval of more than 24 hours between that letter and this. But my darling wont be anxious: I trust to her bravery.

How satisfactory it is to have an account of your first two nights—and how delightful to have so splendid an account. Oh, how tenderly, how yearningly, I love that brave, perfect little mother and those precious babies! I would lay down my life for them. My happiness turns upon theirs. *Please* be careful, my sweet one: don't sew too much!

I went in to uncle Tom's church yesterday afternoon, but had only a moment or two in which to speak to him: for all his household are in Tennessee and he is staying with one of his elders. I explained to him as well as I could in the time (with other people waiting to speak to him) cousin Minnie's difficulties, but he did not seem to remember his offer and I did not know exactly how to recall it to him. In brief, nothing came of the interview. I may have another chance before it is too late.

I am well, sweetheart, and as comfortable as your absence permits. As for my love for you it is beyond all expression or bounds. I am always and altogether

　　　　　　　　　　　　　　　Your own　Woodrow

Love to all[.] Endorse the Draft "Mrs Woodrow Wilson"

ALS (WP, DLC).
  [1] The textbook in comparative government that became *The State*.

From Ellen Axson Wilson

My own darling,   Gainesville, Oct. 4/87.

Many thanks for your thoughtfulness in sending your letter by special delivery. It reached me promptly last night. What a day of it you *did* have Saturday! I am glad at least that it *was* Saturday so that you could have the next day for rest. Though from the programme announced in this letter—moving and going into town—there was little rest in prospect. Am *so* sorry for your worry about lodgings. Was hoping you would go to Uncle Tom's. Did you decide that it was too inconvenient to be so far from your books &c? All this worry and discomfort of yours makes me more anxious than ever to get back. Am sorry now I told Minnie I would wait for her a few days if she wished. Have heard nothing more from her yet. Stockton intended leaving this morning[1] but was too unwell; he thought last night he was getting "broken-bone" fever. But at noon today he was feeling much better and hopes to get off tomorrow. It was evidently a little more malaria working off; I suppose it will be some time before he gets quite rid of it. Grandfather will remain until Wed. night. He must be back to perform a marriage ceremony on Thursday night,—to his extreme annoyance for he wished to remain another week;—wished it so much indeed that he is thinking of coming directly back. I *hope* he will, for the weather here is glorious now,—just the sort to do him most good after his long trying summer in Sav. And he is improving greatly,—says he hasn't slept so well for years. He is going to Charleston and to see Cousin Jimmie Cozby later on. Yesterday was his birth-day, by-the-way; he was seventy-four.

I paid for the carriage yesterday, it was $3.00,—a dollar a month, no charge for the damage. Good-bye darling, please excuse haste. With a heart *full*, full to overflowing with love— I am dearest   Your own   Eileen.

We are all well and are doing nicely;—had another good night. The powders seem to have done baby good already.

Take care of your dear self, darling, don't get too tired and keep up your spirits.

ALS (WP, DLC).
  [1] For the University of Georgia, where he soon enrolled as an eclectic student.

Two Letters to Ellen Axson Wilson

My own darling,   Bryn Mawr, Oct. 4, 1887

I have just come from a long and exhausting interview with Miss Benneson,[1] the new Fellow in History. I dread these first interviews, and am very glad that this one is over with. Miss B. turns out to be a pleasant small person of a mind which it will be very hard, but I trust not impossible, to impress—a mind which has been pressed so often by other things at every point at which you press it that it yields in a *habitual*, acquired way rather than in the way you wish. She seems to herself, evidently, to have heard something of that sort before at the very opening of your remark and so takes it to be what she has heard before to the end, or is only a little confused by something in its course which does not quite exactly tally with what she expected. She seems to talk largely out of her memory; her travels overshadow her reasoning powers; her knowledge of the world makes her ignorant of conclusions which interpret the world,—&c. &c. But she is amiable— 'not wilful,' she says—has some wholesome awe (quite diverting of course to me) of what is expected of her at Bryn Mawr, and can, I confidently expect, be dominated. But, dear me, what a strain & a bore it is to be all the year dominating. Dominating Miss [Jane] Bancroft cost me sore, as you know. Miss [Lucy] Salmon needed only constant encouragement—but that amounted to carrying her on my shoulders. I'm *tired* carrying female Fellows on my shoulders!

But you are coming to me, sweetheart,—that's the balm of hope that cures all my ills. What can I not stand or be or accomplish with my Eileen by my side! When I think of you, my little wife, I love this "College for Women," because *you* are a woman: but when I think only of myself, I hate the place very cordially: for you are the *only* woman hereabouts of your genuine, perfect sort —the only woman anywhere of your perfect title to be worshipped by men—by all who love a nature cultured through and through and a heart learned in all the inspirations that hearts were created to contain. Oh, how I love—how I worship,—the sweet image of my little wife! It is my glory to be subject to her, to be in everything and at all times   Her own   Woodrow

ALS (WC, NjP).

[1] Cora Agnes Benneson of Quincy, Ill., A.B., University of Michigan, 1878; LL.B., 1880; A.M., 1883, who was only a year younger than Wilson.

My own darling,   Bryn Mawr, 5 Oct., 1887

I divide my day's discourse into 3 parts or heads:

1.   I thought last night that I was to have an adventure to relate to you to-day. I went into town, 'along of loneliness,' in the evening to the theatre, to see "Dr. Jekyll and Mr. Hyde."[1] I came back about midnight to find my boarding house locked up tight. I rang furiously again and again: I pounded repeatedly; I walked around and 'halloo'ed': no response. I stood out in the chill moon-light all alone amidst profoundest silence. I worked away at the problem of getting in for a quarter of an hour and still seemed no nearer its solution. I began to think of walking about in the beautiful night till day-break, and then sitting down and writing you a touching account of my homeless condition. But at the last moment Mary heard my ringing and came and let me in; where-upon I went prosaically to bed as usual.

2.   As stated above, I went to see Mansfield play "Dr. Jekyll and Mr. Hyde." I'm not sure whether I'm glad or sorry that it is to be taken off before you get here. I'd like ever so much to have you see it: it's thoroughly worth seeing, despite absurd additions to the story made by the dramatizer. But it's awful, too. It gave me the shudders which is as much as to say that the *Hyde* part of the man was splendidly done: Jekyll not so well,—poorly in-deed,—partly through the absurdities of the dramatizer, who makes him a young man in love with the girl (not in the original) whose father Hyde murders. The two transformations—from Hyde to Jekyll and from Jekyll to Hyde—were managed with consum-mate success. But I never in my life came away from a play with such unpleasant sensations,—so unsatisfied, unamused, dejected. I doubt whether the piece ought to be played—it's too much of a deadweight tragedy.

3.   The Estradas moved out to-day, and left everything in "apple-pie order." I find no appreciable damage done. They have evidently taken just as good care of our things as was possible: I am thoroughly satisfied, and I am sure you will be. How pretty the dear little house looks: I love it as a home already, and oh, how my beautiful little wife will adorn it! What a sweet nest it will be for us! How glad I am to see this week pass its middle day and hurry me on to next week's joy. Eileen, I love, *love, love* you infinitely, altogether.   Your own   Woodrow

ALS (WP, DLC).

[1] Richard Mansfield played the title roles in Thomas Russell Sullivan's stage version of Robert Louis Stevenson's story. The play had opened in Boston on May 9, 1887.

From Ellen Axson Wilson

My own darling, [Gainesville] Oct. 5/87.

I am so sorry that I must put you off with a mere line again, but it is unavoidable. It is almost too dark to see now, and I ought at this very moment to be helping the baby get through her bottle! She has been *so* bad today that I havn't had a minute for anything much but her. You needn't be afraid of my "sewing too much"! For I am either holding her or "holding myself" by main force while she screams all day. In either case sewing is out of the question. I *never* saw anything to equal her. We don't make any progress at all, though I persevere most faithfully in my efforts to train her. It looks as though she and I would kill each other!

I am so glad, dear, that you are comfortably situated and that you are not going into that lonely house.

But it is *really* dark & there is no light. I *must* stop. We are all well and I love you darling more than tongue can say.

Your own Eileen.

ALS (WP, DLC) with WWhw name and address and sums on env.

To Ellen Axson Wilson

My precious little sweetheart, Bryn Mawr, 10th Mo. 6th 1887

The spirit moves me to write to you here in Seminary 'B'[1]: so I sponge on the College for a piece of paper. I have just been over in 'the' house, giving it an hour or so of sunning and wandering about over it in unrestrained enjoyment of the pleasures of hope. To-morrow or next day I shall begin to arrange actively for house-keeping, devoting the afternoons to preparing for my queen's advent. What shall I do for joy when she comes! There's a certain pathetic, half-painful *sweetness* about our separation, darling—have you never discovered it? Memory and hope take leave to set forth the most perfect repasts: they entertain with every sweet thought of which they are capable—the great *hurt* is the voidness of the present,—and yet how secure is the present even, buttressed as it is by all the past and open towards all the future! What we have been to each other is as much a fact as any present enjoyment could be, and ought to secure our happiness and strength though all else were cut off. It is a great fact in our mental, spiritual histories—the greatest fact by far in mine. Whatever might happen, I could never be anything but what *you* had

made me. Add to this the sweet assurance that the blessed work
of your influence is to go on: that I am to continue to feel your
dear arms about me drawing me towards better things, and ought
I not to be ashamed to chafe because you are to come *next* week
and not *this*? I *don't* chafe, pet, I only feel a quiet pain deep in
the centre of my heart: I only feel a still bereavement marring
my life: I only wait for my full life to return. Meantime I am
far from unhappy,—I am even happy[.] I love and am loved *to
my heart's content*: I am full of the deepest possible joy because
I am   Your own   Woodrow.

ALS (WP, DLC).
¹ In Taylor Hall, which then housed the library.

From Ellen Axson Wilson

My own darling,   Gainesville, Oct. 6/87.
    I must try and write to you betimes this morning while things
are quiet so as not to put you off with nothing or worse than
nothing again today. My conscience has been hurting me very
much for yesterday's note. I had only a moment for writing and
I spent that moment speaking, most unnecessarily, about what
would only worry you. The fact is I had just been having a hearty
cry—keeping kind with the baby, so I "felt bad"; and besides was
too hurried to reflect how my remarks would sound to you. I
don't know what I said now; but whatever it was don't believe a
word of it; for my fatigue and discouragement led me to describe
the case—temporarily to *regard* it—as much worse than it is. The
baby it is true is most emphatic in her protests against my treatment,—is a most determined little gourmand; but she generally
ends by crying herself to sleep; and she sleeps very sweetly. And
she does very well at night. By the way, I think she is going to be,
after a while, like one of those described in "Babyhood" who
"cries to be laid down so that she can go to sleep." She goes to
sleep much sooner and more soundly by herself than in anyone's
arms. I have tried both methods thoroughly and allowed Maggie
to try. Last night for instance I felt as though I couldn't stand
another conflict so I succumbed entirely[,] humoured her to the
top of her bent both as regards feeding and "tending" her. She
would be quiet, perhaps doze a few minutes then fret, then
scream, and so alternately for hours. At last I laid her down; she
screamed lustily for three or four minutes and then fell into a
sweet & sound sleep. She seems perfectly well except that her
actions are still a *little* curdled. Margaret is just as well and sweet

and good as she can be,—altogether a comfort and pleasure. Whenever we ask "where Papa is" she looks all about for you in an eager enquiring way, and sometimes calls you.

I have just received a letter from Rose.[1] She intended to pass through Gainesville on Tuesday and spend the day with me, but Mortimer, Jule's[2] boy is very ill and she can't leave; and don't think she ought to stop here now if she did get off as her baby has been exposed to contagion and might communicate it to mine. I can't make out whether it is measles or scarlet fever. So I am quite disappointed, and anxious too about her baby. Stockton is still too unwell to leave—poor fellow! It seems to be a slow malarial fever, or else it is a heavy cold. He *won't* see the doctor. I feel so sorry for him;—but he says it was "just as he expected"!

I had a scare about *you* yesterday,—brought on by a *telegram*. But it turned out to be from Uncle Randolph about Eddie. By-the-way, I have never told yet of the excitement about him. When I wrote to Uncle R. on Friday I told him fully the difficulties about E's education; and on Sunday came a letter saying he thought Eddie had better go to Sav. for the present,—Aunt Ella was "more than willing to take charge of him,"—and if we thought so too to send him with Grandfather. Well, of course I felt very "blank" and disappointed, but the question of his education with us is such a serious one and Uncle R's plan seemed so much to his advantage that I had about made up my mind to it,—when Stockton came. And I wish you could have seen him! I didn't know he *could* get so excited. He farely "rared" as the natives say. You would have thought Uncle R. was sentencing Eddie to imprisonment with hard labour, instead of offering to take him into one of the sweetest homes I know of. He was going to give up going to college so as to make the money for his (E's) education. "He had never been happy since Father's death and now he was going to Sav. to be bullied by Palmer [Axson] and be more unhappy than ever;—there was never any tyranny like Palmer's over younger boys,—at once so cruel and so mean, &c. &c. And besides E. would never feel *at home* in Sav. anymore than *he* did![""] I suggested mildly that he was putting Ed himself in a rather unenviable light. I sympathized unreservedly in his past troubles; a child had no resource against the unkindness of grown people, but I thought a boy of any spirit might be trusted to hold his own against another *boy*. At least I didn't like to think that he would be so completely cowed and crushed by him. But Stock said that not only was Palmer much older but that Eddie who has a great deal of delicacy would hesitate to resent his treatment in Aunt

Ella's house, often before her very eyes, when she herself never interfered. And that besides it is the simple truth that Eddie *is* more gentle than is good for a boy in this rough and tumble world. Well in short he argued & entreated—I may say *commanded!*—rushed from me to Grandfather, from him to Aunt Lou and back again to me. Eddie was brought in & asked what he thought, and he began to cry at the idea as though his heart would break,—poor little fellow! So G-father was convinced, though of course the Palmer argument couldn't be mentioned to him. The chief consideration with him as with me was that the child ought not to be passed around indefinitely from one to another; it was time for him to be permanently settled, to feel that he has a *home*: And of course that home would naturally and properly be with me. So he G-father decided that he had better go with me now,—"as an experiment," he said; if by next summer no satisfactory solution of the school problem could be found he could *then* go to Sav. Grandfather thinks that considering Ed's peculiar circumstances you or Uncle Tom could easily secure him either free tuition or greatly reduced rates in some good school. He seems quite anxious that the child should be with me. So we wrote to Uncle R. for his final decision & yesterday he telegraphed that I should take him to Phila. I am *very* glad, though my anxiety about his future made me unwilling to take the responsibility of deciding in that way myself.

But I am writing an outrageously long letter, on a subject too that might just as well have waited until next week. Now I must make haste to close.

The check came safely, dear; many thanks for it. Now I am puzzled to know where to keep all this money on my journey. I used to keep it in my bosom but that can't be done now.

Please excuse this scrawl; Margaret has been pulling at me much of the time. Good-bye my darling, remember that we are all well and doing nicely, and that I *love you.* Ah there is no word in any language to say *how* I love you or how I long for you day & night, every moment, 'till it seems as though my heart must break with longing.   Your own   Eileen

ALS (WP, DLC) with WWhw notation on env.: "Phila. Evening Telegraph for Wed. Oct. 5, 1887." Wilson may have been referring to the following articles in that issue: (1) "The Example of America," p. 1; (2) "England's First Citizen [Gladstone]," p. 3; and (3) "The Dutch House of Commons," p. 11.

1 From Rosalie Anderson DuBose. Her letter is missing.
2 Julie Anderson McRae, Rosalie's sister.

To Ellen Axson Wilson

My own darling,   Bryn Mawr, 7 Oct., 1887

How sorry I am that you are having such a dreadful time with that little pet, Jessie! She's just such another Bourbon as Margaret, isn't she? I hope that finally, like Margaret, she may be conquered. The cure in her case is quite complete although we postponed undertaking it so long:—and how *much* happier she is! *That's* the comfort of the whole thing: the dear little pet will be just so much the gladder to live: we will have our abundant reward for our present sufferings. But oh, I am *so* sorry for you, darling! I would give more than the imagination can estimate to be with you so that, instead of your "holding yourself," *I* might hold you: might chase away your tremors with kisses: might hold you close as love itself to my heart! My hourly thought and prayer is that we shall stand in everything *together*, bearing and planning, suffering and rejoicing as one person. Otherwise I shall be bereft and weak. I *need* you, darling; I need you in every movement of my life! Your presence is everything to me. Without you I am morose and beyond healthfulness strenuous; *with* you I am light-hearted and normally strong. Ah, little lady, how sweetly you have fulfilled your promises to me—not your spoken promises (those of course) but the promises your eyes, your person, your *self* made to me. I always wanted a *sun-beam* of a wife—and I have one! She cures my morbidness by being herself incapable of it. She looks my ugly moods out of countenance with her sweet placid eyes. She rests and steadies at the same time that she inspires me. Oh, how immeasureably I love her, how wholly I trust her, how confidently I lean upon her! My darling, if it makes you happy to help me, you ought to be the happiest woman in the world. To have a letter of yours in my pocket—even one of these tantalizing little notes—gives me a calm, secure feeling which is sweeter than words can say.   Your own   Woodrow

ALS (WP, DLC).

From Ellen Axson Wilson

My own darling,   Gainesville, Oct. 7/87.

Once again it is twilight before I sit down to write you. But the baby is'nt to blame this time; she has been sleeping sweetly most of the day. There are several reasons for it, the chief being that I had borrowed an *iron* from one of the ladies here and was rushing to get through today several important "jobs" of sewing which required pressing. Then Stockton has been here,—has just left. He is a good deal better,—hopes to get off Monday. He looks quite pulled down, and is very weak, poor fellow!

You certainly made a narrow escape from a most unpleasant adventure! I am truly thankful that you *did* escape and that I am not to receive that "touching account." Is that the way they treat people at your boardinghouse?—or didn't they know you were out?

I am very glad you saw "Dr Jekyll and Mr. Hyde,"—wish I could have been with you and shared your sensations even though they *do* not seem to have been of the pleasantest. But shall expect a full and particular account when I see you,—especially of the wonderful transformation scene.

I am so delighted to hear such good report of the house! To be sure I had, in order not to be worried about it all summer, fully made up my mind that it was going to be all right; but it is a comfort to *know* it. Ah how *wild* I am to get there!—to be in it! I hope to hear from Minnie tomorrow, and then I can decide positively when to start. We are still getting on nicely and are all well. The baby's bowels seem quite right today.

I love you Woodrow, my darling,—love you 'till it fairly *hurts*,— I am always and altogether   Your own   Eileen

ALS (WP, DLC).

To Ellen Axson Wilson

My precious little sweetheart,   Bryn Mawr, 8 Oct., 1887

You see I am still without my own pen and ink—the pen performances I have sent you have been done with College instruments, as you doubtless have observed; the characters being noticeably erratic. I have not thought it worth while to set up such a permanency as an inkstand here at the boarding house. I went to town yesterday and purchased store-room supplies: coal I buy to-day, not much, however, for there's not money enough in hand at present,—and I find that I cannot get it (coal) through the college. I am as yet in doubt, indeed, as to whether or no I can get it at the college prices. I find Dr. Rhoads not at all interested in the matter: we shall derive little or no pecuniary (economical) advantage from our connexion with this amiable institution: and, that being the case, what sort of advantage *will* we derive? That's the conundrum at present amusing my thoughts. For I *am* beginning to be *amused* by the whole situation. I've put away worry in the matter: for I have recollected of late that we are under an all-wise Providence in all things, and that it is in a way impius to worry about the future. Our plain duty is to care cheerfully and diligently for the present—and in doing so I find that I can be contented.

All the same, however (in a legitimate way), the future is much in my thoughts, and is a great puzzle to me. I have devoted myself to a literary life—and I don't see how a literary life can be built up on foundations of undergraduate instruction. That instruction compels you to live with the commonplaces, the A. B. C. of every subject and to dwell upon these with an emphasis and an invention altogether disproportioned to their intrinsic weight and importance—it keeps you on the dusty, century-travelled high-roads of every subject, from which you get no outlooks except those that are catalogued and vulgarized in every guide-book. You get weary of the plodding and yet you get habituated to it, and find all excursions aside difficult—more and more so. What *is* a fellow to do? How is he to earn bread and at the same time find leisure for thoughts detached from the earning of bread? This is the problem we have to solve, darling—and every new difficulty or perplexity makes me the gladder that I am altogether and irrevocably

Your own   Woodrow

ALS (WC, NjP).

From Ellen Axson Wilson

Gainesville, Oct. 8/87.

What a sweet, sweet little letter is this my darling has sent me today! How I wish I had time and quiet in which to answer it as my heart wishes. I did hope to find the opportunity sometime today, but all sorts of things have prevented, and now it is almost six o'clock—as usual! But I trust I may find time tomorrow morning for a quiet little talk with you. In the mean time, darling, however busy I can *always think* of you, and of all these precious words of love and confidence. That is one delight which *nothing* can interfere with.

. How pleasant it is to think that "the" house is really our *home* now, and that it is only a few days—less than a week—before I shall "go home"! I have finished all my little "jobs" now and am ready and oh! how anxious to start. But as yet I have heard nothing from Minnie. I fully expected to hear today, and am very much disappointed. Monday you know was the day on which she was to come. Am afraid there is still a hitch somewhere. It was rather shabby in Uncle Tom to make that offer and then actually forget all all [*sic*] about it. I suppose it was just an impulse of the moment. But baby has "begun" and I must *finish*! We are all *very* well. Baby seems perfectly right again as to her bowels. Stockton still improving,—expects to get off Monday. With a heart full to overflowing with love.   Your own   Eileen

ALS (WP, DLC).

To Ellen Axson Wilson

My own darling,   Bryn Mawr, 9 Oct., 1887

I have just done what I never did before, so far as I can remember,—I have just allowed myself to be driven from church by disgust at the service. I went to church in a mood to enjoy heartily the service of prayer and preaching which we can usually expect from Mr. Miller:[1] but unhappily that good man was not there. In his place stood a man[2] about my own age whose whole heart, whether he spoke or read, seemed to be in listening to his own sounding and meaningless phrases and to the sonorous ring of his own voice. He prayed flipantly: not a word, I feel sure, went to Heaven—every word made me cold and sick—for I longed to hear a prayer: I am sure I should have recognized one had I heard it. Then came the sermon: a vain man's self-satisfied discussion of the authenticity of the Mosaic authorship. At least so it began: I found I *could* not stay—I felt that I *ought* not to stay—to hear it: I was in a back seat and could slip out unobserved by most of the congregation; and so I came away, with a sort of a *sob* in my heart. I had gone into God's house to feel its sacred atmosphere of worship and rest and had found only the void of a common lecture-hall[.] How profoundly thankful we ought to be that we have Mr. Miller! What is one who is above all things else sensitive to spiritual influences—to the unspoken meanings of personality and of heart's intent—to do when thrown into the congregation of a fellow like this one of this morning, as we are upon any move either of ours or of Mr. Miller's likely (or at least liable) to be! My Sabbath's would be seasons of mortification and torture. I fear I should take refuge in the Episcopal service, to escape preaching.

I can't say how much distressed I have been to hear of dear Stock's renewed sickness. Give him *much* love from me, please.

Sweetheart nothing is so bad but that thinking of you offsets my distress at it. I love you, and ours, *infinitely*, with all my heart and being, *always*!   Your own   Woodrow

Couldn't you sew your money inside your dress in a little bag made for the purpose?

ALS (WC, NjP).

[1] The Rev. Dr. William Hamilton Miller, pastor of the Bryn Mawr Presbyterian Church, 1874-1907. The Wilsons had united with this congregation on December 29, 1886—Woodrow by letter of transfer from the First Presbyterian Church of Wilmington, North Carolina, Ellen by letter from the Rome, Georgia, Presbyterian Church.

[2] His identity is, perhaps happily, lost to history, as neither the records of the Bryn Mawr Presbyterian Church, nor the Philadelphia newspapers, nor the local weekly, the *Bryn Mawr Home News*, yield any clue as to the minister's name.

From Ellen Axson Wilson

My own darling,   Gainesville Oct 9/87

I have heard from Minnie at last and she *is* coming after all—coming tomorrow night. I suppose they did finally settle it to suit her, though she gives no particulars. So now I can decide when to start; and it will be *Wednesday* morning,—that is unless I am very much mistaken;—unless something unforseen happens. I suppose it would be better for some reasons to wait until Thursday but I am in such a hurry: so the washwoman has promised to bring in my clothes on Tuesday, and if she does, & Stockton is no worse off we go. Do you think, sir, you will be ready for us, or is that too soon? What about a cook? Have you heard anything more from Mary? If she doesn't succeed she can cook herself for a day or so until we can get one from town.

Poor Stockton isn't so well today. Late yesterday afternoon on his way home from here he almost fainted and afterwards had a hard chill. He has sent for the doctor at last but hasn't seen him yet. He looks *so* badly again. I am exceedingly troubled about him, though I have been trying to keep his spirits up. He is a good deal discouraged, poor boy! But of course it is always a slow business, getting malaria out of the system; I hope and trust he will gradually improve as the cold weather comes on. I went over this morning as soon as I could get off to see how he was and sit with him a little while the rest were at church. Just as I picked up my hat to leave, in order to write to you, Mrs. Lorance came in from the country. So I had to sit down & make another visit as she is an old friend of Mama's & "had been very anxious to see" me, "was so glad of the opportunity." So as a consequence it was dinner-time when I returned. I have now the two children on my hands & of course cannot hope today for the coveted opportunity to answer these sweet *sweet* letters, yesterdays & the one this morning. But my *heart* answers *dearest* to every word. And after all I *could* not tell you if I tried all day how precious every one of these sweet words is to me. Your wife and sweetheart not only ought to be but *is* the happiest woman in the world. Believe me darling always and altogether   Your own   Eileen

We are all quite well.

ALS (WC, NjP).

To Ellen Axson Wilson

My own darling,   Bryn Mawr, 10 Oct., 1887
    I must put you off with a very little scrap of a note to-day, and that by a later mail than usual: for I have been all day too busy and am now too tired to write even were there time. This morning undergraduate class 9-10; unpacking and putting in the house goods from Rome, things from cottage No. 2, and books from Gainesville, 10-1½; this afternoon preparation and delivery of first graduate lecture (4-5) to a class of *two*, one a *beauty*! After lecture (5-6 ¼) conference with the Fellow about her work (struggle and confusion). Which brings me too the present moment. You can imagine my state of mind and body! But I am well and serene—*and love you more than ever*.
                                Your own   Woodrow

ALS (WC, NjP).

From Ellen Axson Wilson

My own darling,   Gainesville Oct 10/87.
    I am, as you may imagine, very full of "business" today, have been doing all sorts of little things this morning;—(among others, packing the valise experimentally). Have just returned from town where Stock. drove me to get the money cashed, &c. Now Maggie has gone to return the carriage and I am nurse. So you see there is as usual little chance for writing. But then there is little *occasion* for writing much when I am *so* soon to escape from this cruel bondage to pen and ink. What could I write even in answer to *this* letter before me which can not be better *said* three days from now. And yet my heart is so full of the letter that it is hard to resist letting everything else slip and talking it over with you now. Oh my darling, I would give my very life to solve

that problem,—to smooth away the difficulties from your path! How hard it is to be so perfectly helpless, when I feel that I would and could and *must* move heaven and earth on your behalf! But after all, there is Someone else who is not powerless and whom I firmly believe is on your side,—Who has given you a certain work to do and will surely make a way for you to do it. Yes, I have full faith in that "all-wise Providence"! As the old hymn says, "It may not be *my* way, it may not be *thy* way, but be sure that in *His* way the Lord will provide." And then dear I try to find some comfort in remembering that you said it had been a great advantage to you to go over the *history* course *once*; by the same rule will there not be a certain advantage in going once over this other course, especially as your "own" work during that time will consist chiefly in preparing those text-books? I cannot but hope that there will be *some* compensation *somehow*. And I do trust and believe that you will in great measure escape before many years. Certainly you will escape from Bryn Mawr, and even if your work *is* partly undergraduate elsewhere it will be more special and surely not *so* elementary as there.

But I must stop *at once*. I am wanted in several places! We are still well all of us—will start Wed.

Stock. will go the same day—with us as far as Lula.

With a heart full of love believe me, darling always & altogether,   Your own   Eileen.

ALS (WP, DLC) with WWhw name and address on env.

From Marion Wilson Kennedy

My dearest brother: Little Rock, Ark. Oct. 12th 1887.

I am not strong enough to write anything like a respectable letter, so will just say abruptly all I have to say now.

In the first place, I want to assure dear Ellie of my sympathy with her for the loss of her Grandmother. I do feel so sorry for Dr Axson. He is so completely alone now.

Then, Ross, jr.[1] wants me to find out if you are willing to dispose of your Law Library, and if so, at what rate, and what books have you? He may write to you himself today, but I know he is in a great hurry to get the books.

Do write when you have time, and tell us all about yourself, Ellie and the children.

Ross joins me in much love to you all,

Your loving sister,   Marion.

Please excuse this scrawl. Did you receive my other letter?

ALS (WP, DLC) with WWhw sums on env.
  [1] Probably a nephew of Marion's husband.

From Melville R. Hopewell

Dear Sir,   Tekamah, Nebraska. Oct 14th 1887
   We have had some inquiry concerning price & terms on N[2] &
SW 1/4 of SE 1/4 Sec. 22–& NW 1/4 of NE 1/4, and SE 1/4
of NW 1/4 of Sec 27–all in Tp 22-N-R 11 E. Burt Co. Will you
please favor us with price & terms and oblige
                    Yours Truly   Hopewell & Dickinson

ALS (WP, DLC).

From Robert Bridges

Dear Tommy: New York Oct. 18 1887
   I was very sorry for the fate of Edward Coppleston.[1] His story
pleased me exactly, and I was delighted with the crisp intelligence of every page, and the gentle humor. I carefully preserved
your anonimity, and Mr. Burlingame frankly expressed his
opinion of it, (the story) accordingly. He thought it too slight in
structure for the length and elaboration of the plan. Of course I
differed with him—indeed our only serious point of difference in
judgment of fiction is on the relative importance of the plot or
fundamental idea of a story.
   It seems to me that the *Atlantic* would snap up your story
immediately. It is of the kind which their audience will appreciate
thoroughly.
   I am very well and more contented than at any time since
leaving college. Can you not come over to see me sometime this
autumn. I long for a comfortable chat with you.
   You have doubtless heard of Mat Emery's[2] death. His life was
short but he lived it out—the whole round of it that is worth
living—except fame. He had hosts of friends, a good home, some
wealth, a wife and daughter.
   Remember me kindly to Mrs. Wilson.
                    Your Friend,   BoBridges

ALS (WP, DLC) with WWhw names and addresses and notation on env.: "Ans.
Nov. 5/87."
  [1] Bridges was referring to "The World and John Hart," printed at Sept. 1,
1887, which Wilson had signed with the pen name Edward Coppleston.
  [2] Matthew Gault Emery, Princeton 1879, who died on October 10, 1887.

A Confidential Journal

[Oct. 20, 1887-Dec. 29, 1889]
Inscribed on cover:
"Woodrow Wilson *Journal* October 1887 to [blank]"
Contents:
WWhw entries for Oct. 20 and 22, 1887, and Dec. 28 and 29, 1889, all printed at these dates, the 1889 entries in Vol. 6.

Looseleaf notebook (WP, DLC).

From Wilson's Confidential Journal

1887

Bryn Mawr

Oct. 20: Lecturing to young women of the present generation on the history and principles of politics is about as appropriate and profitable as would be lecturing to stone-masons on the evolution of fashion in dress. There is a painful *absenteeism* of mind on the part of the audience. Passing through a vacuum, your speech generates no heat. Perhaps it is some of it due to undergraduateism, not all to femininity.

I have devoted myself to a literary life; but I do not see how a literary life can be built up on foundations of undergraduate instruction. That instruction compels one to live with the commonplaces, the A.B.C., of every subject, to dwell upon these with an emphasis and an invention altogether disproportionate to their intrinsic weight and importance: it keeps one on the dusty, century-travelled high-roads of every subject, from which one gets no outlooks except those that are catalogued and vulgarized in every guide-book. One gets weary plodding and yet grows habituated to it and finds all excursions aside more and more difficult. What is a fellow to do? How is he to earn bread and at the same time find leisure, and (in the toils of such a routine) disposition of mind for thoughts entirely detached from and elevated high above the topics of his trade?[1]

[1] Written earlier in slightly different form in WW to EAW, Oct. 8, 1887.

1887

Bryn Mawr

Oct. 22: Ellie and I at an entertainment given by the students last evening in the Gymnasium. A clever lot of tableaux, acting, recitation, original local hits, &c.—too clever to satisfy, not having body enough to satisfy the palate. The reason I thought discoverable in certain facts patent to the perceptions in all the conversation one was able to start or maintain, after the show was over and ices were being handed. One could not contrive by any means to make that conversation go anywhither. It invariably fell into the topics of society, which always talks about itself. It knows its members and the interesting points about them: and its members are bent upon knowing it. They permit themselves no singularity, but only a relativity. The object of their wit is to make hits, of their invention, to make an impression. And so sociality and individuality become mutually exclusive terms, and the reciprocal accommodations of chatter take the place of speech. Men and women utter, not themselves, but their sense of what is expected of them. It falls out of course, therefore, that things are not seen as they are, but only as they will appear to other people. It is no long way round from this to the reason why such entertainments are a bit flat to the taste. They are not meant to *express anything*. Their only aim is to present a few fancies obvious enough to appeal to some universal appetites of taste. They are planned to be *clever*: and cleverness is froth, not strong drink. It is not their aim to give to the players (the entertainers) any ascendency over their audience, such as the orator gets by force of his individuality but only to get on an equal footing with it, *en rapport* with it. It's public chatter.

I enjoyed the entertainment, but I did not enjoy *myself*: there was nothing to stimulate or recreate *me*.

From Joseph Ruggles Wilson

My precious son—   Clarksville, Tenn. Octr 24 1887

Not having heard from you, or of yours, for now a good while, I have taken it into my heart to feel uneasy. Meanwhile I have been solacing myself with the hope that you reached your home in due season, and that dear Ellie and the children followed in good time and condition. When the General Assemblies shall meet, in May next, they are you know to unite in Philadelphia in a mutual Centennial celebration. For such Celebration I myself care little or nothing, but expect to embrace that opportunity for *calling upon you* at Bryn Mawr and spending thus a more profitable—not to say more pleasing—day than by listening to dreary gush-voicings in the Academy of Music. To see you all within your own home will indeed be a joy.

It was with great astonishment that I read the account of the bottom falling out—or threatening to fall out—from underneath the B. & O. R. R. Co.[1] What effect will the present condition of embarrassment have upon the Johns H. treasury—especially as I notice that the October dividend was "passed"—and that the stock has gone down from 200 to almost 100. Or, is this all a financial scare devised by the new syndicate for the purpose of enabling it to purchase control at a low figure? It looks like it—for surely that great property cannot have collapsed thus in a day! At any rate will your lecture-engagement be affected by the existing complications which threaten to withdraw—temporarily at least— a large share of the University's income? What a misnomer is R. Road "*security*"!

I have been requested—in behalf of the ministers of Louisville —to be one of a number of distinguished (?) men selected from the Northern & Southern Churches who are expected to deliver a series of addresses on Presbyterianism in that city during the months of February & March.[2] I have consented. My subject is "Presbyterianism and Education." Will you not help me with hints?

Your mother is better and worse from day to day—but with no great change on the whole.

The College is prospering. My classes number some eighteen, and are doing well. Dr. [John N.] Waddel is laid aside by a sickness which threatens to be his last—and I am teaching one of his classes—Ecclesiology—much to my distress. All send much love to you both.   Affy yr.   Father.

I did not know until the other day that dear old Mrs. Axson had departed this life. Present to Ellie our heart-felt sympathy.

ALS (WP, DLC) with WWhw figures and notation on env.: "Ans. Oct. 26/87."
    [1] See the New York *Nation*, XLV (Aug. 4, Sept. 8, and Sept. 15, 1887), 82, 181, 200.
    [2] Dr. Wilson delivered his lecture in the Second Presbyterian Church of Louisville on April 13, 1888. See the Louisville *Christian Observer and Free Christian Commonwealth*, April 18, 1888.

Three Letters from Edward Ireland Renick

My dear Wilson,   Washington, D. C., Nov 1, 1887.
    No, I didn't get the place. It had to be given to a poor fellow who didn't get to Congress. But I am very grateful to you.
    Now to business. Let me urge you to have some steps taken to secure the position for which you are so well suited & for whose duties you have such a strong taste—namely the place now vacant & which politicians do not at this stage of proceedings especially care for—Asst. Secretary of State.

I have just to day taken the liberty of mentioning this thing to Walter Page of the *Evening Post*, who is a great admirer of yours.

I have my heart set on this. Will you let me know how you feel about it? I do hope that Mrs Wilson is well & that both of you will get to Washington this winter.

As ever but in great haste

Your sincere friend   E. I. Renick

ALS (WP, DLC) with WWhw sums on env.

Washington, D. C., Nov. 3, 1887.

One more favor, my dear Wilson.

I leave to-night, (summoned by a telegram from my friend Walter Page who has just resigned his position on the *Evening Post* for one in the *Forum* office),[1] for New York with a good fighting chance to get the vacant position on the Evening Post.

Can you at once get a line to [E. L.] Godkin, [Horace] White, [W. P.] Garrison or any of them in my behalf? They know pretty well what I am as a writer, but are ignorant of my disposition, habits &c &c. The main thing is to speak of my steady industry, activity & ambition.

Yours with thanks in advance.   E. I. Renick

ALS (WP, DLC).

[1] Walter Page had just become Manager of the *Forum*.

My dear Wilson,   Washington, D. C., Nov 4, 1887.

The position pays $4,500. It is "Assistant Secretary of State"—really First Asst. but the absence of the word "First" implies that the officer is not the "Second" or the "Third," who always attaches the numeral.

James D Porter, ex-Governor of Tenn. held the place under this administration but resigned about 4 or 5 weeks ago. Mr. Bayard[1] has found great difficulty in filling his place, though it is just now *rumoured* that a Mr. [E. Boyd] Faulkner of West Va (a disappointed Gubernatorial candidate & a bro. of Senator-elect Faulkner)[2] has a chance.

Mr Bayard is a genuine Civil Service reform man—that's a great thing in your favor: he wishes to have thorough gentlemen & scholars. I am inclined to think that he has heard of you.

His second asst. I should inform you, is a "holdover"—A. A. Adee, but his third, is a Univ. of Va man, whom, doubtless, you know—John B. Moore of Delaware, who was, I think, in the law class of '79-80—tho' perhaps the class of '78-9. He entered under Civil Service rules about two years ago as a $1200 clerk.

[W. E.] Faison is now getting $1600 in the same Dept.

I don't know how to advise in reference to best steps. With your consent I might do something & so might Page. But, of course, the direct presentation of your name & merits to Mr Bayard by some one of importance would avail most.

My place in New York concerning which I just now telegraphed you suddenly escaped me due to the objection of the man to whom I would have been an assistant. He insisted upon having some one by trade a newspaper man, thoroughly acquainted with the technique.

Do try to come to see us. Do you mean to say that you, like [E. M.] Gadsden, are the father of two children? Give me their biographies.

You should get the photographs of Gadsden's—they are beauties —why not exchange? You will I trust send me one though I have none to return. I should be very much gratified if you would send me your own photo and—if not asking too much—Mrs Wilson's.

As ever yours,   E. I. R.

ALI (WP, DLC).
 [1] The Secretary of State.
 [2] Charles James Faulkner, United States Senator from West Virginia, 1887-99.

To Robert Bridges

My dear Bobby,   Bryn Mawr, Pa., 5 Nov., 1887.

If I have postponed answering your letter for more than two weeks,[1] it has not been because it failed to warm my heart when it came or because the warmth it imparted has died away, but simply and wholly because I could'nt reply to it at such length as I wished amidst an extraordinary press of lecture-writing. I'm sure you know how much I appreciate your approval of Edward Coppleston's story. It very much more than compensated me for its rejection: for I value your judgments in such matters, as well as in others I might mention, more than I should those of a score of literary authorities. Somehow there has come over me of late a deep desire to do writing of a distinctively literary sort. I have more than one story longing to be told and no less than a dozen essays on literary subjects struggling towards utterance—some of them partly uttered in *ms*. The struggle is with my surroundings, namely my profession, which just now demands every scrap of connected thought or speech that I can produce within days of the ordinary length. My work continues to be new work—six new lectures a week and three recitations. I don't repine in the least. All my lecture production is just now in the line of the two text-books, (one elementary, on the U. S. govt., the other advanced, on govt. in general) which I am preparing for D. C. Heath & Co; and it is moreover immensely helpful, fundamentally, to the higher work, in the general theory and practice of govt., which it is my ambition to do as my chief doing in that line. I am not discont[ent]ed, ∴, not a bit. But I *am* tantalized. To do the work of my fancy, as well as that of my reason—to serve my imagination now and again when it seems impatient of its enforced silence—would be so delightful: and I think so helpful to style and man alike! What makes your praise of John Hart specially sweet and comforting to me is the evidence it seems to afford that these new beckonings are not meant to betray me into mere indiscretion and waste of time. I was a bit afraid to send the *ms.* to *Scribners* because I knew you would recognize the thing's nativity and I was fearful lest *you* should not like it. I don't care for any part of Mr. B's judgment except its authority. Your approval was everything from my mental point of view.

I wish I could come to N. Y. this Autumn: I trust I may be able to,—for "*I* long for a comfortable chat with *you*." But, Bobby, Phila is no further from N. Y. than N. Y. is from Phila., and there's an equal distance between Bryn Mawr and Phila. either way. More-over, we are keeping house this year and we have a room which will be empty for lack of you. Can't *you* run over to see me, if only for a Sunday? I can't believe that an editor is any more of a slave than a young professor without a *barrel* is. And we would be as glad to see you and as eager to keep you as you could wish Fortune to be! Please come, wont you?

There's one sentence in yr. letter that made me feel as 'good' as did the several sentences about our friend E. C's. story. It is this: "I am more contented than at any time since leaving Col-lege." My dear fellow, I am profoundly glad! You have got the emancipation from grind that you wanted: and I know that with that emancipation has come the opportunity for original work that you have coveted. I say hurrah! with all my heart.

No, I had not heard of Mat. Emery's death. I had entirely lost report of him. I am very much pained at the news: for I liked Matt. sincerely.

The last day or two has brought me a curious temptation—you will know how strong a one for me when I state it. It seems that I am pretty generally and favorably known of in Washington and a friend there—not an influential one but a real one—has written to urge that I "have steps taken" to have my name put forward for the vacant (first) Asst. Sec'y'ship of State! He seems to think I'd have a good chance of success, as the office is not much in demand by politicians and Mr. Bayard, who likes gentlemanly, scholarly associates, is finding it hard to fill, since Porter's resignation. Unhappily I don't know a single influential person who would carry my name to Mr. B. I say "unhappily," because, absurd as the idea of my candidacy seems, if there's any chance (there are as young men in the other Asst. Sec'y-ships) I should hate to miss it. I would do my best to get honorably out of my engagements here and accept—for there's nothing I need more just at this present juncture (except a trip to Europe) than an inside seat in some dept. of the fed. govt. And, whether I could accept or not, the offer would be an invaluable card in my present calling—with the Johns Hopkins men, I know, and elsewhere, I am sure. If I knew any steps to take I would take them, just on the chance. It could do no harm. Don't you pity me, with my old political longings thus set throbbing again? Can you advise?

Mrs. Wilson joins me in warmest regards and wish for a visit. As ever,

Your affectionate friend   Woodrow Wilson

ALS (WC, NjP).
[1] R. Bridges to WW, Oct. 18, 1887.

To James Burrill Angell

My dear Sir: Bryn Mawr, Pa., 7 November, 1887

Having had some personal experience of your indulgent temper towards the ambitions of young men, I am made bold to address a few lines to you concerning a thought of mine which you will I feel sure regard as extraordinary, but which will at worst, I hope, only make you smile and think none the worse of me.

A friend of mine in the Treasury Dept. in Washington, wrote me the other day urging me to "have steps taken" to have my name presented to Mr. Bayard for the now vacant post of Asst. Sec'y. of State. My friend is a real friend, tho.' *not* an 'influential' one, being in charge of one of the minor subdivisions of the First Comptroller's Office. He says that Mr. B., who likes scholarly men rather than politicians as assistants, is finding it rather hard to fill the place since Gov. Porter's resignation: and he urges that I am better known—more favorably known—in Washington than anywhere else outside of University circles. I have written to him that I have no claims upon the good offices of any influencial person I can think of.

But there are men as young as I in high places in the Depts., and, if there really is any 'fighting' chance even for me, I am very loath indeed to miss it. And my reasons are such as I am sure you will think proper and honorable. I have sometimes thought of entering the Civil Service Examinations for some govt. clerkship in order to see, if only in that way, the inside of the mechanism I am engaged in studying. I have been restrained, not only by the fact that a clerk's salary would not suffice for the support of my little family, but also by the consideration that such a view of the actual operations of the daily conduct of federal administration as I could obtain from a clerk's desk in one of the departments, would be too imperfect and limited to be of any real service to my thought. But I do want—and *need*—particularly, as it seems to me, at this juncture in my studies,—a seat on the inside of government—a seat high enough to command views of the system. I acknowledge I dread becoming doctrinaire: I dread writing what will be of no practical usefulness—a mere closeted student's view of affairs. I want to handle the practical things of my subject for a time, with an official's diligence:—and *that* is the reason I am tempted by this suggestion of my friend's,— absurd as my candidacy may at first sight appear.

I have written to seek your advice upon the matter because I feel confident that you will understand me and my motive.

There are other reasons for my wish as to taking an office *at this time* which I may mention without impropriety. My teaching here this year lies altogether in the field of political economy, and in my own special field of public law: and I already feel that teaching such topics to women threatens to relax not a little my mental muscle—to exalt the function of commonplace rudiments in my treatment. Before I teach elsewhere I sh. like to mix with the rough practical things again in which I was formerly at home —to recover the proper atmosphere for my studies.

You see, therefore, how earnest my wish in the matter is. I would eagerly accept such an office, could I honorably break off from my occupations here: and I am sanguine enough to believe that I could—though my engagements here, while not so binding as they were when I saw you, still hold me back from instituting an active candidacy, even if I could. You, as a student and a man of affairs both, can give me the advice I need. Would I not be a better professor of Public Law for having been Asst.-Sec'y of State? If so, can you suggest proper dignified means of getting my name mentioned in the proper quarter? Or can you—to be at my boldest—give me in any way your own personal assistance?

Now, for my closing request. If you consider all this an indiscretion on my part, pray regard it as a *mere* indiscretion, due to a young man's eagerness to push himself in the ways of his chief ambitions, and cover it with your indulgence.

With sincerest respect,

Yours very sincerely,   Woodrow Wilson

ALS (J. B. Angell Papers, MiU-H).

From Edward Ireland Renick

Dear Wilson,   Washington, D. C., Nov 7, 1887.

Yours rec'd. I can write but a word. How about Prest. Gilman and others at Johns Hopkins? And have you thought of approaching Mr Bayard through Dr Francis Wharton—the Solicitor of his Dept? You know he is late of Univ. of Penn. & himself an author. Could your father do anything through Hampton, or Ransom?[1]

I can't remember anything concerning Lamar[2] in connection with Cong. Govt. except that my friend W. H. Lamar (now his son-in-law) at that time his private secretary, told me of the interest with which he was reading the book. I shall see W. H. L. at club meeting to-night & say something of the matter now under consideration. Don't permit yourself, old fellow, to get too serious about this. I fear we are very late in the field.

Yours very sincerely   E. I. R.

ALI (WP, DLC).

[1] United States Senators Wade Hampton of South Carolina and Matt W. Ransom of North Carolina.

[2] Lucius Quintus Cincinnatus Lamar, then Secretary of the Interior.

From Melville R. Hopewell

Dear Sir   Omaha, Neb. Nov 10 1887

I think I can sell 600. acres. of your land in Burt Co. being that tract lying in Sections Four & Nine, Town 21-R-11-E- to a party to whom I showed it a few days ago. I think he will give $11.00 per acre for it. He is a man from the East, who wants a tract of land as an investment on the prospective rise and will let me know, in a few days, & will pay cash.

If he takes it, I am of opinion the money put at interest will bring better returns, than the rise in value of the land. Write me at once, whether to make sale, or not, & direct to Tekamah.

Yours &c   M. R. Hopewell

ALS (WP, DLC) with WWhw notation on env.: "Ans. (Yes) Nov. 16/87."

From Robert Bridges

Dear Tommy: New York, Nov 11 1887
I only have time for a few lines to tell you the result of my
inquiry in regard to Secy Bayard.

I saw A. G. Sedgwick today (the Special Envoy to Mexico who
created a sensation.)[1] He must not be quoted in what I say—but
he told me confidentially that Mr. Bayard is susceptible to strong
political influence, and that a man must have good political back-
ing to reach him. S. L. M. Barlow, the lawyer, of this city is said
to be high in his councils. He also told me that the man who
made a *direct application* to him (Bayard) for an office would
be pretty sure *not* to get it. I tried to see J. S. Moore (The Parsee)[2]
but did not succeed.

I am sorry that I cannot give you more definite information. It
would be a good position for reputation and work, and I wish you
all success in the effort. I would that I were a politician that I
might use my *"influence."*

Thank you for your invitation. I shall try to accept sometime
this winter.

Perhaps Chang[3] and his wife will come over to the game on
Nov 19. (Yale-Princeton at the Polo Grounds) My regards to
Mrs Wilson.   Your Friend   BoBridges

ALS (WP, DLC).
  [1] Arthur George Sedgwick, a prominent New York lawyer and an editor of the
New York *Nation* from 1872 to 1905. Sedgwick had been sent as a special agent
to Mexico in 1886 by Secretary of State Thomas F. Bayard to assist the United
States Legation in Mexico City in dealing with an incident involving one A. K.
Cutting. Cutting, an American citizen who edited a newspaper in Paso del Norte,
Mexico, had been imprisoned for libel. Bad relations between Sedgwick on the
one side and the American Minister and Consul-General in Mexico City, Henry
R. Jackson and James W. Porch, on the other side, led to Jackson's and Porch's
recall and widespread recriminations in the American press.
  [2] Joseph Solomon Moore, New York commission merchant, tariff reformer, and
frequent letter-writer to the newspapers. He published a collection of letters to
the New York *World* in 1869 under the pseudonym "Adersey Curiosibhoy, Parsee
Merchant of Bombay," and continued to use the pen name "The Parsee Merchant" in later publications.
  [3] William Brewster Lee.

From James Burrill Angell

My dear Mr. Wilson,   Washington, Nov 12/87
You may be sure I appreciate fully your motives in desiring the
position, of which you wrote me. You may be equally sure that I
should be only too happy to aid you in any way.

Were the vacancy in the Chair of the third Assistant, I should think you might well try for it. But so far as I understand the organization of the Dep't of State, experience in public affairs is essential in the discharge of the duties of the first Assistant, and familiarity with consular and diplomatic business, even with the forms and etiquette of such business is in the highest degree desirable. I suppose that circumstances have not given you the opportunity yet to have that kind of experience. Therefore, to be quite frank, I imagine you would have little chance of obtaining the position.

I am much with the Secretary in these days, and may gain more precise information under auspicious circumstances. Should I learn anything profitable for you to know, I will write you again. Yours very truly   James B. Angell.

ALS (WP, DLC) with WWhw notation on env.: "Ans. Nov. 15/87."

From Edward Ireland Renick

Washington, D. C., Nov 12, 1887.
I lost the trail for a few days, my dear fellow, on account of the sickness of my wife. Now I am writing for a conference with Graves[1] (whom I fear to approach without warning, so busy is he, & so slightly do I know him) and am warming up our friend, the Editor of the Capitol—who, you know, wrote so eulogistically of the book when it appeared.[2] I have not heard from Page, & have tried again. If possible—come & meet old Bayard himself. Stay with us, & (Mrs W. consenting) let us be boys again.
As ever yours   E. I. R.

ALI (WP, DLC).
[1] Edward O. Graves, Chief, Bureau of Engraving and Printing.
[2] The Washington *Sunday Capital*, a weekly newspaper. The editor from 1885 to 1887 was Edmund Hudson. No copy of the issue in which his review of *Congressional Government* appeared seems to have survived.

To James Burrill Angell

My dear Dr. Angell,   Bryn Mawr, Pa., 15 Nov., 1887
I am sincerely obliged to you for your very kind letter of yesterday[.] You have honored me by thoroughly believing in my sincerity.

I of course thought that the duties of the Asst.-Secretaryship were such as one with a pretty thorough *outside* acquaintance with the public business might, with diligence, master: for I can of course pretend to no personal experience in affairs, much less to any acquaintance with the formal etiquette of the diplomatic service. I have already confessed that I wanted the office *in order to learn*, my only readiness being a trained understanding relative to such matters. Certainly, under the circumstances, the place ought to be filled from within the Department, by somebody drilled in its service. I must thank you very heartily for setting me right.

Experience in affairs, I feel, is what I most imperatively need to vivify my chosen studies. A constructive imagination will reach but a little way: even a sympathetic instinct to know cannot gain complete instruction in practical affairs; and, if I have heretofore studied Washington from a distance, it has been simply because I had no choice in the matter. It was a limitation to my work which I keenly felt, but which I had no way of removing. The consciousness of it has, moreover, made me particularly impatient of studious isolation: leading me, perhaps, to magnify its present disadvantages. I love the stir of the world; that stir is what I chiefly desire to study and explain; and I know I cannot sanely explain it from Teufelsdröckh's tower.[1]

I did not know that you were already in Washington. I hope that your labours there will be as pleasant as I am sure they will be successful.

With sincere gratitude and respect,

Yours very truly,   Woodrow Wilson

ALS (J. B. Angell Papers, MiU-H).
[1] Diogenes Teufelsdröckh, of Carlyle's *Sartor Resartus*.

To Lucy Maynard Salmon

My dear Miss Salmon,   Bryn Mawr, Pa., 23 November, 1887

The first sentence of your note of Nov. 19—indeed the sight of the letter itself—brought the blood to my cheeks,—not because of anything I have really done, but at thought of what you must think I had done. 'Miss Salmon,' I acknowledged to myself, 'has an apparent right to think that I have treated her shamefully.'

But, as a matter of fact, my dear friend, my only breach has consisted in not writing sooner to explain. My vacation—so much of it as remained after I wrote to you—brought complete restoration of health neither to me nor to Mrs. Wilson, and I felt that I could read your *mss.*[1] only through the sour eyes of partial illness. Since I came back here I have *until to-day*,—the eve of Thanksgiving—been kept close to my work as I never was before. I am well now & the work does not unduly wear upon me; but I have to husband my resources with all possible care and circumspection.

I have read your *mss.*, however,—have read it with great care, and with increased admiration for the grasp and judgment, as well as for the painstaking and thoroughness, with which it is written. I am sorry that you did not have time to dwell upon your style a little more and sharpen the points of the sentences. The level is a high one, but it is too uniform, and so loses the advantages otherwise to be derived from its elevation. Still that is a matter of detail which you could easily remedy; and if Dr. Rhoads is still of the opinion that there ought to be Bryn Mawr publications, I am of the opinion that this essay of yours ought, with your consent, to open the series.

Have you time to tell me how 'the growth of the national idea' comes on? I have thought of it again and again, and am sincerely anxious to know.

The person here who first told me the news of your election to the Chair at Vassar can tell you also how delighted I was— for I choose the word deliberately: I was delighted—and I wish you 'God speed' with all my heart.[2]

I thoroughly like Miss Bennison.

With warmest regards,

Your sincere friend, Woodrow Wilson

ALS (NPV).
[1] See WW to Lucy M. Salmon, Aug. 10, 1887.
[2] Miss Salmon became Associate Professor of History at Vassar College in the autumn of 1887.

From Robert Bridges

Dear Tommy: New York, Nov 28 1887

I feel pretty sure that Prof. [W. M.] Sloane is the coming man for President of Princeton—or at least Vice-President.[1] I should like to see you have his place as Professor of History. Have you any desire for it? It occurred to me the other day that you might advise with Johnstone[2] and Sloane about it. If I can further the plan in any way please let me know.

In haste BoBridges

ALS (WP, DLC) with WWsh and WWhw on env.: "Preamble: Must not a philosophy of politics, being a philosophy of the life of men in masses, be a philosophy of the obvious? It does not concern the separate action of specially gifted individuals, but the joined action of men united, great and small in the state."
[1] President James McCosh had just announced his intention to retire in 1888.
[2] Professor Alexander Johnston.

To Robert Bridges

My dear Bobby,   Bryn Mawr, Pa., 30 Nov., 1887
   You are the watchfullest, thoughtfullest friend a fellow could have, and I appreciate your friendship more than you can realize.
   I had seen it said in the papers that Prof. Sloane's name was mentioned in connection with the vacant presidency, but I did not know how much or how little that might mean. If he be elected will he retain none of the duties of his present chair?
   When I first read your letter two things occurred to me (1) Ought I to seek a chair merely of 'History' when my special interest and knowledge lie in the field of Public Law and Political Science—the field, pretty much, of Johnston's chair? That question was answered by the Princeton catalogue for '85-'86, in which I find that Sloane is professor of History *and* Political Science and that 'the Science of Politics' and 'Comparative Politics' play as large a part in his class work (which seems quite elastic) as does history proper. Moreover he has only seven hours teaching *per* week (largely text-book work) whereas I have nine and shall have eleven, with from six to eight *new* lectures, per week (Argal, my health is in a very precarious condition).
   (2) Would not Johnston kick against my being made his colleague? His somewhat severe strictures on 'Congressional Government' in the Presbyterian Review[1] would seem to promise as much[.] This query I cannot answer by means of the catalogue.
   Now more directly for myself. If Sloane's work as it appears in the catalogue of '85-'86 is the work or the sort of work I would have, I should be glad—more than that, I should be thankful—to get the place. I almost fear I shall break down in health here if I stay another year; for my work then, though it will be still, as now, immediately on my own lines, will be if possible even more overwhelming than now.
   Only one thing interferes. I am under contract to deliver twenty-five lectures a year at Johns Hopkins this year and the next two. If I took any place I should be obliged to stipulate for leave to fulfil this engagement—which would not necessarily, however, seriously break in upon my regular college work: for the Baltimore men are disposed to make any arrangements as to the times and so forth at which the lectures shall be delivered that will best fit into my other work.
   Last March I signed a contract for three years' work here also: but that contract is no longer binding, for in it the Trustees agreed to give me an assistant—that was the condition upon

which I signed—; but they failed to appoint any one, and I consider myself quite free to enter into any other engagement.

The principal difficulty is, that I should not know, in case Prof. Sloane becomes President, how to set about instituting a candidacy. My acquaintance with Sloane is of the very slightest character and somehow I have got it into my head that he don't think me 'any great shakes.' That may be all a fancy, however: the real trouble is that I would not know how to begin, or, once launched, how to go on, knowing Sloane so slightly and being so in the dark as to Johnston's disposition towards me. My chief advantage would lie in the fact that—as I happen to know, from personal inspection of the crop, there are just the fewest men at present available for such a chair.

You see, then, how the whole case stands with me. I think I shall eventually get a chair of some sort at Baltimore—and Bryn Mawr would be a good place to wait meantime, inasmuch as all my teaching will from this [time] out lie in my own field, of political science. But I have more to do here than I can (probably) stand, and I very much fear that teaching young women (who never challenge my authority in any position I may take) is slowly relaxing my mental muscle; and—in short, I should be delighted to teach at Princeton the politico-historical topics that Prof. Sloane has had. I should doubtless be permitted to impart a more or less individual mould to the course. *But*—where-away lies the right course of action: what is the best initiative? You can best tell me that.

My race for the Washington place did not even reach the stage of actual candidacy; but I satisfied my conscience in the matter, upon which I had set my wits but not my heart. I was very much obliged indeed for your letter on the matter: I knew you could only inform me.

As ever   Your affectionate friend   Woodrow Wilson

ALS (WC, NjP).
   [1] Johnston's review appeared in the New York *Presbyterian Review*, VII (Jan. 1886), 204-205.

From John Franklin Jameson

Dear Wilson: Baltimore, Dec. 4, 1887.
   I've been thinking lately that a congenial theme for you, and one convenient for your attack, if, as I hope, you write an essay for our volume, might be the subject of Chisholm, Executors, vs. Georgia and the origination of the eleventh amendment. The

common field of the essays is to be the constitutional history of the formative period, which will in general be taken as the period 1775-1789. But I take it that we may consider that the canon was not definitely closed until the first eleven amendments had been added, and may include any subject concerning their formation.

The subject of the eleventh amendment is still so vital that I should think its origin would have interest for *you*; and, as a legal subject, of a case in court, *you* have the legal training to treat it. But what I particularly had in mind in addition was, that as a Georgian it might be possible for you to find and give interesting facts not hitherto generally known as to the history of the case; that near you, in the library of the Historical Society of Pennsylvania, are the manuscripts of Mr. Justice [James] Wilson, among which I last June noticed an elaborate treatment of the case, (though to be sure this may prove to be only the MS. of his opinion, which I did not compare it with); and that I have found in Massachusetts biographies some interesting facts as to the movement there toward such an amendment, and believe I can have the use of the papers of Sedgwick[1] and Gore,[2] who forwarded the amendment conspicuously in Congress.

Let me know what you think of this. With the best wishes,
Very sincerely yours,   J. F. Jameson

ALS (WP, DLC) with WWhw notation on env.: "Ans. 18 Jany 1888."
[1] Theodore Sedgwick, Federalist Representative from Massachusetts.
[2] Jameson was probably referring to the Federalist politician, Christopher Gore, who was United States Attorney for the District of Massachusetts in 1794 and did not go to Congress until 1813.

From Robert Bridges

Dear Tommy: New York, Dec 7 1887
I had a talk with Prof. Sloane yesterday. He sails for Europe on Saturday to be gone several months. He is, of course, taking no part in the canvass, and is in the hands of his friends. I could not broach the subject of his successor—when I found how extremely unsettled the whole question of the presidency is. I think it will be well to "go slow" at present, though I shall endeavor soon to have a talk with Moses Taylor Pyne. If Sloane is elected President I hope that your candidacy can be pushed. Please let me know how I can help you at anytime. In haste
Yours   BoBridges

ALS (WP, DLC) with WWhw sums and notation on env.: "The Author Himself," "Influence of the Roman Law on the Law of England—Thos. Edw. Scrutton Camb. Univ. Press, 1885."

A Literary Essay

[c. Dec. 7, 1887]

The Author Himself

Who can help wondering concerning the modern multitude of books where all these companions of his reading hours will be buried when they die; which will have monuments erected to them; which will escape the envy of time and live? It is pathetical to think of the number that must be forgotten, after being removed from the good places to make room for their betters.

Much the most pathetical thought about books, however, is that excellence will not save them. Their fates will be as whimsical as those of the human kind which produces them. Knaves find it as easy to get remembered as good men. It is not right living or learning or kind offices simply and by themselves, but,—something else that gives immortality of fame. Be a book never so scholarly, it may die; be it never so witty, or never so full of good feeling or of an honest putting of truth, and it may not live.

When once a book *has* become immortal we think that we can see why it became so. It contained we perceive a casting of thought which could not but arrest and retain men's attention: it said some things once and for all because it gave them their best saying. Or else it spoke with a grace, a fire of imagination, a sweet cadence of phrase, a full harmony of tone which have made it equally dear to all generations of those who love the free play of imaginative thought or the incomparable music of human speech. Or perhaps it uttered with full candor and simplic[i]ty some universal sentiment; or pictured something in the tragedy or the comedy of man's life as it was never before pictured, and must on that account be read and read again as not to be superceded. There must be something special in its form or substance to account for its unwonted fame and fortune.

This upon first analysis, taking one book at a time. A look deeper into the heart of the matter enables one to catch at least a glimpse of a *single* and *common* source of immortality. The world is attracted by books as each man is attracted by his several friends. You recommend that capital fellow, So-and-So, to the acquaintance of others because of his diverting and discriminating powers of observation: the very tones and persons,—it would seem the very selves—of every type of men, live again in his mimicries and descriptions. He is the dramatist of your circle; you can never forget him, nor can anyone else; his circle of acquaintances can never grow smaller. Could he live on and retain perennially that wonderful freshness and vivacity of his, he must become the most famous guest and favourite of the world. Once again: Whoever has known a man shrewd to see dispassionately the inner history, the reason and the end, of the combinations of society, and eloquent to tell of them with a hold on the attention which he gained by a certain quaint force and sagacity resident in no other man, must be able to understand why men still resort to *Montesquieu*. I suppose that there must be circles who have known some fellow of infinite store of miscellaneous lore who has greatly diverted his acquaintance by a way peculiar to himself of giving it out item by item as if it were all homogeneous and of a piece, and by his unexpected application of it to out-of-the-way unpromising subjects, as if there were in his view of things mental no such disintegrating element as incongruity. Such a circle would expect *Burton* to be loved of the world. And so of those who have known a man of a simple, calm, transparent character, untouched by storm or perplexity, whose talk was full of such serious, placid reflection as seemed to mirror his own reverent heart, and which, though often prosy, was oftener touchingly beautiful because of its nearness to nature and the open truth of life; or of those who have felt the thrill of personal contact with some stormy peasant nature full of strenuous, unsparing speech concerning men and affairs: such people can tell you why a *Wordsworth* or a *Carlyle* has firmly established a right to be read always. In every case there is *originative personality*. Not mere origination: that may be mere invention, which in literature has nothing immortal about it; but origination which derives its character from the originator, which is his substance given to the world,—which is himself outspoken.

Individuality does not consist in the use of the very personal pronoun I: it consists in self-expression, in tone, in method, in attitude, in point of view; it consists in saying things in such a way that you will yourself be recognized as a force, an influence, in saying them. Do we not at once know Lamb when he speaks; and even stiffer Addison, does not his speach bewray and endear him to us? His personal charm is less distinct, much less fascinating than that which goes with Lamb's thought, but a charm he has, sufficient for immortality. In Steele the matter is more impersonal, more mortal. Some of Dr. Johnson's essays, you feel, might have been written by a Dictionary. It is impersonal matter that is dead matter. Are you asked who authored a certain brilliant, poinant bit of political analysis? you say, Why only

Bagehot could have written that. Does a wittily turned verse make you hesitate between laughter at its hit and the grave thought contained in its deeper, covert meaning? Do you not know that only Lowell could do that? Do you catch a strain of pure Elizabethan music and doubt whether to attribute it to Shakspere or to another? Do you not *know* the authors who still live?

The noteworthy thing about such individuality is that it will not develope under just any star or in just any place: there is an atmosphere wh. kills it and there is an atmosphere which fosters it. The atmosphere which kills it is the atmosphere of sophistication, where cleverness and fashion and knowingness grow: cleverness which is froth, not strong drink, fashion which is a thing assumed, not a thing of nature, and knowingness, which is naught.

Of course there are born, now and again, as tokens of some rare mood of Nature, men of so intense and individual a cast that circumstance and surroundings affect them no more than friction affects an express train. They command without even the consciousness that to command costs strength. These cannot be sophisticated: for sophistication is subordination to the ways of your world. But these are the very greatest and the very rarest: and it is not the greatest and rarest alone who shape the world and its thought. That is done also by the great and the merely extraordinary. There is a rank and file in literature even in the literature of immortality, and these must go to school to the people about them.

It is the number and charm of the individualities in it that give distinction to the literature of any country. We turn any whither to know men. The best way to foster literature is to cultivate the author himself,—a plant of such delicate growth that special soils sre [are] needed to produce him in his full perfection. The conditions which foster individuality are those which foster simplicity, thought and action from self out, naturalness, spontaneity. *What are these conditions?*

In the first place a certain helpful ignorance. It is best for the author to be born away from literary centres, where are bred the sophistications of learning. It is best to start out with your thinking not knowing how much has been thought and said about everything. A certain amount of ignorance will insure your sincerity, will increase your boldness, and shelter that genuineness which is your hope of power. Not ignorance of life, but that may be learned in any neighborhood; not ignorance of the greater laws that govern human affairs, but they may be learned without a library of historians and commentators, by imaginative sense, by seeing better than by cramming; not ignorance of the infinitudes of human circumstance, but knowledge of these may come to a man without the intervention of universities; not ignorance of ones self and of one's neighbour, but innocence of the sophistications of learning, its research without love, its knowledge without inspiration, its method without grace; freedom from its shame at trying to know many things, as well as from its pride of trying to know but one thing; ignorance of that faith in small confounding facts which is contempt for large reassuring principles.

Our present problem is, not how to clarify our reasonings and perfect our analysis, but how to reënrich and reënergize our literature. It is suffering, not from ignorance but from sophistication and self-consciousness. Ratiocination does not keep us pure, create us earnest, or make us individual and specific forces in the world. Those inestimable results are accomplished by whatever implants principle, quickens with inspiration, fills with purpose and courage, gives outlook and makes character. Reasoned thinking does indeed clarify the mind's atmospheres, and lay open to its view fields of action; but loving and believing, sometimes hating and distrusting, often prejudice and passion, always the many things called the one thing Character, *create and shape* the acting. Life quite overtowers logic. Thinking and erudition alone will not equip for the great tasks and triumphs of literature: the persuading of other men's purposes, the entrance into other men's minds to possess them forever. Culture broadens and sweetens literature, but native sentiment and unmarred individuality create it. Not all of mental power lies in the region of *thinking*. There is power also in passion, in personality, in simple, native, uncritical conviction, in feeling. The power of science, of system, is executive, not stimulative. I do not find that I derive inspiration, but only information, from the learned historians and analysts of liberty; but from the sonneteers, the poets, who speak of its spirit and high purpose, who know nothing of the historical method and obey only the high methods of their own hearts.

Simple unschooled feeling, native thought, and direct, undoubting purpose are still world-forces less than none. It is your unhesitating, intent, headlong man, who has sources in the mountains, that digs deep channels for himself in the soil of his times, and expands into the mighty river that becomes a landmark forever; and not your 'broad' man, sprung from the schools, who spreads his shallow extended waters over the wide surfaces of learning, to leave rich deposits, it may be, for other men's crops to grow in, but to be himself dried up by a few score summer noons. A man thrown upon his own resources and become a conqueror of success before being thrown with the literary talkers; the man grown to giant's stature in some rural library and become exercised there in a giant's prerogatives before ever he is laughingly told, to his heart's confusion[,] of scores of other giants dead and forgotten long ago; the man grounded in hope and settled in conviction ere he has discovered how many hopes time has seen buried, how many convictions cruelly given the lie by fate; the man who has carried his youth into middle age before going into the chill atmosphere of *blasé* sentiment; the quiet, stern man who has cultivated literature on a little oatmeal before thrusting himself upon the great world as a prophet and seer; the man who pronounces new eloquence for England with the rich dialect in which he was bred; the man come up to the capital from the Provinces,—these are the men who people the mind's world with new creations and give the sophisticated learned of the next generation names to conjure with.

If you have a candid and well informed friend among city lawyers, ask him where the best masters of his profession are bred, in the country or in the city? He will reply without hesitation, 'In the country.' You will hardly need to have him state the reason. The country lawyer has had to study all parts of the law alike, and he has known no reason why he should not. He has not had a chance to make himself a specialist in any one branch of the law, as is the fashion among city practitioners; he has known no reason why he should do so: there would not have been enough special cases to occupy or support him if he had. He has dared attempt the task of knowing the whole law, and yet without any sense of daring. In his own little town, in the midst of his own little library of authorities, it has not seemed to him an impossible task to explore all the topics that engage his profession: the guiding principles, at any rate, of all branches of the great subject were open to him in a few books. And so it often happens that, when he has found his sea legs at home and ventures, as he sometimes will, upon the troublous and much frequented waters of city practice, in search of more work and larger fees, the country lawyer will once and again confound his city-bred brethren by discovering to them the fact that the law is a many-sided thing of principles, and not altogether a one-sided matter of technical rule and rigid precedent.

It would seem to be necessary that the author who is to stand as a distinct and imperative individual among the company of those who express the world's thoughts should come to a hard crystalization before subjecting himself to the tense strain of cities, the dissolvent acids of critical circles. The ability to see for oneself is attainable, not by mixing with crowds and ascertaining how they look at things, but by a certain aloofness and self-containment. The solitariness of some genius is not accidental, it is characteristic and essential. To the constructive imagination there are some immortal feats which are possible only in seclusion. The man must heed first and most of all the suggestions of his own spirit; and the world can be seen from windows overlooking the street better than from the street itself.

Literature grows rich, various, full-voiced largely through the repeated re-discovery of truth, by thinking re-thought, by songs re-sung, by the re-telling of the story of life. The song of human experience grows richer and richer in its harmonies, and must grow until the full accord and melody are come. If too soon subjected to the tense strain of the city a man cannot expand: he is beaten out of his natural shape by the incessant compacting press of men and affairs. It will doubtless turn out that the unsophisticated man has more force and literary skill even than the trained *littérateur*. For one thing he has a fresher contact with old literature. He reads, not for the sake of being acquainted with this or that author, with no thought of going through all his writings and 'working him up,' but as he would ride spirited horses, for love of the life and motion of it.

A general impression seems to have gotten abroad that the last of the bullying, omnicient critics and reviewers was buried in the grave of Francis Jeffrey, and it is becoming important to correct the misapprehension. There never was a time when there was more superior knowledge, more specialist omnicience among reviewers than there is to-day: not pretended superior knowledge but real,—Jeffrey's was very real of its kind. For those who write books one of the special, inestamable advantages of lacking a too intimate knowledge of the 'world of letters' consists in not knowing all that is known by those who review books, in ignorance of the fashions prevalent among those who make canons of taste. The modern critic is a leader of fashion in the knowing circles of literary centres: he breathes the air of a literary worldliness.

If your book be a novel, your reviewer will know all previous plots, all former motives and situations; you cannot write anything absolutely new for him: why should you try? If it be a poem, the reviewer's head already rings with the whole gamut of the world's metrical music; he can recognize any simile, recall all turns of phrase, match every sentiment: why seek to please him anew with old things? If it concern itself with the philosophy of politics, he can and will set himself to test it by the whole history of its kind from Plato down to Henry George. How can it but spoil your sincerity to know that your reviewer will know everything? Will you not be tempted of the devil to anticipate his judgment by pretending to know as much as he?

The literature of creation naturally falls into two kinds: that which interprets nature or man, and that which interprets self. Both of these may have the flavour of immortality, but the former not unless it be free from self-consciousness, and the latter not unless it be naïve. No man, therefore, can create after the best manner in either of these kinds who is an habitué of the circles made so delightful by those interesting men, the modern literati, sophisticated in all the fashions, ready in all the catches of the knowing literary world which centres in the city and the university. He cannot be always simple and straightforward. He cannot be always and without pretension himself, bound by no other man's canons of taste in saying or conduct. In the judgment of such circles there is but one thing for you to do, if you would gain distinction, you must 'beat the record'; you must do better than they have yet been done certain definite literary feats. You are pitted against the literary 'field.' You are hastened into the paralysis of comparing yourself with others, and thus away from the health of unhesitating self-expression and directness of first-hand vision.

It would be not a little profitable if we could make correct analysis of the proper relations of *learning*, learning of the critical, accurate sort, to origination,—of learning's place in literature. Although learning is never the real parent of literature, only sometimes its foster-father, and although the native promptings of soul and sense are its best and freshest sources, there is always the danger that learning will claim in every court of taste which pretends to jurisdiction exclusive rights as the guardian and preceptor of authors. There is constantly an effort a-making to create and maintain standards of literary worldliness, if I may coin such a phrase. The thorough *man of the world* affects to despise natural feeling; he does at any rate *actually* despise all displays of unguarded emotion. He has an eye always on the world's best manners, whether native or imported, and is at continual pains to be master of the conventions of society: he will mortify the natural man as much as need be in order to be in good form. What learned criticism essays to do is to create a similar *literary* worldliness, to establish fashions and conventions in letters.

I have an odd friend in one of the Northern counties of Georgia, a county set off to itself among the mountains, but early found out by refined people in search of summer refuge from the unhealthy air of the southern coasts. He belongs to an excellent family of no little culture, but he was surprised in the midst of his early schooling by the coming on of the war; and education given pause in such wise seldom begins again in the schools. He was left, therefore, to 'finish' his mind as best he might in the companionship of the books in his uncle's library. These books were of the old sober sort, histories, travels, treatises on laws and constitutions, theologies, philosophies more fanciful than the romances encased in neighbour volumes on the same shelves. But they were books which were used to being taken down and read: they had been daily companions to the rest of the family, and they became daily companions to my friend's boyhood. He went to them day after day because theirs was the only society offered him in the lonely days when uncle and brothers were at the wars and the women were busy with tasks about the house. How literally he made those dignified volumes his familiar cronies! He never dreamed the while, however, that he was becoming learned; it never occurred to him that everybody else did not read just as he did, in just such a library. He found out afterwards, of course, that he kept much more of such company than did the men with whom he loved to chat at the post-office or around the fire in the village shops; but he attributed that to lack of time on their part, or to accident, and has gone on thinking that all the books that come within his reach are the natural intimates of men. And so you will hear him in his daily familiar talk with his rustic neighbours draw upon his stores of wide, quaint learning with the quiet colloquial assurance 'They tell me,' as if books contained current rumour; and quote the poets with the easy unaffectedness with which one would cite a common maxim of the street. He has been known to refer to Dr. Arnold of Rugby as 'that school-teacher over there in England.'

I treasure the image of this simple, genuine man of learning, as the image of a sort of master-piece of nature in her own type of erudition, a perfect sample of the kind of learning that might beget the very highest sort of literature, the literature, namely, of unsophisticated, authentic individuality. It is only under one of two conditions that learning will not dull the edge of individuality, first if one never suspect that it is creditable or matter of pride to be learned, and so never become learned for the sake of becoming so, or, second, if it never suggest to one investigation as better than reflection. Learned investigation leads to many good things, but one of these is not great miterature [literature], because learned investigation commands, as the first condition of its success, the re-pression of individuality.

His *mind* is a *great comfort* to every man who has one; but *hearts* are not often to be so conveniently possessed. They frequently give trouble: they are straight-forward and impulsive and can seldom be induced to be prudent. They must be schooled before they will become insensible, they must be coached before they can be made to care first and most for themselves: and in all cases the mind must be their schoolmaster and coach. *They* are irregular forces; but the mind may be trained to observe all points of circumstance and all motives of occasion.

I presume that it is considerations of this nature that must be taken to explain the fact that our universities are erected entirely for the service of the tractable mind, while the heart's only education must be got from association with its neighbour heart, and in the ordinary courses of the world. Life is its only university. Mind is monarch, whose laws claim supremacy in those lands which boast the movements of civilization, and he must command all the instrumentalities of education.

At least such is the theory of the constitution of the modern world. It is to be suspected that, as a matter [of] fact, mind is one of those modern monarchs who reigns but does not govern. That old House of Commons, that popular chamber, in which the passions, the prejudices, the inborn, unthinking affections long ago repudiated by mind have their full representation, controls much the greater part of the actual conduct of affairs.

To come out of my figure, reasoned thought is, though perhaps the presiding, not yet the regnant force of the world. In life and in leterature it is subordinate. The future may belong to it; but the present and past do not. Faith and virtue do not wear its livery; friendship, loyalty, patriotism do not derive their motives from it. It does not furnish the material for those masses of habit, of unquestioned tradition, and of treasured belief which are the ballast of every steady ship of state, enabling it to spread its sails safely to the breezes of progress, and even to stand before the storms of revolution. And this is a fact which has its reflection in literature: there is a literature of reasoned thought, but by far the greater part of those writings which we reckon worthy of that great name is not the product of reasoned thought but of the imagination and of the spiritual vision of those who *see*,—writings winged not with knowledge but with sympathy, with sentiment, with *heartiness*. Even the literature of reasoned thought gets its life, not from its logic, but from the spirtt [spirit] and inspiration which are the *vehicle* of its logic. Thought presides; but sentiment has executive powers, and the *motive* functions belong to feeling.

"Many people give many theories of literary composition," says the most natural and stimulating of English critics, "and Dr. Blair, whom we will read, is sometimes said to have exhausted the subject; but, unless he has proved the contrary, we believe that the knack in style is to write like a human being. Some think they must be wise, some elaborate, some concise; Tacitus wrote like a pair of stays; some startle us as Thomas Carlyle, or a comet, inscribing with his tail. But legibility is given to those who neglect these notions, and are willing to be themselves, to write their own thoughts in their own words, in the simplest words, in the words wherein they were thought. . . . Books are for various purposes—tracts to teach, almanacs to sell, poetry to make pastry, but this is the rarest sort of a book, a book to *read*. As Dr. Johnson said, 'Sir a good book is one you can hold in your hand, and take to the fire.' Now there are extremely few books which can, with any propriety, be so treated. When a great author, as Grote or Gibbon, has devoted a whole life of horrid industry to the composition of a large history, one feels one ought not to touch it with a mere hand—it is not respectful. The idea of slavery hovers over the 'Decline and and [*sic*] Fall.' Fancy a stiffly dressed gentleman, in a stiff chair, slowly writing that stiff compilation in a stiff hand: it is enough to stiffen you for life,"[1] etc. to like humourous import, and suggestive of like needed conclusions as to naturalness. This, after all, is the central and important point, the preservation of a sincere, unaffected individuality.

The problem is to prepare the best soils for mind, the best associations and companionship, the least sophistication. We are busy nowadays finding out the best ways of fertilizing and

[1] From Bagehot's essay "Hartley Coleridge" in his *Literary Studies*. [Eds.' note]

stimulating mind; but that is not quite the same thing as discovering the best soils for it, and the best atmospheres. Our culture is by preference of the reasoning faculty as if that were all of us.

Is it not the instinctive discontent of readers seeking stimulating contact with authors that has given us the present passionately spoken dissent from the standards set themselves by the realists in fiction, dissatisfaction with mere recording observation? And is not realism working out on itself the revenge its enemies would fain compass? Is not Mr. Howells ceasing to write literature as rapidly as he succeeds in producing the effects of realism? Must not "April Hopes" exclude from their number the Hope of Immortality?

The Rule for each man is, Not to depend on the education which others organize or prepare for him; but to strive to see things as they are and *to be himself as he is*. Defeat lies in self-surrender.[2]

WWT MS. with WWhw additions and emendations (WP, DLC).

  [2] Several clues strongly indicate that Wilson wrote this essay in about December 1887. The most convincing is that "The Author Himself" is of course a redraft of "The Eclipse of Individuality," written after Wilson's unsuccessful attempt to put the latter into fictional form in "The World and John Hart." Secondly, the essay was typed on the half sheets that Wilson used so frequently while at Bryn Mawr. Thirdly, the handwriting of the emendations and of two additions is that of late 1887 and early 1888. Fourthly, Wilson wrote the title "The Author Himself" on the envelope of Robert Bridges' letter to him of December 7, 1887. Finally, Wilson, referring to "The Author Himself," wrote to Bridges on September 22, 1891: "It was something that I had had in my desk for two or three years."

  The text printed above differs slightly from that of the article printed in the *Atlantic Monthly*, LXVIII (Sept. 1891), 406-13, and reprinted in Woodrow Wilson, *Mere Literature and Other Essays* (Boston, 1896), pp. 28-49. The copy that Wilson sent to the *Atlantic Monthly* via Horace E. Scudder on May 19, 1891, is missing, but Wilson undoubtedly made a new copy of the essay, tightening and improving the text as he typed.

From Joseph R. Wilson, Jr.

My dearest brother: Clarksville, Tenn., Dec. 7/87

  I am more busy than ever with my college duties at present,[1] for the December speaking comes off in about two weeks and I am on the list of speakers. I finished my speech about a week ago and am now commiting it. I am rather anxious as to my first attempt at public speaking, but everything has to have a beginning sometime or other and it will do me more harm than good to put the evil day off. I will let you know about my success (or failure). I am now a member of one of the Literary societies, and take considerable interest in society matters. I am Secretary, which, of course, gives me a little work to do. I like such work, however, so it is not a burden to me.

Christmas is coming, and with it a week holiday. I mean to have as pleasant a time as possible during that week, for we will be obliged to work hard after Christmas, for Intermediate examinations. I believe no one has told you of Dr. Waddel's departure. He has been quite unwell for some time, and is now wintering in Florida according to his doctor's advice. This throws extra work on some of the faculty. Father has one of his classes. I understand he expects to resign *next June*. This is a secret now, however.

Mother's health has not been good of late, and I am anxious to board for two or three months so as to give her a rest from household cares and worries. We cannot see our way clear at present to break up house keeping. Mother has been somewhat better for the last day or two, and we hope she will regain her former strength.

We have some new neighbors now in the Lurton house—the McKeages of Brooklyn. It is quite a large family and somewhat noisy. There are *four* young ladies in the household, and I have found them very pleasant indeed. They are Presbyterians which makes this hill on which we live quite a Presbyterian hill.

Father and I are both pretty well. We heard from sister Marion last evening and she has not been very well of late.

Mother and Father join me in unbounded love to dear sister Ellie, the two little ones, and your self.

Your aff. bro.   Joseph.

ALS (WP, DLC).
¹ That is, as a student at the South-Western Presbyterian University.

To Richard Heath Dabney

My dear Heath,   Bryn Mawr, Pa., 18 Dec., 1887

If your ears have burned or you have had other symptoms of being thought about since that too far-off time when letters last passed between us—it was me! Both during the summer and since our term opened here I have been head over ears in work—during the summer getting together material for a course of 25 lectures on 'administration' which are to be delivered (2 a week) at the Hopkins from February on; and, since we began again here, preparing six new lectures and three recitations a week—so that I have had no time to let anybody know that I was thinking about them, or that I was even so much as alive.

Still, I *have* had means (independent of leisure) of enjoying the 'Memorials of a Southern Planter.'[1] Mrs. Wilson has been reading it with keenest zest and has delighted me with constant retailings of its contents. What a dear thoughtful fellow you are to think of me so practically in such matters! I thank you from the bottom of my heart. That is certainly a grandfather[2] to be proud of, my dear fellow—as noble a figure as I know of—and as nobly *Southern*—bless the dear old section as it was before the 'Money Devil' entered into it! I wish all the North could read that book: with all its artless—and yet, in the result, artistic—detail, and open their hearts to receive its truth. There were not many men like Mr. Dabney, I must believe; but he was, nevertheless, a type:—a type of what I fear this country will never see again—a type of the *chivalrous* gentleman—a type of the sort of man whom if the nowadays industrial world could match with a dozen or two of a like humane, noble sort there would be no labour problem: whose conscience was the only kind of arbitrator between master and workman that will ever bring peace and coöperative friendship.

The address that came with the book was Bloomington, Ia., as of old: so they did not turn Holmes out after all?[3] I was buried in a little Georgia town all summer and heard nothing about anything. Well, that opens our old subject again. What *would* you take to come here and take charge of the history (Greece, Rome, France, England, U. S. or modifications as agreed upon)—ten hours a week, in a place where the authorities strongly wish lectures to bear as large a proportion as may be to text-book recitations? I did not get an assistant for this year (the consequence being that only political science—no history—is being given this year) and our ill success in finding any such man as we wanted (the salary that was offered being what it was) has set the people here upon the idea of importing somebody from England. The plan does not grow upon me much and I think I shall 'kick'; but in any case you would be my first choice. We can offer more this time. The talk is of $1,200, but I think an effort might bring it up to $1,500. A man could live easily by himself on $1200; but there's no avoiding the fact that this is an outrageously expensive place to live—as well as a difficult place to get house-room to live in—and nobody ought to venture to come here *married* on a cent less than $1500—with promise of a timely advance. I want to put the thing as frankly as possible, because I am extremely anxious to get you here—and if I succeed I wouldn't for my life have you disappointed through my instrumentality. The advantage of coming here would be a geographical, atmospheric advantage, not at all a pecuniary advantage: for the biggest salaries they pay here are small when judged by the cost of living.

Let me have your views in full, therefore, old fellow—and a full account of yourself—if you come east for the Xmas holidays cant you give us just a scrap of your time one way or the other? It would do me an immense deal of good—you could see the place—and—it would be jolly! The next best thing—though next by a long remove—would be a long letter from you.

Mrs. Wilson sends her warmest regards and her added prayer that you will come and I send all the old-time affection of

Your all-the-time chum,   Woodrow Wilson

ALS (Wilson-Dabney Correspondence, ViU).
  1 Susan Dabney Smedes, *Memorials of a Southern Planter* (Baltimore, 1887). Mrs. Smedes was R. H. Dabney's aunt.
  2 R. H. Dabney's grandfather, Thomas Smith Gregory Dabney, the subject of Mrs. Smedes' book.
  3 See R. H. Dabney to WW, Feb. 3, 1887, n. 1, and Dec. 28, 1887.

Two Letters from Richard Heath Dabney

Dear Tom: Richmond, Virginia. Dec. 27th, 1887.

Although this is the holiday season, I am extremely *busy* with the not unpleasant labor of *enjoying myself*; for, not to speak of my chief pleasure here, (that of being with my sweetheart for a good part of the day) I am staying at the house of my cousin, Mrs. Bagby, and have other friends in the city with whom I have to spend a good deal of time. Hence I shall not spend much in telling you how greatly I enjoyed your warm and cordial letter, but, leaving that to your imagination, shall go on to "business."

Old fellow, I need hardly tell you how highly I appreciate your steady friendship for me and your renewed offer of a position at Bryn Mawr. If I were still "heart-whole & fancy free" with no definite matrimonial intention, I should not hesitate a moment about accepting a place with you at $1,200. Not only would it be a heart-felt pleasure for me to live in the same place with an old & tried friend like yourself, but I should regard the mere intellectual contact with you as of the highest value for me in my studies. But, as I am engaged to be married, the case is somewhat altered. I have been waiting a long & weary time for my wedding, and should be exceedingly loath to wait any longer than the summer. I am therefore afraid that I should be unable to accept a salary of $1,200 at so expensive a place as Bryn Mawr. Last year I got only a thousand dollars at Indiana Univ., but receive pay at the rate of thirteen hundred this year, and shall get fifteen hundred after the middle of this academic year. There are good prospects, I think, of a still further increase, and as the cost of living at Bloomington is moderate you will easily understand how I—longing, as I do, to get married—could hardly make up my mind to take a smaller salary at a more expensive place.

Still, I have such a loathing for [David Starr] Jordan, who is as contemptible a rascal as I ever met, and such contempt for Hoosierdom in general that, even if you were not at Bryn Mawr, I should be strongly tempted to get there. It is true that I don't take strongly to the *female* feature of the college, as I don't think many women take much interest in History & Political Science; but the other advantages are so great that if the authorities will offer me $1500 with a prospect of increase I *think* I should accept the offer, in spite of the high cost of living. First, however, I should like to ask you something about the price of board etc. in *Philadelphia*. My friend Dr. [Hans Carl Günther] von Jagemann (Prof. of Germanic Languages at Ind. Univ.) with whom I believe you are acquainted, tells me that several of your professors live in Philadelphia and go out to the college every day on the Pennsylvania R. R. trains. What do you think of this plan? How do board, house-rent & living in general in Philadelphia compare with the same in Bryn Mawr? How many minutes' ride from Phila. is Bryn Mawr, and what is the cost per trip with commutation ticket?

I wish I could accept the cordial invitation of Mrs. Wilson & yourself to pay you a visit before my return to Bloomington; but my time here is so short and the attraction so great that I fear I must forego the pleasure of seeing you for a still longer time. . . .

I shall leave here on Sunday night to return to Louisville & then to Bloomington where work begins on the 4th of Jan'y.

Yours most sincerely   R. H. Dabney.

Dear Tom: Richmond, Va. Dec. 28th, 1887.

I knew there was something I wanted to tell you yesterday, but I couldn't think of it to save my neck, owing to the frequent interruptions which knocked pretty much every idea out of my head. I intended, namely, to say a word or two about the University of Virginia and Mr. Holmes. There was a desire (as you perhaps have heard) on the part of some members of the Board to give the faculty a very considerable shaking up and to remove Schele, Holmes & Garnett (Page having resigned in the Spring without being asked to do so.)[1] Mr. Schele, however, made a big fight for his place by writing to all the friends he had in the state & elsewhere & getting them to give him their support. This plan succeeded, as did also the efforts of two members of the Board to keep Mr. Garnett in his chair. Mr. Holmes acted with great dignity and declared himself ready to resign if the Board considered his resignation necessary to the welfare of the University, but they decided to leave him in his place—being induced to do so, I hear, chiefly through pity for his many misfortunes. I have always myself felt a profound sympathy for the poor old fellow, and am glad the Board decided not to set him adrift in his old age. If they would pension him as Prof. Emeritus, it would be all right, but I don't think it would be right to turn him out without a pension. In regard to my own prospects, I will say that I still look upon the old *alma mater* as the ultimate goal of my hopes and shall keep my eye upon the chair there with a view to succeeding Mr. Holmes whenever he should be removed through death or other causes. My chances will, I hope, be all the better two or three years from now than they would have been last summer, and certainly I have a better chance of getting a full professorship there than at any other prominent Eastern institution—owing to the influential friends I have in the state. I have a scheme in my head at present which, I am in hopes, will improve my chances of a place there or elsewhere, and will tell you of it when my plans take a little more definite shape.

How are you getting along with your proposed works on Political Science for D. C. Heath & Co.? I shall look forward to their appearance with great pleasure.

[W. P.] Trent is here for the holidays & is expecting to derive great profit from your lectures on "Administration" at the Hopkins. I wish I could be there to hear them also.

With best regards to Mrs Wilson & wishes for a happy New Year to you both (also to Miss W.), I remain

Sincerely yours,   R. H. Dabney.

ALS (WP, DLC).
    [1] Maximilian Schele de Vere, Professor of Modern Languages; James Mercer Garnett, Professor of English Language and Literature; and John Randolph Page, Professor of Agriculture, Zoology, and Botany.

From George Howe, III

Dear Uncle   Columbia S. C. Jan 3rd 1888
    Mamma is very anxious to hear from you and hear all about your Christmas. We had a very jolly Christmas ourselves. All

day Monday we shot fire-crackers and at night we had a great many fire-works.

Wilson[1] and I recieved a great many preasants most of them were books.

We had ten days holiday and enjoyed it very much. We go to school to Miss Helen McMaster and are very much pleased with her. We have just been studing our lessons for tomorrow. I like my history better than all other studies. Geography comes next. I cannot *stand* spelling.

Mamma has not been very well but is better now. She met a lady the other day who lives in Columbia who asked about Aunt Ellie. She told Mamma that she was a sort of cousin of aunt Ellies. She was a Miss Milligan of Augusta. Her name now is Mrs Bell.

Give my love to Aunt Ellie, Margaret, and my other little cousin, none of us know her name. Please write as soon as you get a chance.

Your nephew   George Howe.

ALS (WP, DLC) with WWhw notation on env.: "Ans. Jany. 16, 1888."
  [1] His brother, James Wilson Howe.

From Albert Shaw

My Dear Wilson: Minneapolis, Jan. 4th, 1888.

I wish you a happy New Year. Will you have the kindness to read the enclosed circular letter, (which I have been delayed in sending out), and will you not further have the goodness to help me by coming into the symposium? I'm not trying to do anything large or ambitious, but simply to get a few clear, brief statements from economists. I think my plan is feasible, and I believe it will be successful if the gentlemen I address will only consent to toss me off something informal and simple, in about such style as they would talk to a class. I shall be disappointed if you do not give me at least something. Choose your own point of view, of course. A few paragraphs about our present system from the administrative side would be acceptable. I am glad to know that you are to lecture at Baltimore. I hope that your lectures will eventually appear in book form. With the warmest wishes for your happiness and prosperity I am as ever yours,

Albert Shaw.

ALS (WP, DLC). Enc.: Albert Shaw to "My Dear Sir," Dec. 21, 1887, printed letter soliciting contributions to a volume on national taxation and revenue from economists "who are well known as writers and instructors."

From Herbert Baxter Adams

Dear Dr. Wilson: [Baltimore] Jao. [Jan.] 6, 1888.

Can you not arrange your lectures so as to give three or four of the more popular ones in Hopkins Hall on Fridays, beginning March 2 and continuing during that month.[1] Gould is to do so on Tuesdays in that month upon the subject of Social Statistics of large cities. We want, if possible, to give our public courses a municipal tendency with reference to reform work in this city, not merely governmental reform *but social and charitable reforms*. Don't put yourself out overmuch, but if you are likely to have one thing more suitable than another for a Baltimore audience, please let me know of it. We have you down for Administration in general, & you can make what you please of it. It will be a very good point for you to get in four lectures in Hopkins Hall, and I should advise you to put in your best work there. The boys up stairs on Saturday morning and at other times can take the plainer food.

Please write me at your convenience as to topics. The general arrangement will suffice for the present.

Very truly,   H. B. Adams

TLS (WP, DLC) with WWhw notation on env.: "Ans. Jany 13/88."
    [1] Wilson gave two public lectures at the Hopkins in 1888. Notes for them are printed at March 2 and 16, 1888.

To Albert Shaw

My dear Shaw,   Bryn Mawr, Pa., 12 Jany, 1888

I have taken you at your word and written off an *impromptu* on the tariff question. I have been almost afraid to look it over, for fear I should have my first words, thus dashed off, 'sicklied o'er with the pale cast of thought,' and should keep the thing to give it a revision for which I have absolutely no time. I should say substantially the same thing in the end, anyhow, and, since I am sincerely anxious to serve you in any way that you may wish me to, I send this off in the same instant heat I have composed it in. I am sure that if you think what I have written not suited for the purpose for which you intend it or if, on any ground, you think it not worth printing, you know me well enough to know that you can withhold or destroy it without in the least touching my pride or arousing anything but my gratitude.

It delighted me to see your handwriting again. I have been

waiting all these months to learn the effects on your mind of my statements in answer to your questions as to the mental desirability of a professor's life. I wish you would join the under-paid but, intellectually, very free company of teachers. Nobody is so much needed in our ranks as 'the likes o' you,' men who have thought *in* the world as well as *about* it—men in whom neither the practical nor the theoretical predominates, but whose thoughts maintain a stable equilibrium.

No, I'm afraid my lectures on Administration will have to stay over the fire for some time before they are 'done' enough to put before the public in a book. They have been 'prepared' but not yet sufficiently *thought out*. In haste, but with much affection,

Your sincere friend,   Woodrow Wilson

ALS (Shaw Coll., NjP).

An Essay on Economics

[*c. Jan. 12, 1888*]

Taxation and Appropriation

Probably a very considerable majority of the thinking people of the country are of the opinion that some sort of revision of our present tariff laws ought to be undertaken. Those laws were passed under very exceptional circumstances; they are full of complexities and absurdities of the most irritating and unnecessary sort; and they yield a revenue greatly in excess of the needs of the government, as well as at some points altogether unnecessary for purposes of protection. So ripe are they for alteration, indeed, that probably the more far-sighted even among those who are most benefited by them would prefer to endure considerable reductions of their present advantages—if only the changes made gave promise of permanency of policy—rather than continue to undergo the constant alarms of legislative tinkering with which a perpetuation of the anomalies and extravagances of the existing system is sure to vex them. The question is, What sort of a revision; on what lines and for what purposes?

No discussion of the interior defects of our present tariff laws would be adequate which did not go into their details; and probably very few besides treasury experts could handle those details with any confidence. For those who look at the tariff from the outside, in its general features and in its bearings upon the general questions of federal finance, interest centres in the three facts of a protective policy, an enormous surplus, and a choice between license taxes on whiskey and tobacco and import duties as sources of revenue. At heart the tariff question is a question of taxation, and such a question of taxation as carries with it some of the most momentous questions of government. The existence of a revenue greatly in excess of the needs of the government is generally looked at almost exclusively in the light of its influence on Congress; a more suggestive view of it may be had if it be considered in its effects upon the political habits of the people at large. Of course, with unlimited sums of money awaiting its vote, Congress will be constantly under an almost irresistible temptation to spendthrift habits of appropriation. It may be expected to look about diligently for thorough means of spending the immense income at its disposal. It is even under a sort of financial constraint to spend. Not to spend is to allow money to be piled up in the treasury; and no extravagance can be worse in its financial results than that. The whole case is bad enough; but apparently betterment is past praying for so long as the surplus exists.

Look now at the other side of the picture, the relations of the people to their government. Money is being spent without new taxation; and appropriation without *accompanying* taxation is as bad as taxation without representation. The people do not feel, any more than Congress feels, that the money expended so lavishly *is being* extracted from the pockets of commerce and the professions. It was, so to say, extracted a long time ago, when the tariff laws were enacted. The policy of protection is neither here nor there, when the matter is looked at from this point of view. That policy was fixed upon long ago; so far as present legislation is concerned taxation is based upon no policy at all—there is no taxation. Congress and the people are accepting a fact; they are not choosing a course of action.

In order to the preservation of political health under a popular constitution, taxation and appropriation must go hand in hand. There is as much need, and the same need, that taxation should be annually renewed, annually re-originated, as that appropriations should be annually renewed and re-originated. If protection be considered a legitimate object of taxation, it may annually be declared so, just as taxation to meet the running expenses of the government is; and it ought, if sound political views are to prevail, to be thus annually voted an object of taxation. The destination of the revenue so raised ought also to be every year determined; the revenue, over and above government expenses, ought to be applied to some particular object every year, to the last dollar that it is safe to promise in advance of the verification of calculations. Nobody claims that protection is equally desirable and beneficial at all times for all countries, as the payment of debts and their interest is. The conditions of the trade and industry of a country change from decade to decade, and even from year to year, and tariffs ought to be sensitive to such changes. If the tariff be the embodiment of a just policy, as it is, untouched and inflexible from year to year, how much more just might it be made by careful modifications periodically undertaken!

At any rate, *the people ought to be made to feel their fiscal policy all the time*; otherwise they will never give regular or adequate head to it. And there would seem to be no room for doubt that the country *feels* the whiskey and tobacco license tax much more than it feels the duties on imports. It shows consciousness of the one, habitual unconsciousness of the other. These license taxes, then, are the best indirect taxes that can be laid, for a double reason: they are taxes which the people—or at any rate a very talkative and imperative part of the people—feel that they are paying; and they fall upon articles of luxury, not upon articles of necessity.

An ideal financial policy is easy enough to describe and wish for; it has hitherto in the world's experience proved a very difficult thing to attain to. Such a policy would have, to suit the United States at present, one special feature: it would not hasten the payment of the national debt, because haste in that direction under existing circumstances would involve more inconveniences, both financial and political, than advantages of any sort. Such a policy—an ideal financial policy—would include for every state the joining hand to hand of appropriation and taxation; would make them inseparable parts of one and the same policy. Whatever may be taken as the ground and measure of taxation—whether the expenses of the government plus protection, or the expenses of the government only—that ought also to be made the ground and measure of appropriation. No nation, if it is to retain the acute sense of responsibility which ought always to accompany the exercise of the financial functions of the body politic, ought ever to have a policy of taxation without having a policy of appropriation of exactly the same proportions; or ought ever to let the two policies lose their proper sequence, which is, appropriation first, taxation afterwards; or ought ever to decide on taxation for a longer period than that for which it votes appropriations. The only way to bring Congress to sober and conscientious ways of spending money is to insist that it assume the responsibility of raising, by its own distinctly adopted plans, the money which it spends; and the only way in which to interest public opinion in every spending vote is to put a taxing vote alongside of it. If, therefore, the financial policy of the country is to be really and effectually reformed, Congress must not be allowed to stop at recasting in some way the present tariff; it must be forced by a steady public opinion to marry the two sides of its fiscal policy, to tax as openly and as often as it spends.

There is another, an administrative, side to the subject. We can never tell whether or no we have an economical administration until appropriation and taxation be brought within sight of one another. There can be no standard of expense while there is no standard of revenue. Economy can be nothing but a matter of mere good conscience among the heads of departments so long as there is no question at all of having to ask the people for money. It will become a matter of careful and watchful policy only when it involves calling on the stockholders for fresh subscriptions.

WOODROW WILSON.

Printed in Albert Shaw (ed.), *The National Revenues* (Chicago, 1888), pp. 106-11.

From Richard Heath Dabney

Dear Tom: Bloomington, Indiana. Jan. 14th, 1888.

I wrote you two letters from Richmond during the holidays, but as I have heard nothing further from you I suppose that your Board of Trustees have not yet met or taken any action in my case. Still, as von Jagemann tells me that he thinks the Bryn Mawr trustees probably meet about once a month like those of Johns Hopkins, I imagine that a meeting cannot be very far off, and I wish accordingly to add a word or two to what I have already said.

When you wrote to me last January you told me that "associates" were usually engaged, I believe, for one or two years. Does this mean that the trustees would hold rigidly to his contract an associate who, we will say, had agreed to stay with them two years, and would positively refuse to release him in case he should see a chance in the meantime of getting a better position? You know already that I have a Univ. of Va. bee in my bonnet. Mr. Holmes is a friend of mine and once told Charley Lindsay that he wanted me to be his successor. For this and for other reasons I think that when the chair at the Univ. does become vacant I should stand a better chance at least of being elected than any other man as young and as obscure as myself. But you appreciate, of course, that here is a chance for me that should by no means be thrown away. Now, I think it likely enough that Mr. Holmes may still live for several years, and I *don't think* it probable that the question of turning him out will be re-opened next June. Still, there is no telling what *may* happen, or *when* it may happen; and I don't want to have my hands tied when the time does come. Suppose, for instance, that your Board should meet in a few days from now & offer me a position at Bryn Mawr, & that I should accept. Suppose, further, that in June the chair of History at the Univ. were to become vacant from whatever cause. Between you & me, could I honorably get out of my engagement at Bryn Mawr?

Do you believe that a married couple could get two good rooms and board for $12 a week in *Philadelphia*?

In case the Board are unwilling to give me $1500, you might say to them that I would at any rate take into consideration an offer of less, though I hardly think I should accept.

When will your works with D. C. Heath & Co. appear? I am about to make a small venture in the book line myself. In fact I am expecting the arrival, in a day or two, of the first proof-sheets of a small volume on the "Causes of the French Revolution," to be published shortly by Henry Holt & Co.[1]

With regards to Mrs Wilson

    I remain, thou very ass,

    Thine illimitably idiotic chum   R. H. Dabney.

ALS (WP, DLC) with WWhw notation on env.: "Ans. Jan 20/88."
[1] *The Causes of the French Revolution* (New York, 1888).

From Herbert Baxter Adams

Dear Mr. Wilson: Baltimore, Md. Jan. 19, 1888.

The President thinks that the second two of your proposed lectures will be best adapted to our municipal and sociological needs in Baltimore. The two are, I believe, Comparative Snstems [Systems] of Municipal Organization and Municipal Government in large cities. The dates have not been precisely fixed, but probably your two public lectures will not come before the last of March or early in April. I think your plan of familiar talks upon the subjects suggested is altogether excellent.

           Very truly,   H. B. Adams

TLS (WP, DLC) with WWhw notation on env.: "Ans. 3 Feby/88."

To Richard Heath Dabney

My dear Heath,   Bryn Mawr, Pa., 20 Jan'y, 1888

I have not written to you before because things have been at a standstill with reference to the Associate question; and I can now do little more than chronicle that fact. The authorities wish to wait till they can hear more about some English candidates, concerning whom Canon Creighton[1] has written them, before taking action; and I am waiting, to oppose, with what efficacy I can, an English appointment, so long as we can do as well as we could wish in America. You may be sure that I will bear in mind all you have said anent your candidacy, and conduct your case accordingly.

The question you put about the probable stiffness of the Trustees in holding a man to his agreement of service for a definite term of years is a 'mighty' interesting one—to all of us here, as well as to you: I wish I could answer it. I can only state probabilities. One of our number got a good offer and resigned; the trustees offered him a better salary and the privilege of accepting it without signing a new agreement; he stayed and is now serving without any written contract—a free man. That is the outside history of the case: I don't know its inside history. I conclude from it that the 'powers that be' would not prevent a man who was determined to leave. They would hardly, I *suppose*, be so shortsighted. It would not hurt for one to ask point blank about the matter before signing, I think. But it's a '*mighty*' interesting question.

I am pretty sure, from the inquiries I have made, that it would *not* be possible to get board such as you would have for $12.00. The lowest figure for first-class board would probably be from $16.00 to $18.00. If the scheme of building cottages to be rented to the Professors, which is now under consideration, be carried out, there will doubtless be rooms for you out here at rates somewhat below what it would cost you to live in town and pay $5.00 per month car fare. But I intend to extend my inquiries and can probably give you more certain figures hereafter.

I've put off speaking about your book, my dear fellow, to the last of my sheet, but not to the last of my thought. I am indeed delighted that you are going into print, and through the medium of such a tip-top house! You're a brave chap to make your first venture in that much discussed field (your Washington and Lee lectures?)[2] but I'm not afraid. I look forward to finding the little volume first class as I look forward to rising and taking a little nourishment to-morrow. Hurrah and hurrah!!

With sincerest regards from us both, I am, oh thou illimitable idiot, in haste and affection

Thy very assinine chum,   Woodrow Wilson

The D. C. Heath books will probably be out next winter—*I hope*[.] They're now on the stocks in a somewhat advanced stage of construction.

We were deeply disappointed, old fellow, that you did not stop with us 'Xmas vacation—but we appreciated the reason.

W. W.

ALS (Wilson-Dabney Correspondence, ViU).
¹ Mandell Creighton, Canon of Worcester, Dixie Professor of Ecclesiastical History, Cambridge University, and editor of the *English Historical Review*.
² Dabney's book, *The Causes of the French Revolution*, was based on lectures that he delivered at Washington and Lee University in the spring of 1886.

Classroom Lectures Notes

[Feb. 1, 1888]
Inscribed (WWhw) on first page: "Bryn Mawr, Pa, 1 Feby"
Contents:
WWhw and WWsh notes for lectures on the history of economic thought from Bastiat through the nineteenth-century classical school.

Loose sheets (WP, DLC).

Wilson's Copy for the Bryn Mawr Catalogue, 1888-89

[*c. Feb. 1, 1888*]

HISTORY.

The courses indicated suggest the topical plan of instruction which is to be followed. The histories of Greece and Rome are taken as representative of ancient history, those of France and England as representative of mediaeval and modern history; and in following those special lines the work of the classes will consist largely in the preparation by individuals of reports on specific topics and important episodes in the histories studied. These reports will be founded, not only upon the text-books used, but also upon all the standard authorities available.

Constant text-book drill will be combined with instruction by means of frequent lectures, whose object will be to give life to the narrative of the text-book used in recitation, by recounting the most important contemporary events in the history of other countries, and by pointing out the chief and most memorable characteristics of the periods studied, as well as the philosophical connection of leading facts and tendencies. The general purpose of the lectures will be to group and explain facts separated in the narrative, subordinating them to broader views of history.

The courses on the Italian Renaissance and the German Reformation will be lecture courses.

Each year's work will be introduced by a brief course of lectures on the philosophy of history and on methods of study.

First Year.
(*Ancient History—Minor Course.*)

I. History of Greece. *Five hours a week on alternate weeks during the first semester.*

In this course, lectures are given on such topics as the reforms of Solon and of Cleisthenes, the causes of the Persian invasion, the character and influence of the Confederacy of Delos. As the history of the popular states of Greece turns largely upon the individual characters and influence of leading men, class reports are required on the antecedents, lives, and work of the principal statesmen, dramatists, and orators.

II. History of Rome. *Five hours a week on alternate weeks during the first semester, and five hours weekly throughout most of the second semester.*

In this course the lectures deal with such topics as the sources of Roman history, the causes, means, and ends of Roman conquest, Roman provincial administration, agrarian troubles, the characters, aims, and reforms of the Gracchi.

In both courses, text-book drill is made prominent, but more especially in Roman history, because the internal history of Rome, down to the time of the empire, turns upon class struggles and consequent legal and constitutional reforms which can be mastered in no other way.

The plan of conducting work in both Greek and Roman history simultaneously, the two courses alternating with each other, week by week, is adopted in order that the histories of the two countries may run parallel up to the point where Greek history is merged into Roman by conquest, with a view to enable the student when hearing lectures to perceive for herself contrasts and likenesses.

III. European History from the fall of the Western Empire to the establishment of the Empire of Charles the Great. *Lectures five hours a week during the last week of the second semester.*

Second Year.
(*Modern History—Minor Course.*)

History of France. *Three times weekly, on alternate weeks throughout the year.*

History of England. *Three times weekly, on alternate weeks throughout the year.*

Italian Renaissance and German Reformation. *Twice weekly during the first semester.*

Lectures on special topics in American History. *Twice weekly during the second semester.*

The topics selected for the lectures on American history will be such as the following: the foundation of the colonies; the contest between England, Spain, and France for the possession of America; contrasts in colonial life and manners; the causes of the Revolution; the second war with Great Britain; the great westward migration; the Missouri compromise; the history of parties, with special reference to the rise and influence of the Federalist party.

Either year of the major course in history may be taken separately as a minor course.

Two years of history may be taken without the course in political science, by electing one year of history as a minor course and a second year as a free elective.

Group. History and Political Science. Students that elect this group may take, as required studies, instead of one year of science and one year of history, one year of science and one year of any language (Greek, Latin, English, French, German, Italian, or Spanish).

POLITICAL SCIENCE.

First Year.
(*Minor Course.*)

Elements of Political Economy. Modern Socialism and Communism. *Three times weekly throughout the year.*

Comparative study of the political institutions of the United States. *Twice weekly throughout the year.*

Second Year.
(*Minor Course.*)

History of Political Institutions. (Lectures.) *Twice weekly throughout the year.*

English and American Constitutional History. (Lectures.) *Three times weekly during the first semester.*

American State Constitutions. (Fifteen lectures.) *Three times weekly during the second semester.*

European Political Revolutions. (Twenty lectures.) *Three times weekly during the second semester.*

The courses of the first and second years will be given alternately, and may be attended in reverse order.

ADVANCED COURSE IN HISTORY AND POLITICS.

Graduate Courses.   The following advanced course in History and Politics has been given by Dr. Woodrow Wilson, to graduate students, in the year 1887-88. It has been planned not only with reference to the needs of those that desire to prepare themselves to be teachers in these branches, but also as a useful preparatory course for students that are looking forward to special studies in law.

1st Semester.

The History, Functions, and Organs of Government. Fifty lectures. *Four times weekly.*

2nd Semester.

    1. Nature and Influence of Roman Law. Ten lectures.

    2. Comparative Constitutional History. Twenty-five lectures.

    3. Growth of Modern Nationalities. Eight lectures.

    4. History of Political Economy. Ten lectures. *Four times weekly.*

These courses of lectures are a fuller treatment of the topics discussed by Dr. Wilson in the graduate course given by him at the Johns Hopkins University.

Throughout the year one hour a week is given to the meetings of a Seminary at which reports will be read of graduate work done privately upon topics collateral with those of the lectures.

In the year 1888-89 the following graduate courses will be offered.

1st Semester.

Theories, Methods, and Problems of Administration. *Four times weekly.*

2nd Semester.

    1. Nature and Influence of Roman Law. Ten lectures.

    2. Comparative Constitutional History. Twenty-five lectures.

    3. Growth of Modern Nationalities. Eight lectures.

    4. History of Political Economy. Ten lectures.

It is planned to give one hour a week throughout the year to the meetings of a Seminary at which reports will be read of graduate work done privately upon topics collateral with those of the lectures.

The modifications of the course in subsequent years will be announced at a later time.

Printed in *Bryn Mawr College. Program. 1888* (Philadelphia, 1888), pp. 38-41.

To James E. Rhoads

[Bryn Mawr]

My dear Dr. Rhoads,   Wednesday morning [c. Feb. 1, 1888]

I send back, by my little brother,[1] the plans you were kind enough to let me have on Saturday last.[2] I am sorry to have kept them so long: we wanted to see the house itself before parting with the paper description.

The reality does not seem to us quite so attractive as the plan. There is a rather too obtrusive appearance of cheapness about the finish of the house. In most respects, however, it promises to be comfortable enough. When I can see you I should like to make some minor criticisms: this morning I am engrossed by lecture-preparation.

Mrs Wilson tells me that you said the rent of a house of the kind now under consideration would probably be $375.00. My experience of the expense of house-keeping out here makes it, so far as I can now see, almost imperative that I should not let my rent bills exceed thirty dollars per month: I think it would be wisest, therefore, for me to leave the matter open for a few days longer in order to visit some houses in the neighbourhood which are advertised at rates quite within my reach.

With sincere regard,

Very truly Yours,   Woodrow Wilson

WWTLS (President's Files, PBm).

[1] Edward Axson.

[2] As this letter soon makes clear, the College was building houses to rent to the faculty.

To Sophia Royce Williams

My dear Mrs. Williams,   Bryn Mawr, Pa., 2 Feby., 1888

I appreciate very deeply indeed your kind letter of Tuesday: if anything could add to my regret at withdrawing from the Club, it would be the necessity of doing so despite suggestions to the contrary prompted by such cordial friendship as yours. For, though your note set me to reviewing the matter in my own mind, I still feel that resignation was the only wise course. For the next four months I am to lecture both here and in Baltimore; my time and thoughts will be entirely engrossed; and it will be quite beyond my choice to be anything social or 'human': I must live inside my tasks, in hope of some future deliverance. Under such circumstances my connection with a Club like the 'Contemporary'[1] could at most be only formal, and I am sure that I ought not to reconsider my resignation. Two babies furnish Mrs. Wilson with an unanswerable argument for her own withdrawal.

With renewed acknowledgements of your cordiality and thoughtfulness for our enjoyment, and with warmest regards from us both for yourself and Mr. [Talcott] Williams,

Very sincerely Yours   Woodrow Wilson

ALS (in possession of Henry Bartholomew Cox).
[1] The Contemporary Club was organized in Philadelphia in 1886 on the model of the Nineteenth Century Club of New York, about which see D. G. Thompson to WW, Nov. 7, 1886, n. 1. The members of the Contemporary Club, originally limited in number to one hundred, met several times each year for lectures and discussions on various topics. Among the charter members was Walt Whitman. Mrs. Talcott Williams was the first secretary. In the Wilson Papers, Library of Congress, there is a receipt by Horace L. Traubel, Treasurer, dated March 14, 1887, for payment of initiation fee and dues for 1887 by Professor and Mrs. Woodrow Wilson.

From Edward Day Page

Dear Sir: New York Feby 3rd 1888.

A branch of the American Economic Association has recently been organized, with a membership of upwards of thirty, in Orange, N. J. Its plan is the same as that of the Springfield Association, with whose operations you are probably familiar.

The Executive Council of the Orange Association, consisting of Mr Arnold Tanzer, Prof. Charles Sprague Smith if [of] Columbia, and the undersigned, are arranging for a series of papers on economic subjects, to be read and discussed before the Association at its meetings on the second Monday of each month. The Council begs to invite you to contribute such t [a] paper at one of its meetings in the future, and if agreeable to you will be happy to learn from you the title and approximate length (in time) of any paper or papers which you would be uilling [willing] to contribute. It is inteuded [intended] that the paper to be read should not exceed one hour in delivery, but it is also believed that shorter papers, say of half or two-thirds that length would also be desirable, if [of] course dependent upon the nature of the subjec[t] discussed.

The plan of the Associationl like that of the Connecticut Valley branch of course precludes the offer of distinct compensation; but it is understood that traveling expenses in both directions will be defrayed, and that entertainment for the night, will be provided for. The Association is composed of New York business and professional men, residents of Orange and vicinity, and all interested in the study and discussion of economic questions.

Trusting that I have not presumed too much in making this request, and that I shall have the pleasure of hearing from you favorably in thi[s] connection,

I am   Yours very truly,   Edw'd D. Page.

Prest. Orange Economic Assn.

TLS (WP, DLC) with WWhw notation on env.: "Ans. Feby. 8/88."

From Herbert Baxter Adams

My dear Dr. Wilson: Baltimore, Md. Feb. 9, 1888
I believe your first public lecture is to be on Friday March 2, at 5 P.M., in Hopkins Hall. The notices are not yet printed, but I shall send you a copy in a day or two. Gould begins before the Seminary on Friday of this week and will continue in a class-course on Tuesdays at 4 P.M. Can you open before the Seminary Friday evening at 8 next week, the 17th? From the numerous engagements of our graduate students I am inclined to think that your Friday's lecture had for the present better be given, as above, before the Seminary at 8 P.M. The second lecture can follow Saturday morning at 10 o'clock. Of course your two public lectures on Fridays occur at 5 P.M. and take the place of class lectures on that day. If possible send me a list of your subjects, or at least the first two or three of them. We have advertised as public lectures the two that I mentioned in my last letter and I believe they come in successive weeks, but am not quite sure until I see the printed notice.

Very truly,   H. B. Adams

TLS (WP, DLC) with WWhw notation on env.: "Ans. Feby 11th/88."

A Course Examination

Politics.

February 10th, 1888.

I.

Explain the origin of the State and of Law, and the probable genesis of the ancient City.

2.

Describe the medieval State and discuss (a) the transition from the medieval to the first form of the modern State, (b) the evolution of the present form of the State, giving the chief characteristics of the latter.

3.

Draw carefully the distinction between a Confederation and a Federal State.

4.

How did the political history of the colonies prepare for us of necessity a federal state, combining union and nationality with complete local self-government? Answer fully.

5.

How do our state constitutions differ from the federal Constitution, and what arrangements have state and federal constitutions in common for securing a strict observance of constitutional limitations? Whence did they derive the idea of such an arrangement?

6.

Describe the early character of the Union, the growth of the national idea, and the present character of the Union.

WWT MS. (WP, DLC).

From Melville R. Hopewell

Dear Sir,   Tekamah, Neb. Feby. 11th 1888

The trade we expected to make, with New York parties, in selling your land @ 11.00 per acre in Secs. 4 & 9-21-11- fell through. The 80. acres in Sec. 10-21-11- I have prospect of selling @ 10.00 per acre, and other parties have asked price of land in Sec 9-[.] I think what land you have in Sec. 9- may be sold @ 10.00 per acre. Am not sure. There is no apparent appreciation in the selling value of land. It is difficult to say, when there will be a rise, but it seems, to me, there should be. I do not think the land I have mentioned can be sold now for more than 10.00 per acre, usual terms. If you want that let me know, and we will see if sale can be closed.

I thought I had paid your taxes for 1886—but it seems—not—as I find tax against your lands, for 1886,   59.

our chge—   1
———
$60.

On the same lands, for 1887, which are now due and payable, the tax is much greater being, $91.46

our chge   1
_____

$92.46

If you forward me sufficient to pay one or both, will forwrd receipt. Expecting to hear from you soon, I am

Yours Truly   M. R. Hopewell

ALS (WP, DLC) with WWhw notation on env.: "*Ans.*"

To Herbert Baxter Adams

My dear Dr. Adams,   Bryn Mawr, Pa., 11th, Feb'y, 1888.

I have received your letter of Feb'y 9th. Is it your purpose to give me charge of the Seminary on the evenings when it will be necessary for me to deliver my lectures? It would hardly be fair, would it, to impose my lectures on the Seminary as a Seminary,— on you, i. e. and Dr. Ely, and Dr. Jameson? They are to be class lectures, of course, not original contributions such as would be suitable for Seminary discussion,—put in my own way, certainly, but made out of the ordinary materials out of which all lectures must be made. In brief, though I should be glad to have the full Seminary attend if they wished, I shall not put forth very much, aside from mere forms of presentation and points of view, for which I should feel that I had a claim to command the attention of other specialists. It would be very agreeable indeed to lecture before the Seminary, and I am entirely at your service, but I do not want to bore you.

I enclose a topical outline of my class course, as you request.[1] I hope it is what you wanted.

Very Sincerely,   Woodrow Wilson.

WWTLS (H. B. Adams Papers, MdBJ).

[1] It is missing. Perhaps it was based upon the announcement printed at Feb. 17, 1888.

From John Franklin Jameson

Dear Wilson: Baltimore, Feb. 12, 1888.

I shall be very glad indeed to leave the topic I spoke of entirely at your mercy,[1] and ought to have written so before; I sincerely hope you will be able to write us something upon it.

Meanwhile, I should like to enlist at least your sympathy in another plan. It seems to me that, placed where we are, we ought to be doing something for Southern history, getting our men to work at it, etc. In order at once to stimulate such work and to furnish materials for it, I propose to make a collection of books upon the subject, which, with what we now have, shall form an Alcove of Southern History and Biography in the library of our department. For this purpose I want to get a fund of $1000. This can't, under present circumstances, be got from the university. So I have resolved to ask the aid, first, of those former students of the university, from Southern states, whose interest has been mainly in the work of our department, and secondly, of its Southern friends in Baltimore. Can I not count upon you? I know that the object is one which will have your warmest approval, and shall be very glad if you find it possible to make some subscription upon the blank enclosed.

Believe me,   Very truly yours,   J. F. Jameson.

ALS (WP, DLC) with WWhw sums on env. Enc.: hw subscription form for donation.
[1] See J. F. Jameson to WW, Dec. 4, 1887.

Wilson Launches His Lectures on Administration at the Johns Hopkins

[c. Feb. 17, 1888]

Announcement of the three years course:

1. In the lectures of the first year, I shall dwell only incidentally upon general principles: only sufficiently to maintain the proper *atmosphere* for our study. My principal object will be to erect the *material scaffolding* for future discussions of principle, by making you familiar with the *machinery of govt.* actually existing in the leading countries of the world at the present day, as well as with their *general historical derivation.*

To this end, I shall describe and discuss separately the (a) *central govts*, (b) the systems of *local government* now in vogue among ourselves and abroad, and (c) *Admin. Justice.*

First, however, I shall, in three or four lectures, clear the ground, and the air, with brief discussions of introductory topics such as the *Functions of Govt.*, the *Nature, Field, and Method of Admin. Study*, and a concise statement of some leading *General Principles & Questions of Administration.*

2. In the lectures of the second year, I shall discuss the administration of *ordinary civil*, as contradistinguished from administrative, *Justice*; then, specializing in the field of local government, I shall consider, throughout some ten lectures, the various methods, problems, and ends of *town and city govt.*; and, finally,

I shall examine particularly the performance by the state of such special functions as *sanitation, poor relief, the* care of incapables, and *the regulation and facilitation of trade and intercourse* (railroads posts and telegraphs, in short.)

3. I shall thus have left, for the lectures of the third year of our course, the special topics *Finance* and *Education*, and the general subjects, *Reorganization, Responsibility, Control.*

It is my purpose to make the course of each year stand upon its own legs as a complete course, and yet to join the lectures of the three years together *in a progressive order,*–progressive from the existing machinery to the standing problems, the general tests, and the essential principles of Administration,–*from form to meaning.*

WWhw MS. (WP, DLC) with WWT notes on verso of pp. 4 and 5.

Notes for Two Classroom Lectures at the Johns Hopkins

[c. Feb. 17, 1888]

Lecture I.
The Functions of Government.[1]

It must greatly assist us in gaining an adequate knowledge of the objects and the machinery of administration, to get firmly in mind at the very start as complete a conception of the general province of govt. as may be gotten without going into discussions so extended as finally to divert, instead of merely preparing our examination of govt. as an operative organism. We must know what, in the main, the functions of govt. are before we can go on with advantage to Administration's narrower qus. as to the way in which they are to be performed.

So much for the attitude we sh. occupy towards the study of Administration. Let us turn now to the study itself. We are getting higher for our prelim. view. How get highest? It seems necessary to look at Adm. from the very high ground of the inquiry *What are the functions of government?*

(1)–Necessary, in the first place, because it is only by regarding the magnitude and scope of the tasks of government that we can get a just conception of the importance and domain of Administration, whose problems concern always the best ways of accomplishing governments tasks and duties.

(2) Necessary, in the second place, because it gives us a

[1] There is a one-page WWhw outline of this and the following lecture on the functions of government in WP, DLC.

glimpse of that which we so much need to know, in differentiating the laws of *Administration* from the laws of *business*, namely the actual distinctive character of the State, the organism whose activities we are about to discuss.

What, (then,) *are the functions of government*? What tasks does govt. habitually undertake?

The qu. has its own difficulties and complexities: it cannot be answered out of hand and in the lump, as the physiologist might answer the qu., What are the functions of the heart? In its *nature* govt. is one: but in its *life* it is many: there are govts. *and* govts. When asked, what are the functions of govt? we must regard individual differences and ask in return, of *what* govt? Different States have had different conceptions of their duty, and so have undertaken different things. They have had their own peculiar origins, their own characteristic histories; circumstance has moulded them; necessity, interest, or caprice has guided them. Some have lingered near those primitive institutions which all once knew and upheld together; others have quite forgotten that man ever had a political childhood and are now old in complex practices of national self-govt.

Notice then one moment a single general point about the nature of this question. It is obviously *a simple question of fact*; and yet there is a very prevalent notion that it is a question of *opinion*. Over and over again it is to be found confounded with that other very different question, What *ought* the functions of government *to be*?—a question which it is quite out of our way to answer at present. It must be content to abide the chance of finding itself answered among the inferences to which a knowledge of what government actually does must lead us: as thus: What government *does* must find its roots in what government *is*: and what government is must determine what government ought to *do*. We are evidently beginning at the right end of the whole matter by first asking for the facts,—the only conclusive evidence.

It will contribute to clearness of thought as well as to many parts of our future discussions, to observe the functions of govt. in *two groups*:

   1. *Constituent* functions
   2. *Ministrant*   ”

Under the *Constituent* I would place that usual category of governmental function, *the protection of life, liberty, and property*, together with all other functions that are *necessary to the civic organization of society*,—functions which are *not optional* with governments, even in the eyes of strictest *laissez faire*,—which are indeed the very bonds of society.

Under the *Ministrant*, I would range those other functions (such as education and the care, say, of forests) which are undertaken, not by way of *governing*, but by way of advancing the general interests of society,—functions which *are* optional, being necessary only according to standards of *convenience* or *expediency*, and not according to standards of *existence*, which assist without constituting social organization.

Note: **The objective, practical nature of this distinction.**

I. Constituent:

(1) The keeping of order and providing for the protection of persons and property from violence and robbery.

(2) The fixing of the legal relations between man and wife and between parents and children.

(3) The regulation of the holding, transmission, & interchange of property, and the determination of its liabilities for debt or for crime.

(4) The determination of contract rights between individuals.

(5) The definition and punishment of crime.

(6) The administration of Justice in civil causes.

(7) The determination of the political duties, privileges, and relations of citizens.

(8) Dealings with foreign powers, the preservation of the state from external danger or encroachment.

These will all be recognized as functions which are obnoxious not even to Mr. Spencer, and which of course persist under all forms of government.

II. *Ministrant.*

It is hardly possible to give a complete list of those functions which I have called Ministrant: the following general classification will suffice, however, for the purposes of the present discussion.

(1) The regulation of Trade and Industry.

Under this head I would include the coining of money and the establishment of standard weights and measures; laws against [']forestalling and engrossing' &c.; as well as the great matters of tariffs, navigation laws, and the like.

(2) The regulation of Labour.

(3) The maintenance of thoroughfares, including state management of railways, and that great group of

undertakings which we embrace within the term 'Internal Improvements' or 'The Development of the Country.'

(4) and very similar in principle, The maintenance of postal and telegraph systems.

(5) The manufacture and distribution of Gas.

(6) Sanitation.

(7) Education.

(8) Care of the Poor and Incapable.

(9) Care and cultivation of forests, and like matters, such as the stocking of rivers with fish.

(10) Sumptuary laws (prohibition, &c.)

There may be room for qu. as to whether some of these functions which I have classed as *Ministrant* might not quite as properly have been considered *Constituent*; but I must here simply act upon my own conclusions without rearguing them, acknowledging by the way that the line of demarcation is not always clear.

It is hardly necessary to prove that these are all actual functions of government,—our discussion must turn, rather, on the diversities and likenesses observable in the practice of them.

As regards the *Constituent* functions which I have enumerated, diversities of practice are, among *modern govts*, I take it, few and unessential.

Very marked differences in the manner and extent of their exercise exist, however, as between ancient and modern govts.— differences which are the more important because they have borne as their fruits widely divergent differences of conception as to *the nature of the State*.

Take, for example, *the State's relation to property*, in which the divergencies between ancient and modern political practice are, (among the functions now under consideration) perhaps most emphasized.

The modern state casts safeguards about property, prescribes the titles by which it shall be held and the forms for all contracts which affect it, and also very materially limits freedom of disposition on the part of owners. In brief, it regulates property rights by general law.

The ancient state went very much further. It reserved, where it did not exercise, the right to *administer*, as itself ultimate *proprietor*, the estates of its citizens. It did not stop at mere general regulation, meant to serve the convenience of the individual:

it regarded the individual as having no rights independent of the State's parental will.

This was true in gen of all ancient states[.] What I would emphasize is the diversity of practice wh., nevertheless, existed underneath this common idea.

Sparta, consistent, logical Sparta, may serve as our base and standard of observation, the type of exaggerated state functions. [It] furnishes the most noteworthy example of this antique conception of the relations of govt. to property. In the earlier periods of her history at least, besides being censor, pedagogue, drill-sergeant, and house-keeper to her citizens, she was also their *landlord*. There was a distinct reminiscence in her practice of the time when the family was the only state and the only owner of property. She was regarded as the original proprietor of all the land of Laconia, and individual tenure was looked upon as rather of the nature of a *usufruct* held of the State and at the State's pleasure than as resting upon a complete and indefeasible private title.* The Spartans had come into Laconia as conquerers, and the land had been first of all booty; but it was booty of which the Spartan host as a whole,—as a State,—had had the dividing, and it had been the purpose of the early legislation to make the division of the land among the Spartan families as equal as possible. Nor did the State resign its right of disposition in making this first distribution. It remained its primary care to keep its citizens, the favoured *Spartiatae*, upon an equal footing of fortune, to the end that they might all alike be rich in leisure, and so the better able to live entirely for the service of the State, which was honourable, and to avoid engaging in a pursuit of wealth which was dishonourable, since it both withdrew them from their bounden political duties and robbed them of social consideration. The State, accordingly, undertook to administer the wealth of the country for the benefit of its citizens. When grave inequalities manifested themselves in the distribution of estates, it did not hesitate to resume its proprietary rights and effect a reapportionment: no one dreaming, the while, of calling its action confiscation. It took various means for accomplishing its ends. It compelled rich heiresses to marry men without patrimony; and it grafted the poor citizen upon a good estate by means of prescribed adoption. No family was suffered to swell its numbers by adoption without express state sanction; no heiress was allowed to throw herself away on a rich youth; and

* There were special reasons for sustaining such a system. [WW's note]

no landed estate could be alienated either by sale or testament from the family to which the State had assigned it unless explicit legislative leave were given. In brief, in respect of his property, the citizen was both a ward and a tenant of the State.

Through its control of the land, the Spartan State maintained also a semi-ownership of the enslaved population of the country, the Helots. These men, who outnumbered eight or ten fold the *Spartiatae*, their masters, were bound, not to individuals, but to the land: they were slaves of the soil. They could not change service save as inseparable appendages of the estates upon which they served, and they had themselves something of the inviolability of the property to which they were attached. They, together with the land, in a sense belonged to the State. They looked to it for every measure which affected their condition either for better or for worse: for emancipation in reward of such services as they were on rare occasions enabled to render their masters in war, or for new restrictions laid upon them in punishment for turbulence or threatening discontent. The system of secret espionage, too, to which they were subjected, in consequence of the disquieting dreams of insurgent massacre by which their numbers and their distressed condition caused their masters' sleep to be broken, was a branch of the public service: the spies were commissioned by the State, which thus controlled by an absolute authority both the land and its cultivators.

As the Spartan state decayed this whole system was sapped: estates became grossly unequal—as did also political privileges even among the favored *Spartiatae*. But these changes were due to the decadence of Spartan power, and to the degeneration of her political fibre in days of waning fortune, not to any conscious or deliberate surrender by the State of her prerogative as owner guardian and trustee. She had grown old and lax simply; she had not changed her mind.

When we turn to Athens we experience a marked change in the political atmosphere, tho' hardly any change in theory[.] Here men breathe more freely and enjoy the fruits of their labour,—where labour is without reproach,—with less restraint. Even in Athens, however, there remain distinct traces of the family duties of the State. She too, like Sparta, felt bound to dispose properly of eligible heiresses. In order that family properties might not be dispersed, an heiress was offered by the law to her nearest male relative; and even after she was married the law still acted as the superintendent of her fortune, commanding its disposition among her offspring, to the exclusion of her husband. Nor was the parental power of the State confined to the case of heiresses. It did not hesitate to punish with heavy forfeitures of right (*atimia*) those who squandered their property in dissolute living, and even those who, through idleness or vice, would not find means of honourable support. There was as little limit in Athens as in Sparta to the theoretical prerogatives of the State; the freedom of the citizen was a freedom of indulgence rather than of right: he was free because the State refrained,— as a privileged child, not as a sovereign under Rousseau's Law of Nature.

When we shift our view to Rome, we do not find a simple city omnipotence like that of Greece, in which all private rights are sunk. The primal constituents of the city yet abide in shapes something like their original: Roman society consists of a series of interdependent links, the family, the gens, the city; the aggregate, not the fusion, of these makes up what we should call the State: but the State so made up was omnipotent thr. one or other of its organs over the individual. Property was not private in the sense of being individual; it vested in the family, which was, in this as in other respects, an organ of the State. Property had not become state property, because it had remained the undivided property of the family. The father, as a ruler in the immemorial hierarchy of the government, was all-powerful trustee of family estates. Individual ownership there was none.

Early (not imperial) Rome is meant, of course.

We with some justice felicitate ourselves that to this omnipotence of the ancient State in its relations to property the practice of our own govts. offers the most pronounced contrasts; but the point of greatest interest for us in the present connection is this, that these contrasts are contrasts *of policy, not of power.* To what lengths it will go in regulating property rights is for each govt. a qu. of *principle*, which it must put to its own conscience, and which, if it be wise, it will debate in the light of political history: but every govt. must regulate property in one way or another. If the ancient state was regarded as the ultimate owner, the modern State is regarded as the ultimate heir of all estates. Failing other claimants property *escheats* to the State. If the modern state does not assume, like the ancient, to administer their property upon occasion for competent adults, it does administer their property upon occasion for lunatics and minors. The ancient state controlled slaves and slavery; the modern state has been quite as absolute: it has abolished slaves and slavery. The modern state, no less than the ancient, set rules and limitations for inheritance and bequest. Most of its more extreme and hurtful interferences with rights of private ownership govt. has abandoned, one may suspect, rather because of difficulties of administration than because of difficulties of conscience. It is of the nature of the state to regulate property rights; it is of the policy of the state to regulate them *more* or *less*. Administrators must regard this as one of the constituent functions of political society and must give close heed to the ways of its exercise.

Similar conclusions may be drawn from a consideration of the contrasts which exist in the field of that other constituent function which concerns the determination of political rights,—the contrasts between the *status* of the citizen in the modern state and the *status* of the citizen in the ancient state. Here also the contrast, as between state and state, is not one of power, but one of principle and of habit rather.

Modern states have often limited as narrowly as did the ancient the enjoyment of those political privileges which we group under the word *Franchise*. They too, as well as the ancient States, have admitted slavery into their systems; they too have commanded their subjects without moderation and fleeced them without compunction. But, for all they have been so omnipotent, and, when they chose, so tyrannical, they have seldom insisted upon so complete and unreserved a service of the State by the citizen as was habitual to the political practice of both the Greek and the Roman worlds. The Greek and the Roman belonged each to his State in a quite absolute sense. He was his own in nothing as against the claims of his city upon him: he freely acknowledged all his privileges to be but concessions from his mother, the commonwealth. Those privileges accrued to him through law, as do ours; but law was to him simply the will of the organic community, never, as we know it in our constitutions, a restraint upon the will of the organic community. He knew no principles of liberty save only those which custom had built up: which inhered, not in the nature of things, nor in abstract individuality, but in the history of affairs, in concrete practice. His principles were all precedents.

Such examples of the differences existing between ancient and modern political habit as regards this first group of functions, which I have called *constituent*, suffice to give point to the only conclusion which I am interested in drawing at this stage of our discussion

That conclusion is not, that the restraints which modern states put upon themselves in exercising these essential, constituent functions are of little consequence: they are of the greatest consequence and have given rise to many important changes in our conceptions as to the proper nature of the State.

My conclusion is, that it is changes of political habit merely (changes due to historical causes) which have altered political conceptions: not changed political conceptions that have altered political habit. These (constituent) functions owe the extent of their exercise to historical circumstance, not to political philosophy,—above all, not to any change in the *essential* nature of the State. With altered times there would be change in their use; and with change in their use would come corresponding ideas as to the nature of the state. These are indeed *constituent* functions: what the state *does*, that it *is*.

In this field of our inquiry differences of practice are grounded in differences of policy with reference to matters upon which action of some sort by the state is absolutely necessary for the existence of political society.

WWT and WWhw MS. with a few WWsh additions (WP, DLC).

[c. Feb. 18, 1888]

Lecture II.

The Functions of Government.

We last time concluded a brief examination of the practice of govts. in the exercise of their *constituent* functions: we now turn to a somewhat more extended consideration of the practice of govts. in the exercise of what I have called their *ministrant* functions.

When we pass from the *constituent*, or so to say genetic, functions of government to the *ministrant* or optional we evidently pass no conspicuous landmarks: the boundary line is not blazed broad and straight: it must be hard at some points to be sure just where it runs. For even among these ministrant functions there are some which everybody recognizes as habitual with most governments,—and the more readily any function is recognized as habitual the more liable shall we be to regard it as an essential and inseparable attribute of government, instead of, what it may more truly be, only a means of serving social convenience. Generally, however, I think that we may be tolerably sure of the distinction.

The regulation of *Trade* and *Commerce* may well enough be put foremost among the functions habitual to government, and whose proper placing in our classification may therefore be made matter of doubt. Have not all governments habitually regulated trade and commerce? Yes, unquestionably; and yet only in the earliest times was that regulation necessary to the existence of government. In the most remote periods of which history has kept any recollection the regulation of trade and commerce seems to have been indispensable to separate political being; the only way in which communities could preserve an independent existence and work out an individual development was to draw apart to an absolutely separate existence. Commerce meant contact, contact meant contamination: the only way to develop character and achieve cohesion was to avoid intercourse. Trade and commerce were therefore forbidden, and a national idea cultivated more absolute and jealous than any modern nationalist (except perhaps Henry C. Cary) cd. well conceive. This was, however, only in the earliest formative periods. The ancient classical states had of course already gotten far beyond the stage at which it had been necessary to cultivate character in isolation: with the Greeks freedom to trade had been freedom to develop; and to the Romans one of Tiber's attractions had been its suitable situation and easy use as an artery of commerce. The Greek and Roman regulated trade and commerce, indeed, but rather for the modern purpose of securing advantage to himself as against competitors than with any conscious jealousy as to its possible effects upon his own individuality. It was still more distinctly his purpose to minister to the fiscal needs of the State, and to provide for the assured sustenance of her citizens. Athens, for instance kept her hand constantly on the corn-trade by provisions which forbade any citizen or resident of Athens to take part in any enterprize for carrying corn to any market but the Athenian; and in times of scarcity or distress corn was dispensed from public graneries either gratuitously or at less than the market price.

The *Roman* corn-laws are famous, playing a prominent part, as they do, in the politics of the troublous times when the Republic was giving way under chronic revolution. But even before politicians began to bid for the favour of the populace by largesses of corn, it had been part of Roman police administration to take care that the city market should be steadily and plentifully supplied with good grain at reasonable prices, and public authority had always used such means as suggested themselves for securing abundant harvests either in Sicily or in Asia Minor.

Sparta long clung to old prejudices about trade, as she clung to everything else that was old, and forbade her citizens any direct part in it. She of course permitted the unenfranchised portion of her populace to engage in it, however, and took care, like her contemporaries, that it should bring abundance of such fare as she deemed morally and physically wholesome to the tables of her households and her public messes.

In the *Middle Ages* the unreasonable exactions of feudal lords fettered commerce, except where the free cities could by militant combination keep open to it an unhindered passage to and fro between the great marts of North and South.

As the medieaval states emerge into modern times we find trade and commerce handled by statesmen as freely as ever, but according to the reasoned policy of the mercantilist thinkers, not with mere cupidity and caprice.

In the modern time there is regulation still, but no longer as a matter of course quite,—rather as a matter of real or supposed convenience, with a thought, in the background at least, that all states might abandon regulative measures, as some have done, and still bring no revolution upon the world of politics. In brief, if the habit of regulating such affairs of enterprise once had firm hold upon all governments, its grasp has now been much relaxed. It is, however old it may be, a habit which may be discarded without doing any violence to the essential constitution of government,—in other words, it is optional, or, as we have agreed to say, *ministrant*, not *constituent*; and it has passed through every stage of practice, from the constituent through the paternal to the merely convenient.

Take now the second among the Ministrant functions, viz., the regulation of *Labour*. This is of course a topic which just now holds the eyes of the world: we turn to it with an interest vigilant to know everything that may be known about it[,] being conscious, as we are, that we stand at the very storm-centre of the universal debate as to the relations of the State to Labour

Is it a constituent or a ministrant question, within the meaning of our classification? Is the State concerned with it as a State or only by reason of considerations of mere social convenience? The relations of one occupation to another would seem to be the secrets of class; the connexion between master and workman must apparently affect very vitally many of the strictly constituent associations of society. Certainly all governments have regulated Labour. By Greek and Roman the labour of the handicrafts and of agriculture,—all manual toil, indeed,—was for the most part given to slaves to do: and of course law regulated the slave.

In the Middle Ages the labour which was not agricultural and held in slavery to feudal masters was in the cities, where it was rigidly ordered by the complex rules of the guild system,—as was trade also, and almost all other like forms of making a livelihood. Where, as in England, labour in part escaped from the hard service of feudal tenure, the State stepped in with its persistent 'statutes of labourers' and tied the workman to one habitation and to one rate of wages. 'The rustic must stay where he is and receive only so much,' was its command.

Apparently, however, all past regulation of labour was but timid and elementary as compared with the labour legislation about to be tried by the governments of our own day. The birth and development of the modern industrial world has changed every aspect of the matter: and this fact it is which reveals the true character of the part which the State plays in the case. The rule would seem to be this, that In proportion as the world's industries grow must the State advance its efforts to assist the industrious to advantageous relations with each other, not that they may keep the peace among themselves so much as that they may none of them unnecessarily starve and none be trodden to death. In other words, it is the part of the State to assist rather than to govern in this case. The State might live, though the weak should perish. Competition will grind the thriftless and the yielding, not those who survive and rule: assistance by the government of those who need assistance is a thing of grace merely, and not of the law. Formerly perhaps the State did deal with labour as with a tool of political administration; but now it seeks to regulate it with the single view of assisting society to steady and healthy ways of daily business. It is significant in this connexion that the tendency to regulate labour rigourously and minutely is as strong in England, where the State is considered the agent of the citizen, as it was in Athens where the citizen was deemed the child and tool of the State, and where the workman was a slave. The drift of policy is everywhere towards a wider and stricter watchfulness of the State over the relations of master and workman, and over even the health and comfort and moral well-being of the wage-worker. Even when restrictions are withdrawn from the interchange of commodities they are multiplied with reference to the interchange of personal services; and governments now interest themselves to see that those who render certain sorts of personal services shall have healthful dwellings and an unburdened youth, limited hours of work and holidays now and again in which to shake off the dust of toil from mind and body. Factory laws, ten-hour laws, infant and female labour laws, all restrictive in a more or less extensive way of contracts for work, or prescriptive of the conditions under which work is to be done, are nowadays accepted as normal acts of legislation, alike in republics and in monarchies; and, if we are to credit the manifest signs of the times, their number is to grow.

This function of government is so *ministrant* that it has been stigmatised as socialistic. Factory laws are not made because the government owns factories and employs men and women in them, but because some of its citizens who are engaged in private business own factories and employ men and women in them, and because these citizens are so eager in their pursuit of private gain that, were there no hindering law, they would employ tender children and frail women in their workshops to the destruction of youth and health. To these government feels obliged to say, 'Take care; you may employ men for such a length of time each day, and women for a reasonable term in occupations which do not too greatly tax their strength; but children below a certain age not at all,—and all in moderation.' In the same spirit governments undertake to inspect mines and try to carry out artisans' dwellings acts and workmen's insurance acts: one and all measures of guardianship rather than of government.

Not essentially different in principle are those measures, so rapidly increasing, by which government is undertaking to regulate the business of *corporations*. In all such cases government is leaving the duties demanded for mere political self-preservation and is undertaking those which are desired for the ease and effectiveness and moderation of private enterprise. It is adding to the maintenance of the State and of just political principle the energising of society and the promotion of just social relations within the workshop and the counting-house.

The maintenance of Thoroughfares may be said to have begun with permanent empire, i.e. to say, for Europe, with the Romans. For the Romans, however, it was a matter first of moving armies, only secondarily a means of serving commerce; whereas with us the highway is above all things else an artery of trade, and armies use it only when commerce stands still at the sound of drum and trumpet. The building of roads may therefore be said to have begun by being a constituent function and to have ended by becoming a ministrant function. But the same is not true of other public works, of the Roman acqueducts and theatres and baths, and of modern 'internal improvements.' They, as much as the Roman tax on old bachelors, are parts, not of a scheme of government, but of plans for the advancement of other social aims,—for the administration of society. Because in her conception the community as a whole was the only individual, Rome thrust out as of course her magnificent roads to every quarter of her vast territory, considered no distances too great to be traversed by her towering acqueducts, deemed it her duty to clear river courses and facilitate by every means both her commerce and her arms. And the modern State, although holding a deeply modified conception of the relations of government to society, still follows no very different practice; and if in many instances the great iron highways are turned over to private management it is oftener for reasons of of [sic] convenience than for reasons of conscience.

Similar considerations of course apply in the case of that modern instrumentality, the *pub-letter-post*, in the case of the still more modern manufacture of *gas*, and in the case of the most modern *telegraph*. We cannot consider the management of any one of these necessarily an affair of government, unless, like the ancients, we make no distinction between *government* and *society*. Convenience and economy command the control of such instrumentalities by government; but political principle is silent. These are among the ancillary, not among the natural and essential, functions of government. Still, whatever be the abstract principle underlying such cases, the modern, no less than the ancient, government unhesitatingly takes a hand in administering the conveniences of society.

Not essentially different are the facts as to the other ministrant functions which I have enumerated.

Modern governments, like the Roman government, maintain *sanitation* by police inspection of baths, taverns, and houses of ill-fame; by drainage, by hospital relief, by water supply, by quarantine, and by a score of other means.

In *education*, though *we** have compulsory army service, we have nothing so thorough as the Spartan discipline;—nor had Sparta's contemporaries, so far as we know. They, like ourselves, were without need for such a system. For Sparta her discipline was an absolute necessity: for the Spartans were a handful of hated conquerors in the midst of a multitude of hating slaves. There was sore need that the chief energies of the State should be bent to the production of shapely, sturdy women and lithe, laconic men, in whose education only rude music, only the use of simple stringed instruments and a taste for the songs of war, softened the steady drill of sense and sinew. In Athens, on the

* View not confined to U.S. [WW's note]

other hand, the relations of man to man were legal only and peaceable, not forcible and hostile. She contented herself therefore with the education of the theatre, the athletic contest, the pnyx, and the market place. She was no nearer than is the modern State to the Spartan practice.

Still the idea held in view in Athens was as little like the modern idea of education as was the *principle* which obtained in the Spartan discipline. In both Greek cities the citizen was educated altogether for the State, not at all for himself, so far as the State's participation in the matter was concerned. The Spartan education was simply a wholesale training of public servants.

In the modern State, on the contrary, the citizen is educated for himself, that he may himself command and develop his native faculties and aptitudes: the advantage which will assuredly accrue to the State as a result of the elevation of its citizens to the point at which they can view the horizons of education is, though one of the great motives for the establishment of public education, still an affair in the background, an indirect result which the State leaves it to the civic virtue of the individual to make real. In other words, education when taken in hand by the ancient governments, was part of the general administration of the State; with us it is the assistance which the State renders to the life of the individual.

In *Sumptuary* laws ancient States far outran modern practice. In Athens the Senate of the Areopagos was, in the early days at least, an almost omnipotent inquisitor into the private morals of the citizen, and it was clearly recognized that, outside the sacred and inviolable limits of the sanctuary of family worship, the State might command and discipline as it chose. Heavy forfeitures of right (*atimia*), for instance, were visited upon such offences against private good morals as a dereliction of duty toward parents

In Rome any act which could be said to come within the vague category of a "violation of order"—and order in Rome included moral order,—brought the man or woman who committed it within reach of magisterial fines. The public officer assumed not only to punish witchcraft and like unblessed practices, but also to discipline for immoralities of private conduct. The Censor could visit men guilty of outrageous acts with partial or entire disfranchisement; and early republican simplicity made it imprudent to expose to his eye too much silver plate.

Modern States have of course foregone all such attempts to make citizens virtuous and frugal by law; but even we have our prohibition enactments; and we have had our fines for swearing.

We have now taken some sort of survey of the wide field of governmental action: we have been on the lookout for *diversities of practice* as between State and State; but we have found these diversities, though numerous, hardly fundamental. Apparently it is safe to say with regard to the functions of government taken as a whole that, even as between ancient and modern States, uniformities of practice vastly outnumber diversities of practice.

But of the uniformities presently: let us dispose first of the diversities, examining them for their thought.

B.   Diversities of Conception:

Even though the practice of governments from age to age does not emphasize contrasts between governments of the ancient omnipotent and governments of the modern constitutional type, we are sure that wide contrasts of theory do separate the one from the other.

In no ancient polity was there any conception of individual rights as contrasted with those of the State. The citizen was merged in the political body to which he belonged; and it was everywhere the dominant thought that the citizen lived first of all for the State, only secondarily and subordinately for himself. Public duty was all and in all to every man who sought to abide by the traditions of his city. This thought is strikingly visible in the writings of Plato and Aristotle, not only in what they say, but also and even more in what they do not say. The ideal Republic of which Plato dreams is to prescribe the whole life of its citizens; but there is no suggestion that it is to be set up under cover of any new conception as to what the State may legitimately do; it is only to make novel experiments in legislation under the *old* conception. Aristotle's objection to the utopian projects of his master is not that they would be socialistic (as we should say), but merely that they would be unwise. He does not fear that in such a Republic the public power would prove to have been exalted too high; but, speaking to the policy of the thing, he foresees that the citizens would be poor and unhappy. The State may do what it will; but let it be wise in what it does. There is no one among the Greeks to deny that it is the duty of the State to make its citizens happy and prosperous: nay, to *legislate* them happy, if legislation may create fair skies and kind fortune: the only serious quarrel is as to what laws are to be tried to this end.

In Rome principles were equally extreme, tho' in some respects differently cast. That superior sense of law which made the

Romans singular among the nations of antiquity showed itself in respect of the functions of government in a more distinct division between public and private rights than obtained in the polity of the Greek cities. An examination of the conception of the State held in Rome reveals the singular framework of her society. The Roman family did not suffer that complete absorption into the City which so early eclipsed the Greek family. Private rights were not individual rights, but family rights: and family rights did not so much curtail as supplement the powers of the community. The family was an indestructible *organ* of the State. The father of a family or the head of a gens was in a sense a member of the official hierarchy of the City,—a lesser king, as the king—or his counterpart, the consul—was a greater father: there was no distinction of principle between the power of king or consul and the power of a father; it was a mere difference of sphere, a division of functions. A son was, for instance, in some things exempt from the authority of the City only because he was in those things still subject, because his father still lived, to the dominion of that original State, the family. There was not in Rome that separation of the son from the family at majority which characterized the Greek polity, as it now characterizes our own. The father continued to be a ruler, an hereditary State officer, within the original sphere of the family life: the large sphere of individual privilege and property.

This essential unity of State and Family furnishes us with the theoretic measure of state functions in Rome. The Roman burgess was subordinated, not to the public *authority* exactly, but rather to the *public order*, to *the conservative integrity of the community*. He was subject to a law which embodied the steady unbroken habit of the State-family. He was not dominated, but merged

From Mommsen:

"The nations of Italy did not merge into that of Rome more completely than the single Roman burgess merged in the Roman community" (I:578, 579).

Speaking of the extraordinary integrity of republican Rome, which sank the individual in the whole, he calls the period between the last of the kings and the first of the Emperors a "five-hundred years' interregnum of extraordinary deeds and ordinary men" (I:580)

Contrasting Greece and Rome, "When the two great nations, both arrived at the height of their development, began to mingle in hostile or in friendly contact, their antagonism of character was at the same time prominently and fully brought out,—the total want of indiv[id]uality in the Italian and especially in the Roman character, as contrasted with the boundless variety, lineal, local, and personal, of Hellenism" (I:578)

"In the Roman commonwealth there was no special dependence on any one man, either on soldier or on general, and under the rigid discipline of its moral police all the idiosyncrasies of human character were extinguished. Rome reached a greatness such as no other State of antiquity attained; but she dearly purchased her greatness at the sacrifice of the graceful variety, of the easy abandon and of the inward freedom of Hellenic life" (I:581).

The range of state power in ancient times, as a range broken only by limits of habit and convenience, is well illustrated in the elastic functions of the Roman Senate. With an unbroken life which kept it conscious of every tradition and familiar with every precedent, with established standards of tested experience and cautious expediency, it was able to direct the movements of the compact society at whose summit it sat as the brain and its consciousness direct the movements of the human body; and it is evident from the freedom of its discussions and the frequency of its action upon interests of every kind, whether of public or of private import, that the Roman State, in its several branches of family, tribe, and city, was one, and that its prerogatives were limited by nothing save religious observance and fixed habit. Of that individual liberty which we cherish it knew nothing.

As little was there in Greek politics any seed of the thought which would limit the sphere of administration by principles of inalienable individual rights. Both in Greek and in Roman conception government was as old as society,—was, indeed, nothing less than the express image and embodiment of society. In government society lived and moved and had its being. Society and government were *one*, in some such sense as the spirit and body of man are one: it was through government, as through mouth and eyes and limbs, that society expressed its life. Society's prejudices, habits, superstitions did indeed command the actions of government; but only because society and government were one and the same, not because they were distinct and the one subordinate to the other. In plain terms, then, the functions of government had no limits of principle, but only certain limits of wont and convenience, and the object of administration was nothing less than to help society on to all its ends: to speed and facilitate all social undertakings. So far as full citizens of the State were concerned, Greek and Roman alike was what we should call a *socialist*; though he was too much in the world and had too keen an appreciation of experience, too keen a sense of the sane and the possible, to attempt the Utopias of which the modern socialist dreams, and with which the ancient citizen's own writers sometimes amused him. He bounded his politics by common sense, and so dispensed with the 'rights of man.'

Individual rights, after having been first heralded in the religious world by the great voice of Christianity, broke into the ancient political world in the person of the Teuton. But the new politics which the invader brought with him was not destined to establish at once democratic equality: that was a work reserved for the transformations of the modern world. Meantime, during the Middle Ages, government, as we conceive government, may be said to have suffered eclipse. In the feudal system the constituent elements of govt. fell away from each other: society was drawn back to something like its original family groups; conceptions of rule narrowed themselves to small territorial connexions. Men became sovereigns in their own right because they owned land in their own right. There was no longer any conception of nations or societies as wholes: union there was none,—but only interdependence; allegiance bowed, not to law or to fatherhood, but to ownership. The functions of government under such a system were simply the functions of proprietorship, of command and obedience: "I say unto one, Go, and he goeth; and to another, Come, and he cometh; and to my servant, Do this, and he doeth it." The public function of the baron was to keep peace among his liegemen, to see that their properties were enjoyed according to the custom of the manor, (if the manor had been suffered to acquire custom on any point,) and to exact fines of them for all privileges, whether of marriage, of coming of age, or of making a will. The baronial conscience, bred in cruel, hardening times, was the only standard of justice, the baronial power the only conclusive test of prerogative.

And this was between baron and vassal. Between baron and baron the only bond was a nominal common allegiance to a distant king, who was himself only a great baron. For the rest, there was no government, but only diplomacy and warfare. Government lived where it could and as it could, and was for the most part divided out piecemeal to a thousand petty holders. Feuds were the usual processes of justice.

The monarchy which grew out of the ruins of this disintegrate system concentrated authority without much changing its character. The old idea, born of family government, that government was but the active authority of society, the magistrate but society's organ, bound by society's immemorial laws, had passed utterly away, and government had become the personal possession of of [sic] one man. The ruler did not any longer belong to the State; the State belonged to him:—he was himself the State, as the rich man is his possessions. The Greek or Roman official was wielded by the community: not so the king who had swept together into his own lap the powers once broadcast in the feudal system: he wielded the community. Government breathed with his breath, and it was its function to please him.

The reaction from such conceptions, slow and for the most part orderly in England, sudden and violent, because long forcibly delayed, on the Continent, was of course natural and indeed inevitable. When it came it was radical; but it did not swing the political world back to its old ideas: it turned it aside, rather, to new. It became the object of the revolutionist and the democrat to live his own life: the ancient had had no thought but to live loyally the life of society. His virtues were not individual in their point of view, but social; whereas our virtues are individual in their motive, social only in some of their results.

In brief, the modern State has largely *de-socialized*. The modern idea is this: The the [sic] State no longer absorbs the individual, but only serves him: the State, as it appears in its organ, the Government, is the representative of the individual, and his representative only within the definite commission of constitutions; while for the rest each man makes his own social relations. 'The Individual for the State,' has been reversed and made 'The State for the Individual.'

Such are the diversities of *conception* separating modern from ancient politics. And yet we have not found, because we could not find that the diversities of *function* existing between the States of old and the States of to-day correspond with the change of conception which has passed through political thought: apparently the new ideas have not been able to translate themselves into altered functions, but only into somewhat *curtailed* functions: breeding rather a difference of degree than a difference of kind.

III.   Uniformities of practice and conception:

Our discussion has brought us to this conclusion, then, that there is no real uniformity of conception observable as between ancient and modern politics, but that there is a very full uniformity of *practice*. Under what new formulas, then, are we to combine the new-time conceptions of the modern State with its old-time practices? Even under the most liberal of our constitutions we still meet government in every field of social endeavour. Our modern life is so infinitely complex, indeed, that we may go great distances in any field of enterprise without once receiving either direct aid or direct check from government; but that is only because every field of enterprise is vastly big nowadays, not because government is not somewhere in it; and we know that the tendency is for governments to make themselves everywhere more and more conspicuously present.

Still we are conscious that we are by no means in the same case with Greek or Roman: the State is ours, not we the State's[.] Perhaps we may say that the matter stands thus: what has changed is not the activities of government, but only the morals and the conscience of government. Government may still be doing substantially the same things as of old; but an altered conception of its responsibilities deeply modifies *the way in which it does them.* Social convenience and advancement are still its ultimate standard of conduct, just as if it were itself still the omnipotent impersonation of society, the master of the individual: but it has adopted new ideas as to what constitutes social convenience and advancement. Its aim is now to aid the individual to the fullest and best realization of his individuality, instead of merely to the realization of his *sociality*: its plan is to create the best and fairest opportunities for the individual; and it has discovered that the way to do this is by no means *itself* to undertake the administration of the individual by old-time futile methods of guardianship.

This is indeed a great and profound change, and we shall find it commanding many parts of our discussions of Administration. It will furnish us with our touchstone of wisdom and expediency.

But our way shall, on the other hand, be not a little illuminated by the fact, plain enough now to the open-eyed, that the functions of government are still, when catalogued, found much the same both in number and magnitude that they always were. Government does not stop with the protection of life, liberty, and property, as some have supposed; it goes on to serve every convenience of society,—its sphere is limited only by its own wisdom, alike where republican and where absolutist principles prevail.

It is customary to speak of Administration as if it were merely the *business* side of government,—as if the organs of a government were to be tested by the same standards of propriety and efficiency by which we test the organs of a great commercial corporation. But it seems to me that, notwithstanding the very large and important element of truth which this view embodies, little but confusion of thought can result from its adoption as a guiding view. The state *is not a body corporate,—it is a body politic*: and rules of good business are not always rules of good politics. Between money-making and political liberty there are radical differences. The State in a large and increasing measure shapes our lives: and a body which shapes our lives must have many principles of organization necessarily unknown to a body which controls only a portion of our money. The State creates conditions for *all* our activities: the business corporation only gives direction to a part of our economic energies; it is absurd to apply the principles of economics merely to the tasks of politics. Business-*like* the administration of govt. may and should be— but it is not business. *It is organic social life.*

The way in which it occupies that sphere is our subject, the subject of *Administration.*

WWT and WWhw MS (WP, DLC); marginal headings omitted.

From E. W. Peterson and James R. Foree

Dear Sir: Tekamah, Burt Co., Neb. Feb 18th 1888

We can sell an odd forty acres of your land in Tp 22 R. 11 over there towards the river at $10.00 if that is still your figure. $100 cash, $100 in 1 yr. $100 2 yrs and $100 3 yrs. 8% or 9%, you to pay us the costomary commission 5% for selling. There is another party here whom we may get to make an offer on some of your land but he is not ready yet. Hoping to hear from you soon we are   Yours Truly   Peterson & Foree

ALS (WP, DLC).

From Charles T. Dickinson[1]

Dear Sir   Tekamah, Neb. Feby 20 1888

On Feby 11/88, Mr Hopewell wrote you in reference to some land in Sec 10-21-11[.] Since then we have had some inquiry about land in Sec 22-22-11. Parties would like to buy but we have no prices on this land. Would you please send us price & terms on the following, NE. of SE. & W2 of SE. 1/4 22-22-11[,] the NW of NE- and SE. of NW- of 27-22-11- and oblige.

Resp yrs—Hopewell & Dickinson

ALS (WP, DLC).

     1 Charles T. Dickinson, attorney at law, successor to Hopewell & Dickinson.

Notes for Two Classroom Lectures at the Johns Hopkins

[c. Feb. 24, 1888]

III.

Comparative View
No very sharp contrasts of function either
among unitary or among federal governments
as regards central administration.

1. *Accounting* and *Audit* systems:
    (*a*) *U. S.*: Auditors—Comptrollers—Secretarys—Register
        —Treasurer.
    (*β*) *England*: Comptroller and Auditor-General of the
        Exchequer, an officer independent of the Treasy, is cus-
        todian of the Revenues. Must satisfy himself of the
        passage of a Ways and Means Act covering the amount
        asked for for any purpose. "There must, moreover,
        be presented to him one or more royal orders authorizing
        the Treasury to apply the supplies granted to the Crown
        by the Ways & Means Act, in conformity to the parlia-
        mentary vote. . . . This done, he grants to the Treasury,
        on its application, a general credit on the Exchequer
        accounts at the Bank of England to the amount limited
        by the votes; and the Treasury, operating upon that
        credit, issues orders to the Bank to transfer money to
        the account of the Paymaster-General, by whom it is
        paid out, as required, to the different services.["] (Traill
        [*Central Government*], 43, *et seq.*)

So much for current disbursements: now for audit of past
expenses:

A special *Audit Department of the Civil Service*—part of the
permanent organization of the admin. "Examines the accts and
vouchers of the entire expenditure. Is supervised by a special
annual Committee of the Commons—constituted with a view to
the business capacity and experience of the members—wh. goes
very thoroughly over all the accts.

    (*γ*) *France*: Besides control and audit in the Depts., a special
        Chamber of Accounts, *acting as a Court*.
    (*δ*) *Prussia*: *Oberrechnungskammer* (Supreme Chamber of
        Accounts) whose members have the tenure and respon-
        sibility of judges: its president nominated by the
        Ministry of State: other members by president with
        countersignature of president of Ministry of State. Over-

sight and revision of accts. of all depts. of income and expenditure + oversight of the state debt and of acquisition and disposition of State property. Judicial guardian of the laws relating to revenue and disbursement.

(ϵ) Switzerland has not yet sufficiently differentiated legislative and executive functions, nor sufficiently developed the latter, to have a distinct system of audit such as exists in France and Prussia.

The contrast is: *Official* vs. *Judicial* Audit.

e.g. Old English Exchequer with its barons, its Pipe Rolls, &c. This system supplanted by *Audit Dept.*

2. *Administrative Integration:*

(a) Relations of Ministers to *head* of the Executive.
Our president and governors have colleagues.
France's president has only indirect power.
Same with England's sovereign—*formal* integration.
Germany, the Emperor *vice* the Chancellor is the real guiding head: the source and centre of authority.

(β) The Administration and the Ministers.
With us only "the Cabinet"—whatever its functions may be—(chiefly political, not administrative). In the States not even so much.
In *Prussia*, a *Staatsministerium* (instead of Stein's proposed Council) wh. is French Council of Ministers + French Council of State. Coördinated with this a (revived) *Council of State.*

(γ) The Administration and the Legislature
Administrative bearings of Relations bet. Executive and Legislation.

e.g. Appropriations—French Budget Committee—Our own appropriations Committees.

e.g. Erection and modification of Depts.—internal changes, &c.

e.g. Financial and commercial policy—admin. ques. generally.

U.S.: Isolation + irresponsibility $\therefore$, irresponsibility.*

Eng.: Leadership + responsibility.

France: Partial leadership + entire responsibility.

Prussia: Leadership without responsibility.

Switzerland: Do. [ditto]

Administrative results: ?

* Note: We have no central govt. in the U. S. (as dist. i.e. from local and forming integration of local)[.] We have either direct govt. (e.g. fed. P. O.) or mere boards (e.g. Labor Statistics)[.] Neither the fed. nor the state govts. furnish what, in other systems[,] is central govt. [WW's note]

In *England* a Cabinet of greater solidarity and more strictly *administrative* control (tho' a "Treasury minute" is required for any redivision of business among the Depts.[).] *No judicial body.*

In *France* a *Council* of Ministers (*administrative* oversight, distribution of business among Depts. &c) as well as a *Cabinet* of Ministers (*political* oversight)[.] Each Ministry, too, has its "Cabinet" (*Council* of heads of sub-depts)[.] Then there is the *Council of State*—the Supreme admin. court—and judicial decider of admin. *conflicts.*

> *Chalmers:* Such was once the case in Eng.
>
>> Complete centralization once universal in Europe[.] Eng. coming half way to meet the European govts., wh. are extending local self-govt. Eng. finding that laws will not admin. themselves *uniformly* throughout a number of local, detached units. That *police (order) finance, sanitation* need central *guidance,*—just as we have long known that *education* does.

This is the *tendency*: *Concentration,* if not *Centralization*: guidance if not control: This is the tendency wh. we must scrutinize and *appraise.*

This is the problem: *Re-integration*: system with flexibility; freedom with control; administrative cohesion without administrative tyranny. This is the problem to solve which we must address ourselves.

WWhw MS. with some WWsh (WP, DLC).

[c. Feb. 25, 1888]

IV.

Central and Local Government:—
General Questions and Principles.

We can best get at the general questions and principles of Administration by way of the distinction upon which I purpose hanging the scheme of my lectures: the distinction, namely, between 'central' and 'local' government.

It is noteworthy that that is *a quite modern conception,* that which distinguishes between 'central' and 'local' government, and the distinction my [may] be made to serve as in some sort a *guage of political development.*

> I. In *Greece and Rome all* government may be said to have been central,—or local, according to the period or the point of view taken. For the isolated Greek cities it was both in one. In Rome it was first both, then central: the establish-

ment of the Roman Empire gave rise to the distinction *in fact*, if not *in principle*,—though the government of the world was Roman; only certain narrow privileges of local autonomy remained.

The Roman process of government:

(a) Methods of the *republican city*.

(b) Methods of the *Empire*.

The Middle Ages saw central government destroyed, and all government made local:

Character and process of *Feudalism*.

Rise of *the free cities*.

Modern times have seen the *reintegration* of central and local government,—where it has not seen local government altogether swamped by central power. W.C. [wherein consider]:

i. *France*, typifying the reëstablishment of Roman principles in the principles of modern monarchy. The Roman idea was *Singleness, organic oneness* of state life—The Germanic idea, on the other hand, was, *vitality, independent vitality*, in loosely connected *parts*.

ii. *England*. Logical process from local development and privileges to personal ditto, and to central union.

[Rudolf] *Gneist* on the progress of England from organic complexity to individual atoms,—disintegration

iii. *Systems of the United States*.

Logical outcome of European (English) tendencies,—the progressive forces freed from the reactionary.

The emphatically local character of government in most parts of colonial America in the early days.

Generalization: Modern times have seen the reintegration of government restored, *as a prelude* to a *new differentiation*, set afoot after a less chaotic, anarchic fashion than that of the Middle Ages.

How shall the functions of government be divided?

They *have been* divided by *history*, by great processes of politics which moved quite regardless of this question.

Now, however, *they may be* divided by *art*,—at least by legislation. *We need*, therefore, *a principle of division*.

Advantages of effective central regulation: *Certainty, Uniformity, Despatch, Efficiency*.

Disadvantages: A *too great* uniformity, a *too absolute* despatch, an *inexorable* certainty and efficiency.

Suggested principles:

1. All *Law* must be *centrally given*, because legal *principles* must be *universal and uniform*; there need be centralized *administration* of those principles only through appeal

    Here, however, a careful distinction between *law-giving and ordinance-making* is vital and essential. The *latter* may be *local.* (By-laws) *Police?*

2. '*Knowledge* must be centralized; *power* may be localized' (*Mill*, &c.) 'Knowledge' includes *system* (?), *auditing*, &c.

    There should be easy resort to central authorities for all really needed assistance,—even, for instance, in detecting local maladministration, malfeasance, &c.

3. *System* is good, but *life* is better. Extent to which system may be carried without crushing out life(?)

    Local differences ought to be regarded (in old countries at any rate).

    "Life' = liberty;—and liberty is not possessed in every case of local self-government. E.G. Indian and Russian village communities (see *Chalmers*, "Local Government") But it may be the result of *more complex, artificial, self-conscious organization.*

WWT MS. (WP, DLC).

Charles McLean Andrews[1] to Elizabeth Williams Andrews[2]

My dear Mama,   [Baltimore] Feb 26. 88.

. . . I have added two more hours to my historical course and dropped one in English. The new lectures are on Administration by Woodrow Willson of Bryn Mawr, author of "Congressional Govt." and promise to be one of the best lecture courses of the season. They are to extend over three years of which I will be on hand for two. Willson is an original thinker and a clear lecturer and we feel we are growing under his instruction. . . .

Your loving Charlie.

ALS (C. M. Andrews Papers, CtY).

[1] Born Wethersfield, Conn., Feb. 22, 1863. A.B., Trinity College, 1884; Ph.D., the Johns Hopkins, 1889. Taught at Bryn Mawr College, 1889-1907, becoming Professor of History there in 1898. Professor of History, the Johns Hopkins, 1907-10. Farnam Professor of American History, Yale University, 1910-31. President, American Historical Association, 1925. A pre-eminent historian of the colonial period of American history. Died Sept. 9, 1943.

[2] Andrews' mother.

To Lucy Maynard Salmon

My dear Miss Salmon,   Bryn Mawr, Pa., 29th Feby., 1888

Just as your note of the 7th[1] came I was plunged into the stream of my work at the Hopkins, and getting the new stroke of the new swimming has absorbed my energies quite to the exclusion of all letter writing.

It was very kind of you to think of our library in connection with the extra set of John Adams: our little collection is, as you know, in a position to appreciate such favours; but in this one item at least you have overestimated our poverty. We have Adams's Works. It's Hamilton, among the old, standard worthies, whom we lack—because we want the new (Putmans) edition, which we cannot get. I notice that the *catalogue* price of Adams is $30.00.

The Vassar (history) letter in *"University"*[2] made my heart warm. Hurrah for the huge success! I am just as glad as I am *not* surprised!

Mrs. Wilson joins me in warmest regards.

Very sincerely Yrs.,   Woodrow Wilson

ALS (NPV).
  [1] It is missing.
  [2] R. C., "Vassar," *University*, 1 (Feb. 8, 1888), 92-93. This letter, dated Poughkeepsie, New York, February 4, 1888, described the course work of the History Department at Vassar College.

From Francis Amasa Walker

Dear Prof Wilson   Boston, March 1 1888

Many thanks for your letter, just rec'd.

I am much disposed to think that the gentleman I have in view is the best man I could name for the place: and, on the other hand that the place wld be excellently suited to his tastes & plans. I will communicate confidentially with his friends. He is presently in Europe, preparing to return this summer.

His name is Williston Walker—he graduated from Amherst; studied in the Theological Seminary at Hartford, married the daughter of Prof Mather[1] of Amherst; and is now taking his Ph.D. degree in Germany.[2] His father is the Revd. Dr George L. Walker, of Hartford. Dont be alarmed by the apparent excess of theological relatives—the young man is sensible, liberal, judicious, humane and manly. He is a gentleman of some private means.

Yours truly,   Francis A. Walker

ALS (WP, DLC) with WWhw notation on env.: "Ans. 3/19/88" and WWhw
research notes concerning city government.
¹ Richard Henry Mather.
² At the University of Leipzig, from which he received the Ph.D. in 1888.

To Daniel Coit Gilman

Dear Mr. Gilman,   Balto. Mch. 2, '88.
Your note of yesterday was brought me from the Post Office
just as I was boarding my train at Bryn Mawr. I am extremely
sorry to be unable to accept your kind invitation, but I promised
last week to meet some friends at dinner this evening at Mr. T. K.
Worthington's¹ with whom I am staying.
With sincere regrets,
Very truly Yours,   Woodrow Wilson

ALS (D. C. Gilman Papers, MdBJ).
¹ Thomas K. Worthington, Wilson's former fellow-student at the Hopkins.

Notes for a Public Lecture at the Johns Hopkins

[March 2, 1888]
Lecture I: *Systems of Municipal Organization.*

It is too late in this age of cities to dwell upon the importance
of the subject of municipal organization. Its looms so big in
every quarter that there are not a few thoughtful reforming
people among us who regard it as the only subject worthy of
present consideration. It almost seems as if city government,
instead of national government, were to be the field of experiment and revolution for the future.

I shall not tarry to tell you, ∴, why the subject of municipal
organization is important. I shall, instead, endeavour to point
out, (1) in the first place, the difference between its old importance and its new importance; (2) in the second place, the difference between city government in the past and city government
in the present; and, (3) in the third place the various systems of
city organization now in vogue, hoping to have a few moments
left, just before the end of the hour, to make a few brief comments upon the wide survey we shall by that time have taken. It
is not given to any one to make thorough analysis of so great a
topic in 60 minutes; but we may hope even in that brief time
to get at least a framework for thought and study.

1. First, then, for the contrast between the old-time and the
present importance of the subject of municipal organization. No
topic in politics may be made fit for thorough digestion without

a liberal infusion of *History*: and the topic we have now in hand is specially in need of such an infusion,—is, indeed, utterly indigestible without it.

In ancient times the problems of city government had no *separate* place as a minor class of the problems of government in general. Their place, on the contrary was at the centre of the topics of politics[.] The City and the State were one and the same thing, and city government was the whole of government. You remember that Athens was Attica; that Sparta was Laconia; that 'Corinth' and 'Thebes' were the names of cities playing the rôle of states; that Greek colonies were independent town-sovereignties for the rule of which the mother cities neither had nor could imagine any machinery; that Rome stood in the midst of her dependencies (until imperial times) as the whole state, the only state; that Roman citizenship away from Rome herself meant protection against oppression merely and commanded privileges of political action only in the assemblies of the city herself; that the only way Rome could at first devise for ruling her provinces was to spread out over them the tentacles of her city constitution, making her consuls pro-consuls, her praetors pro-praetors, continuing her town officers as provincial officers. You remember that, when this city constitution snapped asunder under the too great strain of such practices, it was not possible to substitute any vital, any self-sustaining, civic organization, but that the world had to be held together by the hand of soldiers, ruled and compacted by the methods of soldiers. The most striking part of the result may be seen [in] Italy. Rome had linked Italy together, as she conquered it, by means of a net work of roads whose *nucleae* were towns,—some conquered from free races and made dependent, others established as military colonies. The stages of her government had been marked, not by the progressive degrees by which Italy was brought into connexions of national organization with the dominant city, (Rome never knew any national organization) by [but] by the several degrees of dependence or independence enjoyed by the loosely articulated links of this town system. The rule was, not only city govt. at the centre but also city govt. throughout the Roman possessions. Hence what followed and gave character to the politics of the Middle Ages in Italy. When Roman dominion fell apart in Italy, it fell apart into towns. And not in Italy only, but also up the Rhone, along the Rhine—wherever Rome had built her permanent camps, placed her colonies, or developed old settlements,—wherever she had given her characteristic touch. Till the Teutons came the history of govt. may be said to have been the history of towns.

The influences which were first to surround the cities, so to say, with a political system spread abroad and rural, and then to subordinate cities to nations, came from beyond the Rhine. Here again I must merely remind you of what ensued: of what we call the *feudalization* of Europe. Round about the municipalities, which still retained their Roman organization little altered, the Teuton established his territorial sovereignty: that system by virtue of which a man was ruler because he was an owner of wide estates. Towns were dominated by the baronage, by castles and men-at-arms set over against them; and new towns gathered, as skirts, about the rural strongholds of the lords of the soil. In France the next step was the gathering of the scattered elements of the feudal sovereignty in the person of a king: and he, as supreme overlord, both possessed and ruled the State—ruled it *because* he possessed it. And thus was the first great *nation* of Europe created. Germany and Italy retained the disintegrate organization of feudalism: Spain struggled against foreign foes and internal divisions. But everywhere new soil had been made for government. It had spread wider than the municipalities and it no longer depended upon them to serve as its pillars. The cities still bribed or forced neighbour lords to let them live their own lives; but they one after another found themselves being crushed between the greater masses of feudal might on either side of them. The times were fast ripening when cities would be merely local features instead of heart-centres of government.

You have somewhat the same history, in small, in our New England colonies. There are towns of Mass., of Ct., and of Rhode Island which antedate the wider political organization of those states as truly as Cologne antedates France and Hamburg Germany. The first colonies there were towns; the first towns were states; but now Plymouth is a mere piece of Mass., Providence and Portsmouth are *in* R. I., New Haven is a town of Ct. These are all towns of the olden time for which questions of municipal organization were not distinguishable from questions of state organization. Very different in origin are the towns of the modern time: the *Manchesters* and *Birminghams*, the *Chicagos* and *Minneapolises*. They were never states: they are merely places where an industrial, trading population has come to a head: they are subsequent, not antecedent, to the nation,—centres but not commonwealths. They do not constitute and give life to the

State: the State, on the contrary, creates and gives life to them.

Here, then, lies the cardinal difference we have been seeking between the old-time significance of municipal organization and its significance for us at the present day, and for the near future. Cities, as political organizations, once grew; once acted with a life and an origination all their own; were once self-created, self-acting, self-complete. They are now none of these things: they are now created and directed by the State, wh. is vastly greater and higher than they; they are subordinate pieces, not independent wholes; they have confined and specialized, not general and universal, functions.

Accordingly, the contrast between the ancient and mediaeval town and the modern is the contrast bet. *life* and *mechanism*. The centre of interest has shifted: towns have become *agents* instead of *principals*.

So much for the historical outline: now for the differences wh. it shows us to exist between past city govt. and present city govt. Self-ruling cities first represented a form of govt., a species of state; next, in the Middle Ages, they represented a form of privilege; last, in our own day, they have come to represent only a form of *duty*, and a department of administration.

Let me explain and illustrate: the most matter-of-course thing to our thought nowadays is, that a city should have a charter; but as a matter of fact a charter properly represents a by-gone order of things, a discarded political system.

How charters were granted:

   —They stood upon much the same footing as grants of jurisdiction and privilege to the barons.
   —They were granted by the Kings of *France* (a) to secure the towns as allies against the baronage; (b) to secure money.
   —Granted by European *barons* for money or for peace
   —Granted by *English* sovereigns for money or political support.
   —In every case sought as a boon, granted as a gift of privilege—*The charter stands for disintegration.*

We confer charters, not as grants of privilege, but as *means of organization*; among us, too, of the modern time, they are sought not as boons but as conveniences, as means of organization, rather than as instruments of liberty. They still, however, in a very real sense, *disintegrate*: they are means for making the several parts of govt.,—the local parts,—independent of of [*sic*], instead of interdependent upon, each other. Besides, the charter has lost its life-blood: the deep interest in self-govt. wh. prompted the citizen to every sacrifice to obtain and maintain it, when self-govt. was the only body of liberty.

Think of the vivid interest of the mediaeval citizen in the powers, the privileges, the immunities of his city!

Now, however, there is no such interest: the charter *is a convenience*: liberty does not at all depend upon it: it increases rather than decreases taxation. *Its use has become a duty.*

Hence *system* is displacing charter,—system by means of wh. municipal govt. is being made part of general schemes of local govt. and local govt. linked into a centred net-work—a net-work of nerves centring in the central brain, the central government.

Most logical form of this organization in *France*:—France, where charters once had their best illustrations, and where many cities run back to the Roman time, and retain traditions of the Roman organization.

French System

1. *Department* [*sic*]—*Prefect* and General Council ⎫
2. *Arrondisement*—sub-prefect, and council ⎬ *Const. Ass. and Napoleon.*
3. *Canton*—electoral district ⎭
4. *Commune*—smallest administrative division of the country, and unlike the Arrondisement and Canton, as vital an organism as the Dept.

   The commune either urban or rural—greater number of course rural (total 36,105) but same organization in both kinds.

   Mayor + one or more assistants—elected from its own midst by *Municipal Council*.

Course of *decentralization of choice*: (1) appointment by Minister of Interior or by Prefect. (2) appointment by do. [ditto] *from Council* (3) smaller communes elect (4) 1882 larger communes elect.

No decentralization of administrative responsibility, however. Mayor direct representative of the Minister of Int. Prefect may override or suspend him. Minister *ditto*, &c. Executive may even remove[.] Municipal Council also dependent: Its acts await ratification—It may be suspended—By decree may be dissolved.

Single executive responsibility: The mayor and his assistants do not constitute an executive board: the mayor's assistants are not his colleagues. He is head of the communal govt: they have their duties assigned to them by him.

Police and other subordinate officials of Commune appointed
by the mayor: but in all cases his appointments need the confirmation of the Prefect; and in communes with over 40,000
inhabitants his make-up of the police force must be ratified by
decree.

Though in many of its relations a sub-division of the Dept.,
the Commune is *overseen* direct from Paris—is in reality a division of France rather than a division of the Dept., so far as vital
administrative connexions are concerned.

Prussian System

Does not yet serve so well as an example of system because
it is, as yet, only *in process* of systematization: local govt. in
Prussia is compounded of old and new—of the creations of history and the creations of *Stein*.

Stein more conservative than the Constituent Assembly and
Napoleon—The *Province* retained.

(1) *Province—obsolescent*
(2) *Govt. District*
(3) *Circle*, or County
(4) *Township*
(5) *Town-commune*⎫Distinction made bet. town and country
(6) *Rural-commune*⎬

Somewhat various organization of the town-communes because of historical conditions, sensibly regarded

All types of Executive ⎧ Single executive
⎪ Single executive with colleagues
⎨ Single executive and *boards*, or
⎩ Collegiate executive ⎫ Always a council, more or less pop-ularly chosen.

But the integration is preserved[.] In *finance, police*, and *military* administration there is direct control from Berlin: in these
things the town authorities are agencies of the central govt.

Town govts. have thus a double character: they are at one and
the same time representatives of the authorities at the Capital
and of the citizens at home: and their *responsibility* also is,
correspondingly, a double responsibility.

English System

When we look at Eng. town organization we find ourselves not
far away from our own methods.

A comprehensive view must include

I. *Municipal Corporations*, properly so-called
II *Urban Sanitary Districts*, wh. are simply less developed

municipal corporations—a species of the genus. Sanitary functions standing at the front of their sphere but occupying by no means all of it.

1. *Municipal Corporations Act*, 1835 + amendments (cod. 1882)
2. *Public Health Act*, 1875
>   Petition to Privy Council:
>   Committee—Local hearing and investigation
>   *Charter* and arrangements
>   Constitution ready made in the Act:

Form a   ⎰*Councillors*: 3 years—yearly rotation
single body⎱*Aldermen*: 6 years—triennial rotation ⎱*by Councillors*
Mayor: 1 year   ⎰

Franchise: *Ratepayers*—7 miles residence
Councillors also elect Clerk, Treasurer, and other officers
Powers of the Corporation *subtracted* from *County*, &c
     E.g. *Justice*

Centring of govt.—*system* of govt.—appears in the superintending functions of the *Home Office* and the *Local Govt. Board*.

Home Office: superintends the constabulary, oversees to a limited extent the local magistracy and the admin. of prisons, advises the Sovereign with reference to the granting of pardons, and is the instrument of Parliament in carrying out certain statutes restricting at some points the employment of *labour*.

Local Govt. Board: is, in effect, the Eng. Dept. of the Interior. It is charged with supervising the admin. by the local authorities of the kingdom, "of the laws relating to the public health, the relief of the poor, and local govt."—duties more important to the daily good govt. of the country than those of any other dept.

Police oversight of the *Home Office*
     The Police system in England.

Financial and sanitary oversight of the *Local Govt. Board*
>   "In each instance, when a loan is required by a municipal corporation, the controlling authority [the Local Govt. Board][1] is to be applied to for its consent. A local inquiry, after due notice, is then held, and if the loan is approved, a term of years over wh. the repayment is to extend is fixed by the central authority." (*Bunce*)[2]

Municipal corporations, however, are free from the Local Govt. Board's *audit*, to wh. other local authorities are subject.

[1] WW's brackets.
[2] J. T. Bunce, "Municipal Boroughs and Urban Districts," in J. W. Probyn (ed.), *Local Government and Taxation in the United Kingdom* (London, 1882), pp. 271-318. [Eds.' note]

Urban Sanitary Districts
(1) Initiative of Local Govt. Board
(2) Initiative of residents (*owners* and *ratepayers*)
"Carved out of rural districts according to exigencies of population."

Diff. bet. municipal corporations and Urban Sanitary Dists. a diff. of local preference and legal convenience rather than of size, &c.

Difficulties of extending borough boundaries: towns *pieced* of with Urb. San. Dists., ∴ .

"Nowhere, from one end of Eng. to the other, do we find an instance (Nottingham alone excepted) of a large borough which is municipally self-contained, and consequently self-governing."

Urban Sanitary Dist takes its constitution from Public Health Act, 1875
A *board* elected by the ratepayers
Board has sanitary and, in large part, *town powers.*

American System

A general *scheme of law*; but no *organic integration*
Statutory (or constitutional) *counties, townships, boroughs*, &c.

A scheme of law (meant to operate of itself.) is necessarily *inflexible*. This most apparent in the matter of taxation—that point of delicacy and sensitiveness, with regard to wh. *some* general control is unquestionably necessary. We have *control by general enactment* % of taxation % of loan, &c.

General scheme of law extends in most states (?) to the lesser
Towns:
Pennsylvania boroughs incorporated by County *Court of Quarter Sessions.* The process.
New York villages: self-incorporated—ready-made—by statutory process—Record with county court.—appeal to County Judge.
Cities stand upon a different footing. They are specially chartered. These charters necessarily differ more or less, and necessarily differ *arbitrarily*
Two features:
(1) For the rural and small town units of local govt., system, but self-operative system: system by statute instead of system by administration.

(2) For cities, the old plan of separate, *disintegrate* organization by special charter.

Extensive abnegation of central govt.

We have in no part of our system either *Concentration* of [or] *Centralization*.

Growth of federal and local functions (expenses being the criterion) and tendency to squeeze out the *State* govts.

Through legislation and the courts state govts. touch our local systems, of course, at every point. But *through administration* they touch them scarcely at all

N. Y. State supervisers—board for equalization of taxes and State education—types of almost the only sort of administration our states undertake.

Our State officers are, so-to say, local officers acting at the capital in superintendence of the central conduct of the central machinery of the common govt. The administration of the laws outside the capital is controlled entirely by local officials locally elected, and whose responsibility is only to their constituents, not to the central authorities

E.g. *Balto. police.* There is here no *system* of central control, like that of a minister of the Interior or a Home Office—no organic integration of police administration coupled with public responsibility on the part of the central minister

It is only a hand thrust into Baltimore local politics.

WWhw MS. (WP, DLC).

From Joseph Ruggles Wilson

My dearest Son—   Clarksville, Tenn., Mar. 5, '88

If I did not detest explanations—because they carry confessions; and apologies—because they are not always up to Bible truth—I would cover this initial page with such remorseful lamentations over my epistolary neglects you-ward as would go to show that I had done rather a good thing than otherwise *not* to write! Certainly my silence has had the effect of furnishing you with an excuse for silence: and if I were to spread before you all my reasons for dumbness, I am apprehensive that you would copy some of them as a cloak for yours!—or invent other and worse ones! But you know that I love you and I am sure of your love in return—and love when genuine does not need many words, or frequent, to declare that its depths are always deep: it is the superficial that babbles: the false that asseverates and swears. Yet, after all, it does sound sweetly when the heart, climbing to the mouth, tumbles forth in what may be only the broken stammerings of a blood-warm affection. Thus it has a grammar and a dictionary of its own, which, never studied, is nevertheless perfectly known to itself and all its kindred: its one verb (irregular often) being "I love"—always in the present tense indicative active and calling for no persons except the first and the second: and its one adverb, "forever"—and out of these two what eloquences it weaves and what aphonies it tolerates! A third word its dictionary contains; but a word which is now so much abused as almost to forbid its use in such a connection— "*trust*"—or better, trust*ful*, in order to lift it somewhat away from the odors of "Standard Oil" and the many other stenches of poverty-making monopoly!

That, however, which I particularly wish to say is that I fear we made a mistake in taking up our residence in this place. It now seems to me that to spend another winter here will—for one or both of us—be to spend our last one. You know how your dear mother suffers from the cold weather—and as for myself I have had hardly a well day since the bleak season set in: being afflicted with an almost perpetual cold and racking cough that sometimes tears me up by the very roots. About the middle of January I narrowly escaped an attack of pneumonia. Besides, the experiment of a theological school here is bound to prove a failure—and soon—because (1) I have no colleagues, or as good as none in this department (2) The reopening at Columbia[1] turns the attention of students towards an old institution which has a name and a history (albeit not always a good one) (3) There is slender likelihood of an endowment for my chair: and the salary—which individuals pledged the bulk of for only 3 years —is even now hard to collect and will be impossible perhaps next year. (4) There is no effort, or almost none, made to push the claims of theological schooling at this obscure point (independently of pecuniary considerations)—so that on the whole discouragement lowers all around the horizon of my prospects. I am not indeed rendered unhappy by it—but am sorely puzzled as to the future: especially how is the *health* difficulty to be conquered? I trust in God, yet He does not work miracles for the relief of His people. In view, therefore, of the possibility of our leaving here in search of a milder climate, I entreat you to hasten the sale of the residual western lands that the proceeds may, with what else we have, be invested for such an income as may serve to keep us from drowning outright. I will be able no doubt, should the worst here come to be realized, [to] get some work to do which will pay something. Now don't let yourself suppose that I am *oppressed* by the fears I have thus confided to you: for I am not. Only I feel that I am (variously) in a false position, and it would be a relief could I honorably escape.

Enough about *me*. I turn to what is brighter viz: you and yours. I know indeed what your burdens are, what your perplexities; I will not add, your forebodings, for I hope that you have none, as surely you ought not to have with your youth, your talents, your reputation, your everything with which the great Father has gifted you. Before this you must have been to Johns Hopkins a-lecturing; and I am anxious to learn how you have fared.

One thing further:—don't you *dare* to return me the bit of money I loaned to you—or I will send it right back.[2] Let it be for a gift to your mother's namesake—or for anything you please: but I will have none of it. On the contrary how I wish I could add to it, and make it something worth while.

Love, both distributive and concentrated, to all and each of you and your dear ones—love more than can be told—from us all.

Your affectionate   Father

ALS (WP, DLC).

[1] The troubles growing out of the controversy over Dr. Woodrow had led the Board of Directors of the Columbia Theological Seminary to close that institution in 1886. It re-opened in September 1887, with fourteen students matriculating.

[2] See JRW to WW, Sept. 22, 1887.

From Edwin Lawrence Godkin, with Enclosure

Dear Sir,   New York, March 5, 1888

I enclose a letter sent me to be mailed to you, by Mr. James Bryce of London. As I have undertaken to find some one to take your place, in case you you [*sic*] are unable to comply with his request, will you kindly let me know what your answer to him is, so as to save time, and thus greatly oblige

Yours truly   E. L. Godkin.

E N C L O S U R E

From James Bryce

Dear Sir   London Feb. 25 [1888]

Our common friend Professor [Jesse] Macy who is now in London has encouraged me to make a request to you, which I have the less hesitation in doing because we have many common friends at Johns Hopkins, and because I know your Congressional Government so well and value it so highly that I seem to know you.

I am preparing and hope in few months or so to publish a book on the government and institutions of the U. S. There are, I find, some topics here and there which ought to be briefly dealt with, but which I feel scarcely competent to deal with myself: and on these I have received chapters written by American authorities. Mr. Seth Low of Brooklyn & Prof. [Frank Johnson] Goodnow of Columbia College have written such chapters for me.

I venture to ask you whether you could write a short chapter on the Women's Suffrage Question in the U. S. I do not know how you feel towards it yourself, but am sure you would treat it in an impartial and philosophical spirit. What I should desire is a short account of its present position, of the arguments used for and against it, of the kind of view which sensible Americans, men and women, take of it, and of the prospects of its being carried. It would of course be also desirable to mention how far the experiment of giving political votes to women has succeeded in the Territories where it has been tried (has it been adopted in any State?) and also what is the result of women's suffrage in school elections, if you happen to have any data as to these last mentioned points. But they are secondary. A chapter as long as 15 pages of your "Congressional Government," would be long enough. I would of course print it in my book under your name: and if you could write it, I would like to have it by April 4th or so. With many apologies for the liberty I take in thus writing, believe me to be

Very faithfully yours,   Bryce

ALS (WP, DLC).

To James Bryce

Dear Sir,   Bryn Mawr, Pa., 6th March, 1888
Your kind letter of Feby. 25 reached me this morning, enclosed in a note from Mr. Godkin of the *Nation*.

I am sincerely gratified that you should wish to entrust to me the preparation of any part of the work from which every student of our institutions is expecting so much of instruction and suggestion. Both because you wish it and because I should so greatly profit by such an association, I strongly incline to undertake the chapter you propose. But the hard, untoward fact is that it is just now impossible. Had I made *any* independent investigation of the question, had I any conclusions on the subject already in hand in the rough, it is possible that I might produce such a brief statement as you suggest without too great delay for your purpose; but in this matter I suffer from that most radical of all maladies, 'the lack of preliminary information'; and, being just now held captive by an amount of work and a number of engagements quite up to the top of my capacity for performance, I dare not entertain propositions looking towards more work. I am sincerely sorry that I cannot serve you in this matter: every consideration would prompt me to try were it possible.

Allow me to thank you again for your kind letter, and to express the hope that another opportunity may offer for being of some assistance to you.

Very sincerely Yours,   Woodrow Wilson

ALS (Bryce Papers, Bodleian Library).

Two Letters from Melville R. Hopewell

Dear Sir   Omaha Mch 7th 1888

Your letter inclosing draft to pay taxes for 1886, was rec'd, & I directed treasurer to make receipt, but left Tekamah before it had been done. Possibly Mr Dickinson may have forwarded it to you. If not I will attend to it in a few days, on my return.

I notice what you say in regard to selling land at $10, and think you are right. While land has been dull in Burt Co. for some time, there being but little demand, our excellent crops, & the general prosperity of our farmers, consequent thereon the past year, ought to work a revival, and I think it will. There is no richer or more desirable land than yours anywhere, except that it is rather low, and inclined to be too wet, in rainy seasons. The Ditch for the drainage of all the bottom land, is doing good work, but it remains to be seen, whether of a wet season, it will keep the land sufficiently dry, for cultivation.

Your land in Sections 4 & 9, Tp 21, R 11, lies in a body, and is liable to be wanted by some one for a large ranch. It would not therefore I think be good policy to sell off small portions of it, say, 40, or 80, especially if it cut into the main body, even if you could get price asked. I make these suggestions for your benefit.   Yours Truly   M. R. Hopewell

Address all letters to me at Tekamah. I am there once a week.

ALS (WP, DLC) with WWhw notation on env.: "Ans. 3/19/88" and WWhw and WWsh notes on the government of Berlin. Enc.: two calling cards of Melville R. Hopewell, Judge, Third Judicial District of Nebraska.

Dear Sir   Tekamah, Neb., Mch 10 1888
    I wrote you a line a few days ago from Omaha. On my return to day I find the tax receipt has not been forwarded to you, as I supposed it had. I now inclose same, being tax receipt for the year 1886, covering all your land in this county. If there should be an omission, call my attention to it. I also inclose a map of your land in Sections 4 & 9-21-11. You will notice on 40. acres, the NW 1/4 NE 1/4 Sec 4- corners or rather projects from the rest. We are offered 11.00 per acre cash. I believe I would sell it, as the sale of this will not injure sale of bal. in any way. If you conclude to do so send deed to —— Fuller. You can leave initials blank as I do not recall them & will fill in
                        Yours &c   M. R. Hopewell

ALS (WP, DLC) with WWhw notation on env.: "Ans. 3/19/88."

From Munroe Smith

Dear Prof. Wilson: [New York] 1888 Mar. 11
    Have you anything in hand, or in your mind, that could be worked into an article for the Political Science Quarterly? We find it hard to get good articles on political history, public law, & administration.
    The P. S. Q. is doing so much better than was expected, that we are not obliged to ask our contributors, any longer, to work for the pure love of science.
                        Yours very truly   Munroe Smith

ALS (WP, DLC) with WWhw notation on env.: "Ans. 3/19/88."

From Robert Bridges

My dear Tommy: New York, March 12, 1888.
    The enclosed circulars fully explain the scheme for the Class Memorial which was inaugurated at the little dinner we attended together a few weeks ago. I need not say anything more to you about it as I know your hearty sympathy with all that the class does. . . .
    I hope that I shall see you before you go South for the summer. I am sorry that Sloane was not elected President;[1] especially so as it spoils our little scheme in regard to his successor as Professor of Political Science. I have many things to say to you and hope that I may soon have an opportunity. Can you not come

over to the Alumni meeting on Thursday evening, March 16th? With kindest regards to Mrs. Wilson, I am

Truly your friend,   Robert Bridges

P.S.—Chang writes today that he is the father of a lively boy— and everybody is doing well. I have a great stack of letters to write to the boys, or would add a long personal postscript. RB

Hw and ALS (WP, DLC) with WWhw notation on env.: "Ans. 3/26/88." Encs.: A. W. Halsey *et al.* to members of the Princeton Class of 1879, printed form letter dated Feb. 13, 1888, and Harold Godwin, *The Proposed Class Memorial*, both appealing for funds for '79's decennial memorial—a bronze statue or relief of Dr. McCosh to be executed by Augustus Saint-Gaudens for a fee of $12,000.
[1] Francis L. Patton was elected President of the College of New Jersey on February 9, 1888.

Notes for a Public Lecture at the Johns Hopkins[1]

[March 16, 1888]

II.

The Government of Cities:
Berlin.

The modern city PART of a System.

Its *Reason for Existing* industrial, commercial, not political.

Chiefly a Business Corporation, therefore, having the management of vast amounts of private property.

But it is a *Political Body as well*: it has important functions as an organ of government.

The Mediaeval vs. the Modern City as a body politic:

The mediaeval city, as a State, *controlled* the commercial or political *policy* by which its sucess was assured or its hurt effected. Its guild govt. secured success by independent political organization and policy.

The commercial *interests of a modern city*, on the other hand, *depend upon outside powers*, upon legislatures, R. R. corporations, etc. Its public works, and its contributions (by way of franchises or money) to corporate undertakings (like the building of a railroad) are its only self-originated contributions to its own success.

Not necessary to state the points now most mooted touching the organization of city government, the general questions as to

[1] In the Wilson Papers, Library of Congress, there are two documents closely related to this outline of Wilson's second public lecture: (a) a WWT MS. with WWhw emendations with the heading "Berlin," which is Wilson's digest of Rudolf Gneist, "The Government of Berlin," *Contemporary Review*, XLVI (Dec. 1884), 769-94; and (b) a WWhw draft of the outline printed herewith.

No text of this lecture seems to have survived. However, Wilson's lecture at Brown University on January 18, 1889, an extensive report of which is printed at that date in Vol. 6, was based on the outline printed here.

the distribution of official powers; as to Mayors, Boards, Councils, and their respective responsibility

There is now more instruction to be gotten out of another question, which approaches the subject from quite a different point
of view. Viz.,

WHO SHALL PARTICIPATE in the government of our cities?

We have been seeking new *devices*, new mechanism: is it
not possible that we need *a new point of view*, even *a new
analysis of self-government*?

Do our citizens in our great cities govern themselves?

Why, then, Committees of One Hundred,[2] why the distance
of the voter from govt. his outside position?

Ballot-government vs. Self-government. Govt. by acquiescence
or refusal vs. govt. by action.

Parellel case: money contribution vs. charity *work*.

Voting and eternal vigilance even (how much more spasmodic vigilance!) are not self-government.

Why have we so much Socialism except because the real business of govt. is not understood by many? Has Socialism
ever attained any great development except in countries
where the mass of the people are not accustomed to handling affairs? *Socialism easy for the voter, hard for the
administrator.*

Establish, therefore, self-government; make the voter an
administrator. Take your committees of One Hundred
into your govts; convert their transient zeal into permanent duty: harness the community to the State. 'No man
shall have a right who is not faithful to a corresponding
duty.'

Berlin.

Not a foreign, but rather an English, at heart a Pan-Teutonic,
example of city government.

Berlin only the most perfect flower of the Prussian municipal
system, which rests upon the principle of *citizen coöperation
plus technical official training and long tenure.*

(1) Minority of trained and salaried officials in every Board
of Aldermen.

(2) Gradation of the franchise according to duties.

(3) Personal union of Executive and Legislature and of these
with citizens in executive work.

The Court of Mayor and Aldermen

2 A Baltimore reform group.

The Town Council
Select Citizens
Citizen Coöperation in
    Poor Relief   Education
    Guardianship   Summary and mercantile trials.
    Arbitration   Assessment.

WWT MS. (WP, DLC).

From Catharine Milligan McLane[1]

Dear Sir,   Baltimore March 17th 1888
    As one of your audience on Friday March 16th at Hopkins Hall, may I take the liberty of asking for answers to the following questions, which several, besides myself, wish answered.
    Is there any English translation of Professor Gneist's writings on English administrative systems &c.
    Is there any English article or description of the "communal orphan councillors" who in Berlin have charge of orphans, their disposal, education, &c.?
    Is there any English article describing in detail the working of the Poor Law Relief Ward Committees in Berlin?
    Of course these are not the only features in the Berlin System which interests us,[2] but they were the special departments which we thought might, on investigation, help us in suggesting reforms in charity work
               Yours truly   Kate M. McLane

ALS (WP, DLC) with WWhw notation on env.: "Ans. 3/19/88."
  [1] A pioneer social worker and leader of reform movements in Baltimore until her death in 1927.
  [2] The Charity Organization of Baltimore.

From Melville R. Hopewell

Dear Sir   Tekamah, Nebraska, Mch 17 1888
    I wrote you a few days since, to make deed for 40 acres, in Sec 4-12-11- @ 11.00 per acre: I now write to say don't do it. On investigation, I find, that it can be sold for more to another party, and this last man—talks as if he would want 160. off the north end, or perhaps, more. I have leased grass for this season for $100, to be paid middle of April. When paid I will pay taxes for 87, & forwrd you.   Yours &c   M. R. Hopewell

ALS (WP, DLC) with WWhw notation on env.: "Ans. 3/23/88."

To Munroe Smith

My dear Prof. Smith,   Bryn Mawr, Pa., 19 March, 1888

I am sincerely sorry to say that I have nothing in hand which could be made available for the *Political Science Quarterly*. My Muse is just now 'doing chores' only, so to speak; in other words, class work for the time absorbs my entire energies; and it is not class work for which proper *Quarterly* stuff is needed. What I may have 'in mind' there's no time to work up at present. But you may be sure that I will be very willing to let you see any articles of a suitable nature that my future leisure,—should such a thing be vouchsafed me,—may produce. With warmest regards,
Yrs. very sincerely,   Woodrow Wilson

ALS (*Political Science Quarterly Papers*, NNC).

To Robert Bridges

My dear Bobby,   Bryn Mawr, Pa., 26th. March, 1888.

I hope that you will excuse a machine-written letter, if I myself operate the keys, in view of the fact that much recent use of the pen has greatly fatigued and cramped my hand. You'll get along easier with the reading of the epistle, anyhow, if you consent to its production after this fashion.

I wish that I could name some handsome amount as my contribution to the class monument subscription, and I mean to make as big a gift as lies within my present resources; but all that I can *promise* without peradventure is $25.00. I want to give more than that, and if by the first of January next I should have more to give I will of course give it. If, for instance I should have anything accepted by a periodical for publication, I will regard the memorial fund the proper destination for what I get for the article.

I wished very much that I could go to the Alumni dinner in N. Y. and hear the speech of the President-elect; but the snow blockade was only one of many causes for my absence.[1] What impression did you get of Patton; I did'nt see anything in the published summary of his speech either to like or to dislike.

I am in the midst of my course of Hopkins lectures now, & consequently harder at work than ever. I heard from one of the Hopkins Trustees week before last, incidentally, that Sloane is a candidate for the vacant Latin chair at Columbia, and I am, as you may suppose, not a little interested to know if that be so.

Do you happen to have heard anything about it? Dr. Thomas, my informant, seemed quite well informed on the matter. He spoke of Sloane as a "prominent candidate" for the place, and as one of the men most likely to get it. It seems to me rather improbable, somehow. Sloane, I understood, preferred History to Latin; and, besides, he is identified with Princeton through the [Princeton] Review.

We got a big piece of the great storm down here; were blockaded for some time; and were altogether quite miserable for a season, but the college suffered no loss but that of a chimney, and we came through quite well and serene. Did you have any exciting experiences?

Hurrah for Chang and his boy. Give him my congratulations when you write.

This is all for this time, for this is a tremendously busy season with me, as you may suppose, with its duties both in Baltimore and here; but I am going to write again soon, and I shall certainly try to see you before I go away for the summer. With warmest regards from Mrs. W., and all the oldtime affection from myself,   Yours as ever,   Woodrow Wilson

WWTLS (Meyer Coll., DLC).
  [1] Wilson was referring to the great blizzard of '88, which lasted from March 11 through March 13.

To Richard Heath Dabney

My dear Heath,   Bryn Mawr, 26 March/88
  I am full of disappointment about the way things have gone here. These Trustees here—or, at any rate, those who guide them, —are so parsimonious that there is no prospect at all of my having a competent assistant within any reasonable period—unless a man of independent means who don't care for salary can be had! They have come *down* in the amount which they offer, instead of going up—as they *could* do, for all I can see—and as beyond question, of course, they should do, to make it worth anybody's while to come to this expensive place. They now purpose offering, at the most, $1100 for the first, $1200 for the second year of a two years' engagement. And of course this shuts you out. I could not with decent regard for the duties of friendship advise you to come for a dollar less than $1,500 (the sum I had the first year)[.] I could not have lived on that the second year, with a child: it then took every cent of $2,000; and I could not pretend to keep house now—or, for that matter, to board com-

fortably—with *two* babies, were I not getting an additional $500 for the Johns Hopkins. With the present resources of the college there can be no great advance in salary; and to accept less than enough at first would be to risk continuing with less than enough. Less than enough to marry and live rationally on, I mean of course, for I am speaking to your case—not to that of a starving bachelor. Oh, I am beyond measure disappointed! I shall hence-forth be all the more eager for the turning up of a chance to get a chair of public law or the like somewhere else.

I have received your book and have dipped into it enough to feel that you can afford to wait for openings in the east. I am presently going to have a few days of 'Easter vacation' in which to read the little volume through; but I have already read enough of it to be sure that it is what I expected—*tip top*. Accept my heartiest thanks for it, my dear fellow,—I shall prize it doubly—for your sake, as well as for what everybody else will find in it, clearness, fulness, skilful speed of treatment. But more of it hereafter. You already have my hearty congratulations.

Mrs. W. joins me in warmest regards to you.

Affectionately Yours,   Woodrow Wilson

ALS (Wilson-Dabney Correspondence, ViU).

From Richard Heath Dabney

My dear Tom: Bloomington, Indiana. April 1st, 1888.

I believe I was already in your debt when your letter arrived the other day; but, as I have been very busy, & am still so, I trust that you will excuse me both for my delay in writing and for the brevity of my epistle now that I have at length taken up my pen.

I need hardly tell you how I regret the impossibility of my being your fellow-worker at Bryn Mawr, but I can hardly say that I am surprised at the result of your Board's deliberations. For I have doubted all along very strongly whether they would be willing to give me $1,500 with the promise of an increase the next year—which is the very least that I could have accepted without giving up the hope of getting married for an indefinite period.

Well, we must wait to see what will turn up. Meantime I hope that you will succeed in finding the chair of public law which you desire. As for myself, I am already on the scent of another position. A chair of History has, viz., been just established at the Univ. of the City of N. Y., and is to be filled in June. The announcement was made in the papers just two days ago, and my father sent me a clipping from the N. Y. *Times* on the subject, which I have just received. He has already written to Dr. Howard Crosby & told him that I should be a candidate, and referred him to you & Prof. Price;[1] mentioning also that I had just published a book, and adding that I could send him plenty of testimonials in case he felt sufficiently interested in me, from what you & Mr. Price might tell him, & from what he thought of the book, to desire them. It is perfectly possible that you may receive a letter from Dr. Crosby before you receive this one of mine. . . .

Did you know that Charley Kent took his Ph.D. in English at Leipzig last Summer? He slipped up in the Spring, but tried it over again in the Summer & made it. His dissertation was on "Teutonic Antiquities in Andreas & Elene." He is now at the Univ. of Va. waiting for something to turn up. Both he & Sam Woods asked me after you lately.

With sincere regards to Mrs Wilson I remain,

Very truly your friend   R. H. Dabney.

P.S. And so you are now *doubly* a papa? Well I congratulate you heartily. But it is hard to realize. Was No. 2 a boy or a girl?

R. H. D.

ALS (WP, DLC).

[1] The Rev. Dr. Howard Crosby, formerly Chancellor of the University of the City of New York (now New York University), was at this time pastor of the Fourth Avenue Presbyterian Church in New York and a member of the Council of the University of the City of New York. Thomas Randolph Price, who had formerly taught at the University of Virginia, was Professor of English at Columbia College.

From Melville R. Hopewell

Dear Sir   Tekemah, Neb. Apl 6th 1888

Inclosed please find tax receipt for year 1887, covering lands of your mother in this county, amount being   88.17

The bal—   11.83
_____

Makes amt. recd for grass— $100.00
on your lands, for season 88. I think that perhaps is not too large a fee for the work done in making lease[,] collecting the money, paying taxes &c. If it is will try to make it right hereafter. I am in haste now and will write you again in regard to your land.

Yours Truly   M. R. Hopewell

ALS (WP, DLC). Enc.: tax receipt from Treasurer's Office, Burt County, Neb., dated April 6, 1888.

From Joseph R. Wilson, Jr.

Clarksville, Tenn 4/15 1888
Received at 7:55 AM 4/16

Mother died suddenly father absent but be home tomorrow morning   Jos R. Wilson Jr.

Telegram (WP, DLC).

Four Letters to Ellen Axson Wilson

Arlington Hotel,
My own darling,   Clarksville, Tenn. April 17 1888

As you knew before the receipt of my telegram,[1] I arrived here to find the house shut up and father and Josie gone to Columbia with dear mother's body. My first impulse was to follow; but I find that father left word that it would hardly be worth while for me to come after them—the funeral would be over before I could get there. If I can stand the desolation of waiting here, I will: if not, I will come home. Some word will doubtless come to me in the morning from Columbia. Father and 'Dode' will reach C. to-morrow, Wednesday, afternoon.

Don't be anxious about me. I have stood the journey remarkably well—and am in reasonable spirits. My *darling's* love—and my love for her keep me up—and *will* keep me up. Will write again in the morning.   Your own   Woodrow

[1] It is missing.

My own darling,   Clarksville, Tenn. April 18th 1888

At last I know something definite. A telegram just received from 'Dode' says 'Expect us Friday 8 P. M.' I suppose—I hope—I trust that the 'us' includes sister Annie: this desolate home cannot be set to final rights by any but a loving woman's hand. Meantime I wait, with what fortitude I can. I have learned all the particulars there are to be learned: but I know, my love, that you will be willing to wait till I come to hear them. The pain is so recent that *I cannot write* about it all.

Dear mother's sickness really began on Thursday [April 12]: but it seemed no more than one of her too common attacks. The doctor was summoned Sunday morning; but it was then really too late: he knew nothing of the history of the case—misunderstood it—and did not realize that there was any immediate danger.

At three she died—suddenly—only the servant with her. Josie, at last alarmed, had gone to summon sister to come and care for dear mother. There is nothing to deplore in the management of the case—except that dear mother had not consented to have a doctor frequently before, during the winter. He could then have understood the case and, possibly, have prolonged her life till father and her children got to her. As it was, it was too late. There was probably 'congestion of the liver.'

Everybody has been abundantly kind. But, darling, I can't write about it—my heart is almost broken. By the time this reaches you dear father and Dode will be back. Meantime I am *perfectly* well, and am sustained every moment *by you*, by my treasure of love, my little wife at home. A thousand kisses for the babies.   Your own   Woodrow

My own darling,   Clarksville, Tenn. April 19 1888
Oh, what a comfort it is to write to you. Even amidst the noise and in the vulgar publicity of an hotel office, it brings home-warmth and comfort to my heart to write words for my sweet wife's eyes—those blessed, blessed eyes which contain all the heaven of this world's happiness for me. Oh, my precious sweet-heart, what would become of me *now*, if you were not mine: how could I bear to see this desolation—the home of my whole life broken up forever—father's home gone—the house standing, within a block of where I sit writing, closed, empty, desolate: because my precious mother is dead. Oh, the infinite pity and bitterness of it! When I think of dear father and Josie, I can almost find it in my heart to upbraid myself that *I* have a sweet home to go to!

As the first shock and acute pain of the great, the irreparable blow passes off[,] my heart is filling up with tenderest memories of my sweet mother, memories that seem to hallow my whole life—which seem to explain to me how it came about that I was given the sweetest, most satisfying of wives for my daily com-panion. My mother, with her sweet womanliness, her purity, her intelligence, her strength, prepared me for my wife. I remember how I clung to her (a laughed-at "mamma's boy") till I was a great big fellow: but love of the best womanhood came to me and entered my heart through those apron-strings. If I had not lived with such a mother I could not have won and seemed to deserve—in part, perhaps, deserved, through transmitted virtues—such a wife—the strength, the support, the human source of my life. Oh, darling, without my mother and you, what would I have been!

I am perfectly well. My spirits are very much improved. I am standing the ordeal very well indeed. They will be here to-morrow evening.　　　　　　　　　Your own　Woodrow.

No letter from you yet—but of course I understand—the later telegrams—and my own—have made you write to Columbia, or wait for further news before writing at all.

Yrs. W. W.

My own darling,　　　　　Clarksville, Tenn. April 20 1888

The last day of my loneliness and waiting has at last Come: oh, *what* a comfort it will be to see dear father and Dode, some one who *knows* what I am suffering. Not that I have been losing in spirits: I am gaining—gaining steadily. I suffer now only from an unspeakable sadness: I have regained completely my usual equanimity. It has helped me to stay in this perfectly new hotel, which I never saw before: inside it I have seen nothing to remind me of home and its desolation. I have been in the house; but of course I could not *stay* in it. I could not have borne that alone, and was not so foolish as to try it. I have diligently cultivated all quiet means of diversion: have written a good many letters, have even tried to compose something: and, although the product has been very small indeed, the mental results have been altogether good. The *storm* is completely past, and I am all the better prepared to meet the dear ones who come to-night. And, oh, my sweet, my matchless little wife, how *everything*—whether sorrow or joy, trial or triumph—seems to conspire to draw me *to you*. Surely my love for you must have been *born* in me, must have begun with my life, so integral a part of my life is it—so naturally have you come into my life and possessed it. You have come all this dreadful journey with me, you have sustained me through this lonely waiting, you have brightened and cheered every moment of the time since I left you. Oh, may God bless and preserve you, Eileen, my precious one. Kiss the dear, dear little ones for me as often as they will let you—and imagine a score, a hundred score of kisses on your own sweet lips. I can form no plans till father comes; but very probably I shall start for home on Monday or Tuesday. Love to Eddie and cousin Mary.

Your own　Woodrow.

ALS (WC, NjP).

From Ellen Axson Wilson

My own darling, Bryn Mawr, April 20/88.

I hardly know whether or no you will get this before you leave;[1] however I will continue to write until I hear from you. And I take for granted you will stay over Sunday, won't you? I *hope* so. I had a long pleasant visit from Uncle Tom [Hoyt] yesterday. He saw the notice of your mother's death in a paper yesterday morning, and came out at once to see you, though he thought it most probable you would be away. Dr. Rhoads also called Tuesday night and was very kind.

I had a hasty note from Stockton yesterday[2] begging me to ask you and then let him know *at once* where he can find any material—facts or discussion—on the subject of *"property qualifications for voting."* He is to take part in a prize debate on that subject and says he has ransacked the college library in vain for anything relating to it, and that time is already pressing. Of course I can't help him. I looked over "Hare"[3] & John Mill on representation but found only passing allusions to the subject. Could you, dear, without too great an effort answer his question from Columbia? Though if he can't get access to the books there I hardly know what good it will do him to know of their existence.

I also had a long letter from Beth[4] in which she tells me distressing news about my friends the Andersons[5]—Dr. [James H.] Thornwell's daughter—you know. She says that Lila is dying of consumption, that Mr. A. has been very ill and Mrs. A. is quite broken down from nursing, and that they are now in Columbia. I should be glad if you would make enquiries about them for me.

You have had no mail except pamphlets &c. One that came yesterday was the catalogue of the University of Mich., with compliments of Mr. Angell. Just think!—they have never filled that vacancy yet; have absolutely *no one*—not even an "instructor["] in political science. In your whole department they have only Dr. Adams[6] in political economy, and one of the men in the ordinary law school who gives a *very* little Roman law! Isn't that disgraceful? In a University whose students number *1667*!

But there! Jessie has wakened prematurely and I must close hastily for I am still on duty in the nursery. I hoped to have time to write a satisfactory letter this morning.

But after all on that subject of which both our hearts are so full it is impossible to *write* "satisfactorily." I shrink from saying *anything* about it, love, because every expression that I can use seems *so* cold, so empty, so entirely inexpressive of the feelings of which my heart is full—full well nigh to bursting. Oh darling, my darling if I only *could* tell you all that is in my heart, if I could but let you know how much I love you!

Give my dearest love to Father, Sister Annie, Josie & all. Margaret seem quite herself again today; we are all quite well. I love you darling as my own soul; and am as ever

Your own Eileen.

ALS (WP, DLC) with WWhw and WWsh case citations on env.
    1 WW did not. EAW addressed this letter to Columbia. It was forwarded from there to Clarksville but did not arrive before WW left for home on April 23.
    2 It is missing.
    3 Thomas Hare, *The Election of Representatives, Parliamentary and Municipal. A Treatise* (4th edn., London, 1873).
    4 Elizabeth Adams Erwin. Her letter is missing.
    5 The Rev. Dr. and Mrs. Robert Burton Anderson. He was pastor of the Presbyterian Church in Morganton, North Carolina.
    6 Henry Carter Adams, a noted economist.

To Ellen Axson Wilson

Clarksville, April 21, '88

Just a line or two to-day, my darling. Dear father, and Dode, and sister Annie have come and we are deep in fixing domestic affairs, arranging the house for its changed uses, and such other engrossments as you can imagine. Our safety lies in keeping thus busy about many things.

I have been thinking of you all day, incessantly: for my heart, my life is in your keeping[.] Love me, oh, love me, darling, for I am   Your own   Woodrow

ALS (WC, NjP).

From Ellen Axson Wilson

My own darling,   Bryn Mawr, April 22/88

I don't know whether mails leave on Sunday or not, but I will write a few lines for Eddie to mail after Sunday-school. Tonight I will write a longer letter. We are all quite well, are having such glorious weather that we could scarcely be anything else. Eddie took us just after we came from church to a place where there are a great many flowers and we came home laden; have eight or ten vases full; so that spring is really here at last. I am *so* relieved, dear, that you too keep well,—have borne so bravely those terrible three days of waiting. I was more glad than I can say to get your last sweet, sweet letter, for I felt—I knew from experience—that it showed the first overwhelming *shock* to be passing away, as you said, & that you could think of the past & present, of our noble mother & our own great loss as God would have us think.

But here is E. to say it is time to go, and I must close abruptly.

Give my dearest love to all, & believe me, darling, that I love *you* with all my heart & soul—with all my nature and am always & altogether   Your own Eileen

ALS (WP, DLC) with WWhw and WWsh bibliographical references on env.

To Ellen Axson Wilson

My own darling,   Clarksville, April 22, '88

To-morrow morning I start for home, and shall be in Bryn Mawr, Providence permitting, late on Tuesday. I don't know at what hour, so you must not be anxious if I should not be there till quite late.

Of course the hours I shall be with the dear ones here are so few that I cannot take time for a long letter; but my darling shall have the message of love which is in my heart for her. There seems to me to be nothing *else* in my heart: I long for you, I yearn for you, my little wife, with a longing beyond description— oh, what an unspeakable delight and comfort it will be [to] have my sweet confidant and counseller in my arms again! I am coming to you, sweetheart, with a new claim on you: my precious mother is gone, and you are now my *whole* earthly stay and support: I am going to ask you to love me more than ever, Eileen, my delight. I seem to have grown older during this week. The sorrow has not 'aged' me. I dont mean that: I mean that a new experience has sunk down deep into my heart, and has made my life more entirely a *mature* life—a *man's*, rather than a boy's life. Don't expect me to be anything dulled or to be permanently depressed: dear mother's memory will, in the long run, have too much of inspiration in it for that: but the life—the home—of my youth is cut off—and now it is you and me, my sweet one.

I am perfectly well; not too tired; not in bad spirits; and altogether   Your own Woodrow

ALS (WC, NjP).

From Richard Heath Dabney

Dear Tom: Bloomington, Indiana. April 22nd, 1888.

The "Indiana University Bulletin" is a publication issued six times during the session (twice each term), and Dr. von Jagemann, the editor-in-chief, has requested me to ask you whether you would write a review of my book for the said periodical. He wants some one outside of our faculty to write it, and I should be greatly indebted to you if you would do it for him. Of course, however, I don't want to put too great a tax upon your time, and so I hope you will not hesitate to decline, if you haven't the necessary leisure at present.[1]

I suppose you got my postal card[2] telling you that the Univ. City of N. Y. scheme had fallen through. So I suppose I must remain a Hoosier for at least another year.

Being in a great hurry, I must close, with kind regards to Mrs. Wilson & the young ones.

Fraternally yours   R. H. Dabney.

ALS (WP, DLC).
   [1] Wilson did not write the review, for reasons which he explained in WW to R. H. Dabney, May 16, 1888.
   [2] It is missing.

From Chester David Hartranft

Dear Sir: Hartford, April 28, 1888.

I understand the name of Mr. Williston Walker has been suggested to you as a candidate for the chair of History. Permit me to commend him most heartily to you. His college course others can testify about better; his Seminary years showed an eager, patient and discriminating student, with special aptitudes and taste for history: it was my pleasure also to direct his private reading the results of which he gave me; our mutual studies would have been pursued further in more analytic directions had I not been called away. Mr. W. supplemented his theological training by a two years or more residence at Leipzig. He cannot fail to be eminent in his work.

Yrs. respectfully,   C. D. Hartranft
Prof. in Hartford Theological Seminary.

ALS (WP, DLC).

Charles McLean Andrews to Elizabeth Williams Andrews

My dear Mama   [Baltimore] May 7, 88.

. . . One of our best courses this semester has been that of Dr. Woodrow Wilson in Administration: It is a live subject treated by a live man. And I am trying to take full notes, for they are very valuable. When completed I shall have them bound as did I those on Roman Law, for they are worth it.[1] . . .

Your loving son   Charlie.

ALS (C. M. Andrews Papers, CtY).
[1] Andrews' notes are missing from his papers.

From Joseph Ruggles Wilson

My precious Son—   Clarksville, May 11th 1888.

To-morrow I start for General Assembly via B. & O. R. R.— purposing to stop over Sunday at Chillicothe—and to reach Baltimore on Tuesday, 15th.[1] My address at B. will be "1024 Calvert Street" care of Mr. W. M. Buchanan (the husband of Julia McCoy). The Assembly will go over to Philadelphia probably on Wednesday night the 23d for the Centennial of 24th.[2] I expect to accompany the crowd, but not for the purpose of hearing the speeches: only for imposing my presence upon dear Ellie and you during a few hours.

I cannot write more now—as I am so soon to start. But I hope that we will be permitted to meet week after next, to talk over all things.

Your sorrowing but affectionate father   yours & Ellie's.

ALS (WP, DLC).
[1] The General Assembly of the southern Presbyterian Church met in the Franklin Street Presbyterian Church in Baltimore, May 17-29, 1888.
[2] To celebrate "exercises commemorative of the erection of the General Assembly [of the Presbyterian Church in the United States of America] in 1788 and the adoption of the Constitution of the Church." *Minutes of the General Assembly of the Presbyterian Church in the United States of America, New Series, Vol. XI, A.D. 1888* (Philadelphia, 1888), p. 75.

From Edward Ireland Renick

My dear Wilson,   [Washington] May 14, 1888.

I was in examination room all day Saturday, from which I went home utterly fatigued & unable to write you an acknowledgment of your very great kindness. Your check was rec'd on that day.[1] For it and for the kind words accompanying it I shall always be very grateful. You have deeply touched me, my dear fellow, by this exhibition of trust & affection. . . .

With kind regards, in which Mrs. R. joins, to you & Mrs Wilson—& wishing that the little ones are well

I am, as ever yours   E. I. Renick

ALS (WP, DLC). Enc.: Renick's note for $100 dated May 14, 1888.
[1] See E. I. Renick to WW, May 10, 1888, ALS (WP, DLC), asking Wilson to lend him $100.

To Richard Heath Dabney

My dear Heath,   Bryn Mawr, Pa., 16 May, 1888

Only a reason of the gravest character, I am conscious, can be reckoned sufficient to justify my apparent neglect of your letter: but, alas, I have such a reason. I have been so mastered by work and sorrow that it has not been possible for me to show in *any* way, to my dearest friends even, that I recognized any claims upon me but the not-to-be-shunned claims of the daily task. On the 15th of last month my dear mother suddenly died—my first news of her condition was news of her death. Your letter came while I was away with my poor bereaved father in Tennessee (I stayed as long as imperative duties here at all permitted); and since I returned I have had work enough to deaden the pain of my loss,—work enough (for it included some of the most difficult portions of my Baltimore lectures) to have almost overwhelmed me under other circumstances. As it was I welcomed it—and I still rejoice in it—for the pull is still intense. My mother was a mother to me in the fullest, sweetest sense of the word, and her loss has left me with a sad, oppressive sense of having somehow suddenly *lost my youth*. I feel old and responsibility-ridden. I suppose that feeling will in time wear off, however, and that I shall ultimately get my balance again. In the meantime I crave your sympathy, old fellow—I need all you can give. And yet the worst of it is not my own bereavement, but my father's, whose daughters are both married, and who, with my college-boy brother, is left practically without a home. My own happy little home seems to reprove me on his account, in my morbid moments.

I have just received and read with thorough agreement your contribution to the 'University Bulletin' on methods of Historical Instruction.[1] I *feelingly* endorse what you have to say concerning the *undergraduate seminar* idea—indeed I endorse *all* you say.[2]

Heath, my dear fellow, it will be possible—wont it?—for you to stop over with us for at least a little while this summer on your way between Richmond and New York, in one direction or the other. My work will not end with the college term, but the strain of it will—and it will be the best sort of recreation for me to have you with me for a while. We have set our hearts on it—don't refuse.

With regards from Mrs. W.,
                    Yrs. affectionately.   Woodrow Wilson

Please give my warm regards to Dr. von Jagemann and explain to him why I could not send the review I would, under any other circumstances, so gladly have written.

ALS (Wilson-Dabney Correspondence, ViU).

[1] R. H. Dabney, "Methods of Historical Instruction," *Indiana University Bulletin,* I (May 1888), 69-74.

[2] Dabney cautioned against a too-hasty introduction of the German seminar method of historical instruction to American undergraduates, on the ground that American college and university students were far behind German university students in their preparation and still needed basic instruction.

From Joseph R. Wilson, Jr.

My dearest brother: Clarksville, Tenn., May. 17/'88.

Your most welcome letter reached me last night, and did me a great deal of good. Please write to me as often as you possibly can, especially while father is away. You *can* do something for me in this way. I hardly give myself a chance to get lonely, as I keep going about constantly, and as I am boarding everything is very much changed about me, nothing being like home. I go up to the house every day to see how every thing is, but dont stay long enough to get the blues.

I expect to run down to Nashville next Saturday week the 26th inst. I will go down in the morning and return at night. There is a big military encampment there during the week. I will have no college duties on that day so I will be free. I have not mentioned it to father for he might be anxious about me, and there is no cause for any-thing of the sort, and I will not neglect any duties by going.

I am looking forward with a great deal of pleasure to my possible trip to Baltimore & Bryn Mawr next month. I hope father will let me go. Ask him for me, please.

I am somewhat anxious about my final examinations, as I have not been able to do any studying since Mother's death. I will probably be excused from my Latin & Greek as I dont expect to study them after this session.

I love you both with all my heart, and think often of the dear folks at Bryn Mawr.

Ask dear sister Ellie to please write to me. I am well with the exception of a cold, and am pretty happy, considering all things.
                    Your devoted Brother   Joseph.

ALS (WP, DLC).

From Richard Heath Dabney

My dear Friend: Bloomington, Indiana. May 22nd, 1888.

You indeed have my sympathy in your sad bereavement. Like yourself, I am at present extremely oppressed with work, and have therefore only time for a short letter; but, if I express my sympathy in few words, it is none the less genuine. Surely no loss can be more irreparable, or can cause a man more poignant grief, than the loss of the mother who has given him birth, who has nursed him at her breast, & who has all her life loved him & cherished him with that maternal love, which, of all loves, is perhaps the purest & the most unselfish. My own mother died when I was too young to feel this grief. I was, in fact, not quite a month old when death overtook her. Still, my father's second wife has been enough of a mother to me for me to realize what a blow it must be to a man to lose his own mother. Yes, my dear friend, you have my deep and heart-felt sympathy. At times, when I have thought of the probability that my father, in the course of nature, would die before myself, my heart has sunk within me and I have shuddered with horror. But how much keener must be *your* grief, now that your beloved mother is really gone—gone, too before you even knew that she was in danger! But cheer up, old fellow! You still have a father & sisters & brother. You still have a wife & children to live for. You also have work to do in the world; and I sincerely trust that ere long the sharp grief which you now feel will fade into a sadly & softly poetic remembrance of the loved one that is gone.

Under the circumstances it was of course out of the question for you to attempt writing a review of my book for the *Bulletin*, but I thank you all the same for the good will with which you would have written the review had it been possible for you to do so.

I am much gratified at your hearty endorsement of my views on "Methods of Historical Instruction" as expressed in the *Bulletin*. The footnote[1] may have shown you that the article was in part intended as a defiance to Jordan, who is not only a humbug in general but has endeavored to force me also into the humbug business. The alleged "original work" which his special students in Ichthyology do is, in my opinion, largely a waste of time.

Well, the happy day is fixed! And, if nothing unforeseen should prevent, my single misery will come to an end on June 19th at St. Paul's Church, Richmond. No invitation-cards will be

sent out, but I need hardly say that it would be a great pleasure
& gratification to me if you—and Mrs. Wilson too—could run
down to Richmond and see me shake off the dust of bachelorhood from my feet. After the ceremony there will be a quiet little
reception at Mrs. Bentley's house of our relatives and intimate
friends. Do you think you could be there? As all my movements
after the 19th of June are as yet undecided, I can't say whether
I shall pass anywhere near Bryn Mawr or not, & cannot therefore
say whether there is any chance of my accepting your kind
invitation or not.

In great haste, & with regards to Mrs. Wilson I remain
Most sincerely yr friend   R. H. Dabney

ALS (WP, DLC) with WWhw notation on env.: "Ans. May 31/88."
¹ It was a footnote on p. 73 of Dabney's article which read as follows: "The
official announcement, that seminary work in history is done at the Indiana
University, was the result of a misunderstanding and was printed without the
knowledge of the professor of history."

A Plan for a School of Public Law¹

[c. May 22, 1888]

Faculty: School of Public Law:

1. Professor of Public Law.
   Subjects: General (Comparative) Public Law.
              Public Law of the Union
              Public Law of the States
              Comparative Legislation.
2. Professor of Constitutional History
   Subjects: General (Comparative) Const. Hist'y.
              Const. Hist'y of the U. S.
              Const. Hist'y of the States
              Const. History of England.
3. Professor of Roman Law and Jurisprudence.
   Subjects: Jurisprudence
              Roman Law
              International Law
4. Professor of Administration and Finance.
   Subjects: Administration
              Justice
              Finance.

WWhw MS. (WP, DLC) with WWsh notations on verso.
¹ As Wilson's letter to D. C. Gilman, printed below, suggests, Wilson may
have drafted this plan in the early summer of 1888.

To Daniel Coit Gilman[1]

Dear Mr. Gilman,   Bryn Mawr, Pa., 22 May, 1888

I delivered the last of my lectures for this year on Administration on Saturday morning last [May 19]. I knew that to call on you to say my farewell for the year during the only hours at my disposal in Baltimore, 'between trains,' would, at this season of the year, this crisis of the semester, be anything but considerate: I am, therefore, driven to adopt this means of expressing to you the enjoyment I have derived from my course in Baltimore, and of uttering the hope that your vacation will bring to you all the rest and recreation that are reasonably to be expected between terms.

I feel that I am deriving not a little mental profit from my connection with the University, and certainly the amount of quiet, earnest interest developed by my lectures among the men in the department has been the source of immense encouragement to me. I believe that I shall work into the sort of influence I most desire to have.

If you do not object to have your vacation leisure so invaded, I should esteem it a favor if you would let me know what your address will be during the summer, so that I may consult you as to the means of securing an endowment for a School of Public Law such as I spoke of at our last interview.[2] Schemes are revolving in my head which I want to formulate this summer and upon which I should wish to obtain your judgment so soon as they take form, in order that the effort to raise an endowment may be set afoot at once, should you approve.

Very sincerely Yours,   Woodrow Wilson

ALS (D. C. Gilman Papers, MdBJ).

[1] There is a WWsh draft of this letter in WP, DLC.

[2] This statement strongly indicates that one of two developments had occurred since Herbert Baxter Adams suggested his plan for a school of public affairs and administration at the Johns Hopkins to Wilson in 1887 (see H. B. Adams to WW, Jan. 25, 1887). Either Adams and Wilson had discussed Adams's plan during Wilson's week-end stays in Baltimore in 1888 and agreed that Wilson should assume main responsibility for maturing the plan, or else Wilson had set out upon his own course and initiative with a different plan for a School of Public Law. Gilman, in a reply which is missing, encouraged Wilson to press ahead and sent his summer address, which Wilson recorded in the pocket notebook described at September 21, 1885, as North East Harbor, Maine.

From Williston Walker

Dear Sir: Leipzig May 28. 1888.

I have this day telegraphed and written to President Rhoads

of your College accepting the appointment to the instructorship in History, subject to the confirmation of the Trustees. In my letter of April 30th I outlined to Pres. Rhoads the course of study I have thus far pursued. He has, doubtless, shown my letter to you and I need not repeat what I there said. The division of work, as laid out in the Program, suits me excellently. I have had no experience in teaching; I am therefore glad that the portions of the work which you had planned to have treated in lectures concern periods to which I have given special attention. The presentation of French History in something like the same fullness of treatment as is given to English History, corresponds also with my own ideas of a proper division of the work.

Of course success in the study of modern History is impossible without a thorough grounding in the details of the main political events of the stories of England, France and Germany; but my aim would be constantly to show the development of civilization and the causes which have made Europe and America what they now are.

May I ask you to write me at your convenience detailing your wishes as to the course of instruction to be pursued in History during the coming year? I shall endeavor to be at Bryn Mawr in time to take part in the entrance examinations—about Sept. 25th—but I fear that it will be impossible for me to meet you before that time. I shall not be ready to pass my doctor's examination here till about Aug. 1st and can hardly reach America before Sept. 15th. My address till Aug. 1 will be here—Emilien Str. 13^{11}, Leipzig.

Very respectfully   Williston Walker.

ALS (WP, DLC) with WWhw figures on env.

To Richard Heath Dabney

My dear Heath,   Bryn Mawr, Pa., 31 May, 1888
I am heartily glad to get the good news contained in your welcome letter of the 22nd. To be married on June 19th! Hurrah! and again hurrah! I speak from the card when I say that you are about to do the very best thing a man—and especially a student, as it seems to me—could possibly do. No one is so sensitive, as a rule, as the student—and there's no cure for sensitiveness like a wife's sympathy,—no strength like that to be gotten from her love and and [sic] trust. Marriage has been the *making* of me both intellectually and morally, and, judging by my own experience,

I look forward to hearing the same pæan from you before many months are gone. Of course a fellow's ecstatically happy at first, and all that is genuine and to be cherished—that first feeling of conjugal union; but *afterwards*, as years are added to months, that first ecstasy is succeeded by something even better,—a settled, permeating, sustaining, invigorating sense of strength and completeness and satisfaction which a man, if he be a man, would not exchange for all the wealth and success and fame that the world contains! You can *imagine* all this now: but wait and see if your imagination has done the subject justice. So soon as a fellow begins living *for some one else* he finds himself. In every sense "love is the fulfilling of the law."

You will not charge me with growing sentimental, I know: I am not giving you my sentiments, but my convictions. My bachelor colleagues here think that bachelorhood is freedom,—freedom to buy books, to go to Europe in the summer, to indulge the hundred and one tastes and idiosyncrasies which the student allows himself; and so it is—there's no doubt about it, a wife and family do 'tie a man down.' But when he loses in *extension* he more than makes up in *intension*. He gets an expansion of nature, too, a broadening and sweetening of his sympathies, and a rounding out of faculty such as come in no other way. He loses geographical and pecuniary freedom (if you will allow me the phrases) but *gains* moral and intellectual emancipation!

And now for what I sat down to say: *make your wedding tour include Bryn Mawr*, and convey to Miss Bentley our congratulations, keeping for yourself—the party chiefly to be felicitated—the heartiest good wishes and love of your sincere friends, Mrs and Mr.   Woodrow Wilson

ALS (Wilson-Dabney Correspondence, ViU).

Wilson Reviews His Lectures at the Johns Hopkins

[*c. June 1, 1888*]

Dr. Woodrow Wilson has given twenty-five lectures to twenty-five graduate students upon the subject of Administration.

The course opened with two lectures devoted to a brief historical discussion of the functions of government. It was the object of these lectures to bring Administration out of the field of abstract discussion and give it the practical aspect which it is so desirable that it should wear. Following these, two lectures were given to a consideration of the exact field and nature of Administration and the character of administrative questions, so far as these matters could be suggestively treated at the opening of a course. The ground being thus cleared, the great bulk of the work was devoted to comparative expositions of the structure and functions of the Central Government in France, Prussia, England, Switzerland, the German Empire, and the United States. In the cases of Switzerland and the United States the central gover[n]ments of the States, as well as the structure and functions of the federal administration, were considered.

These were the first-year lectures of a three-years' course and were meant to afford the student a basis for his own study and for the future portions of the course by familiarizing him with the larger parts, the chief functions and energies, of six typical modern governments.

Printed in *Thirteenth Annual Report of the President of The Johns Hopkins University, 1888* (Baltimore, 1888), pp. 72-73.

Wilson Reviews His Course Work at Bryn Mawr

[c. *June 1, 1888*]

History and Political Science.—The course in Political Science was divided into two parts, namely:

I.   A three-hour course in Political Economy was given, which consisted of text-book drill in the elements of political economy, and in the history and analysis of modern French and German Socialism. The text-books used were Professor F. A. Walker's "*Political Economy,*" and Professor R. T. Ely's "*French and German Socialism in Modern Times.*" Full comment was made on these texts by the instructor; articles in current economic journals bearing upon topics developed in the class room were read and discussed; and passages in standard works, like Bagehot's "*Economic Essays,*" Jevons's "*Money and the Mechanism of Exchange,*" Mill's "*Political Economy,*" and Professor Cairnes's latest work, were brought to the attention of the class, either by the instructor or through class reports.

II.   A two-hour course on the Government of the United States was given. This course consisted of lectures only. It was prefaced by a sketch, in about ten lectures, of the origin and development of government, such topics being discussed as the following: The Origin of Government; the Organization and Fundamental Ideas of the ancient State, both Grecian and Roman; the Rise and Character of the Mediæval State; the accumulation of all feudal powers in the hands of a king, who, like the kings of France, in a feudal sense owned his realm, and who, by virtue of possession, was absolute ruler in his own private right; the transformation of the polity of a possessing king into that of a controlling people; the dependent (colonial) State; the modern federal State, with its contrasts to both the ancient and modern Confederation; etc. In the lectures on the Government of the United States the instructor traced the colonial preparations for our present forms of government, both state and national; showed how the Constitution of the Union was made (and made wisely) by a selection of provisions from tested colonial charters and constitutions, except in the one particular of the Electoral College, which was imported from an alien system, and which was immediately to break down; gave as clear an exposition as possible of the general features of the federal system; and added to this a systematic scheme of the state goverments, laying special emphasis on *local* government, in its New England, Southern, and mixed (Western) types. The single endeavor which ran through the whole course as its connecting thread was to make the essential unity of our system of government appear,—to show that it is one system, not several,—that the governments of the States and the government of the Union are but several parts of one frame of Government, together constituting a single organism.

Graduate Course.—A graduate course of lectures was given four hours a week throughout the year, on the history of government, the comparative public law of modern states, viewed historically, and on modern constitutions.

Printed in *Bryn Mawr College. The President's Report to the Board of Trustees, for the Year 1887-88* (Philadelphia, 1888), pp. 20-21.

From John Monroe Van Vleck[1]

My dear Sir: Middletown, Conn., June 6, 1888

Permit me to resume our too brief conversation of last week,[2] and to ask whether you can now give a more definite indication as to your willingness to accept a place here than you then felt yourself able to do.

I hope to meet a committee of our Trustees early next week, and it would be a gratification to me if I could know, before that time, what your decision would probably be. Your lectures at Johns Hopkins University could, I think, be easily provided for. The more serious question in the minds of the Trustees will undoubtedly be the risk of another change in the department at the expiration of your present engagement at Baltimore. With a good man, and with continuity of work, we think the conditions are favorable for building up here a department of History and Political Economy which will add much to the strength of the college, and will satisfy a very generous ambition on the part of the head of the department. Still, I do not think it impossible that it will be deemed best to offer you the place even with the risk of losing you soon.

I do not ask you to expose yourself to any disagreeable candidacy for the place. Any communication which you may make to me will be received with whatever *confidence* you wish to have attached to it. The time remaining before the meeting of our Trustees is, however, very short, and for this reason it is desirable that I should know at as early a day as possible what is practicable for us.　　　　Very truly yours　J. M. Van Vleck.

ALS (WP, DLC) with WWhw notation on env.: "Ans. June 7th & 10th/88."
¹ Born Stone Ridge, N. Y., March 4, 1833. A.B., Wesleyan University, 1850. Served at Wesleyan University as Adjunct Professor of Mathematics, 1853-57; Professor of Mathematics and Astronomy, 1858-1904; Vice-President, 1890-1903; and Acting President, 1872-73, 1887-89, and 1896-97. Died Nov. 4, 1912.
² Van Vleck seems to have conferred with Wilson in Bryn Mawr or Philadelphia about the possibility of Wilson's going to Wesleyan University.

To John Monroe Van Vleck

My dear Sir:　　　　　　　　　[Bryn Mawr, Pa., June 7, 1888]

I have just received your letter of June 6th, and hasten, as you request, to make a provisional answer.

I may say at once that I shall be very strongly inclined indeed to accept the chair at Wesleyan, should the trustees offer it to me. The character and conditions of the work at Middletown, as you described it, give [it] very decided attractions for me. The only difficulties in the way of my saying without reserve that I would accept are these: I must see the men at Baltimore as to what arrangements of time would be feasible there for my course in administration; and I must to a certain extent disclose and discuss the situation with the authorities here at Bryn Mawr so that, in case I should leave them, they may not be left suddenly, without warning. In brief, I must consult with all who have claims upon me.

I do not anticipate any serious impediments: but of course I could not give a categorical answer to your question without first taking all the bearings of the situation. I must therefore only assure you now of my strong inclination to accept. I am in the midst of the examinations here now, in the very toils of the work, and will not be out of them until Saturday [June 9]. On

Saturday I will run down to Baltimore, and on Monday, in order to meet your desire to know by the first of the week, I will telegraph you a statement of something a little more definite than now given.

As for the probability of my being taken away by the Johns Hopkins, that is a matter extremely indefinite both as to time and manner: there is really no definiteness about their pecuniary prospects; and all that I know as to their attitude towards me is that they would like to have me if they could afford to create another chair. The matter, very likely, will stand at this for many years.

Of course I should like you to make use of this communication as you would wish a similar communication from yourself, made under like circumstances, to be used. I leave it to your discretion and sense of delicacy, which I feel that I can trust.

Very sincerely yours,   Woodrow Wilson

Transcript of WWshLS (draft) (WP, DLC).

To James E. Rhoads[1]

My dear Dr Rhoads,   Bryn Mawr, Pa., 7th June, 1888

Negotiations have been opened with me to ascertain my willingness to accept a chair of Political Science and History at one of the oldest and most reputable of the New England colleges, at a salary of $2500 for eight hours work a week, with full opportunity to continue my course at the Johns Hopkins (by means of a six weeks leave of absence). Of course I fully realize the attractions of my place here, and my interest in the college would lead me to further in every possible way its prosperity; but my duty to my little family makes it even more imperative that I should seek rapid advancement in my profession in point of salary, amount and character of work, &c, and I shall feel obliged, therefore, to accept the call which will almost certainly be extended to me, unless our trustees here can very much increase my present salary, upon which I have, this year, found it impossible to live.

I know that you know me well enough to be sure of the spirit in which I make these statements. You will, I am confident, believe that in taking this course I am simply following what I feel to be my plain duty.

Very sincerely Yours,   Woodrow Wilson

ALS (WP, DLC). There is a WWsh draft of this letter in WP, DLC.
  1 Wilson did not send this letter and probably had an interview with Dr. Rhoads instead.

From Edward Ireland Renick

My dear Wilson:　　　　Washington, D. C., June 15, 1888.

I inclose a Treasury draft for $20.00 which will reduce my indebtedness a little. I had hoped to send the whole $100. but I was disappointed of some money which I had been expecting. As I can, I shall send other installments. And with each goes, my dear fellow, warm thanks to you for your kindness, & the best of good wishes for your prosperity. . . .

Wishing very much that we can contrive to see you all in some way, I am with best regards to Mrs Wilson—

As ever yours,　E. I. Renick.

ALS (WP, DLC) with WWhw notation on env.: "Ans. June 19/88"; WWhw shopping list; and WWhw note: "*Law & Ethics*　Law unquestionably expresses moral judgments—but it is not Ethics."

From John Monroe Van Vleck

My dear Sir:　　　　Middletown, Conn., June 16, 1888

You have doubtless expected before this time some reply to your letters and telegram. A suddenly undertaken journey immediately after their receipt, from which I returned only last evening, must constitute my apology

I regret that I have been unable to get a meeting of the committee to which I referred in my former note. One was appointed in N. Y. yesterday, but only two out of five Trustees were on hand. I am arranging for another to be held, probably, on Thursday—certainly on a day on which all will promise to be present. I will communicate with you immediately thereafter. The judgment of those whom I saw was in harmony with mine, that an arrangement could be easily and very satisfactorily made, which would permit the fulfillment of your engagements at J. H. U. I have no doubt the others will be of a similar mind

In the mean time, or later, before the meeting of our Board of Trustees would you not like to make a run up here and see for yourself how the place looks, and those who are in it? I hope to be in Princeton on Wednesday, and shall be glad to meet you if you are also there.

In great haste,

Very sincerely yours　J. M. Van Vleck

ALS (WP, DLC).

From Thomas Dixon, Jr.

Dear Wilson: Boston.[1] June 21, '88.

What are you doing this year with yourself & how are you doing it? I think of you often & wonder how you are getting on. Write me a letter and tell me about yourself. Also tell me something about Bryn Mawr. I've two little sisters to go to college in fall & don't know where I want them to go exactly. Had thought of Bethlehem Pa somewhat as my wife went there. Dewey (D. R.) & Levermore are here at Inst. Technology you know.

Fraternally yours,   Thomas Dixon, jr.

ALS (WP, DLC).
[1] Dixon was at this time pastor of the Dudley Street Baptist Church of Boston.

From John Monroe Van Vleck

My dear Sir: New York. June 21, 1888

I was very sorry to miss connection with you at Princeton yesterday.[1] I had two or three persons looking for you, but got no tidings of your "whereabouts" till you were gone. Our Committee met this morning, with every member present. I am very glad to say that they unanimously and very cordially united with the Faculty of Wesleyan in recommending you for the Chair of History and Political Economy. In this action which is what I have confidently expected from the beginning, they have construed your letters and telegram as signifying readiness on your part to accept the position. If we have been in any degree too confident concerning this will you be so kind as to communicate with me promptly, by telegraph?

The election by our Board of Trustees will be on Tuesday or Wednesday next. I think there is no doubt in the minds of the Committee that there will be a ready concurrence in our recommendation.

We should be glad to see you in Middletown before Commencement if convenient and agreeable to you. In great haste

Yours truly   J M Van Vleck

ALS (WP, DLC).
[1] Wilson went to Princeton with his uncle-in-law, Dr. Thomas A. Hoyt, to attend Dr. Francis Landey Patton's inauguration as twelfth President of the College of New Jersey on June 20, 1888. For Wilson's account of this affair, see WW to R. Bridges, Aug. 26, 1888.

From the Minutes of the Executive Committee of the
Bryn Mawr Board of Trustees
[June 27, 1888]

1.   At a meeting of the Executive Committee held at 228 S.
3rd St, Phila, 6 mo. 27, 1888, there were present, Philip C.
Garrett, Chas. S. Taylor and James Whitall.

2.   The following statement presented by Dr Rhoads[1] and
agreed to as correct by Dr. W. Wilson in a conversation held by
them 6 mo. 23, 1888, was read.

> Notes of a Statement made by Dr Woodrow Wilson to be
> presented to the Trustees of Bryn Mawr College, given
> on *the 23rd of 6th mo.* 1888.

First, Dr Wilson submits his letter to Dr J. E. Rhoads, dated
June 22nd, 1888 to be found on file in Letter Files.[2]

Second. He proposes that the Trustees of Bryn Mawr shall
offer him a salary of $3000. a year for an indefinite period,
the engagement to be subject to a call at any time to another
institution.

Third. Dr Wilson does not feel himself bound by the agreement signed March, 1887, for the following reasons[:] The
contract says that he should have an Assistant "as soon as
practicable," in conversation before the time of signing the
contract the term "practicable" was explained by Dr Rhoads
to mean financial ability to make the appointment, and he
acted on that information in signing the contract. That during
the summer following he received a letter from Dr Rhoads
stating that it was "practicable" so far as means were involved
to make the appointment; of which the accompanying is a
copy.[3] Dr Wilson replied to this letter advising strongly the
appointment of E. C. Lunt, and after finding the appointment
was not made[4] considered himself freed from the obligation
of the contract, & so now feels wholly absolved therefrom.[5]
Dr Wilson stated this view in conversation with Dr Rhoads on
the subject some months since, perhaps in April last. At the
time of the conversation Dr Rhoads quite repudiated the
thought that the reason assigned by Dr Wilson made the
contract invalid, because (1st) E. C. Lunt was to have lectured on Ancient History and yet felt himself that he was not
fully competent for the task; because (2nd), there were no
students in the college who could not defer their courses
in History for a year, and because the expense seemed, on
final consideration, an unwarrantable one. At the time of the

interview, just referred to, Dr Wilson said he was unwilling to make any engagement that would prevent him from accepting a more advantageous offer made him elsewhere, but Dr Rhoads urged the binding force of the agreement, and stated that we expected Dr Wilson to continue next year and with this understanding on Dr Rhoads part the interview closed. Dr Wilson states that he did not expect to be considered as continuing under this contract, but he did expect to continue for the coming year at the rate of salary he had received the past year, the engagement terminable at such time before the actual work of the College shall begin next fall as would, in his judgment allow time for finding a successor; the time Dr Wilson thinks is ample before autumn to find such a successor, and he feels perfectly justified in making the above proposition to the Trustees.

It should be added that Dr Rhoads did discuss the subject of the appointment of E. C. Lunt with the Executive Committee and for the reasons above indicated no action was taken.

3.   Upon a full consideration of the whole subject the Committee have concluded that the contract between Dr Woodrow Wilson and the Trustees is binding upon both parties to it. That under any view of the case the engagement for the coming year would be valid: The time allowed to find a successor fit to take the head of the Department of History is very insufficient, and if the Trustees are to find that any or all of its officers who had made engagements for the ensuing year, withdraw from them after the close of the College year, it will be impossible to carry on the College efficiently, or to fulfil published offers of instruction. In the present case, students intend coming to complete their courses in Political Science, with the full expectation that the instruction of last year will be continued; and Dr. Williston Walker also is coming with the expectation that Dr W. Wilson will be his colleague and adviser.

The Committee therefore feels obliged to decline Dr W. Wilson's proposal to annul the contract.

Hw entry, "Minutes of the Executive Committee of the Board of Trustees of Bryn Mawr College," bound ledger book for period Jan. 10, 1884-March 9, 1894 (PBm).
    1 J. E. Rhoads to M. Carey Thomas, June 23, 1888, ALS (Presidential Files, PBm), repeats Dr. Rhoads's statement to the Executive Committee.
    2 This letter is missing.
    3 J. E. Rhoads to WW, Aug. 25, 1887.
    4 J. E. Rhoads to WW, Sept. 8, 1887.
    5 Wilson made this point in WW to R. Bridges, Nov. 30, 1887.

From James E. Rhoads

My Dear Doctor Wilson,   Bryn Mawr, Penna.—6 mo. 27, 1888.

The Executive Committee of the Trustees of the College met this afternoon, the earliest time at which they could be called together after our interview, and your statement as assented to by us, together with a copy of my letter about the appointment of E. C. Lunt, were laid before them. I endeavored to present your view of the case as fully as I could, and left the decision to them with no other explanations on my part than those referred to in our conversation on the 23rd.

After very thoughtful deliberation the Committee made the following minutes:

"The following statement presented by Dr Rhoads and agreed to by Dr. Wilson in a conversation held by them 6 mo. 23, 1888, was read;

(Then follows the statement)

Upon a full consideration of the whole subject the Committee have concluded that the contract between Dr Woodrow Wilson and The Trustees is binding upon both parties to it.

That under any view of the case the engagement for the coming year would be valid; the time allowed to find a successor fit to take the head of the Department of History is very insufficient, and if The Trustees are to find that any or all of its officers who have made engagements for the ensuing year break them after the close of the College year, it will be impossible to carry on the College efficiently, or to fulfil published offers of instruction.

In the present case students intend coming to complete their courses in Political Science with the full expectation that the instruction of last year will be continued; and Dr. W. Walker also is coming with the expectation that Dr. W. Wilson will be his colleague and adviser. The Committee therefore feels obliged to decline the proposal of Dr Woodrow Wilson to annul the contract."

Your letter of this afternoon[1] reached me on my return from the city, and I will lay it before The Executive Committee as the representative of The Trustees as soon as I can readily do so, unless I hear that you have another wish in the matter tomorrow morning.

In making the above minute The Executive Committee have, I think, endeavored to act in the most dispassionate manner, and simply expressed their judgment as men of business and of long experience in the affairs of Colleges. The difference of view between you and them arises, I believe, from no lack of sensitiveness of honor or conscience on either part, but strictly from the exercise of judgment in a question of business.

I am yours very sincerely,   James E Rhoads

ALS (WP, DLC) with WWhw names and addresses of P. C. Garrett and James Whitall on env.
1 This letter is missing.

From Marion Wilson Kennedy

My dearest brother—   San Antonio, 6/27/88

Why do we not hear from you or Ellie? I know you are very busy, and so is Ellie, no doubt, but I do so long to hear from you both. As you see, I am here in San Antonio—, all alone this time,—in an "Infirmary" for sick women. All that can be done, in the way of kind attention, has been done for me, during the nearly four weeks I have spent here; but I am *very, very* lonely, and seem to feel our great loss more every day. They tell us, dear Father seems much changed, but stands his trouble grandly, of course. I was very ill for about a week, not long after getting here. Had "inflamation of the coating of the liver," and neither the doctor nor I thought I was going to get well, part of the time. I was amazed to find that, after thinking and praying over it one entire night, I felt *quite content* to leave the result in God's hands. I urged the doctor not to send for Ross, until he knew I would not last much longer, and so he never knew of my illness, until all danger was past. I managed to prop myself on my arm long enough to write a little note each day, in which I said nothing about myself at all. I would not run such a risk again, for anything, just because no one knows how suddenly the end may come, as with our precious Mother. I have a good deal of heart trouble, anyhow, and that complicates matters somewhat.

I am too warm and lazy to write any more just now. Have just written to Father, and must write, some time during the day, to Annie. How was she looking, Woodrow? I can't get her to tell me about herself at all.

Write soon, please, to the address given at the head of this epistle. Tell me of something good to read, please. I am lonely and homesick.

With warmest love to you all and kisses for the babies,

Your loving sister,   Marion.

ALS (WP, DLC) with WWhw notation on env.: "Ans. 7/10/88."

From Joseph Ruggles Wilson

My precious Son—   New York Thursday 28th June 1888

Your letter, received yesterday, did me a world of good. Its assurances of love on the part of the dear three now within your home were not indeed *needed*, but they were most timely to my wearied heart. In time I *may* succeed, with God's help, in throwing off the awful burden of that solitude which the decease of your mother laid upon me; but meanwhile nothing enables me to support the pressure so much as the affection of our children: and whilst I *know* that I have this in full measure yet the occasional assurance of it, as in your dear letter, is not amiss. God bless you all.

I am about to leave for Saratoga, where my stay will be indefinite, but I foresee that it cannot be long, for I hate the *place* although dependent upon the *waters*.

My address will be Drs. Strong Circular St. Saratoga. If I shall stop elsewhere I will let you know at once.

Love unmeasured to our darling Dode, and also to our sweet Ellie.   Your affec   Father.

ALS (WP, DLC) with WWsh and WWhw notations on env.

To the President and Trustees of Bryn Mawr College

Sirs: Bryn Mawr, June 29th., 1888.

I hereby tender my resignation of my position as Associate Professor of History and Political Science in Bryn Mawr College, for the purpose of accepting an offer made me by the Trustees of Wesleyan University, Middletown, Ct. The offer from Middletown is of the most generous character. It includes a salary of $2,500 for eight hours' class work per week, with the privilege of moulding the work in such a way as to give prominence to the special topics of instruction in which I am most particularly interested, and with six weeks' leave of absence each year for the delivery of my course of lectures at the Johns Hopkins University. The terms of this offer, coupled with the fact that at Wesleyan University my classes would be composed almost exclusively of men, who from the nature of the case are necessarily much more directly interested in the topics of Political Science than women are, have made me feel that to accept it would be both to secure more advantageous conditions of work and to widen my field of usefulness. I have therefore given my assurance to the authorities at Middletown that I would accept.

I would not of course have felt at liberty to entertain proposals of this nature from any quarter had I thought the contract still binding which was made between the Trustees of Bryn Mawr College on the one hand and myself on the other in the Spring of 1887.[1] A year ago overtures were made to me by President Angell of the University of Michigan touching my willingness to accept the chair made vacant by Judge T. M. Cooley's appointment to the Inter-state Commerce Commission.[2] I at once told Dr. Rhoads of the contents of President Angell's letter, and went into Philadelphia to meet President Angell with the full understanding between Dr. Rhoads and myself that I would take no step whatever in the matter without previous permission had from himself and the Trustees of the College. Dr Rhoads gave President Angell to understand that I could not be released; and the whole matter fell through. Of course I felt deeply chagrined at losing a possible opportunity to succeed Judge Cooley; but I knew that Dr. Rhoads had acted entirely within his right, and I had nothing therefore to say. I mention these circumstances, of course, only in order to indicate what my course would have been, in the present instance, had I still considered myself bound by any definite agreement.

But in the present case the circumstances were very different. It was one of the express provisions of the contract signed in the Spring of 1887 that an Assistant should be appointed in History "as soon as practicable."[3] I regarded that provision as a condition precedent to my acceptance of the contract. Before I consented to the execution of the contract in this form the phrase "as soon as practicable" was explained to me to mean as soon as *pecuniarily* practicable, and I was told that there was at least one candidate for the position then under consideration who would be accepted for temporary appointment should no more fully equipped man be found who would take the place for the salary which would probably be offered. It was upon this understanding that I signed, taking the risk of a lack of pecuniary ability on the part of the College to appoint an Assistant, but, so far as the contract was concerned, taking no other risk of a failure in that particular. When therefore, before the opening of the college year just passed, the first of the three years affected by the contract, I was assured that the College had money enough to warrent the appointment, and that a man had been found competent to teach modern history, the branch most important to the political science courses, and that he would be appointed if I so advised, and when, notwithstanding my urgent advice that the appointment be made, it was not made, I felt that there had been a palpable breach of an essential part of the contract; whereby I was released from further obligation under it: though of course I was convinced that the breach had not been made in any spirit of bad faith.

I had felt fully justified in giving the advice I did give concerning the appointment of Mr. E. C. Lunt,[4] the gentleman thought of, because it had not been proposed that the Assistant should be asked to give instruction in both modern and ancient history: the courses in ancient and modern history were intended to alternate from year to year in any case; modern history both promised to attract larger classes than ancient history could be expected to attract and was more important than ancient history to the success of the political science courses; and I felt sure that, should modern history be offered, a large number of students would be found ready to take it, notwithstanding the fact that none had announced an intention to take ancient history. As regards the desire of students to have the modern history course given, if in no other point, my judgment was abundantly justified by the event.

I resumed my work in the College in October, 1887, under the full, the matter-of-course presumption that, being released from my obligations under the contract, I was serving under a provisional arrangement, such as is customary in the usage of most colleges and which was in no way directly affected by the agreement made in the previous Spring, and I continued under that impression until the early Spring of the present year, when, in a consultation to which I had been summoned by Dr. Rhoads in order to discuss the courses for next year, and the appointment of an assistant, I found that he had not been viewing the case as I did. I therefore, immediately availed myself of this opportunity to state very distinctly my view, and although he did not assent to it, we came to no definite understanding, and I supposed that the question would be opened again. When it was not re-opened, I took it for granted that I was to stay without any agreement for a specific time, as I had expressed a decided wish to do; and it was under that impression, of course, that I encouraged the idea of a call to Middletown, which was first broached to me in the early part of the present month, June, 1888.

Since the question of my resignation has been under discussion[,] being anxious to be assured that my view of the case was perfectly well grounded, though of course with no thought whatever of making the question a subject of litigation, I have been careful to obtain the deliberate opinion of a lawyer, and I believe that, so far as the legal aspects of the case are concerned, I have made no mistake. The case, as it presents itself to my mind, however, is not a case of merely formal departure from the conditions of work which I contemplated when I signed the contract, but is on the contrary much more than that: it is a case of the most serious derangement of my own courses for two out of the three years which the contract was meant to cover. The failure to appoint an Assistant for the year just closed will even more seriously affect the work of the department during the next college year than it has affected it during the past year, inasmuch as none of the new students who will then have entered the classes in political science will have had an opportunity to get the preliminary instruction in modern history which will be indispensable to successful study in the course. The absence of an Assistant has permanently changed the conditions of my work; and has made the position which I hold much less desirable than it would otherwise have been.

I realize that the time seems to be late for offering a resignation; but that circumstance is of course unavoidable, and would be so in case of an election by any one of a great majority of the colleges in this country. The boards of trustees of most of our colleges meet only once or twice during the year, and generally make their selections for vacant chairs at the usual Commencement season, which is a week or two after the close of our own term. It is only at this time, therefore, except in case of an invitation from some one of the few colleges which elect at any earlier date, that I could notify your honorable body of a call to another institution. I have very little doubt, from my own knowledge of the field of choice, that my place could without difficulty be filled, for the salary which I have received from the College, within the next three months.

It is, therefore, with a profound conviction of the rightfulness of my course that I now tender my resignation, and in the confidence that your honorable body will see the justice of acquiescing in my withdrawal. I am virtually committed to the authorities of Wesleyan, and I cannot regard myself as committed to remain at Bryn Mawr; but I earnestly hope that I may with the full consent of its Trustees be permitted to leave the College in which my first work as a teacher has been done with so much both of profit and of enjoyment to myself.

With sincere respect,   [Woodrow Wilson]

WWTL (copy) (WP, DLC). Att.: WWT copy of contract with Bryn Mawr College, March 14, 1887.

1 Printed at March 14, 1887.

2 See J. B. Angell to WW, April 9, 1887, and WW to J. B. Angell, April 12, 1887.

3 In the WWT copy of the contract attached to this letter, Wilson typed within brackets, following the phrase "as soon as practicable," the following: " 'as soon as practicable' is interlined in the handwriting of Dr. Rhoads, being inserted, I understood him to say, by himself—W.W."

4 Of the letters concerning Lunt, we have only J. E. Rhoads to WW, Aug. 25 and Sept. 8, 1887.

From John Monroe Van Vleck

My dear Sir: Middletown, Conn., June 29, 1888

Your letter of the 27th was received yesterday morning, and your telegram came to hand at a late hour of the afternoon. The day was too busy a one with me to admit of any reply except with the brevity of a telegram, and illness today compels me to almost equal brevity.

I am extremely sorry to know that there is trouble where I had least anticipated it. As I understand the case I do not see any ground, legal or moral, on which they can contest your right to resign. It is my sincere hope and belief that they will speedily relieve you of all embarrassment in the matter.

As to the situation here, I can not refrain from saying that it would be peculiarly—I may say, *extraordinarily* unfortunate, if you should fail to accept. There is no subject to which we have given so much attention during the last six months as to the proper manning of our three vacant departments. The result attained seems to be eminently satisfactory to all the progressive friends of the college. Your own election was not only unanimous, but exceedingly cordial. Such unanimity could not have been secured, however, unless I had been able to assure the Trustees of your readiness to accept the place if it should be offered to you. Under the circumstances, with our Board of Trustees gone, and no chance to fill the place otherwise, I am sure that you will appreciate not only the disappointment which your failure to come would produce among our friends, but also the very delicate position in which I would personally be placed.

Let me assure you, however, that I say this with no wish to add the weight of a straw to the burden which you may already be carrying, but only because I feel that you ought to know the situation as fully as possible. I have all confidence in your integrity and straight-forwardness in the matter, and therefore state the case frankly.

Would you like a personal interview? I shall be in New York

on Monday and Tuesday.[1] If you can meet me there a telegram
to this place tomorrow or Sunday will reach me, and I will
appoint time and place. With kind regards to Mrs. Wilson, I am
Sincerely yours   J. M. Van Vleck

ALS (WP, DLC).
  [1] Wilson met him in New York on one of these days. Among other things, they
talked about housing for the Wilsons in Middletown.

From Edson Wyllys Burr

Dear Sir,   Paterson, N. J. June 30 1888
    I have the honor to inform you that, at the Annual Meeting
of the Board of Trustees of Wesleyan University held June 28th
1888, you were unanimously elected to the [Hedding] Professorship of History and Political Economy.
    With the best wishes for your greatest enjoyment and success,
I am   Yours Very Truly,   Edson W. Burr
                        Secretary, Board of Trustees.

ALS (WP, DLC) with WWhw notation on env.: "Ans. July 10/88."

James E. Rhoads to Martha Carey Thomas

My Dear Friend,   Bryn Mawr, Pa. 6 Mo. 30. 1888.
    There was no quorum at the Board Meeting today, & without
action it was adjourned to 6th day next at 2 P.M. the earliest
date at which it appeared possible to have a quorum present.
    Dr Wilson has taken friendly legal advice, and is assured that
his position is sound, that the case would be carried in a court
in his favor. He meets the statement about the year being one
for Ancient History by stating that he urged the apptmt of Lunt
to teach Modern History from the class entering last autumn.
He says he has acted in perfect good faith throughout the while,
never imagining that he was bound by the contract after he discovered that Lunt was not appointed, but took it for granted the
Trustees found that Lunts appntm was undesirable to them &
did not act, but in good faith also released him from his written
agreement.
    He holds that he has acted as a man of honor, education, and
conscience should have acted throughout, but admits some indiscretion in not making sure that what was so obviously right to
him was equally so to the Trustees. . . .
    I am truly thy friend,   James E Rhoads

ALS (President's Files, PBm).

From James E. Rhoads

My Dear Doctor Wilson,   Bryn Mawr, Penna. 7 mo. 6, 1888.

The Board had before it this afternoon your letter of resignation and the facts bearing upon the case as a whole, after which they adopted the following minute, using in the closing part of it the language of your letter as most expressive of their view of the subject:

["]Resolved, That it is the unanimous judgment of the Board that the contract between The Trustees and Dr. Woodrow Wilson is binding upon both parties to it, but inasmuch as Dr. Wilson entertains a doubt as to the validity of the agreement, The Trustees acquiesce in his withdrawal from the College."

I would repeat here what I have said to you in conversation that I entertain the fullest confidence that you are acting in accordance with your convictions of right, and wish to add the expression of my very warm regard for you, my high estimate of your talents, and expectation that a most useful career lies before you.

I would have called this afternoon were it not that I have reached home rather late and wearied with the heat.

Very sincerely yours,   James E Rhoads

ALS (WP, DLC).

Thomas Alexander Hoyt to Ellen Axson Wilson

My Darling Ellie,   Phil— July 7th [1888].

I failed again yesterday to see Mr. Jenkin.[1] I left the papers with Mr. Hinckley, a special friend of Mr. J—. They will confer together, & write Woodrow.

Meanwhile Mr. Hinckley wants the names of the Trustees: he thinks that he & Mr. J— may bring to bear on them, some personal influence: He will write Woodrow, I think for the names. His address is R. H. Hinckley, Esq. 204 South 5th St.

Love to all from all—   Ever fondly—   T—

ALI (WP, DLC).

[1] Dr. Hoyt wrote "Jenkin" and must have meant "Jenkins," as there was no Jenkin listed in the Philadelphia city directory for the years 1887-89. Perhaps he was one of the following lawyers by the name of Jenkins listed in the directory for 1888: Andrew T., Owen B., and Theodore F.

From John Monroe Van Vleck

My dear Professor: Middletown, Conn., July 10, 1888

The intelligence conveyed by your telegram of Saturday was exceedingly gratifying not only to myself but to all of my colleagues. I beg to assure you of a cordial welcome from our entire college community.

Is it not about time that you and Mrs. Wilson should come up here, and see the place you are to live in? Since our last interview, I have made some inquiry concerning houses for rent, and have found, as I suggested would be the case, that they are very few. The introduction into our little city, within the last few months, of two new manufacturing enterprises has made rents unusually scarce. There are at present, however, three houses in the immediate vicinity of the college either of which, if acceptable to you, could without doubt be engaged this week. One of them has just been vacated by our recent instructor in Latin. It is a small and very modest house, entirely without style, but well situated, cosy and comfortable. It is warmed by a good furnace, is provided with a good kitchen range, or rather, stove, also with cold and hot water in the kitchen and bath-room. The rent is $325. It offers more comfort for the money than any other house now unengaged. The principal objection to it, besides its unpretentiousness is the lowness of its ceilings. It is, in fact, an old house recently renovated. There are, however, two or three applicants for it, and it will doubtless soon be rented. What do you say to the proposition that you come and look the ground over this week, and see whether this or either of the other houses mentioned would suit you?[1] If you think favorably of it, please come directly to my house, with or without notice in advance of your arrival, as may best suit your convenience. Most of my family are just now nestled among the White Mountains; but one of my daughters [Clara] is at home with me, and joins cordially in the invitation. I need not say that her gratification and mine will be more than doubled if Mrs. Wilson and the little one accompanies you.

Sincerely yours   J. M. Van Vleck

ALS (WP, DLC).

[1] The Wilsons went to Middletown, saw Van Vleck, and looked at houses on July 13. See J. M. Van Vleck to WW, July 14, 1888.

From D. C. Heath and Company

Dear Prof. Wilson: Boston, Mass. July 10, 1888.
Our Western agent writes that the State of Ky. has just added Civil Government to the course of study for country schools. He is very anxious that we should make a book for such purpose. Will your small book[1] be adapted to such schools, and when will it be ready? There never was a better time to put it on the market then just now. We have been asked to take Mr. Dole's book for such use.[2] We send a copy with this. Do you think it would answer such purpose?
                    Very truly yours,   D. C. Heath & Co.

TL (WP, DLC) with WWhw notation on env.: "Ans 18 July."
[1] Wilson's projected high school text in American government.
[2] Charles Fletcher Dole, *The Citizen and the Neighbor* . . . (Boston, 1884).

From Robert Bridges

Dear Tommy: [New York, c. July 12, 1888]
I am glad to see that you are going to Wesleyan—always provided that it shall not interfere with your taking a place at Princeton, which must come eventually. The Princeton men come from sections of the country which take more naturally to politics than to literature. You could do an immense amount of good there. The men have some enthusiasm and some belief, and are apt to have more staying qualities in practical politics than the New Englanders.
I shall start on my vacation Aug 3 and hope to be away till Aug 26. I am anticipating a first rate time—part at home and part in the Adirondacks. Talcott may join me in the woods. Could you not come with us? . . .
My kindest regards to Mrs. Wilson and the family.
                    Your Friend   Robert Bridges

ALS (WP, DLC) with WWhw notation on env.: "Ans. Aug 26/88."

Three Letters from John Monroe Van Vleck

My dear Professor: Middletown, Conn., July 14, 1888
I regret to say that the Executive Committee seemed so reluctant to make any reduction of the rent of the Westgate house[1] that I did not think it best to *press* them to it. I did not believe that you would wish me to, any further than I did. The expenses of the college are considerably increased for the coming year,

and will be in excess of the ordinary income. They are consequently slow to consider propositions for diminution of income, even when they are slight. I will explain further when I see you again.

I have visited the Butler[2] house again, and have thereby made one discovery, and corrected a blunder which you and I were making in our last conversation about the house. The discovery was that the back room of the second story, the one behind the bath room, has a register in the wall, connecting with the Baltimore heater in the dining room.

The blunder to which I allude was in planning for you and your children to occupy the two *middle* bedrooms—if I may so term them. There is no direct communication between these two rooms, and they could not, therefore, be conveniently so used. There is a narrow door, however, between the front bedroom and the one that is directly over your proposed study. You and your family could, therefore, occupy these two rooms, and the remaining room would then be your guests' chamber. As the house is arranged, I think that this would for other reasons be the better disposition of these three rooms.

The objections to this house, besides its smallness, would then be two: 1st, that the room to be occupied by the little boy would not be warmed by either furnace or Baltimore heater; 2nd, that the servants' room could be entered only through the bath-room, or the boy's room. You are just one too many to make the house a perfect fit.

To sum the whole matter up, I am more disposed than I was yesterday to advise you to take the Westgate house, although the rent is somewhat larger than you would like it to be. If the immediate outlay should occasion you any inconvenience, I am very sure that this could be easily provided for in a way which would not be distasteful to you.

But I must not be officious in the matter. Pardon me if I have already been so, and show your forgiveness by presenting my sincere regards to Mrs. Wilson

Very truly yours   J. M. Van Vleck

[1] A large house at 106 High Street, so-called because it was occupied by Wilson's predecessor in the Hedding chair, the Reverend George Lewis Westgate. As the documents will soon reveal, this was the house that the Wilsons rented.
[2] A house on High Street, now numbered 150, owned by Earle Butler.

My dear Professor: Middletown, Conn., July 16, 1888
Your note of Saturday came to hand this morning. I have

made inquiry as to the probable cost of board for your family at three places, but from none of them do I get an approximately definite estimate. So much depends on the number and quality of the rooms that you would want, as to make the people of whom inquiry was made shy of figures. Indeed it is doubtful whether any of them would be able to give all the rooms that you would need satisfactorily situated. Assuming that this can be done, however, I fancy that the prices would range from twenty five to thirty dollars per week for your entire family including a nurse. Possibly in the house which I think would be most satisfactory the charge would be a little in excess of thirty dollars.

The cost of washing at a laundry would be seventy five cents a dozen. If done by the week, as ours has sometimes been done, by some private party, it would probably cost $2.00 or $2.25 a week.

I have had a conversation with Mr. Butler, who agrees to wait till tomorrow for an answer. He thinks that the room for which no heating is provided will be sufficiently warm for a sleeping room. It is on the south side of the house and is so situated with respect to the other rooms as to prevent it, he thinks, from becoming at any time very cold. In considering the adaptability of this house to your needs, possibly it would be well that you should take account of the fact that there is a room in South College, adjoining to the one which you will probably use for your lectures, that will be at your service for a study. It is heated by steam, for which an annual charge of $20.00 is made, but no rent is expected. By using this[,] one of the rooms on the first floor of the house could be made available as a bedroom.

As to the college house [the Westgate house], I have today consulted three of the Executive Committee, and find that they are willing to put a good cooking stove, with proper water connections into the kitchen. If you take this house, you will therefore be relieved of the larger part of the expense which constituted one of your objections to it.

Sincerely yours,   J. M. Van Vleck.

My dear Professor Wilson: Middletown, Conn., July 19, 1888
You will doubtless remember that, from the spot where you and I met Prof. Winchester,[1] on College Street, I pointed out to you a new house which may possibly be for rent next spring: also, that directly across the street from where we were standing was a brick house—a double one—in one half of which Prof.

Conn[2] had begun his housekeeping. In the latter house, on the side *not* occupied by Prof. Conn, lives a pleasant lady, Mrs. L. C. Vinal who takes boarders. She is the owner of the house. If she decides to stay in it another year, of which there is at this moment some doubt, she will be glad to board you and your family. Her price would be, I fancy, about $25.00 a week. The rooms are not large, but you could probably have three rooms besides the one to be occupied by the nurse.

If Mrs. Vinal concludes to vacate her house, she will be glad to let it for $450 furnished; or $375, unfurnished.

The present occupant of the first-mentioned house likewise takes boarders. It is possible that she may have sufficient accommodation for all of you, yet she did not seem so confident of it when I saw her the other day. I presume that her prices would not differ much from those of Mrs. Vinal.

Perhaps you will remember still another house which was the subject of a little conversation between Prof Winchester and ourselves, he having heard of it as a house that might possibly be for rent. It is very pleasantly situated on High Street, next north of the Club House which we visited along with Winchester. The tenant of this place is Rev. Mr. Tuck,[3] a retired Congregational minister. It is not impossible that you may get in there. If so, you will probably have better rooms, but will have to pay a higher price. Mrs. Tuck's price for a single boarder is $8.00 a week, Mrs. Vinal's $6.00.

The addresses of the persons whom I have named are with sufficient definiteness as follows:—

Mrs. L. C. Vinal, 125 College St.

Mrs. A. C. Stevens, College St.

Rev. Mr. Tuck, corner of Court and High Streets

All of these are near the college. There is still another place at which I have made inquiry, but too distant from High Street for your consideration at present.

I wish that I could say something reliable about the quality of the table at either of these places, but I can not. What little I have heard concerning them, however, has been favorable.

Allow a single suggestion. If you think seriously of boarding, I would advise you to make another trip to Middletown before deciding upon it. You will, I am sure, be much better satisfied if you see in advance the rooms you are to occupy and the parties with whom you are to live, than to engage at a venture. And if you do make us another visit for the purpose of determining this important but vexatious question, can't Mrs. Wilson arrange to accompany you. Please remember that my house and those who are in it are at your service; and I am sure that Clara will have no heartache if Mrs. Wilson comes with you.

Sincerely yours   J. M. Van Vleck.

ALS (WP, DLC).

¹ Caleb Thomas Winchester, born Montville, Conn., Jan. 18, 1847. A.B., Wesleyan University, 1869. Served Wesleyan University as librarian, 1869-85; Professor of Rhetoric and English Literature, 1873-90; and Olin Professor of English Literature, 1890-1920. Author of many books and articles on English literature and literary criticism. Prominent Methodist layman. Died March 24, 1920.

² Herbert William Conn, Assistant Professor of Biology.

³ The Rev. J. Webster Tuck, formerly pastor of the Third Congregational Church in Middletown, who lived at 150 High Street.

From Thomas Alexander Hoyt to Ellen Axson Wilson

Capon Springs. Hampshire Co
My Darling Ellie,   West Virginia July 20, 1888.

Through Mr. Hinckley, I learn that the Trustees have yielded, & that Woodrow is free to accept the Chair in the Wesleyan. Hence I draw the sad inference that you will be going soon to Middletown. While I rejoice in the promotion of your dear Husband, it is a real grief to me & to all of us, to lose you & Him from our vicinity. It has been a joy to have you so near me; you are very dear to me; Woodrow's companionship has been exceedingly agreeable. . . .

I try to console myself with the reflection that the change will be advantageous to Woodrow in his Profession, & that you will be happier because of it.

In view of his leaving, I think it might be well for Woodrow to meet Mr. Wanamaker.¹ The understanding I had with him was that on my return, I would introduce Woodrow to him; but now I fear this will not be practicable.² If Woodrow thinks he will have time & would like it, I will give him a letter to Mr W—, with whom he can talk over the proposed chair at Princeton. . . .

With prayers, & blessings & kisses, Sweet Ellie.

Ever fondly yours,   T. A. H.

ALI (WP, DLC).

¹ John Wanamaker, the Philadelphia merchant and philanthropist.

² For the meaning of this reference, see WW to R. Bridges, Aug. 26, 1888.

From Moses Stephen Slaughter¹

My dear Dr. Wilson,   Phila. July 25th 1888.

A remark of yours on last Saturday in regard to teaching boys Caesar has led me to think that you might have something to suggest which would be helpful to me in trying to give my boys next year an intelligent understanding of that author.

As a Professor of History of course you have some means of knowing what is needed in that line from the Latin preparatory course, and if it is not too much trouble to write it out I wish you would give me some idea of what ought to be done for the student aside from his text-book study of Roman history.

Perhaps it is not possible to specify but from the way you spoke I thought you had a well-grounded grievance against the methods in preparatory work.

Very Truly,　　Moses S. Slaughter

ALS (WP, DLC) with WWhw notation on env.: "Ans. Aug 2/88" and WWhw sums and card game scores.
　¹ Instructor in Latin at Bryn Mawr, 1887-88, who went to the Collegiate Institute in Hackettstown, N.J., in the autumn of 1888. He became Professor of Latin at the University of Wisconsin in 1896.

From John Monroe Van Vleck

My dear Professor Wilson:　　　Middletown, Conn., July 26, 1888
　　Your letter of yesterday is received. I am glad to know that you will visit Middletown again before deciding on your plans for the next year. Permit me to advise that you do so as soon as may be convenient, for two reasons.

First, I fear that you may not find satisfactory accommodation at either of the places I mentioned in my former note. I have heard today that Mrs. Vinal has engaged one of the rooms that she talked of letting you have, for the whole of the next year. If this is so, I am very confident that she will be unable to give you the amount of room that you will need. I have similar fears, also, about the other places. None of the parties in question have large houses. Possibly neither of them, at the best, will be able to meet your views. But if any of them can, it will be to your interest to have the matter settled before other engagements are made.

Second, I am liable to leave home any day *after* Wednesday next. That need not prevent you from coming to my house at whatever time you make your visit here, for some members of my family will be at home all of the time, and will be ready to render you any assistance that may be in their power. Still, I have a fancy that I can serve you better than they, and consequently prefer that you come, if possible, before I go away. Why not spend Sunday with us? We, New Englanders, don't transact business on that day, unless we have to; but you could be ready for an early start at your business on Monday morning, and would be fortified for it, I have no doubt, by your previous experience of a Puritan Sabbath.

If that houseful of company should chance to leave you before that time, we shall allow ourselves the hope of seeing Mrs. Wilson also.   Very truly yours   J. M. Van Vleck.

ALS (WP, DLC).

From Jacob Henry Hager

                      Appletons' Cyclopædia of American Biography,
Dear Sir: New York, 28 July 1888
Will you have the kindness to fill out enclosed form, adding any facts that might prove of interest in writing a brief sketch of your career for above work. Please give year and place of publication of your "Congressional Government" with those of any other works you may have issued, and greatly oblige[1]
          Your Obedient Servant   J. Henry Hager.   S.

ALS (WP, DLC) with WWhw notation on env.: "Ans. 1/8/88 [8/1/88]."
   [1] Wilson's biographical sketch appeared in *Appletons' Cyclopædia of American Biography* (6 vols., New York, 1889), VI, 558.

From John Monroe Van Vleck

My dear Professor: Middletown, Conn., July 30, 1888
I am glad to learn that you have decided to keep house. From the first I have been very doubtful about you getting satisfactory accommodation at either of the boarding houses which I have mentioned to you, and my conviction has been that your final decision, if you should come here and look the ground over, would be what it now is.

The Bagnalls[1] have been notified that you are to take possession of their home on the first of September. Will you wish to move into it promptly on that day? There may possibly be a little painting in the interior or other minor repairs needed which will make it desirable that the house be unoccupied for a day or two after the Bagnalls go out. The outside needs a coat or two of paint which, if you have no objection, we will withhold till after your arrival. The autumn is a better season for out-door painting than the summer, and besides you will probably have a preference as to color which it will be our wish, of course, to gratify.

If I can be of any service to you in advance of your coming, please consider me as at your call. I shall probably go to New

Hampshire for a short vacation, by the latter part of this week; but all letters of importance will be promptly forwarded to me

Very truly yours   J. M. Van Vleck

ALS (WP, DLC).
    1 The Rev. and Mrs. William Rhodes Bagnall, who lived in the Westgate house from 1886 to 1888.

From Martha Carey Thomas

My dear Professor Wilson,   Bryn Mawr, Pa. [c. Aug. 1, 1888]

I must apologize most sincerely for my mistake. I misread Dr Rhoads note. I understood him to say you and Mr. Bourne[1] had *finished* your interview & I was afraid I was keeping you there to listen to me talk to Mr Bourne.

I trust you will forgive what must have seemed an unpardonable rudeness   Yours very truly   M. Carey Thomas
6/P.M.

ALS (WP, DLC) with WWhw draft of reply on verso of letter.
    1 Possibly Edward Gaylord Bourne, who had been an instructor at Yale, 1886-88, and was an instructor in history and economics at Adelbert College, 1888-90.

To Martha Carey Thomas

My dear Miss Thomas,   [Bryn Mawr, c. Aug. 1, 1888]

Of course I was struck by your very unusual manner this afternoon, and could not help feeling that there must be some explanation of it which was quite hidden from my self. But you may be sure that after reading your note just received, I will think nothing more of it.   Very sincerely Yrs.

WWhwL (draft) on verso of M. C. Thomas to WW, Aug. 1, 1888.

A Note on the Democratic State

[c. Aug. 1, 1888]

One notable advantage of the Democratic state with a view to organic wholeness and all-round adjustment & development: all interests will have representation & a voice. The state will not have to depend for its progress upon the eye or upon the limited knowledge of a 'Government': but will itself direct, from many sides (through great endeavour, but finally with solid success) its own course of conduct & development

WWhw note on recto of printed announcement of the annual meeting of the American Economic Association for 1888 and membership invitation (WP, DLC).

To Moses Stephen Slaughter

My dear Mr. Slaughter,   Bryn Mawr, 2 Aug./88

Your letter of July 25 has been crowded to the wall by numerous engagements, literary and other; but it has not by any means been forgotten.

I did not mean to throw any very weighty charge at the head of the ordinary teacher of Caesar in what I said when you were out here: I have no 'firstly, secondly, thirdly' on the matter. But my meaning, though simple, was real, and 'meant business.' The whole matter stands in my mind thus: Boys like generals, like fighting, like accounts of battles: if, therefore, they could be given a just conception of the reality of this man Caesar—could see him as a sure-enough man (who in his youth, for instance, a fop and a lady-killer, was yet in his full age an incomparable commander and a compeller of liking, nay, of devotion, on the part of the rudest soldier—was himself a lover to strategy and force); if they could be made to realize that these Commentaries were written, in many parts probably, in the camp (on some rude stool, perhaps,—the noises or the silence of the camp outside) when the deeds of which they tell were fresh in the mind—perhaps also heavy on the muscles—of the man who was their author as well as author of their history—if, in short, they could be given a fellow-feeling, an enthusiasm, or even a wonder for this versatile fellow-man of theirs, reading the Commentaries would be easy, would be fun—and their contents would never be forgotten, I should say. Maps help to give pictures of the fight: if the boys could be gotten to *play* at the campaigns it would be a capital help: *anything* to dispel the idea that Caesar wrote grammatical exercises in hard words!

I conclude from your speaking of plans for interesting 'your boys,' that you are going to New Jersey and not to New York. I am sure I wish you all the good fortune in the world.

Mrs. Wilson joins me in kindest regards to your sister and yourself, and in the sincere hope that Miss Slaughter is quite well again.   Cordially Yours,   Woodrow Wilson

ALS (WP, DLC).

From John Franklin Jameson

My dear Wilson: Winchester, Mass., Aug. 4, 1888.

I congratulate you sincerely on your translation to a place so much more congenial and advantageous as Wesleyan is likely to prove. I shall be glad to have you so near as Middletown; and, in prospect of that, have a little plan to unfold.

I propose, next winter at Brown, to get up a course of public university lectures in my department.[1] I conceive that it might be a good plan to utilize for that purpose the researches which men have been making for our common volume of essays, and have a course of lectures by them upon points in the development of the constitution of the United States. This will be timely this winter, and will not be too serious for a Providence audience. Six of the men will be in New England this winter, and one or two others can come up. I think each one will be able to make an edifying and interesting popular lecture upon the subject on which he has been working.

I do not yet know that this scheme can be carried out. I do not know what can be promised the lecturer as a fee; (something like twenty dollars, I expect). But I should like to ask whether you feel disposed to consent to give one of these lectures, on the subject of your essay, or something growing out of it. Also, have you found time to make progress with the essay itself? Believe me   Very sincerely yours,   J. F. Jameson.

ALS (WP, DLC).
[1] Jameson had just been appointed Professor of History at Brown University.

From Franklin Henry Giddings

Dear Sir: Springfield, Mass. Aug. 6, 1888
Dr. Rhoads has just notified me of my appointment as Lecturer on Political Science at Bryn Mawr, and he suggests that perhaps I could secure the house that you have been occupying. May I trouble you to speak to the owner about it or to put me in communication with him? I have a wife and two children and we very much prefer to keep house in a quiet way by ourselves than to board.

If you will do me this favor I shall feel very greatly obliged.
                    Yours Very Truly,   F. H. Giddings.

ALS (WP, DLC) with WWhw notation on env.: "Ans. Aug. 14th/88."

From James Woodrow

My dear Woodrow: Philadelphia, Aug. 15, 1888.
I doubt whether this will find you at Bryn Mawr; but as I do not know your movements, I send it at a venture, to say that I

am here at Hotel Lafayette, 825. I heartily congratulate you on your election to the Wesleyan. I should be glad some day to hear from you just how much of a promotion it is.

It sounds queer that any one of the blood should be connected in any way with *Wesleyanism.*

With love to Ella,

Your affectionate Uncle,   James Woodrow.

ALS (WP, DLC) with WWhw notation on env.: "Ans. 19 Aug/88."

Two Letters from J. R. Wilson

Sir   Philadelphia, Aug 16th 1888

I am in receipt your communication re your brother[1] & it pains me to have to state to you my great surprise to learn that such a contemptible fellow should be in any way related to a professor of Bryn Mawr College.

The fact that he left you my letter to answer without acquainting you with his conduct affords another proof of his baseness.

He not only opened the letter but had the meanness to read its contents through & then grossly insulted the writer of it (a young lady) by writing her a letter in reply, after which he forwarded the letter on to me. It is a serious matter between the lady's family & myself. For your sake I should feel sorry to have to publish such a betrayal of honor, or in better language such scoundrelly proceedings. Nevertheless, I am constrained to demand an ample apology in writing. Otherwise, within one week hereafter, I shall hand the whole disgraceful affair over to the newspapers. Leaving you to communicate with your brother,

Very truly   J. R. Wilson.

[1] Joseph R. Wilson, Jr., had been visiting the Woodrow Wilsons in Bryn Mawr at this time.

Sir,   Philada. Aug 17th 1888

Since your brother is "a mere college boy" an apology is no longer desired. "The motives which I intemperately assigned" were for a man of sense or at least in years. Your own exalted opinion of the boy combined with your feasible deductions viz: mere thoughtlessness, out of a false sense of "fun" are sufficient excuse—and under the circumstances, I wish the whole affair erased and mutually forgotten—at the same time trust that Master J. R. Wilson will profit by this early lesson.[1]

Very truly   J. R. Wilson

ALS (WP, DLC).

1 "I wrote to J. R. Wilson as you advised, copying your letter almost exactly. I have not received an answer yet. I think a *gentleman* would answer such a letter. Possibly he will yet." J. R. Wilson, Jr., to WW, Aug. 25, 1888, ALS (WP, DLC).

From Edward Ireland Renick

My dear Wilson,   Washington, D. C., August 17, 1888.

I have been trying for some time to get an opportunity to answer your letter which gave me so much entertainment, but the weather has been so very oppressive that "after hours," I keep as still as possible and free from all work or worry. However, I drop in to say that I had hoped to send you another check ere this, but it will have to be deferred until the 1st prox., unless, indeed, I hear from you that this will be inconvenient. I am again keeping house and am thus enabled to practise greater economy, but rigging up anew was somewhat trying. I am unable to convey to you the fulness of my appreciation of all your kindness & confidence.

I hear of your call to the Wesleyan. How about its acceptance. Princeton, Harvard and the "Johns" will be soon seeking you. Of this I feel sure. Indeed, I am unable to realize that I—a veritable "stick in the mud"—have such friends as you & [Walter H.] Page & a few others & yet remain groping as I do. I am sometimes comforted by thinking that it might be slightly different if more leisure & physical vigor could be gained by me. . . . [W. E.] Faison we have with us always—and we value him highly, but he is not "alive" on many subjects. Page runs down for a few days & gives us a year's refreshment. Can't you, won't you, somehow, sometime, do us a good turn & come with your folks to this city & be our guests? With our love to yourself & family, I am,

As ever yours   E. I. Renick

Would there be any impropriety in using your last letter so as to make a *note* (I mean one of the "notes" of books) in the *Nation?*[1]

That seems a big undertaking—that book—& I am impatient to get at it. It will, I think, be not only valuable, but very salable, if you have succeeded as in the other book (Cong. Govt) in putting your views in popular style. I read your letter to several "dem literary fellers" who are all interested in it & in you.

E. I. R.

ALS (WP, DLC) with WWhw notation on env.: "Nation July 26/88 No. 1204" and shopping list. Wilson was probably referring to a letter from Dr. von Holst in the *Nation* of this date, p. 71.

[1] Renick referred to Wilson's letter to him of June 19, 1888, which is missing, in which Wilson described *The State*. No "notes" in the New York *Nation* near this date suggest that Wilson encouraged Renick to write a notice of *The State*. No doubt Wilson vividly remembered the nearly disastrous biographical sketch of himself that Renick wrote for the *Nation* soon after the publication of *Congressional Government*. See the biographical sketch printed at Feb. 26, 1885, and Wilson's comments on it in WW to ELA, Feb. 27, 1885, both in Vol. 4. However, in March 1889 Wilson seems to have used Renick as the conveyor of his own, Wilson's, very favorable advance notice of *The State* to the *Nation*. See H. E. Scudder to WW, March 25, 1889, n. 1, Vol. 6.

From Thomas Alexander Hoyt

My Dear Woodrow,   Capon [Springs, W. Va.], Aug. 21st [1888].

Pardon my delay, wh. is due to a severe attack of rheumatism, contracted here: writing is still painful.

Call on Mr. Wanamaker, at 13th & Chestnut—go up to his private office—& see him.[1] I hope for good results in the future.

I regret that we will not see you before you leave: but you must stop with us when you pass through to Baltimore.

Give best love to Ellie & the Babies. I wish you much success at the "Wesleyan."

Let us hear from you. Give kind regards to your Father, & the young man, if still with you. Love to Eddie.

Affectionately yours   Thos. A. Hoyt

ALS (WP, DLC).

[1] WW to R. Bridges, Aug. 26, 1888, indicates that Wilson did not call on Wanamaker at this time.

To Robert Bridges

Dear Bobby,   Bryn Mawr, Pa., 26 Aug., 1888.

I fear I have taken a liberty hardly justified by even a friendship like ours in failing for so long to answer your letter[1] asking if I could not join you in the Adirondacks (here it is the *last day* of your vacation!); but this has been for me a summer utterly unfit for letter-writing—a summer of visitors, work, and preparation for moving: and I have been confident that you would not misunderstand. Although I can say without exaggeration that I have thought of your letter almost every day, I have allowed various imperative demands upon my time to take precedence of the writing of an answer to it until now I find myself in a 'packed-up' house on the eve, almost, of our move to Ct. We have had company with us all summer (relatives);[2] I have been obliged to put my text-book into shape for publication next winter—knowing that I would have no time after beginning work at Middletown;

and I have filled all intervals with preparations for leaving—an immense job! I would have given not a little to be able to go to the mountains with you: but you see that, under the circumstances, it was not to be thought of.

No, my going to Middletown will not interfere at all with my future acceptance of a call elsewhere. I have engaged for no definite term whatever. A little scheme which is a-brewing here has been confidentially imparted to me, wh. I am going to venture to tell you about, knowing that you will see how important it is to keep it a secret for the present, lest it should miscarry, and yet wishing you to know and, if you have anything to suggest, advise. My wife's uncle, Rev. T. A. Hoyt, who is pastor of the old 'Chambers church' in Phila., went up to Princeton with me to hear Patton's address (he is a great friend of Patton's & of Princeton's), and came away enthusiastic. He was particularly impressed with the boom Patton gave political science.[3] A week or so later, he dined with John Wanamaker (who sent his sons to Princeton, you know, being a great Presbyterian) and told him what Patton had said. 'Do you know,' said Mr. Wanamaker 'I should like to endow such a chair as that.' They talked the matter over, Dr. Hoyt not in the least discouraging the idea, you may be sure, and Dr. H. suggested that he take *me* to see Mr. W. sometime, as a chap specially conversant with collegiate needs in such matters, and discuss the whole matter at length. Mr. W. assented: and in the Fall Dr. H. and I are to spend an evening with Mr. W.

Thus the whole matter is inchoate: Mr. W. thinks he would like to do a handsome thing for Princeton; and, if we do not prematurely 'give him away'—if we let him keep the initiative, he will doubtless do it. He keeps most of the notions he takes. There is certainly good ground for hope; tho' none as yet, perhaps, for confidence. If he does endow, he will probably, from all indications, endow just the sort of chair I want—in which case I shall certainly be a candidate. Keep it close and give me any points that may occur to you for the interview.

We start for Conn. on next Saturday, Sept. 1st.—shall stop somewhere on the Ct. coast to give our goods & chattels time to reach Middletown (about a week), and then go on ourselves.[4] The term is to open on the 13th of Sept.

I have been working a good deal this 'vacation', but have not overtaxed myself, I believe, and am rather anxious than otherwise to be at work in the class-room. I have for a long time been hungry for a class of *men*.

I sincerely hope, old fellow, that your vacation trip has quite set you up for the winter's pull. I think of you constantly, and confidently: for your successes have seemed to me like mere illustrations of natural laws. I am in a hurry to see you in Burlingame's place, or the like.

Middletown is not quite so far (either in time or money) from New York as Bryn Mawr is and so soon as ever I get a *barrel*—a year now, I hope, at the outside—I trust you shall once in a while see me.

With warmest regards from Mrs. Wilson, and all the old-time love from myself,

Yours affectionately,   Woodrow Wilson

ALS (WC, NjP).

¹ R. Bridges to WW, July 12, 1888.

² Eddie was of course living with the Wilsons at this time. Stockton Axson and Joseph R. Wilson, Jr., visited the Wilsons for an extended period, and Ellen's grandfather, Dr. Axson, visited them for at least a short time. About the latter's visit, see JRW to WW, Sept. 8, 1888, ALS (WP, DLC).

³ See *The Inauguration of the Rev. Francis Landey Patton, D.D., LL.D., as President of Princeton College. Princeton, N. J., June 20th, 1888* [Princeton, N.J., 1888].

⁴ Actually, as subsequent documents and notes will reveal, they stopped in New York on the way, before going to the Connecticut shore.

From Robert Bridges

Dear Tommy: [New York] Aug 28–88.

I hasten to answer your letter before Sept 1st.—though I have not had time to think it over as I should like. It came at a very opportune time for me, as I had just returned from the saddest vacation I have ever had, and needed the voice of an old friend. When I went home on Aug 4 I found my father ill in bed—though everybody had anticipated that he would be around again in a few days. But his vitality had been sadly impaired by four years of invalidism, and did not rally him when his slight illness had been overcome. He gradually sank into unconsciousness and then to a painless death on Aug 7th. His gentleness, affection, and fine courtesy survived to the very end of the journey— qualities which have always seemed the more remarkable to me because his early life and young manhood were full of struggle and hardship in the most humble places. He was strong-willed, vigorous, and stubbornly aggressive in his prime, and yet I can not remember when he was without almost feminine graces of the affections. Almost his last conscious act was to put out his arms for our baby niece and draw her little face to his lips— while his weary features lighted up with a smile which we can never forget.

There are many things about those last days which are even pleasant to remember. I find that for a month or more he had felt that the end was coming. Old friends tell me that of late he often quoted in his broadest Scotch, Lady Nairne's poem:

"I am wearin' awa, Jean
Like snaw wreaths in thaw, Jean
I'm wearin' awa
    To the land o' the leal."

But he said never a word of this at home—and looked ahead for the vacation we were all to have together when I came back. The whole family was to be together for a week and they tell me that nearly every one who passed the porch was told that I was to be home on Aug 4.

I stayed at home till last Tuesday when I started for a three days' walk in the northern Catskills, which put me on my feet. When I was in the heart of the woods I saw a paper announcing the death of Mr. Burlingame's mother—which was a terrible shock to him. He starts on a vacation tomorrow, and needs it very much.

You will pardon me this gloomy narrative, but there is a certain relief in writing it.

The "Scheme in prospect" is one which appeals strongly to me —and if carried out will add much to the value of Princeton for young men who believe there is more in life than the Scotch philosophy dreams of. I am not familiar enough with the present scope of Sloane's and Johnstone's courses to make a suggestion of any value as to the new chair. I do know, however, that what practical young men most need is a knowledge of law-making and the execution of them (laws) when made. If Princeton does not now teach the whole subject of practical legislation, it should be included in the new chair. You have thought more on this subject than I have, and this beclouded sentence will suggest to you what I mean. Most of the young college men who go to the state legislatures are worthless members for a session or two— first, because they know nothing of the means and methods of legislation, and, second, because those means and methods are corrupt or inadequate. [Of course, you will not think that I mean that men should be taught the tricks of parliamentary law, but they should know the nature of laws, and what is necessary to the making of a good law; and the general features of seemingly good laws which are really vicious legislation in principle (e.g. the regulation of city governments by state assemblies.)][1]

When the chair is founded, of course, you are the man for it. I believe that you have enough friends in power, looking after you, to put you there. When the time comes I should write to Bob McCarter whose father is in the Board. I know that Bob has been wishing that you were at Princeton. Pyne I believe is a good friend of yours, and Harlan told me several times that he would speak to Patton about your prospects. Let me know please when you want the word said, and I shall write to Rev. George B. Stewart of Harrisburg (a trustee) who will pay some heed to what I say. Then I can speak to Sam Alexander[2] whom I see occasionally. Perhaps by that time Cyrus McCormick will be on the Board, and you can depend on him to the utmost.[3] He is one of your warmest admirers.

Come to see me soon. I seem to be writing with a leaden hand, and cannot say what I would.

With regards to Mrs. Wilson.

Your Friend   Robert Bridges

ALS (WP, DLC) with WWhw notation on env.: "Ans. Aug. 29/88."

[1] Bridges' brackets.

[2] The Princeton men just mentioned were Robert Harris McCarter, '79; Moses Taylor Pyne, '77; the Rev. Richard Davenport Harlan, '81; the Rev. George Black Stewart, '76; and Samuel Alexander, '79.

[3] Cyrus Hall McCormick, Jr., born Washington, D. C., May 16, 1859. Member of the Class of 1879 at Princeton but was not graduated. Succeeded to the presidency of the McCormick Harvesting Co. upon his father's death in 1884. President, International Harvester Co., 1902-19; chairman, board of directors, 1919-35. Prominent Presbyterian layman and benefactor of the Y.M.C.A. and other causes. Member, Princeton Board of Trustees, 1889-1936. Died June 2, 1936.

To Robert Bridges

My dear Bobby,   Bryn Mawr, Pa., 29 August, '88.

Sure as I am that you do not need to have me *say* that you have my heartfelt sympathy in your great, great loss in order to be sure of it, I am equally certain that the necessity rests upon me to speak out the deep, the heart-deep feeling for you that has sprung up within me since the reading of your letter. Oh, I am so glad that you feel that you can speak of such a grief to me, that I am the proper person by reason of friendship to whom to detail the particulars of those last days of your father's lifetime: and my dear Bobby, you may rest assured that such a narrative is as sacred in my eyes as you could wish it to be. I tried to read your letter aloud to Mrs. Wilson, and could scarcely get through with some passages of it articulately. If I had not seen it all from your point of view, I should still have been deeply moved by the sheer beauty of those last days of your father's. He was of the stuff that most appeals to my love of manly strength and true heart-gentleness. I honor his kind; but particularly I honor him. I am grateful for the glimpses of him you have once and again afforded me. As for your own loss, surely I am qualified to sympathize with you. My dear father is still spared to me, God be thanked; but the death of my mother last Spring went near to break my heart, and has left me with a permanent sense of loneliness, of maimed-ness, such as I could never before have imagined. Think of having a father or a mother whom one could *not* honor and revere! And what a measure that affords of the blessing of being upheld by the memory and example of such a father as yours!

Bobby, I wish I could give you my hand and make you know the sympathy I feel—but I am sure you *do* know it.

Thank you very much for your suggestions *a propos* of the 'scheme': they contain a good point and shall be heeded. As for your suggestions about my election, if &c., they are like yourself and go straight to my heart to join a host of other proofs of your untiring friendship.

Mrs. W. asks to be allowed to add an expression of *her* sympathy with you.

Your affectionate friend   Woodrow Wilson

My address in Middletown will be 106 High Street.

ALS (WC, NjP).

To D. C. Heath and Company

Dear Sirs,   Bryn Mawr, Pa., 30 August, 1888

In accordance with your request for my opinion as to the suitability of Mr. Charles F. Dole's little book "The Citizen and the Neighbor" for use in country and other primary schools, I have examined the book with some care. The plan and contents of the work are not open to serious objection, perhaps, though I am not so sure that that may be said with perfect confidence; but its *style* seems to me entirely to unfit it for the use of young students. It is simple in form, but not in reality. It implies too much in proportion to what it says,—or rather takes for granted too much. For those who know the subjects of which the author treats, what he says is true—and commonplace—enough: for those who do not know those subjects his expositions must necessarily be very obscure—must require much more elucidation, as to the mere meaning of the text than most primary teachers have either the time or the patience to give.

Very truly Yours,   Woodrow Wilson

☞ My address after Sept. 1st. will be *Middletown, Conn.*

W. W.

ALS (Berg Coll., NN).

From Edward Ireland Renick

My dear Wilson,   Washington, D.C., August 31, 1888.

I see in this week's Nation an editorial, "Gen Harrison on Competition," which throws light upon the subject matter of my recent query addressed to you. Perhaps it is your answer to it.

I inclose with my thanks a draft for $20., and will try to send the remaining $60 very soon. I hope payment in this manner does not annoy you. I shall be able, doubtless, to increase the instalment next time. If you should have need of the whole, please advise me & I shall raise it & forward at once.

Hoping to have a reply soon to my last letter I am with our sincerest regards & best wishes to all of you,

Yours as ever   E. I. Renick

ALS (WP, DLC).

INDEX

NOTE ON THE INDEX

THE reader is referred to the Note on the Index to Volume I for a statement of general principles and practices for this series, including the treatment of Wilson's Marginal Notes. The alphabetically arranged analytical table of contents eliminates duplication, in both contents and index, of references to certain documents, like letters. Letters are listed in the contents alphabetically by name, and chronologically for each name by page. The subject matter of all letters is, of course, indexed. The Editorial Notes and Wilson's writings are listed in the contents chronologically by page. In addition, the subject matter of both categories is indexed. The index covers all references to books and articles mentioned in text or notes. Footnotes are indexed. Page references to footnotes which place a comma between the page number and "n" cite both text and footnote, thus: "624,n3." On the other hand, absence of the comma indicates reference to the footnote only, thus: "55n2"—the page number denoting where the footnote appears. The letter "n" without a following digit signifies an unnumbered descriptive-location note.

An asterisk before an index reference designates identification or other particular information. Re-identification and repetitive annotation have been minimized to encourage use of these starred references. Where the identification appears in an earlier volume, it is indicated thus: "*1:212,n3." Thus a page reference standing without a preceding volume number is invariably a reference to the present volume. The index will usually supply the fullest known forms of names of persons of more than casual interest, and, for the Wilson and Axson families, relationships as far down as cousins. Persons referred to in the text by nicknames or shortened forms of names can be identified by reference to entries for these forms of the names.

A sampling of the opinions and comments of Wilson and Ellen Axson Wilson covers their more personal views, while broad, general headings in the main body of the index cover impersonal subjects. Occasionally opinions expressed by a correspondent are indexed where these appear to supplement or to reflect views expressed by Wilson or by Ellen Axson Wilson in documents which are missing.

INDEX